Exceptional Children:

Educational Resources and Perspectives

Edited by

SAMUEL A. KIRK
Professor of Special Education
The University of Arizona

FRANCIS E. LORD
Professor of Special Education
The University of Arizona

HOUGHTON MIFFLIN COMPANY • BOSTON
Atlanta • Dallas • Geneva, Illinois
Hopewell, New Jersey • Palo Alto
London

The photographs in this book are from the following sources:
Howe: Courtesy of Perkins School, Watertown, Massachusetts
Binet: Brown Brothers
Strauss: Courtesy of Mrs. Marie C. Strauss
Head: The Bettman Archive
Terman: Courtesy of Dr. Frederic E. Terman
Itard: Culver Pictures
Gallaudet: Courtesy of Gallaudet College, Washington, D.C.
Braille: Courtesy of Perkins School, Watertown, Massachusetts/Donald
    Dietz, photographer
Phelps: Courtesy of The John F. Kennedy Institute and the Baltimore Sun
Adler: The Bettmann Archive
Graham: Courtesy of Mrs. Ray Graham
Fernald: Courtesy of the Fernald School, University of California,
    Los Angeles
Cover photograph: Arthur Furst, photographer

371.9

K63e

107454

Dec. 1978

Library of Congress Catalog Card Number: 73–11944

ISBN: 0–395–18027–9

Contents

Preface

Practices in special education are undergoing interesting changes and adaptations. These changes have their roots in the influences of the past and the pressures of the present. The editors of *Exceptional Children: Educational Resources and Perspectives* have attempted to assemble articles which represent a balance between glimpses of the past, practices and concerns of the present, and brief "looks" into the future. In a text of this size it is impossible to cover every aspect of special education and to satisfy all the needs of its readers; consequently, articles have been selected which relate to the more significant aspects of each area. It is hoped, however, that the book has sufficient balance among the articles selected to be of value to a wide reading audience.

Insofar as possible, each article has been reproduced in its entirety; any deletions or editorial additions are clearly designated. Aids, such as section headings, explanatory footnotes, and so on, have been inserted to assist the reader, as well as study questions which focus attention upon key points in each article. Articles vary in reading difficulty, with some intended primarily for students with a background in the field and others for those who are less familiar with the education of exceptional children.

The editors are pleased to reproduce certain articles and chapters from texts which are not readily available to most readers. For example, Samuel Gridley Howe's *A Letter to the Governor of Massachusetts upon His Veto of a Bill Providing for an Increase in State Beneficiaries at the School for Idiotic Children* was first published over a hundred years ago. The reader, however, will be impressed with this historic document primarily because of the relevance of Howe's views for today's scene. In a sense, he represents the founding fathers in enunciating their views of the rights of the handicapped in a democracy.

The letter is available in only a few libraries and is generally unknown and unavailable to students in the field.

Another historic publication is from Alfred Binet's *Les Idées modernes sur les enfants*, which appeared in 1911. A section of Chapter Five, *L'Education de l'intelligence*, addresses itself to a current and persistent problem concerning the education of intelligence, which continues to be of great interest in psychology and education today.

Other articles in the book deal with special education and the law, communication disorders, learning disabilities, the intellectually gifted and the mentally retarded, children with auditory and visual handicaps, neurological, orthopedic and other health problems, behavioral disorders, and proposals for restructuring the field.

Each chapter contains a brief sketch of a pioneer whose work was of great significance in the field which that chapter treats. It is hoped that these biographical sketches will assist in giving a historical perspective to the writings in the chapter.

The authors of the articles which have been reproduced here deserve most of the credit for the contents of this volume. Without their creative writings and cooperation in permitting us to reproduce their works, this publication would not have been possible. The simple credit lines in no way express the sincere and genuine appreciation due to them and their publishers.

The editors have drawn extensively upon the articles which have appeared in *Exceptional Children*. Appreciation is expressed for the cooperation of the editor and the Council for Exceptional Children.

Many of our colleagues and associates have advised the editors in the choice of articles. Appreciation is expressed to Ruth Funderburg, Elizabeth Hannah, Audrey Simmons-Martin, George Leshin, Walter Olson, and Lloyd Wright for their constructive and helpful suggestions.

Many of the editorial details and typing of the manuscript were shared by Candace McCarthy and Aldine von Isser, graduate assistants, and

Ilda G. Lord. Their careful work made the assembling of the articles in this volume a much simpler task for the editors.

—SAMUEL A. KIRK
FRANCIS E. LORD
Editors

The University of Arizona

Exceptional Children:

Educational Resources and Perspectives

One

Historical Perspectives

It is impossible to give the reader a complete history of special education in a single short chapter. However, some glimpses can be provided in the space available. We have selected for these glimpses three manuscripts, one published in 1857, one in 1924, and one in 1967. The first one, by Howe, deals with efforts to obtain adequate legislation for the handicapped, the second tells about the organization of the Council for Exceptional Children, and the third deals with the momentous congressional support for handicapped children in the 1960's.

Samuel Gridley Howe, as the "Pioneer Profile" points out, was truly one of the early leaders in special education. As a pioneer in Massachusetts, he sought legislation for an appropriation to establish a residential school for idiotic children (it was the common usage at this time to use the term *idiotic* when referring to mentally retarded children). In this period in history residential facilities, or asylums, as they were often called, were considered the best way to provide care for the handicapped. When the governor vetoed the bill authorizing the appropriation, Howe addressed a letter to him in which he defended in detail the need for a school for idiotic children. The Massachusetts Legislature later overrode the governor's veto. Howe's letter was written in 1857 and incorporates many ideas which have wide acceptance today.

The second article reproduces the presidential address at the first annual meeting of the International Council for Exceptional Children in 1923. During the past fifty years this organization has become a moving force behind the development of all aspects of special education. In 1956, the term "International" was dropped from the name, thus leaving the name "Council for Exceptional Children" (CEC). "International"

1

was dropped for two reasons: (1) by 1956 the Council with its international tag, had become an active unit within the National Education Association, and the illogical structural relationship became apparent; and (2) the Council was trying to obtain federal support for programs for the handicapped, and some members of Congress were confused over the activities of what appeared to be an international organization dealing with national problems. The Council for Exceptional Children publishes *Exceptional Children* and *Teaching Exceptional Children*.

In the third article Edwin Martin, who is presently the Associate Commissioner in charge of the Bureau of Education for the Handicapped, reviews the legislative history of federal support of programs for exceptional children. In the past decade, in particular, the federal role has become very influential. Spearheaded by the leadership within the Division of Handicapped Children and Youth, the U.S. Office of Education, and later the Bureau for the Education of the Handicapped, federal efforts have had a significant impact on the development of services for exceptional children.

Finally, in an Epilogue, brief biographical sketches are provided of the persons who have held the top administrative position in the education of exceptional children within the U.S. Office of Education.

Samuel Gridley Howe
1801–1876

PHYSICIAN
EDUCATOR
REFORMER

Samuel Gridley Howe was born in 1801. He was graduated from Harvard Medical School in 1824. His earlier medical experience was as a volunteer surgeon in the Greek War of Liberation.

Howe was instrumental in organizing what is now known as the Perkins School for the Blind in Watertown, Massachusetts, which he directed until his death in 1876. He trained the deaf-blind Laura Bridgman. This success led, fifty years later, to the education of Helen Keller."

His efforts in the education of the blind and the deaf-blind led him to an interest in the mentally retarded. The Massachusetts Legislature appointed a commission to inquire into the conditions of "idiots" in the state, and Dr. Howe was appointed chairman of that commission. The recommendation of the commission was to establish a state school—which later became the Fernald State School. His letter to the Governor of Massachusetts, included in this chapter, is typical of his philosophy and his drive for services for the handicapped during the beginnings of special education in the United States.

The article by Leo Kanner in Chapter Six supplies some additional details regarding the work of this American pioneer.

1.
A Letter to the Governor of Massachusetts*

SAMUEL G. HOWE

As you read Howe's letter, which was written over one hundred years ago, evaluate his social and educational philosophy in relation to prevailing notions today.

BOSTON, JUNE 30, 1857.

To His Excellency, HENRY J. GARDNER,

Governor of Massachusetts,

SIR:

I address to your Excellency, and through you to whom it may concern, some remarks upon your late extraordinary Veto of a Bill for increasing the number of State Beneficiaries at the School for Idiotic children.

In the exercise of the right belonging to every citizen of criticizing public State-papers, I shall show the illiberal spirit of this one, point out its errors, correct its misstatements, and lessen, as far as I can, its untoward influence.

Lest it should be supposed, that my long official connection with one Public Charitable Institution, and my close relations with others, make me regard all kindred establishments with partiality and so disturb my judgment, let me state some general views.

Experience has lessened the enthusiasm I once felt about such establishments, for it has taught me that they are sometimes created needlessly, sometimes even in violation of sound political economy; and that disadvantages and difficulties are often found in their practical operation, which had not been foreseen by their founders.

---

*This letter was originally published in 1857 by Ticknor & Field, Boston, under the title "A Letter to the Governor of Massachusetts, upon his veto of a bill, providing for an increase of state beneficiaries at the school for idiotic children." It is reproduced here with minor deletions, each of which is clearly indicated. Section headings, which do not appear in the original letter, have been inserted by the editors to aid the reader. *The Editors*

Separation and Not Congregation

In one sense, Public Charitable Institutions, like all prisons and other penal establishments, are evils; and are maintained only to avoid greater ones.

True wisdom and charity teach that in the treatment of the paupers, the infirm, and the criminal, the leading principle should be, *separation and not congregation.*

Such persons are in an abnormal and undesirable condition. Peculiarities of character grow out of it, which are intensified by association, and so classes and clans are formed. The true remedy is disassociation—diffusion in general sound society, and the prevention of classes.

The late movement in our State, by which the paupers were gathered in great State Poor Houses, seemed to be called for by some pressing considerations, but it was in violation of this sound principle.

In many other establishments, the inmates are brought together and treated in classes, not because that is the best conceivable mode, but because it is the best possible one in the present state of society.

Many Institutions, such as the Foundling Hospitals, that were once regarded as wise and good, are now, properly enough, falling out of favor, because suspected of increasing the very evil they were meant to lessen. Others, as Orphan Asylums, Public Reform Schools, and the like, will, I think, be replaced in time by more effectual and truly Christian remedies.

In almost all public, charitable, and penal Institutions, with which I am familiar, serious evils arise from violation of the principle, that we should separate and not congregate.

Being called upon lately to give advice about the establishment of Institutions for the Blind and the Deaf Mutes in a new State, I have counselled a course, different from the one I, myself, followed many years ago. It is to dispense with any great costly building, having common dormitories, dining-rooms, chapel, and the like. To make no preparation for any great common household at all; but to build a simple building, with all the conveniences for instructing classes, and make provision for boarding the pupils in private families. In a word, to reduce the Institution, as we would any machine, to the simplest possible form. This is perfectly feasible in many small towns and villages.

In like manner, if proper occasions should present, I would advise modification of several of our public Institutions; curtailment of operation in some cases, and total discontinuance of the establishment in others.

In the highest possible state of society there will be the fewest penal and charitable Institutions; meantime we must do the best we can with those whose existence is necessary.

I will now consider the question of the abstract right of the poor and infirm to a support, and the correlative obligation of the State to furnish it. I trust that question will not be mooted in Massachusetts until she is so far advanced in civilization as to esteem it a privilege, not a mere duty, to obey the precepts of our Divine Teacher.

These remarks will show that I am not such an enthusiast as to desire any needless multiplication or enlargement of Public Charitable Institutions.

The School Had Legislative Support

I now proceed to the matter of the School for Idiotic Children. Great pains were taken by the friends of that School to induce the members of the last General Court to visit it, and to examine it thoroughly. Many members did do so.

The Joint Standing Committee of House and Senate upon Public Charitable Institutions visited it, and, after giving a patient hearing to the Trustees, they unanimously recommended an increase of the grant made by the State for its support.

The Senate and the House, after due deliberation, and in spite of a general and honest desire for retrenchment, freely voted an increase of 2500 dollars for the current year. This however was not to be an outright gift, for the Trustees had not asked such. It was to be given only on condition that fifteen idiotic children, to be named by the Governor, from among the poor families, should be supported and taught. In other words, the State was to increase the number of her beneficiaries from thirty to forty-five, and pay about three dollars a week for teaching each idiot boy or girl that should be received.

When the bill had been passed through all the forms by the Representatives of the people in the House and Senate, and lacked only the signature of the highest Representative to become a law, I took advantage of the spring vacation to be absent from my post, not suspecting that he would have any motive to thwart the will of the others.

Was It Politics?

I knew indeed that in some States the sacred interests of public Charitable Institutions are often wickedly sacrificed for political purposes, but I did not suspect that in this case there was any thing to endanger them.

I knew too, that a man who lately filled, or rather occupied, a higher office than yours, did once (in order to catch a few votes,) defeat a generous purpose to which Congress had been moved by an heroic woman, and did in cold blood *veto* the noble Bill for the relief of the Insane, known as "Miss Dix's Bill," but I did not apprehend that any Governor of Massachusetts would follow in such footsteps of such a predecessor. I was astonished therefore by learning, on my return, a few days ago, that your Excellency had striven to defeat the will of the Legislature by a Veto, and to forbid the increase of the State's bounty to one of her Charitable Institutions. The Legislature indeed rebuked the interference, and over-rode the obstacle by a two-thirds vote. Under ordinary circumstances this would have so satisfied the friends of the Institution that they could with propriety have held their peace.

If your Excellency had simply withheld your signature and thus defeated the bill; if you could have exercised the *liberum Veto* of the old Polish Diet, and *"Objected,"* without giving reasons; or if you had given reasons without misstatements and slurs, there would have been no need to make public comment on your measure, or to distinguish between your dissent and that of any Representative who voted, Nay.

Veto Statement Misrepresents

But, wittingly or unwittingly, you do really hurl at a Public Charitable Institution a deadly missile in shape of a veto, every material paragraph of which is shotted with a misstatement, and the whole charge rammed down with an unjust and ungenerous insinuation which causes it to make a louder report.

It is hard to believe this was intentional. I hope it was not. It would be a new and sad phase of political action that should show a Governor of Massachusetts using a State weapon to assail and decry a public charitable Institution, and striving to check the people's growing regard and pity for the humblest and feeblest of all classes of the afflicted. It seems like an offense against humanity itself. At any rate, as a friend of the school for Idiotic children, I am constrained to criticize your veto, and point out its various misstatements, its errors of facts, errors of figures, and its consequent injustice. I shall use the occasion, however, to make a few remarks upon the subject of our Public Charitable Institutions generally, and upon this School in particular.

The number and character of Public Charitable Institutions are valuable exponents of the intelligence and wealth, as well as of the moral and religious condition, of a people. Regarded politically, they are exponents of the consideration in which the individual is held by the public. They flourish not in artistocracies, autocracies, or despotisms of any kind, even those miscalled *religious* despotisms. They may indeed be created in great numbers, and sustained by Government, as they are in Modern Rome, but still lack the essentials of true and wise charity. The permanent establishment of any one of them in this country can neither be secured nor defeated by any individual. Several things must combine to ensure its success. There must be a good and needful work to be done; an earnest man who believes it can be done; and a people intelligent enough to see that it really is good and needful, and humane enough to give it moral and material aid.

Why did not the Lying-in-Hospital succeed here? It had ardent friends; it had money; and it was never vetoed by anybody until it vetoed itself. It failed because there was not a needful work for it to do. There were not enough honest women who were so destitute of comforts at home, as to need to go to a hospital for their confinement. The house therefore failed for want of customers.

The existence of the Institutions shows moreover, not only the existence of the unfortunate, but reflects the moral and religous character of the people. There are about as many halt, lame, blind, deaf, insane, and "poor folk" of all sorts, in Egypt, as in England; in Arkansas as in Massachusetts; but how different the number of people who are intelligent enough to see the proper modes of relief, and religious enough to apply them!

There were about as many insane, in proportion to the population, in Massachusetts, two hundred years ago, as there are to-day; but the people did not see the necessity of a Hospital for Lunatics; and the Legislature would hardly have been virtuous enough to pass a bill in aid of one over a veto.

When the noble Horace Mann undertook to create the first State Hospital for the Insane, he found that Governors and Legislators would not take the lead, and so he shouted to the people, until he awakened that sentiment of humanity which always exists, though it may slumber; and as soon as the people heard and understood the claim, they said, Let the hospital be built. There were some open opponents of the measure and many secret ones. There were those who preached economy; and there were croakers of all sorts; but the heart of the people had been touched; and they resolved to have a Hospital. They builded it, therefore, and then went about their business; whereupon the Magnates and the Honorables straightway came forward, and, as is their wont, took the high seats in the synagogue at the celebration.

Public Demands Services

Why are so many other Institutions of public beneficence springing up in our midst? Simply because the moral and religious sense of the people is so far awakened and enlightened, that they are no longer to be satisfied with houses for religious worship, but must have houses for religious works also.

There is here a growing respect for man, as one created in God's image. There is a feeling of brotherhood which reduces to practice the thought of the old heathen, who said, that, because he was a man, every thing human interested him. This feeling is extending even to the poor broken fragments of humanity which we carefully gather up that nothing be lost.

Surely, this feeling should be encouraged, not checked, by all who aspire to lead the people. If we tenderly draw from the sea any human corpse, nay, even the floating limb of a man and give it reverent burial, how much more should we heed the signal of distress shown by any living fellow creature, however infirm and mutilated, who struggles helpless on the great stream of life! The disposition to act thus is innate; and it is peculiarly human. It is the sheet anchor of society; it is the hope of the future; and as it is more or less developed, so are we more or less men.

It has been already so far developed in the people of this Commonwealth that when the Deaf Mutes, the Insane, and the Blind successively claimed kindred and help, the claim was cheerfully allowed, and the help heartily given. And when at last the poor Idiot asked that something be done for him too, the only hesitation arose from the doubt whether his sad lot could be lightened by the hand of the State.

The history of this new claim is particularly interesting because it shows that our people act wisely and cautiously even when moved by a warm and generous impulse. About twelve years ago, some persons, encouraged by success in attempts to teach children who were apparently beyond the reach of instruction, conceived a plan of improving the condition of Idiots, and brought the subject before the Legislature. By an order of the House of Representatives, January 22, 1846, a committee of five members was named, "to consider the expediency of appointing Commissioners to inquire into the condition of Idiots in this Commonwealth, to ascertain their number, and whether anything can be done for their relief, and to report to the next General Court."

In March, 1846, the Committee reported, "that there is no adequate provision by law for the relief, care and treatment of idiots in the Commonwealth."

They set forth strong reasons for the belief that the condition of those unfortunates could be greatly improved. Among other evidence, they gave that of Dr. Woodward, the eminent physician of the State Lunatic Hospital, who said: "My opinion is, that nearly all idiots can be made better; the physical condition and personal habits of the lowest order can be improved, and those possessing more mind can be trained to usefulness, and some can be taught to read, write, and labor advantageously, and be useful and happy." The Committee closed by recommending the appointment of three Commissioners to make a thorough investigation of the subject, and report the result.

The Commissioners were appointed, and reported in part March 31, 1847, and made a full and final report, (Senate Document No. 51) February, 26, 1848.

This report embodied the greatest amount of information ever collected upon the subject. It gave a minute and accurate description of five hundred and seventy-four idiots.

The Legislature was convinced that something should be done by the State, but resolved to do it experimentally. By an Act approved May eighth, 1848, there was appropriated "a sum not exceeding two thousand five hundred dollars a year for three years, for the purpose of training and teaching ten idiotic children, to be selected by the Governor and Council, provided an arrangement can be made with any suitable institution now patronized by the Commonwealth for charitable purposes," etc.

The task was undertaken by the Institution for the Blind, and was performed satisfactorily.

In the meantime, an institution had been incorporated and organized under the title of the Massachusetts School for Idiotic and Feeble-minded Youth; and, at the expiration of the three experimental years, the Legislature doubled the appropriation, by making an annual grant of five thousand dollars a year to the new school.

It soon became clear to all who examined the subject closely, that this institution was really doing a needful work, which could not be done elsewhere, and that there should be a proper building to do it in. The Legislature, therefore, in 1855, voted the sum of twenty-five thousand dollars for such a building.

The edifice was erected in a very short time. The pupils were removed to it during the last year, and more new ones applied for admission than could be supported by means at command.

I claim, then, that the experiment of teaching and training idiots has been carefully and patiently made, and has proved successful, and that this institution has done all that its real friends promised.

True, it has not changed the nature of any born idiot and given him common sense, and no honest and wise persons have pretended that this could be done. But this experiment has done much good in various ways.

It has shown that idiots form no exception to the law that every form of organized life is capable of being changed for better or worse by surrounding influences.

It has rescued some children of merely feeble minds from the imbecility into which they had fallen, either through abuse, or neglect, or unwise treatment;—children who were considered as idiots, and who would have sunk into hopeless idiocy but for the help of this school.

It has given speech to some who were dumb, and who, if left without special aid, would have remained dumb.

It has greatly improved the condition of more than four-fifths of its pupils, as their friends will testify.

They have been put into a higher state of health and vigor.

They have been trained to the command and use of muscle and limb.

They feed themselves, dress themselves, and conduct with decorum.

Their gluttonous and unseemly habits have been broken up.

They have been trained to temperance, cleanliness, and order, until the habits have become as second nature.

Their powers of self-control have been increased, and they strive to make themselves less unsightly and disagreeable to others.

Many have been trained to habits of industry, so that they may at least be less burdensome to their friends.

Idiot Children Must Be Served

Their mental faculties and moral sentiments have been developed by lessons and exercises suitable to their feeble condition, and they have been raised in the scale of humanity.

Finally, a conviction had been produced in many minds, that idiotic children, if they are considered only as belonging to the great class of the insane, should have special care and training; and this conviction is so well founded, that henceforth some establishment for their special benefit will be considered necessary here so long as Massachusetts maintains her present high standard of public morality and Christian beneficence.

This particular school may be crushed, either by reason of the weakness of its friends, or the strength of its enemies, but the charity will reappear in some other form. It has dropped seeds which will surely fructify in the kindly soil of the old Bay State.

Other States Are Providing Schools

Moreover, this sense of duty towards idiotic children has been awakened beyond the borders of our Commonwealth. Measures for the relief of this class of sufferers have been taken in other States, and our institution has contributed not a little in aid of them.

An exhibition of our pupils was given before the Legislature of New York, in reference to which the Hon. Christopher Morgan, Secretary of the Board of Education, wrote as follows:

Albany, March 23, 1852

Dear Sir:

I remember with great satisfaction your visit to Albany with the idiotic pupils under your charge. Previous to your visit, I had regarded the institutions for the instruction of idiots rather as asylums for the improvement of the physical condition of the idiots, than for educational purposes.

A very attentive examination of your pupils convinced me that their physical defects might be, in a great measure, remedied, and their minds cultivated and enlarged to an extent far beyond anything I had imagined,

The exhibition before the Legislature was eminently satisfactory and convincing.

Dr. Baccus, recently a State Senator, and an enlightened and philanthropic citizen of Rochester, labored with zeal and fidelity, though unsuccessfully, to establish an institution for idiots in this State. Very soon after your visit to Albany, a law was passed for an establishment of an institution for idiots; an appropriation of six thousand dollars a year, for two years, was made, and the institution is now in successful operation in the vicinity of this city, under the judicious management of Dr. Wilbur.

It may now be regarded as permanently established, and to your visit more than anything else, are we indebted for this noble charity, so creditable to the liberality and benevolence of the State.

Very respectfully and truly yours,

CHRISTOPHER MORGAN

To the Superintendent of the School for Idiotic Children, Boston, Mass.

The Governor wrote as follows:

"Your visit to our Capitol last winter, was of great service. We feel that we are much indebted to you, for the success of the measure thus far, and hope we may have the benefit of your experience and counsel, in carrying our plan into practical operation.

You must remember that we are now beginners in the good work, and, until we have had some experience of our own, we must look to the East for light and information."

Since that time the State has appropriated seventy-five thousand dollars for a building which has been erected at Syracuse. It, moreover, granted two hundred and fifty dollars a year for each beneficiary.

In Pennsylvania, a School was organized by one of the former teachers in the Massachusetts School. It has been since adopted by the State. A grant has been made for a building, and an allowance of three hundred dollars a year was made for each beneficiary.

A school has just been established in Ohio, and is now in operation.

Rhode Island has made provision for educating idiotic children, and several have been sent to our School.

Preparatory measures have been taken in Connecticut. The subject has been before the Legislature, and will doubtless terminate in provision by the State for the care and training of idiotic children.

Veto Message Has Errors

Such, in brief, is the history and results of an institution, a Bill for the further extension of the benefits of which Your Excellency attempted to defeat by a *Veto*, which I now proceed to examine.

(*Here follow four pages in which Howe examines and refutes the Governor's allegations of unwarrantable cost per pupil.* THE EDITORS)

Instances of this fearful visitation are found, indeed, in all classes, the rich as well as the poor, but chiefly among the latter, and for these this School was intended.

Citizens Want Public Institutions

It is for the many, not the few; for the poor, not the rich. It is a State School, and therefore necessarily public and cheap. Now as people naturally dislike to have their children's infirmity known, most of those who can afford to do so, get instruction for them at home, or else send them to the excellent School at Barre, where the minimum charge is double the ordinary charge at the State Institution, and even then, gives but a moderate profit.

If it had been true, therefore, that private individuals do not send children to this School, it would have been unfair and unkind in your Excellency, to put forth the statement that it was from lack of confidence in it.

Why do the rich prefer to send their friends who have become insane, to the McLean Asylum, or to the private Hospital at Pepperell, or Dorchester, rather than the State Hospital? Surely, not because they lack "confidence" in the latter.

But the statement in this paragraph of the veto, is as incorrect as it is uncalled for and unkind.

There are "private individuals" who prefer public Institutions to private ones, for the reason, that they are less liable to abuse. Ours has from the very outset had among its pupils the children of wealthy parents. Eminent men, [and among them the Governor of a great State,] have had confidence in the benefits of the Institution, and kept their children in it for years. They have been required to pay an extra price, and so help the School to take children of the poor at lower rates.

The Reports of the Institution have repeatedly stated that the grant from the State did not suffice for its support, and that the lack has been made up by receiving a few pupils at higher rates. The Reports of the Treasurer have proved this. In some years about half of the whole income has been from private pupils. Moreover, the very Report from which extracts were made for your Excellency's veto, would have shown the true state of the case, if carefully examined for the purpose of finding it.

The Trustees there say, (House Doc. 212, pp. 4, 5,) "We have taken private pupils from this and other States, who paid more than the bare cost of their maintenance, and this profit has been appropriated to the support of an increased number of the poor children of Massachusetts. Besides, it may be stated that the services of the superintendent and physician have been both gratuitously rendered, and thereby the means of educating the poor have been still further increased."

Again, the Auditors say, p. 16, "the annual appropriation from the State has been $5000; the average annual income from private pupils has been $2140.64."

If it be urged that it is still true that "no considerable number of private persons have had confidence," etc., the answer is plain, to take private paying pupils in any considerable number would exclude the poor.

The last paragraph of the Veto is as follows, "Under these circumstances an earnest desire to prevent any unnecessary expenses, constrains me to withhold my sanction from this resolve."

This is marvellous indeed!

When there are so many perennial leaks from the Treasury to be stopped, it is passing strange that a great pother should be made over such a driblet as this appropriation, to a Charitable Institution, of $2500 for a single year.

The Veto is a great State engine, and, when an enormous breach is made, which threatens to swamp the Treasury, then it may properly be brought out, like a great steam pump. To do this may be sublime, at least in sound; but to ring the alarm-bell, and get up steam merely to stop such a leak as three dollars and a quarter a week for supporting and educating fifteen idiotic children,—that borders rather on the ridiculous.

You Failed to Visit the Institution

I cannot conceive of any private objection, which your Excellency has to the School, or to the system of training and teaching there used, because you cannot be familiar with it.

The law makes your Excellency Chairman ex-officio of a Board of Visitors, and prescribes that their duty shall be "to visit and inspect said Institution, (School for Idiots,) as often as they may see fit," etc. Your predecessors did see fit to inspect the School closely, and some members of the present Board have conformed with the law; but your Excellency has not yet "seen fit" to do so. Notwithstanding repeated invitations, you have never visited the School, that I can learn, and I have made diligent inquiry.

This seems the more extraordinary because it is within my knowledge, that, in regard to some public institutions, you have shown uncommon and praiseworthy diligence in learning the details of their management, the character of the officers, and the like, so as to be able to protect the interests of the State.

There must have been other motives for this State Paper, than that which appears on its surface; and because it is a State Paper, any citizen may well inquire what they could have been.

A straw is worth something as a wind-gage. In some states the minds of men are so possessed by party spirit, that, in the canvass for votes, and the rush for office, the interests of Public Charitable Institutions are usually disregarded, and sometimes even ruthlessly sacrificed. In Massachusetts, such establishments have, time out of mind, been considered as near akin to religious ones, and therefore held sacred. But there are lamentable signs that even this saving virtue is to be lost in the old Commonwealth. The taint of the harpy's foot is perceived, even in our sacred places. Would that your Excellency, as a young man and as a reformer, would see to it that the taint does not spread!

Thus far, I have dwelt only upon the faults of commission in this Veto. There are great ones of omission also.

Hostile to the Spirit of Humanity

It is a State Paper which touches the action of the Commonwealth upon a question of humanity. Its effect is to stem that tide of feeling in favor of the unfortunate, which has been slowly but steadily rising and spreading among the people, and moving them to a wise and generous system of relief. It is the first public protest against continuance in that system, and yet it has no word of sorrow for the necessity of a change.

It is a State paper which touches the condition and prospects of more than a thousand hapless persons in our borders, all of them, in one sense, "little children," whom the State should suffer to come nigh unto her, and the Governor forbid them not,—but surely not without some kindly word of sympathy. The Veto, however, has no such word of sympathy for them. True, the poor creatures are unconscious of their sad infirmity, but its shadow darkens a thousand humble households, where little of sunshine ever comes, and which little the spirit of this Veto would make less.

Finally, it is a State paper which urges a rich and growing Commonwealth to retrenchment of expenses, but shows no consciousness of the moral obliquity she would manifest in leaving unlessened a score of extravagances, and beginning her retrenchment with her "charity fund."

When a rich and noble man is forced to curtail his expenses, he first cuts down his allowance for luxuries, next his allowance for the comforts of life, but never lessens that for religious and charitable purposes, until he can give a reason to God and his conscience for so doing. And shall the State be less noble than her noblest son?

I have done what I proposed to do with regard to this extraordinary State paper.

I have shown that it is hostile to the spirit of humanity and of Christian charity which characterizes our beloved State; that it abounds in errors, and leads to false inferences; that every material paragraph contains at least one misstatement; that these could not have been made if the Report upon which they seem based had been examined with care and candor; that your Excellency has not shown interest enough in the School for Idiots to obey the law which requires you to inspect it; and that your Veto breathes a spirit which, if caught by the Legislature, would not only crush that Institution, but injure other charitable establishments.

I have done what seemed a duty, though an unpleasant one. I have striven to do it in a proper and respectful manner, though I confess that it has not been easy to keep down all indignation, when thinking of those unfortunates who cannot think or act for themselves, and some signs of it may have escaped me.

I have the honor to be, with due consideration,

Your Excellency's Obd't Serv't,

S. G. HOWE.

2.
President's Address: First Annual Meeting of the International Council for Exceptional Children*

ELIZABETH E. FARRELL

What group of exceptional children seemed neglected to the first president of the International Council for Exceptional Children?

This is the first annual meeting of the International Council for the Education of Exceptional Children. The formation of this organization is a cause for congratulation on the part of those who look forward to the day when public education will again become a matter of the education of individuals and will cease to be a part of the vast factory system which characterizes our civilization, in education as in other things.

The International Council was formed in August of last year, by teachers who were students in the Summer School of Teachers College, Columbia University, and whose work was in the field of special education. In the Department of Special Education that summer about two hundred teachers representing practically every state in the union and five foreign countries joined in the organization meeting. When the word went out that a professional body of teachers interested in the teaching of exceptional children had been brought together, applications for membership were made by school administrators, superintendents, supervisors, school board members and others to the number of approximately five hundred.

It is reasonable to ask whether it is necessary to organize another professional group of teachers. With the National Education Association representing the professional teachers of the country, it might be thought undesirable to multiply organizations. The fact is that no organization

From *Proceedings of the First Annual Meeting of the International Council for the Education of Exceptional Children* (Cleveland, Ohio, 26-27 February, 1923), pp. 3-9. Reprinted by permission of the Council for Exceptional Children.

*The word "international" was dropped from the title of the Council in 1956 as explained in the introduction. The Council was organized in the summer of 1922 by teachers who were enrolled in special education classes at Teachers College, Columbia University, under the direction of Elizabeth Farrell, supervisor of ungraded classes in the New York City schools. The Council now has a membership of over 40,000, including 13,000 students majoring in special education from 200 colleges and universities. There are over 800 local chapters throughout the United States and Canada. The Council has recently organized The Foundation for Exceptional Children, a nonprofit organization designed to promote research and innovative programs and to protect the legal, educational, and human rights of children.

which exists meets the need that we in the field of special education feel. Teachers in training believe that a special organization is essential. Such matters as these will come up for discussion: Shall gifted children be advanced rapidly through the grades or shall they have an enriched curriculum? Shall the factor of maturity and social fitness be taken into consideration in promoting pupils, as well as their intellectual capacity? Shall gifted children be taught by the same methods as other children or is there a more scientific method of approach?

Can dull and defective children learn academic work, or shall their training be mainly motor? It is commonly believed that they cannot learn to manipulate the symbols of knowledge. Yet we all know dull and defective children who do learn to read and spell and do arithmetic. Their ability to do work of this kind is stimulated by teachers who know something of the genetic character of modern courses of study, teachers who know that the academic work we offer to children is really the result of somebody's actual experience. It seems certain that dull or defective children can develop to the full measure of their mental ability in fields other than the field covered by motor training. It will be the business of the International Council to throw light on this subject.

If it is necessary to justify further the existence of this organization, it can easily be justified by the wave of enthusiasm that is sweeping the schools of this country because of the intelligent work of the clinical psychologists. As a result of their work, it is possible to make closer and more accurate classification of school children. Instead of having children classified on the basis of chronological age, it is now possible, because of the work of psychologists, to classify children on the basis of their ability to learn. In all progressive schools, classes for gifted children as well as classes for stupid children are being organized.

The efforts of sociologists and child welfare workers have convinced the public that children should not be sent to institutions for this education. This has made it necessary to make different provisions for the deaf and the blind. Therefore, in progressive school systems, provision is made for the deaf child who formerly was obliged to leave the protecting care of his family and live in an institutional school, if he was to be able to manage life with the handicap of deafness. This is true, also, of the blind child.

The feebleminded child previous to the work of the clinical psychologist was thought to be an improvable person whose development could be effected, if at all, in institutions for the feebleminded. The pre-delinquent child was treated in much the same way. The House of Refuge, the Protectory, the Reform School, were the institutions of learning to which he was sent.

With the growth of scientific knowledge, the institutional care of children with special handicaps seemed to be unnecessary. The organization of the Crane School for the Deaf in Chicago is one of the early steps in providing special education in public schools for exceptional children. The

McCormick Open Air School in the same city is one of the latest steps taken in this special field. Now we have in all of our larger cities, special schools or special classes for the blind, the deaf, the tubercular, the undernourished, the cardiac and other types of children who, in one way or another, vary from the normal in their physical makeup.

The greatest advance in the organization of special classes has been made for those children whose intellectual power is markedly below the average required in the regular graded school as it is organized at present. Early in the development of this particular branch, we find Springfield, Massachusetts, Providence, Rhode Island, Cleveland, Ohio, Chicago and New York pointing out the way.

In the days of Seguin it was thought necessary to segregate in special institutions children who were feebleminded. The result of this segregation was the entire neglect of children suffering from minor degrees of intellectual inferiority. Only the obvious cases of mental deficiency could be recognized. This is evidenced in the names given to institutions for children of this type. They were called idiot asylums, asylums for idiots and imbeciles. Such places harbored children whose inferiority was very marked. Because of this segregation in special institutions, society in general established wrong attitudes and developed wrong ideas about this group. The kindness in human nature and not the intelligence of human nature seems to have characterized the attitude of society toward these unfortunate children. Prevalent ideas were that they could be sheltered only; that no useful function could be served by them; that they were to be happy at whatever cost.

When the epoch-making work of Binet was given to the world in 1904, educators were given a measuring rod which proved in a new way that children are different. This measuring rod made it possible to determine the mental age of a child. This mental age really determines what a child can do rather than the chronological age which was formerly the criterion. Binet proved that the difference in children was one of degree and not of kind as Seguin had thought. He proved that the feebleminded were not a different species but were merely less gifted in intellectual power than the average person.

The work of Terman and others in the field of clinical psychology has perfected the work of Binet. They have made it possible for us to determine with more than a fair degree of accuracy, the intellectual power of any individual. The result of this work has served to point out to school administrators that between the average child who is able to do the work of a given grade and the idiot, there is a vast army of children varying in infinite degree in their ability to accomplish satisfactorily the work of the traditional school. It has become a part of our professional jargon to refer to the dull normal, the borderline, the moron as well as the imbecile and idiot. With this increase in knowledge has come a change in our attitude toward this group, toward its usefulness, toward its training and toward its right to educational opportunity of the kind demanded by the intellectual power that characterizes it. The clinical psychologists have shown us that the difference between individuals, is a difference in degree of power and not a difference in kind of power. Since this is true, educational training must be designed to meet individual differences. With scientific data at hand, school authorities are no longer justified in providing a standardized course to be completed in a standardized period of time by all the children in the community.

Besides pointing out to educators that children at the low end of the scale have not the ability to do the work prepared for average children, psychologists have also shown us that children at the high end of the scale differ in ways that are just as remarkable, and that, because of such differences, they too need a course of study which differs in essential particulars from that offered to the average group. We have, therefore, in very recent years, organized special classes for children who differ in physical makeup and special classes for children who differ in mental makeup.

The third group of children, those who are anti-social or who show a tendency in this direction, are still to be considered. The anti-social tendency suggested by truancy is one to which school authorities have already given some attention. In a large number of states the law requires the establishment and maintenance of parental or truant schools. Up to the present time, the children who find a place in such schools have been selected because of non-attendance at school. Little thought has been given to the reason for this non-attendance. Perhaps this statement is a trifle broad. Perhaps a desirable modification would be to say that in the large majority of cases, non-attendance has been blamed upon the home. This attitude is changing. We are now beginning to blame non-attendance upon the school. There are today teachers who look forward to the time when school officials in all matters of non-attendance will question first the school opportunity given to the child. It is not too much to say that in a great majority of cases children are truant from school because the school they attend does not bring them the satisfaction of achievement which is necessary for each one of us to feel if we are to persist in the work at hand.

Truancy must be considered as a by-product of school organization. School administrators must give the same kind of attention to this by-product that captains of industry give to the by-products in their special fields. When you recall that the richest factor in the coal mining industry is the utilization of the by-products of that industry, which a few years ago were discarded, it is not too much to say that education will repeat this experience, and that the human wealth in the community will be greatly increased as we train to usefulness and constructive endeavor the children who are truants, who are incorrigible, who are the obvious failures of our school system.

Such changes in education demand and rest upon a professional staff of trained and skilled teachers. Our great universities and teaching centers have already undertaken the training necessary in the field of special education. Harvard University offered the first university course for the training of teachers of blind children. New York University, Columbia University, The University of Toronto and the University of California were quick in their appreciation of the needs of such teachers. Courses that provide the scientific background for special education are now offered in many universities. Large numbers of teachers are studying the psychology of exceptional children; neurology; the measurement of intelligence; abnormal psychology and similar subjects. Such study relates to education as a science. But education is an art as well as a science and in this phase of study the teacher finds less offered by the universities.

While it is true that atypical children learn in the same way as do average children, yet it is also true that success in teaching certain children to read, for example, is dependent upon having at hand for use, material so organized that the individual idiosyncrasies in the learning abilities of children may be used to their advantage. Such organization of subject-matter and such technique of teaching is part of the art of teaching. Universities and training centers for teachers in the field of special education must provide opportunity for teachers to see and practice teaching as an art. Opportunity must be given also for such teachers to cultivate in themselves the art of teaching.

The International Council for the Education of Exceptional Children will be the clearing house of knowledge useful to teachers in their special fields. The Council will be for teachers the authoritative body on questions of subject-matter, method and school or class organization. At its annual meeting it hopes to present ideas proved to be useful in the training of exceptional children. The Council hopes to stimulate the teaching of children at least to the extent that psychologists have stimulated classification on the basis of intellectual power. The Council will stand back of its membership in demanding high professional qualifications for those designated to serve in its fields. It will demand freedom for its members as practitioners. It will promote the idea that educational work, whether in institutions or in public day schools, must be in the hands of and directed by men and women trained in the science and the art of education. It will demand as a super-structure on this foundation professional training in the particular field which attracts the worker. The training of children, the Council believes, is not a by-product of any other profession. It cannot be carried on successfully and economically except by those who have been trained.

The Council seeks the cooperation of allied sciences and professions. It is hoped that a Year Book will be published. This will depend upon our financial condition and upon the nature of the information to be published.

The organization of the International Council for the Education of Exceptional Children is a significant event. With modesty and great humility all its members accept the responsibilities of their calling. They hope that because of their efforts public education in this country will become less machine-made and more individual; that the schools of this country will use the ability of each pupil group to its maximum; that the school will fit its burden to the back which bears it; that it will bring the opportunity of successful achievement to every child. In doing this it will make of the weakest of our brothers a useful unit in the social fabric. It will return to the community human wealth now beyond our power to reckon.

Elizabeth E. Farrell was director of undergraduate classes of New York City Schools and was the summer session instructor at Teachers College, Columbia, of the two classes from which most of the founders of the Council were selected.

3.
Breakthrough for the Handicapped: Legislative History
EDWIN W. MARTIN, JR.

Room EF 100, in the East Front of the Capitol, is in a political sense, "no man's land." Near the Rotunda and between the House and Senate wings, belonging to neither body, it would be dissected by a line through the middle of the Capitol. In keeping with the formal ritual which is so much a part of the legislative branch, there are separate entrances into each end of the room along the rear wall so that Senators and Representatives can enter and leave through distinct passages in the direction of their chambers. In fact, however, most legislators enter through the double doors in the center of the wall nearest the middle of the Capitol. The separate exits are more likely to serve the practical rather than ritualistic rite of ducking an ardent persuader sitting in the lobby on benches near the main doors.

Twice in the less than 14 months between late October, 1966, and December 15, 1967, members of the House and Senate committees responsible for educational legislation came to Room EF 100 to form a conference committee. These conferees were charged with resolving differences in the 1966 and 1967 Elementary and Secondary Education Act amendments which, among their many purposes, promised to change dramatically the course of education for handicapped children in the United States.

The Senate conferees, led both years by the chairman of their Education Subcommittee, Oregon Senator Wayne Morse, and the House conferees, led by the chairmen of the Education and Labor Committee (in 1966, New York Representative Adam Clayton Powell; in 1967, Kentucky

---

From *Exceptional Children* 34 (March, 1968): 493-503. Reprinted by permission of the author and *Exceptional Children*. Copyrighted by the Council for Exceptional Children.

Representative Carl Perkins), faced the complex task of resolving conflicting aspects of their respective versions of the same bill. In many instances, these involved complex distribution formulas and changes affecting the basic nature of programs. Inseparably bonded to these conflicts were powerful emotional and political factors, such as church-state issues, civil rights, state's rights, school busing, etc. In this context, amendments affecting the lives of the minority group known as handicapped children attracted little attention from the press. People vitally interested in the education of handicapped children, certain members of the conference committee and their staffs, professional groups and their members, and persons operating programs within the government which serve these children, worked, watched, waited, hoped, and eventually exulted over what they knew were major breakthroughs for handicapped children.

The breakthroughs of 1966 and 1967 were the high points of the legislative accomplishments of almost a decade, and of efforts toward these accomplishments of many people over a much longer period of time. The following sections present reports on the development of this federal legislation affecting education for handicapped children and reports on some of the factors which were integral to its development (See Table 1).

The First Step

PL 83-531—THE COOPERATIVE RESEARCH ACT

The 531st Bill to be approved by the 83rd Congress and the President, thereby earning for itself the label "Act," was signed by President Eisenhower on July 26, 1954. It was described as "an act to authorize cooperative research in education," and it made provisions for a program of grants to be given to institutions of higher learning and to the states providing for cooperative support of educational research, surveys, and demonstrations, and for the dissemination of information derived from educational research.

One indicator of the attitudes toward federal aid to education held at that time may be found in the fact that this Act remained unfunded until 1957. That year, of the $1 million appropriated, $675,000 was earmarked to be spent on research related to education of the mentally retarded. This action of the Congressional Appropriation Committees set into being a research program which, with the help of some timely transfusions, is still alive. It also represented the first sign of recognition by Congress of the need for categorical aid for the education of handicapped children since the beginning of federal support for Gallaudet College in 1864 and the American Printing House for the Blind in 1879. In contrast to later programs initiated by new authorizing legislation, this research program was initiated through the Appropriations Committees directing the use of general funds for educational research into this specific area. The support of key men on the Appropriations Committees, particularly the late Representative John E. Fogarty from Rhode Island and Senator Lister Hill of Alabama, was to be an essential factor in almost every phase of the latter development of education legislation benefiting handicapped children.

PL 85-905—CAPTIONED FILMS FOR THE DEAF

On September 2, 1958, "An Act to provide in the Department of Health, Education, and Welfare for a loan service of captioned films for the deaf" was signed into law. The Captioned Films program was primarily aimed at the cultural enrichment and recreation of deaf persons, although its educational implications were apparent. Its passage in 1958 was another evidence of increasing concern on the part of the government for the welfare of handicapped persons. However, the greatest contributions of this program to the sequence of development of educational legislation were to come from later amendments in 1962 and 1965 (PL 87-715 and PL 89-258). These amendments broadened this program into an amazingly flexible and productive comprehensive instructional media program for the deaf, involving research and development, production, acquisition, distribution, and training of teachers to use media. This successful program provided a model for legislation in 1967, extending these benefits to all handicapped children requiring special education.

PL 85-926—TRAINING OF PROFESSIONAL PERSONNEL

In its statement of purpose, PL 85-926 was "to encourage expansion of teaching in the education of mentally retarded children through grants to institutions of higher learning and to state educational agencies." Aimed primarily at training professional personnel who would, in turn, train teachers to work with mentally retarded children, PL 85-926 was perhaps the most significant of the early legislative accomplishments.

Research in education of the retarded had begun to receive support during the previous year under the general provisions of the Cooperative Research Act, but continuing support under this program was not definite, as later events were to prove. Captioned Films for the Deaf, signed four days earlier, was not primarily an educational act; its main thrust was recreational and cultural.

PL 85-926 was developed in the Congress at the same time the National Defense Education Act was under study, and they were signed by the President within a week of each other. NDEA was the landmark legislation which established federal support for individuals pursuing higher education. It established a precedent which almost simultaneously was elaborated upon by PL 85-926 to offer categorical support for education of the handicapped. With this new authority, the pace of legislative support quickened.

PL 87-276—TEACHERS OF THE DEAF

During the 87th Congress the next step was taken with the approval of a new Act which authorized support for training teachers of the deaf.

Whereas the earlier mental retardation program focused on leadership personnel, this program appealed to Congress because of its emphasis on classroom teachers. With the establishment of programs of support for training in the areas of mental retardation and the deaf (including a spread of support from undergraduate trainees through leadership training), the momentum gathered strength for the expansion of this training authority to include other major areas of handicapping conditions requiring special education. Each new building block made the wall stronger and provided a base for new construction.

Throughout the struggle to gain passage for these programs, the forces interested in this legislation continued to grow in strength and experience. Members of Congress who were sympathetic and influential were enlisted in the cause. CEC and other groups dedicated to serving handicapped children stirred their memberships to work with the Congress. They provided testimony and other information necessary for legislative study and, above all, urged support for the new bills. Philosophical differences had to be set aside, at least temporarily, as in the instance of "oral" and "manual" groups interested in deaf education uniting behind PL 87-276.

Most importantly, handicapped children had help from people with professional expertise in legislation, who recognized that special programs were necessary, and who knew how to help them. Key members among these professionals were Patria Winalski Forsythe of the Department of Health, Education, and Welfare; Jack Forsythe, Charles Lee, and Roy Millenson, professional staff of the Senate Labor and Public Welfare Committee; and Russell Derrickson, Robert McCord, and Charles Radcliffe of the House Education Committee staff. Attempts to list key figures in developing legislation will inevitably leave out too many people who have played important roles, yet it would be inaccurate in even the briefest account to fail to identify these usually anonymous people who as resources have provided strength for legislation for handicapped children. Frequently legislation needs powerful support, financially or in numbers of affected voters in order to win approval. Legislation for the handicapped has had to succeed primarily on its basic appeal for compassion, and on the efforts of its expert friends.

The momentum established as these first programs were developed, the growing strength of the "legislation for education of the handicapped team," plus the heightened public interest in handicapped children stimulated by President Kennedy, set the stage for the next phase of development.

Public Law 88-164 and the Division of Handicapped Children and Youth

I am glad to announce at this time that we are establishing a division in the US Office of Education to administer the teaching and research programs under this Act. This will be called the Division of Handicapped Children and Youth.

With these words, President Kennedy signed PL 88-164, and programs for education of the handicapped reached an administrative high water mark. The Division brought together in one unit the Captioned Films program, an expanded teacher training program, and the new research program in education of the handicapped established by PL 88-164. Dr. Samuel A. Kirk was chosen by the President to establish the Division.

A history of legislation concerning education of the handicapped must inevitably involve, to some extent, the administrative structures charged with the operation of programs. This is true because of the traditional governmental response to new programs—that is, a new program begets a new administrative unit. There is almost a one to one correlation between the level of the administrative unit formed and the degree to which the program is valued by the administration establishing it. (This pattern has been readily perceived by Congress, and upon occasion the legislative branch has indicated its interest in a program by creating, by statute, an administrative structure at the level it feels appropriate. One example, of course, is the Bureau of Education for the Handicapped, to be discussed later.) This pattern had been borne out by the development of programs in the area of special education which, by one name or another, had been a part of the Office of Education since its earliest days. For most of those years, special education was a one or two person program primarily charged with gathering and disseminating information. These programs were frequently located near the bottom of the administrative hierarchy. The first significant change in that pattern had come with the initiation of the professional training and Captioned Films programs when, for the first time, Office of Education personnel had the authority to disburse money as part of their attempt to assist in the development of educational programs for the handicapped. The financial resources increased OE's prestige and impact on the professions involved. A new division, second only to a Bureau in the Office of Education hierarchy, brought new strength and significance to the programs for which it was responsible.

PL 88-164, SECTION 301—TRAINING PROFESSIONAL PERSONNEL

Section 301 of the Mental Retardation Facilities and Community Mental Health Centers Construction Act of 1963 amended PL 85-926. It combined the earlier training authorities for professional personnel in the areas of retardation and deafness, and authorized grants to institutions of higher education and to state education agencies. Under the new definitions of this section, personnel could be trained to provide special education, speech correction, and related services to handicapped children, i.e., "mentally retarded, hard of hearing, deaf, speech impaired, visually handicapped, seriously emotionally disturbed, crippled or other health impaired children, who by reason thereof, require special education."

The basic training legislation, PL 85-926, has been amended twice since its major revision by PL 88-164. In each case, the amendments have extended and increased the authorizations for training personnel, but have not changed the nature of the proven program. The most recent change in authority was enacted as part of the 1967 Mental Retardation Amendments, PL 90-170. In this legislation, the authorization was extended through Fiscal Year 1970, and increased to $55 million. Congressional support for this vital program has been based on recognition of its effectiveness. Since its beginning, more than 32,000 awards have been made to support individuals on full or part time study.

PL 88-164, SECTION 302—RESEARCH AND DEMONSTRATION PROJECTS IN EDUCATION OF HANDICAPPED CHILDREN

This legislation authorized the Commissioner of Education to make grants for research and demonstration projects relating to education for handicapped children to

States, State or local education agencies, public and nonprofit institutions of higher learning, and other public or nonprofit educational or research agencies and organizations.

Later in 1965, PL 89-105 added to this authority a section permitting the construction, equipping, and operation of facilities for research and related purposes, including demonstrations, dissemination activities, and training of research personnel.

The necessity for a special research program with its own funds, specifically aimed at education of the handicapped, was demonstrated by the declining support for mental retardation under the Cooperative Research Act. In 1957, 61 percent of funds spent under this Act were spent in the area of retardation. In 1958, the amount was 54 percent. The following year the "earmarking" was removed, and by 1961, only 9 percent of the funds were being spent on projects in the retardation area. By 1963, the percentage was down to 5 (Kirk, 1966).

The message that categorical legislation was necessary to protect the interests of handicapped children was once more reinforced, and the research provisions of PL 88-164 came into being. The demonstrated operational effectiveness of the resulting program and its creative leadership has led to the rapid growth of support from $1 million authorized in 1964 to $18 million authorized for 1970.

REORGANIZATION

Eighteen months after the Division of Handicapped Children and Youth was formed in July, 1965, it was disbanded, caught in USOE's overall reorganization which had been brought about by the giant new responsibilities which accompanied passage of the Elementary and Secondary Education Act of 1965. This action was no reflection on the Division or its leaders, Samuel Kirk and his successor Morvin Wirtz. In fact, under their leadership, the Division received a Presidential citation and a superior service

Table 1. BASIC FEDERAL LEGISLATION FOR EDUCATION OF THE HANDICAPPED, 1957–1967

YEAR	AUTHORITY	PURPOSE
1957	PL 83-531. Cooperative Research	Action of the Appropriations Committee earmarked for the retarded approximately 2/3 of the $1 million appropriated.
1958	PL 85-905. Captioned Films	A program of captioning films for cultural enrichment and recreation of deaf persons.
	PL 85-926. Professional Personnel	Grants for training leadership personnel in education of the mentally retarded.
1959	PL 86-158. Professional Personnel	Added authorization for support grants to institutions of higher learning.
1961	PL 87-276. Teachers of the Deaf	Grants for training basic instructional personnel in education of the deaf.
	PL 87-715. Captioned Films	Provided for the production and distribution of films.
1963	PL 88-164, Section 301. Professional Personnel	Expanded authority to train personnel for handicapping conditions not previously covered; "hard of hearing, speech impaired, visually handicapped, seriously emotionally disturbed, crippled, or other health impaired," were added to mentally retarded and deaf.
	PL 88-164, Section 302. Research and Demonstration	Grants for research and demonstration projects in the area of education of the handicapped.
1965	PL 89-36. National Technical Institute for the Deaf	Created a new source for higher education for the deaf.
	PL 89-105. Professional Personnel and Research	Extended basic authorities, allowed development of research and demonstration centers.
	PL 89-258. Captioned Films	Expanded authority, allowed development and distribution of other media and equipment in addition to films.
	PL 89-313. State Schools	Amended Title I, ESEA to provide grants to states for children in state operated or supported schools for the handicapped.
1966	PL 89-694. Model Secondary School for the Deaf	Created a model high school in Washington, D.C.
	PL 89-750. Education of Handicapped Children (Title VI, ESEA)	Grants to states for preschool, elementary, and secondary school children; National Advisory Committee; Bureau of Education for the Handicapped.
1967	PL 90-170. Mental Retardation Amendments of 1967	Extended basic training authority, added new authority for training personnel and for research in area of physical education and recreation for handicapped children.
	PL 90-247. Amendments to Title VI, ESEA	Regional Resource Centers; Centers for Deaf Blind Children; expansion of Media Services; grants for Recruitment and Information dissemination; earmarking 15 percent Title III of ESEA for handicapped children; intramural research and contracts for research; increased funds for state schools; changes in Title VI grants-to-states formula and authorizations.

award from the Secretary of Health, Education, and Welfare. (Kirk's leaving the Office of Education to return to Illinois after he completed his agreed upon stay has been immortalized in the classic pun of Representative Hugh L. Carey, Chairman of the Ad Hoc Subcommittee on the Handicapped, who told the 1966 Convention of The Council for Exceptional Children that it was a "case of separation of Kirk and State.")

Special education, the minority group, had once more been caught in the philosophy of the greatest good for the greatest number. Under the new organization, the programs for training, research, and Captioned Films were placed in separate administrative units. Programs continued to be operated as effectively as possible, but attempts to coordinate were not always successful and, in general, the new administrative structure seemed to dissipate the sense of active leadership in the national effort to improve education for the handicapped. While creation of the Elementary and Secondary Education Act indirectly contributed to a plateau in the growth of federal support for education of the handicapped in the administrative dimension, its programs did provide new support. In addition, its passage added new strength to the momentum of federal aid for education and to the concept of categorical aid for minority groups.

THE GREAT CONGRESS—FIRST SESSION 1965

The 89th Congress felt strongly that it had a mandate from the people to enact into law the major goals of the Kennedy and Johnson administrations. President Johnson had received 61 percent of the votes in his election the previous November, the highest percentage of votes received by any President. There were strong majorities in both houses of Congress, and the time had come to face what the President called "our ancient enemies, illiteracy, disease, poverty, and bigotry."

Of the many programs developed and approved by the Congress and the Administration—programs aimed at the cities, at the aged ("medicare"), etc.—none outranked in brilliance the Elementary and Secondary Education Act of 1965, PL 89-10. Its final passage, with its programs of assistance to children in disadvantaged areas (including handicapped children), new instructional materials, centers for innovation and research, and support for strengthening state educational agencies, was precedent shattering not only in its educational implications, but also in the brilliance of its legislative drafting and strategy which succeeded in overcoming the traditional barriers to federal aid to education.

PL 89-313—AID FOR EDUCATION OF HANDICAPPED CHILDREN
IN STATE OPERATED INSTITUTIONS

As ESEA became implemented, children with handicapping conditions shared in its benefits. Projects under Title I reached handicapped children in low income areas through local education agencies. Title III provided support for some excellent new programs under its provisions for supplemental centers and its support for innovative programs. Provisions from the other titles also offered some help. It was apparent, however, that the basic thrust of ESEA was toward the economically disadvantaged or the general educational community, and that more direct sources of support for the handicapped would be necessary.

On November 1, 1965, a major step was taken toward this goal through a provision of PL 89-313. While this law was primarily concerned with school construction assistance in major disaster areas, Section 6 of that Act amended Title I of ESEA to provide support to state agencies which were directly responsible for educating handicapped children. Until this amendment, Title I worked through local educational agencies; thus, state operated or supported schools for the deaf, retarded, etc., which were not a part of a local school district, were not eligible for Title I benefits.

This provision has had a profound impact on the educational programs in schools and institutions for the handicapped, by providing new teachers, equipment, supplemental personnel, diagnostic facilities, etc. In numerous cases, children who had been receiving only custodial care began to participate for the first time in educational training.

In addition to its educational implications, the PL 89-313 amendment may be seen as another precedent, a building block toward the total construction of categorical aid for education of handicapped children. As early legislation for training teachers of the retarded and deaf led to broader authorities, so this provision for educational services to institutionalized children paved the way toward broader provisions of service to children in day schools.

PL 89-36—THE NATIONAL TECHNICAL INSTITUTE FOR THE DEAF ACT

The great educational challenge presented by deafness, the effectiveness of people interested in this area, and the success of the training and Captioned Films programs, all have combined to develop a special awareness and receptivity in Congress for educational programs benefiting the deaf. This favorable attitude has been an important component in the expansion of programs to include other areas of handicapping conditions.

For 100 years, Gallaudet College in Washington, D.C., has been the only institution in the world designed specifically to provide post-secondary education for the deaf. While Gallaudet's liberal arts program has won plaudits from educators around the world for its successes, modern society increasingly calls for people with technical and professional training. This need, coupled with declining employment possibilities for the deaf, was documented by national conferences and workshops, the Babbidge report (Advisory Committee on Education of the Deaf, 1965) to the Secretary of Health, Education, and Welfare, and by Congressional hearings.

On June 8, 1965, President Johnson signed the National Technical Institute for the Deaf Act (PL 89-36) authorizing the Secretary of Health, Education, and Welfare to enter into an agreement with an institution of higher education for the establishment and operation of a postsecondary technical training facility for young deaf adults. This agreement had subsequently been made with the Rochester Institute of Technology, in New York.

With these new programs and an expansion and extension of the authorities for the Captioned Films, training, and research programs, the first session of the 89th Congress closed. It was a session which produced new programs, extended authorities, and strengthened momentum, thus setting the stage for the next major era.

The Carey Committee and Title VI, ESEA

In the spring of 1966, Congress decided it was time to take a closer look at federal programs for education of the handicapped, to consolidate gains, and to build a foundation for the future. Representative Hugh L. Carey of Brooklyn, New York, was named Chairman of a Special Ad Hoc Subcommittee on the Handicapped of the House Committee on Education and Labor. A similar House of Representatives Study Committee headed by Congressman Carl Elliott of Alabama, had held nationwide hearings in 1959 and 1960, and while no legislation was forthcoming in that session of Congress, many of the items discussed became part of later Acts. Representative Carey, a prime mover in the development of ESEA, had been a supporter of programs for the handicapped, taking an active part in introducing and gaining passage of PL 89-313 and the National Technical Institute, among other programs.

For a total of nine months, the Carey Committee examined the situation, hearing witnesses from federal programs, professional groups, and state and local agencies. Over 1,000 printed pages of testimony and supplemental information comprised the record of this examination. By August the pattern was clear, and on August 4, 1966, Mr. Carey introduced the Handicapped Child Benefit and Education Act (HR 16847). Following the pattern of ESEA, it provided for grants to the states for education of children in the elementary and secondary schools, grants for the purchase of instructional materials, support for innovative programs, and policies to strengthen state departments in the special education area. In addition, it proposed: (a) expansion of the Captioned Films for the Deaf program to include development and distribution of instructional materials for all types of handicapped children; (b) new programs for recruitment and distribution of information; (c) expansion of research and training authorities; (d) a Statutory National Advisory Committee on Education of the Handicapped; and (e) as a central organizing force, a new Bureau within the US Office of Education specifically for education of the handicapped.

Although this bill was received by the professions with great enthusiasm and anticipation, it was not slated to be passed. Of the thousands of bills introduced each year, only a relatively few pass through the hurdles of subcommittee and committee hearings, debate on the floor before the full House or Senate, and reconciliation of differences by a joint conference committee, to achieve final approval by each House. Among the many factors which influence the fate of a bill, perhaps the most critical is whether or not the Administration approves it, not only in concept, but in timing. Is it a planned part of the President's budget? How much will it cost? These are important practical factors to be weighed, in addition to careful analysis of its ingredients from the program operation point of view.

While the interest of the Administration in education of the handicapped was clear, the combination of cost and timing factors soon made it obvious that while the concept was approved (with the exception of the statutory bureau), the time was not ripe for full scale approval of the Carey Bill. However, within 15 months, every major feature of the Carey Bill had become part of the law, passed as amendments to the Elementary and Secondary Education Act.

PL 89-694—THE MODEL SECONDARY SCHOOL FOR THE DEAF ACT

In its study of federal programs for the handicapped, the Carey Subcommittee was struck by the report that there was not a single high school in the country for deaf children which was comparable in quality to a first class high school for hearing children.

This fact was especially impressive in light of the recent passage of the National Technical Institute for the Deaf legislation. In addition, Gallaudet College authorities testified that only 8 per cent of deaf children attended college, as compared with over 40 percent of hearing children, and they pointed to inadequate high school education as a major factor.

Representative Carey and Senator Hill introduced and gained passage for legislation which created a Model Secondary School for the Deaf, which would be built on the campus of Gallaudet College and would serve children from the District of Columbia and nearby states. The school was planned to serve sufficient numbers of children in order to offer a full curriculum and the normal extracurricular activities of high schools. The success of this model may pave the way for future schools in varying regions of the country.

PL 89-750—TITLE VI: EDUCATION FOR HANDICAPPED CHILDREN

When it had become apparent that the Carey bill would not be able to gain Congressional approval, the House had already passed its version of the Elementary and Secondary Education Act Amendments of 1966, but the Morse Subcommittee on Education of the Senate Committee on Labor and Public Welfare was just beginning its study. When that subcommittee finished its deliberations and reported the 1966 ESEA amendments, Senator Morse had successfully added a new Title VI, Education of Handicapped Children. As part of the total ESEA package, its chances of at least partial success were excellent.

The new Title proposed a program of grants to the states for the initiation, expansion, and improvement of programs for educating handicapped children in preschool, elementary, and secondary schools. It proposed to set up a national advisory committee on handicapped children for the

Commissioner of Education, and it called for the creation of a bureau within the US Office of Education to provide coordination and leadership for programs affecting handicapped children. This proposal to create a bureau became the center of controversy.

The Carey hearings had brought into focus the feeling among professionals that programs for the handicapped had suffered since the dissolution of the Division of Handicapped Children and Youth. Some of the most colorful aspects of the Carey hearings revolved around differences in philosophy between those setting policy for programs in the Office of Education and the Committee Chairman, whose beliefs had practically unanimous support from people in the professional fields involved. The Senate Committee's studies reinforced support for a new bureau.

Administration resistance to the bureau centered around three factors: (a) its statutory nature overruled a usual prerogative of the Executive Branch to plan its own administrative structure; (b) it could possibly set a precedent for the establishment of bureaus for other special interest or minority groups within education; and (c) it would take the research in education of the handicapped program out of the Bureau of Research, thereby undoing the organizational pattern of the Office of Education in which all research activities were under this one structure.

And so the stage was set for the first Conference Committee meeting which was referred to at the opening of this article. If the bureau was not going to be accepted by the conferees, the US Office of Education would probably establish a new division, but in all likelihood the program of research in education of handicapped children would remain in the Bureau of Research. With a new bureau, education of the handicapped would reach full parity with the other programs of the US Office of Education and, for the first time, specialists in education of the handicapped would be at top policy making levels within the Office. There was debate. At the end of the first day of the conference, the general impression was that the bureau was out of consideration, but when the conference ended, Title VI was intact. Senator Morse made a strong statement on the floor of the Senate calling for quick action to establish the program. Within two months, the bureau was established by Commissioner of Education, Harold Howe, II.

The 1967 Legislative Package

In the jam packed first months of the Bureau's operation, the logistics of transferring people, selecting the new Associate Commissioner who in turn selected his staff, the beginning of the new Title VI grant programs, and all the necessary and intricate demands of a continuing government program tended to obscure temporarily the significance of the new legislative proposals which would be part of the Administration's suggestions for 1967 amendments to ESEA. The great excitement of the previous year's hearings and the creation of Title VI and the new Bureau threatened to make new programs slightly anticlimactic.

This perspective was not shared by Bureau personnel and the HEW and Congressional legislative experts who had been developing legislation for the handicapped year by year. The Administration's proposed program to: (a) develop regional resource centers; (b) to provide support for recruitment of personnel and dissemination of information; and (c) to expand the target group of the Captioned Films program, were seen as a heightened commitment to education of the handicapped. Almost all of the previous legislation had been stimulated by Congress, not suggested by the Executive Branch. In addition, there seemed to be a readiness in Congress to move forward from last year's achievements. Congressional support in both Houses was bipartisan, Democrats and Republicans alike expressing interest in providing equal educational opportunity for every handicapped child.

The Education and Labor Committee in the House quickly approved these new provisions for the handicapped, and the bill moved to the Senate for consideration.

The bill that emerged from the Senate Committee, was approved by the full Senate, and went to the House-Senate Conference, included not only these Administration provisions, but added new ones. In all, it was the broadest program of benefits for the education of the handicapped ever to reach this legislative stage. Its provisions would affect every facet of the program of the Bureau of Education for the Handicapped: manpower, research, media, and direct support for children in the schools. In summary, it provided for the following:

1. *Regional Resource Centers.* These centers would assist teachers and other school personnel by providing education evaluation and assistance in developing specific educational programs and strategies. While providing direct services to children and parents, the basic aim of the resource centers would be to work with teachers in meeting the extraordinary challenges presented by handicapped children.

2. *Recruitment and Information.* Under this provision, grants or contracts could be awarded to develop programs for recruiting pesonnel into the field of education for the handicapped and related educational services. Awards could also be made for the development and distribution of information about these programs to parents, teachers, and others.

3. *Expansion of the Media Program to Include All Handicapped Children.* This new program would serve the educational needs of children who are mentally retarded, seriously emotionally disturbed, speech impaired, visually handicapped, crippled, or those having other health impairments, in addition to those deaf or hard of hearing children who are currently benefiting. The program provides for research, acquisition, production, and distribution of media, and for training teachers and other persons in the use of educational media with handicapped children.

4. *Centers and Services for Deaf Blind Children.* This program provides for the establishment and operation of centers for deaf blind children. The centers would provide comprehensive diagnostic and evaluation services; programs for education, adjustment, and orientations; and consultative services for parents, teachers, and others working with the deaf blind. In addition, centers would include research and training programs, where appropriate.

5. *Programs for the Handicapped under Title III of ESEA.* A major source of new support for innovation and for implementation of the newest in educational knowledge in programs for the handicapped would be made available by specifying that 15 percent of Title III funds must be used for programs and projects in the area of education for the handicapped. This provision, effective in Fiscal Year 1969, would provide approximately $30 million during that year for projects which will help bridge the gap between research findings and application in everyday classroom activities.

6. *Increase in Title I Funds for Children in State Schools (PL 89-313).* Title I of ESEA would be amended to provide increased support for education of children in state operated or supported schools for the handicapped. Under the new formula, states receive maximum grants on behalf of these children. This change provides approximately $9 million in additional support in Fiscal Year 1968.

7. *Research and Demonstration.* The program for research and related purposes in education of the handicapped would be extended and expanded to include authority to train research personnel, conduct research, and to award contracts for research, in addition to the current authority under which grants have been available. A new intramural authority would be used to help evaluate the effectiveness of federal programs for education of the handicapped when support for research under the grant and contract method is not practicable.

8. *Changes in Title VI Grants to States Program.* New provisions would allow Title VI grants to be made to the Department of Defense on behalf of handicapped children in schools operated by that department and to the Department of Interior on behalf of children on Indian reservations serviced by schools operated by that department. A change in the grants-to-states allocation formula provides that no state shall receive less than $100,000 or 3/10 of one percent of the appropriation for Title VI grants to states, whichever is greater. This provision is designed to give each state a grant large enough to insure that Title VI programs in that state will be of sufficient quality and magnitude to offer a reasonable possibility of effectiveness.

PL 90-170—Physical Education and Recreation for the Handicapped

While the 1967 amendments to ESEA were in the final stages of development, the 1967 Mental Retardation Amendments were passed, becoming PL 90-170. In addition to extending the 85-926 program, as noted earlier, the Act added a new Title V to the Mental Retardation Facilities and Community Mental Health Centers Construction Act of 1963. This new authority provides support for training professional personnel and for research and demonstration activities in the area of physical education and recreation with mentally retarded and other handicapped children. In language and intent, the new Title parallels the basic training and research authorities for education of handicapped children, and will provide new resources for development in this area.

FINAL APPROVAL

The legislative process involved in securing passage for the 1967 ESEA Amendments progressed slowly. Finally, Congress was in the last week of its session and rumors were that ESEA would be carried over into the next session to begin in January of 1968. Protests were heard from educators around the country, who had been waiting for funds through ESEA programs until the formulas were revised by these amendments, and they wanted final decisions. People interested in education for the handicapped wanted the new programs signed, sealed, and delivered, recognizing that new legislative proposals are never secure until passed. Finally the President and Congressional leadership were able to move the bill along.

The conferees accepted every new proposal to benefit handicapped children. It was not accidental. Much hard work had been done in the nearly 12 months since the session had begun in January of 1967, and, in fact, during the past decade. The full House and Senate approved the conferees' actions, in the last half-hour before adjournment on December 15th. President Johnson's signature completed the process and the 1967 ESEA Amendments became PL 90-247.

The Future

Throughout this discussion, we have traced the development of new authorities and programs. The separate and distinct appropriation process has not been stressed, but, in the final analysis, appropriations are "where the action is."

Converting these new authorities into successful operating programs will require support funds, not only for the grants to be awarded, but for the staff to administer the programs, to oversee their operation, and to cooperate with the grantees in evaluating their effectiveness.

While the glamour and excitement is in the new authorization bills, the power is in their funding. Beyond this, the final meaning of the legislation and the fulfillment of its promise are in the efforts of professional people, teachers, and related specialists who give it life through their successful work with children.

REFERENCES

ADVISORY COMMITTEE ON EDUCATION OF THE DEAF. *Education of the deaf: a report to the Secretary of Health, Education, and Welfare.* Washington: US Department of Health, Education, and Welfare, 1965.

KIRK, S. A. *Hearings. Part I.* Ad-hoc Subcommittee on the Handicapped. House Committee on Education and Labor. 89th Congress, Second Session. June 15, 1966. Washington: US Government Printing Office, 1966.

Edwin W. Martin, Jr. is Associate Commissioner, Bureau of Education for the Handicapped, United States Office of Education, Washington, D.C.

4.
Epilogue: Special Education Leaders in the Office of Education

The U. S. Office of Education was established in 1867 with the primary responsibility of collecting and disseminating information relating to education. It appears that little attention was given to the problems of the education of handicapped children until 1930, when a staff member interested in special education was appointed. Her title was Specialist—Exceptional Children and Youth. A chronology of this position is detailed below. In 1956 the role of the Office was changed somewhat with the beginning of substantial federal support for research and for the training of professional personnel.

Elise H. Martens

Senior Specialist in the Education of Exceptional Children, 1930-1946

Chief of Section, Exceptional Children and Youth, 1946-1950

Dr. Elise H. Martens was the first professional to assume a major role for special education in the Office of Education and the first person to be designated Chief of the Section. She promoted the interests of the field through national conferences, public appearances, and special publications. In the 1930's only about a third of the states' education agencies had even one specialist concerned with handicapped children on their staffs. During her tenure no federal funding from the Office was available for training personnel or for other special programs. Dr.

Martens' home state was California, where she was at one time a student of the late Dr. Louis Terman at Stanford University (See "Pioneer Profile," Chapter 5.)

Arthur S. Hill

Chief of Section, Exceptional Children and Youth, 1950-1953

Upon the retirement of Dr. Martens, Arthur Hill was appointed to fill her position as Chief of Exceptional Children and Youth with responsibility for both the handicapped and the gifted. Mr. Hill was a graduate of the University of Wisconsin at Madison and of Wayne State University. He served as a school psychologist in the Detroit Public Schools, and at the time of his appointment was Director of Pupil Adjustment and Secondary Education in the Des Moines Public Schools. Mr. Hill left the Office of Education to become Director of Special Education for the United Cerebral Palsy Foundation.

Romaine Pryor Mackie

Chief of Section, Exceptional Children and Youth, 1954-1963

Dr. Mackie, who had served as a Specialist in the Office since 1947, succeeded Mr. Hill as Chief of Exceptional Children and Youth in 1954. Before coming to the Office of Education, Dr. Mackie served on the teacher education staff of both Columbia University and Hunter College of the City of New York. In her native state of Ohio she began her work as a teacher of the mentally retarded and later served as a principal of a special school for the handicapped. In addition to serving as a national leader, Dr. Mackie was also very active in international programs for handicapped children.

Samuel A. Kirk

Director, Division of Handicapped Children and Youth, 1964

In 1963 Congress elevated the services for the handicapped to the status of a Division within the Office of Education. President John F. Kennedy was influential in bringing about the legislation and in recruiting the Director for the newly created office. At a White House meeting on October 31, 1963, when S. 1576 was signed, the President announced the appointment of the first Director as follows:

"I am glad to announce at this time that we are establishing a new division in the United States Office of Education to administer the teaching and research program under the Act. This will be called the Division of Handicapped Children and Youth, and will be headed by Dr. Samuel Kirk, who is now Professor of Education and Psychology and Director of the Institute of Research on Exceptional Children at the University of Illinois. He will bring the kind of leadership, experience and wisdom we need to meet the challenges the many problems present."

Dr. Kirk, who was on leave from the University of Illinois, recruited an able staff and organized a service which won a presidential citation at the completion of his leave. Dr. Kirk returned to his post at Illinois, and he now resides in Tucson, Arizona, where he is a professor of special education at the University of Arizona.

Morvin A. Wirtz

Director, Division of Handicapped Children and Youth, 1964-1965

Deputy Assistant Commissioner, Office of Disadvantaged and Handicapped, 1965-1967

Dr. Wirtz succeeded Dr. Kirk when the latter returned to his position as Director of the Institute for Research on Exceptional Children, University of Illinois. Dr. Wirtz had been the Superintendent of the Special School District, St. Louis County, for six years prior to going to Washington. His doctoral work was done at the University of Illinois. Dr. Wirtz became Deputy Assistant Commissioner, Office of Disadvantaged and Handicapped, when the Division of Handicapped Children and Youth was abolished through a new reorganization within the Office of Education. He is now Associate Dean, College of Education, Western Michigan University, Kalamazoo.

James J. Gallagher

Associate Commissioner, Bureau of Education for the Handicapped, 1967-1969

Through congressional action (PL 89-750) the Bureau of Education for the Handicapped was created in 1966. Dr. James Gallagher was selected as the first Director of the newly created Bureau. Dr. Gallagher, whose preparation was as a child and clinical psychologist, had received his doctorate from Pennsylvania State University and later taught at Michigan State University. During the fifteen years he served on the staff of the Institute for Research on Exceptional Children, University of Illinois, he established a national reputation for his leadership ability, competence in research, and skill and effectiveness as a graduate instructor. Following his Washington assignment he became the Director of the Frank Porter Graham Child Development Center, University of North Carolina.

Edwin W. Martin, Jr.

Associate Commissioner, Bureau of Education for the Handicapped, 1969-

Dr. Martin served as the Deputy Associate Commissioner of the Bureau of Education for the Handicapped for two years prior to his appointment to the position of Associate Commissioner. He had served as an assistant to Congressman Hugh Carey and in this position helped to work out the legislation which led to the organization of the Bureau. Dr. Martin received his doctorate in speech pathology from the University of Pittsburgh and was Associate Professor of Speech Pathology and Co-Director of the Speech and Hearing Clinic at the University of Alabama before going to Washington.

Two

Special
Education
and
the
Law

Education has long been considered a right for children in America. During the past hundred years numerous questions have been raised in the courts over the interpretation of this right, especially as it relates to compulsory school attendance. Empress Zedler, in her article which follows, "Public Opinion and Public Education for the Exceptional Child—Court Decisions 1873-1950," traces the major court cases which have established the right of handicapped children to public school education.

During the past ten years numerous cases concerning the rights of handicapped children have been filed and adjudicated in our courts. Many of these cases grew out of civil rights issues, such as equal protection under the law and the right of due process. Among the specific issues were many problems relating to placement—including the validity of tests employed, policies and procedures of assigning children to special classes, and the right of periodic review. A major challenge has been made against the use of intelligence tests with children from minority groups, and the courts have been asked to rule on the segregation imposed by attendance in a special class. The article by Ross, DeYoung, and Cohen describes these and other representative court cases in more detail.

The final short article by Abeson reviews some of the current governmental actions on laws which extended services to the handicapped.

In recent months there have been other court cases which could not be summarized in Abeson's article. In 1971 the Pennsylvania Association for Retarded Children vs. Commonwealth of Pennsylvania case was of great significance since the court ordered the public schools to provide education for certain severely handicapped children for whom provision had not been made. An overseer was appointed to see that the schools complied within a designated period.

The case of Peter Mills vs. Board of Education of the District of Columbia is considered by some attorneys to have far-reaching consequences. The U. S. District Court outlined procedures for adequate due process to be followed when a child is transferred to or placed in a special program. In addition, procedures controlling or limiting suspension or expulsion from schools were prescribed in detail. Because of the importance of the Mills case, the court report which contained the Judgment and Decree is reproduced in Appendix A.

Educational legislation is not effective unless children eligible to benefit from the laws are identified. Therefore it seems appropriate in this chapter to recognize in the "Pioneer Profile" the work of Alfred Binet, the French psychologist and educator who devised the first popular test of mental abilities for the express purpose of finding children who needed special training.

Alfred Binet
1857–1911

PSYCHOLOGIST
SPECIAL EDUCATOR
TEST DEVELOPER

In 1904 the Minister of Public Instruction of
France appointed a special commission to formulate methods of identifying mentally retarded
children in the public schools since the State
wished to establish suitable school programs for
such children. Alfred Binet, a psychologist, was
named to this important commission and distinguished himself with the tests he devised. Much
of his success in constructing useful measures
was due to his insightful notion of intelligence.
He conceived of intelligence as a combination
of general cognitive abilities such as identification of objects, meaning of terms, and the ability
to repeat verbal stimuli. This view was in contrast
to the then prevailing atomistic conception of intelligence as a collection of specific sensory and
motor abilities. Binet and Theodore Simon published their first scale for measuring general intelligence in 1905. A revision followed in 1908,
and again in 1911. Although the term *mental age*
was first employed by Binet, the concept of *intelligence quotient* (IQ) was suggested later by
William Stern, a German psychologist. In Chapter
Six the reader will find an English translation
of a fascinating discussion on the education of
intelligence taken from Binet's text, *Les Idées
modernes sur les enfants.*

5.
Public Opinion and Public Education for the Exceptional Child—Court Decisions 1873–1950

EMPRESS YOUNG ZEDLER

What types of conditions led to school exclusions during the period described in the article? How valid, in your opinion, were these reasons for exclusion?

The right of the exceptional child who is mentally or physically handicapped to equal opportunity for education with other children, regardless of deviation has evolved from a gradual but decided change in public opinion during the last three-quarters of a century. Policies affecting the attendance of such children in public schools have been the direct outgrowth of "play of public opinion and the political complex of pressure and agitation" upon the administrative, legislative and judicial organs of government. It is the purpose of this paper to trace the "rise of the handicapped child"[1] in education, from a state of degradation to one of understanding and acceptance, by studying the court decisions which have been made regarding such children in the public schools. They reveal a gradual, though not uniform, progress of public sentiment through three steps. First, decisions show the belief that school attendance is a *privilege,* to be awarded or withheld at the discretion of school authority. Secondly, they show opinion that school attendance is a *right for all children.* Finally, legal processes reflect public belief in the *right of a child to an education suitable to his individual needs.*

School Attendance a Privilege

The state confers upon all children the privilege of attending public school, in so far as such attendance contributes to the welfare and the safety of the state itself. "Since attendance at the state schools is essentially a privilege and not a right, the state may authorize its agents to exclude all children who do not meet the requirements established by the state. Consequently, a school board usually has the implied power to reject applicants for admission who do not conform to the reasonable and necessary requirements established by the board."[2]

Although an examination of Nineteenth Century court decisions reveals

From *Exceptional Children* 19 (February, 1953): 187-198. Reprinted by permission of the author and *Exceptional Children.* Copyrighted by the Council for Exceptional Children.

a few incidents of school boards being required to provide accommodations for all children legally entitled to attend school, and who desire to do so,[3] the preponderance of decisions rendered upheld, and thereby strengthened, a school board's right to reject and expel deviate children whose presence in the school was presumed to "impair its efficiency or interfere with the rights of other pupils." The only redress from such rejection was to prove that the school board or school committee had acted unreasonably. And the reasonableness of a school board's action was generally conceded by the courts.

The school boards were protected against court action in questions of right to admission in Massachusetts in 1873 when the court ruled that action must be taken against the city or town and not against the school committee.[4] And when such action was brought by a parent in Massachusetts in 1901,[5] demanding instruction in public schools for his child, the court ruled:

> The right given every child by statute to attend public school is not unqualified, but is subject to such reasonable regulations as to numbers and qualifications of pupils as the school committee shall from time to time prescribe.

Privilege of School Attendance—
The Deviate Child

The same trend is found when cases are examined which involve the principle of eligibility of the atypical child to attend school. In the late Nineteenth and early Twentieth Centuries the courts usually left the establishment of a pupil's eligibility to attend school entirely to the local boards and administrators.

In the case of Ward v. Flood in 1874,[6] the court ruled that:
A principal of a public graded school may refuse to admission a child who has not sufficient education to enter the lowest grade of such a school. That the emphasis was upon "general effect upon the school" and that no importance was placed upon the individual in 1893 is shown in the decision of the supreme judicial court of Massachusetts in the case of Watson v. City of Cambridge.[7] In this case, the court ruled that the decision of a school committee was final as affecting good order and discipline, as it related to rights of pupils to enjoy school privileges. The plaintiff in the case, who was asking for reinstatement in the public schools of Cambridge, was a mentally retarded child who was described thus:

> Appears from statements of teachers who observed him, and from certificates of physicians, that he is so weak in mind as not to derive any marked benefit from instruction, and further, that he is troublesome to other children, making unusual noises, pinching others, etc. He is also found unable to take ordinary, decent, physical care of himself.

The court ruled that the committee acted in good faith in expelling such a child. This decision was justified by citing precedent established in a former case,[8] where the court had upheld a school committee's expulsion of a child whose behavior consisted of acts of neglect, carelessness of posture in his seat and recitation, tricks of playfulness, inattention to study and regulations of the school in minor matters.

Further emphasizing conformity and intolerance of any type of individual deviation, the court stated that there was no difference between the mischievous and mentally retarded child.

> The only difference between the acts of disorder in that case and this is that in this the behavior resulted from incapacity and mental weakness of the plaintiff, and in the other they were willful or careless—the result in part of youthful exuberance of spirits and impatience of restraint or control. They were alike in their general effect upon the school; and the reasons for giving the school committee, acting in good faith, the power to decide finally a question affecting so vitally the rights and interests of all the other scholars of the school, are the same in both cases. . . .

The court would not go so far as to review the case, saying:

> Whether certain acts of disorder so seriously interfere with the school that one who persists in them either voluntarily or by reason of imbecility, should not be permitted to continue in the school is a question which the statute makes the school committee's duty to answer; and if they answer honestly, in an effort to do their duty, a jury composed of men of no special fitness to decide educational questions should not be permitted to say that their answer is wrong.

There is seen in the latter statement of the court a foreshadowing, as early as 1893, of the need for "special fitness to decide educational questions." But recognizing no such person nor body of persons as possessing such "fitness," the court in 1893 could not question the power of the school committees to protect "the rights and interests of all other scholars" by excluding alike from school those pupils who made unusual noises, and pinched others, as well as those who were exuberant of spirit and careless of posture when seated! Such was public opinion in 1893.

As late as 1941 in Massachusetts little change is noted in judicial opinion as to eligibility of the deviate child to attend school. In 1937[9] the court interpreted the statute giving the school committee general charge of public schools as also giving the power to exclude pupils of such intellectual capacity or weakness of mind as to interfere with the progress of others. In a case in 1941[10] the court ruled:

> The power of a school committee to exclude children from school is very broad and is to be exercised for the best interests of the pupils of all the people. It may be exercised where there is no misconduct on the part of the children excluded.
> Failure of a child to maintain a standard of scholarship may justify exclusion, though such act is not misconduct.
> Fact that attendance of a child wholly independent of such child's misconduct would impair efficiency of the school may be sufficient ground for exclusion.

In cases thus far examined which involve deviate pupils, the court's practice seems to have been to affirm their expulsion and exclusion from the regular schools on the principle that school boards evidenced no arbitrary action or palpable abuse of statutory powers by declaring the presence of such children harmful to the best interests of the school. But elsewhere, a definite trend toward attention to the individual is noted in court decisions.

The Right to School Attendance

In Missouri in 1927[11] general welfare is made secondary to the rights of the individual pupil:

The right to attend public school is fundamental, and cannot be denied except for general welfare.

By 1934 the ever increasing importance of administrative agencies in determining the nature of the handicapped child's right to admission and instruction is demonstrated by the court's decision in a case in Ohio.[12] In this case it was held that the local school board's exclusion of a child of low mentality, merely on the basis of tests prescribed by the state department of education, was unauthorized. Final determination by the state department of education of the child's low mentality was held to be essential before the child could be legally excluded from the public school. This decision is so far removed from the earlier precedent of leaving the child's right to admission or instruction entirely to the discretion of the local board, that it bears careful scrutiny.

The case involved an 8-year-old child, X——Y——, who was brain injured at birth and admittedly subnormal. In September 1931 the board of education of Cleveland Heights had opened the Superior Opportunity School for children retarded because of low mentality. Classes had been in operation during 1931-32 and 1932-33. These, the child had attended.

On Nov. 14, 1932, the board adopted a resolution that:

Pupils now enrolled in the school having intelligence quotients below 50 be retained in the organization until the end of the current school year, but that beginning with September 1973, all pupils below 50 IQ and special or custodial types be excluded; and further that the present group of pupils of this type be segregated from all other school pupils at an early date. . . .

The board ruled that this retarded child was not to be admitted to the Superior Opportunity School in September 1933.

The father claimed that the child was in the compulsory school age of 6-18 years, and that his expulsion was contrary to Statute 7762-7 of the General Code of Ohio.

The board of education claimed under this section that the department of education of the state can prescribe standards, examinations, or tests to determine if children are incapable of profiting substantially by further instruction, and that further, the General Code of Ohio Statutes states:

School boards, in conducting the schools have wide discretion with which the courts will not interfere in absence of abuse.

Claiming that it had exercised sound discretion in ruling that any child of school age with an IQ of 50 or below by the Revised Binet, is incapable of profiting by schooling, the board held that it had not shown abuse by excluding X——Y—— who had an IQ of 47 and who had shown no progress over two or three years of school attendance.

Justice McGill wrote in his decision:

Apparently this is a case of first impression in Ohio and counsel have been unable to find a case anywhere in the United States which gives the right to exclude from all educational facilities any child within the prescribed ages upon the basis of an intelligence test. It is, therefore, necessary to look to the provisions of the statutes of Ohio with reference to the right to refuse this child admission to the schools, and to seek to determine the intent of the legislature.

The judge noted that there had been sharp conflict of evidence concerning the results of IQ tests given this child: in September 1932 an IQ of 44 was obtained; in November, 47; in October 1933, 55. Henry H. Goddard, expert witness, testified that one child with an IQ of 40 might be more educable than another with an IQ of 50.

Section 7762-7 of the General Code of Ohio provides that:

A child of compulsory school age may be determined to be incapable of profiting substantially by further instruction as follows: The department of education may prescribe standards and examinations or tests by which such capacity may be determined, and prescribe and approve the agencies or individuals by which they shall be applied . . . . no child shall be determined to be incapable of profiting substantially by further instruction if the department of education shall find that it is feasible to provide for him in such district or elsewhere in the public school system, special classes or schools, departments of special instruction or individual instruction through or by which he might profit substantially, according to his mental capacity as so determined. . . .

The result of each exam or test made hereunder, with the recommendation of the agency or individual conducting the same, shall be reported to the department of education, which shall have power to make the determination herein authorized. If a child be determined hereunder to be incapable of profiting substantially by further instruction, such determination shall be certified by the department of education to the superintendent of schools of the district in which he resides, who shall place such child under the supervision of a visiting teacher or of an attendance officer to be exercised as long as he is of compulsory age. . . .

The records of the case show that after the board of education of Cleveland Heights determined that this retarded child was unable to profit substantially by further education, the matter was submitted to the state department of education at Columbus. At first the state department approved exclusion of the child, but later revoked its approval, and finally passed the entire matter back to the local school board.

The court ruled:

(1) There is no doubt but that school boards in the exercise of their powers have a wide discretion, and that courts will not interfere with that exercise of sound discretion in the absence of an abuse thereof.

It is to be borne in mind, however, that not only compulsory attendance is required by our laws, but also that the right to attend our public schools belongs to the people. Education for all youth . . . is considered so essential that between certain ages, children must attend our schools.

(2) The question arises as to where the authority to exclude a child of low mentality is vested. The question in this case is whether or not this child was legally refused admission to the schools. A careful study of section 7762-7, General Code leads us to the conclusion that . . . a determination of the question must be finally made by the department of education, which counsel for the board of education concedes means the state department. In this case the department of education made no final determination. Without such final approval or determination by the department we think that this child was not excluded in accordance with the provisions of the statute. . . .

In this case of first impression in Ohio, the rights of a deviate child to be considered in the light of his individual differences were safeguarded by the courts only because the state board of education had refused to exercise a power expressly granted it by statute, and had attempted to delegate this power to another body, namely the local school board. This particular power of determining a child's educability could not legally be delegated. Therefore, it was illegal for the child to be excluded on any orders other than those of the state department of education.

Thus is revealed a shift in interpretation of the atypical child's right to admission to the public schools, from a liberal acceptance of a local board's discretion as to what does or does not contribute to the welfare and safety of the state, toward a policy of turning to experts for evaluation of individual differences and their influence upon the welfare of others.

The Child's Right to Instruction Suitable to His Need

It is a recognized power of school boards to designate the particular school which a pupil shall attend. The pupil must attend the school to which he is assigned[13] unless the courts find that the board has acted arbitrarily or shown palpable abuse in the exercise of its discretion. Neither convenience of the school's location nor personal preferences of the child or its parents are factors to influence the assignment to a particular school.[14]

Defective children have long been considered candidates for special schools. The philosophy behind the creation of such schools and the assignment of pupils to them has undergone a definite change in the third and fourth decades of the Twentieth Century. Children were first assigned to special schools to protect the interests of the common schools by removing "undesirable" pupils from them. Slowly but definitely the concept of the duty of society toward the deviate individual has been reflected in the assignment of such a pupil to the special school appropriate for his adequate education. This change in social philosophy is clearly shown in the court decisions of two cases: one in Wisconsin[15] in 1919 involving a cerebral palsied pupil, and the other in Iowa[16] in 1950 involving a deaf pupil. So clearly do these two cases indicate the shift of public or state emphasis from general welfare to the welfare of the individual that they bear detailed examination.

The Wisconsin case clearly involves a cerebral palsied boy, although he is never so labeled. The records of the supreme court of Wisconsin, of April 29, 1919, describe him thus:

(R—— T——) 13 years of age on March 27, 1918, a resident of the city of Antigo for 11 years, has been a crippled and defective child since his birth, being afflicted with a form of paralysis which affects his whole physical and nervous make-up. He has not the normal use and control of his voice, hands, feet and body. By reason of said paralysis, his vocal cords are afflicted. He is slow and hesitant in speech, and has a peculiar high, rasping and disturbing tone of voice, accompanied with uncontrollable facial contortions, making it difficult for him to make himself understood. He also has an uncontrollable flow of saliva, which drools from his mouth onto his clothing and books, causing him to present an unclean appearance. He has a nervous and excitable nature.

This is an unmistakable description of a child who received a brain injury prior to or at birth. The diagnosis is further strengthened by the fact that he "did not walk until 6 or 7 years of age." His educability is further verified by the court records which state that:

He entered the first grade of Antigo public schools when he was 8 years old. He continued in the Antigo public schools until he was through the fifth grade in 1917. It appears that he is normal mentally and that he kept pace with the other pupils in the respective grades although the teachers had difficulty understanding him, and he was not called upon to recite as frequently as others for the reason that he was slow of speech, requiring more time for him to recite than the other pupils.

With no apparent interest in an individual who could advance with his classmates in spite of such handicaps, who could successfully participate in school activities one year after he learned to walk, the school board claimed that "his condition and ailment produce a depressing nauseating effect upon the teachers and school children; that by reason of his physical condition he takes up undue portion of the teacher's time and attention, distracts the attention of other pupils, and interferes generally with discipline and progress of the school."

The city of Antigo maintained a day school for the instruction of deaf persons or persons with defective speech. With no attempt to diagnose nor to determine the etiology of this boy's speech disorder, and with no recognition of a difference in therapy and education between the deaf and those with other types of speech disorders, this hearing boy was placed in the special school with deaf children in the fall of 1916 by the school authorities. He remained for five weeks and then of his own volition transferred to the Fourth Ward public school. In the school year of 1916-17 a representative of the state department of public instruction visited the Fourth Ward school and protested the boy's presence and recommended his removal to the school for the deaf and speech defectives. The boy refused to move and was upheld by his parents. In September of 1917, the Second Ward public school refused to accept him as a pupil. The parents appealed to the superintendent for reinstatement of the boy. The superintendent turned the matter over to the school board, which in turn asked for advice from the state superintendent of public instruction. No definite advice was received from this latter official, whereupon the school board never reinstated the boy.

That a definite pressure group was beginning to form in favor of the individual rights of the deviate pupil is shown in that [the] case was tried before a jury, and the municipal court of Antigo issued a writ of mandamus ordering the reinstatement of R—— T—— in the common public school. The board of education appealed the case and it came before the supreme court of Wisconsin.

The statutes of the state of Wisconsin which applied in this case were:

(1) The rights of a child of school age to attend the public schools of the state cannot be insisted upon, when its presence therein is harmful to the best interests of the school.

(2) Where a school board, acting under Laws 1889, vol. 2, c. 197, para. 101 subd. 5, took a child with defective vocal organs and speech out of the public school and removed him to a day school maintained under St. 1917, para. 41.01 for the instruction of deaf persons or persons with defective speech, its acts will not be interfered with by courts, unless it acted unreasonably.

The principle of law which the supreme court was called to rule upon was whether or not the board had acted unreasonably in the use of its discretion. The court held that the local board had not been unreasonable in removing the boy from the public school, thus reversing the judgment of the municipal court with instructions to dismiss the petition.

The majority opinion was written by Judge J. Owen as follows:

... The duty confronting the school board was a delicate one. It was charged with the responsibility of saying whether this boy should be denied a constitutional right because the exercise of that right would be harmful to the school and to the pupils attending same. He should not be excluded from the schools except for considerations affecting the general welfare. But if his presence in school was detrimental to the best interests of the school, then the board could not, with due regard to their official oaths, refrain from excluding him, even though such action be displeasing and painful to them. The record discloses no grounds for the interference of courts with its action.

The dissenting opinion of the court was written by Justice J. Eschweiler, and marks a new trend in judicial interpretation of what constitutes arbitrary action by a school board. It said:

I cannot agree with the result arrived at in the majority in this case for two reasons:

First. Because even under the rule of law adopted by the majority as to the power vested in the school board, it was still a question for the jury as to whether or not there was an unreasonable interference with the plaintiff's rights; there being no evidence that as a fact this boy's presence did have any harmful influence on the other children.

Secondly. Because I believe there is no such exclusive power intended to be vested in such school boards. Those who drafted the Constitution of this state evidently intended to secure to every child a substantial and fundamental right to attend the common schools. Art. 10, para 2, Const. . . .

I think the burden was properly laid, by the instruction given by the trial court to the jury in this case, upon the defendants, to show that their action was a reasonable exercise of their statutory duty. If they were unable to convince a jury to that effect, their order should be set aside.

This dissenting opinion is interesting in that it clearly calls upon an administrative body, the school board, to yield to public opinion, the will of a jury. It also questions the phrase "harmful influence," and implies that since the "nauseating effect" of uncontrolled drooling and slow hesitant speech in no way infringes upon the constitutional right of other children to enjoy free schooling, there is no legal basis for withholding such right from the drooling speech-handicapped child. Thus is revealed the beginning of the educational philosophy of individual differences and the objective attitude, which was to mature in the unanimous decision of all justices in a case in Iowa in 1950.[17]

In March of 1950 the supreme court of Iowa received the case of the state board of education in re Petty v. Petty et al. The facts of this case are directly opposed to those of the Wisconsin case in 1919. In the older case, the plaintiffs are seeking to have a school board compelled to allow a child to pursue his education in the school which will give him the best opportunity to reach the limits of his capabilities. In the more recent case a school board is seeking to have the parent allow the child to be placed in the school which will best fulfill this child's educational needs. In both cases the court decided in favor of the board, but the two boards represent opposite poles of public opinion.

On July 21, 1947 a representative of the state board of education in the state of Iowa filed an application for commitment of Z———, aged 8, a minor child who was deaf, to the state school for the deaf. Such commitment is provided for in the statutes of Iowa, 299.18:

> Children over seven and under nineteen years of age who are so deaf or blind (or severely handicapped) as to be *unable to obtain an education in the common schools* shall be sent to the proper state school; therefore, unless exempted, any person having such a child under his control or custody shall see that such child attends such school during the school year.
>
> The State Board of Education may apply to the district court to compel such attendance.

In August of 1947 a hearing in the district court resulted in requiring that the parents of Z——— take him to the school for the deaf before September 8 or 9, 1948, and that the child attend as provided for under the compulsory educational statutes relative to handicapped children. This was not a quick decision reached at the time the child became of school age. The court records show that a representative of the state board of education had given consideration for several years to the problems of this child's education. This representative had seen the child first at the age of three years. At her suggestion and that of the county nurse and county superintendent of schools, the parents had taken the child to the University of Iowa's hospital in Iowa City on October 22, 1945 for an examination of the child's hearing and an estimate of his educability. The records of the state board of education show that its representative, after a thorough investigation of the home life and educational opportunities afforded this child, recommended that he be sent to the school for the deaf.

However, the farmer parents of Z——— refused to follow the orders of the district court and instead placed the child in a rural school near his home for his first schooling of a preliminary nature. The defendants appealed from the decision of the district court and the case reached the supreme court of Iowa. The appellants contended that the appellee had not proved the deaf child was unable to "obtain an education in the common schools," and therefore he might attend the school in Decatur County near his home.

The principle of law involved in the case was whether or not this deaf child could obtain an education in the common schools. There was no mention of the rights of other pupils in this case. The entire proceedings hinged upon this child's ability to be best educated in the light of his handicap.

When the child started to school he was taught by a high school graduate who had had no special training for instructing the deaf. This teacher gave testimony that it was his opinion that the child could obtain an average education in the country schools. The testimony was sharply challenged by a state's witness, the superintendent of the school for the deaf, who asked searching questions as to the methods of teaching being used with this child. This expert then testified that the methods used by the teacher were not the proper ones to educate a deaf child. From testimony presented, he stated the teacher was apparently unfamiliar with the correct method of teaching such an individual. He also stated that the instruction of a deaf child was a highly technical process and that special instruction was necessary to develop use of the English language by a deaf child.

All the justices concurred that the decision of the district court should be affirmed. An order was issued compelling the parents to send their child to the school for the deaf. This decision is historic in establishing the right of the deviate child to an education. It was as follows:

1. "To obtain an education in the common schools" as applied to the facts in this case should not be considered generally but must be applied to the specific problem.

To obtain an education for a normal child with the facilities presented in an average school would mean one thing, but to obtain an education for a handicapped child, particularly one who is deaf, would mean another thing. A child who has a physical defect necessarily must receive a different type of instruction than one who is not handicapped. . . .

The fact that the child has no hearing necessarily requires that he have a more specialized type of education than a normal child or individual. To fail to provide a handicapped child with all the known educational opportunities within his reach would necessarily result in his being at a disadvantage in meeting the problem of making a living and enjoying the privileges of a reasonable education. Under the circumstances, education in this child's case should be of such nature as to develop his self-reliance and make him nondependent on his family or the state. The common schools which he would have to attend are shown not to possess the facilities which would develop this self-reliance and ability to adequately provide for himself as he grows into maturity and manhood.

3 & 4. Although the primary question involved in this appeal is whether the child could be provided with proper educational facilities in the common schools . . . the rule heretofore universally announced in such cases to the effect that the best interests of the child should be considered is also applicable in our determination of the case. It is our conclusion that the best interests of the child would be served by his attendance at a school where education could be adequately developed in the light of his handicap. We believe . . . that the state is justified through its Board of Education, in seeking to educate the child here in question to the best of its capabilities in a state institution. This does not mean the child is being taken from the parents and that they are being deprived of his custody. It merely means the state is desirous of helping them. . . .

Thus through court decisions relative to the handicapped child, the various stages in the American concept of the state and the law have been revealed. No sooner had the civil liberty of the individual been secured and his privilege of attending school been established, than emphasis began to shift from the few to the many. School boards began to withhold from any child who was deviate, the privilege of adequate education, and the courts upheld such action as reasonable because of "general welfare," "rights of others," "discipline and progress of the school." Then the second stage of awareness appeared, the concept that all children, regardless of disability, have a right to educational facilities. Now, in the mid-Twentieth Century, the courts are reflecting in their decisions regarding the mentally and physically handicapped child a third stage—the right of a child to an education suitable to his abilities. It is a flowering of the American legal and social concept, establishment of a cultural, educational, and economic base under the individual, upon which individual liberty may rest more securely, a base that will make possible the further release of human personality through the establishment of richer opportunities for individual development.

Empress Young Zedler is Professor of Special Education, Chairman of the Department of Special Education, Southwest Texas University, San Marcos.

NOTES

1. WENDELL JOHNSON, S. F. CARTER, AND OTHERS, *Speech Handicapped Children,* 3rd ed. (New York: Harper and Row, Publishers, 1967).
2. NEWTON EDWARDS, *The Courts and the Public Schools* (Chicago: University of Chicago Press, 1933), p. 500.
3. In re Board of Education of Zanesville, Ohio, N.P. 564, 5 Ohio S. and C. P. Dec. 578.
4. Leacock v. Putnam, 111 Mass. 499.
5. Alvord v. Inhabitants of Town of Chester, 180 Massachusetts 20, 61 N. E. 263.
6. Ward v. Flood, 48 Cal. 36, 17 Amer. Rep. 405.
7. Watson v. City of Cambridge, 157 Mass. 561, 32 N. E. 864.
8. Hodgkins v. Rockport, 105 Mass. 475.
9. Nicholls v. Mayor and School Committee of Lynn, 7 N. E. 2d 577, 297 Mass. 65, 110.
10. Committee v. Johnson, 35 N. E. 2d 801, 309 Mass. 476.
11. Constitutional Article II 1, State ex rel. Roberts v. Wilson, 297 S. W. 419, 221 Mo. App. 9.
12. Board of Education of Cleveland Heights v. State ex rel. Goldman, 191 N. E. 914, 47 Ohio App. 417.
13. Freeman v. Franklin Township 37 Pa. St. 385.
14. Williams v. Board of Education, 79 Kan. 202, 99 Pac. 216, 22 L.R.A. (N.S.) 584.
15. State ex rel Beattie v. Board of Education, City of Antigo, 172 N.W. 153, 169 Wis. 231.
16. In re Petty, State Board of Education v. Petty et al., 41 N.W. 2d, 672.
17. Cf. note 16.

6.
Confrontation: Special Education Placement and the Law
STERLING L. ROSS, JR.
HENRY G. DeYOUNG
JULIUS S. COHEN

Some typical court cases are reviewed here.
Consider the cases and evaluate the implications
at the end of the article.

In the nation's public schools, classes for the educable mentally retarded have unwittingly become burial grounds for many children from environments that have not prepared them for the demands of the schools. The educational system has consistently ignored pleas for change to make school experience more relevant to children who may be neither highly motivated nor achievement oriented or who come from culturally different backgrounds. In an effort to make the educational system responsive to the children's needs, concerned parents have turned to the courts. In recent years a groundswell of litigation has arisen, attacking the criteria currently used to label and place children of racial and cultural minorities in special programs. Such intense judicial activity has important implications for educators concerned with the seriousness of the present situation and highlights the need for immediate change.

The Arguments
The following arguments are levied most often against current placement procedures.

For many children, testing does not accurately measure their learning ability. Intelligence tests are generally standardized on white, middle class student populations, are heavily verbal, and contain questions more easily answerable by white, middle class students. These three factors coalesce to produce IQ scores which are based primarily on cultural and/or socioeconomic backgrounds of the students and are not a true indication of learning ability. The tests discriminate against children of racial and cultural minorities and are therefore in violation of the equal protection clause of the 14th Amendment to the United States Constitution.

From *Exceptional Children* 38 (September, 1971): 5-12. Reprinted by permission of the senior author and *Exceptional Children*. Copyrighted by the Council for Exceptional Children.

The reader's attention is called to the Judgment and Decree from the Mills case, which is reproduced in Appendix A.

The administration of tests is often performed incompletely. Even if proper testing instruments existed, many of the present public school personnel are not adequately trained to administer the tests nor qualified to interpret the results properly. The skilled tester must be aware of the cultural backgrounds of the children and be alert to the anxiety created by the testing situation and to any inability to understand directions because of language problems. Hence, an examiner technically may be able to administer a test and yet obtain results which are not an accurate indication of the child's abilities.

Parents are not given an adequate opportunity to participate in the placement decision. Most school codes require that the parents be notified when the decision to place the child has been reached, and some codes require that a hearing be held before placement. However, parents often are not notified when their children are placed in a special class and are almost never given a formal opportunity to be heard before the placement decision is reached. When parents are involved, it is usually in an effort to obtain their agreement to a decision which the professionals have already made.

Special education programming is inadequate. Once a child is placed in an educable mentally retarded class, there is little chance that he will leave it. Insufficient attention is given to the development of basic educational skills and retesting occurs infrequently, if ever. Contributing further to the lack of upward mobility is the student's poor self image which is reinforced by such placement and contributes to the self fulfilling prophecy of low achievement.

The personal harm created by improper placement is irreparable. Special class placement becomes a basic factor in a self fulfilling prophecy, frequently relegating the victim to an economic, educational, and social position far below that which he has the ability to achieve. The social stigma surrounding the label "mentally retarded" remains with the individual his entire life. Obtaining a job may be difficult if not impossible, and even if adequate employment is found, the psychological damage created by improper placement persists.

The Developing Case Law

The following cases form the nucleus of the growing body of case law in the area of special class placement.

Culture Biased Tests

In *Hobson v. Hansen* (1967) Judge Skelly Wright held that the "tracking" system of educational placement in the Washington D.C. public schools was illegal since it was a violation of the equal protection clause of the United States Constitution. He therefore ordered the abolition of the track system. Under this system students were given the *Sequential Tests of Educational Progress* (STEP) and the *School and College Ability Tests*

(SCAT) in the fourth grade and the *Stanford Achievement Test* (SAT) and the *Otis Quick-Scoring Mental Ability Test* in the sixth grade. The students were then placed in an honors, general, or special (educable mentally retarded) curriculum primarily on the basis of test scores. Judge Wright found that in the Washington D.C. schools there were a disproportionate number of black children in special classes and attributed this inequitable distribution to culture biased tests:

The evidence shows that the method by which track assignments are made depends essentially on standardized aptitude tests which, although given on a system-wide basis, are completely inappropriate for use with a large segment of the student body. Because these tests are primarily standardized on and are relevant to a white middle class group of students, they produce inaccurate and misleading test scores when given to lower class and Negro students. As a result, rather than being classified according to ability to learn, these students are in reality being classified according to their socio-economic or racial status, or— more precisely—according to environmental and psychological factors which have nothing to do with innate ability [p. 514].

The chief handicap of the disadvantaged child where verbal tests are concerned is in his limited exposure to people having command of standard English. Communication within the lower class environment...typically assumes a language form alien to that tested by aptitude tests [p. 480].

Other circumstances interact with and reinforce the language handicap. Verbalization tends to occur less frequently and often less intensively. Because of crowded living conditions, the noise level in the home may be quite high with the result that the child's auditory perception—his ability to discriminate among word sounds—can be retarded. There tends to be less exposure to books or other serious reading material—either for lack of interest or for lack of money [p. 481].

Once in a certain track the student is locked in because of infrequent retesting, the student's poor self image, and the teacher's preconceived ideas of the student's academic abilities. Judge Wright noted:

The real tragedy of misjudgments about the disadvantaged student's abilities is, as described earlier, the likelihood that the student will act out the judgment and confirm it by achieving only at the expected level. Indeed, it may be even worse than that, for there is strong evidence that performance in fact declines ....And while the tragedy of misjudgments can occur even under the best of circumstances, there is reason to believe the track system compounds the risk [p. 491].

Therefore, relying on *Brown v. Board of Education* (1954), the court held that the tracking system and its methods irrationally separate students on the basis of race and socioeconomic background and thereby violate their right to an equal educational opportunity. On appeal, the District Circuit Court of Appeals in *Smuck v. Hobson* (1969) affirmed the lower court's decree abolishing the track system.

DISCRIMINATORY INTERCLASS GROUPING

Since *Hobson,* California has become the battleground over intelligence testing and educational placement. On January 22, 1970, *Spangler v. Board of Education* (1970) was decided in the United States District Court for the Southern District of California. The court found that there was a "racial imbalance" in the student bodies and faculties of the Pasadena school district at all levels. It attributed the racial imbalance to conscious policies and practices on the part of the school district to maintain disproportionate racial distributions. One such practice was discriminatory "interclass grouping" based upon intelligence tests and teacher's recommendations. Without contest by the defendant, it was admitted that the intelligence tests used were inaccurate and unfair:

The racial effect of the grouping procedures generally in use in the District is to increase segregation. At every secondary school a higher percentage of Black than white students is in slow classes in every subject matter, and a higher percentage of white than Black students is in fast classes . . . . The racial segregation that exists within integrated schools as a result of interclass grouping doubtless has numerous causes, not all of which are treated in the record. . . . One is that grouping assignments are based in part on scores obtained on achievement and "intelligence" tests. As the District's Assistant Superintendent for elementary education acknowledged, such tests are racially discriminatory, based as they are primarily on verbal achievement [p. 159].

LANGUAGE BARRIERS TO ADEQUATE PERFORMANCE

In *Diana v. State Board of Education,* filed in the District Court for the Northern District of California in February 1970, nine Mexican-American public school students, ages 8 through 13, claimed that they had been improperly placed in classes for the mentally retarded on the basis of inaccurate tests. Each plaintiff came from a family in which Spanish was the predominant or only spoken language. In the first and second grades the children were given the Stanford-Binet and Wechsler intelligence tests. On the basis of IQ scores so derived, they were placed in educable classes. The plaintiffs argued that (a) the tests relied primarily on verbal aptitude in English thereby ignoring learning abilities in Spanish and (b) the tests were improperly standardized by testing only white, native Americans and therefore related in subject matter solely to the dominant white, middle class culture. This inherent culture bias discriminated against the Mexican-American plaintiffs.

Citing *Brown v. Board of Education* (1954), the Civil Rights Act of 1964, and Article 9 Section 5 of the California Constitution, the plaintiffs contended that the Federal government and state of California guarantee every citizen the right to an equal educational opportunity. The case was settled in February 1970 by a stipulated agreement which set forth the following practices to be observed in the future.

1. All children whose primary home language is other than English must be tested in both their primary language and English.

2. Such children must be tested only with tests or sections of tests that do not depend on such things as vocabulary, general information, and other similar unfair verbal questions.

3. Mexican-American and Chinese-American children already in classes for the mentally retarded must be retested in their primary language and must be reevaluated only as to their achievement on nonverbal tests or sections of tests.

4. Each school district is to submit to the state in time for next school year a summary of retesting and reevaluation and a plan listing special supplemental individual training which will be provided to help each child back into the regular school class.

5. State psychologists are to work on norms for a new or revised IQ test to reflect the abilities of Mexican-Americans so that in the future Mexican-American children will be judged only by how they compare to the performance of their peers, not the population as a whole.

6. Any school district which has a significant disparity between the percentage of Mexican-American students in its regular classes and in its classes for the retarded must submit an explanation setting out the reasons for this disparity.

In February 1971, *Covarrubias v. San Diego Unified School District* was filed with the Federal District Court for the Southern District of California on behalf of 12 black and 5 Mexican-American pupils in classes for the educable mentally retarded. The plaintiffs rely on the attack in the *Diana* case on the culture bias of the Stanford-Binet and Wechsler intelligence tests and the resultant denial of the right to an equal education. In seeking money damages under the Civil Rights Act of 1871, they argue that the defendant school district, its officers and agents, conspired to deprive plaintiffs of the equal protection of the laws. In addition, an injunction is sought to prohibit the continuation of special education classes in San Diego until valid testing methods are devised and correctly administered.

Though *Covarrubias* resembles *Diana* in the legal arguments presented, two significant differences are apparent. First, *Covarrubias* introduces money damages as a possible remedy under the Civil Rights Act of 1871, though the elements of conspiracy may be difficult to prove. Second, any revision of current testing methods based on *Diana* must also recognize the cultural influences of the ghetto environment in determining a student's learning ability.

PARENTAL PARTICIPATION AND PRIOR HEARINGS

In 1968, 11 Mexican-American public school children, ages 5 through 18 years, filed a complaint (*Arreola v. Board of Education*) in the Superior

Court of Orange County, California, seeking an injunction to prohibit the continuation of special classes for the educable mentally retarded until the following reforms are instituted: (a) a hearing is provided before placement as required by the due process clause of the 14th Amendment to the United States Constitution and Article 1, Section 13 of the California Constitution, (b) the IQ tests used to determine placement must recognize cultural differences among students in general and the Mexican-American plaintiffs in particular; and (c) the classes for the mentally retarded provide an educationally meaningful curriculum and periodic retesting.

After *Diana* the plaintiffs' request for more appropriate testing methods appears to be moot. The real thrust of *Arreola* is its demand for parental participation in the placement decision. Before the decision to specially place a child has been made, the parents must be notified and given a formal opportunity to challenge placement. The plaintiffs' argument for a due process hearing was supported by the United States Supreme Court's ruling in *Wisconsin v. Constantineau* (1971). The Court held that a Wisconsin law requiring the posting of the names of alleged problem drinkers in taverns and package stores for the purpose of preventing the sale of liquor to them constituted stigmatization serious enough to require prior notice and hearing before posting. Justice Douglas writing for the Court found the Wisconsin practice to be a violation of the due process clause of the 14th Amendment:

Where a person's good name, reputation, honor or integrity are at stake because of what the government is doing to him, notice and an opportunity to be heard are essential. "Posting" under the Wisconsin Act may be to some merely the mark of illness; to others it is a stigma, an official branding of a person. The label is a degrading one. . . . Only when the whole proceedings leading to the pinning of an unsavory label on a person are aired can oppressive results be prevented [p. 4129].

In educational placement litigation, the plaintiffs are arguing that the label "mentally retarded" is a stigma, "an official branding of a person," the imposition of which requires notice and a prior hearing.

Compensation for Damages

In Boston, *Stewart v. Phillips* presages the most far reaching revision of current testing methods. The complaint was filed in the Massachusetts Federal District Court in October 1970 and delineated three classes of plaintiffs; (1) all poor or black Boston public school students who are not mentally retarded but have been improperly placed in special classes for the mentally retarded; (2) all poor or black students who are mentally retarded and have been denied placement in educational programs created for their special educational needs; and (3) all parents of students placed in classes for the mentally retarded in the Boston public schools who have been denied opportunity to participate in the placement decision. The class (1) and (2) plaintiffs argue that the improper placement of students who are poor or black on the basis of tests which do not accurately measure the learning ability of these students and the denial of educational programs for their specific educational needs abridge their right to the equal protection of the laws as guaranteed by the 14th Amendment. Class (3) plaintiffs argue that the denial of the opportunity to be heard in relation to the placement of their children in classes for the mentally retarded deprives them of their right to due process of the law in violation of the 14th Amendment.

In so arguing, the plaintiffs seek $20,000 each in compensatory and punitive damages and ask that no student be placed in a special class until a Commission on Individual Educational Needs is established consisting of members appointed by the Commissioner of Education, the Commissioner of Mental Health, the President of the Massachusetts Psychological Association, and the Mayor of Boston. The purpose of the Commission would be to oversee the administration of a battery of psychological tests rationally related to an accurate determination of a student's learning ability, to devise educational programs to meet the individual education needs, to insure that the tests be administered by qualified psychologists, and to establish consultation procedures by which parents might participate in the placement of their children.

The plaintiffs in *Stewart* have gone one step beyond *Covarrubias* in asking that IQ tests recognize not only the influence of the black culture in determining learning ability but that they also be sensitive to the influence which poverty has on educational potential. The creation of a Commission on Individual Educational Needs would provide for the continuing revision of special education long after the specific needs which prompted this litigation were satisfied.

ELIMINATION OF RACIAL SEGREGATION

Finally, in response to the United States Supreme Court's mandate to integrate the nation's schools immediately, Sunflower County, Mississippi, proposed that it use intelligence tests to place students in certain schools. Under the plan, beginning in September 1969, children in the first three grades were given the *California Test of Basic Skills*. Those who ranked in the top quarter in test scores were sent to the nearest of three schools. This included all the white and 38 of the black children. Children in the lower three-quarters were sent to the nearest of five schools. This included the remaining 4,100 black children and no white children.

On August 13, 1970, the Court of Appeals for the Fifth Circuit affirmed the District Court's review of the plan which ordered that the assignment of students based on the achievement testing program be rescinded at the close of the 1970 school year. The Court of Appeals held that any use of intelligence tests to maintain a dual instead of a unitary school system is prohibited as inconsistent with recent Supreme Court decisions.

Implications

Special education procedures serve to highlight institutional racism in many school systems. Many minority group children are systematically deprived of their rights to an education. Mercer (1970) examined the process of special placement in the public schools of Riverside, California. She found that three times more Mexican-Americans and two and a half times more Negroes than would be expected from their percentage in the population tested at an IQ of 79 or below on the *Stanford-Binet Intelligence Test.*

Dunn (1968) postulated that minority children constitute well over half of those enrolled in this country's special education classes:

... there are approximately 32,000 teachers of the retarded employed by local school systems—over one-third of all special educators in the nation. In my best judgment, about 60 to 80 percent of the pupils taught by these teachers are children from low status backgrounds—including Afro-Americans, American Indians, Mexicans, and Puerto Rican Americans [p. 6].

Hall (1970) claims there are possibly 15 times as many black children as white in classes for the mentally retarded based on the Jensen report (1969). Franks (1971) found, in an examination of 11 Missouri school districts, that learning disability programs are predominantly composed of white, middle and upper social status children, while educable classes contain disproportionate numbers of black children. The racial breakdown in the educable classes was 34.21 percent black, 65.79 percent white. In the learning disability classes it was 3.22 percent black, 96.78 percent white.

Disproportionate numbers of minority group children alone would not support the argument that educable classes are failing to provide a meaningful educational experience. However, the negligible number of black children who return to general classes bears out the contention that special classes are failing. In a recent study Chenault (1970) found that once placed in an educable class, it is less likely that the black child will leave the class than the white:

The exit pattern for EMR students placed in special classes was found to vary as a function of race. This finding is indicative of a school policy which basically retains Black students in special classes once they are diagnosed and placed. Caucasian students, on the other hand, were found to have access to exits such as transferring to parochial schools, moving from the school district, or entering the job market [pp. ix, x].

Educators must examine their use of intelligence test scores. Intelligence tests have been under attack for their unfair treatment of racial and cultural minorities for many years. Intelligence test scores and the other criteria currently used for special placement are separating out those children of ethnic and socioeconomic minorities whom the educational system has determined do not possess the necessary skills to achieve success in this white, middle class society. Such children are then relegated to classes containing disproportionate numbers of minority children. The likelihood that their school created handicaps will be remedied and that they will be replaced in the regular class is exceedingly small.

Some test publishers have joined in the criticism. However, when facing attacks on the culture bias of tests, the response is not always in terms of test reform. Instead the argument is presented that tests are merely performing the job assigned to them by general education. Lennon (1964) said:

Let me offer you an analogy that may help in evaluating this issue of test fairness. If we take a youngster who has suffered malnutrition over a period of years . . . and put him on a scale, we may well discover that he is ten, or fifteen, or twenty pounds underweight. We do not then say the scale is biased because of the deprivation the child has suffered. We take this information as currently and accurately descriptive of an important fact about this child—a fact that can be used to his advantage in planning a program calculated to make up for the deficiencies in his earlier care. . . . I suggest to you that this is the way of looking at a test score. The test is giving us a piece of information about a child's performance here and now, which information if properly used, can be extremely helpful in planning the educational endeavors of the child [p. 9].

Educators will not be able to continue to hide behind the indefensible and inexcusable use of intelligence test scores as the primary basis for identifying, labeling and placing children in special classes. The psychologists' defense has been that it is not the problem of the instrumentation but rather the way in which the results have been used. The educators' defense is that while test scores might not be the best indicators of mental retardation, they are the most easily attainable and accurate predictor of school achievement. These arguments overlook the fact that the results are not meaningful since minority group children were not represented in the sample group on which the norms were based and that the application of such instruments to them deprives them of their basic rights. Perhaps what should be recognized is that while trying to weigh the child, a ruler rather than a scale is being used.

The interaction of the child and his environment must be examined carefully in every diagnostic workup. Pathology may reside not in the child but in the school. In such situations, behavior judged as maladaptive by one set of norms may be appropriate and necessary. The ease with which the white controlled educational system has applied the instrument, the label, and the stigma of special class placement on minority children is a function of institutionalized racism in the school setting. Educators "know" that black kids are dumb; the tests "prove" that they are dumb; and then the special education programing ensures the kinds of behaviors through which such children can demonstrate that they are dumb. Diagnostic attention must be given to the personnel and to the system before any child or group of children is relegated to other than regular educational experiences.

University training of educators and psychologists must be revised to meet the demands of consumers. During the preparation of this paper, the authors had extended contacts with faculty from many universities and with a great number of students from a variety of disciplines. There was a wide range of awareness about the litigation and its implications. However, primary concern of the majority of faculty was training more psychologists to administer the standardized tests and teachers to work with children in segregated classrooms. Unfortunately, many of the university students reflected the same values. Even programs that were moving beyond this were not fully integrating what must be done to improve special education programming, to break the cycle of built-in discrimination and failure in many public school students, and to prepare professionals able to develop and apply alternating approaches to child needs.

There will be accountability for program decisions. It is obvious that educators and psychologists must have a greater concern about the negative effects of the separation of a child from the mainstream of education. Such movement is seen by the courts as a deprivation of rights and it is becoming increasingly evident that due process must be followed in such cases. Parents must be active, informed participants in the decision making process. Special class placement must be demonstrated as an effective tool to assist the child in his education, and placement must not be a one way, school life sentence. Routine review and reevaluations, improved programing, and relevant experiences must be available, and their value to the child must be demonstrated.

Maintaining the status quo will be costly. A final implication of the court cases is that the continuation of the existing practices may cost money. The cases which are asking for compensatory and punitive damages have not as yet been decided. However, if the $20,000 being requested for each plaintiff in the *Stewart v. Phillips* case in Boston is awarded, this will cost the Boston school system millions of dollars. Lest the individual professional feel somewhat apart from this, there has been some discussion of malpractice suits directed at individual practitioners who, because of their own roles in the identification, labeling, and placement process, do in fact engage in improper, unethical, or negligent treatment which results in real damage to the child.

Conclusions

The rapid growth of litigation indicates that parents of minority group children have become increasingly dissatisfied with the criteria used to determine special class placement and with the level of educational programing their children receive after placement. Generally, school systems have been unresponsive to pleas for change, so the parents have turned to the courts. Parents have not been alone in voicing their dissatisfaction. Increasingly, the use of intelligence tests, the viability of special education programing, and the relevance of the total school experience are coming under attack by professionals. Of great concern is the unfair treatment of racial and cultural minorities and the growing realization that educable classes are not remedying deficiencies in children.

The response of the profession must not be merely to protect itself but to serve the needs of children. The response to a court order to prevent inappropriate placements and to remove children from special classes must not result in dumping those children into regular classes without providing for their special needs. Responsible educators must devise special approaches and programs to assist such children within the regular class framework. The actions of the professionals should not focus on behaviors to protect themselves and their systems from court suits; emphasis must be on those actions which modify practices, improve programs, and serve as efficient and effective responses to the needs of individual children.

While litigation indicates the seriousness of the present situation, a basic question is raised: Who will direct educational reform, judges or educators? Judge Wright expressed his reluctance to make educational decisions in *Hobson:*

It is regrettable, of course, that in deciding this case this court must act in an area so alien to its expertise. It would be far better indeed for these great social and political problems to be resolved in the political arena by other branches of government. But these are social and political problems which seem at times to defy such resolution. In such situations, under our system, the judiciary must bear a hand and accept its responsibility to assist in the solution where constitutional rights hang in the balance [p. 517].

Educators have a final opportunity to lead in the change, rather than have it imposed. Such leadership will require a careful reexamination of the behavior of school staff rather than school children. Each individual must examine his own role and his own contribution to a system which frequently is repressive, discriminatory, culturally and racially biased, and not responsive to the needs of children. Such a critical assessment is essential to the establishment of a personal accountability for what is done to children in schools. People, rather than systems, hurt other people. Each educator must decide whether he will continue dealing with the symptoms or start working on the cause.

REFERENCES

Arreola v. Board of Education, 160 577 (1968).
Brown v. Board of Education, 347 U.S. 483, 74 S. Ct. 686 (1954).
California Constitution, Article 9, Section 5.
CHENAULT, J. *Mental Retardation as a Function of Race, Sex and Social Economic Status.* Doctoral Dissertation, Michigan State University, 1970.
Civil Rights Act, 42 U.S. Code 2000 d, 2000d-1 (1964).

Covarrubias v. San Diego Unified School District, 70-394 Texas Reports (February, 1971).

Diana v. State Board of Education, C-70 37 RFP, District Court for Northern California (February, 1970).

DUNN, L. M. "Special Education for the Mildly Retarded—Is Much of It Justifiable?" *Exceptional Children* 35 (1968): 5-22.

FRANKS, D. J. "Ethnic and Social Status Characteristics of Children in EMR and LD Classes." *Exceptional Children* 37 (1971): 537-38.

HALL, E. "The Politics of Special Education." In *Inequality in Education*. Harvard Center for Law and Education, 16 March 1970, nos. 3 & 4, pp. 17-22.

Hobson v. Hansen, 269 F.Supp. 401 (1967).

JENSEN, A. R., "How Much Can We Boost IQ and Scholastic Achievement?" *Harvard Educational Review* 39 (1969): 1-123.

LENNON, R. T. *Testing and the Culturally Disadvantaged Child.* Boston: Harcourt, Brace, and World, 1964.

MERCER, J. R. "The Ecology of Mental Retardation." In *The Proceedings of the First Annual Spring Conference of the Institute for the Study of Mental Retardation,* Ann Arbor, Michigan, 1970, pp. 55-74.

Smuck v. Hobson, 408 F.2d 175 (1969).

Spangler v. Board of Education, 311 F.Supp. 501 (1970).

Stewart v. Phillips, 70-1199-F (October, 1970).

Wisconsin v. Constantineau, 39 U.S.L.W. 4128 (January 19, 1971).

Sterling L. Ross, Jr. is Program Assistant, Henry G. DeYoung is Program Associate for Program Development, and Julius S. Cohen is Associate Director, Institute for the Study of Mental Retardation and Related Disabilities, The University of Michigan, Ann Arbor.

7.
Movement and Momentum: Government and the Education of Handicapped Children
ALAN ABESON

What happens to handicapped children in this decade will depend a great deal on the roles that the special educator is willing to play outside the school as well as on his behaviors within the school. Our past suggests we have needed to work as citizens, joining with the parents of handicapped children and with other concerned citizens to influence public priorities, urge school boards to support programs, and influence legislators to pass state and Federal laws.

These comments by Edwin Martin (1972), Associate Commissioner of the Bureau of Education for the Handicapped, reestablish the basic concept that the achievement of full educational opportunities for handicapped children lies in the development of a strong legal foundation.

Within the past year major components on this foundation have been advanced. The positive change occurring at all levels of government and involving all avenues of governmental change can only be described as a "movement." This movement is indicated by the introduction and passage of new state and Federal legislation, the delivery of major attorney generals' rulings, the growing establishment by the Federal courts that the right to an education and the right to treatment for handicapped individuals is "unalienable," the availability of increased funds, and the increased attention to the delivery of services for the education of the handicapped by public policymakers. While it must be recognized that all of these activities have to some degree been occurring for years, it is only now that the volume of activity has reached a point where it can be described as a movement. It is the purpose of this article to report briefly on some of these activities and events which are increasingly reshaping the face of special education.

State Law

State legislative activity regarding the education of the handicapped is not new, but in the past 5 years a major resurgence of action has occurred. This resurgence suggests that US Commissioner of Education Sidney Marland's goal, full educational opportunity for all handicapped children by 1980, may not be a fantasy.

From *Exceptional Children* 39 (September, 1972): 63-66. Reprinted by permission of the author and *Exceptional Children*. Copyrighted by the Council for Exceptional Children.

In the past, many states through permissive laws gave school districts the option of serving or not serving handicapped children. Now, however, the passage of mandatory legislation by an increasing number of states is removing this option. To date almost 70 percent of the states have such laws. Recently passed mandatory legislation is more than just requiring the operation of educational programs for handicapped children. In some states such as Tennessee, which recently passed most provisions in the model laws developed by CEC (Weintraub, Abeson, & Braddock, 1971, Ch. 12), new funding formulas, provisions for personnel training, materials, facilities, and guarantees of the rights of handicapped children were established. All these components are necessary to make mandatory legislation effective. Without them quality programs cannot develop.

Other state legislation has progressed beyond the issue of whether or not to require such programs for handicapped children. In response to research findings that early childhood education is essential for all children, especially the handicapped, states are moving toward lowering the minimum entrance age for school to birth, and in some states, this extends to infants with all disabilities (State-Federal Information Clearinghouse for Exceptional Children, 1972). Similarly, in recognition that some handicapped youth may need prolonged preparation to deal with the adult world, some states have extended the maximum age for school eligibility to 21 years or higher.

Traditional services are also being expanded to provide a more comprehensive educational program for handicapped children. School transportation traditionally provided only between home and school is now carrying children to both the public and private sectors where other needed special services are offered. Many states are also enacting laws which allow for the creation of increased numbers and varieties of regional programs. For example regional programs may occur in a simple form with one district paying tuition to another or in a more complex situation with the formation of a school district and board of education with taxing powers solely providing for special education services.

Federal Law

A new subcommittee of the Senate Labor and Public Welfare Committee, called the Subcommittee on the Handicapped, is indicative of the new awareness at the Federal level. One reason for the formation of this subcommittee is the volume of such legislation now being introduced to Congress. Most Federal legislation for the handicapped considered by the Senate will be dealt with by this subcommittee. An example of this awareness is Congressional action requiring that 10 percent of the children served in Head Start programs be handicapped. Among the other items being considered in this session are:

1. Bills (S. 3614 and H.R. 14866) to place a portion of the financial re-

sponsibility for the cost of educating handicapped children on the Federal government. If this bill were to become law, states would no longer be able to claim lack of funds for their failure to educate handicapped children.

2. Bills (S. 3044 and H.R. 12154) to include the handicapped in Title VI of the 1964 Civil Rights Act. If this passes, no recipient of Federal funds could discriminate against the handicapped in areas such as education, employment, and housing and still retain Federal funds.

3. Other major bills concerning child advocacy (S. 1414 and H.R. 10278), child development (S. 3617), vocational rehabilitation (S. 3368 and H.R. 8395), treatment standards for institutions (S. 3759 and H.R. 15729), employment (H.R. 317 and H.R. 11032), and transportation (S. 3495, H.R. 2221, H.R. 1605, H.R. 15051, and H.R. 15074) which have been introduced during this session of Congress.

If the achievement of more and more money is an indicator of progress and this concept is applied to the movement, then progress is being achieved. Appropriations for the education of the handicapped provided by the Congress for this fiscal year contained record increases. Title VI-B of the Education of the Handicapped Act which provides grants to states to initiate, expand, and improve educational services contains the most significant increases.

Attorney Generals' Opinions

Within the past 2 years the realization that the power of the courts to adjudicate inequities regarding the education of the handicapped has become widely recognized. However, another interpretive avenue has gone almost totally unnoticed—the power of attorney generals' opinions. In New Mexico late last year, in response to a question from a state legislator about the legality of the state's permissive special education law, the state attorney general ruled that the law was contrary to the state's constitutional requirements that free education be provided to all children including the handicapped (1971 NMAG 71-125).

Similarly a 1969 ruling by the North Carolina Attorney General stated that:

It is unconstitutional and invalid, therefore, to operate the public school system in a discriminatory manner as against the mentally retarded children and to allocate funds to the disadvantage of the mentally retarded child. Often a mentally retarded child develops fair skills and abilities and becomes a useful citizen of the state but in order to do this, the mentally retarded child must have his or her chance [p. 250].

It is likely that these issues will increasingly come under the scrutiny of legal officers at all levels of government.

Litigation

Perhaps the activity occurring in the nation's courts is the most significant stimulator of the movement. Two recent landmark cases that have been concluded proclaim the right to an education for all mentally retarded children as well as the right to treatment of the mentally retarded and the mentally ill in institutions. In a third action (*Mills v. Board of Education of the District of Columbia*, 1971), the right to an education is established for all children previously excluded from school.

In the now well publicized *Pennsylvania Association for Retarded Children v. Commonwealth of Pennsylvania* (1971) case, a class action suit was filed to obtain and guarantee for all mentally retarded children in the state a publicly supported education. The decision on the Pennsylvania Association for Retarded Children (PARC) case, in addition to guaranteeing the educational rights of mentally retarded children, requires that the child and his family be provided the rights of notice and due process prior to any alterations in the child's educational status. This is in accordance with the 14th Amendment to the US Constitution. At a minimum, these rights require that school districts notify parents of mentally retarded children that an alteration in their educational status is being considered. This knowledge must be imparted before any change can occur. Further, procedures such as the right to counsel, cross examination, presentation of evidence, and appeal, as well as others, must be followed in the placement process. The decision in Pennsylvania has stimulated similar litigation throughout the country, with many additional suits expected by the end of 1972. It is anticipated that many of these civil actions will be brought as class actions on behalf of all handicapped children rather than single disabilities.

Implicit in the litigation movement is that, while handicapped persons should be treated in as normal an environment as possible, there will always be some persons needing institutional programs. The courts have affirmed that these persons despite their institutionalization also have the right to receive a full treatment program including education. In the case establishing this principle (*Wyatt v. Stickney*, 1971), which focused on Partlow State Hospital for the Mentally Retarded in Alabama, the US District Court judge issued a set of minimum standards for the adequate treatment including education for all Partlow residents. This case, like PARC, is being duplicated throughout the nation and also, like PARC, will open doors to education and other services for institutionalized handicapped children.

Public Awareness

The movement to obtain quality education for all handicapped children has in itself momentum which generates signals to the public and its policy makers which in turn sets the stage for action by public bodies. This momentum has now reached a pitch that requires public policy makers to be aware and to act.

The passage of law at both the state and Federal levels, the rulings of attorney generals, and judicial activities have received considerable attention in the nation's media. The exposure of conditions at New York's Willowbrook State School for the Mentally Retarded, through a 10 part news series and a subsequent 30 minute special, drew the largest audience for a public affairs program in the history of New York City. The filing of 2 law suits against the state (*New York State Association for Retarded Children et al. v. Rockefeller et al., 1972; Patricia Parisi, Anselmo Clarke et al. v. Rockefeller et al., 1972*) and the involvement of Federal and state officials is testimony to the momentum. In Vermont, after a political action campaign focusing on obtaining increased appropriations for the handicapped, the governor was required by the media to spend a considerable portion of a press conference answering questions about his administration's position on the education of Vermont's handicapped children.

The range of concern is extending to other groups that traditionally have not been involved in education of the handicapped. The Council of State Governments, an organization of legislators and attorneys, annually publishes a book titled *Suggested State Legislation* containing model laws in many areas for consideration by state legislators. In the 1972 edition of this volume the model laws for the education of the handicapped developed by CEC will be included. Of interest is the question posed by the attorneys and legislators from the Council of State Governments' board reviewing the models: Was there a provision to keep handicapped children as close to home as possible to receive their education? Such a provision does exist in the model but what is more important is the question itself and the level of knowledge and concern on the part of "uninitiated laymen" it suggests.

Another measure of this momentum was a recent meeting of 35 chief state school officers sponsored by the Education Commission of the States. Here the participants listened and reacted to a presentation concerning the legal movement pertaining to the education of the handicapped. Also included was a discussion of the model statutes developed by CEC.

Concluding Comments

It was not long ago that many of those interested in the education of the handicapped appeared before public policy making bodies to obtain their assistance in making educational programs available because it was "nice" for governmental bodies to do so. Today the demand for assistance is as great but is sought not on the basis of charity but on the basis of rights.

As indicated, progress is occurring. It has been documented above and it will continue to occur for some time. The significance of this progress will depend on the use of all legal fronts—legislative, administrative, and judicial. Crucial to the ultimate success of these efforts is the opening of doors to progress. The special education community must be prepared to provide quality educational progrms for *all* handicapped children—programs which will not only teach children but will stand the test of accountability.

REFERENCES

THE COUNCIL OF STATE GOVERNMENTS. *Suggested State Legislation.* Vol. 32. Lexington, Ky.: CSG, in press.

MARTIN, E. W. "Individualism and Behaviorism as Future Trends in Educating Handicapped Children. *Exceptional Children* 38 (1972): 517-25.

Mills v. Board of Education of the District of Columbia, Civil Action No. 1939-71 (District of Columbia, 1971).

New York State Association for Retarded Children et al. v. Rockefeller et al., 72 Civil Action No. 365 (E.D. New York, 1972).

NORTH CAROLINA ATTORNEY GENERAL. *North Carolina Attorney General Reports.* Vol. 40. Raleigh, N.C.: State of North Carolina, 1969.

Patricia Parisi, Anselmo Clarke et al. v. Rockefeller et al. (E.D. New York, 1972).

Pennsylvania Association for Retarded Children, Nancy Beth Bowman et al. v. Commonwealth of Pennsylvania. David H. Kurtzman et al. Civil Action No. 71-42 (3 Judge Court, E.D. Pennsylvania, 1971).

STATE-FEDERAL INFORMATION CLEARINGHOUSE FOR EXCEPTIONAL CHILDREN. *Pre-School Programs for the Education of Handicapped Children—Summary Report.* Arlington, Va.: SFICEC, 1972.

WEINTRAUB, F., ABESON, A. R., AND BRADDOCK, D. C. *State Law and the Education of Handicapped Children: Issues and Recommendations.* Arlington, Va.: The Council for Exceptional Children, 1971.

WYATT V. STICKNEY, M.D., Alabama Civil Action No. 3195-N (1971).

Alan Abeson is Director, State-Federal Information Clearinghouse for Exceptional Children, The Council for Exceptional Children, Reston, Virginia. The research presented herein was performed pursuant to a grant from the Bureau of Education for the Handicapped, Office of Education, US Department of Health, Education, and Welfare.

For further information about state and Federal law, rules and regulations, attorney generals' opinions, completed and pending litigation, and other information about government and the education of the handicapped, write the State-Federal Information Clearinghouse for Exceptional Children, The Council for Exceptional Children, 1920 Association Drive, Reston, Virginia 22091.

Three

Specific
Learning
Disabilities

Currently the learning problems of children who have the general abilities to succeed in school, but are not doing so are receiving special attention. Many of these problems are now being classified under the professional term of *specific learning disabilities*. The National Advisory Committee on Handicapped Children of the United States Office of Education advanced the following definition of specific learning disabilities for legislative purposes (1968):

Children with special (specific) learning disabilities exhibit a disorder in one or more of the basic psychological processes involved in understanding or in using spoken or written language. These may be manifested in disorders of listening, thinking, talking, reading, writing, spelling, or arithmetic. They include conditions which have been referred to as perceptual handicaps, brain injury, minimal brain dysfunction, dyslexia, developmental aphasia, etc. They *do not* include learning problems which are due primarily to visual, hearing, or motor handicaps, to mental retardation, emotional disturbance, or to environmental disadvantage.

The introductory article gives a brief historical perspective on the establishment of our present national organization which promotes the welfare of children with learning disabilities. The footnote to the article gives additional details concerning this occasion.

The second article in this chapter, by Doris Johnson, describes treatment approaches for dyslexia, which she defines broadly to include disturbances manifested in a child's inability to comprehend or use a spoken word, to read, write, calculate, or perform certain nonverbal functions. This article will help to introduce the reader to the range of communication problems with which the field is concerned.

In the third article Larry Silver, a physician, reports on a study of over five hundred children with the neurological learning disability syndrome and suggests the possibility of inherited central nervous system dysfunction.

The above readings present the educational and medical points of view and are complementary to each other. It is hoped that the reader will obtain an insight from them regarding the scope of this rapidly advancing field.

Experts in learning disabilities are concerned with the identification and remediation of a wide variety of defects, including deficiencies in such major skills as auditory and visual processing. Velma T. Falck details in the fourth article the important skills in auditory processing. This article illustrates how a complex process may be analyzed for instructional purposes.

The final article, by Chalfant and Scheffelin, invites the reader to look to the future and to define and examine some of the research needs in this area of special education.

The "Pioneer Profile" reviews the contributions of Alfred Strauss in the psychopathology and education of "brain-injured" children.

Alfred A. Strauss
1897–1957

PHYSICIAN
NEUROLOGIST
EDUCATOR

Alfred Strauss is recognized as one of the major twentieth century contributors to the field of learning disabilities. He received his medical degree at the University of Heidelberg, Germany, in 1922. He later engaged in advanced training in neurology and psychiatry at the Psychiatric University Clinic in Heidelberg and at the Neurological Institute of the University of Frankfurt. There he became familiar with Kurt Goldstein's research on brain-injured soldiers following World War I. He proceeded to relate this research to the learning problems of mildly retarded children who showed signs of brain injury.

Shortly thereafter Strauss became Director of the Psychiatric-Neurological Policlinic at the University of Heidelberg, where he also served as Associate Professor of Child Neuro-Psychiatry and as consultant to a number of children's psychiatric and educational services. In 1937, he was invited to come to the Wayne County Training School, Northville, Michigan, to assume the position of research psychiatrist. It was here in collaboration with Heinz Werner, who had also emigrated from Germany, that Strauss did his major research and writing relating to the psychopathology and education of brain-injured children. The cluster of traits which were identified with high frequency among these children became known as the *Strauss Syndrome.*

Appreciation is expressed to Mrs. Alfred A. Strauss for her assistance in the preparation of this profile. *The Editors*

8.
Behavioral Diagnosis and Remediation of Learning Disabilities

SAMUEL A. KIRK

Trace Dr. Kirk's logic, which brought him to suggest the use of the term "learning disabilities" to the organizers of this conference.

I should like to first compliment the organizers of this conference for bringing together lay and professional personnel to discuss a problem that has bothered all of us.

Any group that meets to discuss the problems of children with developmental deficits of one kind or another is facing a formidable task. I say a formidable task because no one yet has been able to present us with a solution to the management and training of these children. If we had a fool-proof solution to the management and training of deviations in children, this meeting would not be necessary. And the fact that there are so many diverse opinions and partial solutions should make this meeting highly interesting and hopefully challenging.

As I understand it, this meeting is not concerned with children who have sensory handicaps, such as the deaf or the blind, or with children who are mentally retarded, or with delinquent or emotionally disturbed children caused by environmental factors. It is concerned primarily with children who can see and hear and who do not have marked general intellectual deficits, but who show deviations in behavior and in psychological development to such an extent that they are unable to adjust in the home or to learn by ordinary methods in school. The causes of these behavior deviations have been postulated as some sort of cerebral dysfunction.

There are two kinds of terms that have been applied to these children, either alone or in combination.

From *Proceedings of the Conference on Exploration into the Problem of the Perceptually Handicapped Child,* First Annual Meeting (Chicago, Illinois, 6 April 1963), pp. 1-4. Evanston, Illinois: Fund for Perceptually Handicapped Children, Inc.

On April 6, 1963, representatives of several associations, each of which was organized to advance the interests of children who had special learning problems, met in Chicago to explore common interests and to establish a single national organization. Dr. Samuel A. Kirk was invited to give the opening address and to assist these organizations in defining a common focus. A portion of Dr. Kirk's address relating to labels and terminology is reproduced here.

Representatives of the Associations for Brain Injured Children and the Fund for Perceptually Handicapped Children convened later during the conference and officially organized a national body, The Association for Children with Learning Disabilities (ACLD). *The Editors*

The first group of terms refer to causation or etiology. We try to label the child with a term that has biological significance. These terms are *brain injury, minimal brain damage, cerebral palsy, cerebral dysfunction, organic driven-ness, organic behavior disorders, psychoneurological disorders,* and a host of other terms. All of these terms refer to a disability of the brain in one form or another as an explanation of the deviant behavior of the child.

The second group of terms refers to the behavior manifestations of the child, and include a wide variety of deviant behavior. Terms such as *hyperkinetic behavior, perceptual disorders, conceptual disorders, Strauss syndrome, social dyspraxia, catastrophic behavior, disinhibition, learning disorders,* and the various forms of aphasia, apraxia, agnosia, dyslexia and a host of other terms which describe the specific behavior deficit of the child.

I know that one of your problems at this meeting is to find a term that applies to every child. Last night, a friend of mine accosted me with the statement, "We're going to ask you to give us a term." I didn't know how to answer his question, and I still do not believe I can answer it because the term you select should be dependent on your specific aims. Is your purpose a research one, or is it a management and training problem?

Research workers have attempted to correlate the biological malfunctions with behavior manifestations. Actually the job of the neurophysiologists and the physiological psychologist is to explain deviations of the brain and their effect on emotional, perceptual, and cognitive behavior, or vice versa, to explain the behavior manifestations by finding the correlated brain dysfunction. This is a research task and of particular concern to the research neurophysiologist and physiological psychologist.

As I understand it, the task of the group meeting today, however, is not to conduct research on behavior and the brain, but to find effective methods of diagnosis, management, and training of the children. From this point of view, you will not be so concerned with the first category of concepts relating to etiology of brain injury or cerebral dysfunction, but with the behavior manifestations themselves and with the methods of management and training of the deviations in children.

Actually, what does it mean to say that one of these children is brain injured? It is actually saying that the overt behavior of a child, *hyperactivity* (which we can observe), *low intelligence* (which we can test), or perseveration, short attention span, or learning disability is caused by a *brain injury* or *cerebral dysfunction* for which we may or may not have adequate neurological evidence. But we have some brain-injured individuals, diagnosed as cerebral palsied, who have obtained M.D. or Ph.D. degrees. We have some definitely diagnosed brain-injured children who are severe mental defectives. We have some brain-injured children who are hyperkinetic (hyperactive) while others with brain injuries are extremely lethargic, under-active, and passive. If we can obtain diverse types of behavior, high intelligence or low intelligence, hyperactivity or hypoactivity, under the same label "brain injury," the label ceases to have diagnostic integrity from the point of view of management and training.

I have felt for some time that labels we give children are satisfying to us but of little help to the child himself. We seem to be satisfied if we can give a technical name to a condition. This gives us the satisfaction of closure. We think we know the answer if we can give the child a name or a label—brain injured, schizophrenic, autistic, mentally retarded, aphasic, etc. As indicated before, the term "brain injury" has little meaning to me from a management of training point of view. It does not tell me whether the child is smart or dull, hyperactive or under-active. It does not give me any clues to management of training. The terms cerebral palsy, brain injured, mentally retarded, aphasic, etc., are actually classification terms. In a sense they are not diagnostic, if by diagnostic we mean an assessment of a child in such a way that leads to some form of treatment, management, or remediation. In addition, it is not a basic cause, since the designation of a child as brain injured does not really tell us why the child is brain injured or how he got that way.

I often wonder why we tend to use technical and complex labels, when it is more accurate and meaningful to describe behavior. If we find a child who has not yet learned to talk, the most scientific description is that he has not yet learned to talk. The labels of aphasia or mentally retarded or emotionally disturbed are not as helpful as a description and may, in many instances, tend to confuse the issue. Instead of using the term hyperkinetic we would understand the child better if the observer states that he continually climbs walls or hangs on chandeliers.

I should like to caution you about being compulsively concerned about names and classification labels. Sometimes names block our thinking. I would prefer that people inform me that they have a child that does not talk instead of saying to me their child is dysphasic. People apparently like to use technical terms. I have received letters from doctors and psychologists telling me that "we are referring a child to you who has strephosymbolia." I would prefer that they tell me that "the boy has been in school two years, and he hasn't yet learned to read even though his intelligence is above average." This description of the problem is more scientific than the label "strephosymbolia," since the latter term itself has a specific meaning. It actually means the child has twisted symbols because of lack of cerebral dominance. But it is used by some people to designate a child who is retarded in reading, regardless of the cause.

Recently, I have used the term "learning disabilities" to describe a group of children who have disorders in development in language, speech, reading, and associated communication skills needed for social inter-action. In this group I do not include children who have sensory handicaps such as blindness or deafness, because we have methods of managing and training the deaf and the blind. I also exclude from this group children who have generalized mental retardation. This approach has led me and my colleagues to develop methods of assessing children, or describing their communication skills in objective terms, in such a manner which gives us clues to management and training. . . .

Samuel A. Kirk is Professor of Special Education, The University of Arizona, Tucson.

9.
Treatment Approaches to Dyslexia
DORIS J. JOHNSON

This article illustrates the common approach of a learning disabilities specialist to problems in this field. As you read the article, pay special attention to the variables identified and to the implied remediation.

At a recent meeting concerned with the education of exceptional children it was suggested that we first define our raw material before discussing approaches to remediation. The point is well taken and should be considered here since the term "dyslexia" is used to represent various conditions. The word itself means an inability or partial inability to read; however, there are many reasons for learning failure so a more specific definition is needed. In our work at the Institute for Language Disorders the term dyslexia is used to designate a subgroup within a larger population of children who have learning disabilities. A child with a learning disability has a disturbance in one or more basic psychological processes such as perception, memory, symbolization, or conceptualization. The disturbance may be manifested in the child's inability to comprehend or use the spoken word, to read, write, calculate, or perform certain nonverbal functions. It does not include those children who have sensory impairments, mental retardation, primary emotional disturbance, nor those who have had limited opportunities for learning. According to this definition, the dyslexic has at least average intelligence, has normal hearing and vision, has had opportunities for learning, and is reasonably well adjusted, despite his difficulties in reading.

The evaluation of children with learning disabilities requires the compe-

From the *International Reading Association: Conference Proceedings* 13 (1969): 95-102. Reprinted with permission of Doris Johnson and the International Reading Association.

tencies of many professional persons including psychologists, pediatricians, neurologists, ophthalmologists, social workers, educators, and others. The primary task of the team is to determine why the child is not learning. The intensive psychoeducational study is designed to explore the ways in which the child learns or fails to learn. It is concerned with learning processes. An important contribution to these studies in the semiautonomous systems concept of Hebb.[1] This concept proposes that the brain is made up of semi-independent systems, and that at times a given system, such as the auditory or the visual system, functions semi-independently from others. At times one system functions in a supplementary way with another, and at times all systems function interrelatedly. Diagnostically and educationally this concept has many implications.[3] Each psychosensory system must be appraised as it functions semiautonomously, in coordination with another system, and as all of the systems function simultaneously. In learning, this means that we try to ascertain whether a child can perceive, remember, and interpret what he hears, sees, or feels. We also explore the ways in which the systems work together. This being the case, we have suggested that three types of learning must be evaluated: (1) *intrasensory* learning requiring only one system such as audition or vision, (2) *intersensory* learning requiring two or more but not all systems, and (3) *integrative* learning requiring all systems functioning as a unit. The study of each type of learning includes measures of perception, memory, symbolization, and other basic psychological functions. Since reading is a highly complex symbol system involving many of these processes, it is understandable that the dyslexics constitute one of the largest subgroups within the learning disability population.

In normal learning all functions and processes seem to be related. If a child hears, we expect him to understand; if he can read silently, we expect him to read orally; if he reads single words, we expect him to read the same words in context; if he spells aloud, we expect him to write. These same assumptions, however, cannot be made in regard to children with learning disabilities. The interrelation of abilities varies greatly in dyslexics as compared with normal children.[5] Some have superior auditory abilities but very poor visual abilities; others, the reverse. Some have adequate intrasensory abilities but poor intersensory or integrative functions. They perceive and remember what they hear or see, but they cannot associate the information from two or more sensory channels simultaneously. Some have adequate input but poor output; they comprehend but cannot express themselves. In some a specific mode of output such as writing or speaking may be impaired. Because of these variations in abilities we must examine the child's performance in relation to the processes that were required. For example, a ten-year-old boy reads silently at the fourth grade level but only at a second grade level orally. An inspection of the processes required for each task indicates that the silent reading test requires only intrasensory visual functions whereas the oral requires both auditory and visual. In contrast, a seventh grade boy comprehends *only* when he reads aloud. He must go through an auditory translation in order to interpret visual symbols. Discrepancies of this type may also be noted in spelling achievement. The processes involved in multiple choice, oral, and dictated spelling tests are so different that children manifest differences of three or four grades, depending upon their specific learning deficits.

A major purpose for analyzing systems and processes is to determine which learning circuits are operative or inoperative. A second is to determine what and how the child should be taught. If a student reads silently, our task is not to teach him to read per se, but to help him "reauditorize" words. Similarly, if he spells better orally we would try to help him "revisualize" letters or form the visual-motor patterns for writing. When working with a dyslexic, we attempt to analyze the child's strengths and weaknesses, and then select methods which correspond with his learning patterns.

In our research, diagnosis, and remediation, we have emphasized another basic concept called *overloading*. Many children fail to learn, or become confused if they are required to assimilate information through more than one system at a time. Some can look and learn or can listen and learn, but they cannot look, listen, *and* learn. The information being received through a given sensory modality impedes integration of the information being received through another. Overloading may be seen clinically in the child's failure to learn, his confusion, his random movements, and occasionally by behavior resembling seizures. The concept of overloading has considerable relevance for teaching dyslexics. If a multisensory or VAKT approach is used inappropriately, learning may actually be impeded.

To explore the factor of overloading in relation to learning, we are engaged in making brain studies. While the child is engaged in learning tasks (intrasensory, intersensory, and integrative), EEG's are taken and analyzed by computer techniques. The presumption is that we will be able to explore the concept of overloading as it relates to dyslexia and other learning disabilities. Hopefully, our educational methods, techniques, and procedures can be more scientifically oriented in the future. Conceivably, research will reveal that some children learn only in the presence of certain well defined conditions of input and output.

Although the goal is to teach all dyslexics to read, the initial approach varies with the nature of the disability. Many fall into one of two major categories—those who are deficient in visual processes and those who are deficient in auditory learning. We have called the former group visual dyslexics. Characteristically they have a tendency to reverse, rotate, or invert letters or transpose letters within words. Some attend to details within words or to the general configuration but not to both. Some have a reduced rate of visual perception. Most have visual memory problems which prevent them from remembering whole words. As Hinshelwood[2] stated many years ago, certain children seem to be capable of storing auditory but not visual images. Because they cannot perceive and remember whole words, we use an elemental or phonic approach in remediation. Letter sounds are introduced (a few consonants and short vowels) and the student blends them into meaningful words. Letter names are not used in the early stages and few if any rules are used. Rarely are associations such as *a* for *apple* used. The objective is to help the student unlock the code, to convert the visual to the auditory as simply as possible. The forms of the letters should be kept constant since the visual dyslexic often finds it difficult to read both upper and lower case print. As soon as he can attack several words consistently, phrases and sentences are presented. A few sight words such as *the, you,* and *I* are introduced in context so the sentences can be natural and similar to the child's spoken language. In this way he can begin to anticipate words while reading. Although some of the current linguistic readers have a vocabulary which is appropriate for this group (with consistent sound-symbol associations), the sentence structure in a few is distorted and confusing; hence, the children fail to acquire meaning.

The basic approach to reading for the visual dyslexic circumvents his basic weakness and capitalizes on the strengths; however, work is also done to improve the deficit. A two-pronged remediation plan is used. The objective is to assist the child in both word attack and instant recognition. In the past we found it was neither beneficial to bombard the deficit nor to raise all skills to a normal readiness level. Thus, the dual plan. However, even when working on a specific deficit such as visual perception or memory, one must consider the most effective teaching circuit. If a child cannot perceive letters in the normal way he probably will not benefit from being given worksheets designed to improve visual perception. The teacher must decide how the materials can be used so that the child can, in fact, see the similarities and differences. At times color cues may be used. In other instances the size of the letters may be increased. In other cases taction (kinesthesis) or extensive verbalization will be used to "lead the child's looking." The techniques are not selected at random, but are based on the child's pattern of strengths and weaknesses.

In contrast to the visual dyslexic, the auditory dyslexic usually cannot learn phonics and therefore is taught to read whole words. Characteristically these children have disturbances in auditory perception, rhyming, blending, analysis, and memory. Although gross discrimination may be adequate, the children fail to perceive sounds within words. Many have difficulty with oral reading. Because of these learning patterns, the children are taught with an intrasensory visual approach during the initial stages of remediation. They are taught a sight vocabulary which consists largely of nouns and verbs, that is words which can be associated with an object, experience, or picture. In this way no oral response is required. While some children benefit from saying the words aloud, others cannot concentrate on the visual image if they also must call up the auditory. Therefore, even when phrases and sentences are first introduced, the assignments are arranged so the child can match them with pictures rather than read them aloud. In some respects the approach is similar to that used in learning a foreign language. Words are often introduced in units such as foods, clothing, or transportation. Since no child can learn every word from visual memory, and since we want to help him with word attack, a dual approach is also used with this group. As soon as a child has a substantial sight vocabulary, every attempt is made to help him with the auditory skills so that he can decode unfamiliar words. Again, the teacher must ask, "How can I facilitate learning?" Consider the possibilities that might be used to improve auditory perception.

One alternative is intrasensory stimulation. Some children cannot listen and look. They automatically close their eyes or turn their heads when working on difficult auditory tasks. A six-year-old, for instance, could take a hearing test only when his eyes were closed. Although some children spontaneously develop strategies for learning, others need assistance from the teacher. Therefore, while working on rhyming, discrimination, blending, or other auditory tasks the child is asked to close his eyes. With this slight modification many can learn to hear similarities and differences in words.

Another possibility is intensification of the stimulus. Some teachers intuitively raise their voices when working with students who have auditory perceptual problems, and, in doing so, facilitate learning. Occasionally we give children portable, binaural amplifiers to use during brief periods of instruction. When the sound is amplified through the headsets, many can perceive units within words that they cannot detect under ordinary listening conditions. A seventh grade boy improved substantially in spelling when he decided to wear the amplifier while the teacher dictated words in class.

Frequently teachers utilize cues from other sensory modalities. For example, various types of visual aids are beneficial. Some auditory dyslexics were able to perceive the rhyming parts of words only after they saw the similarities in their sight vocabularies. After children learned to match pictures with words, the teacher placed the words in groups, asking the children to find those that looked the same at the end. Following this procedure, they began to hear the similarities.

Other children profit from watching the position of the tongue, lips, and jaw of the speaker. Those who cannot hear the difference between words such as *pin* and *pan* are directed to watch the mouth of the speaker. On the other hand, some cannot follow a sequence of movements and are not aided by this type of visual clue.

Some students profit from taction or kinesthesis while working on auditory perception. However, again the nature of the stimulus will vary. Some learn to feel the position of the tongue and lips when they say words themselves; others feel cut out letters or words; others write the letters and learn to discriminate differences. In all instances the basic question raised by the teacher is, "How can I balance the input simulation to modify the child's behavior?"

Some children present totally different learning patterns. They may be deficient in both auditory and visual learning processes and, therefore, will not respond to any of the methods described here. Some will need more taction and possibly a multisensory approach. In any case we stress the need for selection of methods by choice, not chance. Every attempt is made to analyze the child's style of learning and match it with appropriate methods and procedures. This being the case, teachers need to be familiar with many approaches and particularly with the integrities required for learning according to each. Critical questions pertaining to methods include the following:

1. What is the nature of the input stimulation? Is it primarily visual; does it combine auditory and visual stimulation; are all sensory channels used simultaneously?

2. What is the expected response from the child? Is he expected to match figures or to mark something? Is he expected to give an oral response? Does he need to know how to write?

3. What is the nature of vocabulary? On what basis were the words selected? How controlled is the vocabulary? Do the words have a consistent phoneme-grapheme relationship? How many meaningful words are used (specifically nouns and verbs)? Is the vocabulary useful to the student?

4. What is the nature of the sentence structure? Is it similar to the child's language? Is the sentence length beyond the range of his auditory memory span?

5. What is the nature of the content? Is the material in keeping with the child's level of experience and interest?

6. Does the method require deductive or inductive thought processes? Does the child work from the whole to the part or from the part to the whole?

In addition to the preceding questions the teacher analyzes reading books for other factors such as the size of print, the amount of material on a page, variations in letter case and size, spacing between words and lines, length of story, and nature of the pictures or illustrations.

These constitute but a few of the variables to consider when teaching dyslexic children. Others include level of intelligence, language, and experience. As we learn more about children and about learning processes, undoubtedly more variables will be included in the plan. In essence the dyslexic child may be likened to a special type of computer.[4] The computer has a potential capacity for processing information. However, it will not function properly unless fed with a particular program which satisfies the necessary criteria for production. A program which fits one computer will not necessarily work for one of a different type. Furthermore, an incorrect program will be rejected by the computer, and under no circumstances will the processing of information occur with that program. Like the computer, the dyslexic child will process information only when "fed" with the proper program. Although we have countless variables to control (and match) when dealing with something as complex as the human brain and the reading process, the years ahead can be exciting as we do try, in fact, to study and program the variables in a more systematic fashion.

REFERENCES

1. HEBB, D. "The Semi-Autonomous Process: Its Nature and Nurture." *Am Psychol*, 18:1, 16-27, 1963.
2. HINSHELWOOD, J. *Congenital Word-Blindness*. London: H. K. Lewis, 1917.
3. JOHNSON, D. AND MYKLEBUST, H. *Learning Disabilities: Educational Principles and Practices*. New York: Grune, and Stratton, 1967.
4. KATZ, S. "Teaching Techniques for Dyslexics." Unpublished paper, Northwestern University, 1968.
5. ZIGMOND, N. "Intrasensory and Intersensory Processes in Normal and Dyslexic Children." Unpublished doctoral dissertation, Northwestern University, 1968.

Doris J. Johnson is Associate Professor, Department of Communication Disorders, Program in Learning Disabilities, Northwestern University, Evanston, Illinois.

10.
Familial Patterns in Children with Neurologically-Based Learning Disabilities

LARRY B. SILVER

As you read this article, try to assess the possible role of inherited central nervous system dysfunction among children with learning disabilities.

The Neurological Learning Disability Syndrome and Its Definition

About 30 years ago there was an accelerated effort to refine the differential diagnosis of children with educational difficulties. Werner and Strauss sought to account for divergent patterns of functioning in a population of mentally defective children by classifying children as having or not having extrinsic damage to the nervous system based on the background histories of the children. Comparison of the cognitive and emotional behaviors of the two groups revealed that, despite considerable overlap, the group with a history of perinatal or later childhood nervous system damage contained a larger proportion of children who were hyperactive, emotionally labile, perceptually disordered, impulsive, distractible, and abnormally rigid and perseverative than the group with no such history. It was to the children with these peculiar patternings of behavioral organization that the term "brain damaged" or "brain injured" came to be applied, and with it came the concept of "the brain-damaged child."

This label, unfortunately, remains the most popular. As Eisenberg notes, "to many physicians, 'organic brain injury' conveys irreversibility and hopelessness . . . and mention of 'brain' in a diagnostic context suggests to parents tumor, trauma, and operation, all with grim overtones" (p. 63).

Later, as more children with these problems were recognized and evaluated and as less evidence was found to confirm brain damage and more evidence suggested subtle disturbances of the nervous system, the emphasis was shifted from brain damage to the possibility of dysfunctioning or immaturity of the central nervous system. The primary area of learning was considered to be the cerebral cortex; thus, a new diagnostic label began to be used, "minimal cerebral dysfunction" or "minimal brain dysfunction." Clements felt that, "with our limited validated knowledge concerning relationships between brain and behavior, we must accept certain

From *Journal of Learning Disabilities* 4 (August/September, 1971): 349-58. Reprinted by permission of the author and *Journal of Learning Disabilities*.

categories of deviant behavior, development dyscrasias . . . as valid indices of brain dysfunction" (p. 6).

Birch, in summarizing this classification confusion, noted:

One major obstacle to knowledge has been the tendency to consider the problem of the "minimally brain-damaged" child as a problem in the singular. The essential inadequacy of the term "brain damage" for the purpose of classification derives from the contradiction between its singular form and the plurality of content which it seeks to embrace. As Birch and Demb, Laufer and Denhoff, and Wortis have pointed out, brain damage may vary with respect to etiology, extent, type of lesion, locus, duration of damage, rate at which damage has been sustained, time of life and developmental stage at which the injury has occurred, and the syndromes of dysfunction that may result. In point of fact there is not a minimally brain-damaged child but rather many varieties of brain-damaged children. [p. 4]

Until our knowledge of brain and behavior clarifies the issues, it is best to avoid a label which connotes an understanding of etiology, pathogenesis, or site of pathology. The learning problems are primarily neurologically based, not emotionally or culturally based, not retardation. In addition, there is no one entity, but rather a group of related signs and symptoms. The best purely descriptive label is the suggested "neurological learning disability syndrome."

Children with this type of learning disability have problems in relating to their environment and in receiving, processing, storing, retrieving, and expressing information. Because of the frustrations they face in trying to cope, they may develop secondary emotional problems.

Concerning the interaction with their environment, many are *hyperactive*. There appears to be an imbalance between the excitatory and inhibitory motor processes. Many parents report that their child with this syndrome was more active even *in utero*. This activity appears to be purposeless; it is as if the muscles are in continuous motion and the child has to find an excuse for this motion. Paradoxically, the hyperactivity decreases with the use of a psycho-stimulant but increases with the use of a central nervous system depressant.

Another area of dysfunction which creates problems in coping with the environment is the child's difficulty in selectively filtering stimuli. Normally, sensory inputs are monitored at a lower brain level and certain inputs are selectively forwarded to the cortex. This allows, for example, an individual to ride a noisy train and selectively block out auditory stimuli so that he can listen to one conversation, yet hear the conductor call his stop. This child does not have so efficient a "filtering system." He is frequently at the mercy of his environment, receiving different stimuli simultaneously and at the same intensity. Consequently, he is *distractible*. All stimuli compete for his attention. In the classroom he may try to concentrate on one task but be quickly distracted by a child walking by or by a noise in the hall. When he returns to his work he has lost his place or pattern of thought. Because of the distractibility he cannot concentrate successfully on any one task for very long. All stimuli seem to interfere; the result is a *short attention span.*

Another area of environmental difficulty has to do with occasional *perseveration,* an inability to stop a theme. The child may see a picture of trees, begin to discuss the topic, and be unable to end. Regardless of the change in topic or picture, he will continue to concentrate on trees.

Specific learning disabilities have not yet been described here. Yet, it is apparent that any child with hyperactivity, distractibility, a short attention span, and occasional perservation would have difficulty in the process of acquiring knowledge.

The specific learning problems may be at any or all levels of learning. He may have central perceptual problems in interpreting visual, auditory, tactile, or kinesthetic stimuli. Following this input, he may have difficulty in sequencing, abstracting, or other aspects of integrating the data. Or, after integrating, he may have difficulty in storing the data (memory) or in retrieving this information. Even if the information is received, integrated, and stored, he might have difficulty expressing the information through muscle output (motor) or word output (language).

Another possible problem for the child with learning difficulties can have to do with his availability for learning. Many of these children appear to be "in-and-out." During some minutes, hours or days they seem to assimilate and retain everything taught. During other periods of time, nothing seems to be learned or remembered. This feature does not appear to be a seizure-like state.

This child has difficulty coping with stress. He is emotionally labile; his frustration tolerance is low. Impulsivity is compounded by apparent poor impulse control.

To summarize, children with this syndrome *all have* one or more of the following primary dysfunctions and, in addition, *may have* one or more of the following secondary dysfunctions. Certain observable behavioral difficulties are also noted: *Primary Dysfunctions*: perceptual learning disability, integrative learning disability, memory learning disability, output learning, disability (motor and/or language). *Secondary Dysfunctions:* hyperactivity, distractibility, short attention span, perseveration. *Altered Behavior:* inconsistent availability for learning, emotional lability.

The Problem of Etiology

This syndrome has been well defined; however, the etiology is far from understood. Pasamanick and Knobloch hypothesize that there is a spectrum of disorders caused by perinatal brain damage, the most severe forms causing fetal or neonatal death, cerebral palsy, epilepsy, or mental deficiency, and the less severe forms (depending on the location and extent of damage) causing a variety of learning and behavioral disorders.

Abrams feels that the syndrome reflects a delayed and irregular maturation pattern. Such irregular development of the total individual may be secondary to chemical, genetic, metabolic, emotional or other still unknown factors. In another paper, I have proposed a neurochemical imbalance in the ascending reticular activating and limbic systems as the etiologic factor in one group of children with the neurological learning disability syndrome (Silver).

The brain is a complex organ and many types of minimal dysfunction can occur. The child with the neurological learning disability syndrome has a specific cluster of dysfunctions. As suggested by Birch, maybe there is no one etiology for this syndrome, for there are several ways in which brain function can be compromised. In some cases there may have been subtle perinatal brain damage; in some cases there may have been a circulatory, toxic, or metabolic embarrassment during a critical period of prenatal development; in some cases a stress to the nervous system during the critical early years of life (trauma, fever, encephalitis, etc.) may have resulted in the dysfunction. The study reported on here was designed as a pilot exploration of the possibility that in some cases with this syndrome an inherited central nervous dysfunction, not brain damage, is the etiologic issue.

Procedure

This study was formally begun in September 1967 at The Willis School for Educational Therapy, a special program for children with learning disabilities. The 556 subjects were selected from the total past and present population of students at this school: all those for whom there were diagnostic data confirming the diagnosis of neurological learning disability syndrome, as defined above, and who tested on the WISC or Binet as having at least average intelligence.

A special questionnaire for the parents was introduced into the diagnostic evaluation of each new child at the school. Then I reviewed the information on the questionnaire with the parents at the time of the interpretive conference. It included the following:

1. Child's age, sex, birth order, and if adopted.

2. History of pregnancy and delivery (previous miscarriages, Rh factor, prematurity, prenatal and perinatal difficulties).

3. Medical history of the child (illnesses, hospitalizations, neurologic problems, EEG abnormalities, history of a temperature over 105°).

4. History of mother, father, sibling (or siblings) having similar learning difficulties as a child.

5. Developmental history of child (motor, language, psychological, and social development; history of sensitivity to noise or sound).

6. History of impulsivity (enuresis, temper tantrums, stealing, firesetting, sneaking and hoarding food).

7. History of medication for the child.

These data were collected on the 184 children selected for the study from September 1967 through September 1969. At the same time all records of the school from January 1965 through September 1967 were reviewed, and although these records were less complete, enough information was available to be able to include 372 of these children, using the same criteria as for the other group.

To further explore whether the learning disabilities were inherited, a special project was designed separate from the questionnaires and records review to find out if any of the parents who reported a school-age history of similar learning difficulties still had evidence of such problems. A random group of 50 children in this study and their parents were selected for further testing. Twenty-five of these children were selected with a positive family history of learning disabilities. The 50 children and their 100 parents were given a battery of diagnostic tests covering visual-perceptual, spatial, visual-motor, and fine motor areas, but not auditory perception, language, memory, or integrative skills. The test battery included the Bender-Gestalt, Gottschalk Embedded Figure—form for adult (Witkin, 1950), or child (Goodenough and Eagle, 1963)—Rod and Frame (Witkin, 1954), Laterality (Culver et al., 1963), and Purdue Pegboard.

From the initial conception of this study, limitations in data collection and data accuracy were apparent. Data on the child were based on parent reporting. Copies of all consultations and evaluations were obtained and used, but the early history was based on the parents' memory. Once the parents understood their child's learning and language disabilities, they were asked if either of them had had similar difficulties as a child. These data, too, could not be as objective as data produced by a search of the elementary school reports might have been, but that was not feasible. Whenever parents reported that another of their children had similar difficulties, that child (or children) was seen for an evaluation if possible, or his school records were reviewed. Thus, the history of a similar language disability in either of the parents or in a sibling was, in large part, subjective data.

Prior to September 1967, questions on familial patterns were not asked; the data for that period were based on information volunteered by the parents. Since no parent had been asked if he or she had had a learning disability, the fact that anyone spontaneously volunteered such information was significant. In fact, it was the frequency with which this information was volunteered that led me to explore the possibility of a familial pattern.

Results

Of the 556 children included in this study, 372 were evaluated on the basis of school records from January 1965 to September 1967, and 184 were evaluated at the time of admission to the school between September 1967 and September 1969. The findings, by factors investigated, will be presented initially and then discussed.

Sex: 77.3 percent of the children were male, a 3.4:1 ratio of boys to girls.

Adoption: A total of 36 children were adopted. According to the most current national statistics available for both adoption and live births in the United States (for the year 1965) there were 3,760,358 viable births (U.S. Bur. of Census, 1967b) and 142,000 registered adoptions (U.S. Bur. of Census, 1967a) in the country that year. Thus the national incidence of adoption is one child for every 26 live births. The 36 adopted children in this study population is 1.68 times the national norm.

Family history of learning disability: This information was available for 319 of the 1965-67 families and for 170 of the 1967-69 families. Only in the latter group were the parents specifically asked about this issue. Families in which the mother, father, sibling, or siblings had a history of learning disabilities were as follows: 1965-67: 78 families, or 24.4 percent of the sample; 1967-69: 67 families, or 39.4 percent of the sample; total: 145 families, or 29.6 percent of the sample. See Table 1 for specific breakdowns of the data.

For a family chart that clearly reflects a familial trend for learning disabilities, see Figure 1. The maternal grandfather was described as having trouble learning and being "dyslexic." The maternal grandmother was described as having "years of problems with reading." A maternal uncle and a paternal uncle were described as having similar disabilities. Each of these two uncles had two children with similar disabilities. The child in this study had two brothers with similar problems.

Twins: There were four sets of twins, all fraternal. In one set, both twins

Table 1. Family Member with a Similar Learning Disability

Family Member	Sample Group	Total Numbers	Percent of Sample
Father	1965-67	19	6.0
	1967-69	33	19.0
	Total	52	10.0
Mother	1965-67	17	5.0
	1967-69	21	12.0
	Total	39	8.0
Sibling	1965-67	42	13.0
	1967-69	34	19.0
	Total	76	15.0
Siblings	1965-67	22	7.0
	1967-69	3	2.0
	Total	25	5.0

had the neurological learning disability syndrome. In the other three sets, the fraternal twin did not have learning difficulties; however, in each case another sibling did have this syndrome.

Birth order: The birth order is shown in Table 2.

Education of parents: A bachelor or graduate degree was held by 35.5% of the fathers and 19.1% of the mothers (see Table 3).

For the following data, enough information was available in the records of the 1965-67 group for both groups to be combined and all 556 children (1965-69) studied.

Previous history of miscarriage: In the cases with a positive family history of learning disabilities, six mothers, or 4 percent had had a previous miscarriage. In one case the mother was Rh negative and the child was Rh positive (middle child). In all six of these cases an older sibling, born prior to the miscarriage, had the neurological learning disability syndrome.

In 23, or 7 percent of the cases without a family history of learning disabilities the mother had had a previous miscarriage. In three of these cases there was a potential Rh incompatibility. One mother had toxemia and one hemorrhaged throughout the pregnancy while carrying the child included in this study. Five children were born prematurely and required oxygen at birth.

Rh factor: Nineteen, or 13 percent of the cases with a positive family history of learning disabilities had a potential Rh incompatibility—that is, Rh negative mother, Rh positive child. In one of these cases, the mother had had a previous miscarriage. In 11 of the 19 cases either an older sibling

Figure 1. FAMILY HISTORY OF LEARNING DIFFICULTIES, T. J.

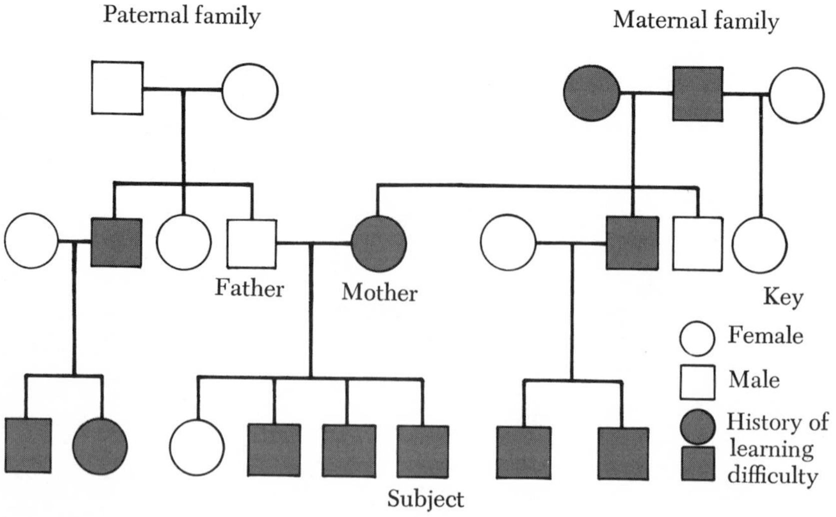

Paternal family   Maternal family

Father   Mother

Subject

Key

◯ Female

☐ Male

● History of learning difficulty

had the neurological learning disability syndrome or the child in the study was the only child.

Thirty-three or 10 percent of the cases without a family history of learning disabilities had a potential Rh incompatibility. Eleven of these children were the first born or only child; 22 were the middle or youngest child. In four of the latter group the mother had had a previous history of a miscarriage.

Prematurity: Seven (5 percent) of the children with a positive family history of learning disabilities were born prematurely. In no case was there a potential Rh incompatibility. Six of these children had a sibling, not born prematurely, with the neurological learning disability syndrome. The seventh had a father with this syndrome.

In the group without a family history of learning disabilities, 20 cases (6 percent) were born prematurely. In four of these cases there was a potential Rh incompatibility but no previous history of a miscarriage. Three of the mothers had toxemia during pregnancy and one hemorrhaged during the fourth month of pregnancy.

Maternal complications during pregnancy: Three of the mothers (2 percent) with a positive family history of learning disabilities had difficulty during pregnancy (toxemia). In addition, six mothers required a Caesarian section for delivery (reason not known). In all nine of these cases a sibling or siblings of the child in the study had the neurological learn-

Table 2. Birth Order Percentages

	First Born	Middle Child	Last Child	Only Child
1965-67	28.5	34.3	31.1	6.1
1967-69	38.6	33.2	21.7	6.5
Total	31.8	33.9	28.0	6.3

Table 3. Education of Parents by Percent

		Less Than HS	HS	Some College	College Degree	Graduate Degree
Father	1965-67	18.9	23.9	25.6	15.7	15.9
	1967-69	12.4	19.7	23.8	19.7	24.4
	Total	16.7	22.5	25.3	17.1	18.4
Mother	1965-67	16.9	38.4	28.8	12.7	3.7
	1967-69	10.6	34.1	30.6	20.6	4.1
	Total	14.5	37.0	29.4	15.3	3.8

ing disability syndrome; there were no maternal complications during these other pregnancies.

Sixteen of the mothers (4 percent) without a family history of learning disabilities had complications during pregnancy (12 had toxemia and 4 had bleeding during the middle trimester). In addition, five required a Caesarian section (reason not known).

Neonatal distress: In 17 of the cases (12 percent) with a positive family history of learning disabilities, respiratory distress was noted at birth and oxygen was required. Only one was premature. In 15 of these 17 cases the child had a sibling or siblings with the neurological learning disability syndrome; none of these siblings had a history of perinatal distress.

In the group without a family history of learning disabilities 39 cases (11 percent) were noted in which oxygen was required at birth. Thirteen of these cases were born prematurely.

Medical history: In two of the cases with a positive family history for learning disabilities (less than 2 percent) there was a concomitant medical problem. One child had congenital heart disease (intraventricular septal defect, mild) and one had pyloric stenosis (surgery at age 4 weeks).

In 54 of the cases (16 percent of the sample) without a family history of learning disabilities a previous medical problem was reported: history of skull fracture with concussion, 4; history of encephalitis, 4; history of febrile convulsion during the first year of life, 6; history of seizure disorder, 25 (18 grand mal, 7 petit mal); congenital heart disease, 2; cerebral vascular accident, hemorrhage, 1; esophageal atresia with surgery, 1; information not available, 10.

Previous history of temperature over 105°: Forty-six of the children (32 percent) with a positive family history of learning disabilities had such a past history. Four had a sibling with the neurological learning disability syndrome (no information available on their medical history). Sixty-four, or 19 percent of the cases without a family history of learning disabilities had such a history.

Delayed motor development: Eighteen (13 percent) of the children with a positive family history of learning disabilities had a delay in motor development (sitting, standing, walking). None was born prematurely. In 14 of the 18 cases the child had two or three siblings with the neurological learning disability syndrome. Data were not available on the motor development of these siblings.

Eighty (26 percent) of the children without a family history of learning disabilities had a delay in motor development. Thirteen of these children were born prematurely.

Insufficient information was available on the child's sensitivity to noise or touch during the first year of life; thus, no assessments of these factors was possible.

Familial pattern by sex: The sex pattern in these cases in which there was a positive family history of learning disabilities is shown in Table 4.

Impulsivity: The entities considered to reflect difficulty with impulse control were enuresis (after age four), temper tantrums, stealing, firesetting, and sneaking and hoarding food. This information was available on 208 of the 556 children. There were no differences between those with and those without a family history of learning disabilities. One hundred twenty-seven of the total population (61 percent) had a history of one or more of these symptoms. Of these, two had all five, three had four of the five, nine had three of the five and 16 had two of the five symptoms. Table 5 shows the breakdown, by sex, of the number of chldren with each of these symptoms.

Medication: Seventeen (13 percent) of the children with a positive family history of learning disabilities and 34 (11 percent) of the children without that family history were on psychostimulants (34 on dextroamphetamine and 17 on Ritalin). Eight children of the former group and 87 of the latter were on other medication (anti-convulsants, anti-anxiety, anti-psychotic, thyroid).

In addition to the above studies on the 556 children, a separate project was done to explore whether any parents still showed evidence of a learning disability. Fifty children were selected for specific testing. Twenty-five

Table 4. POSITIVE FAMILY HISTORY OF LEARNING DISABILITIES BY SEX OF CHILD

FAMILY MEMBER WITH SIMILAR DISABILITIES	CHILD WITH SYNDROME	
	Boys	*Girls*
Father	19	0
Mother	7	2
Sibling	26	17
Siblings	21	0
Mother and Father	5	1
Mother and Sibling	10	7
Mother and Siblings	2	2
Father and Sibling	15	1
Father and Siblings	4	0
Mother, Father, and Siblings	1	0
Total	110	30

Table 5. NUMBER OF CHILDREN WITH SYMPTOMS SUGGESTING IMPULSIVITY

	BOYS	GIRLS
Enuresis	51	14
Temper Tantrums	53	9
Stealing	14	2
Firesetting	17	0
Sneaking/Hoarding Food	14	4

of the children were from the group with a positive family history of learning disabilities and 25 were from those without this family history. These 50 children and their 100 parents were given the following battery of tests: (1) Embedded Figure (adult or child's forms); (2) Bender-Gestalt; (3) Rod and Frame; (4) Laterality; and (5) Purdue Pegboard.

Although the children's results reflected their individual learning disabilities (visual motor, spatial, motor, visual perceptual, etc.), none of the parents did below average on any test. Each test was rank ordered from best to worst performance for the child, mother, and father. The rank-order coefficient (Spearman Rho) was not significant in each case.

Discussion

This study was designed as an initial attempt to explore the possibility of a familial pattern for children having the neurological learning disability syndrome. There were limitations and some of the data were more subjective than one would like. A more extensive study with matched controls is recommended.

Because specific information was asked for on the 1967-69 group of children studied, these data were more complete than those for the 1965-67 group. The fact that the percentage of families with a positive history of learning disabilities was greater in the later group than in the earlier group is felt to reflect the specific effort made to obtain this information rather than any increase in incidence.

The difference in data is most apparent in the findings of the families with a positive family history. For the 1965-67 group 24.4 percent of the children had a sibling, siblings, mother, or father with similar learning disabilities; whereas, in the 1967-69 group 39.4 percent had a similar finding. Although the total study population showed a positive familial pattern in 29.6 percent of the cases, it is strongly felt that the true incidence is closer to the 40 percent figure.

None of the twins in this study was identical. It is of interest to note that in the three sets where both twins did not have similar learning disabilities, another sibling did.

A large percentage of the parents completed college or graduate school. It is felt that this reflected the type of parents who would be concerned about their child's academic difficulties and who would pursue a private program for this child. There was no significant difference in the level of education obtained by the parents in the group with a family history of learning disabilities than in the group without this family history.

Brain damage due to central nervous system embarrassment during the prenatal or perinatal period is frequently inferred as the etiology of this syndrome. It is important to note that in each of the families with a positive history of learning disabilities the information suggestive of central nervous system stress was made less significant by the family data. Where there was a previous miscarriage, an older sibling (born before the miscarriage) had similar learning disabilities. Further, six of the seven children with a positive family history who were born prematurely had a sibling, not born prematurely, with learning disabilities; the seventh had a father with a similar history of academic difficulties. Also, all nine of the mothers from the positive family history group who had maternal complications during pregnancy had another child (or children) born after an uncomplicated pregnancy with similar learning disabilities. Finally, 15 of the 17 children with a positive family history who had respiratory distress requiring oxygen at birth had a sibling (or siblings) born without perinatal stress who also had learning disabilities. Such data strongly suggest that prenatal or perinatal embarrassment is not a contributing factor in producing this syndrome.

The importance of a potential Rh incompatibility (mother Rh negative, child Rh positive) is not clear but does not appear to be a contributing factor. Eleven of the 19 children in the group with a positive family history either had an older sibling with similar learning disabilities or was the only child born in the family. An analysis of potential Rh incompatibility, birth order of the child, and previous history of miscarriage showed no clear relationships.

The significance of the child's experiencing a temperature of 105° is also not clear. Unfortunately, the data did not show the age at the time of the fever, and it is possible that the critical issue, if any issue exists, could be the age of the child at the time of this stress. The cause of the elevated temperature was not available; possibly in some cases the underlying illness was as important as the fever.

Fourteen of the 18 children with a positive family history and a delayed pattern of motor development had at least two and in one case four siblings with a similar developmental history, suggesting the possibility of a familial pattern of motor maturation lag. None was born prematurely.

Although a clear pattern of a family trait is noted, the syndrome could not be characterized as sex-related; it was not possible to distinguish any definite relationship between this syndrome and either parent. Most of the girls in this group had no parent but did have a sibling or siblings with similar learning disabilities; almost half of the boys had a parent with a past history of similar difficulties (fathers more than mothers).

Almost two-thirds (61 percent) of the children for whom this information was available showed suggestive evidence of impulse disorder. With some, there was more than a suggestion; almost one-fourth (24 percent) of the group had a history of two to five of the symptoms. The significance of the sex differences and the possible psychodynamics involved are the topics of a study in progress.

Few (just 12 percent) of the children were on psychostimulants. There was no relationship between these children and the children with impulse difficulties. An accurate assessment of clinical hyperactivity was not available in this study.

The specific test battery given 50 children and their parents did not test auditory perception, language, memory, or integrative skills. It is difficult to conclude, therefore, that no residual of a learning disability exists by the time of adulthood. The data do suggest that there was no difficulty with visual-perceptual, visual-motor, or fine motor difficulties by adulthood. A more extensive study which includes matched normal controls is needed.

Conclusions

The neurological learning disability syndrome is just that, a syndrome, a cluster of findings frequently appearing together. As noted earlier, there is no one etiology for this syndrome for there are several ways in which brain function can be compromised. In some cases there may have been subtle perinatal brain damage; in some cases there may have been circulatory, toxic, or metabolic embarrassment during a critical period of prenatal development; in some cases stress to the nervous system during the critical early years of life (trauma, fever, encephalitis, etc.) may have resulted in the dysfunction.

The findings of this study strongly suggest another possibility for some of the children with this syndrome. A dysfunctioning nervous system may have been inherited. A strong familial pattern does exist in 30-40% of the cases in this study. Even though some of these children had prenatal, perinatal, or postnatal difficulties, the data suggest that these difficulties were not a contributing factor in producing this syndrome, for siblings without a history of such difficulties also had learning disabilities.

The clinical findings in this syndrome are too consistent and too similar from child to child for me not to question the concept that random trauma or embarrassment occurring at various times during the fetal or post-delivery maturation of such a complex organ as the central nervous system is the etiological factor. When considering the problems of hyperactivity, distractibility, and perseveration, such an overview of multiple etiologies becomes even less tenable. The clinical picture in these children is too consistent.

I believe that further studies will clarify the frequency of this syndrome as a familial trait and the infrequency in which it is due to central nervous system damage. As research sophistication permits further neurophysiological studies, it is probably that genetically determined physiologic dysfunction rather than tissue damage will be found to be the etiologic factor for the neurological learning disability syndrome.

ACKNOWLEDGMENTS

This study was supported in part by a Research Fellowship from the Trubeck Family Fund. The author wishes to acknowledge the cooperation and assistance of Mrs. Elizabeth Willis and her staff at the Willis School for Education Therapy.

REFERENCES

ABRÁMS, A. I. Delayed and irregular maturation versus minimal brain injury. Recommendations for a change in current nomenclature. *Clin. Pediatrics* 7 (June 1968): 344-49.

AMERICAN ORTHOPSYCHIATRIC ASSOCIATION. *Bender-Gestalt Test.* New York: Grune and Stratton, 1946.

BIRCH, H., ed. *Brain Damage in Children, The Biological and Social Aspects.* Baltimore: Williams and Wilkins, 1964.

BIRCH, H. G., AND DEMB, H. The formation and extinction of conditioned reflexes in "brain-damaged" and mongoloid children. *J. Nervous and Mental Diseases* 129 (1959): 162-169.

CLEMENTS, S. *Minimal Brain Dysfunction in Children.* NINDB Monograph No. 3, Washington, D.C.: U.S. Department of Health, Education, and Welfare, 1966.

CULVER, C., et al. *Recent Advances in Biological Psychiatry. Proceedings of the 18th Annual Convention and Scientific Program of the Society of Biological Psychiatry.* June 1963.

EISENBERG, L. Behavioral manifestations of cerebral damage in children. In H. BIRCH, ed., *Brain Damage in Children, The Biological and Social Aspects.* Baltimore: Williams and Wilkins, 1964.

GOODENOUGH, D. R., AND EAGLE, C. J. A modification of the embedded figure test for use with young children. *J. Genetic Psychology* 103 (1963): 67-74.

JOHNSON, D. J., AND MYKLEBUST, H. R. *Learning Disabilities: Education Principles and Practices.* New York: Grune and Stratton, 1967.

LAUFER, M. W., AND DENHOFF, E. Hyperkinetic behavior syndrome in children. *J. Pediatrics* 50 (1957): 463-74.

PASAMANICK, B., AND KNOBLOCH, H. Syndrome of minimal cerebral damage in infancy. *J.A.M.A.* 170 (1959): 1384-87.

PURDUE RESEARCH FOUNDATION. Purdue Pegboard. Chicago: Science Research Associates, 1957.

SILVER, LARRY B. A proposed view on the etiology of the neurological learning disability syndrome. *J. Learning Disabilities* 3 (1971): 123-33.

U.S. BUREAU OF THE CENSUS. *Current Population Reports,* Series P-25. Nos. 368-369. Washington, D.C.: U.S. Government Printing Office, 1967. (a)

U.S. BUREAU OF THE CENSUS. *Statistical Abstract of the United States: 1967* (88th ed.) Washington, D.C.: U.S. Government Printing Office, 1967. (b)

WERNER, H., AND STRAUSS, A. A. Pathology of figure-background relation in the child. *J. Abnormal and Social Psychology* 36 (1941): 236-48.

WITKIN, H. A. Individual differences in ease of perception of embedded figures. *J. Personality,* 1950: 191.

WITKIN, H. A., et al. *Personality Through Perception.* New York: Harper, 1954.

WORTIS, J. A note on the concept of the "brain-injured child." *Amer. J. Mental Deficiency* 61 (1956): 204-06.

Larry B. Silver, M.D. is in the Department of Psychiatry at Rutgers University Medical School.

11.
Auditory Processing for the
Child with Language Disorders
VILMA T. FALCK

The reader will learn from this article how an important ability, such as auditory processing, may be analyzed and instructional units prepared for use in training specialists to remediate developmental language disorders.

During inservice programs, special educational personnel have been helped to develop instructional units with emphasis on the learner and the learning act. Units of work are carefully organized to be completed by students in structured learning and teaching environments.

It has been helpful for teachers to learn to manage specific programs related to auditory processing which were selected as one important element of concern for the child with language disorders.

The following information is distributed to special education personnel to serve as a basis for their development of units of work.

Auditory Processing

I. Signal Reception
  A. Auditory Sensitivity
    1. Function: Being able to respond to pure tone audiometry within normal limits and to hear faint sounds at all necessary pitches or frequencies.
    2. Malfunction: Being inattentive; watching faces; misunderstanding (all auditory processes may be impaired).
    3. Programing possibilities: Supplying medical care and audiological help (hearing aid, lipreading instruction, special seating, speech therapy); referring child to speech and hearing specialist.

  B. Auditory Localization
    1. Function: Being able to determine direction and distance of a sound in space and to focus on place where stimuli originated.
    2. Malfunction: Not knowing source or direction of sound;

From *Exceptional Children* 39 (February, 1973): 413-16. Reprinted by permission of the author and *Exceptional Children*. Copyrighted by the Council for Exceptional Children.

being slow to respond to which child in the classroom is talking to group.

3. Programing possibilities: Indicating direction from which sound comes or originates; increasing awareness to various sources of sound in varying locations and distances, e.g., pointing to a whisper from each of four corners; practicing listening skills with stereophonic equipment as the sound of a train transfers from the left to right earphone.

II. Signal Analysis and Acceptance

A. Auditory Scanning—Attention

1. Function: Being able to screen sensory impulses; being aware of a wide variety of acoustic stimuli in the environment but being tuned in to an auditory world (psychoneurological process of selecting only a portion of the available stimuli while ignoring, suppressing, or inhibiting other stimuli).

2. Malfunction: Being inattentive; saying "huh" frequently; requiring repetition of the teacher's instructions; focusing on part of a phrase.

3. Programing possibilities: Increasing attention by planning instructional units of auditory stimulation that will attract attention; varying physical intensity of sound; contrasting or changing auditory background; using repetition, novelty, motivation, and/or personal contact.

B. Figure-Ground Choice

1. Function: Being able to focus awareness on stimuli of choice; tuning in sounds which one wants to hear and filtering them from a background of other sounds.

2. Malfunction: Being easily distracted by background noise (child cannot ignore bulldozer outside window and accurately sort out teacher's words); being unable to follow teacher's instructions in a noisy classroom.

3. Programing possibilities: Developing instructional units which increase in level of difficulty; turning background sounds on and off to help child select relevant from irrelevant sounds; building up tolerance to distractors; helping child discriminate, i.e., differentiate figure or wanted sounds.

C. Discrimination

1. Function: Detecting gross or fine differences among sounds; detecting differences and similarities between environmental sounds, speech sounds, and voice qualities which reflect emotions.

2. Malfunction: Being unable to discriminate between a telephone and a door bell, between the sound /b/ and /p/, the words *bass* and *bath,* or between various inflections in a voice; making errors such as *pisgetti* for *spaghetti* or *Band-Aid* for

banjo ("I went to Alabama with a Band-Aid on my knee");
making phonic errors in spelling, grammar, and speech.

3. Programing possibilities: Developing units of work to allow practice in the identification of the meaning of *oh* to connote "you surprised me," "I made a mistake," or "I misunderstood"; helping the child understand that one cannot separate what he may say from how he says it; building units of experience to help the child hear the differences between similar sounds (/d/, /t/, and /p/); discriminating between initial or final sounds in words by spacing words for contrast.

D. Auditory Closure

1. Function: Being able to rapidly and accurately recognize words in an unorganized, incomplete, mutilated, or distorted field or amid distracting and confusing noise, i.e., any unwanted sound; having conscious or automatic closure.

2. Malfunction: Being unable to blend syllables; omitting words when repeating sentences; not understanding defective or foreign speech easily; not supplying missing parts of words which are distorted.

3. Programing possibilities: Developing instructional units which provide practice with analysis and synthesis of words; filling in missing part or closing gaps when auditory unit is incomplete; sequencing a series of listening tasks to develop blending of tones, words, and sounds; practicing recognition of separate parts of a word and production of a whole word when sounds are spoken at ¼ and then ½ second intervals.

E. Auditory Monitoring (Feedback)

1. Function: Being able to rapidly recognize differences in auditory stimuli. There are four kinds of auditory monitoring:

   a. Recognition—ability to detect differences in what is heard as produced by others (as in discrimination).

   b. Comparative cognition—ability to detect differences between an accepted norm and self production (interaction). Examples of a malfunction would be a teacher saying *rake* and a child responding *wake,* not realizing that he produced the word differently and a child saying *mycon tree* for *my country* and not realizing it.

   c. Simultaneous cognition—ability to monitor differences in self as produced by self. An example of a malfunction would be that the child says *mafrigerator* and does not realize he has said it incorrectly even though he knows the word.

   d. Delayed cognition—ability to detect self made errors after a time duration. Examples of malfunctions would be that the child does not reauditorize, i.e., cannot realize he gave an incorrect answer and that he transposes words or letters even though he understands the difference, never catching his mistakes (he may say, "I went town down," for which a normal response would be for him to laugh at his error).

2. Malfunction: Having malfunctions in any type of auditory monitoring (such as those described above).

3. Programing possibilities: Developing instructional units to establish discrimination skill which always require cognition and recognition.

III. Signal Retention

A. Immediate and Delayed Auditory Recall

1. Function: Being able to have an accurate hold on stimuli which will allow rapid or delayed processing; being able to retain or recall. (This factor does not necessarily involve language processing.)

2. Malfunction: Not recalling numbers or letters presented to him; following oral directions poorly; not knowing his name, address, or birthday.

3. Programing possibilities: Developing units of work increasing numbers of digits, syllables, words, and ideas; using rhymes and songs and associating visual clues with oral directions and practice with motor responses (many commercially available auditory memory programs can be used).

B. Memory for Meaningful Material (Memory for Ideas)

1. Function: Being able to store auditory information on a permanent basis in language coded form and to derive meaning from verbally presented material.

2. Malfunction: Being unable to follow standard classroom direction, to focus attention, to remember orally presented stories, to pay attention during oral reading, or to apply meaningful concepts to stories or other information presented to him; being unable to retrieve words though he recognizes them.

3. Programing possibilities: Reinforcing with other sensory channels all new information presented to the child; practicing attention maintaining techniques; using visual materials to aid recall (many commercial materials are available).

C. Auditory Sequencing in Temporal Order

1. Function: Being able to reproduce a sequence of auditory stimuli in desired order and to cope with temporal rate and order of presented material.

2. Malfunction: Being unable to follow several directions; having trouble with sound blendings; being unable to relate phone numbers; being unable to recognize first and last sounds in words and phrases; making errors such as saying "the cat chased the dog" instead of "the dog chased the cat"; being unable to determine or infer adequate meaning from the

sequence of words: "he went home and played ball is not the same as he played ball and went home."
3. Programing possibilities: Varying temporal rate of presentation of stimuli; reproducing sequences in imitation of tapping, singing, and speaking; analyzing a series of sounds into separate units; synthesizing separate sounds into wholes; helping the child retain order with consistent color codes and sizes of materials which accompany temporal sequences.

IV. Signal Synthesis and Integration
A. Auditory Association—Semantic Concept (Language)
1. Function: Being able to relate, organize and internally manipulate auditory symbols in a meaningful way (this is based on a cross filing system, with the statistical concept being based on memory storage retrieval); being able to remember connections between meaningful units with understanding and being able to interpret them.
2. Malfunction: Being unable to follow conversation; seeming not to listen or understand; not recognizing last with first names of friends, family names, and positions (e.g., who is oldest in family); giving poor responses in word association.
3. Programing possibilities: Tape recording short questions requiring single concept short answers (verbal and nonverbal); building vocabulary by having the child listen to brief descriptions of simple pictures of objects; developing sequences of pictures into more complex associations and having the child make a motor response when he recognizes certain words or phrases; developing units of work with similar or identical letters or sounds as clues, e.g., all foods which begin with sound /p/; having the child select the object appropriate to the directions in a sequence, e.g., what runs, has four legs, hurts his foot, cries, etc.; varying men and women's voices and known and unfamiliar voices.

B. Auditory Comprehension
1. Function: Being able to integrate what has been heard and to derive meaning from verbally presented material.
2. Malfunction: Seeming less intelligent than tests indicate; being unable to get the point of a joke; having difficulty with reasoning and seeing relationships between what is heard; having a poor vocabulary which is not easily developed with normal help techniques.
3. Programing possibilities: Developing suggestions cited in auditory association area; using techniques to build associations with words which lead to an understanding of the various uses of these words, e.g., when one word has various meanings such as the words *run, off,* and *chair;* varying voice sources: woman, man, relative, friend, or stranger.

V. Signal Convergence and Divergence
  A. Creative, Innovative, Evaluative Cognitions via Auditory Channel
    1. Function: Being able to generate information from memory storage in response to given need in order to achieve unique or best outcome, e.g., writing music, telling a story, and making comparisons.
    2. Malfunction: Having difficulty predicting a story from its title, choosing a title for a story, and completing sentences in other than highly predictable ways.
    3. Programing possibilities: Developing techniques for encouraging children to use divergent and convergent thinking; helping children evaluate or judge excellence; building in quality values by recording music on tape in varying degrees of harmony and dissonance; helping the child play with word rhymes, absurdities which he must recognize and respond to with an appropriate selection of pictures.

Vilma T. Falck is Associate Professor, Division of Continuing Education, Graduate School of Biomedical Sciences, The University of Texas at Houston.

12.
Directions for Future Research in Learning Disabilities

JAMES C. CHALFANT

MARGARET A. SCHEFFELIN

This article points out a number of fruitful areas for research and development in learning disabilities. Which of these areas should be pursued to give the profession the greatest immediate benefits? Long-range benefits?

Focus and Direction

There are at least five general stages in advancing the status of knowledge in any discipline: (1) recognition that a problem exists; (2) active investigation and identification of possible factors, which may be contributing to the problem; (3) synthesis of relevant information; (4) translation into practical application; and (5) dissemination of knowledge.

The review of research which is presented in this report represents an attempt to synthesize relevant research findings. This chapter is intended to highlight the major problem areas in which research is needed.

(1) Precise descriptions of specific observable behaviors related to dysfunctions in learning.
(2) Procedures for recording these behaviors.
(3) Procedures for educational assessment and diagnosis.
(4) Prevalence and incidence.
(5) Effective remedial or compensatory methods of intervention.
(6) The efficient delivery of services to children.
(7) Prevention.
(8) The nature of learning.

In order to seek the answers to these problem areas it will be necessary to mobilize resources at the Federal, State, and local levels of government. A decision to commit money, personnel, and facilities must be made at each of these levels. The magnitude of the problem is such that it will probably require a "total push" effort by Federal, State, and local agencies to mount an attack which carries with it any probability of success. A hierarchy of these commitments is outlined as follows:

From *Central Processing Dysfunctions in Children* (1969) pp. 135-46. Bethesda, Maryland: United States Department of Health, Education, and Welfare. Reprinted by permission of the authors.

1. Passing legislation which provides financial support.
2. Coordination of Federal, State, and local agencies.
3. Training qualified personnel.
4. Providing facilities and equipment.
5. Gaining access to preschool and school-age populations.
6. Researching the problem areas.
7. Field testing.
8. Demonstration and dissemination.

Without a definite commitment to support long-range research efforts, it will not be possible, nor is it realistic, to expect resolution of the research needs presented in this chapter.

For purposes of organization, these research needs will be discussed under the following headings: (*a*) "Screening, Identification, and Referral"; (*b*) "Assessment and Diagnosis"; (*c*) "Intervention"; (*d*) "Mobilizing Community Resources"; and (*e*) "The Need for Basic Research." It should be noted that if the reader desires a more detailed discussion of research needs, he should refer to the appropriate chapter and section. This chapter is intended only to provide a brief overview of the more salient research needs.

Screening, Identification, and Referral

Figure 1 is a flow chart which represents the administrative procedure by which most school districts identify, assess, and refer children who have difficulty in school. Staff members who participate in the formal screening program for the pupil population usually include

Figure 1. FLOW CHART FOR THE IDENTIFICATION, ASSESSMENT, AND REFERRAL OF CHILDREN WHO HAVE DIFFICULTY IN SCHOOL

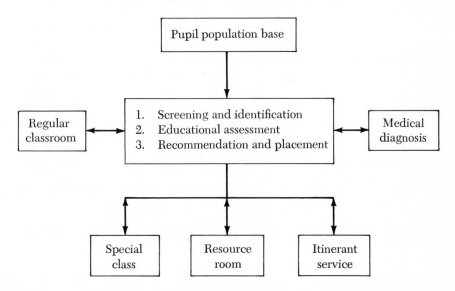

classroom teachers, school physicians and nurses, school social workers, guidance and counseling personnel, speech correctionists, and school psychologists. Formal screening programs are designed so that all the children in the school system are tested every 2 or 3 years. Teacher referrals supplement the more formalized screening program. Children who do not have obvious problems are returned to their regular classes. If a child with a problem is not identified by the screening program, his teacher will make the referral when the child experiences difficulty in the classroom.

Children who are identified by the screening program as having learning problems are referred for individual testing or examination to provide more detailed information upon which an educational recommendation can be based. In some cases it may be necessary to refer a child to the family physician, audiologist, otolaryngologist, pediatrician, or other medical specialists. A child might be placed in a regular classroom and receive an itinerant service such as individual counseling, speech correction, or remedial reading. He might also be placed in a special education class.

These procedures for screening, individual evaluation, recommendation, and placement meet the needs of the majority of children with educational problems, but they are neither sufficient nor adequate for diagnosing specific learning disabilities or for making recommendations for specific remedial instruction.

At present, there seems to be some confusion with respect to the specific population in question. This confusion is reflected by the terminology and definitions in use and the diversity of problems upon which emphasis is placed in the literature. These differences should not be surprising because professionals in special education, speech correction, psychology, child development, and neurology and other branches of medicine are frequently called upon to deal with these problems. Differences in background, theoretical orientation, and professional responsibility probably account for many of the differences in terminology and definition.

Because the characteristics exhibited by children with learning disabilities are diverse, there is no consistent behavioral pattern which identifies the group in question. This complicates the development of a definition which is descriptive of the group in question. Identification and definition are further complicated in that many of the behavioral symptoms found among children with learning disabilities are also found among normal or bright children who experience no difficulty in learning. Early identification is difficult because a learning disability may not become obvious or manifest itself until the child is of school age and attempts to read, write, or compute arithmetic problems.

In order to identify more clearly the children who have central processing dysfunctions, it will be necessary to identify the specific observable behaviors or clusters of behaviors which are symptomatic of these dysfunctions. These observable behaviors should eventually include the anatomical, neurological, and physiological symptoms as well as the psychological and educational symptoms related to difficulty in learning.

When specific behaviors or behavioral syndromes have been identified, it will be possible to develop checklists and other recording systems for use by classroom teachers. The systematic application of checklists should increase the number of referrals by classroom teachers. There is need to develop these behavioral checklists for different age levels, preschool through high school, to help account for sequential development of specific skills by different age groups. Such checklists would include observable behaviors which are indicative of central processing dysfunctions in: (a) auditory, visual, and haptic processing; (b) synthesis of sensory information; (c) storage or memory; and (d) the processing of symbolic information in auditory language, reading, writing, and arithmetic and mathematics.

When the kinds of disorders in question are clearly identified, it will be possible to launch controlled prevalence studies at local, state and national levels. This information will enable school administrators to estimate the number of teachers needed to serve the population and permit institutions of higher education to project staff and facility needs for teacher preparation programs.

Assessment and Diagnosis

The assessment and diagnosis of central processing dysfunctions is difficult to accomplish because the analysis, synthesis, storage, and manipulation of symbolic information take place in the brain, or what is commonly referred to as "the little black box." Central processing is not accessible for direct observation and must necessarily be inferred from behaviors which are accessible to observation. The functions of the brain are very complex and the present status of knowledge with respect to what goes on in the brain is limited.

Because the brain of a living individual is not readily accessible, autopsy and animal research have been used to study the psychological effects of brain damage. Generalizations from animal research have obvious limitations with respect to comparing the functioning of the brain of the animal with the brain of the human. Animals do not suffer with the type of learning disability observed in humans—i.e., specifically those having to do with language. Any information on this problem must be derived from the human. Although animal studies cannot help with problems such as language, they can elucidate certain learning mechanisms. There is only now beginning to be a strong effort to study the differences of the effects of brain injury in immature versus adult animals.

While pathological examination of the brain is an important research area, there are several methodological problems in studying the psychological correlates of the brain lesions. Since learning disabilities are studied most prominently in children, the likelihood that such an individual will die and be available for anatomical examination of the brain at post mortem is unlikely. In other instances where there is an accidental death, those interested in the autopsy are probably unaware of the fact that the child suffered from a learning disability, and the brain has not been studied from this point of view. If enough people are sensitive to this rather crucial need, it will be possible to obtain anatomical specimens.

Another problem is the relative inadequacy of the methods for examination of the brain. We are not dealing with gross brain damage. If physical damage exists it must be of the most subtle type. It may ultimately require the ability to make quantitative studies of neuronal populations in the brain to determine the anatomical substrate of the learning disability. There is also a lack of correlation between the individual who has studied the child and the individual who has the opportunity to examine the brain. Another complication is that other injury to the brain may have occurred during the time intervals between the initial trauma, testing of the subject, and the autopsy. Finally, the degree to which it is possible to make inferences about children based on research evidence obtained from adults is open to question.

In the past, research effort focused upon localization of brain function, while comparatively little research was directed toward the difficult task of studying interaction within the brain. There is need to study the behavioral implications of brain injury as related to the type and extent of lesion, duration of the lesion, the age at which the lesion was sustained, and how lesions in one area of the brain affect the functioning of intact areas of the brain.

At present, most educators take the position that knowledge of brain damage does not tell them what to do. The rationale is: (a) the educator cannot fix the brain, (b) he does not know what he would do differently if he knew that the brain was damaged, and (c) inferences about brain damage or problems which lie within the brain tend to stop attempts at remedial work on the assumption that the damage and its behavioral consequences are permanent. The educator, therefore, finds it more helpful to observe the situation under which learning failure occurs, then attempt to arrange procedures and materials differently than the child has experienced. This educational approach bases new ideas and new techniques on empirically demonstrated theories of learning. If the child fails on one program, then try something else!

The fact remains, however, that there may be conditions arising from within the child that will interfere with particular remedial approaches. Some of these conditions may be remediable through certain kinds of training. Other conditions may not be remediable. In these cases it may be necessary to devise compensatory methods for learning. Also, certain conditions may be alleviated through surgery or drug therapy. In any case, there is need to pinpoint the behaviors which are related to dysfunctions in the brain and study their prognosis and responsiveness to different kinds of treatment programs. This kind of information hopefully will provide a more systematic approach to teaching, lead away from a trial-and-error philosophy, and provide a more efficient and effective approach to dealing with learning disorders. Until educators and the medical profession can find the links between organic pathology and treatment, educators should continue to focus their service efforts on observable behaviors, but their research efforts should include interdisciplinary exploration with the medical profession and active participation in increasing the status of knowledge in this complex problem area.

The remainder of this section will highlight the research needs with respect to the: (a) analysis of sensory information; (b) synthesis and storage of sensory information; and (c) the processing of symbolic information.

THE ANALYSIS OF SENSORY INFORMATION

Both basic and applied research is needed if effective procedures are to be developed for the assessment and differential diagnosis of dysfunctions in the analysis of sensory information. Basic research is needed to identify the mechanisms for processing auditory, visual, and haptic stimuli. This will require study of the psychological, neurological, biochemical, and physiological correlates to these central processes.

There is need, also, to examine the traditional distinction made between central and peripheral disorders. For example, there is need to study: (a) the functioning of the eye as an adjustor; (b) the eye as a transducer; (c) the cerebral cortex as a central processor; and (d) to clarify the interrelationships between these mechanisms. Hopefully, this kind of basic research will lead to more efficient and effective medical and surgical procedures for prevention and contribute to the improvement of procedures for educational assessment and treatment.

Because the educational assessment and diagnosis of central processing functions are largely dependent upon observable behavior, there is need to provide more detailed descriptions of the behavioral symptoms which are characteristic of: (a) normal functioning at different age levels and (b) dysfunctions in processing auditory, visual, and haptic information. For purposes of both differential diagnosis and treatment, research is needed to link behavioral symptoms with neurological, biochemical, and physiological correlates. This kind of information will make it possible to develop more discrete procedures for diagnosing auditory, visual, and haptic dysfunctions.

Auditory Processing. It is often difficult to identify the causes of auditory processing disorders, because different etiological factors are often characterized by many of the same behavioral symptoms. Failure to respond to auditory stimuli may be due to peripheral deafness, central deafness, mental retardation, severe emotional disturbance, aphasia, or auditory imperception (Myklebust, 1954).

A thorough differential diagnosis often requires diagnostic skill and training beyond that of the individual practitioner. The otolaryngologist, pediatrician, neurologist, psychiatrist, psychologist, audiologist, speech pathologist, and educator all have specific contributions to make to the diagnostic team. There is an urgent need to improve the diagnostic procedures for disorders of auditory processing. The use of precise descriptive terms will help facilitate communication between disciplines. One of the basic steps that should be taken to provide detailed and comprehensive descriptions of the behavioral responses to auditory stimuli, which are characteristic of peripheral and central deafness, mental retardation, emotional disturbance, aphasia, and disorders in the central processing of auditory stimuli.

For example, a child whose mental ability is severely limited may not respond normally to auditory stimuli. It is necessary, therefore, to examine the child's total pattern of behavior to ascertain whether or not mental retardation is a contributing factor. There is some evidence that auditory behavior tends to be consistent with mental age and that the mentally retarded seem to respond better to meaningful test stimuli, than to the more abstract pure tone test (Myklebust, 1954). There is need, however, to develop diagnostic procedures to further differentiate mental retardation from other etiological factors.

For example, children with peripheral hearing losses have been found to use their residual hearing in a consistent and meaningful manner (Myklebust, 1954). In contrast to the consistent responses of children with peripheral hearing losses, the behavioral responses to auditory stimuli made by auditory aphasic children tend to be inconsistent and disintegrated (Monsees, 1961).

According to Myklebust (1954) the inconsistent and disintegrated behavior of aphasic children is due to their apparent difficulty in attending and integrating auditory input. Myklebust points out that inconsistent responses to auditory stimuli are not caused by shifts in sensitivity, but by shifts in the ability to attend and integrate. Response consistency and the ability to integrate auditory stimuli seem to be two important variables in differentiating the child with a peripheral hearing loss from the child with an auditory aphasia. There is need to develop specific procedures for measuring these variables and obtaining clinical information.

There is need, also, to evaluate the effectiveness of various classes of auditory stimuli as well as the response modes of the subjects. Research should examine the processing of auditory stimuli which varies along different acoustic and presentational dimensions. This kind of applied research should lead to greater efficiency in selecting stimuli, mode of input, and method of indicating response, which in turn should lead to improved diagnosis.

In summary, research is needed to explore procedures for evaluating auditory processing disorders such as: Differentiating sound from no sound; sound localization; discriminating sounds varying on one acoustic dimension; discriminating sound sequences varying on several dimensions; auditory figure-ground selection; and associating sounds with their sources. The use of precise terms will help facilitate communication of these behaviors, and the recent advances in electronics should be of assistance in studying many of these problems.

Visual Processing. There are a number of ocular-motor tasks which are critical for the central processing of visual information. These include such tasks as distinguishing light from no light, seeing fine detail, scanning, and tracking. Central processing tasks include activities such as developing visual-spatial relationships, discriminating object qualities, differentiating figure-ground, completing visual wholes, and recognizing objects. Research is needed to provide more accurate descriptions of both ocular-motor and cognitive tasks and to study the relationships between these tasks.

The question of whether or not there is a common visual perceptual factor or several separate factors remains unresolved. Attempts to study this question are complicated by the fact that the perception of printed words, individual numbers, groups of digits, or geometric forms represent different visual perceptual tasks which make slightly different demands upon the visual processing mechanism.

There is need to develop more effective procedures for the screening and identification of visual processing dysfunctions. Unless the child is referred to an ophthalmologist, it may be very difficult, if not impossible, to identify subtle visual problems such as structural anomalies, refractive errors, and muscle imbalances, or problems in color vision, depth perception, binocularity, dominance, or other central dysfunctions. If gross indicators of possible central visual disorders can be identified by simple behavioral tests, it may be possible to develop screening techniques for use by school personnel. These techniques should provide additional specific information for use in referrals to ophthalmologists for diagnosis.

Haptic Processing. There is comparatively little information with respect to the assessment of haptic processing. There is need to acquire a more thorough understanding of the system or subsystems which process cutaneous and kinesthetic stimuli, and the kinds of information which are obtained through integrating cutaneous and kinesthetic sensory input. Future research efforts should attempt to develop systematic procedures for the diagnosis of haptic processing disorders.

One apparent problem in the assessment of haptic processing is the use of auditory language in the test procedures. If the subject has difficulty in following directions or is unable to express himself, the language deficit may confound the test results.

THE SYNTHESIS OF SENSORY INFORMATION

The synthesis or integration of sensory information represents one of the most exciting and highly complex areas for future research. Much of the previous research has attempted clinical investigations of single functions while attempting to control for other functions. While this kind of research is urgently needed, further research efforts should not ignore the synthesis of sensory information. For example, a child may be able to process auditory information on task A, process visual information on task B, but when task C is presented, the child may be unable to process auditory and visual information simultaneously. This example represents a breakdown in intersensory integration. The simultaneous or successive processing of multiple sensory stimuli and the storage and retrieval of sensory information are two important problem areas which should be investigated.

Multiple Stimulus Integration. There is comparatively little research concerning the integration of multiple stimuli. The complexity in studying the processing of multiple stimulus integration has undoubtedly been a factor which has limited research efforts to date. There is need to learn more about the intersensory and intrasensory processing systems for multiple stimuli. What constitutes these systems? How do they develop? How do they function? What are the educational, psychological, physiological, neurological, and biochemical correlates which are related to these systems?

At present, there are only a few procedures which have been used to assess dysfunctions in this very complex area. This is unfortunate since so many school tasks make demands on the processing of multiple stimuli. Research is needed to develop more precise methods for assessing the intersensory and intrasensory integration of multiple stimuli.

Memory. In the absence of definitive information about the psychological, neurological, and biochemical factors which contribute to the storage and retrieval of information, several theories have emerged to attempt to provide an explanation of the memory phenomenon.

There are several issues which need to be explored. Are memory disorders usually specific or general? Are the memory dysfunctions described in adults characteristic of memory dysfunctions found among children? Is memory global or molecular? How does sensory memory differ from intellectual memory? How does memory process relate to memory product? What is the difference between storage, screening, and retrieval of information? Research is needed to identify the psychological and physiological processes which involve the storage and retrieval of symbolic information.

At the present time, comparatively little is known about the process by which memory is stored in nervous tissue. There is need to conduct research on neurophysiological changes which occur in the brain when something is learned. There are several questions which need to be explored. What is the nature of anatomical or biochemical changes at the synapses along the neural pathways? What kinds of chemicals found in the brain are most important for learning? To what extent does the amount of various chemicals affect the rate of learning? Is the ratio of one chemical to another an important factor? Do chemical imbalances in the distribution of chemicals in different areas of the brain create problems in storage and retrieval?

Procedures for assessing the memory function typically rely upon recall and reproduction tasks, after-image and memory span, delayed response, the effect of aspiration level, and the application of learning strategies to facilitate remembering. Assessment procedures should take into account the nature and quantity of the material to be learned, whether or not the material is meaningful, the specific steps necessary to learn the material, the amount of time necessary to learn the material, activities which are introduced during the retention period and the duration of retention. Instead of relying upon digit or word span, perhaps educators should begin thinking of assessing memory in terms of specific school tasks where recall and recognition are required for achievement in specific content areas.

SYMBOLIC OPERATIONS

The processing of symbolic information is the basic task the school demands of all children. To succeed in school a child must be able to acquire, retain, and use auditory language; read, or decode graphic symbols; write or encode graphic symbols; and solve problems in arithmetic and mathematics. In addition to obtaining information about the kinds of behavioral errors in performing symbolic operations, future research should attempt to learn more about the brain mechanisms and the psychological correlates which underlie failure to acquire, retain, and use symbolic information. This section will present a brief summary of the research needs with respect to auditory language, reading, writing, and quantitative concepts.

Auditory Language. During the past few years, there has been increased interest in determining the developmental sequence in which the universals of the English language are acquired. While linguists are providing a steadily growing body of information with respect to the children's utterances, disagreement exists concerning the manner in which children acquire the language code, and the impact of various dysfunctions on language acquisition. There is need, therefore, to clarify the developmental sequence or sequences for acquiring a first language and to study the effects of central dysfunctions on this developmental sequence. Research should attempt to identify the brain mechanisms which underlie language functions, and those central processing operations which play a role in the attainment of auditory language. Methods for assessing performance on various subtasks need to be developed for both the normal and atypical populations.

Reading. Future research in the assessment and diagnosis of reading disorders should result in a thorough analysis of the reading act including: (a) a description of terminal reading behaviors; (b) the conditions under which they occur; (c) the identification of specific subtasks which are necessary to achieve these terminal behaviors; and (d) a hierarchical sequence for the subtasks. Also, attention should be directed toward the elements of the graphic language code, particularly the graphic shapes, the space direction sequence, and spelling.

Failure in reading has been linked with a number of physical and psychological correlates incuding sensory deficiencies; low intelligence; low verbal ability; dysfunctions in auditory, visual, and kinesthetic perception; memory disorders; integrative dysfunctions; poor laterality; emotional disturbance; and genetic factors. The extent each of these variables is related to success or failure in reading is not clear. There is need to determine the extent to which a deficiency in any of these correlates affects the acquisition of reading skills as well as determining the results of various combinations of dysfunctions.

Research into diagnosis of reading difficulties should include medical considerations as well as educational and psychological assessment. There is need to develop administrative structures to maximize cooperation in interdisciplinary assessment and diagnosis.

The diagnostic program should distinguish between children who have failed, the child who is in the process of failing, and the child who might be expected to fail prior to instruction in reading.

For the child who has failed, research is needed to develop more effective procedures for estimating reading potential, determining reading level, describing the behavioral symptoms of faulty reading, and examining the physical and psychological correlates to reading failure.

There are no systematic procedures for identifying the child who is beginning to fail. There is need for more systematic procedures for measuring progress in beginning reading and describing the reading behaviors of the children. Checklists, for example, may help teachers make early judgments about the behavioral symptoms of these children who are beginning to fail so that early referral and intervention can take place.

For the child who might be expected to fail, the need for assessment procedures leading to the prediction and prevention of reading failure is especially crucial. The identification of correlates to reading at an early age and the development of procedures for measuring these correlates appears to be a promising area for future interdisciplinary investigation. The concept of reading readiness has led to the development of tests for reading readiness. Yet, one's concept of reading readiness depends upon one's definition of beginning reading. Ready to do what? There is need to devise specific tests for the various subtasks which make up the reading act or are necessary for beginning reading activities.

Writing. Encoding written language symbols requires the intent to communicate, formulation of the message, retrieval of graphic-language symbols which correspond to selected auditory-language signals (spelling), and organization and execution of the graphic-motor sequence. A problem at any one of these levels will interfere with communication through writing. The assessment and diagnosis of writing disorders must be considered within the larger contexts of both the language and the perceptual-motor areas. It is important for the diagnostic procedure to differentiate between dysfunctions in the ideational use of language and the visual-motor execution of thoughts onto paper.

Future research should investigate those factors which may contribute to the problem. These include: (*a*) developmental deviations; (*b*) psychomotor aspects such as paralytic disorders, ataxia and apraxia, (*c*) visual processing; (*d*) auditory processing such as dysnomia, syntactical aphasia, receptive aphasia, reauditorization of letters, auditory sequencing, syllabication, and sound blending; (*e*) discrepancies between spoken and written language; (*f*) reading and written language; (*g*) speech handicaps; (*h*) social or emotional disturbance; (*i*) poor auditory acuity; (*j*) cultural deprivation; and/or (*k*) instructional factors. The correlates to the writing process need to be identified more clearly. There is need, also, for descriptions of dysfunctions in the language system, visual-perceptual system, and motor symptoms which interfere with the encoding of graphic language symbols.

Quantitative Concepts. The present status of research suggests that a number of different cognitive abilities are probably involved in comprehending the structure of numbers, performing concrete arithmetical operations, and developing abstract quantitative concepts. In addition to general intelligence, at least four other factors seem to be related to the attainment of quantitative concepts: spatial ability; verbal ability; problem-solving ability; and neurophysiological correlates. There is need to identify other factors or subfactors which are related to the acquisition, retention, and use of quantitative concepts.

There is need, also, to devise comprehensive tests and procedures for the screening, identification, and diagnosis of children who have difficulty in arithmetical and mathematical operations. These diagnostic instruments should measure those correlates which are relevant to specific kinds of learning tasks and lead to appropriate intervention techniques.

Intervention

At present there is a comparatively small number of school districts which are effectively meeting the needs of children with learning disabilities. Several reasons may account for this. First, a factor which has impeded special programs has been the necessity within the school system for mass production. Overwhelmed by increasing numbers of students, the schools have had to provide the best they can for the average individual. There is still serious question whether our best effort at this time is toward upgrading the general level of instruction by providing the regular classroom with flexibility to meet the varied needs and abilities of varied children, or whether we should focus on special education for those with special disabilities. At the moment we are heavily committed to mass production.

Second, the group in question has not been clearly defined. Third, there is a shortage of professional personnel trained in diagnosis and remediation. Fourth, there are only a few techniques for screening, and the tests for differential diagnosis which pinpoint disabilities are crude. Fifth, remedial methods based on the educational diagnosis are in the process of being developed. Sixth, in the past, these children have not been identified accurately and have been placed in special education classes which do not provide educational programs designed for their needs. Many children with learning disabilities have been placed in classes for the retarded, despite the fact that they have normal abilities in many areas. Appropriate educational intervention might remove some of them from the classification of mental retardation. In some instances, children who cannot recognize objects or printed letters or words are placed in classes for the visually handicapped. It is even more common, however, for the child to remain in the regular classroom where the teacher does whatever she has time to do.

It is difficult to secure local, State, or Federal support for an educational program in which the group of children in question has not been well defined, where the educators have differences of opinion on some of the key issues, and the status of knowledge is diffuse and controversial. There are several steps which need to be taken to resolve these problems:

1. Establish a definition that is meaningful to those who work with the group in question.
2. Construct effective tests for the early identification of children with learning disabilities, and for pinpointing areas of deficits which lead to remediation.
3. Develop remedial techniques for specific kinds of learning disorders.
4. Train psychological examiners who are interested in educational problems and who have had some exposure to remedial teaching methods.
5. Train diagnostic teachers and supervisors who have knowledge of test practices and developmental, corrective, and remedial techniques.
6. Field test teaching methods, and new ways of utilizing personnel.

SELECTING REMEDIAL OBJECTIVES

In reviewing the research on remediation, it is rather surprising to note that the objectives of educational intervention are not clear. Is the objective normalcy? Near normalcy? Academic success? Changes in test scores? Modification of specific behaviors? Unless the teacher designates specific objectives or a series of sub-objectives, and specifies criterion standards for having learned, it is difficult to determine the effectiveness of remedial programs.

There are several viewpoints with respect to educational intervention. One point of view is that the purpose of remediation is intended to ameliorate a psychological deficit, usually defined in vague terms, which will enable the child to generalize the ability to other behaviors. A second point of view is that remediation should be directed toward training a specific skill. It may be more to the point to ask if it is possible to train one and not the other. In other words, as we train behaviors, are we in fact training the substrata of basic skills?

There is some question whether time should be invested in attempting to ameliorate the deficit area or to teach through the asset areas and strengthen compensatory behaviors. Is such a dichotomy possible in actual practice? In most cases the teacher is confronted with both the assets and deficits and must deal with both during instruction.

THE RATIONALE FOR EDUCATIONAL PLANNING

A principle of educational planning which has gained wide acceptance, at least on a verbal and written level, is that remedial approaches should be based on an educational diagnosis. The assumption, here, is that by pinpointing the nature and/or the correlates of the learning disability, the teacher will have a rational basis for selecting a particular remedial method. How is this differential diagnosis accomplished?

1. Standardized Tests: The traditional approach to remedial planning is to administer a series of standardized tests which are intended to give some indication of achievement levels, intellectual capacity, and psychological functioning.

2. Structured Observation: More recently attention has been directed toward structured observation as the basic methodological entity.

3. Diagnostic Teaching: A third and related approach to educational planning is the concept of diagnostic teaching. When formalized tests fail to provide sufficient information about the area of difficulty, remediation then becomes part of the diagnostic process. The concept of diagnostic teaching is based on the assumption that effective teaching procedures contain many of the same procedural sequences which are found in effective diagnostic procedures. Children are placed in one or more carefully controlled learning situations and taught over a period of time.

4. Neurophysiological Correlates: A fourth approach to remedial planning is examination of the neurophysiological correlates to behavioral disorders. At present, educators seem to be somewhat impatient with the medical profession, because knowledge of these correlates ". . . does not tell us what to do with the child."

It is true that educators possess only a few remedial alternatives, and it is true, also, that the medical profession is trying to improve the status of knowledge. Research has demonstrated that changes in ability and personality accompany brain lesions. Although knowledge of brain injury will not tell the teacher what to do, it might help the teacher anticipate future problems, particularly if the condition is progressive and cannot be arrested. Knowing the age at which a lesion was sustained is an important consideration. One would expect a lesion sustained by an infant to have different effects than a lesion occurring in the brain of a young child, or an adult. In some cases, knowledge of the nature, location, extensiveness, and duration of the damage may be relevant to the behavioral sequences. At present, the relevancy of brain lesions to behaviors is not clear. Another important consideration is how much spontaneous recovery is it reasonable to expect over a given period of time? These areas should be targets for future research.

The educator cannot afford to overlook the potentialities for treatment that future research in biochemistry or neurophysiology might bring. Medical or surgical intervention procedures or drug treatment may eventually prove to be some of the most effective ways of meeting the needs of many children.

Future research needs are clear. We need to improve the technology for standardized testing, structured observation, diagnostic teaching, and medical diagnosis. Unless we improve the status of our technology we will not be able to fulfill the ultimate goal of diagnosis—to obtain the maximum amount of useful information with respect to etiology, prognosis, and treatment.

5. Temporal Considerations: Other aspects of educational planning include temporal instructional considerations. The decision of how much time to allocate for remedial instruction is often based on the availability of the teacher, and not on the needs of the child. Most research studies in remediation have been conducted on a short-term basis. Is 20 minutes to an hour a day for 2, 3, or even 5 days a week sufficient time in which to bring about marked change? How many months or years will be required? Are we talking about 6 weeks, 6 months, or 6 years? There are little data which help the teacher determine either the length of each session, the number of sessions per day per week, or the total duration of remedial intervention. Time is critical to remedial programming, and there is need to acquire more definitive data for specific kinds of disorders.

It is important to note that any social institution, such as our educational system, has an obligation to provide a built-in evaluation for any new program or method which it proposes to introduce. With billions of dollars being spent for education, the taxpayer is entitled to a cost benefit analysis in terms of the manpower and expenses required to mobilize a new program against the money saved through the lack of school repeats, and the social and economic consequences of learning failure.

6. Instructional Setting: Remedial programs are being implemented in special classes, resource rooms, and through itinerant teachers. There is need to determine when one approach is more appropriate than another for a particular child.

7. Multiple Disabilities: The child with learning disabilities seldom presents a picture of a single clear-cut disorder. It is more common to find children with several disabilities. The presence of multiple disabilities not only complicates the task of assessment, evaluation, and diagnosis, but makes remedial planning even more difficult. Much of the research literature is concerned with a specific kind of learning disability. In many cases the remedial program is focused on only one aspect of the child's problem, while other aspects remain neglected.

There is need to develop teaching approaches for use with children who have multiple problems. It is doubtful that the child has time for us to deal with one problem at a time. In addition to developing a rationale for selecting remedial priorities, we need to develop remedial approaches which will permit multiple attack on multiple disabilities. This will not only require flexibility and versatility in the individual teacher, but will require collaborative programs between different disciplines as well.

In the past, many remedial approaches were developed by clinicians or master teachers. Clinicians are very knowledgeable and have had a long history of working with children, but they tend to be service oriented. The clinician says, "I'm a clinician, not a researcher. I like to spend time working with children and dealing with their problems." The clinician is not particularly interested in measurement. He is too busy working with people. As the clinician gains experience, he refines and records his procedures, and a book is eventually written. Thus we have a remedial approach with very little evidence or data to back it up. In the absence of objective data, the teacher or administrator may use the procedure in an inappropriate situation and charges are leveled that the procedure is ineffective. When controversy arises, the researcher, who is concerned with measurement, comes on the scene and starts to explore the efficacy of the procedure under different situations. Educational research has typically been conducted with groups on a short-term basis.

Attempts to study learning disabilities have not been very successful because the groups in question do not represent single clinical syndromes. Also, much of the research has often focused on a small number of discrete variables, while other potentially significant variables have been omitted from investigation.

In order to better understand the nature of different kinds of learning disabilities, and their amenability to different remedial procedures, there is need to break with traditional group studies and study the learning problems of individual children in depth. A longitudinal $N=1$ case study approach offers promise for finding specific answers for specific problems. When a number of case studies have been compiled on a specific problem, it may be possible to formulate hypotheses which lead to future research efforts. Placing case study data on IBM cards will further facilitate data retrieval as well as the study of interrelationships between different variables. The interdisciplinary graphic description of individual subjects may provide one of the most fruitful approaches to this complex problem area.

There is need, also, to develop more precise descriptions of teaching procedures. One of the major problems in remediation is that it is very difficult to describe what goes on during the teaching process. We have to have accurate descriptions of teaching procedures so that teachers can replicate teaching procedures. Thorough reporting should include a description of the tasks which are presented in terms of stimulus input, information about the subject, and a quantitative and qualitative description of the responses.

The mobilization of local, State, and Federal resources is necessary to provide needed services for children. There is comparatively little research, however, with respect to the organization, administration, and supervision of programs for children with central processing dysfunctions. Research priority has not been placed on administrative problems in mobilizing resources. Instead, research priority has been directed toward: (*a*) describing the emotional, physical, social, and cognitive characteristics of children with dysfunctions; (*b*) developing procedures for assessment; and (*c*) refining teaching techniques and methods.

DESCRIPTIVE STUDIES

There is need to conduct descriptive studies which describe how administrative units have attempted to resolve problems in providing services. What are the basic philosophies upon which these programs are founded? What policies have been found to be successful? What procedures for screening, identification, and placement of pupils have been developed? What are the criteria for teacher selection? What kinds of supervisory services are needed? How can in-service training programs be implemented successfully? What kinds of legal and financial arrangements are effective?

For example, the concept of the regional center is one approach which has been used to resolve many of the demographic and economic problems inherent in establishing services for children with learning disabilities. It would be helpful to have descriptions of the programs between school districts or counties. By joining together, two or more school districts or counties increase their pupil population base and provide sufficient numbers of children to justify needed services. Being a contract of policy, a cooperative program is better assured of being both continuous and stable, reducing the per capita cost for the program, permitting the sharing of space and facilities, and creating a situation which will attract competent staff and supervisory personnel. There is need, however, to conduct descriptive and evaluative studies of different kinds of administrative arrangements.

NORMATIVE DATA

Normative data studies are needed at the local, State, and national level. Research would include such things as the characteristics and prevalence of central processing dysfunctions; the kinds of services and facilities which are available as well as the number which is needed; information about the recruitment, training, placement, and retention of personnel; expenditures for program support; and staffing patterns and staff utilization. Correlational studies will provide knowledge of the interrelationships of the many variables with which administrators must be concerned.

For example, one of the first steps in mobilizing local or State resources for program support is to study the nature and extent of the problem and determine what kinds of educational services are needed to meet the needs of the children. A study of the nature and extent of the problem requires the adoption of a criteria which can be used to identify children with specific learning disabilities and an extensive screening effort for establishing prevalence. A thorough statewide prevalence study should utilize all local and State personnel who can contribute to the screening and identification process. Normative data will provide a basis for planning and program evaluation.

PROGRAM EVALUATION

Program evaluation studies are needed to provide information about the effectiveness, efficiency, and appropriateness of different administrative approaches to solving administrative problems. Few administrators have attempted to apply evaluative methods to programs which have been implemented. The evaluations which have been done are in retrospect. The probability of an objective appraisal is increased by selecting goals, procedures, and evaluative techniques before the program or the study begins. Evaluative studies have potential impact on policy, procedures, and legislation. This kind of research approach may be termed "action research."

For example, research is needed to evaluate the different kinds of educational services which are being offered. At present, there seem to be three administrative approaches to providing services for children with learning disabilities. Special classrooms have been established which require the teacher to provide instruction in all academic areas as well as attempt to do remedial work with the basic disability. Being all things to these children is a difficult responsibility to fulfill. The homogeneous grouping of children in classes and integrating them back into the regular school program also poses major problems.

The resource room offers a second alternative for the teacher. School buildings with large enrollments can support resource rooms for remedial work. Children remain in the regular school program and report to the resource room for remedial training. The teacher may meet with individual children or small groups. A third alternative is the itinerant teacher who travels from one school to the next. The question that needs to be answered is, "Under what conditions should these alternative educational techniques be used?"

Another problem area that needs to be investigated is that of teacher preparation. It would be helpful if professionals from different disciplines would sit down together and conduct an objective, impersonal task analysis of the specific subtasks which are necessary to provide needed services. Knowing the specific tasks which need to be accomplished will make it possible to estimate the minimal amount of training necessary to accomplish each task. This information will give universities and school systems an objective basis for establishing training programs which can train larger numbers of personnel in as brief a time period as possible.

The eventual outcome of this approach may be a gradual restructuring of professional roles which will hopefully provide great efficiency in the effective use of personnel in our schools. It is important, therefore, that our schools maintain sufficient flexibility to field test the effectiveness of personnel who have been trained in innovative programs. This may require school districts to create new and innovative job positions in order to evaluate the effectiveness of a particular service.

There is need to study the effectiveness of different approaches to teacher preparation. Preservice training in learning disabilities is being conducted at different levels. Several universities are beginning to explore the feasibility of training remedial teachers at the undergraduate level. There is some question, however, whether the 120 hours of a bachelor's degree curriculum provides sufficient time for the undergraduate student to attain basic competencies with normal children as well as children with learning disabilities. The 4-year remedial teacher would probably work under close supervision and execute or carry out educational programs which are prescribed by their supervisors and those who have attained greater competency in assessment, evaluation, diagnosis, and educational planning.

It should be noted that most university programs are presently training remedial teachers at the master's degree level to work as tutors, itinerant teachers, resource room teachers, or special class teachers. These programs emphasize the interpretation of test results, ongoing assessment, and extensive remedial training. A sixth year of advanced clinical training prepares personnel to work as diagnostic teachers. Training programs at several universities provide advanced practicum in assessment, evaluation, and diagnosis and remedial procedures; supervisory experience; and the opportunity to work as a consultant with school districts which are developing programs.

Students at the doctoral level are being prepared for teacher training, research, and leadership roles in service agencies. Doctoral programs also include advanced clinical practicum courses in assessment, educational intervention, learning theory, and statistical procedures.

The problem of providing effective in-service training programs provides another potential area of study. In-service training for teachers of children with specific learning disabilities often have limited value in changing teacher behavior. Workshops and extension courses on week nights usually consist of lectures and an exchange of information and experiences between teachers. There is need to investigate the use of videotape, films, various content, and time of workshops to determine the most productive approach to in-service training.

PREVENTION OF LEARNING FAILURE

At this point in time, we probably know more about learning failure than we do about the learning process itself. It is very difficult to talk about the prevention of central processing dysfunctions when our present state of knowledge is limited. Before effective procedures for prevention can be developed and put into action, it is necessary that we: (a) obtain precise descriptions of specific observable behavior related to the central processing dysfunctions; (b) develop procedures for educational assessment and diagnosis; (c) determine the prevalence and incidence of these problems; (d) develop effective remedial or compensatory methods of intervention; and (e) find ways to deliver services to children at an early age.

The Need for Basic Research

If we are to make major inroads on this problem of prevention, it is essential that we learn more about the learning process. This means that a major thrust should be made in areas that are sometimes classified under the term "basic research." Basic research has been shown to have the effect of accumulating the "critical mass" of information necessary for a quantum leap in several scientific disciplines. It is important that the knowledge obtained from basic research in learning and the knowledge obtained from studying children with learning disorders be integrated, in order to establish educational programs for preschool children which would hopefully contribute to preventing and/or ameliorating central processing dysfunctions.

Despite the fact that present knowledge is limited, it is important to begin studying and working with the preschool population. It is encouraging to note the recent attention and financial support given to the education of preschool children and to prenatal care. This kind of effort should contribute toward the development of educational programs for early intervention and prevention.

REFERENCES

MONSEES, E. Aphasia in children. *Journal of Speech and Hearing Disorders* 26 (1961): 83-86.
MYKLEBUST, H. *Auditory Disorders in Children.* New York: Grune & Stratton, 1954.

James C. Chalfant is Professor of Special Education at the University of Arizona in Tucson. Margaret A. Scheffelin is a member of the staff of the California State Department of Education, Sacramento.

Four

Communication Disorders

Speech Pathology is one of the older disciplines in special education. Since man is differentiated from animals fundamentally through language and speech, attention to communication defects has prevailed since Aristotle.

Numerous texts are available to the reader that describe the pathology and correction of speech disorders. Indeed, there are specialized publications that treat such disorders as aphasia, cleft palate, stuttering, articulation disorders, etc. Consequently this chapter does not attempt to duplicate these writings.

The lead article describes the range of opportunities available to persons who wish to know more about the field of speech pathology and audiology as a career. These are presented in the form of biographies of individuals working in a wide variety of settings—hospitals, schools, clinics, and other agencies. Bown's article, which follows, discusses the role of the speech clinician in the public schools. He points out that specialists tend to become more and more specialized in our society and advocates a wide range of services for therapists. His views may not be shared by many specialists. Nevertheless, expanding roles are being widely advocated for certain specialists, such as the general resource teacher and the school psychologist.

Articulation disorders are the most common speech defect among school-aged children and the prevalence is age related. In the third article Morency, Wepman, and Hass discuss developmental articulation inaccuracies in the early school years. This longitudinal study assesses the relevance of therapy for young children.

Problems of language development are discussed in the last two articles of this chapter since much attention is currently being given to this phase of communication. The first article, by Daisy Jones, describes the range of problems found among school children, indicates which have significance, and provides helpful educational suggestions. In the second article, Valletutti discusses some of the unique aspects of language development for mentally retarded children. The nature of common language problems is discussed and teaching suggestions are made.

The "Pioneer Profile" in this chapter is that of Henry Head, an English physician whose significant research on aphasia following World War I greatly influenced the study of communication.

Henry Head
1861–1940

PHYSICIAN
NEUROLOGIST
SPEECH PATHOLOGIST

Henry Head was a prominent English physician whose pioneer research on language disorders is well known in this country. His two volumes (approximately one thousand pages) entitled *Aphasia and Kindred Disorders of Speech,* published by the University Press, Cambridge, England (1916) has had a profound influence upon the development of the science of speech pathology. He is also credited with two volumes of studies in neurology which appeared in 1926.

Head defined aphasia as a disturbance of "symbolic formulation and expression." He developed a four-fold classification of aphasia: verbal, syntactical, nominal, and semantic. His subjects were twenty-six aphasics, nineteen of whom were World War I veterans who had suffered from head injuries and/or shell shock. He derived information from the theories of Hughlings Jackson and from his own penetrating observations and the results of the unique tests which he devised. Head followed the progress of his patients for years and eventually published detailed profiles in the two volumes referred to earlier.

Head, like other pioneers cited in this volume, was trained in medicine. He was graduated from Cambridge in 1892 and became a member of the Royal College of Physicians of London in 1901. In 1927, he was knighted and is referred to in England as Sir Henry Head. The University of Edinburgh awarded him an L.L.D. degree in recognition of his distinguished work.

13.
Career Profiles in Speech Pathology and Audiology
AMERICAN SPEECH AND
HEARING ASSOCIATION

The following composite biographies present a cross section of careers in Speech Pathology and Audiology. While no one of these descriptions represents an actual member of the profession, together the sketches indicate the potential for career achievement in Speech Pathology and Audiology.

Definition

The profession of Speech Pathology and Audiology is concerned with communication competency as manifested in speech, language, and hearing. It is devoted to the study and management of disorders, normal development, and cultural-ethnic influences in human communication. It provides clinical services for children and adults and performs related basic and applied research.

Some members of the profession concern themselves primarily with speech and language disorders, others with hearing disorders; nevertheless, these disorders are so interrelated that professional competency requires familiarity with all. Such terms as speech correctionist and speech and hearing therapist have been used to identify the workers in this profession; however, the American Speech and Hearing Association recommends the use of *Speech Pathologist* (or *Speech Clinician*) and *Audiologist*.

Veterans Hospital

Edward Andrews, Ph.D., is an audiologist in a Veterans Administration Hospital. He received both his M.A. and his Ph.D. from the department of Speech Pathology and Audiology in a large university.

Dr. Andrews divides his time between patients and research. In the hospital clinic he administers a wide variety of tests designed to determine precisely a patient's hearing level, to identify the most likely site of damage to the auditory system, to describe the amount of social disability resulting from the patient's hearing loss, and to predict potential benefits

---

From *Speech Pathology and Audiology—Career Information.* Revised ed. Washington, D.C.: American Speech and Hearing Association, 1971.

from use of a hearing aid or special training. He counsels patients to help them understand their disabilities. If a hearing aid is necessary, he assists with the selection of a suitable one. He helps the patient learn to use the aid, develop more attentive listening habits, and use visual cues which can fill in the blanks left by hearing loss. If the hearing loss can be treated surgically, Dr. Andrews assists the surgeon pre-operatively by describing the extent and kind of hearing loss. After the operation he conducts studies to determine the amount of improvement.

Contact with war veterans has given Dr. Andrews a particular interest in the effects of noise on hearing. His current research project deals with the physiological changes in the internal structure of the ear that may be attributable to prolonged exposure to high noise levels such as gunfire, industrial noise, or amplified music. Because of his published work in this area, he is frequently called upon to lecture on noise pollution and its control.

Public Schools

John Kovac, M.A., accepted his present position as speech, hearing, and language clinician with the board of education of a suburban community after earning his master's degree in Speech Pathology and Audiology at a state university. He is one of 15 clinicians in a well-staffed and supervised special education program.

Mr. Kovac is assigned two schools to which he makes regular visits. At the beginning of the school year he identifies all children in these schools who have speech, hearing, and language problems. Each child is studied thoroughly to describe the nature and extent of his communication problem and to determine his need for special services. Mr. Kovac frequently confers with other professional people in the school system and in the community regarding the children with whom he is working. He counsels parents to help them understand and assist in alleviating their children's speech, hearing, or language problems.

During a typical day, he may work with a kindergarten teacher to help some pupils who are slow in speech and language development, with a group of children from the upper primary grades who have difficulty producing specific speech sounds, with a child whose speech difficulties result from cleft palate, with a child who has severe problems in all aspects of language usage, with a group of junior high school students who stutter, or with individual hearing-impaired children who can succeed in regular classes if they have extra help in speech, language, and speechreading.

The director of school speech and hearing services meets once a week with Mr. Kovac to discuss his cases and a department research study on the effectiveness of programmed language-development techniques with mentally retarded children. In addition, Mr. Kovac participates in a weekly in-service workshop on the correlation of reading competency and the development of speech and language skills in children.

College Instruction

Erica Hansen, Ph.D., is a university faculty member in the division of Speech Pathology and Audiology. After receiving a master's degree in Speech Pathology and Audiology, she worked for two years as a public school speech and hearing clinician and three years on the staff of a community speech and hearing center. She then returned to the university to earn her doctoral degree.

Each semester Dr. Hansen teaches two or three courses in various aspects of Speech Pathology; she also supervises student clinicians in the university's speech and hearing clinic. Through clinic demonstrations she helps her students develop skills in the evaluation of speech, hearing, and language disorders and in counseling and remedial procedures. She directs the research of students working toward their M.A. and Ph.D. degrees. She is currently assisting with plans to establish a branch of the university speech and hearing clinic in a multi-ethnic area of the city near which the university is located. The proposed satellite clinic would make services more available to that portion of the community and enable students to become familiar with cultural language differences.

Dr. Hansen's own research efforts are aimed at obtaining a better understanding of deviant verbal learning patterns among children with speech disorders. Specially programmed teaching machines are used to obtain objective data which compare normal verbal learning rates and patterns to the rates and patterns demonstrated by children with speech disorders.

State Consultant

Al Williams, M.S., is the speech and hearing consultant for a state health department in the southeast. He received his master's degree from a state college and was employed as a school Audiologist before accepting his present position. One of the main functions of his department is to insure the provision of high-quality service at reasonable cost equally throughout the state. His department's programs are supported through monies allocated by the federal government to each state and by state support from taxes. Mr. Williams keeps abreast of any federal legislation which may affect program funding, and he also reviews any proposed state legislation relating to speech, hearing, and language services.

His staff of Speech Pathologists and Audiologists takes a mobile van throughout the state to provide speech, hearing, and language screening. This screening program may result in referral of clients to other agencies, purchasing of hearing aids, or contracting for diagnostic and therapeutic services at multidisciplinary centers. Mr. Williams is using information gained in his staff's screening programs to support the expansion of state speech, hearing, and language programs, according to a comprehensive plan developed in cooperation with his state board of education counterpart, representatives of county education and health departments, and directors of clinical facilities in the state.

He hopes also to develop speech and hearing services in state institutions, particularly juvenile detention centers and chronic disease hospitals.

Industrial Research

Gordon Baker, Ph.D., is a specialist in communications on the staff of the research division of an electronics corporation. The work for his M.A. and Ph.D. degrees involved a cooperative program between a university's school of engineering and its department of speech sciences. For his doctoral research, Dr. Baker investigated selected aspects of electronic simulation of human speech sounds.

Dr. Baker's current research is concerned with the reception and storage of speech signals in computer systems. A wide variety of future uses is seen for business and industry when his present techniques are refined. Portions of his work, published in scientific journals, have already contributed to the knowledge of the nature of speech sounds.

School of Medicine

Elizabeth Stevens, Ph.D., holds a university appointment jointly in the departments of physiology and otolaryngology and the division of Speech Pathology and Audiology in the school of medicine. While working on her master's degree in physiology, she became interested in nerve and brain functions, particularly as related to hearing. Throughout her Ph.D. program she combined majors in physiology and Speech Pathology and Audiology.

Although presently she lectures to medical students and graduate students on her fields of specialization, most of her time is devoted to research in the neurophysiology of hearing. Currently she is working on a series of studies in which electrodes are painlessly implanted in the brains of laboratory animals to measure the type and degree of electrical discharge at various levels within the brain when the animals are stimulated by sound. In this way valuable information is acquired about the reactions of various brain centers to sound impulses.

Dr. Stevens and other members of the Speech Pathology and Audiology staff provide consultative services to the university hospital in a long-term project to evaluate methods of testing infant hearing.

Private Practice

Sam Frasier, Ph.D., is in the private practice of Speech Pathology and Audiology. He holds ASHA's Certificate of Clinical Competence in both areas. He has had several years of clinical experience in diagnosing and treating voice, speech, and language disorders. He also provides audiological testing services, auditory training, and speechreading. His well-equipped private office is located in a medical building where he has the opportunity for contact with physicians and psychologists who refer patients to him and to whom he refers patients.

Dr. Frasier practices in a medium-sized town in an area where there are limited clinical facilities. He schedules part of his time to provide diagnostic and therapeutic services for selected cases from the local schools on a contractual basis. He receives referrals of patients through hospitals and physicians from several counties in his part of the state. Since speech services for adult aphasics are nonexistent in his geographic area, he consults with these patients and their families and provides treatment where possible. He also sponsors a laryngectomy club which meets one night a month in his office. This club provides continuing supportive help for many laryngectomees who do not have access to clinical services in their community.

As a prominent professional member of his community, Dr. Frasier has been a leading proponent of adding the full-time services of a speech and hearing clinician to the public schools and of building a needed regional diagnostic and clinical facility. He frequently speaks to community groups that are considering these proposals.

Rehabilitation Service

Dorothy Miller, M.A., is a Speech Pathologist in the rehabilitation division of a county hospital for the chronically ill. She completed work for her M.A. in Speech Pathology and Audiology and became a Speech Pathologist on the staff of a large city hospital. During several years of retirement while raising a family, Mrs. Miller kept up her professional interests through volunteer work at a local community clinic, through reading professional journals, and through membership in her state speech and hearing association. Later she began taking additional course work at a nearby university in the treatment of aphasia; now she is working toward her Ph.D. in Audiology while serving part-time on the county hospital's staff. The hospital hopes to expand its audiologic services; currently patients requiring such services are referred by Mrs. Miller to a neighboring university hospital.

Mrs. Miller is a valued member of a team of specialists concerned with the rehabilitation of patients who have had disabling illness or injury. She works with men and women who have suffered losses in language usage or disorders in speech production following strokes or head injuries. She also works with young adults who have had cerebral palsy since birth and with patients who have had successful surgery for cancer of the speech structures. Another facet of her duties is helping the patients' families understand these disabilities. With her assistance, patients may overcome their difficulties sufficiently to return to their families and live productively in their communities.

Community Clinic

David Stern, M.A., took several courses related to Speech Pathology and Audiology while he was an undergraduate. He then attended a private college to complete his master's degree in Speech Pathology. His first position as a Speech Pathologist on the staff of a community speech and hearing center involved him with many other community agencies; for example, when he worked with a child who was hard of hearing, he also had to work with the public school system to obtain proper school placement for the child. He found he had a growing interest in the problems of administering a community agency and wanted to acquire the skills needed to deal with other agencies, with the public, with volunteers, and with professionals in other fields. A fellowship permitted him to spend another year at the university, taking courses in social work and in Speech Pathology and Audiology. He organized and became director of a new community speech and hearing center in a rural area where previously there had been no speech and hearing services.

The agency provides a wide variety of rehabilitative services. These include direct assistance to children and adults with speech, language, and hearing disorders, a preschool program for hearing-impaired children and their parents, and special recreation activities designed to promote improved social adjustment among adolescents and adults with severe hearing problems. The center has begun a pilot research program in early case finding and diagnostic teaching for preschool children with language disabilities.

Mr. Stern and his staff work closely with the board of education, the public health department, and local civic and medical agencies to plan and provide comprehensive services for persons with multiple disabilities. He and his staff also carry on a program of public education to increase the understanding of speech and hearing problems and to encourage people to seek needed help.

Frank Atkins and Lois Chavez are graduate students at a western university. Mr. Atkins' military experience as a medic led him to seek information about the effects of brain injuries on speech and language. He has become increasingly interested in the early detection and prevention of communication disorders in children. His faculty advisers have helped him select courses and clinical practice cases to expand his experience in the areas in which he is interested. He plans, upon graduation, to work in a community clinic in a predominantly Black area. His wide experience in speech, hearing, and language disorders should make him a valuable member of the diagnostic and treatment team.

Miss Chavez is a member of the National Student Speech and Hearing Association, and she attends professional meetings and workshops whenever her school schedule and budget permit. She financed part of her education through the cooperative study program as an assistant in a federal agency office which provides funds for programs and projects in

Speech Pathology and Audiology. After she completes her graduate work she may decide to take additional course work in administration or go directly into a doctoral program.

Mr. Atkins and Miss Chavez, like many students and professionals in Speech Pathology and Audiology, bring to their profession a breadth of experience, intellectual curiosity, and a desire to serve. They will be able, upon completion of appropriate training and clinical practice, to enter existing programs or to create job opportunities where none may now exist.

History and Trends

Before the twentieth century there were few services for individuals with speech, hearing, and language disorders, except for several special schools for deaf children and the occasional efforts of individual physicians and teachers. In Europe the early growth of the profession was closely allied to medicine. In America, however, the initial impetus came from speech, education, and psychology. A separate professional identity emerged in the 1920s when speech and hearing services were initiated in some public school systems; university programs were developed to prepare clinicians and researchers in Speech Pathology and Audiology; and a national organization (now the American Speech and Hearing Association) was founded.

During World War II, hearing, speech, and language retraining became an important part of military rehabilitation programs for the many servicemen who suffered speech and language impairments caused by head wounds, or hearing losses resulting from exposure to noise. Professional horizons broadened as electronics and communication systems produced new techniques for research and new ways to assist children and adults with communication disorders.

In the 1950s and 1960s, recognition of the need for Speech Pathologists and Audiologists led to increased federal funding for training and research programs throughout the country. A number of states passed legislation that specifically provided for the needs of handicapped children, including those with speech, hearing, or language disorders. Medicare and Medicaid provisions, under which payment for certain services by qualified Speech Pathologists and Audiologists can be reimbursed, also contributed to the growing demand for services. Project Head Start and similar programs have informed the public about the effects of early deprivation on the speech, hearing, and language of young children. The public also became increasingly aware of the need for diagnostic and remedial speech, hearing, and language services for children born in the aftermath of rubella epidemics.

14.
The Expanding Responsibilities
of the Speech and Hearing Clinician
in the Public Schools

J. CLINTON BOWN

This article argues in favor of broadening the range of the services of the speech therapist. As you read the article, try to assess the validity of the suggestions set forth.

The expanding responsibilities of the speech and hearing clinician in the public schools are discussed within the framework of (1) his role in defining his own educational responsibilities; (2) the emerging duties of the resource, remedial, and learning disability teachers and speech and hearing clinicians, and educational implications; (3) the traditional role of the sensory-motor technician as contrasted to his emerging role as a specialist in communication disorders; (4) evaluating and remediating communication and achievement problems with regard to channels, processes, and levels of communication; (5) important guidelines for planning remedial activities; (6) defining responsibilities for a team approach; (7) his responsibilities toward a speech improvement program in the classroom; and (8) the necessity for him to expand his role from that of a sensory-motor technician to that of a specialist in the area of communication disorders.

Speech and hearing programs are changing, sometimes radically, in public schools throughout the country. Although a speech and hearing program should be tailored to the policies of the local school system, there remain these questions: How much responsibility for role definition lies with the speech and hearing department in a school district and how much with administrative superiors in special services and special education programs? Moreover, how much help should the national organization (American Speech and Hearing Association) offer to the local clinician in defining his job?

Boundaries separating the speech and hearing clinician from the resource teacher, the learning disability teacher, and the remedial reading teacher seem to be disappearing. The current procedure in some school districts is to group children with IQs of 80 and above who have communication problems (in listening, speaking, reading, writing, thinking, and

From *Journal of Speech and Hearing Disorders* 36 (November, 1971): 538-42. Reprinted by permission of the author and *Journal of Speech and Hearing Disorders*.

arithmetic) into a special class for part of the day. The teacher is considered a resource, educational handicapped, remedial, or learning disability teacher. His duties may also include assessing and aiding the educable mentally retarded children. The teacher is not itinerant but functions only within one school. His qualifications include an understanding of the language code (phonology, morphology, syntax, and semantics) and of its channels of communication (listening, speaking, reading, and writing). One or more resource teachers can be placed within a school according to need.

Will eliminating duplication of services reduce the need for speech clinicians? How will speech and hearing clinicians function if programs such as the ones just described are developed? Will they function as remedial specialists working with hard-core articulation, voice, and stuttering problems? Will they be utilized as specialists assisting the resource teacher? Will they become resource teachers? Will clinician aides and volunteers handle most of the mild articulation problems, with supervision from the master clinician, thus leaving the speech clinician free to handle severe problems or to assist the resource teacher in this task? The role of the speech and hearing clinician may, in part, be defined by district administrators, and if speech and hearing clinicians wish to function in a public school setting they will probably have to obtain more extensive training through general and special education departments at the university level.

Public school clinicians are at a crossroads. They must fit into the local district philosophy and policies but should be included in formulating their emerging role.

In the past, public school clinicians have primarily emphasized the diagnosis and remediation of problems in the following categories: (1) phonation (voice disorders), (2) rhythm (stuttering, etc.), (3) articulation (phonological competence), and (4) hearing (detection and perception levels). The clinician's emerging role should include more diagnosis and remediation in the areas of linguistics and semantics, to aid those children who have difficulty understanding and producing the structure and meaning of language. Some public school clinicians have considered the phonological aspects of expressive language as their sole responsibility, not realizing that articulation is only one facet of oral expressive language, which is, again, only one part of the communication behavior of the child. This has resulted in their treating articulation problems synthetically, apart from the context of language development.

One of the primary reasons for the lack of intensive work with children who demonstrate severe communication problems is an excessive caseload of articulation problems. According to Irwin (1953) and Bingham et al. (1961), approximately 80% of the children seen by public school speech clinicians fall into this grouping. However, according to Van Riper and Erickson (1969), from 47% to 60% of the children who demonstrate articulation problems in first grade will show normal articulation by the time they enter third grade, without having received professional help.

Presently, there are measuring devices available to help the public school clinician screen out those children who will probably obtain normal articulation by maturation alone. One is Van Riper's Predictive Screening Test (Van Riper and Erickson, 1969). More time and emphasis can then be spent on the severely handicapped child with articulation or language disorders.

When selecting his caseload, the speech clinician should ask the following questions: (1) Does the child have an emotional reaction to his communication effort? (2) Does the child's speech and language interfere with communication? (3) Does the child's communication problem interfere with classroom achievement?

The emerging role of the speech clinician in the public school setting should be oriented toward the total verbal communication behavior of the child, with emphasis upon its influence on the child's social and academic achievement. The clinician will not neglect the phonological or sensory-motor aspects of language development (articulation), or the phonatory and rhythmic aspects, but will diagnose, prescribe, and treat directly the total aural-oral communication disorders of children. Moreover, the clinician should help the child to develop aural-oral proficiency (phonological, grammatical, and semantic receptive and expressive skills) in order to prevent reading and writing problems. Also, where these factors influence the communication disorder, the clinician should assist and consult with the classroom teacher, remedial teacher, and psychologist in the identification, diagnosis, prescription, and remediation of visual-perceptual, visual-motor, visual-memory, and visual-associational problems. Arithmetic, gesturing, and nonverbal motor and general behavior skills may also be included as communication skills. These skills should be assessed, along with the verbal communication skills, to realize a comprehensive evaluation of a child with a communication disorder.

Evaluation and remediation of verbal communication disorders should include assessing strengths and weaknesses in (1) channels of communication (auditory, visual, and tactile-kinesthetic input and oral and manual output); (2) processes of communication, including reception (detection, recognition, discrimination, verbal acceptance and interpretation, and concept recognition), expression (concept formulation, semantic, grammatical and phonological-graphic codification, motor patterning, and response), and association (the integration or transduction of reception and expression at all levels of organization); (3) levels of organization, including (a) detection and response; (b) perceptual-motor matching, consisting of perceptual awareness, motor experimentation, and patterning; (c) temporal-spatial perception, including sequencing or chaining of verbal content of the input and output; (d) phonological-graphic, grammatical, and semantic acceptance and formulation of a message, utilizing predictive and evocative mechanisms based upon the redundancies of language; and (e) categorizing-abstracting or conceptual formulation level, consisting of nonverbal and verbal (semantic) concept recognition, deliberation, and recall for expressive purposes. A monitoring or feedback system is operating at each level, and short- and long-term storage and retrieval are utilized in the theoretical construct.

When planning remediation based upon a theoretical construct or empirical knowledge, the clinician should ask himself the following questions: (1) Are principles of learning theory and desirable learning conditions present in the remedial setting? (See Gagne, 1965, for a discussion of types of learning and their educational implications—signal, stimulus-response, verbal and nonverbal chaining, multiple discrimination, concept, principle, and problem-solving learning.) (2) Has the clinician the skills necessary to utilize task analysis and behavioral objectives? (3) Are remedial methods and procedures integrated with classroom and home activities, and are remedial materials based on the child's curriculum? (4) Is there an awareness of critical periods or readiness stages in language development, and are they utilized when planning remedial activities? (5) Does the clinician utilize a synthetic (part to whole) or analytic (whole to part) approach to remediation (Van Riper and Irwin, 1958; Backus and Beasley, 1951)? Does one approach work better than the other with certain age groups and severities of problems? Is remediation being initiated in a noncommunication or communication setting? (6) Is there an awareness of the influence of general body coordination and perception and other nonverbal behavior upon communicative skills (Cruickshank, 1966; Kephart, 1960)? (7) Does the clinician apply principles of linguistic theory (rules governing the linguistic code and reference system) to the diagnosis and remediation of communication problems (Smith and Miller, 1966)? (8) Are self-hearing or discrimination-of-own-error techniques utilized in articulation therapy, rather than discrimination of error sound as spoken by external model? Also, are all channels (visual-auditory-tactile-kinesthetic) utilized when engaging in remedial training? (9) Does the clinician understand the influence of motivation and mental health upon the child's learning?

The evaluation and remediation of the child's communication problem should be carried out by a team when feasible. The team should consist of the classroom teacher, speech and hearing clinician, remedial teacher, principal, learning disability teacher, psychologist, educational diagnostician, parents, social workers, physicians, and nurse. Although responsibilities would overlap, they should be defined. The child with a communication disorder may be diagnosed as being emotionally disturbed, cerebral palsied, hard of hearing, aphasic, or learning disabled. However, the principal concept to remember is that the prescription is more important than the classification since the former leads to behavior change.

It is hoped that children who demonstrate mild phonological problems will be benefited by a speech improvement program in the classroom, carried out by the classroom teacher assisted by the speech clinician. The clinician could help the classroom teacher integrate speech improvement into classroom programs through demonstrative activities and supplementary teaching, such as phoneme recognition, discrimination, and production; recognition and production of the normal prosody of speech; acquaintance with the speech mechanism and the importance of using correct speech; and the use of stories, dramatic play, poems, and games to instill carry-over of correct sound production into everyday speech. The clinician could also help develop a speech improvement curriculum employing the same types of activities and utilizing clinician aides and volunteers to help implement it.

In conclusion, the speech and hearing clinician in the public schools needs to expand his role from that of a sensory-motor technician to that of a specialist in communication disorders, for several reasons:

1. The supply of clinicians is catching up with the demand in certain school districts because of an increasing number of clinicians graduating from universities and a stabilized or decreasing student population. As a result, more intensive help for severe problems now appears feasible.
2. Eighty percent of the clinician's caseload is made up of articulation problems, and half of these children will probably obtain normal articulation by third or fourth grade without help. Moreover, most of the ones who will obtain normal articulation by maturation alone are probably not upset about the status of their speech delay.
3. Some types of disorders, such as cleft palate, do not occur frequently in the schools.
4. Clinician aides and volunteers can function as sensory-motor technicians with the supervision of a master clinician.
5. Some administrators do not consider most articulation problems as handicaps; as a result, limited funds and distribution units are allotted to other special education programs that have children with greater deficits.
6. If the "resource" teacher concept catches on, there would be a decrease in demand for clinically trained specialists as opposed to curriculum-oriented specialists.
7. The speech and hearing clinician should consider himself not only a skilled technician but also a specialist working primarily to diagnose and remediate oral-aural communication disorders. If he is to receive a professional's salary, he must carry out a professional's role.

ACKNOWLEDGMENT

The author wishes to thank Gordon Low of Brigham Young University for the concept of the speech clinician as a resource teacher. His lectures provided the motivation for this article.

REFERENCES

Backus, O. L., and Beasley, J. *Speech Therapy with Children*. New York: Houghton Mifflin, 1951.

Bingham, D. S., Van Hattum, R. J., Faulk, M. E., and Mayper, L. R. Program organization and management. *J. Speech Hearing Dis. Monogr. Suppl.* 8 (1961): 33-49.

Cruickshank, W. M., ed. *The Teacher of Brain-Injured Children: A Discussion of the Bases for Competency*. New York: Syracuse University, 1966.

Gagne, R. M. *The Conditions of Learning*. New York: Holt, Rinehart, & Winston, 1965.

Irwin, R. B. *Speech and Hearing Therapy*. Englewood Cliffs, N.J.: Prentice-Hall, 1953.

Kephart, N. C. *The Slow Learner in the Classroom*. Columbus, Ohio: Merrill, 1960.

Smith, F., and Miller, G. A., eds., *The Genesis of Language—A Psycholinguistic Approach*. Cambridge, Mass. and London, England: MIT, 1966.

Van Riper, C., and Irwin, J. V. *Voice and Articulation*. Englewood Cliffs, N.J.: Prentice-Hall, 1958.

Van Riper, C., and Erickson, R. A predictive screening test of articulation. *J. Speech Hearing Dis.* 34 (1969): 214-19.

J. Clinton Bown is Communication Disorders Specialist in the Salt Lake City Schools, Salt Lake City, Utah.

15.
Developmental Speech Inaccuracy and Speech Therapy in the Early School Years

ANNE S. MORENCY

JOSEPH M. WEPMAN

SARAH K. HASS

As you read this article, consider the possible contributions of the speech therapist to the education of young children with speech problems.

A previously reported study (1) discussed some of the various types of articulation inaccuracy that are likely to be found among children in the early grades of the elementary school. The study showed that the kind of errors children make in articulation depends on the cause of the difficulty. The investigation focused on a type of difficulty that is by far the most prevalent at this early age. The difficulty can be attributed to no known physical or emotional handicap and for this reason has in the past been called a *functional speech defect*. Teachers raise questions about the learning ability of children who have this difficulty particularly when classroom activities are centered on the teaching of reading. Speech correctionists often find that their case loads consist almost entirely of children who have functional type problems. However, the study showed that the children in public school speech therapy classes who had no known physical or emotional problem to account for their inaccuracy seemed to be not defective in speech, but just slower than their peers in acquiring accurate speech. The findings of the previous study suggested that the term *developmental articulation inaccuracy* would be more appropriate than the term *functional speech problem* or *defect*. However, it seemed advisable to test further the developmental aspect of this type of speech inaccuracy by investigating whether speech therapy hastens children's ability to produce accurate consonant sounds over a period of time.

The present research was undertaken to explore this area of developmental speech inaccuracy in a three-year longitudinal study (2).

All the children, with certain stated exceptions, who entered the first grade of two schools in a suburb of Chicago were studied. The two schools were situated in the same middle-class socioeconomic area and drew their school children from adjacent sections of the suburb.

From *Elementary School Journal* 70 (April, 1970): 219-24. Copyright © 1970 by University of Chicago Press. Reprinted by permission of the senior author and the University of Chicago Press, Publishers.

The children, who were all Caucasian, were tested at the beginning of first grade and at the end of second and third grades. Children were excluded from the study if they had previous first-grade experience, if they had inadequate and uncorrected visual or auditory acuity, if they had an intelligence quotient below 80 as measured by the Lorge-Thorndike Intelligence Tests (group tests administered routinely by the schools), if they had a physical disability such as cleft palate that might cause an articulatory problem, if they moved out of the school system some time during the three years of this study. Initially 250 children were studied; 177 of them met all the criteria.

Each child was given the Dual Modality Test of Articulation, which is described in more detail elsewhere (3). The test provides four stimuli (two visual and two auditory) for each consonant sound appearing in the initial position in English. Since /th voiced appears in no picturable form in the initial position, the test has eighty-six individual stimuli—forty-two visual and forty-four auditory. The order of presentation on the test form is the order in which children usually learn consonant sounds according to the inquiry conducted and reported by Templin (4). The examiner recorded each response on the test form. Responses were recorded verbatim. With a verbatim record it was possible to learn how many errors of each type—substitutions, distortions, or omissions of individual sounds—each child made.

Figure 1, which lists the sounds in the same order as the test form, shows the number and the per cent of children who made errors on each sound. Without exception the errors were made on sounds that are near the end of the list—the last ten sounds of the Templin ordering. The importance of the finding shown in Figure 1 is that the errors occur among the sounds that are acquired later rather than along the entire list of sounds. This finding demonstrates and confirms a finding of our previous research (1).

To study the effectiveness of speech therapy in correcting this particular pattern of speech inaccuracy, the children were divided into three groups on the basis of the results of an articulation test in first grade. The results showed a definite clustering of children who made six or more errors on the Dual Modality Test of Articulation. These children formed the experimental group. The children who made five errors or fewer than five errors on the Dual Modality Test of Articulation became the normal, or control group. There were 111 in this group. Few of these children made more than one or two errors in all, although it is possible to make four errors on each sound tested. All the errors were substitutions.

The experimental group, which was made up of children who made six errors or more, was further divided into Groups A and B corresponding to the school the children attended. Group A, which had thirty-four children, was assigned to speech therapy, but therapy was withheld from Group B, which had thirty-two children. These children generally made two or more errors per sound.

The co-operation of the speech department of the school district was enlisted to select children for speech therapy in first grade, using the customary criteria of the department. The two assessments—one based on the number of errors made on the test and one based on the independent evaluation of the speech therapists —selected the same children with only two exceptions.

Figure 2 shows profiles of the errors made by Groups A and B over the three years of the study. The profiles represent no major change from the profiles of the total population shown in Figure 1, but are more severe extensions of those profiles. This finding further supports the idea that the speech inaccuracies of the children in the experimental group were the result of a common developmental phenomenon rather than a speech defect. There was a rapid decline in the number of children in both Group A and Group B who showed errors between the beginning of the first year and the end of the second year of the study, when the children were tested the second time. This finding further supports the idea that a developmental process is at work. Group A and Group B were compared at the end

Figure 1. Number and Per Cent of 177 Children Who Made Two or More Errors on the Dual Modality Test of Articulation Taken the First Year of Testing

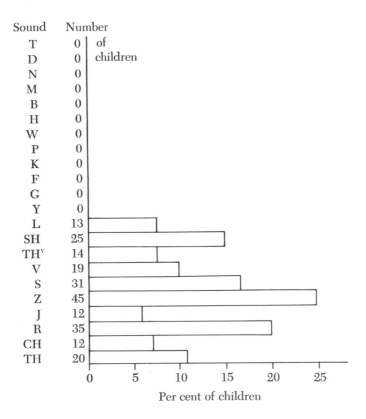

Sound	Number
T	0
D	0
N	0
M	0
B	0
H	0
W	0
P	0
K	0
F	0
G	0
Y	0
L	13
SH	25
THᵛ	14
V	19
S	31
Z	45
J	12
R	35
CH	12
TH	20

Per cent of children

of the three-year period of the study. Group A had fewer children making errors in articulation than Group B did. However, the number of children in either group who made errors on the various sounds is small, as Figure 2 shows, and not sufficient to justify therapy for children whose

Figure 2. Number and Per Cent of Children in Groups A and B Who Made Two or More Errors on the Dual Modality Test of Articulation, for Each of the Three Years of the Study

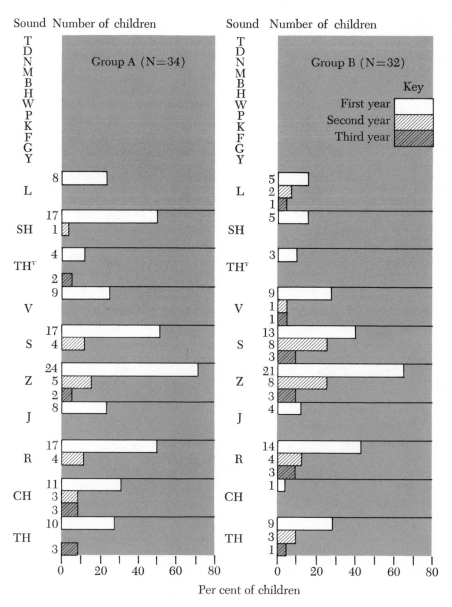

errors are of this type. Table 1 shows, as the earlier study did (1), that the variety of errors made in the first year is noticeably greater than in the second and third years.

The minimal change between the end of the second year and the end of the third year indicates that by the end of second grade most of the children had overcome their inaccuracies of pronunciation. At the end of third grade only a few children still had difficulty.

The study confirms another finding of the original 1967 study discussed earlier (1). As Table 1 shows, the predominant type of misarticulation during the initial survey was simple substitution. The sounds substituted were in most instances the earlier developing consonants that the children had learned. The sounds substituted were never phonemes the child had not yet used accurately. The distortions listed in Table 1 are in all cases single occurrences, and seemed to be caused by not-yet-complete transition from the incorrect substitution to the correct articulation of the phoneme. Therefore, it appears that the more familiar, earlier discriminated sounds provided the base for substitutions.

Errors characterized as lateral lisps were made only in the first year, only by children in the experimental groups, and only by four children. The /th/ substitution for /s/ and /z/, generally described as a simple lisp, was not uncommon in the first year of the experimental group. As Table 1 shows, the lisp was not present in the second year. In the third year, however, the /th/ substitution was again prominent. An explanation for this deviation from a steady, developmental progression was found when children were studied on an individual rather than a group basis. A few children acquired the /th/ substitution for /s/ and /z/ for the first time in the third year. The simple lisp is thought to have several causes. Dental and occlusive problems, which commonly occur at the ages of six and seven, provide a physical basis for some errors of this kind. This type of lisp is also frequently related to emotional immaturity that manifests itself in "baby talk," a common misnomer for the articulatory error. The lisp is not viewed here as developmental in nature.

The results of this study, then, confirm the reality of developmental articulation inaccuracy and make possible a more detailed description of this type of problem. All the articulation errors were among the sounds that are acquired last by all children. The predominant type of error was the consonant-for-consonant substitution. A few errors were approximations of the sound intended. The number of articulation errors declined rapidly with age during the early school years. The simple and lateral lisps are not included in the developmental articulation pattern of inaccuracy.

The value of speech therapy for children who evidence a developmental pattern of misarticulation as they are entering first grade seems highly questionable in the light of the small number of children who made errors on the various sounds at the end of third grade, regardless of whether they received therapy. These children are not impaired and therefore should not be considered defective in speech. They are, we believe, at

Table 1. SOUND SUBSTITUTIONS MADE BY THE NORMAL POPULATION AND BY THE EXPERIMENTAL GROUPS FOR ALL THREE YEARS OF THE STUDY, LISTED IN DESCENDING ORDER OF FREQUENCY OF OCCURRENCE*

SOUND	SUBSTITUTION	
First Year	By Normal Population	By Experimental Population
L	W, Y	W, Y, N, ?
SH	None	S, TH, ?, Lateral
TH'	D	D, Z, V, T, ?
V	B, W	B, W, F, TH
S	None	TH, Lateral, ?
Z	None	TH, S, G, Lateral, ?
J	D, K	D, G, T, B, Lateral, ?
R	W	W
CH	None	SH, T, Z, TH, Lateral, ?
TH	T, P	F, S, T, ?
Second Year	By Normal Population	By Experimental Population
L	None	W, F
SH	?	?, S
TH'	TH, S	None
V	B	B
S	?	?
Z	S	S, ?
J	D	None
R	W	W
CH	SH	SH, ?
TH	F	F
Third Year	By Normal Population	By Experimental Population
L	None	W
SH	None	?
TH'	F	F
V	B	B
S	?	TH, ?
Z	S	S, TH, ?
J	D, Omit	D
R	W	W
CH	SH	SH
TH	F, ?	F, ?

* TH' = TH voiced
TH = TH unvoiced
? = approximations

Errors occurred only on last ten sounds of Templin ordering. Previously acquired sounds are not shown. See Figures 1 and 2.

the lower end of a normally developing process: they are delayed in developing articulatory accuracy, but their development follows the normal pattern, of acquisition and, according to the concept of a developmental norm is age appropriate. Case selection based on guidelines provided in this study might well free the speech therapist to work with children who have more impelling speech and language problems such as those caused by the pathological conditions (for example, cleft palate) or to assist the child whose language is delayed. In addition, case selection along the lines described here would avoid the negative psychological effect that speech therapy sometimes has on children who are subjected to it when corrective procedures of this kind are unnecessary.

NOTES

1. MORENCY, ANNE; WEPMAN, J. M. and WEINER, P. S. Studies in speech: developmental articulation inaccuracy. *Elementary School Journal* 67 (March, 1967): 329-37.
2. This study was partially supported by the Department of Health, Education, and Welfare, Office of Education, Project No. 2225, Contract No. 4 10 006.
3. MORENCY, ANNE. Studies in articulation: The construction of the dual modality test of articulation. Unpublished Master's thesis. Chicago: University of Chicago, 1962.
4. TEMPLIN, MILDRED C. *Certain Language Skills in Children.* Minneapolis: University of Minnesota Press, 1957.

Anne S. Morency, Joseph M. Wepman, and Sarah K. Hass are faculty members at the University of Chicago.

16.
All Children Have Language Problems—Which Ones Are Special?
DAISY M. JONES

Language is probably the most important single learning the child will experience in his entire life. Much of that learning has already taken place long before the schools ever see him. Some of the learning is advantageous to him and some may be a distinct disadvantage. It is the part which is disadvantageous to him with which we are chiefly concerned at this time.

The five- or six-year-old comes to school with enough vocabulary and enough knowledge of the structure of language to enable him to communicate in some manner. This communication may be inadequate from our point of view, but it has served his needs up to now, and therefore may seem quite adequate to him. If pointing or grunting will satisfy his needs, if single words or short terse phrases will suffice, if vulgarity and profanity will get his point across, if silence will protect him from a hostile environment, if faulty grammatical construction will communicate, then that is the language he has learned. It is when those around him speak a different language, or attempt to teach him to read and write in language patterns to which his ear is unaccustomed that he begins to have problems. Whether it be a different language, faulty language usage, or lack of language, he still has a problem. Our job is to identify the problems, study the evidence, then get busy helping him do something about it. Doing something about it may be as much an adjustment on our part as helping him make the adjustment to our language or our expectations.

Identifying the Problems

Some problems are physical, some are emotional, some are cultural and for some children, they may be a combination of all these factors. What we will do about them depends on the nature of the problem, its causes, and the child's potential for adjustment.

Physical Problems show up in many ways. A listless child who has a weak body and limited stamina may refrain from using language merely because of *lack of energy*. Another cause of inadequate language may be *hearing loss* merely because there is no language reception to trigger language expression. *Speech defects* may be caused by abnormalities in the organs of articulation. These kinds of difficulties need the attention of

From *Elementary English* 46:6 (October, 1972) 836-41. Copyright © 1972 by the National Council of Teachers of English. Reprinted by permission of the author and publisher.

specialists in the medical profession and therapy from trained experts. The teacher is in the front-line position to spot the difficulties and to refer the child to the appropriate specialist. She is also in a position to lend support to the child's efforts and to follow through with recommended procedures. Anything she does that ignores the problem or aggravates it may do more harm than good.

Emotional Problems show up in the child's social relations. The kind that erupt in the form of *aggressive behavior* usually get deserved attention because the teacher is forced to deal with the outer symptoms if she is to create a learning atmosphere, not only for the child who is disrupting, but also for the rest of the children in the classroom. The overly aggressive child may demonstrate his language problems through monopolizing the conversation, talking incessantly, talking louder than anyone else to gain attention, using undesirable language, demanding to be heard, interrupting others, and sometimes displaying physical force to win the limelight. Treatment may call for curbing the outpouring of language, suppressing the undesirable language, or substituting more suitable language.

The kinds of emotional problems that exhibit themselves through *inhibitions* are less likely to disturb the teacher or the rest of the children in the classroom. The withdrawn child may want very much to say something but may be unable to do so. If he has lived in an adult world where he has been told to "Shut up!" where he has had his ears boxed for talking out of turn, where nobody listens to him, then he may have learned long ago that it is safer to keep still than to risk the consequences. To draw him out through the use of language may call for a long and patient effort. If he has heard adults remark, "He's so bashful," "He won't talk," or "You can't understand him," then he has learned to accept himself as one who is bashful, won't talk, or can't speak so he can be understood. If he has a parent or sibling who always answers for him without giving him a chance, he will learn to wait and let them do it. If there is an older person who always does it over because he can't "measure up," eventually he gives up and just lets them do it. He never learns to speak adequately. He never outgrows "baby talk." Drawing out the inhibited child may take more effort on the part of the teacher than curbing the overly aggressive child. And what's more the withdrawn child is more likely to be overlooked, because unlike the aggressive child, he doesn't disrupt the routine or "bother the teacher."

Cultural Problems are more school related when it comes to the language skills. Some children lack adequate language merely because they have had a sparse background of *experience*. Others may have had plenty of experience, but not the kind approved by the school, therefore, their language, adequate as it may be, is totally unacceptable in the classroom. Still others may bring to school an adequate background of experience but an inadequate background in language suitable for speaking and reading experiences being presented in an all-English-speaking setting, not because their language is necessarily inadequate or bad, but just different. This includes the child who comes from a home or a community where a *different language* or *dialect* is used. Sometimes his speech is unintelligible to his peers and his teacher, and sometimes it is merely regarded as "funny." If his accent or his colloquialisms bring forth laughter or jeers from his listeners, he soon dries up in self-defense.

Accumulating the Evidence

The alert teacher will be observant in identifying language problems. They show up in speech patterns and habits. They show up in language facility and vocabulary. Sometimes it becomes necessary to make a few notes on individuals in order to objectify the problems and deal with them constructively. We might consider the types under the headings of non-lingualism, mono-lingualism, bi-lingualism, and non-standard-lingualism. Let's examine them one at a time.

Non-lingualism is evident in the child who does not or will not talk. Sometimes he refrains from talking in self-defense. Sometimes he has not had the opportunity to learn to talk for reasons mentioned earlier. Whatever the cause, if he does not, or will not talk, the problem is pretty special. Obviously you can't teach him to improve his language usage until he first learns to use language. You can't teach him to read in any language until he can first understand and use a language. I know a story of a young teacher who had a little girl in her room who had not yet spoken that first word by Christmas. In desperation the teacher came back after the holidays with a lovely doll which she showed to Erma and said, "When you talk to me the doll will be yours."

Erma held out her hands and said, "Give me."

The teacher handed the little girl the doll and smiled saying, "What will you call her?"

That did the trick. Once the valve was opened the words gushed forth like a flood. It wasn't long before Erma was talking and reading freely. Apparently she had been *absorbing language* all along but just couldn't relax and let go. When she found she could, the rest came easily. Unorthodox as the technique may seem it does illustrate a point about the inhibitions of the child. Was she non-lingual or merely inhibited? In either case the start was necessary. Exposure alone won't do. The child must have a reason for *communicating*.

Mono-lingualism presents no particular problem as long as the one language the child uses is familiar to his peers, his parents, and his teachers. It becomes a problem when he speaks only one language and that is not a language which can be understood by those around him. I knew a little Vietnamese orphan who was sent to this country by an adoring GI. The new foster mother welcomed him with open arms but could not communicate with him through language. The child had a voluminous and expressive language but there was no communication. Frustrations and exasperations were exhibited in screaming and tears. A few days later when the GI returned by a later plane the child subsided because he had someone with whom he could communicate. As a four-year-old he quickly picked up the English he was hearing and changed rapidly from a mono-lingual to a bi-lingual child.

Bi-lingualism is evident in the child who communicates effectively in *more than one language*. These children are not as numerous as we would like to think. Many so-called bi-lingual children are actually mono-lingual, or sometimes non-lingual. Just because they have learned to com-municate sketchily in a language other than English does not make them bi-lingual. A truly bi-lingual child is not a major problem. He is gifted. He can often make a contribution in the classroom by *acting as an interpreter*, between his parents and his teachers, or between the teacher and other children in the room who are limited to one language, not the language the teacher speaks.

I am reminded of a sixth grade girl I encountered in a classroom in Panama. Along with some dozen or so other visiting educators, I was tour-ing the school. We spoke no Spanish. The attractive head mistress spoke no English. But the alert black eleven-year-old with tight braids handled both languages with ease. She acted as our interpreter and the head mis-tress invited her to follow us. I asked the girl where she learned both lan-guages and she responded, "At home." Then I asked if her father was in the military service and she said, "No, he works on the base." I didn't press the matter further. Draw your own conclusions.

Non-standard-lingualism is evident in the child who speaks English but in such a unique way that his speech is either unintelligible or unaccepta-ble. He is at an even greater disadvantage than any of the above because he thinks he can communicate but finds his efforts rejected or condemned. This leads to frustration that curbs his speech and delays learning.

Colloquialisms and *dialects* may seem "funny" especially if they are un-familiar to the rest of the group. This often happens to the newcomer or the child who comes from a sect which tends to remain aloof.

Slang and sometimes *profanity* and *vulgarity* creep into the language of the young child. Such expressions are used as a matter of course, and the younger speaker may not even know his language is unacceptable. He may get his language from older siblings and pick up colorful expressions which seem quite adequate to him. He may hear adults use profanity and vulgarity to punctuate their speech and not necessarily recognize it as "bad." He may let foul language or profane expressions trip glibly off the end of his tongue. He seems to know the words but not the "tune," be-cause his profane expressions lack the emphasis or inflection usually ac-companying strong feeling. If such language, non-standard though it may be, is rejected by the teacher, or an issue is made of it, the child may be led to feel that his language is not only inadequate but "bad," and since he has no other to substitute he may just "dry up."

Mannerisms accompanying language may interfere with communica-tion. Unless they are obnoxious they may be merely colorful and expres-sive. The teacher should be alert for excessive grimacing, squinting, violent bodily movement, and such mannerisms accompanying speech.

Deciding What to Do About It

Identifying language problems and accumulating evidence to support their existence will be of little value unless the teacher is ready to do something constructive to help the child. That's the point at which we identify problems that are special enough to need attention.

If a language problem is merely colorful, temporary, unique, interesting, or immature, we may be wise to accept it, help the child grow and mature, and watch for improvement.

But if a language problem is objectionable, persistent, distracting, and growing, then we may be wise to investigate it and help the child overcome it.

Doing something to help is more important than either identification of the problem or determination of the cause. To know that it exists, to say so to the child or his parents, to blame his environment, or his lack of ability only recognizes the problem but does little or nothing to guarantee improvement.

To isolate or not to isolate is one significant question. Shall we put him in a *special group* with other children exhibiting similar problems, or leave him with the total group? There are different opinions on this. One point in favor of separation is that there may be more time to concentrate on the problem and apply specific remedial measures. Of course we take the ill patient to the hospital and give him the care he needs to correct his ailment, but we don't keep him there indefinitely. The child with the speech or language problem may need *special attention*, but there are also dangers in pointing out his case as special.

If he enjoys the attention he gets from being special, he may perpetuate the problem in order to continue the attention he enjoys.

If he resists the notoriety, he may dry up to avoid what seems embarrassing to him.

No one solution is suitable for all children with language problems.

To begin with the environment might be worthy of consideration. If the child is rejected perhaps we could work with those who are doing the rejecting rather than with the one who is being rejected. *Accepting a child* with a different language and making him feel welcome is a first step. *Soliciting help* from the rest of the class in teaching him English may be a genuine learning experience for them as well as for the new-comer. They will learn a lesson in human empathy and at the same time may pick up a bit of the new language which may broaden their own knowledge. If he is isolated the others won't benefit from what he might contribute to the group. Since language is for the purpose of communication, he needs someone with whom to communicate. Isolating him removes the opportunity to communicate. Perhaps ALL or NEITHER is not the answer. Can he be grouped with others with similar problems without permanent isolation? Language calls for group situations. Who is in his group? If it is only those with problems like his, he never hears any other type of language and may never know that others "speak a different language." He must have a different pattern to imitate if he is going to adjust to a different world.

To identify the conditions is a first step. It is more important how a child is treated in the group in which he finds himself than what group he is in; therefore these conditions seem evident:

—If he is *rejected,* he will either rebel and clamor for the attention he wants or dry up the fountain of speech.

—If he is severely *corrected* or *criticized,* he will either become subservient and try to conform or fall by the wayside.

—If he is *accepted* and *encouraged,* he will learn to accept himself as well as others and, hopefully, make adjustments that will enhance his ability to use language as a means of communication.

—If he is helped through positive *suggestions* and *examples,* he will tend to "follow suit," and merge with his social environment.

To make suggestions for action in dealing with a child with special language problems is a positive approach. Consider these:

—First, *accept him* as he is and for what he is.

—Second, *study him* and his problems. Determine what language he uses and how well he uses it. Identify his differences and his inadequacies.

—Third, *look into his background.* Find out how he "got that way."

—Fourth, *let him experiment* with language through talking and expressing his ideas. Let him retell stories, dramatize telephone conversations, relate experiences, express wants, and converse with his peers.

—Fifth, *talk with him* to show an interest, to provide an opportunity for him to use the language he knows, and to provide him with appropriate patterns to imitate.

—Finally, *work for growth* and improvement, not perfection.

To establish goals is the next step. If you set *perfection* and *conformity* as the goals, you are reaching for the stars. It is doubtful if any of us ever reach that goal. *Perfection* is a debatable standard both from the standpoint of what it is and when it is attained. *Conformity* is an impossible standard because there are so many variations in language usage that what is conformity in one setting may not be conformity in another.

If you set *growth* as the goal, all can attain that. Begin with the most obvious and take one step at a time.

If the child is *non-lingual* you may have to resort to bribery or other unorthodox methods to open the fount. Getting him to talk is the first step. It may call for alleviating fears, assuring him of support, or freeing him from corrections. You can't improve language until some language exists. It's like the mountaineer who was asked, "Do you want molasses on your pancakes?" and he replies, "How can I have mo' 'lasses until I've had some 'lasses?"

If the child is *mono-lingual,* and the language he speaks is not the same as those around him, then obviously some means of communication must be found. Learning English as a second language may be difficult for him but help is abundant. Sometimes the children can do more about it than the teacher. Accept him. Help him. Enjoy the new learning with him. Help him see that others may know something they don't know. Capitalize on his extra ability. Record progress and laud efforts.

The child who is *bi-lingual* should be treated as a decided asset in the classroom. Make him feel that his extra abilities are not only to his advantage but to the advantage of the rest also. Encourage him to maintain both languages for the rest of his life.

The child who uses *non-standard-English* including colloquialisms and dialects, slang, profanity, and objectional mannerisms is often reflecting his background. He shows his own inadequacies. To make him feel even more inadequate only aggravates the issue. Give him plenty of good examples. Accept him and lead his peers to do likewise. Encourage him to imitate a more acceptable pattern.

To recognize diversity leads the child to see that he may have several languages. What is acceptable in the home may not suffice in the classroom. What he says on the playground, in the alley, on the street, or among his peers, may lack the elegance by which his language is judged in the educated world. What language he uses may vary with the environment. All of us have several languages. It is not so much a matter of which one is *right* and which ones are *wrong* as which one is *appropriate* under the circumstances.

There are situations in which a nod of the head may be sufficient for purposes of assent. There are situations when a simple one-word response is better than a verbose monologue. There are situations in which Spanish, or French, or German, or Navajo, or perhaps even pidgin English might be more readily understood than elegant and refined English. And sometimes the attitude of the listener might be as important as the understanding of the language itself. The child who goes home from school criticizing the language of his parents has lost something in human relations that an "A" in English will never replace.

Yes, all of us have language problems. They become *special* only when they interfere with the basic purpose for using language, that is, communicating. The first questions to ask is:

"Did he communicate?"

Then we may follow that with other questions such as:

"Was communication effective?"
"Could it be made more effective?"
"If so, how?"
"And how can we help him?"

Daisy M. Jones is Professor of Education at Arizona State University, Tempe, Arizona. This article is the text of an address given by Dr. Jones at the 1971 NCTE National Convention.

17.
Language of the Mildly Mentally Retarded: Cognitive Deficit or Cultural Difference?
PETER VALLETUTTI

How do you weigh the relative importance of the cognitive factors vs. the environmental factors in explaining the poor language patterns of the retarded?

Man develops implicit theories of human behavior in order to rapidly evaluate others. Social intelligence is to a large extent measurable by how well behavioral stereotypes are incorporated into functional judgments of people. Rapid judgments are based on a variety of visual and auditory inputs, which include speech, size, shape, color, and physical attractiveness (McKeachie, 1952; Myerson, 1963; Secord, 1958). These intuitive diagnoses incorporate a wide range of human characteristics to which personality and behavioral correlates are assigned.

Speech is one of the most telling stereotypic clues to an individual's social class membership. Judgments of individual worth are often based upon grammatical and syntactic conformity. On the other hand, Shaw's *Pygmalion* and its various adaptations illustrates how the modification of speech behavior may facilitate social mobility. Many non English speaking immigrants in America waited several generations before the assimilation of standard speech patterns made it possible for them to become socially mobile. Such foreign accents, however, are viewed positively as evidenced by the success of English and Viennese actors. On the other hand, the linguistic attempts of other nationality groups are often denigrated as broken or pidgin English. What accounts for the differential selection process is not the concern of this article although the existence of this selection factor emphasizes the arbitrariness of such judgments.

Socioeconomic Factors

A substantial majority of functionally retarded persons come from the lower socioeconomic areas of the community (Dunn, 1963; Johnson, 1961; Sarason, 1959). Thus members of the middle class, with some logic, develop implicit theories which equate deviant speech patterns of low socioeconomic groups with low intelligence. The

From *Exceptional Children* 37 (February, 1971): 455-59. Reprinted by permission of the author and *Exceptional Children*. Copyrighted by the Council for Exceptional Children.

stereotypic judgment that socioeconomic status is closely related to speech and language patterns is supported in the literature (Beckey, 1942; Bernstein, 1960; Cohn, 1959; Deutsch, 1967; Gesell & Lord, 1927; Hockett, 1950; Irwin, 1948a and 1948b; John, 1963; McCarthy, 1954; Mowrer, 1958; Raph, 1965; Schiefelbusch, 1963; Stevens & Heber, 1964; Templin, 1953; Weaver, Furbee, & Everhart, 1960). Whereas homes which provide superior linguistic models are more likely to produce children with superior linguistic development, and whereas a majority of the functionally retarded come from lower socioeconomic backgrounds, the speech function of the mildly retarded may stem not only from intellectual factors but may also be a product of impoverished or restricted language models. Language defects are generally judged by middle class standards, and defects found in the lower class groups may merely represent deviations from these standards rather than retarded development.

The speech deficits of the economically disadvantaged have been compounded and perpetuated by at best a paternalistic and at worst a brutally aggressive majority through years of educational deprivation and social isolation. In light of the many variables and their interactions relevant to intelligence (e.g., the environmental contributions to cognition, the effects of intelligence on language development, and the effects of language on cognition), it is difficult to sift out significant factors and meaningful interactions. Two provocative and related questions arise, however: (a) Does the speech and language of the mildly retarded reflect cultural difference and/or cognitive deficit? and (b) Does cognitive deficit result from nonstandard speech patterns and/or genetic inadequacy?

Causes of Speech Defects

Those authorities who have questioned whether mental retardation is a direct cause of speech defects have suggested a number of other possibilities.

. . . There are many other aspects which do more to explain the patient's defective or absent speech than his intellectual subnormality: for example. . . there is a higher incidence of hearing loss amongst feebleminded patients, there are the physical concomitants of such conditions as mongolism, cretinism and congenital syphilis; poor family environments may result in neglect of dental and other physical abnormalities which may have an adverse effect on speech and the emotional deprivation of the institutionalized child may be an important factor in retarded speech [Penwill, 1961, p. 395].

MALADJUSTMENT

Problems of maladjustment are considered by Schlanger (1953) to be a significant etiological factor in speech defects among the retarded. The maladjustment often seems to be more closely associated with reactions to environmental pressures than with congenital or organic predisposition. According to Berry and Eisenson (1956), linguistic inadequacy rather than speech deficiency causes lack of intelligence and this may result in the development of inferiority feelings which may be manifested in defective speech. Wood (1957) warned that although the symptomatology of behavior might suggest that mental retardation is the causal factor for delayed speech development, further evaluation might indicate that such factors as hearing loss, emotional disturbance, or language disorders may be the true cause of delayed speech.

SOCIAL CLASS

Because most of the functionally retarded are found among the lower socioeconomic levels, the relationship of social class to speech development and defect should be considered. Irwin (1948a) conducted a pioneer series of studies on the relationship of family occupational status and speech development. He compared infants of laboring men with infants of professional, business, and clerical workers and found no significant differences in amount of vocalization during the first year and a half of infancy. After infancy, however, he did find a significant difference in the frequency of utterance of speech sounds in favor of the higher occupational groups. In another study (1948b), an analysis of variance yielded significant differences between two socioeconomic groups in favor of the higher level. Milner (1951) indicated that the correlation between language and socioeconomic status is somewhere between .78 and .86. Beckey (1942), Gesell and Lord (1927), McCarthy (1954), Stevens and Heber (1964), Templin (1953), and Weaver, Furbee, and Everhart (1960) all reported a marked relationship between socioeconomic status and linguistic development.

The question of whether the speech and language of the mildly retarded reflects cultural difference and/or cognitive deficit cannot be answered at this time. The interaction of environment and intelligence is inextricably interwoven and a reliable answer may never be found. Nevertheless, assigning inferior status to individuals who speak a nonstandard dialect is an arbitrary decision by the culturally biased majority which may contribute further to the handicap. In order to counteract the many negative effects of such a critical perspective, some educators have adopted a liberal approach which stresses the positive attributes of nonstandard language with its vitality, precision, and effective peer group communication (Reissman, 1962; Shaw, 1948; Whorf, 1967).

The Liberal Approach

George Bernard Shaw expressed the liberal viewpoint when he spoke of the English speech of several nationalities.

Chinese traders, Negroes, and aboriginal Australians, who have to learn English as a foreign language, simplify it much further, and have thereby established what they call business English, or as they pronounced it Pidgin. The

Chinese, accustomed to an uninflected monosyllabic language do not say I regret that I shall be unable to comply with your request. 'Sorry no can' is quite effective, and saves the time of both parties. When certain Negro slaves in America were oppressed by a lady planter who was very pious and very severe, their remonstrance, if expressed in grammatic English, would have been 'if we are to be preached at let us not be flogged also: if we are to be flogged let us not be preached at also.' This is correct and elegant but wretchedly feeble. It says in twenty-six words what can be better said in eleven. The Negroes proved this by saying 'If preachee preachee; if floggee floggee; but not preachee floggee too.' They saved fifteen words of useless grammar and said what they had to say far more expressively [Shaw, 1963, pp. 117-118].

The liberal approach emphasizes the relationship aspect rather than the cognitive aspect of language. Social and linguistic success may be found in polydialectical fluency which is emphasized in the liberal approach. A person in our society is increasingly called upon to communicate across a wide variety of social, occupational, and ethnic levels. He must learn to value not only the speech of white middle class America but also subgroup idioglossia (Shuy, 1966).

The Conservative Approach

On the other hand, conservative evaluators note the inflexibility and cognitive confusion of lower class idioglossic language patterns and the frequent unintelligibility of its articulation. Bernstein (1961, 1964) theorized that the speech of lower class adults follows a linguistic code that is ideally suited to maintaining social relationships but which is poorly suited for sharing familiar experiences and opinions, for analysis and careful reasoning, for dealing with anything hypothetical or beyond the present, or for dealing with anything very complex. A similar viewpoint was expressed by Bereiter and Englemann (1966). They pointed out a further characteristic of lower class language:

The speech of the severely deprived seems to consist not of distinct words, as does the speech of middle class children of the same age, but rather of whole phrases or sentences that function like giant words [p. 34].

These giant words are not taken apart by the child and recombined and transformed from statements into questions and from imperatives to declaratives. For example, for such children the sentence, "He's a big dog!" is considered to be a single word, "Hebidaw." As a result the child cannot transfer either the single word or the concept "big" to another sentence. Generally, however, educators have ignored the effects on cognition of deviant speech patterns such as those identified by Bereiter and Englemann. Instead they have been preoccupied with language as it relates to communication and have been especially obsessed with the relative social acceptability of various dialects. Educators are now increasingly focusing on the poor, the culturally different minorities, and the unassimilated and have emphasized the social value rather than the cognitive aspects of good English. A different priority ordering is essential.

This article proposes an evaluation of language which alternates between the opposing conservative and liberal perspectives. It supports a view which assigns educational priority to the cognitive function of language and assigns a minor role to social acceptability. Aspects of language critical to the development of intelligence should be identified and differentiated from those aspects which are benign dialectical differences. Those aspects of speech vital to thought processes must be taught; those errors of language which interfere with cognition must be identified and remediated.

At the same time, the educator is not ethically justified in interfering with those aspects of language which do not damage the cognitive processes and which perhaps facilitate intragroup communication. Delineating those aspects of languages which carry cognitive value and afford fluency and precision becomes essential.

Beginning language is primarily a matter of establishing associations for arbitrary symbols which name common objects and people, actions, and qualities. Arbitrary symbols are group specific and possess little intrinsic cognitive value except through associative linkage. Only when time, quantity, and relativity are attached to these names do language and thought pass beyond the primary stage of association and into a higher level which includes symbolic relationships of number, tense, and degree. Errors and confusion in this sphere may retard cognitive development and inhibit more sophisticated communication.

Oral and written language involves four linguistic systems each of which contributes to the development of acceptable words, phrases, and sentences:

1. Phonological (sound features);
2. Semantic (meaning);
3. Syntactic (word order);
4. Morphologic (tense, person, number, case).

Cognitive Confusion

Every dialect, whether standard or non-standard, must be analyzed in terms of these four systems to examine what its organized patterns are. If one employs the criterion that the child's cognitive development is most critical, then the pronunciation "bafrom" for "bathroom" would represent a benign dialectical difference since its dissimilarity to any other common word would prevent cognitive confusion.

On the other hand, pronouncing the writing implement "pen" as though it were the item in a sewing basket—"pin"—would confuse the child who must somehow differentiate between two vocal utterances acoustically similar but denotatively dissimilar. The tendency for some older children and younger adults from lower socioeconomic groups to ask the question, "Do you have an ink pin?" appears on the surface to be an example of nonstandard redundancy pattern while it may in actuality be an attempt to receive the correct response. "Chimbley" for "chimney," "g'rage," for "garage," and "punkin" for "pumpkin" would be unlikely to cause cognitive confusion. Omitting the final consonant of a monosyllabic word such as "bat" however, will result in a wide range of proliferating homonyms (back, bad, bath, bag, bash, ban, bass).

Logical Patterns

Nonstandard dialect may possess its own logic, logic which may be somewhat foreign to standard English. In standard English, one way of indicating a predicate adjective is with a form of the verb to be. In the nonstandard dialect, one way of predicating an adjective is without the verb to be. For example, "He busy" changes in meaning when "be" is inserted so that the expression reads, "He be busy." In dialect the rule is that for a short-term state, or an immediate situation, the expression should be, "He busy." If it is a long-term state, a habitual action or pattern, the expression should be, "He be busy." If someone says, "Why doesn't your uncle come to visit us today?" "He busy" would mean something came up to deter him. "Because he be busy" would mean the uncle always has some reason for not visiting.

In some nonstandard dialects, pluralization is another example of deviant but logical speech patterns. For example, "I got four bruvva" for "I have four brothers" is a logical variation. Four apparently takes care of the pluralization. But this same deviant speech uses the plural s in "It belong to my bruvvas" because here nothing else shows that it is plural. Thus, in this case, there is less redundancy in the nonstandard dialect without loss of accuracy of meaning (Stewart, 1966).

A very logical mistake like "thunk" or "thinked" for a past process may be considered a benign dialectical difference because the child is using a past form that is not standard, but accurately indicates that reference is being made to something which happened in the past. A different past form was used, in this case a nonstandard one. The essential criterion is whether person, tense, or number have been indicated in some way, not necessarily the standard way. If person, tense, or number is not indicated in any way, then cognitive confusion is bound to occur. Correction of cognitively critical deviant patterns must take precedence over attempts to correct more benign dialectical differences.

Classroom Implications

Time is the most critical constraint in curriculum development. The teacher has so little time to effect change, to stimulate growth, and to make his work significant. He must establish priorities in his teaching to maximize his effect. Time is also critical on a developmental basis for each child. The early years have pervasive and significant effects on language and cognitive development. The teacher must not waste irretrievable time in correcting benign dialectical differences which clash with prevailing speech patterns. Time may be given to benign deviations from middle class speech only after efforts have been concentrated on improving cognition of lower socioeconomic children through significant language remediation. Perhaps then the incidence of mild mental retardation among this group may be diminished. In reality, mild mental retardation among the poor may be a result, in part, of cognitive confusion resulting from illogical deviant language patterns. A curriculum intervention of the nature described above is researchable and may produce definitive answers to the question of whether the higher incidence of mild mental retardation among the lower socioeconomic group results not so much from cognitive deficit as cultural difference.

REFERENCES

BECKEY, R. E. A study of certain factors related to retardation of speech. *Journal of Speech Disorders* 7 (1942): 223-49.

BEREITER, C. & ENGELMAN, S. *Teaching Disadvantaged Children in the Preschool.* Englewood Cliffs, N.J.: Prentice-Hall, 1966.

BERNSTEIN, B. Language and social class. *British Journal of Sociology,* 1960, 11, 271-76.

BERNSTEIN, B. Social class and linguistic development. In A. H. HALSEY, J. FLOUD, & C. A. ANDERSON, eds., *Education, Economy and Society.* New York: Free Press, 1961.

BERNSTEIN, B. Elaborated and restricted codes: Their social origins and some consequences. *American Anthropology* 66 (1964): 1-34.

BERRY, M. F. & EISENSON, J. *Speech Disorders: Principles and Practices of Therapy.* New York: Appleton-Century-Crofts, 1956.

COHN, W. On the language of lower-class children. *School Review* 67 (1959): 435-40.

DEUTSCH, M. *The Disadvantaged Child.* New York: Basic Books, 1967.

DUNN, L. M. Educable mentally retarded children. In L. M. DUNN, ed., *Exceptional Children in the Schools.* New York: Holt, Rinehart & Winston, 1963.

GESELL, A. & LORD, A. E. A psychological comparison of nursery school children from low and high economic status. *Pedagogical Seminary and Journal of Genetic Psychology* 34 (1927): 339-56.

HOCKETT, C. F. Age grading and linguistic change. *Language* 26 (1950): 449-57.

IRWIN, O. C. Infant speech: The effect of family occupational status and of age on sound frequency. *Journal of Speech and Hearing Disorders* 13 (1948): 320-23. (a)

IRWIN, O. C. Infant speech: The effect of family occupational status and of age on use of sound types. *Journal of Speech and Hearing Disorders* 13 (1948): 224-26. (b)

JOHN, V. P. The intellectual development of slum children: Some preliminary findings. *American Journal of Orthopsychiatry* 33 (1963): 813-22.

JOHNSON, G. O. The education of mentally handicapped children. In W. M. CRUICKSHANK and G. O. JOHNSON, eds., *Education of Exceptional Children and Youth.* Englewood Cliffs, N.J.: Prentice-Hall, 1961.

McCARTHY, D. Language development in children. In L. CARMICHAEL, ed., *Manual of Child Psychology.* New York: John Wiley & Sons, 1954.

McKEACHIE, W. J. Lipstick as a determiner of first impressions of personality: An experiment for the general psychology course. *Journal of Social Psychology* 36 (1952): 241-44.

MILNER, E. A study of the relationship between reading readiness in grade one school children and patterns of parent-child interaction. *Child Development* 22 (1951): 95-112.

MOWRER, O. H. Hearing and speaking: An analysis of language learning. *Journal of Speech and Hearing Disorders* 23 (1958): 143-53.

MYERSON, L. Somatopsychology of physical disability. In W. M. CRUICKSHANK, ed., *Psychology of Exceptional Children and Youth.* Englewood Cliffs, N.J.: Prentice-Hall, 1963.

PENWILL, M. Speech disorders and therapy in mental deficiency. In A. B. D. CLARKE and A. M. CLARKE, eds., *Mental Deficiency.* Glencoe, Ill.: Free Press, 1961.

RAPH, J. B. Language development in socially disadvantaged children. *Review of Educational Research* 35 (1965): 389-400.

REISSMAN, F. *The Culturally Deprived Child.* New York: Harper & Row, 1962.

SARASON, S. B. *Psychological Problems in Mental Deficiency.* New York: Harper & Row, 1959.

SCHIEFELBUSCH, R. L. Introduction. *Journal of Speech and Hearing Disorders* 18 (1953): 339-49.

SCHLANGER, B. B. Speech examination of a group of institutionalized mentally handicapped children, *Journal of Speech and Hearing Disorders* 18 (1953): 339-49.

SECORD, P. F. Facial features and inference processes in interpersonal perception. In R. TAGIURI and L. PETERULLO, eds., *Person Perception and Interpersonal Behavior.* Stanford: Stanford University Press, 1958.

SHAW, G. B. Preface to the miraculous birth of language. In A. TAUBER, ed., *George Bernard Shaw on Language.* New York: Philosophical Library, 1963.

SHUY, R. W. Dialectology and usage. *Baltimore Bulletin of Education* 43 (1966): 40-51.

STEVENS, H. A. & HEBER, R. *Mental Retardation: A Review of Research.* Chicago: University of Chicago, 1964.

STEWART, W. A. Nonstandard speech patterns. *Baltimore Bulletin of Education* 43 (1966): 52-65.

TEMPLIN, M. C. Norms on a screening test of articulation for ages three through eight. *Journal of Speech and Hearing Disorders* 18 (1953): 323-31.

WEAVER, H. C., FURBEE, C., & EVERHART, R. W. Paternal occupational class and articulatory defects in children. *Journal of Speech and Hearing Disorders* 25 (1960): 171-75.

WHORF, B. L. A linguistic consideration of thinking in primitive communities. In J. B. CARROLL ed., *Language, Thought, and Reality.* Cambridge, Mass.: MIT Press, 1967.

WOOD, N. E. Causal factors of delayed speech and language development. *American Journal of Mental Deficiency* 61 (1957): 706-08.

Peter Valletutti is Professor and Director of Special Education, Coppin State College and Assistant Professor of Pediatrics, Johns Hopkins University School of Medicine, Baltimore, Maryland.

Five

Intellectually Gifted Children

The four articles in this chapter deal with representative aspects of educating the able children and youth. A number of states have enacted laws that authorize special programs and services for gifted children, but the special class, which has been a common instructional arrangement in most areas of special education, is not widely practiced for gifted children. Rather, a number of unique instructional arrangements have been developed, which are described in detail in most texts relating to educating exceptional children. Currently there is widespread interest among both laymen and professionals to extend the educational opportunities for able children and youth in our society. The importance of able leadership and creative talent in a democracy must not be underestimated.

The first selection is a report of the Policies Commission of the Council for Exceptional Children on goals for educating the gifted. This statement is intended to stimulate judicious planning for gifted children in American schools.

The influence of the home is recognized as a major factor in stimulating the development of the abilities of gifted children, but most of the educational writing deals with the school and its challenge in adequately serving the gifted. The second article, by Kathleen Dewing, discusses some of the relationships between the home influences and the development of creativity in children.

The third article reports on a survey of the opinions of gifted students regarding school practices. The study was made in the San Diego Unified School District where an extensive program for gifted students has been provided for the past twenty-five years. This interesting report provides some guideposts for curriculum development as well as suggestions for classroom instruction.

The final article, by Paul Torrance, describes the changing concepts in the education of the gifted. Most schools today prefer to serve children who express their unusual abilities in any one of several ways: high academic abilities, unusual artistic skills, musical talent, leadership ability, etc. Torrance discusses some of the complications of this multi-talent concept of giftedness.

Lewis Madison Terman is internationally known for his longitudinal studies of the development of gifted children. Since he was clearly the United States' most distinguished scholar in the study of gifted children, it is appropriate to honor him as a pioneer in this chapter.

Lewis Madison Terman
1877–1956

PSYCHOLOGIST
EDUCATOR
TEST DEVELOPER

Dr. Louis Madison Terman was internationally known for his pioneer work in revising and standardizing the Binet intelligence test in 1916, and for his extensive studies of gifted children. His longitudinal studies, summarized in *Genetic Studies of Genius,* greatly influenced the development of school programs for able children. Both of these achievements were significant in the field of special education.

As a farm youth, Terman borrowed money to obtain a college education, including his Ph.D. degree. At age fifteen he entered normal school and later taught a one-room rural school. He earned both his bachelor's and master's degrees at the University of Indiana. His interest in psychology led him to go to Clark University to study under G. Stanley Hall, who was a distinguished child psychologist. Terman's graduate research related to his early major interests— mental testing and gifted children.

From the Los Angeles Normal School, where he was an instructor for four years, he went to Stanford University as an assistant professor of education in 1910. Later he became head of the department of psychology. It was in this position at Stanford that he distinguished himself as a scholar, researcher, and writer. His longitudinal studies of gifted children were initiated in 1921 and continued until his death thirty-five years later.

18.
A Policy Statement on
Education of the Gifted

The 1971 Delegate Assembly, in approving a statement of basic commitments and responsibilities to exceptional children, affirmed "that every person is valuable in his own right and should be afforded equal opportunities to develop his full potential."

Failure to act to meet the educational needs of the gifted is not only a denial of democratic right, it is a serious subtraction of potential effort for society as a whole. When the educational system fails to recognize and provide for his unique characteristics, the gifted child often develops patterns of boredom, of lazy scholarship, and a disastrous belief that all problems can be solved easily, an attitude that ill befits the urgent complex problems of a troubled world. A system that is ignorant of or indifferent toward his needs does damage not only to the gifted child but thereby renders future society the poorer.

The Position of the Special Educator

Special education for the gifted is not a question of advantage to the individual versus advantage to society. It is a matter of advantage to both. Society has an urgent and accelerated need to develop the abilities and talents of those who promise high contribution. To ignore this obligation and this resource is not only short sighted, but does violence to the basic concept of full educational opportunity for all.

When professional educators tend to move from one enthusiasm to another, and when educational systems tend to react primarily to urgent problems and crises, the needs of gifted children are too often overlooked. Because the gifted are always with us, their education does not arouse prompt professional fervor. And because their neglect represents a subtle long term wastage rather than a present threatening issue, educational systems channel their energies in other directions. But the commitment of The Council for Exceptional Children to equal educational opportunity for all to develop their full potential places a continuing responsibility for the gifted upon its members.

Special educators should vigorously support programs for the gifted, as consistent with their concept of the need for special assistance for all exceptional children. Such programs should reflect both the cognitive and noncognitive needs of the gifted.

From *Exceptional Children* 40 (September, 1973): 73-76. Reprinted by permission of Maynard C. Reynolds, Chairman, Council for Exceptional Children Policies Commission, and *Exceptional Children.* Copyrighted by the Council for Exceptional Children.

This paper derives from earlier position papers by Ruth Martinson, Willard Abraham, and James Gallagher. The Commission gratefully acknowledges the special contributions of Fred A. MacKinnon in constructing this statement.

Identification

Children with outstanding talents and abilities[*] can be identified before school entry, and even more readily in the primary grades. Further, gifted children are to be found in all parts of society, no social segment possessing a monopoly. With even present incomplete means, in-depth search for gifted children results in the identification of many from minority elements, from disadvantaged sectors of the population, and from isolated geographic areas.

Broad search for and early identification of its gifted within all social groupings should be hallmarks of an adequate educational system.

Articulation and Continuity

For various reasons, including the readier accessibility of certain age groups to traditional kinds of assessment, school systems have tended to make special provision for their gifted during the middle school years. Special education opportunities have less frequently extended through high school and post high school years. Because recent emphases upon the importance of preschool education for exceptional children are largely focused on the needs of the handicapped, gifted children are being overlooked in this period as well. Yet evidence from research studies affirms that the intellectual abilities of the gifted are manifest at all age levels.

A program of special education for the gifted should provide continuing and appropriate educational experience from preschool into adult years.

Educational and Administrative Provisions

In a very real sense, the problem of educating the gifted resides in the discrepancies which exist between his educational needs and the educational reality of the organization within which he attends school. If the advanced capacity of the gifted is taken seriously, the usual school arrangements must be altered.

At the same time it should be recognized that no single administrative plan or educational provision is totally appropriate for the gifted. Certain administrative and instructional arrangements may provide settings in which the gifted can perform more adequately. In the final analysis, however, the task is one of accommodation to the needs of the individual.

New arrangements and new provisions must be utilized, including freedom to pursue interests which might not fit the prescribed curriculum, op-

---

[*] "Gifted and talented children are those who are capable of high performance as identified by professionally qualified personnel. These are children who require different educational programs and/or services beyond those normally provided by the regular school program in order to realize their full potential in contribution to self and society. [US Office of Education. *Education of the gifted and talented.* Vol. 1: Report to the Congress of the United States, Washington, D.C.: USGPO, 1971, p. ix]."

portunities for open blocks of time, opportunities for consultation with resources external to the classroom, including adults who are not teachers, and opportunities to bypass those portions of the curriculum which have been absorbed in the past by the individual. These kinds of arrangements must go on in all educational settings and procedures for the gifted, whether in the regular classroom or in highly specialized situations.

Special education for the gifted demands both differentiation within special programs in terms of individual needs and differentiation between programs for the gifted and those for others.

Preparation of School and Leadership Personnel

The identification of the legitimate needs of the gifted and an understanding of the problems which accompany unmet needs necessitate specialized preparation for all school personnel who deal with them. Of the adults in the school its teachers have the greatest impact, but other school personnel affect the gifted directly and indirectly. These persons also require preparation.

Specialized preparation for professionals teaching the gifted should be provided just as specialized preparation is provided for those who teach other exceptional children. Such preparation should include short term workshops, conferences, and summer session courses. More importantly, it should include year long programs of study designed to promote a comprehensive understanding of the gifted, along with the consideration and evaluation of various provisions for them.

School counselors and school psychologists play an important role in identifying the gifted and in interpreting their needs to teachers, parents, and other school and community personnel. School librarians and specialist teachers also need preparation so that they may better recognize the uniqueness of gifted children and provide opportunities in keeping with their special needs.

School administrators must have some specialized understanding of the gifted in order to evaluate programs in relation to needs and, where indicated, to alter school arrangements. School administrators who are cognizant of the needs of the gifted can affect greatly their opportunities for learning.

Beyond the local level appropriately prepared leadership personnel should be provided at state, provincial, and national levels. Without such leadership special education for the gifted risks restriction to isolated local efforts, however good, and thus failure of broad realization.

Special preparation is required for those educators who have specific responsibilities for educating the gifted. Teachers and other professional educators who work with the gifted need special training in both program content and process skills. Such training should be recognized by appropriate certification in the case of teachers and should receive the general support of local, state, provincial, Federal, and private interests.

Demonstration Programs

The preparation of school personnel in the education of the gifted should be carried out in settings which permit opportunities to examine relevant research and to observe innovative administrative provision and exemplary instruction. This requires extensive library services, ongoing research or access to such research, and most important, centers in which teachers may observe and try out new styles of teaching, appropriate to the education of the gifted.

Special model or demonstration programs should be established to illustrate to educators and others the kind and range of innovative program efforts that are possible for gifted students.

Research and Development Centers

At several locations throughout the country, learning centers of the kind in existence for professionals working with other types of exceptional children should be developed for those who work with the gifted. If at such centers projects are conducted in cooperation with local school systems, the effect could be a substantial increase in the rate of change toward individualized, pupil centered programs for gifted students within public school structures.

Research and development resources should be focused on the needs of the gifted in order to develop new methodologies and curricula and to allow educators and others to evaluate current and proposed methods.

Parents and the Public

In the past the gifted have been at least as much misunderstood by parents and the public as have the handicapped, and at the present time are probably the least accepted of all exceptional children. Since gifted children are relatively successful in school, and since typically they have neither visible physical disabilities nor learning handicaps, little public concern is extended toward their education. The public as a whole tends to be indifferent both toward its obligation to promote their education and the social benefits to be derived from it.

Another reason for seeking greater public awareness lies in the increasing extent to which educators are looking beyond the school's doors for learning experiences for students. This is true for all students, but it is particularly true for the gifted. The community's resources may provide for the gifted student far more meaningful learning opportunities than the school is able to arrange within itself. But if the community's adults are unaware of the nature, range, and power of his intellectual interests, his learning environment is significantly less rich than it should be.

The educational needs of the gifted warrant planned programs of public information particularly at the local community level. Special educators should accept this responsibility as an important part of their professional involvement.

Although programs for the gifted can sometimes be initiated at relatively modest cost, it is important that funds for this purpose be earmarked at local, state or provincial, and national levels. Principal expenditures should be directed toward the employment of leadership personnel, the development of methods and programs, and of particular importance at the local level, the preparation of persons for the support and implementation of such methods and programs in the schools.

The importance of optimal educational services for the gifted merits the spending of funds in appropriate amounts toward this end by all levels of government, as well as by other sources.

19.
Family Influences on Creativity:
A Review and Discussion
KATHLEEN DEWING

What parental attitudes and practices seem to foster the development of creativity in a child? Do you agree or disagree with the suggestions set forth in this article?

During the last twenty years, psychologists have re-examined the role of parents in fostering intellectual growth. Hunt (1961), Hebb (1949), and many others have questioned the concept of fixed intelligence, and have extensively explored the effect of deprived and enriched environments. Hess's work on material teaching styles is particularly relevant; he has argued that the most important factor in cultural deprivation is a lack of meaning and precision in the mother-child communication system (Hess, 1965; Hess & Shipman, 1965). Other nonintellective factors in academic success have been identified, notably the "achievement motive" (Atkinson, 1958; McClelland, et al., 1953), which has been shown to have its origins in early training by parents and in middle-class status.

Parallel with these developments, research into creativity has heavily underlined the interaction between cognitive abilities—e.g., fluency, flexibility, etc.—and certain personality and environmental factors. As

From *Journal of Special Education* 4 (Fall-Winter, 1970): 339-404. Reprinted by permission of the author and the *Journal of Special Education*.

knowledge about creative people was accumulated, it became apparent that persons from completely different spheres—artists, chemists, writers, physicists, psychologists, biologists—showed some similar personality traits (Barron, 1963; Cattell, 1963; Roe, 1952; Stein, 1963). Broadly speaking, these traits culminated in tendencies to interact with the environment in particular ways, to be open to and anxious for new experiences, to employ internal frames of evaluation, to be able to tolerate uncertainty, and to reject the security of established attitudes, preconceived notions, majority opinions, and accepted norms.

Much of the impetus for these studies came from the writings of personality theorists like Maslow (1954), Rogers (1951), Fromm (1941), May (1953), Murphy (1947), and Schachtel (1959). Their ideas were adapted for research programs by students of the creative personality, particularly at the Institute of Personality Assessment and Research (IPAR) at the University of California. The findings of these programs, now well documented (Barron, 1963; MacKinnon, 1962), have considerable educational implications.

The IPAR discoveries that "original" persons prefer complexity and are more independent in their judgments can be used by educators and parents as bases for refraining from attempting to structure the experiences of creative children too highly, encouraging self-evaluation, accepting such traits as self-assertion, "feminine" interests, and poor impulse control, and rewarding a wide range of performance.

These principles have been extensively applied in the educational sphere by Torrance (1963, 1965, 1967), who has demonstrated that the creativity of school children may be raised or lowered by environmental and cultural factors.

Many other investigators have demonstrated experimentally that "creativity" can be influenced by varying environmental conditions (cf. Denkler & Mackler, 1964; Gerlach, et al., 1964; Malzman, Bogartz & Breger, 1958; Osborn, 1953; Parnes & Meadow, 1963).

In spite of this, there has been relatively little systematic research into the effects of parental attitudes, child-rearing practices, mother-child communication patterns, and other family variables on the development of creativity in children. Reported findings are often incidental to the main research, and are usually based not on direct observations but on retrospective reports by adults who are judged to be creative for one reason or another. This review attempts to piece together such information as is available, and to indicate certain consistencies in it.

Parent variables of importance in the development of creative children appear to be: (1) an unpossessive relationship which encourages the child to be self-reliant and independent, (2) permissive child-rearing methods, and (3) diverse and intellectual interests of parents.

The unpossessive nature of the parent-child relationship which permits creative children emotional "separateness" and freedom to develop independently was particularly noted by Weisberg & Springer (1961) in a study of the family structures of 32 gifted fourth graders. Correlations between creativity test scores ("Alternate Uses; Tin Cans" and "Ask and Guess" tests from the Minnesota battery) and family life styles indicated an:

> ... optimal family pattern ... not an overly close family unit, with little clinging to each other for support. Conformity to parental values is not stressed in the child, for instance. Nor is it a particularly well-adjusted marriage. ... There is open, not always calm, expression of strong feeling ... when the child regresses the behavior is accepted by the parents without discomfort [Weisberg & Springer, 1961, p. 559].

A similar picture is presented by the Dreyer & Wells (1966) investigation of the families of 24 four- to five-year-olds. Creativity, again measured by tests from the Minnesota battery, was related to greater emphasis on individual divergence and expression of feeling in the home and to less value consensus and more role tension, as defined by the Farber (1957) index of marital integration, between the parents. Essentially, these variables involve agreement between husband and wife on ten domestic values ranked for importance to family success (value consensus) and lack of agreement between husband and wife on ratings for self and spouse on ten personality traits (marital role tension).

Domino (1969) also describes a characteristic lack of emotional closeness in the mothers of creative high school males. He concluded: "These mothers are perceptive individuals, alert to the needs of others, informal, tolerant and observant. ... Yet these socially desirable characteristics are counterbalanced by a degree of indifference and detachment [p. 182]."

The tendency for family ties to be not very close has been reported in many retrospective studies, where data has been collected from creative adults about their parents' child-rearing attitudes. Stein (1963) found that the creative compared with the non-creative chemist was typically "exposed to greater complexity in parent-child relationships which he resolved successfully early in life by detaching himself from others [p. 225]." Eiduson (1958), in a study of artists, reported that they were "lonely and isolated as children, dissociated from family ties." Psychoanalytic writers have described the early severance of family ties in the lives of particular creative individuals (Freud, 1916; Greenacre, 1958). Roe (1953) claimed that physical and biological scientists developed early a way of life requiring little personal interaction. MacKinnon (1962) stated that the parents of creative architects showed "extraordinary respect for the child and confidence in his ability to do what was appropriate," and granted him "unusual freedom in exploring his universe and making decisions for himself." The architects recalled a lack of emotional closeness with their parents, and the absence of strong pressure toward a particular career. There was a high incidence of "distinctly autonomous mothers leading active lives with interests and sometimes careers apart from their husbands." Lucas & Dana (1966) constructed a rating scale based on the MacKinnon results, and found that high, moderate, and low creative groups differed as expected with respect to those aspects of childhood experience which MacKinnon suggested contribute to creativity. Drevdahl (1964), in a study of psychologists, says that the creative individual "was given a good deal of freedom and personal responsibility at an early age with the largely unenforced expectation that he would behave in a creditable manner. There was an apparent element of emotional coolness in family relationships" (p. 179).

Getzels & Jackson (1962) and Dewing (1968) also found more mothers with jobs outside the home in their groups of creative children. The Getzels & Jackson study of gifted high school children reports parental information which is firsthand, not secondhand, but it confuses the issue by an artificial dichotomy between "highly intelligent" and "highly creative" students (both groups drawn from a sample with a mean IQ of 132). The parents of the former are said to be more "vigilant," critical, and rigid, the parents of the latter more permissive. We are left to wonder whether these opposing traits cancel each other out in the parents of the large group who are high on both creativity and intelligence. However, the study provided inspiration and suggestions for many subsequent investigations, and the relationship between non-authoritarian parental discipline and creativity has been established by several other workers (Balagtas, 1969; Datta & Parloff, 1967; Dewing, 1968; MacKinnon, 1962; Shapiro, 1968; Watson, 1957).

A relationship between permissiveness and creativity was reported by Nichols (1964) as part of a large-scale project carried out on National Merit Scholarship finalists. Parents of creative students were also found to be less anxious for their children to conform or possess socially desirable traits, more anxious for them to be self-reliant, able to defend themselves, and ambitious (Nichols & Holland, 1963).

A variable of considerable importance is the intellectual climate of the home. Schaefer & Anastasi (1968), in a study of 400 high school boys, emphasized the strong intellectual and cultural orientations of creative students and reported that "their familial background was not only academically superior, but the parents tended also to provide models of interest and creative expression in the student's field." College education was more frequent among parents of creative students, especially among mothers. In a subsequent study of high school girls (Anastasi & Schaefer, 1969), they again found a relationship between creativity and cultural level of the home, assessed in terms of parents' artistic and literary hobbies, number of musical instruments in the home, quality of reading material, etc.

Skager, Schultz & Klein (1965) reported that creative achievement of college freshmen was related to intellectual discussions in the home, and not to the father's occupation or education, size of the home, or number of possessions. Dewing (1968) found that mothers of creative 12-year-olds had more formal education than mothers of equally intelligent non-creative children. Neither educational level nor occupation of the fathers was related to creativity. However, in a study of high school students (Rivlin, 1959), the education of both parents was related to teacher-rated creativity.

Dauw (1966) developed a life experience inventory in conjunction with Torrance (de Young, Torrance & Dauw, 1964) as part of an investigation of high and low creative senior high school children. Fathers' occupation and education, and mothers' education, were significant variables for girls but not for boys. Position in the family showed some relationship to creativity in boys. Fathers of creative daughters encouraged them to be more independent, and also engaged in more hobbies and activities with them, as did mothers of creative sons. The discipline in the home was less strict for creative children of both sexes.

Ravenna Helson (1965, 1966, 1967) conducted a study of women who had had strong imaginative and artistic interests in childhood, which she showed to be an enduring syndrome associated with rated creativity in adulthood. Creative girls were judged to identify more closely with their fathers than the non-creatives, and the fathers themselves were strongly intellectually oriented. Barron (1969), reviewing the Helson findings and an earlier investigation of creative Vassar women under the direction of Nevitt Sanford, commented, "Parents of the more creative women characteristically had intense artistic and intellectual interests, placed an especially high value on moral principles, and were effective and successful persons [p. 112]."

Conversely, lack of intellectual stimulation in the home may be related to low creativity. Vernon (1969) reported low originality and low flexibility scores on Torrance tests in a sample of 10- to 11-year-old children from the physically barren and culturally isolated Hebridean islands, although oral fluency scores were slightly above average. He concluded, "Since this was not due to any lack of linguistic fluency, it suggests that their rural and home environments tend to restrict creative imagination [p. 158]."

Discussion

In general, studies of the family backgrounds of creative persons may have somewhat different emphases, but there is little contradiction in the main findings. The most important factors seem to be non-authoritarian discipline, diverse and relatively intellectual interests, and a parent-child relationship which is not overly dependent.

It is interesting that cross-cultural and historical investigations have also demonstrated a relationship between authoritarian, repressive societies and lack of creativity (Dye, 1964; Hagen, 1964; Lembright & Yamamoto, 1965; Straus & Straus, 1968; Torrance, 1963).

"What is honored in a country will be cultivated there." Plato's statement has been thoroughly substantiated in a long series of research studies by Torrance and his co-workers (*op. cit.*). Creativity in the classroom has been shown to vary markedly with the teaching methods and value systems of particular teachers. In a study of 114 teachers in the public and private schools of 14 states, non-creative teachers were found to value time, orderliness, respect for authority, the child's responsibility to the group and to the teacher, preservation of their own self-images, and the importance of information (Myers & Torrance, 1961). Perhaps of even greater significance is Torrance's general conclusion: "The weight of present evidence indicates that fundamentally man *prefers* to learn in creative ways—by exploring, manipulating, questioning, experimenting, risking, testing and modifying ideas, and otherwise inquiring [Gowan, Demos & Torrance, 1967, p. 57]."

REFERENCES

ANASTASI, A. & SCHAEFER, C. E. Biographical correlates of artistic and literary correlates in adolescent girls. *Journal of Applied Psychology* 53 (1969): 267-73.

ATKINSON, J. W., ed. *Motives in Fantasy, Action and Society*. Princeton, N.J.: Van Nostrand, 1958.

BALAGTAS, T. M. The relationship between parental attitudes and children's creativity in rhythmic movements. *Dissertation Abstracts* 29 (1969) (12-A): 4304-5.

BARRON, F. *Creativity and Psychological Health: Origins of Personal Vitality and Creative Freedom*. New York: Van Nostrand, 1963.

BARRON, F. *Creative Person and Creative Process*. New York: Holt, Rinehart and Winston, 1969.

CATTELL, R. B. The personality and motivation of the researcher from measurements of contemporaries and from biography. In C. W. Taylor and F. X. Barron, eds., *Scientific Creativity: Its Recognition and Development*. New York: Wiley, 1963.

DATTA, L. E. & PARTOFF, M. B. On the relevance of autonomy: Parent-child relationships and early scientific creativity. *Proceedings of the 75th Annual Convention of the American Psychological Association* 2 (1967): 149-50.

DAUW, D. C. Life experiences of original thinkers and good elaborators. *Exceptional Children* 32 (1966): 433-40.

DENKLER, R. & MACKLER, B. Originality: Some social and personal determinants. *Behavioral Science* 9 (1964): 1-7.

DEWING, K. Creativity in children: The influence of parental characteristics. Unpublished doctoral dissertation, University of Western Australia, Nedlands, Western Australia, 1968.

DE YOUNG, E., TORRANCE, E. P. & DAUW, D. C. Life Experience Inventory, revised high school form. Minneapolis: University of Minnesota, 1964.

DOMINO, G. Maternal personality correlates of sons' creativity. *Journal of Consulting and Clinical Psychology* 33 (1969): 180-3.

DREVDAHL, J. E. Some developmental and environmental factors in creativity. In C. W. Taylor, ed., *Widening Horizons in Creativity*. New York: Wiley, 1964.

DREYER, A. S. & WELLS, M. B. Parent values, parental control and creativity in young children. *Journal of Marriage and the Family* 28 (1966): 83-8.

DYE, M. E. An enquiry into creativity and its nurturing climate: An exploratory study. *Dissertation Abstracts* 25 (1964): 320.

EIDUSON, B. T. Artist and non-artist: A comparative study. *Journal of Personality* 26 (1958): 13-28.

FARBER, B. An index of marital integration. *Sociometry* 20 (1957): 117-34.

FREUD, S. *Leonardo da Vinci: A Psycho-Sexual Study of Infantile Reminiscence*. (Trans. by A. A. Brill) New York: Moffat, Yard, 1916.

FROMM, E. *Escape from Freedom*. New York: Holt, Rinehart and Winston, 1941.

GERLACH, V. S., SCHULTZ, R. E., BAKER, R. L. & MAZER, G E. Effects of variations in test directions on originality test response. *Journal of Educational Psychology* 55 (1964): 79-83.

GETZELS, J. W. & JACKSON, P. W. *Creativity and Intelligence: Explorations with the Gifted Child.* New York: Wiley, 1962.

GOWAN, J. C., DEMOS, G. D. & TORRANCE, E. P. *Creativity: Its Educational Implications.* New York: Wiley, 1967.

GREENACRE, P. The family romance of the artist. *Psychoanalytic Study of the Child* 13 (1958): 9-43.

HAGEN, E. E. *On the Theory of Social Change.* London: Tavistock, 1964.

HEBB, D. O. *The Organization of Behavior.* New York: Wiley, 1949.

HELSON, R. Childhood interest clusters related to creativity in women. *Journal of Consulting Psychology* 29 (1966): 352-61.

HELSON, R. Personality of women with artistic and imaginative interests: The role of masculinity, originality, and other characteristics of their creativity. *Journal of Personality* 34 (1966): 1-25.

HELSON, R. Personality characteristics and developmental history of creative college women. *Genetic Psychology Monographs* 76 (1967): 205-56.

HESS, R. D. Maternal teaching styles and educational retardation. In E. P. Torrance and R. D. Strom, eds., *Mental Health and Achievement.* New York: Wiley, 1965.

HESS, R. D. & Shipman, V. C. Early experience and the socialization of cognitive modes in children. *Child Development* 36 (1965): 869-86.

HUNT, J. McV. *Intelligence and Experience.* New York: Ronald, 1961.

LEMBRIGHT, M. L. & YAMAMOTO, K. Subcultures and creative thinking: An exploratory comparison between Amish and urban American children. *Merrill-Palmer Quarterly* 2 (1965): 49-64.

LUCAS, F. H. & DANA, R. H. Creativity and allocentric perception. *Perceptual Motor Skills* 22 (1966): 431-7.

McCLELLAND, D. C., ATKINSON, J. W., CLARK, R. A. & LOWELL, E. L. *The Achievement Motive.* New York: Appleton-Century-Crofts, 1953.

MACKINNON, D. The nature and nurture of creative talent. *American Psychologist* 17 (1962): 484-95.

MALZMAN, I., BOGARTZ, W. & BREGER, L. A procedure for increasing word association originality and its transfer effects. *Journal of Experimental Psychology* 56 (1958): 392-6.

MASLOW, A. *Motivation and Personality.* New York: Harper and Row, 1954.

MAY, R. *Man's Search for Himself.* New York: Norton, 1953.

MURPHY, G. *A Biosocial Approach to Origins and Structure.* New York: Harper, 1947.

MYERS, R. E. & TORRANCE, E. P. Can teachers encourage creative thinking? *Educational Leadership* 19 (1961): 158-9.

NICHOLS, R. C. Parental attitudes of mothers of intelligent adolescents and creativity of their children. *Child Development* 35 (1964): 1041-9.

NICHOLS, R. C. & HOLLAND, J. L. Prediction of the first year college performance of high aptitude students. *Psychological Monographs* 77 (1963): No. 570.

OSBORN, A. F. *Applied Imagination.* New York: Scribner, 1953.

PARNES, S. J. & MEADOW, A. Development of individual creative talent. In C. W. Taylor and F. X. Barron, eds., *Scientific Creativity: Its Recognition and Development.* New York: Wiley, 1963.

RIVLIN, L. G. Creativity and the self-attitudes and sociability of high school students. *Journal of Educational Psychology* 50 (1959): 147-52.

ROE, A. *The Making of a Scientist.* New York: Dodd, Mead, 1952.

ROE, A. The psychological study of eminent psychologists and anthropologists and a comparison with biological and physical scientists. *Psychological Monographs* 67 (2) (1953): No. 352.

ROGERS, C. *Client Centered Therapy.* Boston: Houghton Mifflin, 1951.

SCHACHTEL, E. G. *Metamorphosis: On the development of affect, perception, attention, and memory.* New York: Basic Books, 1959.

SCHAEFER, C. E. & ANASTASI, A. A biographical inventory for identifying creativity in adolescent boys. *Journal of Applied Psychology* 52 (1968): 42-8.

SHAPIRO, R. J. Creative research scientists. *Psychologica Africana* (1968): Monograph Supplement No. 4.

SKAGER, R., SCHULTZ, C. & KLEIN, S. Quality and quantity of accomplishments as measures of creativity. *Journal of Educational Psychology* 56 (1965): 31-9.

STEIN, M. I. A transactional approach to creativity. In C. W. Taylor and F. X. Barron, eds., *Scientific Creativity: Its Recognition and Development.* New York: Wiley, 1963.

STRAUS, J. H. & STRAUS, M. A. Family roles and sex differences in creativity of children in Bombay and Minneapolis. *Journal of Marriage and the Family* 30 (1968): 46-53.

TAYLOR, C. W. *Widening Horizons in Creativity.* New York: Wiley, 1964.

TORRANCE, E. P. *Education and the Creative Potential.* Minneapolis: University of Minnesota Press, 1963.

TORRANCE, E. P. *Rewarding Creative Behavior.* Englewood Cliffs, N.J.: Prentice Hall, 1965.

TORRANCE, E. P. Toward the more humane education of gifted children. In J. C. Gowan, G. D. Demos and E. P. Torrance, eds., *Creativity: Its Educational Implications.* New York: Wiley, 1967.

VERNON, P. E. *Intelligence and Cultural Environment.* London: Methuen, 1969.

WATSON, G. Some personality differences in children related to strict or permissive parental discipline. *Journal of Psychology* 44 (1957): 227-49.

WEISBERG, P. S. & SPRINGER, K. J. Environmental factors in creative function. *Archives of General Psychiatry* 5 (1961): 554-64.

Kathleen Dewing is a member of the faculty of the University of Western Australia, Perth.

20.
Opinions of Gifted Students Regarding Secondary School Programs

JOSEPH P. RICE

GEORGE BANKS

Which of the suggestions set forth here are also pertinent for the college-level student? As a teacher or prospective teacher, could you support the suggestions made by these gifted students and also play a role in implementing them?

Since 1948, the San Diego Unified School District has developed diversified and exemplary programs for mentally gifted students. Periodic assessment of the special scholastic problems and needs of students with IQ scores in excess of 150 has resulted in the establishment of such experimental programs as ungraded classes in the elementary schools and special groupings and seminars in the high schools. The survey described here is but one of an ongoing process of program evaluation.

This study included 119 junior and senior high school students who were interviewed to gather their opinions and recommendations for changes in their current academic programs. Essentially, these students were asked open ended questions with the following purposes:

1. To ascertain the way in which they would design their own courses of study.
2. To contrast existing curriculum offerings with their ambitions, interests, and aspirations.
3. To discover whether or not students are afforded sufficient opportunity to think.
4. To assess current outlets for creative and intellectual expression.
5. To answer a number of controversial questions, e.g., Do gifted students prefer to be in segregated classes?

From *Exceptional Children* 34 (December, 1967): 269-73. Reprinted by permission of the authors and *Exceptional Children*. Copyrighted by the Council for Exceptional Children.

Procedure

Student interviews were conducted by a state consultant utilizing a prearranged list of discussion questions. A district consultant acted as recorder with occasional administrative personnel attending some of the sessions as objective observers. Students were invited to submit written answers to supplement the oral interviews; approximately 75 percent of the 119 students submitted some sort of written contribution which was considered in the overall compilation of the findings.

As the findings were compiled, an attempt was made to distinguish between the responses of gifted (Binet IQ scores between 130 and 154) versus highly gifted (Binet IQ scores over 155) students, boys versus girls, and junior high versus senior high students. However, responses among these groups tended to be consistent. Exceptions are noted in the results.

Objective measurements of course choice and philosophy of education were obtained by administering specially prepared sets of checklists. The Checklist for Academic Course Choices was empirically structured from lists of courses offered by all high schools in California. This checklist included any academic course actually being offered by any high school in California. These courses were listed alphabetically. Students rated each course according to the following criteria: (a) whether or not their high school should offer it, (b) whether or not they would take the course, and (c) how they estimated its value in comparison with that of other courses.

The Checklist of Possible Purposes for Your School was directly adapted from an earlier checklist used to study junior college students (Rice, 1961). Gifted students rated and ranked 17 simply stated purposes for a school by the criterion of essentiality. This resulted in an hierarchical list of philosophical purposes which could be compared with similar lists made by college students and teachers.

In general, interviewers and objective observers agreed that these techniques resulted in an objective survey of the thinking and opinions of gifted secondary school students.

Selected Findings

Most of the following statements represent majority student opinion. Certain significant minority opinions or dissensions are mentioned where they are appropriate. The findings are reported by categories used in the interviews.

Given freedom, how would gifted students redesign their own curriculum? They would:

1. Demand more freedom in course selection.
2. Eliminate many of the physical education courses (boys and girls), home economics classes (girls), and shop courses (boys).

3. Place more emphasis upon literature, drama, art, and music.
4. Endorse the general education philosophy, yet make provisions for individual specialization by interest area.
5. Add more social sciences to the curriculum. (Early junior high school students differed significantly from the rest of the group by scorning social studies.)

With all responses considered, the following composite word picture might describe the ideal program which gifted students would design for themselves. Their choices of courses, study times, and grade level placement would be flexible. Literally, each student would work at an intellectual level best suited to his individual learning needs. A culturally enriched and diversified curriculum of subject offerings would be about equally divided among the sciences, mathematics, fine arts, foreign languages, and the social sciences.

Students at the junior high school level would choose interdisciplinary seminars such as one which might relate the natural sciences to the social sciences. At the high school level, students would pursue subjects in great depth and to levels now construed to be higher education.

For the highly gifted student, there would be opportunity for advanced placement at any developmental level. Qualitatively different subject matter such as psychology or sociology would be introduced to them at the high school level. Periodic testing procedures would enable students to demonstrate mastery over fundamental subject areas in order to be placed in more appropriate content areas.

Thus, there would be two essential changes in the existing program: (a) flexible programing at all grade levels, and (b) qualitative content changes in subject matter, with more emphasis upon acculturation in subject matter treatment.

Among courses now available, what are the popular academic choices of gifted students? In general, 75 percent or more of the students tended to choose the first courses listed; no course is listed unless 50 percent or more of the students selected it. The courses are presented in descending order of priority:

1. Foreign languages: French, German, Russian, Spanish, and Latin.
2. Language arts: humanities, creative writing, American literature, English literature, modern literature, and oral arts (debate or dramatics).
3. Mathematics: geometry, algebra, calculus, and trigonometry.
4. Science: chemistry, physics, and zoology.
5. Social sciences: psychology, American history, economics, international relations, and ancient history.

Do existing programs challenge students to aspire, think, and develop values?

1. Over 90 per cent believed that the existing curricula were preparing them for college very well and constituted excellent general education programs.
2. Aspirations were not well defined at any level. Only 30 percent of the high school students had thought about a career. The highly gifted students were noted to be more decided concerning aspirations and career choices than the gifted.
3. Most students voiced the need for more open discussion in controversial areas.
4. Mathematics, English, and social science courses, in that order, were prominently mentioned by students as courses in which critical thinking was enhanced. Most students felt that teachers with adequate training were in a better position to "stimulate and motivate the thinking processes."
5. General criticism was expressed about the state textbooks. Also, teachers who "taught chiefly from the textbooks" were castigated. It was generally alleged that state textbooks "played down controversies, did not promote critical thinking and relied upon rote memory processes."

Are there sufficient outlets for creative and intellectual student products?

1. Almost unanimously, the students expressed various needs to create tangible products. A majority indicated that they had already produced some worthwhile product for which they could find no outlet for display, dissemination, or recognition. The product types ranged from practical inventions and many varieties of creative writing to musical and artistic compositions.
2. Outlets for science and literary products were rated as adequate. Such activities as the annual science fair were commended. However, in the literary field, potential authors complained that existing publications "systematically excluded controversial or avant-garde material."
3. Students criticized teachers' emphases upon "purely practical applications." Many felt that teachers "emphasized quantity as opposed to quality." In a constructive way, students felt that more emphasis should be placed upon "situations in which one might have time to think alone." They requested more independence from the school with "opportunities to create what we want as opposed to what the school wants."
4. As a special group, girls more keenly felt the lack of creative outlets and the lack of freedom of choice than did boys. Moreover, the problem appeared to become more acute as the students advanced in school. The girls complained about "culturally loaded determinations about the courses we should take." Also, a majority of the girls seemed to be unwilling to conform to such socially acceptable expectations as having "ladylike behavior or feminine interests."

Should students with different abilities be in classes together or should they be separate?

1. All groups overwhelmingly favored some sort of segregation of gifted students for selected activities. However, marked differences between gifted (Binet IQ scores between 130 and 154) and highly gifted (Binet IQ scores over 155) students were noted.
2. The highly gifted almost unanimously requested completely separate education.
3. There was far more difference of opinion among the gifted students. The majority felt that some separation was necessary, and most felt the need for separate advanced subjects, such as mathematics. However, the majority of these students wanted to retain egalitarian social contacts.
4. The highly gifted were not impressed by the social motive; they tended to reject the notion that they ought to be of assistance to students with lesser ability. The highly gifted freely discussed their intellectual prowess and felt that their extreme difference in comparison with other students warranted extreme differences in the educational provisions they ought to obtain.
5. All groups mentioned selected acceleration procedures as appropriate means of offering gifted students opportunities to obtain advanced work. Most felt that acceleration should be based upon a subject by subject review of capabilities. Junior high school students tended to favor segregated and accelerated classes based upon ability in most subject matter areas. High school students emphasized the need for individualized programs that cut across high school and college level subjects.

What do gifted students deem to be essential purposes for their high school? Ranked in the order of essentiality and priority, gifted high school students would state the philosophical purposes for their high schools as follows:

1. It provides preparation for formal education.
2. It emphasizes the use of the intellect and promotes critical thinking.
3. It promotes social development and maturity.
4. It helps the student develop and appreciate creativity.
5. It helps the student to realistically choose his life's work.
6. It provides academic counseling and guidance.
7. It promotes self understanding and good mental health habits.
8. It teaches basic skills for everyday living.
9. It provides general orientation and guidance programs.
10. It helps develop sound moral and spiritual values.
11. It provides help for the student in solving personal adjustment problems.

12. It promotes the development of aesthetic skills and appreciation.
13. It promotes the democratic way of life.
14. It provides specific vocational education.
15. It prepares young people for homemaking and family life.
16. It promotes international understanding and peace.
17. It provides a program of adult education beyond high school.

Roughly, the first nine priorities listed above received at least a majority endorsement by the gifted students. Proceeding from rank 10 through rank 17 their endorsement decreases; for rank 17, only 20 percent (approximately) of gifted students agreed.

The configuration of purposes chosen by the gifted students in this sample resembled the configurations of priorities agreed upon by college and high school teachers and curriculum specialists (Rice, 1961). It is quite different from the typical statement of educational priorities made by junior college students, normal students, or school administrators. Typically, these latter groups place more emphasis upon such priorities as the democratic way of life, vocational education, and homemaking than do gifted students. In general, school administrators or normal students arrive at priority configurations approximately the reverse of those outlined above for gifted students.

Conclusions and Recommendations

It has been shown that gifted students are capable of providing meaningful insights about the nature of their educational programs. Moreover, gifted students represent an essentially untapped reservoir of imaginative suggestions for program innovation and change. Inspection of their opinions reveals a close resemblance to suggestions made in the literature for programs for the gifted. Substantial unanimity was observed among the gifted concerning many basic questions about their education.

Based on these findings, the following suggestions might be considered by school districts that are planning programs for the gifted:

1. Create special groups of gifted students who would meet during the school day to study curricula including special activities as well as accelerated content.
2. Carefully assess the needs of the local gifted population.
3. Utilize more psychometric data, such as achievement test scores, for the proper scholastic placement of gifted students.
4. Provide special counseling and interview services for the study and treatment of developmental problems which appear as attitudinal disparities among subgroups of the gifted and apparently disturb them just as frequently as any other student group.

5. Establish seminar settings in which controversial issues and problems may be discussed, clarified, and analyzed for value.
6. Reevaluate the worth of nonacademic activities such as physical education in consideration of the true needs of the gifted.

REFERENCE

RICE, J. P. Differing views of institutional aims among college administrators, teachers and students. *California Journal of Educational Research* 12 (1961): 165-72.

Joseph P. Rice is Consultant in Education of the Mentally Gifted, California State Department of Education, Sacramento; and George Banks is Secondary Coordinator for Gifted Programs, San Diego City Schools, San Diego, California.

21.
Broadening Concepts of Giftedness in the 70's*

E. PAUL TORRANCE

What will be some of the skills required of future teachers of gifted children to meet the educational demands detailed in Dr. Torrance's article?

In this country there is widespread belief that every human being has a right to optimum development of his potentialities and that every person possesses a unique set of potentialities, interests, goals, percepts, liabilities, and assets. Yet we have never been able to work up very much support for educational provisions that will give our most gifted children and youths this chance. As we enter the 70's, it is time that we ask some searching questions about the reasons for this state of affairs and develop more valid concepts of giftedness that this country can accept.

Multi-Talent Concepts of Giftedness

To replace concepts of a single type of giftedness, a variety of proposals have emerged. One of the earliest of these came from England. The Education Act of 1944 in England implemented the idea that there are three kinds of intellectual giftedness: a literary or abstract type to be educated at grammar schools, a mechanical or technical type to be educated in technical schools, and a concrete or practical type to be educated at modern schools. Writing in 1958, Sir Cyril Burt, the eminent English educational psychologist, reported that this scheme has not worked out as well as had been hoped.

In the United States, most of the broadened concepts of giftedness offered in the 60's were inspired by Guilford's (1967) Structure of Intellect Model. In this Model, Guilford has offered what amounts virtually to a periodic table of different kinds of intellectual functioning. The Model is complex and incomplete but it has inspired a number of important innovations in the education of gifted children.

Guilford's Structure of Intellect Model remained almost totally neglected until Getzels and Jackson (1962) showed that highly divergent or creative

From *Gifted Child Quarterly* 14:4 (Winter, 1970): 199-208. Reprinted by permission of the author and *Gifted Child Quarterly.*

*Prepared for Northeast Regional Conference for the Gifted and Creative, November 5, 1970, New Haven, Connecticut.

adolescents achieved as well as their highly intelligent peers, in spite of the fact that the two groups studied differed by 23 I.Q. points. In eight partial replications of the Getzels and Jackson study, I (Torrance, 1962) found that if one identified as gifted the upper 20 percent of a given population on an intelligence test alone, he would miss 70 percent of those who would be identified in the upper 20 percent as gifted by a test of creative thinking. Not all of my replications yielded the same results concerning school achievement as did the Getzels-Jackson study. They indicated clearly, however, that there were some terribly important differences between children identified as highly intelligent and those identified as highly creative.

Still almost unnoticed is that part of the Getzels-Jackson study (1962) dealing with two kinds of psychosocial excellence—that is, high school adjustment and high moral courage. It was found that just as the highly intelligent student is not always highly creative, the highly adjusted student is not always high in moral courage. Further, it was found that although students high in moral courage achieved at a higher level than highly adjusted students, the teachers perceived the highly adjusted students as the leaders—as the really worthwhile members of the student body—rather than those high in moral courage. Educators were not ready to accept high moral courage as a desirable kind of giftedness.

By the mid-60's a number of multiple talent models of giftedness were being offered. One of the more powerful of these is the one suggested by Calvin W. Taylor. Taylor's (1968) groupings of talent are based on world-of-work needs and specify at present academic talent and five other important types: creative (and productive) talent, evaluative or decision-making talent, planning talent, forecasting talent, and communication talent. Taylor argues that if we consider only the upper ten percent on each talent group as gifted, the percentage of gifted will increase from ten percent for one talent area to thirty percent across the six talent areas. He argues further that if we limit ourselves to cultivating one of these talent groups, only 50 percent of our students will have a chance to be average (the median) in classes. If all six talent groups are considered, about 90 percent will be above average in at least one group and almost all others will be nearly average in at least one of them.

Taylor believes that we now know enough about measuring and fostering multiple talents to find ways of cultivating most of them in school rather than letting them lie largely dormant. He also believes that in classrooms where multiple talents are cultivated all students will learn more. In other words, by having more pathways through their complex nervous system, students can use several different abilities at one time or another to process information during the school week. He believes this will happen if teachers sharpen their abilities to cultivate these talents and deliberately work across a greater number of these talents with which schools now concern themselves.

Hidden Giftedness of Disadvantaged

During the 60's there was some budding interest in finding "hidden" giftedness, especially among children born and reared in poverty and deprivation. Most of the projects designed to either discover or develop the "hidden" talents of disadvantaged children and youth have been effectively "put down" as quickly as possible. Even those short-lived, always-gasping-for-life projects have taught us much. Furthermore, there have been a few of these such as George Witt's in New Haven that have survived in spite of lack of support from established sources.

Frank Reissman (1962) was one of the first to call attention in any very powerful way to the positive talents of culturally disadvantaged children. He recognized the need for building upon these positives, which he identified as follows:

1. Slow learning gifted children—children who appear "slow" because they are careful, cautious, one-tracked in their way of learning, or physical learners.
2. Hidden verbal ability—very verbal out of school, articulate with peers, and articulate in role playing.
3. Positive attitude toward education, though unfavorable attitude toward school.
4. Enjoyment of and skill in games, physical activities, music, expressive activities.
5. Cooperativeness and mutual aid.
6. Avoidance of strain accompanying competitiveness and individualism.
7. Children's enjoyment of each other's company.
8. Informality and humor.

Building upon Reissman's work and on the basis of four years of exploratory work with disadvantaged children, primarily blacks, I have suggested a set of creative positives which I have found to exist to a high degree among disadvantaged children and upon which I believe we can build successful educational programs and ultimately optimal use of potentialities. These creative positives are as follows:

1. Ability to express feelings
2. Ability to improvise with commonplace materials
3. Articulate in role playing, creative activities
4. Enjoyment and ability in art, drawing, painting, etc.
5. Enjoyment and ability in creative dramatics, dance, etc.
6. Enjoyment and ability in music
7. Expressiveness in speech
8. Fluency and flexibility in nonverbal media
9. Enjoyment and skills in group learning, problem solving
10. Responsiveness to the concrete

11. Responsiveness to the kinesthetic
12. Expressiveness of gestures, "body language," etc.
13. Humor
14. Richness of imagery in informal language, brainstorming
15. Originality of ideas in problem solving, brainstorming
16. Problem-centeredness
17. Emotional responsiveness
18. Quickness of warm-up

I have argued that if one is searching for gifted individuals among disadvantaged populations, he is likely to have better success if he seeks them in the areas identified here than in traditional ways. I have also contended that we should give more serious consideration to careers in the creative arts and sciences for disadvantaged youth than we have in the past. When asked about their aspirations, almost no disadvantaged children express choices in the creative fields (Torrance, 1967). Yet a large share of the disadvantaged persons who have attained outstanding success have done so in creative fields, especially in those where talent has no boundaries and economic advantage has not been a barrier to admission. More important than these considerations, however, is the possibility of building educational and talent development programs on these positives. Special educational programs for disadvantaged children and youth have been compensatory in nature and have emphasized the virtues of uniformity. My proposal is that we recognize and acknowledge as positive these qualities and teach disadvantaged children to use them positively and to build upon them.

Pressures for Uniformity in Programs for Gifted

Earlier, I mentioned the fact that in the main we have relied upon acceleration, enrichment, and special classes as the vehicles by which we have sought to provide more adequate education for gifted children. None of these provisions has ever been very popular with educators or with the public. Major criticisms have been that these special provisions are elitist, undemocratic, and cause children to have inflated self-concepts. A more justified complaint might have been that these programs for gifted children have overemphasized uniformity and standardization. When children have been accelerated it has been to keep them from being too outstanding in their group and to have them learn the standard things that older children are learning. When children have been placed in separate classes, they have almost always been given a uniform curriculum. There has still been one standard, one set of books, one curriculum, and one fiscal policy. In practice, enrichment has been much the same and teachers have not dared wander far from the prescribed curriculum or let the curriculum be different for one child.

Respect for Individuality

The first requirement is that this new concept of giftedness respect each child's individuality and aid him in achieving a healthy, strong sense of identity (Torrance, 1970a). Rather than honoring the cultural assumption that "the good child is a modest child," it must stress the fact that recognition and acceptance of positive characteristics is necessary for self-realization. It must reject the assumption that "man is innately evil" and instead accept the fact that man is born neither good nor evil but with innate potential for determining in large part his "human" development. It must reject the assumption that giving attention to deficiencies motivates proper behavior and instead accept the more realistic belief that giving attention to successful behavior motivates attainment of potentialities.

It must reject the assumption that suffering produces character and instead teach children to cope constructively with predictable stresses. It must reject the assumption that independence is the highest virtue and instead recognize that interdependence is the road to cultural competence and interpersonal satisfaction. It must reject the belief that the only way a person can succeed is to best others and instead recognize that each person is unique and has particular strengths that must be valued. It must reject the idea that there is a superior race, a superior sex, or a superior set of cultural characteristics and instead accept the fact that our strength is in our diversity. It must reject the assumption that the expression of feelings demonstrates weakness and instead accept the fact that the expression of feelings is essential to mental health and to the realization of human potential.

Individuality in the Early Years

This new approach to the education of gifted children must give full recognition to the fact that individuality is established largely in the early years of a child's life and that these early years are critically important in the emergence of a healthy, strong identity and the realization of potentialities. In this new approach, we would start teaching children almost from birth about their own individuality. Almost from birth, children's senses of taste and smell, their reactions to colors and forms, their styles of doing things, their likes and dislikes of sounds, etc. will be sufficiently diverse from those of other children to be striking and revealing. I would agree with Roger J. Williams (1953, p. 73), who maintains that the idea of non-uniformity, if clearly demonstrated to children at an early age, would become an easily accepted commonplace. As the child grows older, he would continue to learn more and more about himself and about the society into which he has to fit (or *misfit*, if need be). However, as Williams argues, it is likely that a child's chances of being a misfit would be decreased if he knows about himself and about society. The gifted and creative child will be inclined to accept his unusualness and will not be psychologically disturbed by it.

Certainly in the primary grades, children would be taught about their individuality. There are certainly pitfalls, and ways and means of avoiding these must be worked out. However, I can see no reason why even small children would not profit from learning about their differences in tastes (colors, designs, music, flowers, food), in motor skills, and in hearing and visual characteristics. I would even teach them about the differences in their intellectual skills. If schools could do this successfully, we would no longer find so many gifted older adults whose potentialities have been wasted because they always thought that they were "below average" or "only average."

When I think about what happens to gifted young people today, it is easy to understand why we have so many cases of wasted potentialities. For example, a college freshman wrote me just a few days ago about a whole series of things that teachers, counselors, and school administrators have done to "put him down" and to pressure him in the direction of uniformity. For example, the counselor who gave him the individually-administered Wechsler Adult Intelligence Scale deliberately showed him another person's test record (pretending it was his) to make him "feel more normal or average." In dealing with this highly intelligent and highly creative young adult, not even a professionally trained counselor was able to acknowledge this college freshman's identity. Such behavior would not occur in this new approach to the education of the gifted.

Open-ended Programs and Methods

To accommodate such an expanded concept of giftedness and creativity as I have described, educational programs and methods must be open-ended. Perhaps the biggest reason why most present programs for the gifted are unsatisfactory is that they have not been open-ended enough really to give gifted children a chance to develop their potentialities. Only open-ended programs and methods can be truly responsive to the abilities, choices, and interests of gifted children. If we know anything for sure about gifted children it is that they are different. They learn different things in different ways, not just quicker. Some think better in numbers than in words, and they perceive and understand mathematical relationships more easily than verbal relationships. Still others are unusually skilled in manipulating spatial relationships and objects but are quite incompetent in literature. The ways in which gifted children differ in the ways they learn are almost infinite since each person is unique.

Open-ended programs and methods of instruction have generally been regarded as dangerous. Such programs and methods of instruction cannot be pre-inspected and certified for safety (or sterility). One never knows where the open ends will lead and this is frightening to the incompetent, the insecure, the unimaginative, and the non-creative. Open-ended kinds of education requires a high degree of creativity of the teacher or who-ever else is responsible for managing the learning-teaching situation. It is extremely interesting to note that the new approaches to individualized instruction are relying upon educational technology. With the various kinds of programmed and computerized instruction that are coming into vogue under the label of individualized instruction, the curriculum specialist and teacher feel that they are in control and are safe. One wonders, how-ever, if this approach genuinely respects the individuality of the child or if it simply guarantees a higher degree of uniformity than ever before. The gifted child, strapped into a piece of educational hardware, may have fewer escapes from coercion than in the most rigid and authoritarian classroom.

For effective learning—or effective behavior of any kind—there must be some structure, some guides to behavior. One must never lose sight of the self-acting nature of the human mind. This is an especially powerful force in the education of creatively gifted children and young people. It is almost as if their creativity plugs them into infinity. No matter how much structure you give the highly creative child, he will want to know about things outside of this structure. He will produce ideas that go beyond the wildest predictions of the teacher or curriculum maker. This is a major reason why the creative child makes the insecure, authoritarian teacher so uncomfortable and is punished so severely by such teachers. It is also the reason the secure teacher who respects individuality finds such joy in teaching such children. Many of a child's guides to behavior come from the way the teacher responds to him and especially to his self-initiated at-tempts to learn. This requires of the teacher the most sensitive and alert kind of guidance possible.

Unfortunately, the whole idea of open-ended education is foreign to the understanding of many educational leaders. During the past ten years, I have tried to develop and test a variety of open-ended instructional materials and instructional methods (Torrance and Myers, 1970; Torrance 1970a). I continue to be surprised at the way these are perceived by some of my colleagues. Recently a colleague who styles himself as a "behavior modifier" remarked to me that he had examined many of the materials that I had developed and that there were in them strong elements of behavior management and behavior modification. What he was unable to see was that everywhere there were in them open ends which give children full opportunity to respond in terms of their experiences, abilities, interests, and motivations and which respect the individuality of each child. What one cannot satisfactorily build into instructional materials is the respon-siveness of the teacher and other pupils to the infinity of responses evoked by the instructional materials. For this and other reasons we shall need more than ever to have well trained specialists to work as teachers, con-sultants, and administrators of programs for gifted and creative chil-dren.

Administrative Arrangements

This open-ended kind of education can take place within a variety of kinds of administrative structure. I would not quibble a great deal whether it involved separate classes, acceleration, or enrichment—or some combination of the three approaches. At the elementary level, some kind of nongraded arrangement might provide a very congenial administrative structure. It would have to be an open-ended enough so that some of the instruction could be done in large groups, some in small groups, and some with single individuals. In many instances, the children would instruct one another. Much work would be done in dyads, working both inside the school building and outside of it.

In many instances, the instruction would be by persons in the community—perhaps not certified to teach but capable of teaching with authority something that even the best qualified teachers are unable to teach. Systematic and deliberate attempts would be made to place children identified as gifted or creative with a sponsor, a creative person in the community who would assume some responsibility for helping the child get a chance to cultivate his potentials. The philosophy to accompany this might be: "You don't get something for nothing but you'll have a chance to work for it."

Identification and Testing

Perhaps I should comment on the matter of identification and the use of tests in the identification of potentialities. In the past I have advocated the use of both intelligence and creativity tests, because I think they help make us aware of potentialities that might otherwise go unnoticed. However, I am not certain that tests will even be needed under the expanded concept of giftedness and creativeness that I have tried to describe. If we start almost from birth teaching a child about his individuality and if the important adults in a child's life recognize and acknowledge his potentialities, there is little need for tests. I realize, of course, that standardized tests may provide a kind of feedback that will be useful in establishing a realistic identity. I also realize that we may never have adequate resources for providing gifted children with all of the opportunities and resources needed for developing their potentialities. For this reason, it might be necessary at times to use standardized tests.

As much as possible, however, I would like to see a shift from the present stimulus-response approach in testing with its standardized tasks to a responsive environment approach in which intellectual and creative potentialities would be assessed in situations which the child initiates. There would be an ongoing process in which parents, teacher, and talent developers would continually be recognizing and acknowledging a child's potentialities. This process would begin very early in a child's life and continue at least through the years of formal schooling if not through career development. This is necessary because the broadened concept of giftedness and creativeness that I have been describing is something dynamic and changing, not something static and predetermined.

One of the features that has disturbed me about many recent and current programs for gifted children is that only well-adjusted, high achieving children have been included. Children exhibiting behavior problems, children who excel in one or two fields but are not well-rounded, children from disadvantaged backgrounds, and children who learn a great deal on their own but do not excel on those things that count on the grade books are usually excluded. Educators have argued that even though these children have high potentialities, the probability of their success is low and that they hold the rest of the class back. Such an attitude, of course, springs from a lock-step concept of uniformity and conformity in programs for the gifted. For several years, I have urged that we be concerned about identifying those potentialities which, if given a chance, will produce outstanding achievement. Giving gifted children in these categories a chance requires that their individuality be respected. It is when attempts are made to coerce them to learn and behave in ways contrary to their individuality that the trouble begins. Williams (1953) contends that millions of potentially fine members of society become criminals who would become useful members of society if we recognized their individuality and were reasonably successful in finding suitable outlets for their creative energies. The broadened concept of giftedness that I have in mind would include all of the categories I have just mentioned.

Ecological Child Psychology

Under this broadened concept of giftedness and creativity, it will be necessary to pay much more attention to the environmental features of both schools and communities. Fortunately, the advent of the 1970's witnesses a burgeoning interest in ecological child psychology. One of the two recommendations of Forum No. 2 (Emergence of Identity) of the 1970 White House Conference on Children will be for the establishment of child-oriented environmental commissions that might operate at national, state, and local levels.

These environmental commissions would develop and disseminate information about environmental conditions favorable to the emergence of strong, healthy identities among children. These commissions would advise, help plan, inspect, and approve construction and renovation of homes, apartments, public buildings, parks, day care centers (preferably child development centers), streets, and the like to meet children's needs. They would encourage studies of the influence of various kinds of behavior settings and environmental conditions on children. Local commissions might organize and operate a children's cultural committee to expand the life space of crowded city dwellers by enabling families in a variety of ways to use the parks, zoos, museums, libraries, and other facilities of the larger community. These local commissions might organize and supervise community centers that provide materials (clay, paper, string, rope, wire, wood, wheels, etc.) and personnel (artists, musicians, carpenters, mechanics, engineers, cooks, writers, etc.) to share their skills and abilities with children.

It may be some time, of course, before we gain wide acceptance of the importance of environmental considerations in homes, schools, and communities in the realization of human potential. In his recent book on ecological psychology, Barker (1968) pointed out that a common view among psychologists is that "the environment of behavior is a relatively unstructured, passive, probabilistic area of objects and events upon which man behaves in accordance with the programming he carries about within himself" (p. 4). On the basis of his ecologically-oriented research, Barker proposes that the environment be viewed as consisting of "highly structured, improbable arrangements of objects and events that coerce behavior in accordance with their own dynamic patterning" (p. 4). Barker and his associates found that they can predict some aspects of children's behavior more adequately from the behavior characteristics of the settings (drugstores, playgrounds, classrooms, etc.) than from knowledge of the behavior tendencies of the particular children.

It takes little imagination to begin thinking of environmental changes in schools, homes, and communities that would facilitate talent development and serve the needs of gifted and creative children. I suspect, however, that there are ways of improving these environments for gifted and creative children of which we cannot yet dream. Thus, we need immediately individuals and groups willing to explore the possibilities and researchers willing to undertake experimental studies of the role of environments as talent developers.

Summary

To summarize, it might be said that the 1950's and 1960's witnessed profound changes in our concepts of intelligence and the functioning of the human mind. One of these changes was a broadened concept of giftedness to include creativeness and other types of ability. Thus far, however, neither professional educators nor the public has found these concepts satisfactory. In an effort to move in the direction of an even broader and a more satisfactory concept of giftedness, I have proposed that we go back and really place credence in our old belief that every human being has a right to optimum development of his potentialities and that every person possesses a unique set of potentialities, interests, goals, percepts, liabilities, and assets. In order to give our most gifted and creative children and youths a chance to develop their potentialities optimally, I have suggested that the following characteristics be incorporated into educational programs:

1. Respect for each child's individuality and aid in achieving a healthy, strong sense of identity.

2. Rejection of those cultural assumptions that are contrary to our new understandings of the nature of man and human development and acceptance of beliefs more in harmony with present knowledge.

3. Recognition of the importance of the early years of a child's life and teaching children almost from birth about their individuality.

4. A continuous process in which both the child and society recognizes, acknowledges, and accepts his potentialities.

5. Identification of potentialities not be limited to what can be learned from standardized tests but including performances initiated by the child in his own environment.

6. Programs and methods open-ended but with adequate structure for guides to behavior.

7. Well trained educational specialists who will emphasize roles as talent recognizers, acknowledgers, and developers.

8. Attention to environmental features in homes, schools, and communities that support and facilitate talent development.

REFERENCES

BARKER, R. G. *Ecological Psychology.* Stanford, Calif.: Stanford University Press, 1968.
BURT, C. The inheritance of mental ability. *American Psychologist* 13 (1958): 1-15.
REISSMAN, F. *The Culturally Deprived Child.* New York: Harper and Row, 1962.
TORRANCE, E. P. *Guiding Creative Talent.* Englewood Cliffs, N.J.: Prentice-Hall, 1962.
TORRANCE, E. P. *Rewarding Creative Behavior.* Englewood Cliffs, N.J.: Prentice-Hall, 1965.
TORRANCE, E. P. Understanding the fourth grade slump in creativity. (Mimeographed USOE Report) Athens, Ga.: Georgia Studies of Creative Behavior, University of Georgia, 1967.
TORRANCE, E. P. *Encouraging Creativity in the Classroom.* Dubuque, Iowa: Wm. C. Brown, 1970a.
TORRANCE, E. P., ed. Preliminary Report: Emergence of Identity. Report of Forum No. 2, White House Conference on Children, Washington, D.C., 1970b.
TORRANCE, E. P. AND MYERS, R. E. *Creative Learning and Teaching.* New York: Dodd, Mead, 1970.
WILLIAMS, P. J. *Free and Unequal.* Austin, Tex.: University of Texas Press, 1953.

E. Paul Torrance is a member of the faculty in the Department of Educational Psychology, University of Georgia.

Six

Mental Retardation

Chapter Six includes articles representing several aspects of mental retardation. Jean Marc Gaspard Itard, the author of the classic *The Wild Boy of Aveyron,* is recognized in the "Pioneer Profile" for his significant contributions to the study of mental retardation over one hundred and fifty years ago.

The first article in this chapter deals with a historic document on the educability of intelligence, published in 1911, by none other than Alfred Binet, the father of mental testing. In the United States Alfred Binet is known as the father of normative mental testing; he has not been known as a special educator. Yet this chapter points out that Binet used mental tests to identify the mentally retarded so that he could organize a special program for them. He labeled his educational program "mental orthopedics." His methods encompass some of our modern systems of cognitive training and his approach utilized many of the activities we now label as "readiness." Many of his statements could well be repeated today, for example, "The pedagogical stupidity of today reaches fantastic proportions."

Interestingly, the early pioneers in special education were frequently doctors of medicine. Their interest in remediation of handicaps led them into the field of education and training. Also, since mental retardation was the principal handicap to receive attention in the nineteenth century, these leaders were primarily occupied with this disability. In the second article, Leo Kanner describes the work of three physicians—Itard, Seguin, and Howe—all of whom were challenged by the educational problems of retarded children. The writings of these three men paved the way for many educational developments.

Seguin, for example, used many techniques which are utilized today under the label motor-perceptual training.

Of the many studies of the effects of preschool education upon the development of intelligence of mentally retarded children, a summary of the investigation by Dr. Harold Skeels has been included in this chapter because of its longitudinal nature. In 1939 Dr. Skeels published a sensational report on early intervention with thirteen retarded children, and twenty-one years later he did a follow-up study of these cases. Space permits only a reproduction of the summary and implications from his recent monograph.

Currently there is a controversy over the best instructional plan for the retarded child. The discussions relate to special class assignment *versus* placement in a regular class with supplementary services. Hammons analyzes the controversy, presents both sides of the debate, and suggests some modifications in current practices.

Texas has a statewide program through Vocational Rehabilitation for the training of mentally retarded youth for employment. The results of two years of their efforts are reported by Strickland and Arrell. Since successful post-school employment is one of the major goals of training of the retarded, a review of such programs is indeed relevant.

In the final article of this chapter, Philip Roos, Executive Director of the National Association for Retarded Children, reviews the practices in the education of the mentally retarded and identifies some of the current, pressing needs. Students who are entering the field of special education should get a perspective of the area of mental retardation from this review.

Jean Marc Gaspard Itard
1775-1838

PHYSICIAN
OTOLOGIST
EDUCATOR

Itard was born in Oraison in Provence, France. As a young man, he decided to enter medical school to avoid military conscription. Although he became an eminently successful physician, his greatest distinction was in the field of the education of the deaf and the retarded.

He served for some time as a member of the medical staff of the Institution for Deaf-Mutes in Paris. He was recognized as an authority on diseases of the ear and on educational procedures for the education of deaf children. However, Itard is best known in special education for his work with the "wild boy of Aveyron." The boy was thought to be about eleven years old when hunters found him in the woods, naked, foraging for acorns and roots. Itard became interested in this child, Victor, and believed special training could make up for earlier neglect. However, after five years of training, Victor did not acquire the ability to handle speech and language. He learned to recognize, write, and even to comprehend the meaning of many words and handled simple social relationships with his teacher. Itard was keenly disappointed with Victor's limited progress and finally was forced to conclude that the boy was mentally deficient.

Itard's work stimulated interest in developing training methods for the mentally retarded and led to improved practices throughout the world. Kanner's article in this chapter provides additional details about Itard's work.

22.
L'Education de l'intelligence
ALFRED BINET

Binet considered his ideas about children to be modern. Which of his views enunciated over sixty years ago do you consider relevant today?

After the evil, the remedy; after exposing mental defects of all kinds, let us pass on to their treatment. In order to present the difficulty in all its magnitude, we suppose that we have discovered with certainty in one of our pupils a grievous incapacity to comprehend what is said in class; the child cannot comprehend well, nor judge well, nor imagine well; though he may not be abnormal, he is nevertheless very markedly retarded in school. What is to be done with him? What is to be done for him?

If nothing is done, if we do not actively and effectively intervene, he will continue to lose time and, realizing the futility of his efforts, will end by becoming discouraged. The affair is very serious for him and, since this is not an exceptional case, for the children with defective comprehension are legion, it may well be said that the question is serious for us all, for society; the child who loses in class the taste for work greatly risks not acquiring it after he leaves school.

Prejudice Against Educability of Intelligence

I regret that I have often found a prejudice against the educability of intelligence. The familiar proverb which says: "When one is stupid, it is for a long time," seems to be taken literally by noncritical teachers; they are completely indifferent to the pupils who lack intelligence; they have neither sympathy nor even consideration for them for their immoderate language in the presence of the children in this connection takes the following trend: "He is a child who will never do anything . . . he is poorly endowed . . . he is not at all intelligent." Too often have I heard these careless words. They are repeated everyday in the elementary schools, and the secondary are not exempt from the charge. I remember that during my examination for the baccalaureate the examiner, Martha, irritated by one of my responses (I had given to a Greek philosopher, by a confusion of words, a name belonging to one of the personages of the *Charactères* of La Bruyère), declared that I would never have a philosophi-

---

Translated from *Les Idées modernes sur les enfants*, Chapter V, Part III, 141-161. Paris, 26 Rue Racine: Ernest Flammarion, Editeur 1911.

Section titles have been added throughout this translation to assist the reader in following the Binet discussion. *The Editors*

cal mind. Never! What a strong word! Some modern philosophers seem to have given their moral support to these deplorable verdicts by asserting that the intelligence of an individual is a fixed quanitity which cannot be augmented. We must protest and react against this brutal pessimism; we shall try to demonstrate that it has no foundation.

Experimental Psychology Is Helpful

Five or six years ago if I had been obliged to discuss this question, I would have had few resources for my argument. I should have shown that instruction and education are often paired and confused; that to receive correct ideas benefits the behavior; that example, imitation, emulation, open horizons; I would have cited from my own experience many instances of people who had acquired a critical mind and freedom in discussion only by the help of others; young people had become less naive, more resourceful, more active after foreign travel or a year of military service; intelligent women whom I have known would have held to the most rigorous religious practices without a suggestion from someone else, usually a man, who opened their eyes. Then, after exhausting the examples, observations and even anecdotes of this kind, I believe that I should have drawn chiefly on the information furnished by experimental psychology. The science is a little dry, but it becomes eloquent when one knows how to interpret the figures. It demonstrates for us, beyond a doubt, that every thought and mental function in us is susceptible to development. Every time that anyone has taken the trouble to repeat methodically work which has measureable effects, it has been seen that the results follow a characteristic curve which merits the name of *curve of progress*. If one learns to use the typewriter, the number of words written in an hour increases; in one case, for example, the subject went from three hundred to eleven hundred after fifty-six days of practice in which he did only one hour of work at a single sitting each day.[1] If one undertakes to cross out certain letters in a text, the speed of the work increases to such an extent that after two hundred and fifty trials, one a day, distributed over two years, a given amount of work required only three minutes although at first it required six.[2] That improvement is the rule; up to this time it has not been contradicted by a reliable experiment, and thousands have confirmed it. Of course, it is not an indefinite improvement, and neither can one think that its rate and extent are indeterminate. They are improvements which are regulated in their ensemble by a law of remarkable fixity; the usual marked improvement at the beginning later diminishes little by little; it even ends by becoming insignificant and, despite the greatest efforts, the moment arrives when it becomes practically equal

---

[1] I. J. Swift. Memory of Skillful Movements. *Psychological Bulletin*, June, 1906.

[2] Bourdon. Récherches sur l'habitude. *Année Psychologique*, XVIII, 1902, p. 327. For a study of the ensemble, consult Thorndike, *Educational Psychology*, p. 80.

to zero. At that time, one has attained one's limit, for it cannot be denied that there is one; the position varies according to the individual, and in each individual according to the function considered. In some cases, many years are necessary to reach it, and further, the gains so made may persist through many years of disuse; Bourdon has seen them preserved through seven years. Now if we consider that intelligence is not a single function, indivisible and of a particular essence, but that it is formed by the union of all the little functions of discrimination, observation, retention, etc., whose plasticity and extensibility have been determined, it will appear undeniable that the same law governs the ensemble and its elements, and that consequently anyone's intelligence is susceptible to being developed; with practice, training, and above all, with method, one arrives at augmenting one's attention, memory, and judgment, and in becoming literally more intelligent than before; that improvement will continue until one reaches one's limit. And I should also have added that what is of consequence for behaving intelligently is not so much the strength of the faculties as the way one uses them, that is, the art of intelligence, and that this art ought necessarily become refined with practice.

That is about the most scientific idea that I should have been able to produce in order to encourage the teachers in the education of the intelligence of their less gifted pupils, and without doubt with these ideas one might have thought it highly probable that the intelligence of a child could be developed. But it would still have been only a probability, and we greatly prefer to have a certainty.

Better Classes for the Abnormal

The recent creation of classes for abnormal children, of which I speak so often and with such pleasure because I have learned so much from them, has given us the demonstration, the certainty which we needed. Here are no debatable arguments, but tangible facts. We admit into these classes not simply children who have not had enough instruction, but those who are really weak in intelligence, for a child must lack attention or comprehension if he is retarded three years in his studies if he does not know at the age of twelve what children in general know at nine. The most exacting tests guard the door to the special classes; we admit only the proven retarded, those who have attended school regularly. It might have been supposed that these children would gain nothing from special instruction, and that these new classes would be one "bluff" added to so many others.

Also, it might have been thought that, since there is no special pedagogy, correctly speaking, and since pedagogy is the same for all, the best teacher could not do any more for these abnormals that one ordinarily does for the normals. Exactly this objection was posed to me in the beginning by the professors for the abnormal. They said: "If there are any new, original methods, show them to us. . . ." And we were obliged to answer that there were none, that they must do in these classes as in the regular ones; and that reply discouraged them. Then we had the surprise and joy of discovering that all these initial fears were useless. At the end of a year we reclaimed, one after the other, all these abnormal pupils; we knew their degree of knowledge at their entrance into the classes because we had preserved their old notebooks. We measured their new attainments and we saw their progress. This progress was already visible in their general appearance; their attitude was less dissembling, their countenance more alert and more attentive, their manner of dressing more careful; but these are only appearances, and appearances may be deceitful. What convinced us was that in rigorously equivalent new dictations they made fewer mistakes; also, they put more expression into their reading, and disfigured the difficult words less; and, finally, in arithmetic especially, in which they had been so weak in the beginning, they had made enormous progress; certain problems in which they had failed pitifully at first, a year before, were now solved with ease. Charmed with these results, but still distrusting myself and my immediate collaborators, I wanted to have recourse to the criticism of others; therefore, I asked a school director to go into our classes for the abnormal every six months and measure, in his own way, the progress actually made in instruction. His estimates and measurements confirmed ours. Decidedly, the improvement was clear, undeniable, and even great. Is a figure required? Let us grant in advance that all the children of a class for abnormals entered it with a retardation of three years in their studies. At the end of a year, on trial, measured again, they showed no more than two years retardation. What does that signify? Let us analyze a little in order to realize this better. If during the year that had just passed these children had remained in their ordinary classes, where they so joyfully lose their time, their retardation would have been aggravated; it would have become, for example, equal to three and a half years. If they had advanced as the normals do in their studies, in a year they would have advanced exactly a year; but they would not have made up the lost time, and their retardation would have remained equal to three years as it was in the beginning. If they diminished their retardation, it is because they benefited more than the normals; if they were only two years retarded instead of three it meant that they had taken two steps instead of one.

We Can Increase Intelligence

It is necessary to anticipate an objection. It will be said: "What you have increased, what you have measured by that precise method, was not the intelligence of the children, it was their degree of instruction. You demonstrate very well the possibility of rapidly teaching the ignorant; you do not demonstrate that their intelligence was increased." Well, these children were not merely ignorant; each one had a mental blemish—weakness of attention, weakness of comprehension, or other deficiency; and it was that blemish which prevented them from benefitting by the instruction given in the regular classes and by the regular methods. Now, that instruction was assimilated; there is the fact; habits of work, of attention, and of effort were acquired; that also is fact, and this second fact is even more important than the first. What is the exact part of instruction and that of intelligence in this final result? It would be extremely difficult to know this, and perhaps useless to try to know it, for the output of an individual, his social utility, and his saleable value depend at the time on these two factors. This child's mind is like a field in which a wise farmer has changed the mode of cultivation; result: instead of wasteland fallow with weeds, we now have a harvest. It is in this practical sense, the only one we can consider, that we say the intelligence of these children was able to be increased. We have increased what constitutes the intelligence of a pupil, the capacity for learning and assimilating instruction.

Special Methods Help Regular Teachers, Too

In front of this so encouraging result, we feel our hopes and our ambitions expanding. We are happy to have concerned ourselves so long with the abnormal. When, with so many good willed people, we first interested ourselves in these unfortunates, it was from a feeling of pity, and also from a desire of social defense, to try to lessen the number of those who will later be useless and who might become burdens; but it was chiefly because we firmly believed that the study of the abnormals would serve the normals, as we see in another field that the study of the insane serves the psychology of the normal individual. We are not deceived. With some variations, the methods that are good for the education of the abnormal will render great service to the normal. One of the best teachers of special classes whom I know, Mr. Roguet, one day said to me with a twinkle in his eyes: "What would I not have accomplished in other days with my pupils, intelligent children, if I had treated them as I have treated these."

Program of Good Instruction

How, then, by what process were we able to fix all these weak and wandering attentions, to open, to force all these closed intelligences? We wish to explain that process now, for it is of capital importance, as everyone understands. But it must not be thought that we are going to write here principles of education which have never before been published. In order to explain the success of these classes, it will suffice to remark that we have been led, partly unwillingly, partly thanks to luck, to avoid some of the most dangerous errors which vitiate present day pedagogy. And what is to be said about it will appear so simple, so commonplace that perhaps a little time and reflection will be needed to grasp its significance.

Adjust to Pupils' Level

The first preoccupation of the teachers was to place the instruction on their pupils' level. They spoke in such a way that they were always understood. If many of these retardates had not profited by the lessons in their former classes, it was partly because of inattention, but chiefly because the lessons went over their heads, were too complicated, too abstract for them; they involved too many preliminary ideas which the children did not have. Let us imagine that we are listening to a lesson in geometry, and that someone explains the hundredth theorem; had we the mind of a Pascal, we should not be capable of understanding it if we do not have the slightest idea of the ninety-nine theorems upon which the demonstration is based. That is a comparison which clearly explains the state of confusion of the mind of an abnormal when he tries to comprehend the lesson that is far beyond him.

Go from Easy to Difficult

By keeping a child in a class that is too difficult for him, one transgresses the great, the greatest principle of pedagogy: it is necessary to proceed from the easy to the difficult. This transgression is universal, it gives rise to the most deplorable errors on the part of teachers who are very intelligent, but absolutely ignorant of pedagogy. For I cannot put it too strongly; today's ignorance of pedagogy reaches fantastic proportions. I am constantly finding that a pupil is engaged in a struggle with a task that is too difficult for him; but the teacher easily consoles himself with the quite gratuitous assumption, "that will keep him busy." Lately I saw a young girl who, for her first work in modeling, was made to copy a bust of complicated movement. "You will have trouble," her professor said to her, "but you will learn a great deal." Why not assign an ignorant person to learn differential calculus? This would be absolutely the same type of error. A little difficulty is a good thing, it is a stimulus for the pupil; but too great a difficulty discourages, disgusts, and makes one lose precious time, and worst of all, forces one to adopt bad habits of work; one is obliged to make incorrect attempts which one cannot correct because one is not capable of judging these; one resigns to the fact of not comprehending them, one works blindly, that is to say, very badly. From this there results a disorganization of the intelligence, while the precise aim of all education is to organize. I have seen the same error on the part of over-zealous parents who were annoyed because a young child was afraid and who wished to cure him of this shameful fault. They were right in wanting to cure him of it, but how poorly they set about it. The true method consists in going from the easy to the difficult; it is, then, necessary at first to give the child occasion for very gentle fears which he will be able to dominate, for the whole thing is included in this, that he must learn self-control; then, in the degree that this power of control increases, the experience will be made more difficult, but by very gradual steps, very cautiously; in this way success is nearly always assured at the end of the apprenticeship. But if one acts abruptly, brutally, without adapting oneself to the strength of the child, more harm than good is done; if one forces him to experience a painful, atrocious fear which he is incapable of dominating, then one gives him the habit of mental disturbance, of mental loss of equilibrium; one teaches him not to react but to be afraid. One of my friends, excessively timid in his childhood, had a doctor father who, in order to render him brave, conducted him into a mortuary chamber, showed him a corpse and made him touch it; the child experienced an emotion of which he still bears a trace; ten years later in Paris, he could not enter the amphitheater and refused to study medicine. We see that, in all these cases, there is an abuse of the same elementary principle of method and prudence.

Also, we understand why the abnormal children who have been admitted to the special classes have gained so much from the instruction. For each class there was an observant teacher who could know each pupil individually because he had only a few, about fifteen. This teacher watched over them and ascertained whether the pupil had thoroughly comprehended the lesson; if he had not, he started over instead of going ahead. A slight effort was required of each pupil, but it was proportionate to the child's capacity, and it was seen to that this effort was actually made. Few things were taught them, but these few, always very elementary, were well learned, well comprehended, well assimilated. To ask of each child only what he is capable of doing—what is more just, what is more simple?

Some Good Methods

So much for the program of the things to teach, it remains to describe the method by means of which one teaches. On this last point also our classes of abnormal children have taught us much. Having children who did not know how to listen, nor to regard, nor to be quiet, we discovered that the first duty was not to teach them the ideas which seemed to us most useful to them, but that first of all, they must learn to learn; therefore, with the help of Mr. Belot and our other collaborators, we devised what were called exercises in *mental orthopedics*: the expression is significant and has become current. One guesses its meaning. Just as physical orthopedy straightens a crooked spine, so mental orthopedy straightens, cultivates, and strengthens the attention, memory, perception, judgment and will. We did not seek to teach the children an idea, a memory, but we put their mental faculties in shape.

Exercises in Immobility

We began with exercises in immobility. It was arranged that once a day, in each class, the teacher should ask all his pupils to strike an attitude and keep it, like a statue, for seconds at first, then a whole minute; the attitude was to be taken instantly, at a signal, then abandoned instantly, at a second signal. In the first trial, they accomplished nothing; the entire class was convulsed with foolish laughter. Then, little by little, they were calmed; the exercise lost its novelty, the children grew accustomed to it. Their self-respect became involved. The honor was to the one who could hold the attitude the longest time. I have seen children who had been turbulent, noisy, disobedient, the despair of their teachers—I have seen, I repeat, these children for the first time make a serious effort and bring into play all their vanity in order to remain immobile; they were, then, capable of attention, will and self-control. What was called the *game of statues* became so popular that the children asked for it. Encouraged by these first results, we had them perform pressure exercises with the dynamometer; each child came in his turn to press the instrument, to learn his record, and to write in his notebook. The dynamometer excited general emulation; it was used once a week during the entire year, and children never became indifferent to it. They were the more interested in it because the teacher took the trouble to draw on a large sheet of paper fastened to the wall the complete curve of the efforts at each sitting; and nothing interested them so much as to watch that curve which gradually rose, from week to week, thus indicating that everyone in the entire class was working on his motor education and, above all, working on it willingly. Then we introduced speed tests consisting of marking with a pen, in the very short time of ten seconds, the greatest number of dots on a paper. This is excellent work for the somnolent ones. In all these exercises the essential thing is to compel the pupil to make an intense effort; it is necessary to excite general emulation. That was accomplished by recommending to the teacher that he give a warm word of encouragement and especially that he make known to the pupils all they had accomplished by means of individual marks and averages which were posted regularly each time on the walls of the classroom.

Develop Motor Skills

I will cite also, in the order of operation, the exercises for motor skill; they were of various kinds. We began by the carrying of bowls full of water; it was necessary to carry them from one table to another without spilling the least drop in the saucer; and it was very difficult, for the distance was long, and the bowls were full to the brim; then we invented complicated exercises with corks. It will be said that this is very little like school; and perhaps an uninformed father who sends his son to school only to have him learn spelling and arithmetic would be surprised to discover that at certain times we had him play statue and that on other days we had him play games with corks. Let us not joke; and beneath the surface, which must often be rendered interesting, gay, and even comic, let us discover the reality. The reality is that these games are nothing but lessons for training the will; modest lessons which are appropriate to the capacities of the child, but which actually force the will into activity; for will is necessary to maintain a fixed position for some time, with steady regard, hand extended without trembling; if a child had no will, he would give in to the slightest suggestion of fatigue and of boredom, he would not remain immobile. Furthermore, to make a vigorous effort to press the dynamometer is painful; the more he presses, the more it hurts the palm of his hand, but also, the harder he presses, the higher the figure he attains. And so on for the other exercises. To give lessons in willpower, to teach children to make an effort and to scorn a little physical suffering, the pleasure of self-mastery, all this is certainly a course of instruction which is as valuable as lessons in history and arithmetic!

Train Habits of Attention

We were too well started to stop. Chance had suggested a new method to us; we sought to extend, to perfect it, and we formed a general plan of mental orthopedy embracing all the mental faculties. Recalling the ancient feats mentioned by Robert Houdin, we wished that our pupils should learn to perceive quickly a large number of objects at a glance; and for that we showed them large boards on which many objects or many pictures were glued; in a very short time the pupil was to regard, study, collect in his mind all these objects; then, with the board hidden, to write from memory the names of all he had seen. According to the always precise directions of Mr. Vaney, we arranged an extended series of these boards with an ever increasing number of objects. Then we desired to give the children habits of observation; we trained them to respond to questions about what they had seen in the street, on the playground, or in the class. Then came memory exercises consisting of the immediate repetition of words, of digits, or of sentences, the number being increased each time; and finally, exercises for the imagination, ingenuity, analysis, judgment . . . I pass. Little by little we succeeded in forming a complete system of mental orthopedics with exercises which varied for each day; these exercises are performed daily in the classes of abnormals; the results are assembled with the greatest care, and we see that the pupils so trained make unexpected progress when we compare the late results with those of the first attempts. An example: In a class of abnormal children the trained pupils had succeeded in perceiving nine objects in five seconds and writing the names from memory; not all accomplish this but two-thirds do. Is it not surprising? Imagine the difficulty. Nine objects, selected at random, were fastened to a board; this board was regarded for five seconds; the child was obliged to return immediately to his place and write from memory the names of these nine objects without forgetting a single one, and without inventing the name of a single object which had not figured on the board.

The adult who witnesses that exercise receives a great surprise! I remember that when the deputies, at the time the law regarding the abnormals was voted on, came to visit our classes, and they saw the exercises; some of them, fascinated, asked to try it themselves; they succeeded far less well than our little abnormals. The results were astonishment, laughter, jokes of their colleagues, and all the comments imaginable. To be a deputy and show himself inferior to a little abnormal. In reality, despite the piquancy of the adventure, it is easily explained. Our deputies did not take into account the intensive training that our pupils had undergone.

Everyone agrees that the exercises are excellent; they favor no particular faculty, but an ensemble; they facilitate discipline, teach the children better to regard the blackboard, to listen better, to remember better, to judge better; they bring into play self-respect, emulation, perseverance, desire for success, and all the excellent sensations which accompany activity; and, above all, they teach the children to will with greater intensity; to will, that is certainly the key to all education; and, consequently, moral education is acquired at the same time as intellectual education; but this is not yet all; and I believe that, by studying with some perseverance these modest exercises which were devised to give tone to some poor abnormals, it will be discovered that the method which inspired these exercises is by no means a special method for a few heedless, debile, and weak-willed children, but that it is a method appropriate to all normals. I will even say, more ambitiously, it is the unique method for all instruction. But on this point it is necessary to explain myself clearly and to avoid all confusion.

AVOID OVEREMPHASIS OF THE VERBAL

The most usual reproach directed at the Old University methods which, braving the most impartial critics, continue to rule supreme, is that they consist of verbal lessons which the professor pronounces, and the pupils hear passively. The lesson so conceived has two defects: it impresses only the verbal function of the student, it gives him only words instead of putting him into relation with realities; and furthermore, only his memory is made to function, he is reduced to a condition of passivity; he judges nothing, reflects on nothing, does not invent, does not produce, he need only retain; his ideal is to recite without mistake, to make his memory function, to know what is in the textbooks, and to repeat it cleverly at the examination. There he is judged by the effect of his speech, by his loquacity, by appearances. The result of this deplorable practice is, in the first place, a lack of curiosity about everything outside of books, a tendency to seek truth solely in books, the belief that one accomplishes original research by leafing through a book, an exaggerated respect for the written opinion, an indifference to the lessons of the outside world of which the pupil sees nothing, a naive belief in the omnipotence of simple formulas, a lowering of the meaning of life, an awkwardness in adapting himself to contemporary existence, and above all else, a routine mind which is sadly out of place in an epoch when society evolves with infernal speed.

Lately, in an investigation that I made on the evolution of philosophical instruction in the lyceums and the colleges, I received from many of my correspondents curious confidences about the mentality of the young people who composed the philosophy classes. They have, I was told, an innate taste for discussion, not the discussion of facts, but of dialectics; they are carried away by the desire for an oratorial joust, for the pleasure of defending any opinion whatever with purely theoretical arguments, without deeply concerning themselves about being in the right. Is it not absolutely certain that the taste for unfruitful dialectics, sophistry, and the abuse of reasoning and of ideas a priori are fostered by that verbalism which the University does its best to propagate?

When they become University students, the pupils keep the habits they acquired at college. If a student has his choice between an hour of a lecture course and an hour of practical work, he decidedly prefers to go seat himself for the instructions; if at the end of a lecture one calls for those who wish to learn to manipulate an apparatus or to study a preparation they are embarrassed; the majority, having written their little notes, ask only to leave; and if one insists one sees them scatter like a circle of idlers before the bowl of the juggler who takes up a collection. It is very difficult to make even the most intelligent understand that what is heard in a lecture can be found again, in even better form, in a book, while the lesson of the laboratory can never be replaced.

What, then, do we demand in the way of reform, and how do we think that we ought to make war on verbalism?

STUDENTS MUST BE ACTIVE

Assuredly we shall not go to the extreme of forbidding the teacher the use of words, but his words ought not to be the essential, the substance of the lesson; they ought to be only an accompaniment, a guide, a support. The mind of the student ought to be placed directly in contact with nature, or with schemes, with pictures reproducing nature, or rather, with both at once, nature and schemes, and speech ought not to intervene except to comment on the sensory impression. Above all, it is necessary that the student be active. Instruction is bad if it leaves the student inactive and inert; it is necessary that instruction be a chain of intelligent reflexes emanating from the teacher, going to the student, and returning to the teacher; it is necessary that instruction be a stimulus, determining the student to act and creating in him reasonable activity, for he knows only what has passed not only through his sense organs and through his brain but also through his muscles; he knows only what he has done. Philosophically, all intellectual life consists of acts of adaptation, and instruction consists of making the student accomplish acts of adaptation, easy at first, then more and more complex and perfect. That is why object lessons, walks, manual training and laboratory experiments are so popular today; they respond to this need of exciting activity in the pupils. Enter a class; if you see all the pupils immobile, listening without effort to an agitated teacher who discourses at length from his platform, or again if you see these children copying, writing, the lecture which the teacher dictates to them, pronounce it bad pedagogy. I prefer a class where I see the children less silent, more noisy, but occupied in performing the most modest task, provided it be a task into which they put a personal effort, a task which is their own work, which requires a little reflection, judgment and discernment.

And thus it is that I return to our exercises in mental orthopedy: for they give a very neat, very clear, very striking example of that new pedagogy which makes the pupil an *actor* instead of reducing him to being only a *listener*. Our plans and methods are only an illustration; and, of course, the illustration is altogether special, conceived for children of a certain age, of a certain degree of intellectual development, of a certain culture; in its technical detail, it is appropriate for them alone. But it is the principle of the method which seems to me to be recommendable.

USE A DISCOVERY METHOD

An objection is going to be made. Without doubt, it will be said, those are excellent methods for training at home, or even in class, the child's mind. Instead of explaining ideas to him, it is better to have him find them; instead of giving him orders, it is better to let him act spontaneously and to intervene only in order to control him. It is excellent for him to acquire the habit of judging for himself the book that he reads, the conversation in which he takes part, the current events everyone is discussing; excellent that he learn to speak, to relate, to explain what he has seen, to defend clearly, logically, methodically his own ideas; furthermore, it is better that he practice making decisions, learn to orient himself while traveling, to plan his days, to imagine, to invent, briefly, to live on his own account and so feel at once the excellence and the responsibility of free action. All that, it will be said, is excellent in extra-academic life on the expressly understood condition that education, reduced to the role of control and check, remains efficacious for correcting errors. But that method, where it is the student who is active and the teacher who is passive, that method of general education—someone will object—can it be applied to instruction? When the pupil has forged his attention, his will and his judgment it will still remain for him to learn the ensemble of subjects prescribed by the program; it will be necessary that he assimilate grammar, arithmetic, geometry and all the rest. Must we not, in order to acquire this knowledge, call on the memory, and thus do we not fall back on the fact that memory is necessarily the base of instruction?

I do not think so. And those who have understood the profound significance of the orthopedic exercises will divine without difficulty that similar exercises could help assimilate any knowledge whatever, for all knowledge resolves itself into action which it has rendered one capable of performing, and consequently it is possible to *learn by doing* according to the favorite formula of American educators. To know grammar does not consist of being capable of repeating a rule, but in being able to express one's thoughts in a correct, clear and logical sentence. To know multiplication does not consist of being able to repeat the definition of such an operation, but to combine any multiplier whatever with any multiplicant whatever and give the correct product. It is then possible always to replace the formula by the exercise, or rather to commence with the exercise and to wait until it has resulted in training and a habit before interposing the rule, the formula, the definition, and generalization.

The general plan of the course of instruction so conceived, according to an active method, has been advocated for a long time by great philosophers.

Useful suggestions are found in the works of Rousseau, in the more systematic ideas of Spencer,[3] and an entire plan, methodical in its execution has been laid out by Froebel for children of the maternal school. In our day, all of that has been said and re-said, perfected through practice by the most competent persons. There are some in France, Balot for language, Queniou for drawing, Laissant for the sciences, LeBon for the living languages and the ensemble of training. In America, there are Dewey, Stanley Hall, and many other educators. We can only repeat what they have said. Teach written language by calling forth many written narratives, by much reading, and by many compositions; the insipid grammar lessons, instead of being placed BEFORE, like obstacles in the path, should not be interposed until AFTER in order to bring out the rules that have already been learned by use. Teach arithmetic by giving problems to be solved; geometry, by constructing things; the metric system by having measurements taken; physics by having small, elementary apparatus constructed and used; esthetics, by showing side by side reproductions of masterpieces and of mediocre works and having the differences discovered, explained, felt; drawing by allowing free drawing and later by replacing that with instructions in the laws of perspective; the living languages by imposing the habit of speaking them and by facilitating the understanding of them.

USE CONCRETE EXPERIENCES

By following this course, we gain an immense advantage; instead of beginning with the general idea, which is incomprehensible and unfruitful for those who do not know its content, we always begin with the concrete experience, the special fact—for an exercise is always special. Thus we follow the easiest way, the most normal, that of progressing from the particular to the general. On the other hand, by having the child act, we lead him to become interested in his work, we give him the precious stimulus of the warm feelings that accompany action and reward the success of his effort; and this stimulus will be proportionately more effective as we more exactly take into consideration his natural activities and his special aptitudes. All, or almost all, children before given any instruction show a taste for singing, drawing, story telling, inventing, manipulating objects, moving them about, changing them, using them to construct; by grafting education and instruction on these natural activities, we benefit from the

---

[3]This lengthy footnote relating to comments on Spencer's methods was deleted. *The Editors*

start already made by nature; nature furnishes the activity, the teachers intervene only to direct it. It is from this double viewpoint that the active method asserts its superiority, and we can say that it reproduces the fundamental law of evolution; by it, the mind of the child is led to pass along the same roads which the soul of humanity has traversed.

23.
Itard, Seguin, Howe—Three Pioneers in the Education of Retarded Children
LEO KANNER

How do you account for the great interest of early leaders, who after all were trained in medicine, in the problems of the education of mentally retarded children?

In discussing the history of the care of mental defectives, it has been customary to cite a few sporadic passages from Greek and Roman literature, from the Bible, the Talmud, and the Koran. The sum total of all those quotations amounts to little beyond the fact that the existence of such persons was known and that occasionally friendliness toward them was advocated. There is no evidence of any specific or organized effort to do anything for their housing, protection, or training. Though kind words were written about idiots from time to time, there was no practical application of any kind throughout the centuries. We encounter a mixture of taunting, neglect, and good-natured toleration.

Then almost suddenly, interest in the education of mental defectives began to flare up in the first half of the nineteenth century, spreading from France and Switzerland to the rest of the civilized portion of Europe and to the United States of America. A number of developments converged to explain this unprecedented spurt. Some of them are closely connected with the ideas with which Rousseau, the Encyclopedists, Pestalozzi and Fellenberg are identified. Those were the times when spokesmen arose who vigorously espoused the causes of thitherto oppressed or neglected groups—the slaves, the prisoners, the insane, the blind and the deaf. It is, as a matter of fact, remarkable that the principal pioneer in the training of idiots in France carried out his work at an institution for

From *American Journal of Mental Deficiency* 65 (1960): 2-10. Reprinted by permission of the author and *American Journal of Mental Deficiency*.

deafmutes and that the first "experimental school" for idiots in America was housed at an institution for the blind. It is also significant that the early sponsors of the education of mental defectives openly declared that they derived much of their inspiration from Jacob Rodrigues Pereire and his accomplishments in the teaching of deafmutes.

The first explorations were undertaken by enthusiastic young men in their early to middle twenties who usually were not encouraged by the established authority. Itard proceeded against Pinel's better judgment, and Seguin had in Esquirol a benevolent, though highly skeptical, friend and mentor. This was, in a way, not surprising in view of the goals that the fervent youngsters had set for themselves. Guggenbühl had set out to "cure" cretins, and Itard originally intended to lead the wild boy of Aveyron on to a normal existence. Both of them failed and yet they and others inaugurated methods and facilities which were soon incorporated in the western civilization.

The whole movement cannot be fully appreciated without a review of the personalities and individual efforts of the men who originated the educational and institutional work with the feebleminded—Itard, Guggenbühl, Seguin, and Howe. A detailed study of Guggenbühl's work has been recently published by this author in the *Bulletin of the History of Medicine* (1959, Vol. 33, pp. 489-502). The following pages are devoted to the contributions made by the other three men.

Jean Marc Gaspard Itard (1774-1838), born at Oraison in Provence, leaped into prominence as one of the originators of the education of the feebleminded because of his efforts on behalf of "the wild boy of Aveyron."

Itard was destined to enter a business career but those were hectic days in France when he had reached the age of settling down for a steady occupation. His country was at war with most of the rest of Europe and, to avoid conscription, he enlisted as an assistant surgeon in a military hospital. He became fascinated by his work, pursued the study of medicine with great zeal, and soon gained distinction as a physician. His first major assignment on the medical staff of the Institution for Deaf-Mutes in Paris directed his interests toward the training of the inmates and toward the scientific study of the organs of hearing and speech. His treatise on the diseases of the ear, published in 1821, is regarded as the historical event which laid the foundation of modern otology.

Shortly after Itard had started on his job at 25 years of age, a young boy, approximately 11 or 12 years old, was brought to the Institution by the Abbé Sicard Bonnaterre, Professor of Natural History at the Central School of the Department of Aveyron. This boy, sometimes referred to as Victor or Juvenis Averionensis, had stirred the fantasy of the philosophers and the scientists of those days. There are different versions of the story about his early background and about the manner of his capture. As reported by P. J. Virey (*Dictionnaire d'histoire naturelle du genre humain*, Vol. XI, 1803, pp. 329-331), a naked child was seen, who ran away from human beings and who roamed through the woods of Caunes in the Department of Tarn, searching for roots and acorns for food. He was caught but escaped soon afterwards. In 1798, he was again caught by three hunters, brought to Caunes, escaped again and lived like a vagabond for six months, "exposed to the cold of the coldest of winters." One winter day, he entered the house of a dyer outside the city of St. Sernin, wearing only the remains of a shirt which had been put on him half a year earlier. They gave him potatoes, which he ate raw, as well as chestnuts and acorns; he refused any other food. He did not speak any language and uttered inarticulate sounds. "Wherever he was, he would answer the calls of nature and had no idea of modesty."

The boy was taken to the Hospice St. Afrique and then turned over to the naturalist Bonnaterre, who in turn got Itard interested in him. Opinions differed about him. Some observers declared him to be a swindler. Philippe Pinel, the famous psychiatrist, decided after an examination that the boy's wildness was a fake and that he was "an incurable idiot, inferior to domestic animals." Still others wondered whether he represented a specimen of what Rousseau had thought were the advantages of "natural existence."

The boy's appearance created considerable controversy and a number of children were recalled who had been reported previously as being discovered after living wildly in the fields and woods, some of them nurtured by animals. The authenticity of some of the sources is questionable. Carl Linnaeus (1707-1778) listed ten such instances as a variety of the genus Homo, speaking of them as homo ferus (wild), tetrapus (walking on all fours), mutus, and hirsutus (hairy): (1) Juvenis lupinus Hessensis, found among wolves in 1544; (2) Juvenis ursinus Lithuanus, brought up by bears (1661); (3) Juvenis ovinus Hibernius, nursed by wild sheep in Ireland (reported by Tulpius, 1672); (4) Juvenis bovinus Bambergensis, found among a herd of oxen (according to Camerarius); (5) Juvenis Hannoveranus, "Wild Peter" of Hanover, found by a Townsman of Hameln in 1724, brought in 1726 to London, where he became a sensation; King George I made a present of him to the then Princess of Wales, who later became Queen Caroline; Swift immortalized him in a humorous production, *It cannot rain but it pours, or London strewed with Rareties;* (6) Pueri Pyrenaici (1719); "a dubious case": Zingg; (7) Puella Transisalana, found in 1717 in the Dutch province of Over-Yssel; (8) Puella Campanica, discovered in the Champagne in 1731; (9) Johannes Leodicensis, or John of Liège (Boerhaave); (10) Puella Karpfensis (1767).

Interest in feral or wild children has by no means subsided. One need only mention the story of Kaspar Hauser (who was made the central figure of a novel by Jakob Wassermann) and the excitement created not too long ago by the accounts about Kamala and Amala, rescued from a wolf den in a jungle near Midnapore, India, on October 17, 1920. R. M. Zingg has made an exhaustive analysis of the extensive literature on "feral man" (*Wolf Children and Feral Man,* New York, Harper, 1939).

When Victor of Aveyron was brought to Itard, the young physician could not accept Pinel's prognosis of irreversibility. He believed that the boy was mentally arrested because of social and educational neglect, that he had acquired idiocy through isolation, a sort of mental atrophy from disuse. He undertook to transfer the boy "from savagery to civilization, from natural life to social life." He set before himself five main objectives; (1) To render social life more congenial to the boy by making it more like the wild life he had recently left. (2) To excite his nervous sensibility with varied and energetic stimuli and supply his mind with the raw impression of ideas. (3) To extend the range of his ideas by creating new wants and expanding his relations with the world around him. (4) To lead him to the use of speech by making it necessary that he should imitate. (5) To apply himself to the satisfaction of his growing physical wants, and from this lead on to the application of his intelligence to the objects of instruction.

Itard labored for five years. He did not achieve his goal and, when the boy "broke out in a wild storm of passion" attributed to puberty, his teacher gave up, feeling that he had failed in his mission. Victor lived for many years in custodial care and died in 1828.

Nevertheless, the French Academy of Science applauded not only the effort but also the fact that the boy, who initially was mute, walked on all fours, drank water while lying flat on the grounds, and bit and scratched everyone interfering with his actions, showed some remarkable changes. He had learned to recognize objects, identify letters of the alphabet, comprehend the meaning of many words, apply names to objects and parts of objects, make "relatively fine" sensory discriminations, and "preferred the social life of civilization to an isolated existence in the wild." The Academy recognized that Itard had made a positive contribution to educational science. He had proved that even a severe mental defective could be improved to some extent by appropriate training. This is a part of the statement issued by the Academy:

This class of the Academy acknowledges that it was impossible for the instructor to put in his lessons, exercises, and experiments more intelligence, sagacity, patience, and courage; and that, if he has not obtained a great success, it must be attributed not to any lack of zeal or talent, but to the imperfection of the organs of the subject upon which he worked. The Academy, moreover, cannot see without astonishment how he could succeed as far as he did, and think that to be just toward Monsieur Itard, and to appreciate the real worth of his labors, the pupil ought to be compared only with himself; we should remember what he was when placed in the hands of his physician, see what he is now; and more, consider the distance separating his starting point from that which he has reached; and by how many new and ingenious modes of teaching this gap has been filled. The pamphlet of Monsieur Itard contains also the exposition of a series of extremely singular and interesting phenomena of fine judicious observations; and presents a combination of highly instructive processes, capable of furnishing science with new data, the knowledge of which can but be extremely useful to all persons engaged in the teaching of youth.

PUBLICATIONS BY ITARD

De l'education d'un homme sauvage. Paris, 1801.
Sur le pneumothorax, ou les congestions gaseuses qui se forment dans la poitrine. Paris, 1803.
Rapports et mémoires sur le sauvage d'Aveyron. L'idiotie et la surdimutité, avec une appréciation de ces rapports par Delasiauve. Préface par Bourneville. Éloge d'Itard par Bousquet. Paris: F. Alcan, 1804.
Rapport faith a son Excellence le Ministre de l'Intérieur sur les nouveaux dévelopments et l'etat actuel du sauvage d'Aveyron. Paris: J. J. Marcel, 1807.
Traité des maladies d'oreille et de l'audition. 2 vol. Paris: Méquignon-Marvis, 1821.

BIOGRAPHICAL DATA ON ITARD

BOUSQUET, J. B. E. Éloge historique de Itard. Paris: Cosson, 1839.

Edouard Onesimus Seguin was born January 20, 1812, at Clamecy in France. He attended the Collège d' Auxerre and the Lycée St. Louis in Paris and then studied medicine and surgery under Itard, who encouraged him to devote himself to the investigation and treatment of idiocy. He acknowledged freely his debt to Itard but, probing beyond the matter of individual relationship, saw in his attitude also the result of influences exerted by "the Christian School" or "Saint-Simonism," which, in Seguin's own words, was "striving for a social application of the principles of the gospel, for the most rapid evaluation of the lowest and poorest by all means and institutions, mostly by free education." In those days, he was certainly in need of both an inspiring mentor and a sustaining philosophy. Little support could be expected from the leading alienists. The great Jean Étienne Esquirol, from whom he sought guidance, declared categorically that educational efforts were useless because "no means are known by which a larger amount of reason or intelligence can be bestowed upon the unhappy idiot, even for the briefest period."

Undismayed by such pessimism, Seguin, at 25 years of age, made in 1837 an attempt to educate an idiotic boy. He worked with him steadily and strenuously for eighteen months, at the end of which his pupil "was able to make better use of his senses, could remember and compare, speak, write, and count." Esquirol was among the first to testify to the success of this venture. On August 18, 1839, he issued a statement in which he gave credit to Seguin, although he subtly defended his own position by referring to the patient as "un enfant . . . *semblable* à un idiot." If we decree that absolutely nothing can be done for an idiot, we can save face by saying that one whose condition has improved must have been a *seeming* idiot. Nevertheless, Esquirol concluded his statement by endorsing Seguin as a person "capable of giving the educational system all the desirable extension."

Seguin began to treat more children at the Hospice des Incurables and at the Bicêtre. At the October 12, 1842, session of the administrative council of hospitals in Paris, a commission appointed to report on the results of

Seguin's work (under the chairmanship of Dean Orfila of the Faculty of Medicine) reached the following decisions: (1) Seguin should be invited to continue his educational methods which he has so successfully applied at the Hospice des Incurables; (2) the director of the Hospice and the alienists should follow the progress and the results of the methods employed by Seguin. On December 11, 1843, a commission, consisting of Messieurs Serres, Flourens, and Pariset, gave a detailed report of their examination of Seguin's work, which they summed up by stating: "Monsieur Seguin has thus opened up a new career of beneficence. He has given to hygiene, to medicine, to ethics an example worthy of being followed. We, therefore, have the honor of suggesting that a note of thanks be written to Monsieur Seguin for the communication which he has addressed to this Council, and that he be encouraged in his charitable enterprise." In 1844, a commission of the Paris Academy of Sciences, appointed at Seguin's request to examine ten of his pupils, declared that he had definitely solved the problem of idiot education. Seguin, in his later writings, referred to the 1842 and 1843 reports as "the twin cornerstones of all the institutions since founded for the education of idiots."

In 1846, Seguin published his classic textbook, which won immediate recognition, was crowned by the Academy, and brought to its author an autograph letter from Pope Pius IX, thanking him for the services he was rendering to humanity. In this work, Seguin set forth the details of his method of the combined physiological and moral treatment of idiots. "According to this method," Seguin wrote in the introduction to a later book, "education is the *ensemble* of the means of developing harmoniously and effectively the moral, intellectual and physical capacities, as functions, in man and mankind. To be physiological, education must at first follow the great natural law of action and repose, which is life itself. To adapt this law to the whole training, each function in its turn is called to activity and to rest; the activity of one favoring the repose of the other; the improvement of one reacting upon the improvement of all others; contrast being not only an instrument of relaxation, but of comprehension also. . . . The general training embraces the muscular, imitative, nervous, and reflective functions, susceptible of being called into play at any moment."

Seguin's fame spread far and wide, and alienists of many nations flocked to Paris to see the work done by him. But just then came the 1848 revolution and Seguin, distrusting the new regime, packed up and emigrated to the United States. He settled in Cleveland as a general practitioner, then moved to Portsmouth, Ohio. In 1860, after a brief interval as head of the Pennsylvania Training School for Idiots and a visit to his native country, he moved to Mount Vernon, N.Y. When, in 1861, the medical department of the University of the City of New York conferred on him the M.D. degree, he made his residence in that metropolis, where he spent the last two decades of his life. Since his arrival in this country, he played a major role as consultant to all who were interested in establishing new residential treatment facilities for retarded children or improving those already in existence. He was in contact with Samuel Gridley Howe, whom he visited for two months early in 1852. In 1873, he went to Europe as United States Commissioner on Education at the Vienna Universal Exposition and published a comprehensive report on his impressions of the contemporary ideas about child rearing, school education, and the care of handicapped children.

In 1876, when six men got together to form the Association of Medical Officers of American Institutions for Idiotic and Feeble-Minded Persons, Seguin was chosen as its first president. This was the nucleus of the American Association on Mental Deficiency.

The last enterprise of his career was the organization of a Physiological School for Weak-Minded and Weak-Bodied Children in New York City.

As a side interest, Seguin occupied himself with medical thermometry, invented a widely used thermometer, and published several books on the subject, one of them (*Manual of Thermometry for Mothers*, 1873) was written for a lay public.

Seguin died October 28, 1880.

PUBLICATIONS BY SEGUIN

Résumé de ce que nous avons fait pendant quatorze mois. Paris, 1839.
Conseils à M. O. sur l'éducation de son enfant idiot. Paris, 1839.
Théorie et pratique de l'éducation des idiots. Two parts. Paris: Baillère, 1841 and 1842.
Hygiène et éducation des idiots. Paris, 1843.
Traitement moral, hygiène et éducation des idiots et des autres enfants arriérés. Paris: Baillère, 1846.
Images graduées a l'usage des enfants arriérés et idiots. Paris, 1846.
Jacob Rodrigues Pereire, notice sur sa vie et ses travaux. Paris, 1847.
Historical Notice of the Origin and Progress of the Treatment of Idiots. 1852.
Idiocy and Its Treatment by the Physiological Method. New York: W. Wood and Co., 1866. (Reprinted 1907 by Teacher's College, Columbia University.)
New Facts and Remarks Concerning Idiocy. New York: W. Wood and Co., 1870.
Medical Thermometry and Human Temperature. New York: W. Wood and Co., 1876.
Psycho-physiological Training of an Idiotic Hand. New York: G. P. Putnam's Sons, 1879.
Vienna International Exhibition, 1873. Report on Education. Washington: Government Printing Office, 1875. Second Edition: Milwaukee: Doerflinger, 1880.

BIOGRAPHICAL DATA ABOUT SEGUIN

BOYD, W. *From Locke to Montessori*. New York: Henry Holt, 1914. Chapter VI: Eduard Seguin, pp. 88-129.
DANA, C. L. "The Seguins of New York, Their Careers and Contributions to Science and Education," *Annals of Medical History*, New York, 6 (1924): 475-79.

Samuel Gridley Howe. Prior to the nineteenth century there was no public or private facility for the care of retarded children on the North American continent. A small attempt was made in 1818 to provide a place for a very limited number at the Asylum for the Deaf and Dumb in Hartford, Connecticut.

The idea of a special residential school for the feebleminded in this country stems from Massachusetts. In July 1848, Hervey Backus Wilber (1820-1883) took into his home at Barre a group of defective children beginning with the 7-year-old son of a distinguished lawyer. At about the same time, Dr. Samuel Gridley Howe was able to convince his contemporaries that the training and education of the feebleminded was a public responsibility.

Howe, born in 1801, graduated from Harvard Medical School in 1824. He volunteered for six years as a surgeon in the Greek war of liberation. On his return to the United States, he collected $60,000, which he personally disbursed in a relief depot at Aegina; soon thereafter, he arranged a refugee colony for exiles on the Isthmus of Corinth. At an early time, he developed an enthusiastic interest in blind and deaf children. He made a trip to England in preparation for the founding of a New England Asylum for the Blind. He was temporarily diverted from his purpose when, asked by Lafayette to carry funds to the Polish revolutionaries across the Prussian frontier, he was caught and imprisoned in Berlin. After his release in April 1832, he took a few blind children into his father's house. Colonel Thomas H. Perkins was so impressed that he offered his house and garden on Boston's Pearl Street as a permanent location of what is known as the Perkins Institution for the Blind, which Howe directed until his death in 1876. Howe developed new methods for the instruction of the sightless and deafmutes and his phenomenal success with one of his pupils, Laura Bridgman (who could neither see nor hear), won him international fame. He was actively associated with Dorothea Lynde Dix in her work for the insane and with Charles Sumner and Horace Mann in the struggle for educational reforms. Together with his wife, Julia Ward (they were married on April 27, 1843), he was an advocate of Negro emancipation. In 1866, appalled by the plight of the Cretans, he went back to Greece and established in Athens a school for refugees from the island.

Howe's profound interest in the handicapped did not fail to include the feebleminded. His daughter, Laura E. Richards, wrote: "In the course of his labors and research in behalf of the blind and the insane, especially the latter, he had been deeply impressed with the sufferings and needs of a kindred class, the idiotic and feebleminded." More specifically, he was led to the first practical steps by his experience with three blind children who were also idiotic and whom he treated "with considerable success." He inferred that, "If so much could be done for idiots who were blind, still more could be done for idiots who were not blind."

Inspired by Howe, Judge Horatio Boyington, then a member of the House of Representatives, moved on January 22, 1846, an order for the appointment of a committee "to consider the expediency of appointing commissioners to inquire into the condition of the idiots of the Commonwealth; to ascertain their number and whether anything can be done for their relief, and to report to next General Court." The order was passed and printed on the same day. A report of the committee, presented on

March 25, urged the appointment of such commissioners, and on April 11, Judge Boyington, Dr. Howe, and Gilman Kimball were chosen.

In the two years following, those three sent circular letters to town clerks and other responsible persons in every community of the Commonwealth, visited 63 towns and personally examined the status of 574 "human beings who are condemned to hopeless idiocy and left to their own brutishness."

On February 26, 1848, the commissioners submitted their first report, written and signed by Howe as chairman. A few extracts will give its flavor:

"Massachusetts admits the right of all her citizens to a share in the blessings of education; she provides it liberally for all her more favored children; if some be blind or deaf, she will continues to furnish them with special instruction at great cost; and will she longer neglect the poor idiots—the most wretched of all who are born to her—those who are usually abandoned by their fellows,—who can never, of themselves, step upon the platform of humanity,—will she leave them to their dreadful fate, to a life of brutishness, without an effort in their behalf? . . .

"The benefits to be derived from the establishment of a school for this class of persons, upon humane and scientific principles, would be very great. Not only would all the idiots who should be received into it be improved in their bodily and mental condition, but all the others in the State and the country would be indirectly benefitted. The school, if conducted by persons of skill and ability, would be a model for others. Valuable information would be disseminated through the country; it would be demonstrated that no idiot need be confined or restrained by force; that the young can be trained to industry, order, and self-respect; that they can be redeemed from odious and filthy habits, and there is not one of any age who may not be made more of a man and less of a brute by patience and kindness directed by energy and skill."

The report made a profound impression. There were a few scoffers, it is true. A caricature was circulated, which represented Sumner and Howe as twin Don Quixotes riding a tilt against various windmills, and one critic remarked: "The doctor's report is one *for* idiots as well as one concerning them."

Nevertheless, the legislature consented to allow $2,500 per annum for three years for the teaching and training of ten idiotic children. A wing was opened on October 1, 1848, at the Perkins Institution to serve as "an experimental school." A competent teacher was found, James B. Richards, who later did pioneering work in Pennsylvania.

Toward the end of the three years, the Joint Committee of Public Charitable Institutions visited the place, reported that "the experiment seems to have succeeded entirely," and suggested that the school be put on a permanent footing. An institution was incorporated under the name of Massachusetts School for Idiotic and Feeble-Minded Youth. A pleasant site was chosen in South Boston in 1855, and the children were moved thither from the Perkins Institution. Howe made daily rounds, examined all candidates for admission, engaged all officers, and prescribed diets, regimen, rules and regulations, discipline and exercises. In 1887, the school was located permanently in Waltham; it is now known as the Walter E. Fernald State School, in recognition of the long services of one of its most distinguished superintendents.

Howe's activities on behalf of the feebleminded were not confined to his home state. In the winter of 1850-1851, he appeared with some of his pupils before the state authorities of New York at Albany, showing what he had done in Massachusetts, and pleading for the establishment of a similar school in New York. As a result, an appropriation of $6,000 annually for 2 years was voted for "an experimental school," which was opened in Albany in 1851 and moved to Syracuse in 1855, with Hervey B. Wilbur as its first director. It is now known as the Syracuse State School. (Howe proved to be more persuasive than Dr. Frederick Backus of Rochester, who had introduced at the 1864 session of the legislature a bill for the opening of a residential school; the bill was passed in one house but failed to carry in the other chamber.) In July 1851, Governor Hunt of New York wrote to Howe: "Your visit to our capital last winter was of great service. We feel that we are much indebted to you for the success of the measure thus far, and hope we may have the benefit of your experience and counsel in carrying our plan into practical operation.

As Guggenbühl deserves the credit for inaugurating the institutional care of retarded children in Europe, so does the credit go to Howe for rendering the same kind of pioneering service in this country. We know that Howe had visited Guggenbühl's Abendberg before he submitted his report in 1848 and that he was full of praise of the Swiss enterprise. We do not know for certain whether he had also been to the Bicêtre (it is certain that his friend Charles Sumner was there) but, when Seguin came to America, Howe invited him to come to Boston. Happily, he wrote to Horace Mann on January 21, 1852: "I have luckily secured Dr. Seguin, formerly the life and soul of the French school for idiots," and on March 15, 1852, he wrote to Charles Sumner: "Seguin has been here two months, and proves to be a man of great vigor of intellect, and full of resources; he has done wonders—but we can hardly keep him."

Howe kept up his concern for the blind, the deaf, the insane, the feebleminded, the slaves, and the oppressed nations (particularly Greece) to the end of his busy life. Oliver Wendell Holmes wrote a touching "Memorial Tribute" to Howe in beautiful verse, from which these lines are taken:

"He touched the eyelids of the blind,
And lo, the veil withdrawn,
As o'er the midnight of the mind
He led the light of dawn."

Howe's example was followed not only by New York State. James B. Richards, his first teacher in Boston, started a private school in Germantown, Pennsylvania; in 1854, the state legislature appropriated $10,000 for its support and in 1859 the school was located at Elwyn, "dedicated forever to the shelter, instruction, and improvement of God's most afflicted children." In April 1857, the Ohio Institution for the Education of Feeble-Minded Youth (now the Columbus State School) was opened. The Connecticut School for Imbeciles was founded in 1858 by Dr. Henry M. Knight (1827-1880); it was supported by private donations, fees, and a small grant from the state, which closed it in 1917 when it established the Mansfield Training School. Kentucky followed in 1860, Illinois in 1865, Iowa in 1877, Indiana and Minnesota in 1879, Kansas in 1881, California in 1885, Nebraska in 1886, Maryland and New Jersey in 1888. Arkansas was the latest to establish such an institution; it opened its Children's Colony in 1955. Nevada and Alaska are the only two states which have no such facilities at present. In Canada, the first school was opened in 1876 at Orillia in the Province of Ontario, intended specifically for low-grade patients.

BIOGRAPHICAL DATA ON HOWE

HARRINGTON, T. F. "Samuel Gridley Howe," in *The Harvard Medical School.* New York and Chicago: Lewis Publishing Co., 1905, Vol. II, pp. 741-53.
PHALEN, J. M. "Dr. Samuel Gridley Howe, a Yankee Cervantes," *Military Surgeon* 88 (1941): 553-55.
RICHARDS, LAURA E. (Howe's Daughter). *Letters and Journals of Samuel Gridley Howe.* Boston: Dana Estes & Co., 1909. Two volumes.
_____. *Samuel Gridley Howe.* New York: Appleton-Century, 1935.
WILLIAMS, F. E. "Dr. Samuel G. Howe and the Beginning of Work for the Feeble-minded in Massachusetts," *Boston Medical and Surgical Journal* 177 (1917): 481-84.

PUBLICATIONS BY HOWE

Report Made to the Legislature of Massachusetts on Idiocy. Boston: Collidge & Wiley, 1848.
Report to Inquire into the Condition of Idiots of the Commonwealth of Massachusetts, No. 51, February 28, 1948.
Second Annual Report of the Doings under the Resolves of the Legislature, May 8, 1948, for Training and Teaching Idiots, January 20, 1851, Senate No. 9, Boston, 1851.
Third and Final Report of the Experimental School. *American Journal of Insanity* 9 (1852): 9, 20.
A Letter to the Governor of Massachusetts upon His Veto of a Bill Providing for an Increase of State Beneficiaries at the School of Idiotic Children. Boston: Tickner & Fields, 1857.
On the Causes of Idiocy. Edinburgh: McLachlan and Stewart, 1858. (Contains an abstract of the first report, the entire supplement, 12 of the original 47 pages of tables, and 20 pages of appendix: excerpts from later reports by Howe.)

Dr. Leo Kanner is Professor Emeritus, Department of Psychiatry, Johns Hopkins University Medical School, Baltimore, Maryland.

24.
Adult Status of Children with Contrasting Early Life Experiences
HAROLD M. SKEELS

Summary

In the original study, the 13 children in the experimental group, all mentally retarded at the beginning of the study, experienced the effects of early intervention, which consisted of a radical shift from one institutional environment to another. The major difference between the two institutions, as experienced by the children, was in the amount of developmental stimulation and the intensity of relationships between the children and mother-surrogates. Following a variable period in the second institution, 11 of the 13 children were placed in adoptive homes.

The contrast group of 12 children, initially higher in intelligence than the experimental group, were exposed to a relatively nonstimulating orphanage environment over a prolonged period of time.

Over a period of two years, the children in the experimental group showed a marked increase in rate of mental growth, whereas the children in the contrast group showed progressive mental retardation. The experimental group made an average gain of 28.5 IQ points; the contrast group showed an average loss of 26.2 IQ points.

The first follow-up study was made 2½ years after the termination of the original study. The 11 children in the experimental group that had been placed in adoptive homes had maintained and increased their earlier gains in intelligence, whereas the two not so placed had declined in rate of mental growth. Over the three-year postexperimental period, the children in the contrast group showed a slight mean gain in IQ but were still mentally retarded to a marked degree. In those children that showed gains in intelligence, the gains appeared to be associated with improved environmental experiences that occurred subsequent to the original study.

In the adult follow-up study, all cases were located and information obtained on them, after a lapse of 21 years.

The two groups had maintained their divergent patterns of competency into adulthood. All 13 children in the experimental group were self-supporting, and none was a ward of any institution, public or private. In the contrast group of 12 children, one had died in adolescence following con-

From Harold M. Skeels, "Adult Status of Children with Contrasting Early Life Experiences: A Follow-up Study," *Monographs of the Society for Research in Child Development,* 31:3 (1966): 54-57. Copyright © 1966 by the University of Chicago Press. Reprinted by permission of the Press and the Society for Research in Child Development, Inc.

tinued residence in a state institution for the mentally retarded, and 4 were still wards of institutions, one in a mental hospital, and the other 3 in insti-

In education, disparity between the two groups was striking. The con-tutions for the mentally retarded.
trast group completed a median of less than the third grade. The experi-mental group completed a median of the twelfth grade. Four of the subjects had one or more years of college work, one received a B.A. degree and took some graduate training.

Marked differences in occupational levels were seen in the two groups. In the experimental group all were self-supporting or married and function-ing as housewives. The range was from professional and business occupa-tions to domestic service, the latter the occupations of two girls who had never been placed in adoptive homes. In the contrast group, four (36%) of the subjects were institutionalized and unemployed. Those who were employed, with one exception (Case 19), were characterized as "hewers of wood and drawers of water." Using the t test, the difference between the status means of the two groups (based on the Warner Index of Status Characteristics applied to heads of households) was statistically significant ($p < .01$).

Educational and occupational achievement and income for the 11 adopted subjects in the experimental group compared favorably with the 1960 U.S. Census figures for Iowa and for the United States in general. Their adult status was equivalent to what might have been expected of children living with natural parents in homes of comparable sociocultural levels. Those subjects that married had marriage partners of comparable sociocultural levels.

Eleven of the 13 children in the experimental group were married; 9 of the 11 had a total of 28 children, an average of three children per family. On intelligence tests, these second-generation children had IQ's ranging from 86 to 125, with a mean and median IQ of 104. In no instance was there any indication of mental retardation or demonstrable abnormality. Those of school age were in appropriate grades for age.

In the contrast group, only two of the subjects had married. One had one child and subsequently was divorced. Psychological examination of the child revealed marked mental retardation with indications of probable brain damage. Another male subject (Case 19) had a nice home and family of four children, all of average intelligence.

The cost to the state for the contrast group, for whom intervention was essentially limited to custodial care, was approximately five times that of the cost for the experimental group. It seems safe to predict that for at least four of the cases in the contrast group costs to the state will con-tinue at a rate in excess of $200.00 per month each for another 20 to 40 years.

Implications of Study

At the beginning of the study, the 11 children in the experimental group evidenced marked mental retardation. The developmental trend was reversed through planned intervention during the experimental period. The program of nurturance and cognitive stimulation was followed by placement in adoptive homes that provided love and affection and normal life experiences. The normal, average intellectual level attained by the subjects in early or middle childhood was maintained into adulthood.

It can be postulated that if the children in the contrast group had been placed in suitable adoptive homes or given some other appropriate equivalent in early infancy, most or all of them would have achieved within the normal range of development, as did the experimental subjects.

It seems obvious that under present-day conditions there are still countless infants born with sound biological constitutions and potentialities for development well within the normal range who will become mentally retarded and noncontributing members of society unless appropriate intervention occurs. It is suggested by the findings of this study and others published in the past 20 years that sufficient knowledge is available to design programs of intervention to counteract the devasting effects of poverty, sociocultural deprivation, and maternal deprivation.

Since the study was a pioneering and descriptive one involving only a small number of cases, it would be presumptuous to attempt to identify the specific influences that produced the changes observed. However, the contrasting outcome between children who experienced enriched environmental opportunities and close emotional relationships with affectionate adults, on the one hand, and those children who were in deprived, indifferent, and unresponsive environments, on the other, leaves little doubt that the area is a fruitful one for further study.

It has become increasingly evidence that the prediction of later intelligence cannot be based on the child's first observed developmental status. Account must be taken of his experiences between test and retest. Hunt (1964, p. 212) has succinctly stated that,

. . . In fact, trying to predict what the IQ of an individual child will be at age 18 from a D.Q. obtained during his first or second year is much like trying to predict how fast a feather might fall in a hurricane. The law of falling bodies holds only under the specified and controlling conditions of a vacuum. Similarly, any laws concerning the rate of intellectual growth must take into account the series of environmental encounters which constitute the conditions of that growth.

The divergence in mental-growth patterns between children in the experimental and contrast groups is a striking illustration of this concept.

The right of every child to be well born, well nurtured, well brought up, and well educated was enunciated in the Children's Charter of the 1930 White House Conference on Child Health and Protection (White House Conference, 1931). Though society strives to insure this right, for many years to come there will be children to whom it has been denied and for whom society must provide both intervention and restitution. There is need for further research to determine the optimum modes of such intervention and the most appropriate ages and techniques for initiating them. The present study suggests, but by no means delimits, either the nature of the intervention or the degree of change that can be induced.

The planning of future studies should recognize that the child interacts with his environment and does not merely passively absorb its impact. More precise and significant information on the constitutional, emotional, and response-style characteristics of the child is needed so that those environmental experiences that are most pertinent to his needs can be identified and offered in optimum sequence.

The unanswered questions of this study could form the basis for many life-long research projects. If the tragic fate of the 12 contrast-group children provokes even a single crucial study that will help prevent such a fate for others, their lives will not have been in vain.

Dr. Harold M. Skeels, deceased, spent most of his professional career in Child Development with the United States Public Health Service. On the basis of his unique research, he received a citation from the Division of Child Development of the American Psychological Association and the Joseph P. Kennedy Award in Mental Retardation.

25.
Educating the Mildly Retarded:
A Review
GARY W. HAMMONS

*This article proposes a middle-of-the-road position
relative to the desirability of special classes for
the mildly retarded. In the light of the analysis
presented, what are your convictions on the
problem?*

A number of recent writings in special education,
this one included, have begun with a reference to Dunn's (1968) article,
"Special Education for the Mildly Retarded—Is Much of It Justifiable?"
Yet, in spite of the multitude of citations, this work was only symptomatic
of a growing disenchantment with emerging practices of special education.
For example, the original efficacy studies of Bennet and Pertsch during the
1930's were undoubtedly initiated as a result of concern for the academic
progress of educable mentally retarded children (Reynolds, 1971). In
addition to comments concerning the numerous efficacy studies, the professional literature in the past decade contains several comments similar to
Dunn's. For example, Blatt (1960) pointed out that no supportable advantages of special classes for this population have been established, and
Johnson (1962) said:

It is indeed paradoxical that mentally handicapped children having teachers especially trained, having more money (per capita) spent on their education and
being enrolled in classes with fewer children and a program designed to provide
for their unique needs, should be accomplishing the objectives of their education
at a lower level than similar mentally handicapped children who have not had
these advantages and have been forced to remain in the regular grades [p. 207].

Connor (1964) expressed concern for the problem of " . . . the practice
of placing children in a special class because they cannot be handled in the
regular programs regardless of their being able to learn the special setting
available [p. 207]." Others, Fisher (1967), Reger, Schroeder, and Uschold
(1968), have questioned the appropriateness of using medically derived
criteria for grouping handicapped children rather than criteria reflecting
their educational and social needs. Prior to publication of Dunn's article,
Schwartz (1968) pondered the growing stress on the establishment of
special classes to the exclusion of specialized education. He further noted

From *Exceptional Children* 38 (March, 1972): 565-70. Reprinted by permission of
the author and *Exceptional Children*. Copyrighted by the Council for Exceptional
Children.

that for secondary level special classes, adaptation has been overlooked in favor of using IQ scores as a placement criterion. A substantial body of research shows (a) serious doubt of the efficacy of special classes, (b) clearly deleterious effects of labeling a child as mentally retarded, and (c) the fact that friends, parents, and work associates of this group do not think of them as retarded.

Focal Point

The reception Dunn's article met represented the culmination of dissatisfaction with current practices more than the response to the contentions he advanced. However, the quantity and variety of reactions have probably surprised even Dunn himself. These reactions have generally taken three forms: (a) support and elaboration of Dunn's contentions, (b) further inquiry into the efficacy studies, and (c) discussion of problems of categorization.

Those writers who have supported Dunn generally reiterate the position that, because of lack of evidence to the contrary, special classes should be abolished for all but the profoundly handicapped. Lilly (1970), for example, said that " ... traditional special education services as represented by self-contained special classes should be discontinued immediately for all but the severely impaired ... [p. 43]." Christoplos and Renz (1969) questioned the justification for special classes for all populations served by the schools, and Johnson (1969) reiterated their point and typified the position of several writers that special classes were initially created to serve a relieving function for regular education and to reduce classroom disruption by exceptional children. Johnson and others (Franks, 1971; Lilly, 1970; Simches, 1970) further contended that these classes are now used by the schools to perpetuate racism.

Efficacy Revisited

Dunn's article also appears to have stimulated renewed interest in the efficacy studies: their design and implications. Often cited as most comprehensive and yet inconclusive, the Illinois study of Goldstein, Moss, and Jordan (1965) has been prefaced by Kirk and analyzed by Guskin and Spicker (1968). Kirk indicated that, even with the excellent methodology of this study, nothing conclusive was established and researchers should concentrate instead on processes by which the retarded develop mentally, socially, and academically. Guskin and Spicker countered:

If we are to agree with Kirk that what we need to study are learning and developmental processes rather than administrative arrangements, the same argument could have been just as legitimately made before carrying out the study. If we demand evidence for the effectiveness of special class arrangements, this study may be the best we have so far, but it is far from decisive [pp. 239-240].

Lilly (1970) attempted to relegate the efficacy studies to obscurity, stating:

To avoid exhaustive argument with regard to research design and confounding variables in these efficacy studies, let us accept the statement that they are inconclusive to date. It must be added, however, that in the true spirit of research they will be inconclusive forever [pp. 43-44].

However, Nelson and Schmidt (1971) analyzed several facets of the issue not considered elsewhere. They concluded:

If there is any sustaining value in the position of those who challenge or uphold the effectiveness of the special class, it must be the systematic examination of the statements which are used to reject or justify special classes. To challenge on any other basis leads to trivial conclusions [p. 384].

Categorization

In addition to renewed interest in the efficacy studies, a related concern appears to be with the problems manifested in categorization of exceptional children. This apparently stems from considerations of the stigma of special classes. Blatt (1971) related that, in spite of long overdue progressive developments, "... children continue to be labeled and stigmatized ... some to be placed in segregated programs while others to be excluded or exempted from public schools [p. 3]." Hurley (1971) echoed, "There are many issues in education today but the 'Hottest' by far is the issue of labeling children and its corollary, the elimination of traditional categories of special education [p. 9]."

Some teacher training institutions are responding to this pressure by redesigning their instructional sequences to deal more with exceptional children on a noncategorical basis, under the justification that most of the techniques demonstrated are applicable to all handicapping conditions. However, some writers (Reynolds & Balow, 1971; Lucus, 1971; Guskin & Spicker, 1968) have suggested that when terminology is used to describe programs and teachers rather than children, communication and programing are thereby improved.

Alternative Proposal

Many of Dunn's contentions have been extensively expanded by later writers. These include:

1. Labeling and categories do more harm than good.

2. The efficacy studies do not support continued existence of special classes.

3. General education has improved its ability to cope with a greater range of individual differences.

4. The existence of special classes protects regular education from facing its failures.

While Dunn suggested several alternatives to special classes, many of his fellow critics have supported only resource room or consultant intervention. Lilly (1971) proposed returning special class teachers and students to regular classes and providing instructional specialists to assist them with their educational problems. He also suggested a three part program that would eliminate failure completely, both on the part of the student and the regular class teacher. This model, which stresses the training of teachers to handle problems rather than to refer them to others, would provide personnel to aid the classroom teacher in coping with exceptional situations. Christoplos and Renz (1969) proposed that many of the same arguments advanced for elimination of special classes for the slow learner also are valid for all other exceptional categories and therefore that total integration of all handicapped students into regular classes should be considered. Hurley (1971), commenting on the issues of special classes and categorization, said, "Since we recognize that we deal with failures of the educational system, we cannot decategorize unless we get involved in the whole system and not just special education [p. 5]."

Not Carefully Read

Recently, however, Johnson (1971) and Lucas (1971) have pointed out that the critics of special classes who credit Dunn's writing (1968) as their inspiration have not read this article well. They pointed out that his position, while not popular at the time, was limited in terms of population affected and that the alternatives he proposed were much more encompassing than only resource room concepts. Both Johnson and Lucas apparently have read the article well; they emphasize that Dunn was concerned primarily with the borderline or mildly retarded and that *some* classes for this population are inappropriate. Johnson and Lucas take exception to the contention of Dunn and others that the existence of special classes provides shelter for regular education from its failure to teach this low group effectively. In fact, several writers have recently exposed inequities in regular education's ability to provide for this population at all. Hurley (1969) stressed that educators have not only been remiss in intervening but have virtually guaranteed repetition of the cycle by this generation's children. Stein (1971) affirmed the contention: "The average child in eighty-five per cent of the Black and Puerto Rican schools is functionally illiterate after eight years of schooling in the richest city in the world [p. 158]." Thus, Dunn's premise that regular education has greatly improved its ability to deal with a wide range of individual differences may not be supportable.

The general conclusion of those who have examined Dunn's contentions carefully, and not necessarily agreed with him, has been that the situation is far more complex than appearances indicate. It has not yet been demonstrated that any one method or strategy is either superior or without redeeming value in educating exceptional children. Furthermore, the general feeling that evidence is not sufficient to indicate any definite stance is well stated by Engel (1969):

In this case it is fallacious to argue for the abolishment of special classes on the basis of the research evidence; the classes exist, the groupings are in effect, but after that we still have to construct new teaching methods before we have anything to assess [p. 382].

While the reasons advanced by critics appear credible and convincing in isolation, they may have a serious flaw in their logic. Frequent justification for replacing special classes with resource teachers or consultants is that the efficacy studies show special classes to be deficient, yet virtually no significant studies are available showing the alternate model to be efficacious. While this might be excused or justified on the grounds that such programs have not existed long enough for proper evaluation and that there is a need to explore this programing experimentally, it is pretentious to expect regular educators to accept or even tolerate consultation from special educators. Smith (1971) succinctly pointed out that special educators traditionally have argued that the best way to handle underachievers is to place them in special classes. Now that this does not seem to be effective, the proposal that special educators serve instead as consultants is like saying, "We were unable to teach them anything, so you get them back. However, we retain the right to tell you how to do it." The possibility of regular education's accepting such a strategy would seem remote.

Furthermore, resource room, consultant, or crisis teacher programs have several serious flaws in their functional design. In striving to justify their existence, teachers in these positions tend to extend their services into all areas of instruction. While this may be sound educationally, it has the net effect of diluting or reducing aid to the populations the concept was devised to serve. Additionally, the tendency of school districts to abandon traditional special classes completely in favor of resource rooms increases the threat of total abolishment of special education. As the financial crisis in education worsens and programs are curtailed, resource room programs are more susceptible to budget cuts than traditional classes, since their demise would not result in educationally difficult students being returned to the regular classroom.

Early Intervention

Most writers, with the possible exception of Reynolds (1971), have ignored Dunn's limitation of attention to only young children, that is, " . . . the emphasis of the article is on children, in that no attempt is made to suggest an adequate high school environment of adolescents still functioning as slow learners [Reynolds, 1971, p. 6]." In addition, the tendency to react as if a crisis exists and to make an immediate unilateral shift or return in educational programming for the slow learner could wel create a crisis. The hazard, as Dunn recognized, is in conceptualizing the situation about a single point in time and making decisions and provisions which are, in effect, only short range responses to a long range problem. As Reynolds (1971) observed, education should consider foremost what each child will be like as a result of the education he receives or should receive and then should consider the most appropriate strategies presently available.

A growing response has been prefaced with concern and agreement in principle, but it requires more realistic and timely strategies than simple abolishment. Johnson and Balow (1971), Reynolds (1971), Lucas (1971), and MacMillan (1971), among others, have reiterated Kirk's contention that the real concern should not be what kind of administrative arrangement best handles slow learners but what is best for them educationally and what system of grouping is best to accomplish this. Johnson further argued that whether this population is considered retarded tomorrow is highly dependent on what is done for them educationally today.

Many writers, in addressing themselves to the question of justification of separate classes for the slow learner, regardless of their point of view, have stressed that the current introspection has been beneficial to special and regular education. Miller and Schoenfelder (1969) expressed this view:

It is quite right and proper that special education not be considered sacrosanct, and that special educators be forced to consider their basic assumptions, premises, and philosophical foundations. Professions seem to take a long, hard look at themselves in this sense only when under critical onslaught. No field which is expanding as rapidly as is special education should be allowed to so grow without having a strong philosophical and theoretical foundation [p. 397].

Stephens (1967) emphasized that the current status of special education is part of an evolutionary process: "... whatever its other virtues, the school has been a survival device which some societies evolved, or borrowed, or stumbled upon, or otherwise acquired during the remote past [p. 37]."

Crossroads

If, indeed, the current controversy is part of an evolutionary process, special education must now be at a crossroads of conflicting courses of action. The transition it undergoes will be highly dependent on forthcoming strategies of special education leadership. To continue current self flagellation and recrimination without adequate provisions for shifting to a more viable position is to risk abolishment of all special education. While this might be more in keeping with the professed goals of some writers (Christoplos & Renz, 1969; Lilly, 1970), it could cause irreparable damage to many programs not involved in the controversy. Thus, professionals must reckon with the forces of change, channeling them into courses of action beneficial to the improvement of education for all handicapped populations.

The present controversy concerning special classes might better be viewed as an opportunity to explore needed changes than as evidence that special education is in the throes of a survival crisis. Increased concern with long range solutions, coupled with more systematic application of research and implementation, would allow for orderly transition. Furthermore, that a major shift in programing is required may not be obvious to all concerned (Nelson & Schmidt, 1971). Thus, special education professionals must seek more empirical evidence of the most appropriate course of action, while continuing to maintain and improve the current level of service to the handicapped. Valletutti (1969) has summarized the situation appropriately:

Segregation or integration is not the critical issue. The values and attitudes of teachers and their effects on the pupil's self-perception and performances are the key questions. Segregation without a program is just a destructive as integration without understanding. Returning to an educational system which ignores the promise and possibility of the special class would disregard the imperatives of educational history, which have mandated an alternative to wide range heterogeneity [p. 407-408].

REFERENCES

BLATT, B. Some persistently recurring assumptions concerning the mentally subnormal. *Training School Bulletin* 57 (1960): 48-59.

BLATT, B. Public policy and the education of children with special needs. *Proceedings of the Conference on the Categorical/Non-Categorical Issue in Special Education*, Columbia: Special Education Department, University of Missouri, 1971. Pp. 49-62.

CHRISTOPLOS, F. & RENZ, P. A critical examination of special education programs. *Journal of Special Education* 3 (1969): 371-379.

CONNOR, F. P. Excellence in special education. *Exceptional Children* 30 (1964): 206-09.

DUNN, L. M. Special education for the mildly retarded—Is much of it justifiable? *Exceptional Children* 35 (1968): 5-22.

ENGEL, M. The tin drum revisited. *Journal of Special Education* 3 (1969): 380-82.

FISHER, H. K. What is special education? *Special Education in Canada* 41 (1967): 9-16.

FRANKS, D. J. Ethnic and social status characteristics of children in EMR and LD classes. *Exceptional Children* 37 (1971): 537-38.

GOLDSTEIN, H.; MOSS, J. W.; & JORDON, L. J. The efficacy of special class training on the development of mentally retarded children. Cooperative Research Project 619. Washington, D.C.: HEW, Office of Education, 1965.

GUSKIN, S. L. & SPICKER, H. H. Educational research in mental retardation. In N. Ellis, ed., *International Review of Research in Mental Retardation*. Vol. 3. New York: Academic Press, 1968. Pp. 217-78.

HURLEY, O. L. A categorical/non-categorical issue: Implications for teacher trainers. *Proceedings of the Missouri Conference on the Categorical/Non-Categorical Issue in Special Education.* Columbia: Special Education Department, University of Missouri, 1971. Pp. 39-40.

HURLEY, R. *Poverty and Mental Retardation—A Causal Relationship.* New York: Random House, 1969.

JOHNSON, G. O. Special education for the mentally retarded—A paradox. *Exceptional Children* 29 (1962): 62-69.

JOHNSON, J. L. Special education and the inner city; A challenge of the future or another means for cooling the mark out? *Journal of Special Education* 3 (1969): 241-51.

JOHNSON, G. O. Why special education for the mentally retarded: A rebuttal criticisms. In *Exceptional Children Conference Papers: Trends and Issues in Special Education.* Papers presented at the 49th Annual Convention of the Council for Exceptional Children, Miami Beach, April, 1971. Pp. 127-34.

LILLY, M. S. Special education: A teapot in a tempest. *Exceptional Children* 37 (1970): 43-49.

LILLY, M. S. A training based model for special education. *Exceptional Children* 37 (1971): 745-49.

LUCAS, C. J. The use and abuse of educational categories. *Proceedings of the Conference on the Categorical/Non-Categorical Issue in Special Education.* Columbia: Special Education Department, University of Missouri, 1971. Pp. 14-22.

MACMILLAN, D. L. Issues. In R. L. Jones (Chm.), Special education for the mildly retarded—How justifiable? Symposium presented at the International Conference of The Council for Exceptional Children, Miami Beach, April, 1971.

MILLER, J. G. & SCHOENFELDER, D. S. A rational look at special class placement. *Journal of Special Education* 3 (1969): 397-403.

NELSON, C. C. & SCHMIDT, L. J. The question of the efficacy of special classes. *Exceptional Children* 37 (1971): 381-84.

REGER, A.; SCHRODER, W.; & USCHOLD, D. *Special Education: Children with Learning Problems.* New York: Oxford University Press, 1968.

REYNOLDS, M. C. What is special education? In R. L. Jones (Chm.), Special education for the mildly retarded—How justifiable? Symposium presented at the International Conference of The Council for Exceptional Children, Miami Beach, April, 1971.

REYNOLDS, M. C. & BALOW, B. Categories and variables in special education. *Proceedings of the Conference on the Categorical/Non-Categorical Issue in Special Education.* Columbia: Special Education Department, University of Missouri, 1971. Pp. 82-96.

SCHWARTZ, R. H. Toward a meaningful education for the retarded adolescent. *Mental Retardation* 6 (1968): 34-35.

SIMCHES, R. F. The inside outsiders. *Exceptional Children* 37 (1970): 5-15.

SMITH, J. O. Personal communication. University of Washington, Seattle, 1971.

STEIN, A. Strategies for failure. *Harvard Educational Review* 41 (2) (1971): 158-204.

STEPHENS, J. M. *The Process of Schooling, a Psychological Examination.* New York: Holt, Rinehart, & Winston, 1967.

VALLETUTTI, P. Integration vs. segregation: A useless dialectic. *Journal of Special Education* 3 (1969): 405-08.

Gary W. Hammons is Lecturer in Special Education, Central Washington State College, Ellensburg, Washington, and a doctoral student in Special Education, University of Washington, Seattle.

26.
Employment of the Mentally Retarded
CONWELL G. STRICKLAND
VERNON M. ARRELL

The purpose of this study was to determine the extent to which educable mentally retarded youth in Texas had found initial employment in the jobs for which they had been trained in the school work program. The Texas school work program is a cooperative effort between the divisions of Special Education and Vocational Rehabilitation of the Texas Education Agency and the local independent school district, to provide classroom instruction and on the job training for public school special education students 16 years of age and older. The specific purposes of the investigation were to determine what percentage of the educable mentally retarded students who had participated in this program had: (a) been trained for the job in which they were employed; (b) been trained for some other job in the same category; (c) been trained for a job in an occupational field which was unrelated to that in which they were employed; and (d) received guidance, counseling, and job placement services, but no specific classroom instruction or on the job training.

Data were obtained from the case files in the Vocational Rehabilitation Division of the Texas Education Agency on those individuals whose cases had been closed between July 1, 1963, and August 31, 1965. A case was considered to be closed if the person had been employed successfully on a job for a period of at least three months. Out of a total of 1950 closed cases, only the files of those who had been enrolled in or had completed the cooperative school work program (1754 cases, or approximately 90 percent) were considered. Of these, only 80.1 per cent, or 1405 clients (977 males and 428 females), were used for analysis, since some of the information was taken from a section of the record which had not been uniformly reported.

Results

The data were organized according to the subdivisions of occupations established by the US Department of Labor (1949). The subdivisions used were those determined by a previous investigation (Strickland, 1964) to be the most common in which retarded youth were being trained. A summary of the findings is included in Table 1.

From *Exceptional Children* 34 (September, 1967): 21-24. Reprinted by permission of the authors and *Exceptional Children*. Copyrighted by the Council for Exceptional Children.

Agriculture and Horticulture Occupations. Ninety-one clients, 81 males and 10 females, were closed in this job category. Sixty-three, or 69.2 percent, were trained on another agriculture or horticulture job. Eighteen and seven-tenths percent were trained on a job in another occupational area. The other 12.1 percent had received no specific training for the job on which they were closed.

Auto Service Occupations. All clients closed in auto service occupations were male. Of the total of 126 employed, 114 (90.5 percent) had been trained for the specific job. Two had been trained in another auto service job, three were trained in an unrelated job area, and 7 had completed no on the job training.

TABLE 1 Employment of Retarded Youth according to Occupational Subcategory, Sex, and Training

Occupational Category	Sex	N	Trained for Specific Job N	Per-centage	Trained for Related Job N	Per-centage	Trained for Unrelated Job N	Per-centage	No Specific Job Training N	Per-centage
Agriculture	Male	81	55	67.9	0		16	19.8	10	12.3
and	Female	10	8	80.0	0		1	10.0	1	10.0
Horticulture	Total	91	63	69.2	0		17	18.7	11	12.1
Automobile Service	Total[a]	126	114	90.5	2	1.6	3	2.4	7	5.5
Cleaning	Male	18	16	88.9	0		0		2	11.1
Pressing,	Female	25	23	92.0	0		2	8.0	0	
and Laundry	Total	43	39	90.6	0		2	4.7	2	4.7
Construction	Total[a]	90	63	70.0	1	1.2	13	14.4	13	14.4
Domestic	Male	49	38	77.6	0		3	6.1	8	16.3
Service	Female	37	26	70.3	0		5	13.5	6	16.2
	Total	86	64	74.4	0		8	9.3	14	16.3
Furniture	Male	14	12	85.8	0		1	7.1	1	7.1
	Female	2	2	100.0	0		0		0	
	Total	16	14	87.4	0		1	6.3	1	6.3
Homemaking	Male	5	0		0		2	40.0	3	60.0
	Female	110	58	52.7	0		27	24.6	25	22.7
	Total	115	58	50.4	0		29	25.2	28	24.4
Hotel and	Male	205	172	83.9	0		10	4.9	23	11.2
Restaurant	Female	70	65	92.8	0		2	2.9	3	4.3
	Total	275	237	86.2	0		12	4.4	26	9.4
Medical	Male	16	11	68.8	0		5	31.2	0	
Service	Female	56	56	100.0	0		0		0	
	Total	72	67	93.1	0		5	6.9	0	
Personal	Male	32	30	93.7	0		0		2	6.3
Service	Female	32	31	96.9	0		0		1	3.1
	Total	64	61	95.3	0		0		3	4.7
Retail	Male	102	90	88.2	1	0.9	2	2.0	9	8.9
Trade	Female	34	32	94.1	0		0		2	5.9
	Total	136	122	89.7	1	0.7	2	1.5	11	8.1
Miscellaneous	Male	239	186	77.8	0		29	12.1	24	10.1
	Female	52	40	77.0	0		3	15.3	4	7.2
	Total	291	226	77.7	0		37	12.7	28	9.6
Totals	Male	977	787	80.5	4	0.4	84	8.6	102	10.5
	Female	428	341	79.7	0		45	10.5	42	9.8
	TOTAL	1405	1128	80.2	4	0.2	129	9.2	144	10.4

[a] In the categories Automobile and Construction all of the clients were male.

Cleaning and Pressing and Laundry Occupations. Forty-three clients, 18 male and 25 female, secured employment in this category. Those trained for the specific job comprised 90.6 percent of the total. Two had trained in unrelated jobs and two others received no specific job training. None of the group had been trained in another job in the same occupational subdivision.

Construction Occupations. All of the 90 construction employees were male. Seventy percent (63 clients) had received training for the specific job on which they were employed. Only one was trained on a related construction job. Thirteen, or 14.4 percent, had training in another occupational area, and the same number had received no job training prior to employment.

Domestic Service Occupations. Domestic service occupations provided initial employment for 86 clients, 49 male and 37 female. Job training for the specific job has been received by 74.4 percent. None were trained on some other domestic service job. Training on an unrelated job had been provided to 9.3 percent, and 16.3 percent had received no specific job training.

Furniture Occupations. Fourteen males and two females were employed on jobs relating to the furniture industry. All except two of the males were trained for the specific job they held. This accounted for 87.4 percent of the total. Of the other two, one had been trained on an unrelated job and the other had received no specific job training.

Homemaking Occupations. Two types of clients were included in this category, homemakers and unpaid family workers. Five males were unpaid family workers, two of whom had received job training in another area. The other three had received no job training. Seventy-nine of the 110 females had established their own homes. Of the total group, 50.4 percent had been trained to be homemakers. Another 25.2 percent had been trained for a job in another field of work. The other 24.2 percent had received no job training.

Hotel and Restaurant Occupations. Two hundred and seventy-five clients were employed in hotel and restaurant occupations. Of this group, 86.2 percent had been trained for the specific job. None were trained on another job in this field. Four and four-tenths percent were trained in an unrelated field, and 9.4 percent received no job training.

Medical Service Occupations. All of the 72 employed in medical service had received some job training. Five, or 6.9 percent, were trained on a job outside the area, while 93.1 percent were trained for the job on which employed. No one was trained on another job in the field.

Personal Service Occupations. Sixty-four clients, equally divided as to sex, were closed on personal service occupations. Three of these received no specific job training. The other 61, or 95.3 percent, were trained for the specific job on which they were employed.

Retail Trade Occupations. The retail trades provided jobs for 136 clients 102 males and 34 females. One had been trained for a job in this area on which he was not employed. Two were trained in an unrelated occupational area, and 11 had received no job training. The remaining 122, or 89.7 percent, were employed on jobs for which they had been trained.

Miscellaneous Occupations. The miscellaneous jobs were those which could not be classified under any of the eleven major groups or were involved only a few times. Two hundred and ninety-one clients were employed on those jobs. Of this number, 226 (77.7 percent) were employed on jobs for which they received training. Thirty-seven (12.7 percent) were trained on unrelated jobs. The other 28 (9.6 percent) had received no job training.

Out of the total of 1405 clients, only four had received training on a different job in the occupational area of the job on which they were closed. There were 129 who were trained for a job in an occupational area entirely unrelated to the one in which they secured employment. This group comprised 9.2 percent of the sample. One hundred and forty-five, 10.4 percent, had received no specific job training for the job on which they were closed.

There was very little difference between the sexes in the percentage that had been trained for the specific job on which employed (males, 80.5 percent; females, 79.7 percent). The percentages of those trained for the specific job on which employed ranged from 50.4 for homemaking occupations to 95.3 for personal service occupations. The percentages for clients who had received no specific job training before closure ranged from nine in the medical service occupations to 24.4 in the homemaking occupations.

Conclusions

The findings of this investigation appear to warrant the following conclusions:

1. It is possible, to a large degree, to determine which jobs can be performed by mentally retarded youth and to secure job training in these occupational areas.
2. For the most part, it has been possible to secure job training in occupational areas which offer future employment.
3. It has been possible to place 80 percent of the students in jobs for which they have been trained.

4. Clients who were placed on jobs for which they were not given specific training were usually employed in an occupational area unrelated to the area in which they were trained.

5. Ten percent of the students had needed only counseling, guidance, and direct job placement in order to become productively employed.

6. The percentage of closures who had received specific job training for the job on which employed was influenced by the nature of the job.

7. The opportunities for training and employment were equally available to both sexes.

REFERENCES

STRICKLAND, C. G. Job training placement for retarded youth. *Exceptional Children* 31 (1964): 83-86.

US DEPARTMENT OF LABOR. *Dictionary of Occupational Titles.* (2nd edition) Washington: US Government Printing Office, 1949.

Conwell G. Strickland is Professor of Education, Baylor University, Waco, Texas, and Vernon M. Arrell is Consultant, Vocational Rehabilitation Division, Texas Education Agency, Austin. This study was supported by a grant from the Baylor University Research Fund.

27.
Trends and Issues in Special Education for the Mentally Retarded
PHILIP ROOS

What new abilities and skills will be required of teachers of retarded children to meet the changing demands described in this article?

The past 20 years have witnessed a great expansion of educational services for the retarded. Goldberg (1969) reports expansion of education for children in residential schools of 100 percent and an increase of 400 percent for children enrolled in public schools. A 1966 survey (Mackie, 1969) concluded that 540,000 children were enrolled in special education programs for the retarded, including 140,000 served in public high schools. By 1967, the total number served had increased to 677,000, of which 9,000 were classified as trainable (President's Committee on Mental Retardation, 1967). Yet is is estimated that only half of the retarded children in need of special education are currently being served (Goldberg, 1969). In 1968 some parts of the country were meeting the educational needs of less than 15 percent of retarded children (President's Committee on Mental Retardation, 1969).

In 1962, 20,000 teachers were teaching retarded children in special classes, but the need was estimated to be for 75,000 (President's Panel on Mental Retardation, 1962). The situation had only slightly improved by 1969, when 34,000 teachers were employed in public and residential schools for the retarded and the need was estimated at 93,000 (Goldberg, 1969).

These alarming shortages of vital services reflect the fact that children's basic right to education has not yet been generally accepted. Many children are still denied services simply on the basis that they are retarded. A 1962 survey (LaCrosse, 1964) revealed that only 16 states had mandatory legislation regarding public school classes for educable mentally retarded children, and only 13 had such legislation for trainable mentally retarded children.

The 1969 decision of the Third Judicial District Court in Utah may become a landmark as a basis for requiring educational services for the retarded by concluding that: "It is ... abundantly clear that the (mentally retarded) plaintiff children must be provided a free and equal education within the school districts of which they are residents. ..." This conclusion

From *Education and Training of the Mentally Retarded* 5 (April, 1970): 51-61. Reprinted by permission of the author and *Education and Training of the Mentally Retarded.*

is in complete harmony with the position of consumer groups, such as the National Association for Retarded Children and the International League of Societies for the Mentally Handicapped, that retarded persons have the same basic rights as all citizens.

Current Trends

DEVELOPMENTAL MODEL

Most professionals working in the area of mental retardation have adopted a "developmental model" of retardation. According to this model, retarded children are considered to be developing individuals with potential for growth and learning. Even the most profoundly retarded are assumed to have some capacity for development. This model, which supports the establishment of training and educational services, can be contrasted with other popular models of retardation which favor destructive strategies for dealing with the retarded (Wolfensberger, 1969). According to the "medical model," for example, retardation is interpreted as a disease best served by a hospital or clinic. This orientation tends to generate submissiveness, passivity, and hopelessness in the individual while insuring a management monopoly for physicians and related professionals (Roos, 1969). The model of the retarded as a "menace" continues to operate against integration of retarded persons into community life and continues to be a basis for denying retarded children and adults access to generic services. The "sub-human model" of retardation has fostered dehumanizing conditions (Vail, 1967) in many residential facilities by suggesting that retarded persons do not share the same basic feelings, sensitivities, and needs with the rest of society.

Concern with these destructive models of mental retardation has been reflected in the enthusiastic endorsement by many professionals of the "principle of normalization" (Bank-Mikkelsen, 1969; Nirje, 1969). According to Nirje: "The normalization principle means making available to mentally retarded persons patterns and conditions of everyday life which are as close as possible to the norms and patterns of the mainstream of society [p. 181]." Although this principle is particularly relevant to residential services, it is also applicable to other community services, including educational programs. It would suggest that whenever possible, the use of generic services would be preferable to specialized services for the retarded.

SCOPE OF SPECIAL EDUCATION

Educational programs for the retarded have primarily focused on the school-aged child. The traditional classifications of "slow learner," "educable," and "trainable" specifically refer to children of school age (Goldberg, 1969). Yet there is increasing recognition of the importance of broadening the scope of special education to include all levels of retardation as well as all age levels.

Increasing evidence of the importance of early cognitive stimulation emphasizes the need to expand educational programs into the preschool years. In view of the retarded child's particular handicap, programs of early education seem particularly crucial if the individual is to be given the opportunity of reaching his maximum potential (Gordon & Wilkerson, 1966; Weikart & Lambie, 1968). Yet in 1948 no preschool classes were reported, and by 1966 only 1,400 retarded children were reported enrolled in such classes (Mackie, 1969).

The Handicapped Children's Early Education Assistance Act of 1968 (P.L. 90-538) was designed in recognition of the lack of viable models for education of preschool handicapped children. According to the US Department of Health, Education, and Welfare (1968):

Research conducted recently indicates at age 4, a child has already developed 50 percent of total intellectual capacity as an adult; by the age of 8, he has attained 80 percent of his capacity. The best time to attack a child's mental and emotional handicaps appears to be the period from birth through the early childhood years [p. 2].

This Act authorized only $1 million for fiscal year 1969, primarily as planning funds for demonstration projects. Authorized appropriations for 1970 ($10 million) and 1971 ($12 million) were designed to establish 75–100 centers. It is too early to detect a significant impact from this program, but competition for the very limited 1969 funds indicates a major interest in developing these types of programs.

To date the majority of early education programs for retarded children have been operated by local associations for retarded children. Yet operation of these programs tends to violate the policy of the National Association for Retarded Children and of the International League of Societies for the Mentally Handicapped, that services should be obtained rather than provided by voluntary associations (Roos, 1969).

Expansion of education programs for retarded adults has probably lagged even behind the preschool programs. Although the validity of "continuing education" for normal adults seems now generally accepted, the relative lack of such programs suggests a continuing belief that the capacity to learn—at least for persons with subnormal intelligence—somehow ceases if a person is over 20 years old. Yet the rapidly changing environment in which most retarded adults must live necessitates continuing education to insure competence in handling problems of daily life.

In general, retarded adults have been assigned to vocational training programs aimed at developing specific work skills or to "activity centers," designed primarily for those considered too handicapped for sheltered workshop placement (DiMichael, 1959). Most activity centers are operated by local associations for retarded children, and many furnish only limited services (Cortazzo, 1968).

Just as education programs are gradually expanding to serve a wider age range, they are also expanding to include the more seriously retarded. Less emphasis on academic skills as the sole responsibility of educators and development of nonverbal teaching methods are contributing to the establishment of education programs for the severely and profoundly retarded (Hollis & Gorton, 1967). Yet there still seems to be a negative relationship between teacher sophistication and degree of student impairment; the more seriously impaired students are taught by the least skilled teachers. Special educators still seem to equate education primarily with the teaching of academic skills.

SUPPLEMENTING TEACHERS

In recognition of the serious shortage of trained teachers, increasing interest has been focused in supplementing professional teachers so as to increase their effectiveness. One method is to involve persons with less sophisticated training in the teaching process (Bowman & Klopf, 1968; Frost & Rowland, 1970). For example, "teacher aides" are becoming common and "master teachers" are being used in a supervising and training capacity (Cruickshank & Haring, 1957; Esbensen, 1966; Blessing, 1967). Volunteers—often mothers of the students being served—are working primarily in preschool, daycare, and adult programs. Trained volunteers have been successful in working with blind and deaf retarded children, conducting language development programs, and monitoring programed instruction (Ludtke, 1969). Involvement of parents as key members of the educational team has been found particularly beneficial (Wildman, 1965; Weikart & Lambie, 1968). For example, Terdal and Buell (1969) reported successfully educating parents in behavior shaping techniques which enabled them to eliminate inappropriate behavior and to develop skills in their child at home. Likewise McKenzie, Clark, Wolf, Kothera, and Benson (1968) described participation of parents in a classroom behavior shaping program.

Teachers are not only being supplemented by other persons, but by mechanical devices as well. The "talking typewriter" (Moore, 1964) has now been used extensively with retarded children and the concept of the autotelic responsive environment on which it is based is being applied in classroom situations (Meier, Mimnicht, & McAfee, 1968). Programed instruction—often using "teaching machines"—continues to be a promising approach to maximizing teacher effectiveness (e.g., Birnbrauer, Bijou, Wolf, & Kidder, 1965; Bijou, 1966; Thomas, 1968). Audiovisual techniques, including films, tape recordings, and television, have been reported to be particularly useful (e.g., Goldstein, 1964; Smith, 1966; Lombardi & Poole, 1968). Much of the specialized equipment becoming available to educators who work with retarded students has been purchased with federal funds derived from Title I of the Elementary and Secondary Education Act (US Department of Health, Education, and Welfare, 1969).

Successful attempts to supplement professional teachers should not be interpreted as minimizing the importance of skilled, trained educators. There is still a need for more teachers. Though new approaches seem successful in optimizing the teacher's impact they cannot replace the teacher himself.

PRACTICAL EDUCATION

Another area of general agreement among educators is to orient educational programs toward practical aspects of life. Traditional academic content is emphasized less than prevocational and vocational preparation (Peck, 1966). School programs are being integrated with vocational rehabilitation services (Younie, 1966; Herk, 1967), and appropriate materials are being developed (Younie, 1967). Combining classroom and work oriented activities has proven to be a successful approach to vocational preparation and work study programs have now been adopted by most states (Shawn, 1964; Peck, 1966). There is increasing recognition that prevocational work study programs must be introduced several years prior to expected graduation from special education programs (O'Connor & Tizard, 1956). Sheltered workshops have been assimilated into the school setting to facilitate transition from the classroom to a working environment (Hill, 1952).

Emphasis on the practical aspects of education has not been limited to vocational preparation of mildly retarded children. Classes for moderately retarded and for very young children are likewise stressing practical aspects of education (Kirk, 1962). Rather than emphasizing acquisition of traditional reading skills, for example, children are taught recognition of signs judged important in daily living. Youngsters are taught skills which have direct value to them or to the school, such as mending clothes, preparing and serving food, or laundering clothing. In short, special classes are attempting to prepare students for productive life rather than for limited academic excellence. More attention is being given to the development of social skills as a prerequisite to successful community adjustment (Goldstein, 1962; Dunn, 1964). Evidence now strongly suggests the vocational success is dependent on social skills (Johnson & Kirk, 1951). Likewise, appropriate use of spare time is becoming a major program objective. Data indicate that inability to find acceptable leisure time activities is a frequent cause for failure to maintain a successful community adjustment (Peck, 1966).

EVALUATIVE TECHNIQUES

Special educators are becoming increasingly disenchanted with evaluative approaches based on traditional intelligence testing (Wolman, 1965; Bechtold, 1967; US Department of Health, Education, & Welfare, 1968). Criticisms have focused primarily on the following issues: (a) performance on popular intelligence tests is affected by variables judged more or less independent of intelligence, such as motivation, sociocultural background, verbal skill, testtaking attitude, and sensory impairment; (b) results derived from most intelligence tests, particularly the intelligence quotient, are not constant throughout an individual's life, but rather tend to fluctuate, at times rather markedly; (c) intelligence tests measure the product of learning rather than cognitive skill or learning capacity; (d) most intelligence tests, by yielding a single numerical score, obliterate the uniqueness of the individual and fail to supply the basis for planning programs aimed at capitalizing on strengths and remedying weaknesses; and (e) most current tasks are poorly suited to very young children and to nonverbal subjects.

Dissatisfaction with traditional evaluative approaches has led to new evaluative strategies. Nonlanguage tests and "culture-fair" tests have been designed to overcome cultural and verbal biases of traditional tests. Instruments yielding a profile of subscores, such as the Illinois Test of Psycholinguistic Abilities (McCarthy & Kirk, 1963), have been heralded as providing a more meaningful basis for program planning than the single I.Q. Likewise the recently developed Adaptive Behavior Check List (Leland, et al., 1968) is proposed as an improvement over the Vineland Social Maturity Scale.

Some approaches to evaluation are placing less emphasis upon the precise, quantified psychometric approach in favor of qualitative observation of performance aimed at assessing the nature of cognitive functioning in the individual. Piaget's approach to cognitive functioning is gaining popularity as an assessment technique, although extensive validity and reliability data are not yet available (Nelson, 1968).

Another qualitative approach gaining popularity is based on determining the readiness of children to establish conditioned responses (Friedlander, McCarthy, & Soforenko, 1967). Operant conditioning situations have been successfully applied to young nonverbal retarded children. These techniques are based on the assumption that the success in learning simple responses through operant techniques relates significantly to learning more complex responses and should be useful in predicting the subject's eventual learning potential. Although the advantage of the evaluative strategies over the traditional psychometric approaches has not yet been demonstrated, continuing experimentation and innovation certainly seem warranted.

Innovations

Unfortunately, evaluation is not the only area of disappointment in the field of special education. A lack of success with current teaching strategies is a serious basis for concern (Kirk, 1962). Little innovation has been noted in curriculum or teaching methodology.

Use of Old Techniques

Approaches which were developed decades ago seem to be regaining popularity. There has been a renewal of enthusiasm, for example, for the Montessori approach to education (Argy, 1965; Gitter, 1967; Orem, 1969) as well as for Piaget's approach to cognitive development (Levitt, 1968). Some of the most encouraging recent work has been based on these approaches. Kirk's emphasis on a remediation approach to education for the retarded continues to enjoy considerable support (Kirk & Bateman, 1962).

OPERANT CONDITIONING PRINCIPLES

Probably the most innovative approach to special education in recent years has been the application of operant conditioning principles (in themselves by no means a recent development) to the education of retarded children (Bijou, 1966). Operant conditioning is applicable to all levels of retardation, including non-verbal and behaviorally disturbed subjects. This approach is useful in developing skills as well as in modifying attitude and motivation (Whelan & Haring, 1966). It has been particularly helpful in altering behavior which would typically lead to exclusion from the classroom (Perline & Levinsky, 1968). Controlled studies are beginning to emerge suggesting that operant procedures may be significantly more successful than traditional approaches with certain types of retarded subjects (Roos, 1970).

One advantage of operant procedures is that they are applicable to a wide variety of subjects including very young and very seriously impaired subjects. They can also be implemented in almost any setting and with relative ease they can be taught to unsophisticated persons and to parents.

REINFORCEMENT

The use of tokens as reinforcers has proved particularly applicable in the classroom (Birnbrauer, Wolf, Kidder, & Tague, 1965; O'Leary & Becker, 1967), but more sophisticated equipment, such as teaching machines and "time out rooms" are being used with increasing frequency (Patterson, 1965).

These innovations in teaching methods have not yet been paralleled by significant advances in the content of teaching (Lorenz, 1953). A recent survey (Fuchigami, 1969) suggests little innovation in curriculum for the retarded, with the possible exception of experimental projects at Teachers College, Columbia University (Connor & Talbot, 1964) and Yeshiva University (Goldstein & Mischio, 1967).

Some Unresolved Issues

INTEGRATION-SEGREGATION

The question of whether to separate retarded children from normal children in schools remains a controversial issue (Dunn, 1964). Positions on this issue vary from segregation into special schools devoted entirely to retarded students to complete integration of retarded students into normal classes (Plowman, Hunter, & Gulliford, 1968; Schwarz, 1968). Intermediate strategies are more prevalent, and generally consist of operating special classes within a public school. Frequently, retarded students are segregated into special classes for certain facets of the curriculum (usually "academic" subjects) while they are integrated into normal classes for other aspects of the curriculum such as physical education and arts and crafts. Tutors or other specialized staff may supplement the regular classes (Dunn, 1964; Guerin, 1967).

A basic distinction is usually drawn between educable and trainable children. Based on the assumption that trainable pupils are usually destined to remain relatively segregated from normal society throughout their lives, they tend to be handled in segregated classes or special schools (Katz, 1967). It has been agreed, as a matter of fact, that public schools are inappropriate settings for trainable students (Goldberg & Cruickshank, 1958). Educable students, on the other hand are more likely to be integrated with their normal peers, since they are expected to function within general society. Furthermore, trainable children are more likely to need specialized services than educables, and hence centralized facilities are more appropriate to develop these specialized services.

Arguments favoring segregation include: (a) it facilitates homogeneous groupings of students with similar disabilities and needs; (b) it allows development of specialized staffs and resources; (c) it offers opportunities for training specialized personnel; (d) it facilitates individualizing special problems; (e) it increases program visibility; (f) it allows development of supportive services and programs; and (g) it improves students' self-esteem by decreasing the frequency of failure experiences.

Arguments supporting integration include: (a) it harmonizes with the principle of normalization by including the retarded in the mainstream of life; (b) it encourages use of generic services; (c) it facilitates generalizing from the classroom situation to other situations; (d) it improves students' self-image by not stigmatizing them as being "special" or "different"; (e) it minimizes the danger of self-fulfilling prophecies derived from labeling and segregating students into classes with limited goals; (f) it is less expensive than specialized services, and it generally allows for wider geographic distribution of services and hence greater accessibility.

Research evidence regarding the relative merits of these strategies remains largely equivocal. Classes for trainable students have usually demonstrated progress in social variables while demonstrating little or no value with regard to development of academic skills (Dunn, 1964). Some studies suggest that educable pupils in segregated classes may show significantly better social adjustment than those taught in integrated classes, while the latter show significantly more academic progress (Kirk, 1962; Dunn, 1964).

Although the issue of integration and segregation remains unsolved, compromise solutions are generally being adopted with apparent success. There is need for further research, carefully evaluating subject variables and refining dependent measures.

SOCIETY CENTERED EDUCATION

Another unresolved issue revolves around the basic locus of control for the education process (Goldberg, 1969). Some have argued that education should be child centered in that each student should be given the opportunity to develop his own goals and to discover his own interests. Others have endorsed a society centered approach, based on the premise that education should strive to mold students into the type of person deemed desirable by the society of which they are members, a process referred to as "adultation" by Doll (1963).

A similar issue has been recognized with regard to programs of early educational intervention. Society centered programs, in which efforts are directed at shaping young children into culturally sanctioned molds, have been contrasted with parent oriented approaches stressing early education by parents (Weikart & Lambie, 1968; Roos, 1969). Roos (1969) concludes his discussion of this issue by stating:

For those societies which cherish individualism and self-determination, the concept of governmental agencies shaping future generations through manipulation of the impressionable young child might be less than tasteful. In such societies, strategies to modify parental child rearing practices—including development of educational skills—might receive higher priority [p. 37].

Conclusion

In summary, although there are more special education programs for the retarded, an alarming number of retarded children remain without educational services. Most professionals seem to agree on the following important points: (a) more retarded children and adults should be included in education programs; (b) a developmental model of retardation is better suited to educational programs than other prevailing models; (c) special education should encompass a broader age range and a wider range of handicap than are currently being served; (d) teachers can effectively be supplemented with less sophisticated personnel and with mechanical devices; (3) special education should be oriented toward practical goals, including vocational preparation; and (f) popular evaluative techniques have serious shortcomings.

Theoretical and methodological innovations have been disappointing. Application of operant conditioning principles seems to be the major new approach to special education. The relative merits of integration and segregation are still being debated, as is the issue of deciding where the locus of control of the education process should be. Further research should help resolve these issues and lead to innovative approaches to educating the retarded.

REFERENCES

ARGY, W. P. Montessori versus Orthodox. A study to determine the relative improvement of the preschool child with brain damage trained by one of the two methods. *Rehabilitation Literature* 26 (1965): 294-304.

BANK-MIKKELSEN, N. E. A metropolitan area in Denmark: Copenhogen. In R. B. Kugel, & W. P. Wolfensberger, eds., *Changing Patterns in Residential Services for the Mentally Retarded.* Washington, D.C.: President's Committee on Mental Retardation, 1969, 229-54.

BECHTOLD, M. L. IQ: Sacred cow or demon. *School and Community* 54 (1967): 15.

BIJOU, S. W. Research in the application of modern behavior theory to the education and training of the retarded. *Community Day Centers for the Mentally Retarded in Illinois*. Springfield, Illinois: Department of Mental Health, 1966, 73-81.

BIRNBRAUER, J. S., BIJOU, S. W., WOLF, M. M., & KIDDER, J. D. Programmed instruction in the classroom. In L. P. Ullman, & L. Krasner, eds., *Case Studies in Behavior Modification*. New York: Holt, Rinehart, & Winston, 1965, pp. 358-63.

BIRNBRAUER, J. S., WOLF, M. M., KIDDER, J. D., & TAGUE, C. Classroom behavior of retarded pupils with token reinforcement. *Journal of Experimental Child Psychology* 2 (1965): 219-35.

BLESSING, K. R. Use of teacher aides in special education: A review and possible applications. *Exceptional Children* 34 (1967): 107-13.

BOWMAN, G. W., & KLOPF, G. J. *New Careers and Roles in the American School*. Washington, D.C.: Final Report for the Office of Economic Opportunity, 1968.

CONNOR, F., & TALBOT, M. *An Experimental Curriculum for Young Mentally Retarded Children*. New York: Bureau of Publications, Teacher College, Columbia University, 1964.

CORTAZZO, A. D. An analysis of activity programs for mentally retarded adults. *Mental Retardation* 3 (1968): 31-34.

CRUICKSHANK, W. M., & HARING, N. G. *A Demonstration: Assistants for Teachers of Exceptional Children*. Syracuse, New York: Syracuse University Press, 1957.

DIMICHAEL, S. G. Vocational rehabilitation and the mentally retarded: A statement of issues. *Preparation of mentally retarded youth for gainful employment*. Washington, D.C.: US Government Printing Office, 1959, 10-19.

DOLL, E. A. Adulation of the special child. *Exceptional Children* 29 (1963): 275-80.

DUNN, I. M. *Exceptional Children in the Schools*. New York: Holt, Rinehart, & Winston, 1964.

ESBENSEN, T. Should teacher aides be more than clerks? *Phi Delta Kappan* 47 (1966): 237.

FRIEDLANDER, B. Z.; MCCARTHY, J. J.; & SOFORENKO, Z. A. Automated psychological evaluation with severely retarded institutionalized infants. *American Journal of Mental Deficiency* 71 (1967): 909-19.

FROST, J. & ROWLAND, G. T. Teaching the disadvantaged. In *Compensatory Programming*. Dubuque, Iowa: Wm. C. Brown Co., 1970, in press.

FUCHIGAMI, R. Emerging curricula for the elementary level educable mentally retarded. *Mental Retardation* 7 (1969): 37-40.

GITTER, L. L. Montessori principles applied in a class of mentally retarded children. *Mental Retardation* 5 (1967): 26-29.

GOLDBERG, I. & CRUICKSHANK, W. M. Trainable but non-educable: whose responsibility? *National Education Association Journal* 47 (1958): 622-23.

GOLDBERG, I. *The Multidimensional Problems and Issues of Educating Retarded Children and Youth*. Paper read at the meeting of the World Mental Health Assembly, Washington, D.C., November, 1969.

GOLDSTEIN, H. & MISCHIO, G. *A research and demonstration project in curriculum and methods of instruction for elementary level mentally retarded children*. Ferkauf Graduate School of Education, Yeshiva University (Final report not ready for distribution).

GORDON, E. W. & WILKERSON, D. A. *Compensatory Education for the Disadvantaged. Program and Practices: Preschool through College*. Princeton, N.J.: College Entrance Examination Board, 1966.

GUERIN, G. R. Special classes or resource rooms? *Mental Retardation* 5 (1967): 40-41.

HERK, I. Developing a vocationally oriented curriculum for the mentally retarded in secondary schools. In *Symposium on habilitating and mentally retarded*. Mankato State College, Mankato, Minnesota, February, 1967, pp. 16-24.

HILL, A. S. *The Forward Look: The Severely Retarded Child Goes to School*. Washington, D.C.: Bulletin No. 11, US Government Printing Office, 1952.

HOLLIS, J. H. & GORTON, C. E. Training severely and profoundly developmentally retarded children. *Mental Retardation* 5 (1967): 20-24.

JOHNSON, G. O. & KIRK, S. A., eds. *Educating the Retarded Child*. Boston: Houghton Mifflin Co., 1951.

KATZ, B. *Meeting the needs of the trainable mentally retarded in a centralized public day school facility through meaningful grouping*. Paper read at the first annual convention of the New York State Association of Teachers of Mentally Handicapped, Inc., November, 1967.

KIRK, S. A. *Educating Exceptional Children*. Boston: Houghton Mifflin Co., 1962.

KIRK, S. A. & BATEMAN, B. Diagnosis and remediation of learning disabilities. *Exceptional Children* 29 (1962): 73-78.

LACROSSE, E. L. *Public School Enrollments for the 1962-63 School Year*. New York: National Association for Retarded Children, 1964.

LELAND, H.; NIHIRA, K.; FOSTER, R.; SHELLHAAS, M.; & KAGIN, E. *Conference on Measurement of Adaptive Behavior: III*. Parsons, Kansas: Parsons State Hospital and Training Center, 1968.

LEVITT, E. VIEWS of cognition in children: "Process" vs. "Product" approach. *Young Children* 23 (1968): 225-32.

LOMBARDI, T. P. & POOLE, R. G. Utilization of videosonic equipment with mentally retarded. *Mental Retardation* 6 (1968): 7-9.

LORENZ, M. H. Follow-up studies of the severely retarded. In M. C. Reynolds, J. R. Kiland & R. E. Ellis, eds., *A Study of Public School Children with Severe Mental Retardation*. St. Paul, Minnesota: Statistical Division, State Department of Education, 1953.

LUDTKE, R. H. & ELLIOT, A. The changing role of volunteers in a residential facility for the mentally retarded. *Mental Retardation* 7 (1969): 13-16.

MACKIE, R. *Special Education in the United States: Statistics 1948-1966*. New York: Teachers College Press, 1969.

McCARTHY, J. J. & KIRK, S. A. *The Construction, Standardization and Statistical Characteristics of the Illinois Test of Psycholinguistic Abilities*. Urbana, Illinois: University of Illinois Press, 1963.

McKENZIE, H. S.; CLARK, M.; WOLF, M. M.; KOTHERA, R.; & BENSON, C. Behavior modification of children with learning disabilities using grades as tokens and allowances as back-up reinforcers. *Exceptional Children* 34 (1968): 745-52.

MEIER, J. H., NIMNICHT, G. P. & McAFEE, O. An autotelic responsive environment nursery school for deprived children. In J. Hellmuth, ed., *Disadvantaged Child*, Vol. II. New York: Brunner/Mazel, 1968, pp. 301-86.

MOORE, O. K. Autotelic responsive environments and exceptional children. In J. Hellmuth, ed., *The Special Child in Century 21*. Seattle, Washington: Special Child Publications, 1964, 87-138.

NELSON, K. E. Organization of visual-tracking responses in human infants. *Journal of Experimental Child Psychology* 6 (1968): 194-201.

NIRJE, B. The normalization principle and its human management implications. In R. B. Kugel & W. P. Wolfensberger, eds., *Changing Patterns in Residential Services for the Mentally Retarded*. Washington, D.C.: President's Committee on Mental Retardation, 1969, pp. 181-95.

O'CONNOR, N. & TIZARD, J. *The Social Problem of Mental Deficiency*. London: Pergammon Press, 1956.

O'LEARY, K. D. & BECKER, W. C. Behavior modification of an adjustment class: a token reinforcement program. *Exceptional Children* 33 (1967): 637-42.

OREM, R. C., ed., *Montessori and the Special Child*. New York: G. P. Putnam's Sons, 1969.

PATTERSON, G. R. An application of conditioning techniques to the control of a hyperactive child. In L. P. Ullman & L. Krasner, eds., *Case Studies in Behavior Modifications* New York: Holt, Rinehart, & Winston, 1965, 370-75.

PECK, J. R. The work-study program—a critical phase of preparation. *Education and Training of the Mentally Retarded* 1 (1966): 68-73.

PERLINE, I. H. & LEVINSKY, D. Controlling maladaptive classroom behavior in the severely retarded. *American Journal of Mental Deficiency* 73 (1968): 74-78.

PLOWMAN, G.; HUNTER, R. N.; & GULLIFORD, R. More thoughts on segregation of ESN pupils. *Remedial Education* 3 (1968): 4-8.

President's Committee on Mental Retardation. MR 67: *A First Report to the President on the Nation's Progress and Remaining Great Needs in the Campaign to Combat Mental Retardation*. Washington, D.C.: US Government Printing Office, 1967.

President's Committee on Mental Retardation. MR 69: *Toward Progress: The Story of a Decade*. Washington, D.C.: US Government Printing Office, 1969.

President's Panel on Mental Retardation. *Report to the President. A Proposed Program for National Action to Combat Mental Retardation.* Washington, D.C.: US Government Printing Office, 1962.

Roos, P. Parent organizations. In Wortis, J., ed., *Mental Retardation: An Annual Review.* New York: Grune & Stratton, Inc., in press.

Roos, P. Current issues in residential care with special reference to the problems of institutional care. In *Symposium on Residential Care for the Mentally Retarded.* Brussels, Belgium: International League of Societies for the Mentally Handicapped, 1969.

Roos, P. Opening address: National conference on residential care. New York: National Association for Retarded Children, 1969, pp. 2-14.

Roos, P. Evaluation of operant conditioning with institutionalized retarded children. *American Journal of Mental Deficiency* 74 (1970): 325-30.

Schwarz, R. H. Toward a meaningful education for the retarded adolescent. *Mental Retardation* 6 (1968): 34-35.

Shawn, B. Review of a work experience program. *Mental Retardation* 2 (1964): 360-64.

Smith, C. The tape recorder in the EMR classroom. *Mental Retardation* 4 (1966): 33-35.

Terdal, L. & Buell, J. Parent education in managing retarded children with behavior deficits and inappropriate behaviors. *Mental Retardation* 7 (1969): 10-13.

Thomas, D. J. Programmed learning and the severely subnormal. In *Studies on the Mentally Handicapped.* London, England: Edward Arnold, 1968, pp. 162-74.

United States Department of Health, Education, and Welfare. Secretary's Committee on Mental Retardation. Handicapped Children's Early Education Assistance Act of 1968, P. L. 90-538. *Programs for the Handicapped.* Washington, D.C., 1968.

United States Department of Health, Education, and Welfare. Secretary's Committee on Mental Retardation. Education programs for handicapped children in state-operated or supported schools. Progress report, 1968. *Programs for the Handicapped.* Washington, D.C., 1969.

Wail, D. J. *Dehumanization and the Institutional Career.* Springfield, Illinois: Charles C Thomas, 1967.

Weikart, D. P. & Lambie, D. Z. Preschool intervention through a home teaching program. In J. Hellmuth, ed., *Disadvantaged Child,* Vol. II. New York: Brummer/Mazel, 1968, pp. 437-95.

Whelan, R. J. & Haring, N. G. Modification and maintenance of behavior through systematic application of consequences. *Exceptional Children* 32 (1966): 281-89.

Wildman, P. R. A parent education program for parents of mentally retarded children. *Mental Retardation* 3 (1965): 17-19.

Wolfensberger, W. P. The origin and nature of our institutional models. In R. B. Kugel & W. P. Wolfensberger, eds., *Changing Patterns in Residential Services for the Mentally Retarded.* Washington, D.C.: President's Committee on Mental Retardation, 1969, pp. 63-171.

Wolman, B. B., ed. *Handbook of Clinical Psychology.* New York: McGraw-Hill, 1965.

Younie, W. J. Increasing cooperation between school programs for the retarded and vocational rehabilitation services: An experimental teaching approach. *Mental Retardation* 4 (1966): 9-14.

Younie, W. J. Developing instructional materials for vocational education of the retarded. In G. E. Ayerers, ed., *New Directions in Habilitating the Mentally Retarded.* Elwyn, Pennsylvania: Elwyn Institute, pp. 67-72.

Philip Roos is Executive Director, National Association for Retarded Children, New York, N. Y.

Seven

Children
with
Auditory
Handicaps

The development of communication is the major
task before a teacher of deaf children. Hence,
this chapter will center its attention upon this
highly specialized problem. There is, and has
been for years, a great deal of controversy over
the various approaches to instruction, which
center primarily around a strict oral system vs.
"manual" or non-oral approaches, and combinations of both systems. An attempt has been made
to include both points of view in the readings.

Audrey Simmons, in the first article, analyzes
the linguistic components of language and applies the oral philosophy to the education of
young deaf children. Her excellent description is
very representative of current trends in language
instruction.

Howard Hofsteater, a deaf teacher of the deaf,
in the second article describes how his parents
taught him reading and language as a young
deaf child. His anecdotal account, which was
written while he was a graduate student at the
University of Illinois, is unusual in that Hofsteater
demonstrated a proficiency in reading and
writing equivalent to a superior hearing person.
There is no doubt that he possessed unusual mental ability and capacity for self-education,
although it is reported that he had no speechreading ability and no oral speech. He successfully completed a master's degree by sitting beside
a student in class who took good notes and
by having the instructors write out for him what
he was supposed to learn in order to pass the
examinations in the courses. The acquisition of
language comprehension by most deaf children
and youth is relatively poor, and this results in

limited achievement in all the language arts. Hofsteater presents an interesting personal testimonial of how he developed high proficiency in language through reading, which he learned from his mother through finger spelling. Some teachers of the deaf would have reservations regarding the general use of the procedures he describes.

Alice Streng's article describes in concrete fashion how the subject matter fields may contribute to the development of the language arts skills of the deaf. The need for interrelating all aspects of the curriculum in individualized, sequential steps is clearly demonstrated.

Currently there is much interest in an instructional approach commonly referred to as *total communication* for the deaf. This procedure combines elements of the oral and the manual approaches into a single system. Richard Brill argues the case for total communication in his article in this chapter.

In a single page Richard McElwain, a college student who is deaf, sets forth some convictions regarding communication which he wrote while a student at the National Technical Institute for the Deaf. His views and those presented in the preceding articles in Chapter Seven represent a balanced treatment of the major problem—communication—in this area of special education.

The double handicap of deafness and blindness provides the most challenging instructional problem in the field of special education. While the hearing of the blind compensates in a major way for the absence of sight and the sight of the deaf compensates for the absence of hearing, the double handicap permits no such compensation and greatly complicates the teaching and learning process. Lars Guldager, of the Perkins School for the Blind, outlines the educational needs of the deaf-blind child in the final article of the chapter. The Perkins School has been engaged for many years in training programs for such children and has been recognized as a leader in the field.

Finally, Thomas Hopkins Gallaudet is profiled as a pioneer in this field of special education. He helped to establish the first American school for the deaf and, along with his sons, greatly influenced the early development of the education of the deaf in the United States.

Thomas Hopkins Gallaudet
1787-1815

MINISTER
EDUCATOR
ADMINISTRATOR

Gallaudet College for the Deaf, Washington, D.C., is the only college for the deaf in the world. Few realize that it was named after Thomas Hopkins Gallaudet, a pioneer in the education of the deaf.

Thomas Hopkins Gallaudet was born in Pennsylvania in 1787. He was educated at Yale and for a time clerked in a law office. In 1812 he went to Andover Theological Seminary and was graduated two years later. During his Andover days he became acquainted with a deaf child and attempted to teach her, since no special schools were available at that time in the United States. His interest in the problems of the education of the deaf eventually caused him to go to Europe to investigate the oral method, which was being used in Scotland where Thomas Braidwood in Edinburgh was reputedly getting good results. Braidwood was secretive about his methods, however, so Gallaudet crossed the Channel to France, where he received assistance and encouragement from educators. He studied at the Institut des Sourdes-Muets and received instruction in manual rather than oral methods. Upon his return to the United States, he established the first American residential school for the deaf, the American Asylum for the Education and Instruction of the Deaf and Dumb at Hartford, Connecticut (1817).

Gallaudet served as the first principal of this school, which opened with an enrollment of only six pupils. Now known as the American School for the Deaf, it is a thriving state residential school enrolling about 500 students.

28.
Teaching Aural Language*
AUDREY SIMMONS-MARTIN

As you read this article, consider the information and skills required of a teacher of the deaf which are not commonly possessed by the regular teacher.

Speech and language are not synonymous terms. Emphasis in teaching the deaf child should be on communication rather than on precision in the early stages of instruction. In teaching aural language it is well to remember the importance of timing, intonation, and rhythm. It is better for teachers to use simple sentences than single words. Intonation is particularly important, as it can change the meaning of a sentence. At the same time, consideration has to be given to syntax. We hear, speak, and respond to language all at once, and all of a piece, so it must be taught this way—particularly to hearing impaired children.

When we begin the education of the hearing impaired child we are besieged by a battery of questions from parents. "Will Johnny talk?" and "When will he speak?" occur with the greatest frequency. With something akin to cathechismal acceptance, they listen to our perennial response, "Of course Johnny will talk, *after* he has acquired language."

When the parents read the literature appropriate to their needs they find the areas of speech and language treated almost as if it were speech *or* language. In fact, there are those who would have us believe that one can exist without the other.

Articles on the subject of language of the deaf tend to dismiss the spoken aspect completely and direct all the attention to the grammar of the written form, which has been shown by psychologists to be of very complex nature for hearing children. On the other hand, if the article that deals with the vocal production of language (speech) appears in our journals, it usually treats only articulatory problems of speech. We may be fostering the speech-language dichotomy by studying only those aspects of language which lend themselves to the tools we have available to measure

Reprinted by permission from *The Volta Review,* 70:1 (January, 1968): 26-30. Copyright © The Alexander Graham Bell Association for the Deaf, Washington, D.C., 1968.

*This talk was delivered at the Southwest Regional Meeting of the Alexander Graham Bell Association for the Deaf, held in Dallas, Texas, Oct. 6-7, 1967.

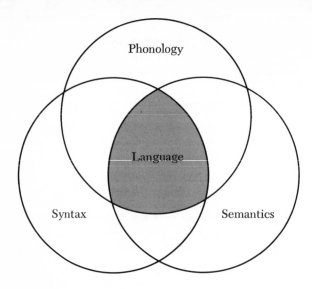

Figure 1. LINGUISTIC COMPONENTS OF LANGUAGE

them, and by dismissing the several aspects that force us to consider the interrelation of the two, because they are elusive.

The concept that language and speech are separate entities may also be inferred when we set aside certain periods for training of speech. Frequently, individual speech teachers concentrate on articulation of single sounds and single words to the exclusion of other aspects. Other teachers may do auditory training in other periods when nonlinguistic noise-generating instruments (bells, whistles, records) provide the stimuli.

The linguists have been telling us for some time that language is both an auditory and vocal process which incorporates phonology, syntax, and semantics as shown in Figure 1.

Linguists agree that the *spoken language* is the language and that its most stable features are phonologic. Syntax and grammar are constantly undergoing change. Look at what is happening to the word *like*. "Winstons taste good like a cigarette should," while ungrammatical, is still language. Certainly the English language is abused, if not changed, with every issue of *Time Magazine.*

Phonology

Consider the three features which make up the phonologic portion of the interrelated aspects of language as shown in Figure 2.

Phonology is the sound or vocal system of the language. It includes the smallest unit in the process as well as the largest. Since children learn from the general to the specific, the smallest units are usually the last to

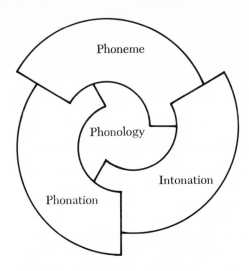

Figure 2. COMPONENTS OF PHONOLOGY

develop in their repertory and with hearing children are not perfected until they are 7 or 8 years old.

Phonemes

The smallest units are the phonemes of the language, which in our case is the English of our region. There are approximately 46 of these phonemes or speech elements which follow a predictable pattern. For example, children deduce at an early age that a vowel usually follows a consonant. Indeed, they have absorbed sufficient information that they observe the rule without ever knowing it exists.

They know, also, that a number of these units must be said in a given interval of time. Frequently, they misarticulate the sounds while giving appropriate timing to their utterances.

Deaf children, on the other hand, may take three to four times longer to articulate each phoneme and distort the relative durations among phonemes (Calvert). It may be that these distortions and inappropriate timings result from the speech teaching taking place away from the rest of the linguistic task. This may also be due to the overemphasis given single words or single sounds.

Sounds that look alike in print and that may be pronounced one way if taught alone or in single words are something quite different when put into meaning-bearing units for language. For example, "see Mabel" is different from "seem able" yet they contain the same phonemes. When we give the child such exercises as *p, t, k, f, th*, we may be failing to provide him with the correct data with which he can induce the consonant-vowel-consonant principle.

Phonation

Phonation, as distinguished from phonemes, has to do with production, in particular the amount and quality. All of us are pleased that our children learn to talk, but there remains a problem that their voices are not always pleasant. Sometimes they are nasal, breathy, or harsh (Hudgins and Numbers).

It has been my experience that if a hearing impaired child has a model to follow with the emphasis on the meaning-bearing unit, the child tends to be relaxed in his imitation patterns. For the severely deaf child, the patterns may be given through multisenory modalities whereas, for the partially deaf child, it may be unisensory. When the stress is on *communication* and less on precision in the early periods of instruction, the child has a purpose for the vocal effort. Given patterns that are meaningful to imitate, the hearing impaired child has less tension in his vocal output.

It may be that some of our activities should be examined. For example, the breath we use to extinguish a candle or to blow tissue paper may be more than the amount of breath we need to use to produce the sounds being taught that way, e.g., *p, t, k.* As a matter of fact, we could produce a large number of spoken words on that same amount of breath.

Furthermore, the timing of utterance can help to improve quality. If a child is encouraged to imitate the teacher's model of the sounds produced in the interval of time in which she spoke them, his speech should have good rhythm and not have a choppy quality.

Normal breath units, of course, are meaning units. It is very desirable that the hearing impaired child imitate normal units from the beginning. This would mean that classroom teaching would use simple phrases made up of several words rather than single words or words in carrier sentences. If the child has at least phrase units to attempt, he can't possibly build the habit of pumping out word by word.

Intonation

This brings us to the third area of phonology, referred to by many linguists as intonation. They have shown that with hearing children, speech production proceeds by patterned wholes instead of by segments. Large patterns of intonation usually develop before the child begins *consciously* to develop the basic speech phonemes. When one listens to a young hearing child, he hears him employing genuine native intonations for statements, questions, and requests entirely without intelligible phonemes, words, or word groups. This is vocal language even though there is no observable meaning to adults, no statement by adult standards, but only the melodic and rhythmic contour-suggesting utterances (Leopold). We have found that when hearing impaired children are encouraged to talk when given meaning-units to follow, they too pass through this phase.

Later, after the child has acquired phonemes, and some meaning-bearing units, he will fill these general configurations of sound with specific words and speech elements.

The child seems to develop linguistic control by working in from larger structural patterns to smaller ones. He understands a sentence because he understands the "Bububu" as different from the "Bububu?" and quite different from "Bububu!" This is not because he has learned a rule that a sentence must have a subject and a verb, or that it must tell something, ask a question, or give a command. Nor is it because he understands a period, a question mark, or a comma. It is because intonation patterns are part of the grammar of his language. Intonation can be meaningful to the hearing impaired child in the same manner it is to the hearing sibling.

Prosodic patterns can tell even more about an utterance than what kind of sentence (statement, question, or exclamation). It can also denote internal meaning as well. For example, note the comma in "John, put the cat out" and its omission in "John put the cat out." These tools of intonation lead to grammar for hearing children and should help hearing impaired children also.

The meaning of a pattern can be altered entirely by the intonation used, e.g., Why did *you* come to Dallas? *Why* did you come to Dallas? Why did you come to *Dallas?* The hearing child derives emotive meaning from the intonation pattern. "The sad girl" and "the happy boy" take on meaning from their intonation before the abstractions, sadness and happiness, are truly understood. It is easier to generalize from the pattern than from the units taken singly.

As teachers, we must not forget that the very prosodic pattern of utterance changes the meaning conveyed by a speaker, for example, contrast the meaning of "Aw, you poor thing" said in sympathy and "Aw, you poor thing" said in sarcasm. Even the part of speech of a word can be changed by its stress pattern. Take the word "contrast" as used above in "contrast the meaning" and then the noun, "They are in sharp contrast." The features of phonology are always a part of the grammatical and syntactical structuring of American English. Intonation, in particular, is basic to our language.

Syntax

The language system is a totality; we hear it, speak it, and respond to it all of a piece and all at once. The aim of our teaching then is to approximate this totality of intake multisensorially, through mastery of the system. Here, space permits me only to direct your attention to the role of function words and urge you to seriously consider them in the early education of the children.

When I gave the students in our teacher education program the bibliography for their course, I marked it as follows:

- Books that must be read
- Books that should be read
- Books that might be read
- Books that could be read
- Books that may be read

The lexical words are all identical, but because of the function words, *must, should, might, could,* and *may,* I know which list will be used. Only one of those words forces the issue. A child who spends most of his time gaining meaning from single words does not have the opportunity to gain control of function words.

Certainly these are words which above all can never be taught in isolation, but only as they structure language—in syntactical patterns. They take on meaning only as they mark the lexical words which receive the primary stress. It is because function words usually get secondary stress that they are omitted from the early speech of hearing children; not only are *a, the, my, am, is, if, up, on, and* low in acoustic power, but they are also low in visibility. Deprived of these words, as the child is who has word lists to master, he may never gain control over these features. This is another reason the hearing impaired child needs meaning units to process through his multisensory vocal mechanism.

A sequence of language teaching in a classroom at Central Institute for the Deaf, where the teacher is following a linguistic program, illustrates this point.

These children were able to imitate a model which was meaningful. The lesson grew from an activity all the children had experienced, the feeding of fish. The teacher gave training in auditory discrimination when she asked the children to identify the sentences they had listened to and seen earlier.

She corrected speech, particularly the faulty "sp" in *spots* and the timing of the sentence, by requiring the child to give a better imitation. She had the child process all the information through his vocal system, thereby helping him store linguistic information for later automatic use. All of these tasks, along with the teaching of concepts and providing opportunities for induction of rules, require a broadened view of language.

REFERENCES

CALVERT, D. R. An approach to the study of deaf speech. In *Report of the Proceedings of the International Congress on Education of the Deaf.* Washington, D.C.: U.S. Government Printing Office, 1963, pp. 242-45.

HUDGINS, C. V., and F. C. NUMBERS. *An Investigation of the Intelligibility of the Speech of the Deaf.* Reviewed in *The Volta Review,* Jan., 1943, p. 42.

LEOPOLD, W. Patterning in children's language. In S. Saporta, ed., *Psycholinguistics.* New York: Holt, Rinehart, & Winston, 1961.

Audrey Simmons-Martin is Director, Aural Rehabilitation, Central Institute for the Deaf, St. Louis, Missouri.

29.
An Experiment in Preschool Education: An Autobiographical Case Study
HOWARD T. HOFSTEATER

As you read this autobiographical case study, try to identify the procedures which the author judged to be most effective.

I

It has always been my belief that the exasperating problem of nonverbalism among deaf infants was quite adequately solved years ago by my parents when they set about giving me approximately the same language background as a normal hearing child possesses upon entering school.

To the best of my knowledge, the program for my education, as conceived and carried out by my parents, was so revolutionary—yet so simple—that it had never been attempted before then, nor since. Although it caused some controversial discussion at the time, no one else seems to have cared to duplicate the experiment on which my parents gambled my entire intellectual life.

At many different times I have been asked to write a detailed account of how I "learned to read," how I was "educated," how I was enabled to express myself freely in English long before the average deaf child possesses a single word in his vocabulary—let alone forms a concept of language as a means of communication. For years I have hesitated to do so, feeling that it would be far more seemly for someone else to write such a piece. But as time slithers by and the teaching profession is still baffled by the problem, I have at long last convinced myself that I should record the details of my so-called education, for the simple reason that this single case history might lead to further research and experimentation with happy results.

II

I was the only child born to Howard McPherson Hofsteater and Ollie Tracy, both deaf. He was 45 years of age and she 40 when I was born on November 22, 1909.

Dad lost his hearing at the age of two when his father, Eli Hofsteater, mislaid his spectacles and could not make out the labels on the bottles

From Bulletin 8, Vol. 3 (February, 1959), Gallaudet College, Washington, D.C. Reprinted by permission of Gallaudet College.

in the medicine chest with the horribly tragic result that he squirted carbolic acid into Dad's ears instead of the earache drops the doctor had prescribed.

Mother became deaf shortly before she was two years old when she crawled through an open kitchen door and plunged down the cellar stairs. Her brother, the late Rev. H. Lorraine Tracy, lost his hearing unnecessarily as the result of a protracted siege of catarrh when he was about ten years old.

Dad had two cousins who were deaf, and there was also a deaf cousin lurking in Mother's family background. All these factors taken together convinced my parents that there was a familial predisposition towards deafness on both sides, and for that reason they decided to forego the pleasures of parenthood. But when I insisted on being born, they accepted the event with good grace, nevertheless.

Both my parents were educated at the Iowa School for the Deaf in Council Bluffs where my mother taught for several years immediately after graduation. My father went on to Gallaudet College (1884-1887), but he left college after his sophomore year when Mr. Harry Simpson, the deaf founder of the Dakota Territorial School for the Deaf, prevailed upon him to accept a teaching position. That was a step Father bitterly regretted to the last, for he was a very proud and ambitious man, and it galled him no end to be forever explaining why he never was graduated from college. While at the Dakota school, Dad founded the school paper, the *Dakota Advocate*.

Shortly after my parents' marriage in 1893, they spent their next eleven years teaching at the North Carolina School in Morganton. While in North Carolina, my father started and edited the *Deaf Carolinian*. In 1907, they moved on to the Alabama School. In 1909 I was born, giving a new twist to their lives.

Stung by the embarrassments of having to explain why he did not finish college and by the feeling that he was not adequately educated, my father went heavily into independent historical study with the result that he became very familiar with ancient and modern history—a fact which had much influence on the nature of my reading.

In the meantime, my mother stuck to her program of adding bits here and there to her self-education as a primary grade teacher. She became an expert with retarded children. She acquired the reputation of being singularly able to salvage "hopelessly retarded children." Children who failed miserably in oral programs, children with mental deficiencies, children who arrived at school at embarrassingly late ages, were invariably turned over to my mother for instruction.

Our financial status was only moderate. In those days teachers were on a very low level of remuneration, but in spite of that, my parents managed to live quite comfortably and to afford the special expenses of my private education up to the age of nine.

To summarize—I was born into a determinedly academic and ambitious atmosphere, for which I am naturally thankful. My parents were unusually conscientious teachers, spending much of their spare time in devising new techniques of teaching. Our home was filled with good literature to which my parents added immeasurably when they were confronted by the special problem of raising a deaf infant.

III

Before a watchmaker's apprentice is introduced to the individual movements in a watch, he becomes thoroughly familiar with the watch as a completely integrated piece of machinery. Proceeding on the same line of thought, it seems advisable first of all to have a general, factual report on my progress from the time my deafness was discovered to the time I completed the elementary and secondary phases of my education.

I deplore my father's failure to keep a diary—outlining his philosophy of education and, at the same time, recording day-to-day occurrences. Such an account would have been invaluable as a case history study—far more detailed and accurate than this introspective essay which is based entirely on my own memory of events and of the things my parents and friends told me in regard to my preschool development. The idea of maintaining a daily record simply never occurred to Dad, for I am dead certain that he would have undertaken such a task with enduring, professional enthusiasm.

Let it be repeated that I was born on November 22, 1909—from a week to ten days overdue, and blue from head to foot. This anoxia was due to strangulation by the umbilical cord, and it still remains to be seen whether or not it affected my mind. Otherwise, there seems to have been nothing out of the ordinary in my development as a baby. My parents always stoutly maintained to me that up to the time I was eight or nine months old, they observed many indications of normal response to sound stimuli, ranging from loud noises to tapping a glass with a spoon, and so forth.

It was then that my father contracted pneumonia in both lungs and I a "heavy cold" as the result of his playing with me on a quilt spread out on the floor in a very drafty room. Oxygen tents had not been invented then, so it was necessary to keep all doors and windows open day and night in order that Dad might gasp his way through to recovery. In the meantime, Mother kept me as warmly bundled up as possible. In their desperate struggle to pull Dad through, neither Mother nor Dr. Sims considered my cold as being dangerous.

Dad and I recovered at about the same time. Immediately thereafter, my parents noticed that I no longer responded to any sound. I was taken at once to several ear specialists who confirmed my parents' worst fears. Our familial predisposition had struck again.

I do not know how long it took my parents to reach a decision as to how they were going to educate me—but once their plan was formulated, they stuck to it stubbornly in the face of considerable criticism, derision and abuse.

Visions of becoming a prosperous business man caused Dad to resign from the Alabama School in 1912 to enter into the printing and rubber-stamp business in Birmingham, Ala., with Osce Roberts—the father of Miss Maumee Roberts, who was my private tutor in speech and lipreading for a period of two or three years.

We moved from our comfortable home in Talladega to the somewhat drab, crowded neighborhood of 50th Street in Birmingham. There were on that street a good many boys of approximately the same age as I, but much tougher. The appearance of a "new boy on the block" who was also "a deaf-and-dumb" freak made me legitimate prey. I got into many fights during the three years we lived there, but I must say that as soon as I learned the hard way how to defend myself, the harum-scarum life in the alleys back of 50th Street proved in the long run to be the most enjoyable and socially educative phase of my boyhood. I had no trouble at all in mixing with the 50th Street boys, with whom I conversed by means of "natural" signs.

When I was six or seven years old, Supt. F. H. Manning offered my parents their old jobs at the Alabama School. Father's dreams of becoming a bloated plutocrat having collapsed, my parents accepted with alacrity—so we moved back to the tranquil and scholarly atmosphere of old Talladega.

However genteel and cultured Talladega was—and still is—it had at that time the foulest, filthiest drinking water in the country. Half of the time between 1916 and 1920, it seems, Dad and I were in bed suffering from an incredible succession of infectious diseases. Generally it was dysentery, or something very close to it. I don't think I have ever gotten over the constant succession of lingering illnesses that beset me during that time. However, it must be conceded that my poor health must have spurred my reading progress, for that was practically the only way I could amuse myself and obtain vicariously the experience I needed.

When my parents were away at school, my care was entrusted to two deaf governesses, one after another. They had no influence whatsoever on my education. They functioned only to cater to my physical needs; however, they were required to converse with me only by spelling on the fingers.

Because of my frail health and because my parents really could not make up their minds what was best for me, I was kept out of school until I was nine years old and allowed to develop freely very much as John Dewey would approve of, but, of course, under the firm, purposeful guidance of my parents. At that time, strong pressure was brought to bear down on my parents by the school authorities with the result that I was enrolled at the Alabama School for the Deaf in January, 1920.

I was placed in the fourth grade in the Oral Department. The following year I was shifted to the seventh grade. After one year in that class, the authorities moved me to the ninth grade. With that class I progressed through twelfth grade and graduation, which explains why I spent only 5½ years at the Alabama School and went on to Gallaudet College at the age of 14.

IV

When I was a college student back home for vacations, Dad, Mother, and I often discussed various phases of my early childhood. After I became a teacher, Mother (Dad died when I was only seventeen years old) and I went into the professional aspects of my early education pretty thoroughly at many different times. Time and again, I would run into people who knew me "back when" and who would tell about seeing me talk on my fingers when I was a little boy and how it usually startled them. My relatives (most of them now gathered to their ancestors) also told me about many incidents. I mention all this by way of explaining how I am able to furnish so much information for the ensuing narrative. Miss Maumee Roberts, whom I have already mentioned, and Miss Eugenia Thornton—who was my beloved teacher for the last two years of my stay at the Alabama School—have also furnished valuable data.

As soon as my parents became convinced that I had irretrievably lost my hearing, they were confronted with the question of what next to do with me. They had before them these precedents established by other deaf parents of deaf children:—

(a) Employing signs for ordinary, practical purposes and leaving language development to properly constituted school authorities. This plan, of course, robs the child of early acquisition of a vocabulary and the concept of words used in proper relationship with others as the universally accepted mode of intercommunication.

(b) Using signs at first and slowly introducing words by means of the manual alphabet as the child grows up. The child then enters school with anywhere between 100 and 500 words in his vocabulary and has that much of a head start.

Neither of these alternatives appealed to my parents. They felt that they could do much better than that in the way of developing me during my early formative years.

Quite logically they argued that if a normal hearing child effortlessly acquires spoken language by hearing it and imitating it, a deaf child should be able to do exactly the same by seeing it used. They saw no psychological—nor physiological—difference between a baby's using its vocal cords, tongue, and lips to imitate spoken language and a baby's using his hands to imitate the movements of finger-spelled words. Furthermore, they maintained that since I had become totally deaf at so early an age that I might as well be considered congenitally deaf, sound would for me be forever only a hazy, mental concept instead of the vivid thing it is to hearing people and to those who lose their sense of hearing at around ten years of age and to those with considerable residual hearing. Therefore, speech and speechreading would be an entirely foreign and artificial means of mental development for me. Carrying their line of reasoning still further, it occurred to them that, since they had committed themselves to some form of manual English, they might as well go the whole hog and use nothing but English through the medium of fingerspelling.

My parents' theories were in direct contradiction with the curious belief then prevailing and which persists to this very day in some quarters. Many people believed that it was dangerous for a child to learn language by any means other than hearing—or its make-shift equivalents—and that resorting to other methods would be "forcing the child" with disastrous aftereffects. I may be very much in the wrong, but I understand that some teachers are convinced that it is impossible for anyone to learn a word until he has previously learned the basic sounds thereof. The word, "airplane," is withheld from a first-year pupil because he may not have mastered at that time the phonetics involved—a, r, pl, a, n—to say nothing about the mechanics of running them together in two syllables. This principle is adhered to in spite of the fact that an airplane is as much a part of the child's environment as a cow, a ball, a dog.

My parents then decided upon this course of action. They would (1) begin at once to talk casually and constantly to me on their fingers, just as hearing people do vocally to their babies—*whether or not I was paying any attention;* (2) talk to me just as naturally as hearing people do when attending to my physical needs, pausing only to emphasize key words tied to my bodily wants and interests; (3) use only fingerspelling between themselves when I was consciously present; and (4) in general, raise me as if I were a normal hearing baby with the sole exception of using the manual alphabet instead of speech.

So, instead of spelling only the word "milk" to me at feeding time, they said something like "Here is your milk—m-i-l-k," or "Howard, it's time for your milk—m-i-l-k," and so on. Apparently from all reliable accounts, the results were astoundingly quick.

Miss Eugenia Thornton, in her letter discussing my early education, writes, "The first vivid recollection I have of you was when you were very young. I am sure I saw you, before that time and many times when you were still a baby, but no other incident stands out clearly. You were lying in your crib. Your mother brought a bottle of milk to you. You reached for the bottle and at the same time spelled "m-k" several times, just as spontaneously and naturally as a hearing baby of the same age would have attempted to say "milk," and perhaps have said "mik." . . . This is not a story that I have heard about you but an occurrence that is clearly remembered."

Then followed *w, w-t, w-t-r, water; p, p-d, pdy, puddy* (custard pudding of which I was inordinately fond throughout my childhood) *c-t, cat; pa; ma; s-g-r,* sugar; *b-n,* banana; *a-pl,* apple; and so on. My parents are authorities for the foregoing information as regards the first few words I learned. While I was stumbling through the spelling of the words that appealed to me right off, the deluge of natural, everyday English continued unabated.

Anyone who knows the manual alphabet appreciates the fact that consonant letters are much more distinctly formed than the vowels. So I believe it was only natural for me to omit vowels at first. Miss Thornton compares this tendency of mine to "lisping" among hearing babies.

No one has ever been able to put his finger squarely on the subtle mental process by which a normal infant shifts from the vocabulary level to the beginnings of connected language. The nearest one can come to doing so is to speculate on the part suggestion for imitation plays. When Daddy leaves for work, Mama says fondly to Baby, "Tell Daddy good-bye," and waves her hand to Daddy. Daddy waves back. Mama takes hold of Baby's hand and waves it up and down. After Baby has been repeatedly told to do so, the miracles of spontaneous hand-waving and "Bye" and "Goo'-by" follow. In general, the same thing happened to me.

Once that mysterious transition is made, development of connected language and thought (the two are inseparable) becomes swiftly cumulative and is limited only by the quality and quantity of the child's experiences and the nature of his environment.

My parents assured me time and again they never had to resort to formal teaching procedures to get me started in free, idiomatic language. I used more and more everyday English because I saw it used all the time and because I wanted to participate. Dad and Mother repeatedly emphasized to me this point:—never did they physically force me to look at their fingers when they were talking to me; nor did they insist on my "copying" consciously or memorizing words or phrases or expressions. They, of course, helped me along when I struck out on my own to imitate.

The idea that whenever they manipulated their fingers in my direction would in some way affect my well-being must have percolated through somehow, for I developed at a rather early age the faculty of *concentrated visual attention*—subject, of course, to my fluctuating desire to listen.

Another interesting thing is this:—I learned the proper sequence of the letters in the alphabet some time after I could spell many words. That is in keeping with good, modern psychology.

I have a suspicion that even my parents were surprised by the extent and rapidity of the language "osmosis" their experiment precipitated. While it gratified and encouraged them, it caused distress among many of my parents' friends and fellow-teachers. They were frankly alarmed, and some of them urged my parents to "cease and desist." And when Dad and Mother serenely went ahead as usual, some people went so far as to accuse them of trying artificially to produce a mental prodigy to satisfy their vanity, and to predict for me either a very early mental breakdown or a career as a Frankensteinian horror. I imagine my parents' feelings were hurt very much and often during that period, but they were convinced they were on the right track.

While I played more or less with the babies in our Talladega neighborhood, my reaction to companionship must have been only middling fair, for my parents never said much about that phase. If I had had brothers and sisters, within close age range, my story might have taken a different direction. It was really not until we moved to 50th Street in Birmingham that I learned to enjoy the company of others of my own age and size. Upon my return to Talladega, my frequent illnesses and growing fondness for books kept me from mixing a great deal with hearing boys of my age. However, I did have a few cronies, all of whom quickly learned to spell on their fingers—and to read fingerspelling. I learned many colloquialisms and Southern expressions from them.

I was naturally introduced to picture books at about the same time as I began to manipulate building blocks intelligently. I became familiar with the printed symbols for various letters through informal play with the blocks. My parents saw to it that I could identify each block with its equivalent on my fingers. At the same time, so my parents said, I was fascinated by the gaudy picture books published at that time. They were huge affairs printed in a lavish medley of colors on pages of indestructible linen. The initials, A-B-C, etc., were sunbursts; so were the illustrations.

My parents began to tell me stories shortly before we moved to Birmingham, and I quickly slid into the phase in which a child insists on a bedtime story as well as stories at various times of the day.

When I asked for a story, Dad or Mother would always drop everything else to gratify me, and my appetite for stories became a great drain on their time and energy. I was pretty badly spoiled in that connection. They would ask me what story I wanted and, unless Dad had brought home a new book, I would ask for one of my old favorites for a repeat just as all children do. Then they would get the book and, with me comfortably snuggled in their laps, "spell aloud" the story. They would hold their hands pretty close to the pages and spell.

At this point, I am afraid it devolves on me to explain a peculiar phenomenon to people who are not thoroughly familiar with the ins-and-outs of the psychology of the bona-fide deaf. It is not necessary for one who is adept in fingerspelling or signs to look directly at the hands of the person talking. He catches the fingerspelling or signs on the outer edge of the cone of his vision while centering his attention on something else. That is why many deaf people have the disconcerting habit of looking straight into the eyes or at the face of the person to whom they are listening, not at his fingers.

With this explanation in mind, one can see how easy it was for me to center my attention on the illustrations and text and, at the same time, get the words as Dad or Mother spelled them out. Spelling out the words close to the pages also had the effect of keeping my attention on the printed pages. This factor probably had something to do with speeding up my reading readiness.

I was about four and a half years or so old when I received such a shock that I can remember every detail of the event. I asked Mother one day to read me the story of Silver Paw—which I knew by heart and which always caused me to cry. It was a very sad story about a puppy that got lost. I got impatient with the rate at which Mother was spelling it out and turned a page before she had finished it. She stopped spelling, but I kept right on and sobbed and bawled through to the end. The next day when I asked for another story, she flatly refused, telling me to go read it myself. I was very much hurt, but I did retire into a nook and read the story. That evening when Dad came home, I rushed to him and asked him to read me a story, only to be rebuffed likewise. That was how I was abruptly weaned away from having stories read to me.

Several interesting points come to light in the foregoing account of how I learned to read.

It was only to be expected that I skipped entirely the "oral reading" phase of the standard learning process. It would have been silly for me to spell out the words, too, while my parents were spelling the stories to me. It would have slowed down the reading so much as to make it tedious and uninteresting. I could follow the story and the spelling at a more rapid and natural speed.

It was very easy for me to stop my parents at any time for explanations or for them to pause and ask me if I knew the meanings of words they were pretty sure were new to me.

I have a theory that, in addition to the concepts I was establishing all along through ordinary conversation and observation, this fast reading contributed a great deal to my unconscious acceptance of the fact that words can have different contextual meanings.

Another important point in regard to my reading is that I dearly loved to dramatize the stories I read. I learned to pretend in a big way from my association with the children on 50th Street. We pretended we were Indians, played cops and robbers and so forth. "Bang!" and we'd fall down dead, and so on. But it was only with Dad and Mother that I dramatized stories. We had quite a lot of fun, although it must have been tiresome at times for my parents.

I recall that, after I got through Little Red Riding Hood, Jack and the Beanstalk, Puss-in-Boots, The Three Bears and the like, I went on to fairyland. I loved the Brownie stories. Thornton Burgess' endless series of humanized animal stories held my interest for quite a while. Aesop's Fables, the Riverside and the Eclectic series of adapted tales, The Raindrop, Greek, Roman and Teutonic myths, and tales of ancient times and heroes led me on and on to the classics. In between, I read a good many stories about Indians, wilderness scouts, the Pilgrims, George Washington, pirates, cowboys, knights, and Boy Scout adventurers. In my imagination, I shot it out with Zane Grey's badmen. Sherlock Holmes was a prime favorite for a long time. My father spent a great deal of time looking through publishers' catalogs and ordering the books he thought I would enjoy. And, too, there was the Carnegie Public Library just across the street from the Alabama School.

The following facts and implications stand out clearly in this case history study:

(1) It is possible to *spell* on one's fingers to a deaf baby and gradually to attract sufficient attention from it for educational purposes.

(2) It is possible for a deaf baby to *identify* important letters and words formed on the hands and, later on, to imitate them.

(3) Sound is by no means the *sine qua non* of the very foundation of a deaf infant's acculturation.

(4) It is easier for a deaf infant to identify and understand something he can see very clearly than something he has to guess at.

(5) It is possible for a congenitally and totally deaf child to achieve through spelling approximately the same amount of "language absorption" that a normal hearing child does, and at the same pace—other factors being equal.

(6) The process used by my parents was exactly like that followed by most educated parents of hearing children except that fingerspelling was substituted for hearing and speech.

(7) It is during the formative, preschool years of a child's life—hearing or deaf—that he should be started on language.

One can with good reason infer from this narrative two things in regard to reading:—(a) It is easier for a deaf child trained exclusively by the manual alphabet to get started in reading than his hearing counterpart because of the elimination of all phonetic difficulties; (b) that would not be true of a deaf child whose sole method of communication during his preschool life was that of signs alone.

It occurs to one that hearing parents of deaf children could very easily make use of the manual alphabet to get their babies off to a flying start and wait until they are about three years old before attempting to introduce them to the alien world of sound. The important thing is to establish a free and easy means of intercommunication between the deaf child and his intimates from the very beginning—not only for the sake of exchange of ideas but also for the sake of alerting as early as possible the deaf child's mind. One can even logically argue that it is easier to introduce speech and lipreading to a deaf child who already has some language than to one who has absolutely no language concepts.

Approximately the same observation was made by Dr. Harris L. Taylor in his article, "The Missing Mind," in the May, 1937, issue of the *American Annals of the Deaf*. To quote him,

I would recall some deaf children of intelligent deaf parents; these children came to school with a mental development far greater than that of other deaf children with approximately equal ability. It was true that these deaf children of deaf parents were developed through the sign language, but it was equally true that they excelled in oral school work. Their school progress was more rapid on account of their development. If so much could be done through the sign language, why could not more be done by using English from the beginning?

Another inference that could be made is that the deaf child who is trained by a medley of signs and finger-spelled words is in a much better position, both mentally and linguistically, to begin school work than one who starts from scratch. *If the signs and words are uniformly used in the same grammatical order as spoken language, the child is vastly that much better prepared.*

VII

The story of how my parents endowed me, a totally deaf child, with practically the same language background that the average normal hearing child enjoys before entering school is of special interest only to myself and to the few who have wondered how it was done. It does establish a few facts, and it does open the way for some discussion. But since (a) it was written from a subjective point of view, and (b) it is an isolated case, it cannot be taken seriously by the profession.

However, if one were to make out a list of at least fifty (one hundred or more would be better) congenitally deaf people with unusually good command of English and—

(1) inquire very closely into the means by which they were enabled to conquer their language handicaps,

(2) prepare a detailed study of each case, presenting all relevant data available,

(3) get as much corroborative evidence for each case history as possible,

(4) point out similarities and differences, and

(5) analyze, draw conclusions and offer constructive recommendations.

then the findings of such a study would carry considerable weight, especially if it were undertaken under the scientific guidance of a responsible educational institute—for example, the Department of Special Education of the University of Illinois. It is my opinion that a research project along that line will more likely than not uncover some highly interesting and significant data on the language problem of the deaf.

Prior to his untimely death, Howard T. Hofsteater was on the staff of the Illinois School for the Deaf, Jacksonville, Illinois.

30.
The Language Arts in the
Curriculum for Deaf Children
ALICE H. STRENG

*What are the types of language experience
which may be provided for the deaf through the
subject matter fields?*

*Language development should be considered an
integral part of the total plan for learning in schools for the deaf. The
subject matter fields are an important part of the curriculum. They can
contribute not only to vocabulary growth, but can also provide opportunity
for clarification of and practice in spoken, written, and read language.
Deaf children must be guided in verbalizing the concepts inherent in the
subject matter fields so as to gain power not only in expressing concrete
ideas, but in thinking and reasoning. The teaching-learning unit may well
be the best way in which to organize learning experiences for children.*

A curriculum is a plan for learning. In the United States, at least, the
curriculum is the way the school takes for preparing its young people to
become productive members of a technological society in a fast-shrinking
world. Such a society tends to foster conformity of behavior and mind and
uniformity of economic and social cultural patterns. Yet, in our society,
importance is also placed on self-actualization and independence of
thinking. The reconciliation of these opposing forces is an important task
for any school, but especially of the school for the deaf as it plans the
learning experiences of its children.

Deaf children have the added burden of not being able to verbalize concepts they acquire without special language instruction. It is perfectly
clear that they can acquire certain critical nonverbal concepts of behavior
from exposure to ordinary life experiences. For instance, a deaf child can
be taught to shun matches by the use of conditioning techniques, but he
cannot understand the reasons nearly as well as his brothers and sisters
who are able to hear verbal explanations of why they should not play
with matches.

The deaf child can learn to look up and down the street for oncoming
vehicles before he crosses it, but he can hardly be expected to deal with
the past or the future comfortably, with cause and effect, with sequences
in time, or with inferences and judgments, and even with his own feelings
if he has no power over words and sentences to express himself.

Reprinted by permission from *The Volta Review*, 70:6 (September, 1968): 127-32.
Copyright © The Alexander Graham Bell Association for the Deaf, Inc., Washington,
D.C., 1968.

Therefore, the curriculum in the schools for the deaf must be designed so that all learning experiences will develop the children's capacity to handle language symbols in conjunction with a system of ideas and concepts best expressed through sentences. In the past, and perhaps even in the present, much confusion has existed in developing continuous and cumulative learning experiences for deaf children because sequence of content, as well as sequence of skill development and competency in language usage as related to thinking processes, have been overlooked.

It seems logical to suppose, then, that all aspects of the curriculum must contribute to the child's knowledge about his growing self and his growing life space, and be closely correlated with his ability to understand and use the language that fits his level of conceptualization.

The Language Arts Program and the Subject Matter Fields

The language arts program in any school will include vocabulary study, acquisition of power to speak and write clearly, and learning to read with understanding. Input of language in schools for the deaf will, of course, vary with the school's philosophy. The choice may be through lipreading and trainable residual hearing, through manual spelling and signs, or combinations of these elements. However, the goals for all programs will be to increase the children's ability to deal with verbal symbols in motor and graphic forms.

It is a foregone conclusion that vocabulary acquisition will be a necessary aspect of the subject matter to be studied. A deaf child's vocabulary begins to accumulate slowly at first but rapidly later. Before long, he is expected to learn 100 or more new words a day if he is to conquer the world of words around him. Not only must he be able to remember the basic lexical meanings of a great many words, but he must know where they fit in the sentence patterns he is learning. Moreover, he must be aware of how the meanings of words change in a wide variety of environments. His task is a monumental one.

Writing lists of words on the blackboard for social studies or science lessons and asking a child to look up these words in the dictionary will build neither concepts nor power to use or remember words. How he acquires vocabulary will depend on the insights his teachers have concerning the learning process in general and a knowledge of his own unique capacity to acquire language.

To expedite the acquisition of vocabulary, there must be: (1) a concerted effort to build and organize vocabulary on meaningful personal experiences or on an experience-related base within the framework of sentence patterns, (2) provision for constant review of vocabulary in order to stabilize it, (3) emphasis on multiple meanings of words, and (4) clarification of the idiomatic use of vocabulary. A plan for learning that is structured so as to include all these aspects is bound to be a good one.

The subject matter fields all have their own vocabularies to be mastered. For instance, the language requisite for modern mathematics, the study of space, the life cycle of the butterfly, world conflicts, riots, and even football games puts demands on the child's ability to acquire sheer numbers of words, to say nothing about their multiple uses. But, acquisition of a body of words is not enough. The use of words in clearly structured sentences is one of the basic goals for all deaf children.

The efficacy of using the subject matter fields as a basis for clarifying and teaching English sentence structures might be questioned by some teachers. If the goal is to teach facts of science, history, or mathematics, and to have the child answer "key" questions about these facts with single words or phrases, English sentence structure has no relevance in this context. But, if the children are to react thoughtfully to their environments, they must be actively engaged in the learning process based on their own activities and experiences.

Hopefully, they will develop a knowledge of sentence structure through daily practice and repetition as they discuss the ideas and concepts with which they come in contact. Correct sentence structure becomes the vehicle by which they can express their thoughts and ideas more precisely and guarantees the use of the vocabulary they are learning.

The Teacher-Learning Unit

I shall assume that the best way to achieve curriculum objectives in the elementary school, at least, is through the teaching-learning unit approach. This approach allows for dealing with individual differences among children not only from the standpoint of their intelligence, their experiences, their values, and their learning sets, but from the standpoint of their competence and understanding of the use of language. The following illustrations attempt to show the relationship of language development and the subject matter fields within the framework of the unit.

Let us envision a group of 8- or 9-year-old deaf children who are participating in one small segment of a larger social studies unit based on the concept that there are likenesses and differences among people. They are familiar with the terms "likenesses" and "differences," so they must be prepared for an understanding of this abstract vocabulary.

The teacher might place a large group of articles on the table and then ask the children to sort them into sets. The sets chosen are "Clothing" and "Toys." The children may easily sort these items into the required two sets. The sets are labeled "Things to Wear" and "Things to Play With," and/or "Clothing" and "Toys." After the children have completed the sorting, the set of toys is discarded and the attention is focused on the clothing. Figure 1 indicates how the clothing is further subdivided into girl's and boys' clothing, with the common items placed in the intersection C.

Another step may be added in showing the children that likenesses and differences refer to other items. Each child is asked to describe himself. In the process, children will learn alternate ways of expressing the same idea.

Leona may write, "I'm Leona. I'm nine years old. I'm four feet tall. I have blue eyes. I have brown hair, I weigh 72 pounds," whereas Larry may write, "My name is Larry. I'm nine. I'm four feet three inches tall. My eyes are brown. My hair is blond. I weigh 80 pounds."

Two children then work together listing sentences under the headings, "How We Are Alike" and "How We Are Different," or "Likenesses" and "Differences." Under "How We Are Alike," they might write, "Our names begin with 'L.' We are nine years old."

Under "How We Are Different," Leona might write, "I am a girl and Larry is a boy. Larry is four feet, three, and I am four feet tall. Larry has brown eyes and I have blue eyes. Larry weighs 80 pounds, and I weigh 72 pounds."

Undoubtedly, they would need help in detecting the subtle differences as found in "Our names begin with 'L,' " as well as in selecting the appropriate sentence patterns.

Figure 1. LIKENESS AND DIFFERENCE SETS

Girls' clothing		Boys' clothing
A	B	C
a dress	gloves	a tie
a petticoat	mittens	a belt
a slip	a long scarf	a shirt
a hair band	knee highs	underpants
tights	a T shirt	trousers
patent leather slippers	sandals	western boots

These clothes are <u>not the same</u> for boys and girls.

These clothes are <u>the same</u> for boys and girls.

These are <u>different</u> for boys and girls.

They are <u>different</u>.

They are <u>alike</u>.

They are <u>not the same</u>.

In order to advance the concept of *likenesses and differences* beyond physical characteristics, children may study different kinds of work done outside the home. One child might say, "My father goes to work every day. He is a plumber." Another might say, "My father works at night. He is a policeman," and a third, "My mother works at Brown and Company. She is a typist."

The generalization they make is that people do different kinds of work. They also understand that the jobs of many policemen, many plumbers, and many typists are similar. All the time, the teacher has stressed sentences using the verb "be" and action verbs in the habitual present tense to illustrate the generalities to be drawn.

At a higher level, the educationally retarded deaf child in a work-study program might be learning a different vocabulary, yet be using the same simple sentence structures. There is infinite opportunity to do so. For example, descriptions of jobs lend themselves to the use of simple sentences:

"Mr. Wyne is the painter in our factory and our Union steward. He listens to our complaints. Mr. Wyne went to high school. He earns $160 a week."

"Mr. Finch is a personnel manager. He hires people for Brown and Company. Mr. Finch went to college. He earns $800 a month."

"Mr. Strong is a patternmaker. He makes patterns for gears. Mr. Strong went to the Technical Institute. He earns $800 a month."

This type of exercise might seem unimportant and irrelevant at first glance, but many deaf young people aspire to grandiose and unrealistic vocational goals. They must be led to understand the variety of educational qualifications and aptitudes required for different kinds of jobs.

It can readily be seen that the sentence structures being used in all instances are the same basic ones used at a lower level: $NP + be + NP$, $NP + be + Adj$, $NP + VP_I + Adv$, and $NP + VP_T + NP$. These structures can be further practiced by relating them to other aspects of the unit. New ones can also be introduced and clarified as requirements demand. Practicing language thus becomes an integral part of every subject matter lesson.

The subject of science lends itself beautifully to the explanation of causality. Children eventually discover relationships between wearing warm clothing and the outdoor temperature. As little children, they may not wish to wear their clumsy wraps and flatly state "No!" when their parents tell them to put them on before they go outdoors. But, understanding of the situation is enhanced if they can ask "Why?"

If they understand the causal relationships, they can understand the language which goes with it, for example, "Why did the balloon go up?" Or they can even ask such questions as, "Why did the goldfish die?" or "Why is it cold at the South Pole?" Countless opportunities to teach sentence structure are inherent in situations involving subject matter. Teachers must be aware of them and utilize the opportunities presented. Every social studies, science, and mathematics lesson must be a language lesson.

Deaf children who know only simple sentence patterns will, of course, have great difficulty in using texts prepared for hearing children. The complex organization of written English will be completely baffling to them. Consequently, teachers of the deaf must be alert to the kinds of transformations and sentence organization to which the children are exposed in the available printed matter. It is incumbent on these teachers to introduce these transformations gradually but consistently into the reading matter they themselves prepare for their classes. Complex structural meanings should become clear because of their introduction in meaningful situations.

On the other hand, children must have intensive instruction and special practice for reducing the highly structured language of texts and reference materials into simpler terms. The subject matter fields offer abundant attractive reading matter that could contribute a great deal toward furthering reading ability in deaf children. Thus the language arts truly become an integral part of the curriculum.

Conclusion

All aspects of the curriculum can and should serve as the basis for language acquisition by deaf children. I believe that the teacher of the deaf will serve his children best by planning the language program in sequential steps and by individualizing the instruction within the framework of large teaching-learning units. A firm foundation of language is the best base on which to build concepts and understandings and to promote thinking and reasoning. Therefore, whether a child is studying science, history, biology, or mathematics, every minute of every day should contribute to strengthening the language abilities of every deaf child in every school for the deaf in the United States.

Alice H. Streng is Professor Emeritus, The University of Wisconsin at Milwaukee.

31.
Total Communication as a Basis of Educating Prelingually Deaf Children
RICHARD G. BRILL

The justification for the use of total communication is presented here. As you read the assumptions, try to weigh the force of the author's arguments against the potential of the oral approach described elsewhere in the chapter.

The education of the deaf is the oldest form of special education in the United States. The first permanent school for the deaf was established in Hartford, Connecticut, in 1817. The education of blind children and the education of mentally retarded children followed many years later than the establishment of programs to educate deaf children. We have much to be proud of in the more than 150 years that we have been educating the deaf, but we also have much to be concerned about. No professional educator that I know of is particularly proud of the general level of education obtained by the huge majority of deaf students. No professional educator is satisfied with the communication skills of the huge majority of deaf students. We all seek something better.

Perhaps much of the lack of progress is due to what is sometimes referred to as the One Hundred Years War or the tremendous controversy in regard to methods of communication in educating deaf children. The two first entirely oral schools for deaf children were established in 1867 so that we can pinpoint with great accuracy the time the war of methods has been carried on.

This One Hundred Years War has been characterized by emotion on the part of both educators and parents, by lack of precise thinking including the understanding of terminology and definition of terms, and finally by lack of perspective in regard to the appropriate relationships between means and ends.

We will start with the description of the child we are talking about and definitions of some terms that are used in this field. We will then proceed to placing the problems in perspective by considering the general objectives we may have. Next, we will consider certain assumptions that have been made in the past. Finally, we will present certain positive reasons for using total communication with deaf children starting with their preschool years and carrying through their entire school program.

From *Communication Symposium* (1970) pp. 7-14. Maryland School for the Deaf, Fredrick, Maryland. Reprinted with permission of author and Maryland School for the Deaf.

As our major concern is the education of deaf children, the most important word to define is that of deafness or the word deaf. Simply stated, a person is deaf who cannot hear and understand connected speech, though such a person may, and generally does, have extensive sound perception. He can hear many sounds when they are amplified sufficiently and he may be able to hear individual speech sounds, but he does not hear enough of the speech sounds to be able to understand connected speech. In contrast, the hard-of-hearing person has a hearing loss but either with or without amplification can understand connected speech. A very simple test to differentiate between the two is to have the individual close his eyes. If such an individual cannot understand someone else's connected speech, then he is deaf. If he can understand it through his hearing alone even though amplified, he is hard of hearing.

Within the general area of the deaf, for educational purposes, we have the very important distinction between those who are prelingually deaf and those who are postlingually deaf. The prelingually deaf child is the child who was born deaf or becomes deaf at such an early age that he never had an opportunity to learn language and to learn speech through his hearing. In contrast, the postlingually deaf child had relatively normal hearing the first two or three years of life at least so that he was able to learn language and learn speech as other children do. For educational purposes, the distinction between the two is tremendous.

In addition I would like to add another category that we might call the pseudo hard of hearing. One definition of pseudo is a deceptive resemblance to a specified thing. This is the child who has a great amount of residual hearing. However, he did not have enough to really learn language and to learn speech through his hearing alone, even when highly amplified, except through quite structured lessons on the part of a qualified teacher. There are some children falling in this category who after they have learned a great deal of language can understand this language through hearing with amplification, but who have very great difficulty in understanding any language or any subject that they have not dealt with before.

It is important to note that the huge majority of the enrollment of most schools for the deaf today is made up of the prelingually deaf child. The postlingually deaf child is really rather rare. This is due to the advances in medicine resulting in very few children becoming deaf as a result of a high fever accompanying typical childhood diseases such as measles, mumps, whooping cough, etc. In the California School for the Deaf where we have 580 children enrolled, 95% of our enrollment is prelingually deaf. We have two children in the entire school who can be identified as postlingually deaf children and we have about 35 children who are hard of hearing. In general, hard-of-hearing children should not be educated with deaf children because the basic educational problem is different and there are many kinds of situations that are neither beneficial to the deaf children in the school nor the hard-of-hearing children in the school when both are attending the same school. However, as a practical matter there are situations where even though the ideal solution to the hard-of-hearing child's problem is not a school for the deaf, it is the only practical solution because there is no other school or agency meeting his needs.

Within recent years the term "hearing impaired" has become prevalent in certain educational areas. The hearing impaired is a global term that must include the prelingually deaf, the postlingually deaf, the hard-of-hearing child at the very least, and possibly in addition to this the pseudo hard of hearing and possibly the aphasic. It is difficult to see how use of such a global and imprecise term can help to clarify the objectives and the responsibilities of a school that has as its primary mission the education of deaf children. We have not infrequent instances of some parents who for one reason or another refuse to refer to the child as a deaf child but always refer to him as a hard-of-hearing child. This, in spite of the fact that the child cannot hear and understand speech through the ear as evidenced by the fact that he has never learned language through hearing. Perhaps because of guilt feelings on the part of the parent, or the inability of the parent to accept the child's handicap, he uses this euphemism when he insists on referring to the child as hard of hearing rather than deaf. One wonders whether some educators may not have equally invalid reasons for insisting that programs always be referred to as programs for the hearing impaired as though this made the whole thing much more modern, rather than using the term deaf, which can have objective specificity. The use of the term "hearing impaired" primarily confuses the issue as far as appropriate educational procedures are concerned.

What are our objectives in educating deaf children? It may be assumed that the objectives we have in educating deaf children are essentially the same as we have for the education of hearing children. These have been frequently cited as the achievement of self-realization, the development of proper human relationships, the attainment of economic efficiency, and the assumption of civic responsibility. Put in another way, this means that each individual must learn to live with himself, he must learn to live with other people, he must attain a particular level of economic efficiency in order to support himself and contribute to society, and he should assume civic responsibility within a community of which he is a member.

The education of deaf children differs from the education of other children even though we have the same objectives, because the teaching of deaf children is complicated by the fact that they do not have normal communication skills. This in turn affects their social, psychological and emotional development as well as their general educational development.

Because of the handicap of deafness and the resulting handicap of communication it is the responsibility of the school to teach communication in all its phases, language, speech, speechreading, reading, and writing. I would add to the list, phases of manual communication also. Communication is but a tool. It is the school's responsibility to teach all of the subject matter and content material it is possible to teach each child in the time available. The school also has the responsibility of teaching the many things concerned with social living which hearing children learn almost subconsciously because of their ability to hear and thus communicate.

Communication then is the core of the problem in educating deaf children. Webster defines communication as intercourse by words, letters, or messages. Also, the interchange of thought or opinions.

In considering the communication problem we are talking about, there are certain distinctions that it is essential to understand. One of these is the distinction between language and speech. Language is a particular symbol system that can be expressed in a number of different ways. Speech is one method of utilizing that symbol system but other methods include writing, printing, and finger spelling. An individual who knows no Italian might read a paragraph written in Italian orally well enough for an Italian to understand what he is saying, if the proper phonetic markings were indicated. The individual reading the paragraph would still not understand what he said himself, because although he was utilizing Italian speech he did not understand the Italian language. Similarly, teaching a deaf child the speech for a particular word does not in any way guarantee that the child knows the language or the meaning of the word.

Another important distinction to be aware of is the fact that we have expressive communication and receptive communication. Without both being present there is no such thing as communication, but we must recognize that they are two different things, and the skills involved are separate in each instance. A person who has normal hearing and suddenly loses his hearing at the age of 20 will have no difficulty in terms of his speech or expressive communication. However, because he cannot hear he may have tremendous difficulty now in his receptive communication because he may not be able to speech read very well. On the other hand, although more rarely, a deaf person may not have intelligible speech and yet may be rather highly skilled in lipreading or in the receptive communication phase. Skill in expression does not automatically ensure skill in reception, nor vice versa.

In any discussion of expressive and receptive communication, most of which is based on language, we should also note that we have internal language as well. This is the ability to handle the symbol system in such a way that cognitive thinking can be carried on by the individual.

In the area of education of the deaf we have certain terminology that is customarily used within this profession, but which is not always completely understood by others who are not directly concerned. It is further confusing because the meaning as used in one place is not necessarily the meaning as used in some other place.

The term "oral communication" as used by educators of the deaf denotes the teaching of speech as an expressive skill to deaf children and the teaching of speechreading as a receptive skill to deaf children. It also means that speech and speechreading are the means of communication used for transmission of thoughts and ideas. The oral educator does not exclude the use of reading and writing but he does exclude the use of any manual communication. In some, but not all oral programs, it is thought that the oral skills should always precede reading and writing.

The term "manual communication" includes both expressive and receptive forms of communication. It also includes two basic systems; one the sign language and the other finger spelling. In actual practice frequently both sign language and finger spelling are used in the same communication.

The terms "combined" or "simultaneous" means of communication generally mean that expressively, speech and finger spelling are used simultaneously or speech and the sign language are used simultaneously. On the receptive end the individual is receiving the message both through lipreading the speech and through reading the signs or finger spelling simultaneously with the lip reading.

In addition to this terminology used to identify methods of teaching and methods of communication, we also have the words used as a method of classifying schools. The pure oral school is the school that completely prohibits the use of manual communication at any time and any place as far as the school is concerned or as far as the children who are attending the school is concerned. Other schools that are not pure oral schools will state that they have oral departments. Sometimes all of the educational departments in such a school are oral. This means that as far as the educational program in the classroom is concerned that they prohibit all manual communication and resort only to oral means of communication. However, in such schools they allow manual communication between children outside of the classroom and frequently will use manual communication in assembly exercises and other group meetings.

Sometimes schools with these oral departments are referred to as combined schools, but in practice there are a number of different patterns that may be in effect in several different schools, each one of which calls itself a combined school. As indicated above, there are certain instances where all of the educational programs are carried on orally but manual communication is allowed outside the classes. In certain other schools there are manual classes established for those children that they generally consider as slow learners while all of the rest of the classes will be oral. In still other schools all of the classes for older children may be conducted as combined classes with both manual communication and oral communication in the classroom while all of the classes for the younger children are exclusively oral. In other schools that have a combined or simultaneous system they may use what is sometimes called the Rochester Method. This means they finger spell and talk simultaneously regardless of whether this communication is in the classroom or on the playground, the vocational department or the assembly hall. The sign language is not part of the Rochester Method. Some schools with the Rochester Method may use this system with the very beginning children and all of the children in the school, and others may still use it only with older children and restrict their younger children to exclusively oral means of communication in the classrooms.

It can be seen from this multiplicity of specific terminology which has different meanings and different definitions in different places that a great deal of misunderstanding has developed because of lack of agreement in regard to the terms being used.

In this long controversy pertaining to methods of communication in teaching deaf children which has been going on for the past 100 years, there has been a lack of objective data obtained through approved scientific methods to form the basis of programs or procedures. Due to this lack of data there have been certain assumptions made which form the basis of the exclusively oral education as practiced by most schools for the deaf in the country, at least as far as their younger children were concerned. It appears now that there is beginning to be a gathering together of scientifically obtained data that disproves these assumptions. Following are eight assumptions listed and accompanying each assumption the reason for now considering it invalid:

1. It has been assumed in oral education that expressive and receptive communication was one global entity. Parents or others who continually refer to their desire that a child be taught orally were completely ignoring the fact that oral communication is not one global skill but is composed of at least two very different types of skills in the expressive and receptive phases. We have a specific understanding of this today and we have a great deal of evidence that the two skills may not be present equally with each individual.

2. Demanding that a child's communication be limited to oral communication ignores completely the laws of individual differences. We know that children are as different in their ability to learn to talk and to learn to speechread as they are in their ability to learn anything else.

3. The distinction between using speechreading as a receptive means of communication when a person had a command of language as opposed to using speechreading to learn a new language was frequently not recognized. Thus the effectiveness of speechreading for the postlingually deaf person is much greater than for the prelingually deaf person. The objectives are different. Even the postlingually deaf person has difficulty in understanding because less than fifty percent of the sounds are visible on the lips. However, he has a language background to fill in the gaps. The prelingually deaf person does not have this background of knowledge in language to fill in the gaps. In addition he has to try to use this highly inefficient input system to try to learn the language. When a large percentage of the enrollment of a school for the deaf was postlingually deaf or hard of hearing, speechreading was frequently a good input system for many of this group. Now that most of the enrollment is prelingually deaf and these children have to learn language, this is a very ineffective input system when used alone.

4. It was assumed that if deaf children used manual communication, particularly the sign language, that this created the confusion in language that deaf children have. When deaf children use mixed up language this is commonly referred to as "deafy" language. The assumption that deafy language results primarily from knowledge of the sign language has been disproved. Deaf children who never knew the sign language also make "deafy" mistakes. An analysis of the small number of clues received in speechreading indicates that a person does not see English on the lips. He sees only a few clues and then has to fill in the rest. Therefore, the deaf child does not see normal English on the lips. Thus speechreading does not result in continued input of straight English, and does not help the child to learn without supplementary input.

5. It has been long assumed that the use of manual communication by a deaf child would make that child less proficient in his own speech and in the use of speechreading. Recent research studies carried on by different investigators in separate parts of the country have disproved this assumption. It has been shown through the studies made by Meadows and by Quigley among others, that the speech of deaf children who have manual communication in their background is no less intelligible or their understanding of speechreading no less proficient than those deaf people who had no manual communication.

6. It has been assumed that if a person had the opportunity to use manual communication he would not attempt to use oral communication. Experience has shown that this assumption is not valid. We have been utilizing manual communication and oral communication simultaneously for years, and we find that our students continue to talk and continue to want others who are proficient in manual communication to talk simultaneously with the manual communication. This means that our students are benefiting by the speechreading in addition to the manual signs or finger spelling.

7. It was apparently assumed that if there were any problems of a psychological and emotional nature as a result of limited oral communication between the child and his parents, that these problems were not as important as trying to be sure that exclusively oral communication was continued. Both experience and research studies show that major psychological and emotional problems result from lack of communication between parents and child. In addition there is some evidence that some children develop further emotional problems when the parents reject manual communication. Because this is a communication method this child uses with other children, the child subconsciously feels that the parent is rejecting him when the parent punishes him for using manual communication.

8. It has been assumed that pure oralism could not exist where any manualism was allowed. This statement has been made by DiCarlo. So while in other areas of great controversy a middle ground has gen-

erally been reached, in this controversy such a middle ground has not been reached because of the assumption that no compromise could be made without losing the entire battle. If the objective is good oral communication skills, then this assumption is not valid because good oral communication skills are attained by many children who utilize a combined or simultaneous method.

These eight assumptions stated above were the basis for three objectives of the exclusively oral educational program. These were: (1) that the major communication method used by deaf people would be primarily oral, (2) that the result of this educational program would be functional as far as the communication skills of most of the deaf children were concerned, and (3) that all deaf people would be primarily a part of what was referred to as "the hearing world."

In actuality we find that deaf people adjust their communication methods according to their own skills and according to the situation in which they find themselves. A deaf person with good expressive communication skills will use them when he is with hearing people. If he does not trust his receptive skills or has very poor receptive skills he will have hearing people write to him. It is not an all or none or an either/or situation as far as a deaf person is concerned. He finds he has to continue to make adjustments.

Unfortunately, the overall oral communication skills of a great number of adult deaf people have not proved to be functional in spite of the fact that nearly all had an oral education during at least their early school years.

And finally, deaf people do not live exclusively in a hearing world, nor do they live exclusively in a deaf world. Deaf people generally marry other deaf people. A certain number of them have deaf children and a larger number have hearing children. Some have other deaf relatives but a larger number have other hearing relatives. Their neighbors are hearing people and generally they are working with hearing people. Most deaf people probably get the biggest part of their social life with other deaf people and most deaf people find that if they are going to be involved in any way in organized religion that this has to be with a group where other deaf people are involved and where means of communication is such that they can understand, which generally means manual communication.

Public residential schools for the deaf that have prided themselves on being combined schools, but have maintained exclusively oral education with their younger children, have been nearly as guilty in contributing uneducated deaf people to our society as pure oral schools.

Assuming that a child could learn expressive and receptive communication orally equally well, ignoring individual differences in young children, attempting to teach a new language through speechreading as the receptive channel of communication, assuming oral skills could not develop if manual communication was allowed in primary classrooms, and disregarding emotional problems that arise out of frustrated communication are all factors that have contributed to the low educational level we are all concerned about and were generally practiced by combined schools as well as oral schools.

The evidence seems quite clear that total communication is what is needed for all deaf people from the youngest years to the oldest. Communication is not speech or speechreading alone. Also, it is not vocabulary building or word recognition alone. Communication is the person's ability to use his language for expressing ideas, needs and feelings. As Meadows points out, a four year old hearing child not only has the vocabulary of from two to three thousand words, but in addition he follows the rules of grammar and syntax that enable him to combine these words in many meaningful ways. The typical deaf child of the same age with exclusively oral communication has only a few words at his command and rarely expands these few words into expressions for additional meanings.

We have general agreement that the early years are tremendously important for all kinds of learning and particularly for the learning of language and communication. This leads to the conclusion that all means should be used to get concepts, ideas, words and expressions into a child's mind so that he will have the tools for communication with others and also the basic tool necessary for cognitive thinking. Studies of deaf children of deaf parents who had manual communication from their earliest years showed these children attain higher levels in school, have better language, and their performance I.Q. averages are higher. Such children had a "Head Start" with communication from their earliest years.

At our school our younger children carry on finger painting, which is not unusual for any group of young children. If an adult tries to interpret what a child means when he draws a picture he has little chance, but if the adult can ask the child what he has drawn the child can generally tell him with a great deal of information about it. By allowing our younger deaf children to use any means of communication including formal signs, informal signs, and in some instances finger spelling, the teacher could generally find out what the child had in his own mind when making a particular painting. Using this as the basis the teacher could then write a story in English in manuscript form for that individual child based on his picture. We believe that this is one of the best means of starting to teach beginning reading. It is only through total communication that this could be carried on.

At the California School for the Deaf in Riverside this year we have had two preschool classes of children between the ages of three and five. We have been teaching them signs and finger spelling as well as speech, speechreading, and word recognition from the manuscript form. We find some three year olds have developed as many as 300 usable concepts manually, while the typical number for a child using exclusively oral means is likely to be about 20 in the same period of time. The mothers come to school one day per week and use the total communication with the children at home. The mothers are highly enthusiastic because they and their children are really communicating.

We have had many five year old children of deaf parents who came to school with a good background in manual communication. When the child is old enough for the manual finger spelling to be meaningful the child will use finger spelling instead of signs when the teacher insists.

Emotional problems may result when a child's mother disappears for several hours and the child has no idea of where she has gone or when she will return. Physically the child may be quite safe with his older brother or with a baby sitter. If the mother can use any means of communication with this child to get across the idea of where she will be and perhaps some idea of when she will return, there is strong likelihood that fewer emotional fears will develop.

One of the most important sequences in every child's learning development is the period of time when he asks the question "why." Sometimes he really wants to know why and other times he doesn't really care, but he merely wants an answer that ensures contact. Without total communication most deaf children never have an opportunity to go through this learning phase. What effect has such a lack had on the development of the deaf child's cognitive powers?

Many articles about education and about teaching frequently emphasize the fact that the good teacher draws out from the individual information that he already knows, or skillful questioning and discussion help the individual to see new relationships that he was not aware of before. All of this is predicated on the assumption that a great deal of ability to use a symbol system is in that student's mind so that the teacher can utilize it. These assumptions are not valid in the case of deaf children. Without hearing and without a knowledge of language the deaf child has not been able to acquire the information and skills for the teacher to draw out. The important thing is to get information into the child's brain so that he will have it to use. It seems logical then to use every channel and every vehicle possible to get all of this mass of information and language into the child so that the teacher will have the opportunity to draw it out again in different forms and in the educative process teach the child to think. This means saturation with total communication.

REFERENCES

BRILL, R. G. A study in adjustment of three groups of deaf children. *Exceptional Children* 26 (May, 1960): 464-66.

BRILL, R. G. Hereditary aspects of deafness. *The Volta Review* 63 (April, 1961): 168-95.

BRILL, R. G. The superior I.Q.'s of deaf children of deaf parents. *The California Palms* 15 (December, 1969): 1-4.

MEADOW, K. P. Early manual communication in relation to the deaf child's intellectual, social and communicative functioning. *American Annals of the Deaf* 113 (January, 1968): 29-41.

MOORES, D. F. Psycholinguistics and deafness. *American Annals of the Deaf* 115 (January, 1970): 37-48.

MORKOVIN, B. Experiment in teaching deaf preschool children in the Soviet Union. *The Volta Review* 62 (1960): 260-68.

QUIGLEY, S. P. *The Influence of* FINGER SPELLING *on the Development of Language, Communication, and Educational Achievement in Deaf Children.* Institute for Research on Exceptional Children, University of Illinois, 1969.

VERNON, M. Mental health, deafness, and communication. *The Maryland Bulletin* 90 (February, 1970): 81-82, 94.

Richard G. Brill is Superintendent of the California School for the Deaf, Riverside.

32.
The Importance of Communication
RICHARD McELWAIN

As a strong oralist, I think it is permissible to use sign languages or fingerspelling, if and ONLY if, they are beneficial. For example, in classrooms in hearing colleges or in any public lectures, you might have an interpreter to translate the topic. This is beneficial for it is known that to lipread everything all day is often a strain and a despairing job. Assuming signs or fingerspelling are essential, let us consider those hearing people who hardly understand this means of communication. If you should approach a hearing individual such as a gas station attendant, store attendants, or policemen, how would you communicate with them in the most efficient way? Oralism is an important and interesting aspect of communication. This method is known to be successful in many respects, but not perfect as yet. What is it? This method enables one to lipread and speak intelligibly to a certain degree. Of course, it cannot apply to every deaf person, due to different environments, upbringing or different school background.

It is realized that not all the deaf can master the oral method, as not all hearing people are brilliant or stupid, but there must be a solution somewhere to the need for better communication. It is a fact that oralism is, and will always be, in great demand for the deaf by the general public and will not die in the near future. So what must be done?

From *The Junior Deaf American* 20 (May, 1969). Reprinted by permission of the publisher.

It is true that I know some manual method, I can carry on a conversation with a manualist, but I am not perfect. It astonishes me somewhat about some deaf individuals who simply refuse to go half way by not moving their lips at all! I was interested enough to learn their lingo in order to be on the same level with them, but was not granted the same courtesy. I am not interested in their vocal speech, but moving lips helps a great deal.

Now back to the hearing individual; what must be done to clear up the barrier between some of the deaf and him? He could learn the manual method all right, but how many hearing people have the time or gumption to bother? The deaf in reality are few in number, therefore the deaf must somehow integrate or communicate with the hearing to their best ability, which very often is reciprocated by the hearing people themselves. It is a sad thing that the deaf must make the first move, but he can show them his ambition to communicate with them one way or another.

I strongly feel that, in the long run, speech and lipreading offer great rewards, especially in everyday life such as in industry, participating in community events, and social affairs. From my experience in industry, employers might tend to be more attentive to employees who can speak and lipread.

Richard McElwain was a student at the National Institute for the Deaf, Rochester, New York, when this article was written.

33.
The Deaf Blind: Their Education and Their Needs
LARS GULDAGER

Evaluate the potential of each of the methods described for the instruction of deaf blind children.
How may instruction be complicated by the presence of associated handicaps?

Laura Bridgman, the first deaf blind child in the world to be educated, attended Perkins School for the Blind in Watertown, Massachusetts, in 1837. Her teacher was Dr. Samuel Gridley Howe, the director of the school. At that time Charles Dickens, who was touring the United States, visited Perkins School and observed Laura being taught by Dr. Howe. Dickens was greatly impressed by what he saw and the visit filled much space in the book he wrote about his trip. The Keller family in Alabama read Dickens' book and wrote to Perkins for help in educating their child, Helen. The Helen Keller story is well known, and will not be reiterated here.

In 1955, the first training program for teachers of the deaf blind was set up at Perkins in association with Boston University. At present, the training program is run in conjunction with Boston College. In 1968, there were 17 teacher trainees including one from Denmark, two from Jamaica, one from England, one from Canada, and one from South Africa.

World conferences in educating deaf blind children were held in 1962 in England, in 1965 in Denmark, and in 1968 in the Netherlands. There are now programs for teaching deaf blind children in the USA, England, Holland, Denmark, Norway, Germany, Australia, Russia, Switzerland, and France, and new programs are being established in other countries.

There are different criteria for admission to deaf blind departments in various parts of the world. One common to all is that the child must have combined visual and auditory handicaps, although the severity of the deficits differ. Although most departments have criteria for admission, they operate with a broad margin of doubt and will accept children on trial who do not quite meet the established criteria.

The deaf blind can be divided into the following groups:

1. Congenital blindness, acquired deafness
2. Congenital deafness, acquired blindness
3. Congenital deaf blindness

From *Exceptional Children* 36 (November, 1969): 203-06. Reprinted by permission of the author and *Exceptional Children*. Copyrighted by the Council for Exceptional Children.

4. Acquired deaf blindness

Some examples of causes are:

1. Congenital blindness, acquired deafness—meningitis
2. Congenital blindness, acquired blindness—retinitis pigmentosa
3. Congenital deaf blindness— congenital rubella
4. Acquired deaf blindness—accidents

One of these causes is generating much concern throughout the world—rubella. During 1963-65 an epidemic of rubella swept the United States and several studies have been made of these so-called rubella children.

Stenquist and Robbins (1967) studied 28 rubella children at Perkins School for the Blind. They described some of the characteristics of these children: thinness, a low hairline with double cowlicks, a bumpy nose with a deviated septum, delicate hands and feet, an almost fanatical obsession with light, a delay in physical progress, unusual pleasure in rocking, lack of recognition of human relationships, little interest in food, and difficulties with toilet training.

In April 1968, the Developmental Evaluation Clinic of the Children's Hospital Medical Center (1969) in Boston studied 46 deaf children with congenital rubella. Their findings, when complete, will be made available to the Advisory Council for the Deaf. The major handicaps observed were deafness, congenital heart disease, cataracts, and gross mental retardation. The 46 children exhibited the following handicaps:

1. Mental retardation—moderate or severe in about 10 percent of the cases. Another 30 percent had low-average intelligence ratings.
2. Behavioral abnormalities—in those not markedly retarded, about 30 percent.
3. Visual handicap—cataracts in 15 percent of the cases. Strabismus occurred in about 20 percent of the cases.
4. Neurologic abnormalities and/or limitations in motor skills—excluding the group of retarded children, about 50 percent had faulty balance, coordination, and control of movement.
5. Congenital heart disease—in about 25 percent of the children, with half of these having serious heart disease.
6. Small size—40 percent of the children were below the third percentile in height.
7. Receptive language problems—this was difficult to evaluate.

Communication with the Deaf Blind

The senses of sight and hearing are normally used as the mediums for communication. One hears an airplane come long before seeing it but one does not know what kind it is before coordinating sight with hearing, "consulting" the brain, and comparing the stimuli with what is stored there.

The deaf blind person has to substitute for these senses—the near senses of touch, smell, and taste. In most instances, however, the deaf blind child has some residual hearing and vision to supplement the near senses. Most children labeled as deaf blind do in fact have some usable sight and hearing.

The following communication systems are used with the deaf blind: (a) speech and vibration, (b) fingerspelling, (c) gestures, (d) sign language, and (e) communication using a machine.

Internationally, in most deaf blind departments, speech and vibration are stressed as the main form for communication. However, there are many children who never will learn to speak and, therefore, must use one of the other systems.

Vibration. (Tadoma Method) This method was developed by Sofia Alcorn with two deaf blind students named Tad and Oma. The sense of touch is used for receptive language. The student puts his hand on the face of the person to whom he is talking. The thumb covers the mouth and feels the movements of the lips, jaws, and tongue. The four other fingers are spread over the cheek and jaw to pick up vibrations.*

Fingerspelling. Each letter in the alphabet has a specific finger position. The letters are spelled into the hand of the deaf blind person and the deaf blind person spells out his ideas to the person with whom he is talking.

Gesture. The normal young child finds movement and language inseparable. To the young deaf blind child, language must also be movement, and there is meaning in language for him only insofar as it includes movement. The natural method of expression should, therefore, be movement for the deaf blind child as well as for the seeing and hearing child. The young deaf blind child may express himself, then, in natural gestures. This spontaneous gesturing is rare in the congenitally deaf blind child and he must be taught to use gestures as one of the first steps in learning language. When the young seeing and hearing child shows his desire for a ball by making a gesture for a bouncing ball, this is an opportunity for adults to present speech for the child. The child should be allowed to use these natural gestures as a road breaker for speech, but later the child substitutes the spoken word for the nature gesture. The same principle holds true for the young deaf blind child: natural gestures are necessary, but not as the final goal.

Sign Language. In sign language, each word has as its symbol a movement of hands and arms. Movements are combined to form a language used mainly by deaf students. In some instances, deaf blind students can use

---

*For an account of this method see: Sophia K. Alcorn, Development of the Tadoma Method for the deaf blind. *Exceptional Children* 11 (January, 1945): 117-19. *The Editors*

this system, but speech and fingerspelling are more often preferred. The movements of sign language are difficult for the deaf blind child to pick up through touch or residual sight.

Communication Using a Machine. Two machines will be mentioned: the Tele Touch machine and the Artificial Ear. The latter was introduced by a Danish firm some years ago and translates sound into vibration patterns in a number of keys. However, it has not yet been adequately evaluated through research.

The Tele Touch machine consists of a typewriter keyboard and a braille cell. The deaf blind person puts his finger on the braille cell; the person talking to him uses the keyboard. For example, pressing "A" on the keyboard makes the braille "A" appear. This system is usually used by deaf and blind people who become handicapped after school age. It can easily be used without specialized training on the part of the hearing and seeing person, who needs only to know how to spell.

The method most widely taught in schools is speech with vibration. In some instances several methods such as speech, vibration, and fingerspelling are combined. It is sometimes necessary to use every available method to communicate with a deaf blind person.

The Educational Process

Developing skills in children starts very early. R. R. Gariepy (1967) tells of a Japanese music teacher who takes his pupils before they are born. He says that it is very important that the parents develop the right attitude immediately. After the child's birth, the parents are asked to play appropriate music to stimulate the infant's abilities to learn.

A newborn baby should be surrounded with the right kind of auditory stimuli. When the baby is mature enough he should be in the middle of the family activities, not left alone all day. Later the child enjoys participating in family activities and helping other family members. For example, the child loves to help mother in her household tasks, so everyday activities can be used as a learning medium.

Later when the child plays soccer, baseball, balances on the curb, climbs trees, and swims, the child really is receiving training in motor coordination, eye-hand coordination, auditory localization, and figure-ground discrimination. He is exploring the potential of the body, training the senses, and learning to judge distance and perspective and coordinate his body movements.

This development is basic for all children. If there has been a gap in the development for whatever reasons, the child is handicapped and needs special attention. It is obvious that the deaf blind child is probably seriously lacking in the above mentioned training. The earlier a deaf blind child can be identified and given direction in skill development, the better.

An important area in educating deaf blind children is language. Following is an example of how one deaf blind Danish girl learned the language symbol for airplane. One morning an airplane passed high over the clouds; she could not see it but had enough hearing to clearly hear the noise. She looked up, pointed to the sky, and looked very questioningly at her teacher, who told her it was an airplane. She now had the first clue; to her at that time an airplane was a noise in the sky. A few days later when a jet fighter passed over the school, the girl heard the noise and said the word for airplane. She had a chance to see it pass over her head and now had the second clue: an airplane was a noise and looked like a bird. A classmate used an airplane to go home and when the girl heard that she became very confused. She did not believe that the student could fit into the bird-like thing in the sky. The next time her classmate flew home, the girl accompanied her to the airport. She saw the airplane land and turn from a "little bird" into a "big thing." Some weeks later she, herself, went to Copenhagen by plane and finally she gained enough clues to complete her concept of the word "airplane."

A Dutch colleague gave an example of how too few clues are often given to develop a concept. In a class for deaf children, he found a picture of a hammer with the word for hammer printed underneath and asked a child what it was. The boy made a gesture for hammer and appeared to know what it was. The two of them went to the woodwork shop but the boy could not point out a hammer, although there were several in clear view. The use of a picture and a natural gesture by the teacher was like starting to build an apartment building on the fifth floor. The child had never had experience with a hammer so that a picture and a gesture told the child nothing.

When building language and experience for the deaf blind child, one must use real things, situations from the child's world, not imitations or situations from preprimers to which the child cannot relate. To teach the child about the mail, for instance, have him buy paper, envelopes, and stamps and write a letter to his parents. While shopping, it is a good idea to take a Polaroid camera and show the pictures to the child right away. On returning to the classroom, they can be used to help write a story about what happened. The child has seen the pictures being taken and can associate with the things. It is more real when the child is in the picture himself, when it is from his own world.

Use a movie camera and the child himself as the "star." One can put a text on it and make worksheets to go with the movie. The children will learn better when they are in the center of the situation and not just reading about a strange storybook child whom they do not care about.

Speech

Before beginning to educate a deaf blind child, one must be sure that his needs have been properly evaluated. The child should be seen, if possible, by a pediatrician, otologist, ophthalmologist, neurologist, audiologist, dentist, and psychiatrist. This is the ideal situation which is rarely realized in practice. When the child comes to speech lessons, he should have been fitted with the proper hearing aids if needed. Some years ago, there was a deaf blind child in Denmark with hearing impairment of unknown degree. In motor training and auditory training classes the child was taught to move her body to sound, first using her whole body, later using parts of the body. Finally she was able to take part in normal play audiometry. The child had not been ready for the test before; it was the teacher's responsibility to prepare the child for such an examination.

Some important factors in the teaching of speech to deaf blind children are:

1. Start as early as possible with prespeech work.
2. Make the child pay attention to the mouth with touch.
3. Use the methods which adapt to both teacher and child.
4. Be sure to use the child's residual hearing and sight.
5. Be sure the child receives maximal help with his individual hearing aid.
6. Teach parents of housemothers what they must learn to help the child.
7. Use visual speech apparatus.
8. Use good amplifiers in individual lessons.
9. Make the child love speech.

Audiovisual Machines

On the market today there are many teaching machines and audiovisual apparatus such as Language Masters, tape recorders, and video-tapes. There are possibilities in these machines for use with the deaf blind. Unfortunately, very few commercial programs, tapes, and films can be used. One must make one's own materials, and they can be a good supplement to the teacher. However, the teacher is still the most important factor in the program.

REFERENCES

GARIEPY, R. R. *Your Child Is Dying to Learn!* Barre, Mass.: Barre Publishers, 1967.
ROBBINS, N. & STENQUIST, G. *The Deaf Blind "Rubella" Child.* Watertown, Mass.: Perkins School for the Blind, 1967.
Developmental Evaluation Clinic of Children's Hospital Medical Center. *The Rubella Study.* 1968.

Lars Guldager is Assistant Principal, Department for Deaf Blind Children, Perkins School for the Blind, Watertown, Massachusetts.

Eight

Visually Handicapped Children

Most people know that the braille system is used by the blind. Few know, however, that Louis Braille, the inventor of this reading system, was himself blind, or that his system was not used by his peers but only became popular after his death. It is appropriate, therefore, to call attention to his work in this chapter concerning visually handicapped children.

Most sighted people are at a loss to know how to react to the common demands made upon them when they meet a blind person. Some are embarrassed because they do not know how to help, or whether or not they should help. William Goodman provides some practical leads for the uninitiated in his interesting article, "When You Meet a Blind Person."

It has been a common practice to distinguish between persons who are blind and those who are visually impaired. Yet it often is surprising to those who are just beginning their study of exceptional children to find that most "blind" or legally blind persons may have usable vision. The term "visually impaired" is used to describe children with greatly reduced visual acuity. In the second article, Benjamin Wolf points out some of the differences in the needs of children with low visual acuity and those of children who lack usable sight.

Limitations in travel imposed by blindness tend to result in greatly reduced experiences for the blind, but since World War II significant progress has been made in teaching orientation and mobility skills to blind children and adults. Paul Schulz examines some of the psychological factors relating to the teaching of travel skills in the third article in this part.

Blindness is often considered more of a vocational and social hardship than a retardant to school learning. The psychological and neuropsychological effects of blindness may be far-reaching. Jerome Cohen reviews some of the effects of blindness on children's development in this chapter.

The age of technology has made important contributions to the education and management of the blind, as the reader will learn from the discussion at a symposium reported by the editors of *The New Outlook for the Blind*. Among the advances are such improvements as increasing the production of braille materials, translation of print into braille by scanners, electronic travel aids, and more rapid reproduction of speech for persons who depend on recordings as a substitute for reading. They are described in the report entitled "The Blind in the Age of Technology: A Public Discussion," which is the final article in this chapter.

Louis Braille
1809-1852

EDUCATOR
INNOVATOR
ORGANIST

Louis Braille, for whom the braille system used by the blind is named, was born near Paris in 1809. His father maintained a shop in the home, where he made harnesses. One day, while handling his father's tools, Louis, age three, accidentally cut his eye with the harness-maker's knife. Infection soon spread to the other eye and in a short time Louis had lost his sight. His parents, with deep affection, took time to help him understand his environment and to assist with his education in the village school where he surpassed his seeing classmates in achievement. At the age of ten, on his own urging, his parents enrolled him in the Paris School for the Blind from which he later graduated and whose faculty he joined.

Few aids existed at that time to assist with the instruction of the blind in reading and writing. Sometimes twigs were used to form letters. A system of embossed letters designed by Haüg was in use, but it was very difficult to read by touch and, of course, was of no help in the task of writing. Braille undertook to adapt a system of dots which had been developed by Barbier. This system had employed twelve dots—two vertical rows, six high. Braille found the mass of dots too difficult to comprehend by touch so he reduced the number of dots from twelve to six— two vertical rows of three each. The Paris school temporarily rejected Braille's new system and did not, in fact, adopt it during his lifetime, so that he was forced to bootleg instruction in it after school hours. However, in 1952, on the centennial of his death, his remains were exhumed and brought to Paris to rest among the immortals in the Pantheon.

34.
When You Meet a Blind Person
WILLIAM GOODMAN

*How many suggestions, new to you, can you gain
from this article that will assist you in your
relations with a blind person?*

During the summer of 1962, while working as a
mobility instructor at the Ohio School for the Blind in Columbus, I had occasion to work with a teenage blind girl near the Ohio State University campus. One day, upon reaching the street corner, she found the curb with her
cane and listened carefully to the traffic sounds, trying to find a break in
the traffic so that she could cross the street safely. As she waited, a foreign
student, perhaps from India, observed her with a solemn, puzzled look.
After a couple of minutes of serious deliberation, he walked over to the
young lady. Without saying a word, he grabbed the tip of her cane and
pulled it horizontally across the street. The girl, holding on for dear life,
followed passively behind her cane!

In this incident, we can see at once the good intentions of sighted people toward blind people and their general lack of information and technique for dealing with them. In a way many of us are foreigners when it
comes to dealing with blind people because, for the most part, we have
little direct contact with them. With this in mind, the aim of this paper is
to provide some ideas, some practical do's and don't's about meeting a
blind person and how to be most helpful, without stepping on each other's
toes—the physical or the emotional ones.

Perhaps you have never met a blind person. This is not surprising since
there are relatively few blind people in this country—perhaps half a million who are legally blind. Of that number, less than 10 percent are totally
blind; the vast majority of legally blind people have a considerable amount
of residual vision. Another reason might be that you have avoided such a
meeting because you were unsure about what to do and what to talk
about.

It may be useful to become aware of some basic differences among blind
people. One basic difference is between those who are totally blind and
those who are partially sighted. Some sighted people mistakenly believe that
only those who are totally without sight are considered blind. Differences
are also related to the time in life when blindness occurred. Those blinded
from birth or during the first five years of life experience blindness as an

From *The New Outlook for the Blind* 64 (June, 1970): 186-92. Reprinted by permission of the author and *The New Outlook for the Blind*.

integral part of their mental and emotional growth. This group is referred to as the congenitally blind. In contrast, those who become blind later in life, known as the adventitiously blinded or newly blind, are faced with the task of integrating blindness into personalities they developed as a sighted person. Some people become blind suddenly as a result of an accident, others gradually over a period of time due to a disease. Of course, there are volumes written on the causes and effects of blindness, and the more information you gain on the subject, the more effective you will be as you interact with a blind person.

Meeting a Blind Person

Meeting a blind person is much like meeting any other person. The same rules of courtesy and tact apply. Common sense is sufficient to cope with most new or sensitive situations. It will also help if you do not assume that a blind person is helpless, that he is either gifted or defective, that he is hard of hearing or an accomplished musician. Blind people are as different from one another as are sighted people. Some have the ability to put you at ease, others do not. Don't let a person's blindness keep you from seeing him as a unique individual, with assets and faults like anyone else.

SHAKING HANDS

When you first meet a blind person, take a little more initiative than you ordinarily might. Begin by making your presence known with a casual hello or other appropriate greeting. Even though you may have met the person before, avoid playing games like "Guess who I am?" It is best to identify yourself right away.

You may wonder whether you should shake hands. This question should be handled just as you would when dealing with a sighted person. One difference is that the blind person who wants to shake hands with you may make only a small gesture, moving his hand slightly upward from his side because he does not know exactly where your hand is or whether you wish to shake hands with him. If you see his hand make such a movement, reach for it, even though it requires you to go more than half way. When meeting a blind child, it is a good idea to reach for his hand even though no gesture is made by the child. This physical contact gives the child concrete evidence of your presence and replaces the friendly smile or nod that he cannot see. This is also a small way to help the child to develop social skills.

SPEAK DIRECTLY TO THE BLIND PERSON

If the blind person is with someone else, do not use his companion as an interpreter for what you want to say to the blind person. Speak directly to the blind person, aiming your eyes and voice at his face. In this way it is easier for the blind person to tell when you are talking to him and it is simply the same courtesy you would extend to the person if he were sighted. Don't raise your voice on the assumption that he is deaf. Speak in a normal, natural tone of voice. It may be a strange experience at first to talk directly with someone who cannot see you. Your reaction might be to say as little as possible because you are not sure that he understands you or how he is reacting to you. This uncertainty is natural and can be overcome in time with experience, once you get into the give-and-take of ordinary conversation.

Talking About Blindness

Regarding the subject of blindness, don't feel that you must talk about it and don't feel that you must not talk about it. If it comes up naturally in the course of a conversation, and both of you feel comfortable with it, go ahead and discuss it. You should avoid expressions of pity and references to blindness as an affliction. This irritates those who are reasonably adjusted to their blindness and discourages those who have not yet reached that stage.

There may be times when you wonder whether a blind person needs your help to get from one place to another. When in doubt, the best idea is to ask the blind person if he would like some assistance. Your question should be in an off-hand manner that does not sound condescending or maudlin. If your offer of help is turned down, do not insist on helping anyhow. You should assume that the blind person knows his own mind—that if he wants your help he will accept it. If your offer is accepted, don't provide any more help than is necessary in a given situation.

Leading a Blind Person

Assuming that you are going to lead a blind person, what is the best way to go about it? Control your natural impulse to grab his arm and push him ahead of you. This arrangement is awkward for both of you. The blind person will have a greater sense of security and direction if he holds on to your arm just above the elbow. You take the initiative in this by asking him to put his hand there and, at the same time, placing his hand above your elbow with your free hand. If a blind person is experienced at being led, it may be sufficient to touch his arm with your elbow and he will automatically reach for it. You can walk with the blind person on either your right or left side, depending on what seems most comfortable for both of you. Needless to say, leading a blind person should be done as inconspicuously as possible, without bringing undue attention to either of you. Although a blind person cannot see the people around him, he senses their presence and their reactions as much as anyone else does.

The arm you use for guiding can be either bent at the elbow or hang straight down, as you prefer; the important thing is to relax your arm. Tension in your arm can be detected by the blind person and this might reduce his feeling of confidence in you as a reliable guide. After all, he is placing his safety in your hands and he will want to know how much he can trust you. So try to relax. With experience you will find that leading a blind person is not as difficult as it might seem at first.

Walk Slightly Ahead

Ordinarily you should walk slightly ahead of the blind person—about one half step. This makes it easier for him to follow the motion of your body. It will also help for both of you to walk in step with each other and fairly close together, but not quite shoulder to shoulder. Don't let the blind person lag a full arm's length behind because it is more difficult to lead him, especially when in narrow passages and when making turns. On the other hand, if he gets too close to you, he is likely to trip over your heels.

Walking Pace

There is no absolute rule about how fast you should walk with a blind person. Here again, use common sense and be sensitive to his needs. If you are walking too fast, you will feel the blind person pulling back on your arm. You should respond to this by slowing down. If you walk too slowly, the blind person may keep trying to walk ahead of you. His idea of a comfortable walking pace may be quite different from yours, especially when walking in unfamiliar territory. However, an experienced traveler may soon grow impatient with a walking pace that is overcautious. When starting or stopping, try to do so gradually and smoothly, avoiding any sudden or unexpected movements. Walk in as straight a line as possible, making turns only when necessary. As you get to know a blind person better, your cues to him become more subtle and less verbal. You will soon develop signals that are passed almost unconsciously between the two of you. You become accustomed to each other and begin to function as a team.

If you happen to be leading more than one blind person at a time, place both of them on one side, the one having the most vision on the outside. At best this arrangement is difficult, for the guide as well as for the blind persons; and so this practice should be used only when absolutely necessary.

Doorways

When walking through a narrow doorway, it is difficult for both of you to move through side by side. You can either turn sideways, so that both of you are sidestepping through in single file, or you can bring your elbow toward the middle of your back; the blind person walks almost directly behind you, but not close enough to step on your heels. If the door needs to be held open, ask the blind person to hold on to it as he passes through. It is a good idea to involve the blind person actively whenever practical, giving him the feeling of participation rather than one of passive dependency. If the door is hinged on the side opposite the blind person, he can either switch to your opposite side or just switch his hand to your other elbow.

As you go through the doorway, try to maintain a steady forward movement, avoiding unnecessary twists of the body which can easily confuse the blind person and cause him to become unsteady. Make sure his fingers don't get caught in the crack of the door as it closes! Keep your eye on your companion until he is completely through the door. Having managed the door safely, don't make the mistake of stopping to talk with the blind person's back to a door that may open unexpectedly. The same applies to having him stand with his back to a flight of stairs—one small step backwards and he would be in trouble.

LOCATING AND AVOIDING OBSTACLES

Since you do take a certain amount of responsibility for the blind person when leading him, it is quite possible that you will feel afraid that he may hurt himself. Perhaps this fear, more than any other factor, can make you nervous and less effective. Within reasonable limits, anxiety is good because it keeps you on your toes, doing your utmost to ensure the safety of the blind person. But it is difficult to be responsible for two bodies instead of just one. Not infrequently you will be looking ahead to locate obstacles, and may not notice that the blind person is bumping into an obstacle that you have already cleared. On the other hand, if you keep your eyes on him too much, you may very well bump into some obstacle yourself. In time you will develop the skill of alternating your vision from looking ahead to watching the blind person. Make sure he has cleared the obstacle before you take your eyes off him.

WHEN HE BUMPS INTO SOMETHING

Inevitably the blind person will bump into something while you are leading. Most of the time these bumps will not be harmful, other than jarring his confidence in your ability to lead. When a bump does occur, don't draw attention to it; assuming there was no real harm done, pass it off lightly. At the same time, try to realize why the accident occurred so you will not make the same mistake twice. There may be times when, for one reason or another, you do not wish to guide a particular blind person. For example, he may become demanding of your services and take them for granted, as something you were obligated to provide for him. When this situation develops, take a firm stand on setting limits on your services as a guide, which are, after all, voluntary.

STAIRWAYS

No doubt during your travels with a blind person you will have to deal with stairways. Approach the stairs head-on rather than at an angle. This gives the person a better idea of a straight direction down the stairs. Also, as you approach the stairs, be sure to mention whether the steps go up or down. Pause when you get to the edge of the first step. Have the blind person touch the edge of the first step with his foot so that he knows exactly where it is before he starts down. You might want to describe briefly how long the stairway is, how wide, and how crowded. As you start down the steps, stay one step ahead of him because this makes it easier for him to follow and he can detect when you have reached the bottom landing, making it less likely that he will mistakenly take an extra step that is not there. While walking down move at an even pace that is somewhat slower than the pace used at ground level. Use these same pointers while going up stairs, still staying one step ahead of him. He may feel more secure, either going up or down stairs, if he holds onto a bannister with his free hand. This is especially true for a newly blinded person, or for someone you are leading for the first time on an unfamiliar stairway.

SITTING ON A CHAIR

Another situation that requires special attention is helping a blind person into a chair. When you reach the chair, place his hand on the seat of the chair and then place the same hand on the top of the chair's back. In this way he can slip into the chair knowing exactly which way it is facing and where the back is. If you put his hand on the back of the chair but not on the seat, there is the danger that he may end up sitting on the floor, not having learned which way the chair was facing. Position yourself near the chair as he sits down so you can help out if he has any trouble. Make sure he has physical contact with the chair before you turn away; don't just say "there's the chair," and then walk away unless you are familiar with the person's abilities. Once he is seated, you may give a verbal description of where the chair is located in relation to other objects and people. This will give him a sense of orientation, especially if you have to leave him alone.

IN AND OUT OF AUTOMOBILES

As for getting seated in an automobile, it is best to give the blind person information so that he can enter it himself, rather than being led into it on your arm. Let him know which way the car is facing by having him touch the hood or the windshield wipers; then have him find the door handle. Be sure to let him open the door himself. With one hand he can hold on to the edge of the roof and duck his head under his hand, thus preventing a head injury on the metal roof. Feeling for the seat with the other hand, he can easily slide into place. For a beginner, stand close by until he completes the operation to make sure that he can handle it. When leaving the car, the hand should go on the roof again, the head being ducked underneath it. If the blind person has a cane, it should be taken into the car only after he is seated; it is then placed upright between his knees. Leaving the car, the cane goes out first. By using this procedure there is less chance of his stumbling over the cane.

AUDITORIUM AND THEATER SEATING

When finding a seat in an auditorium or theatre, the guide leads the blind person in the usual way into the row of seats. Both side-step together until they are in front of their seats and then sit down. Going out of the row, cross in front of the blind person and then lead in the usual manner.

ESCALATORS

Using an escalator is similar to the procedure for walking up and down stairs, except that the idea of a moving stairway can create more anxiety in you and in the blind person. Therefore, more attention and preparation is called for. Let him feel the handrail and then get his feet near the edge of the first moving step. Step on to the escalator with as smooth a motion as possible, watching carefully as the blind person gets his balance and adjusts his feet. Stay one step ahead of him as you would on ordinary stairs; in this way he can feel you level off at the top of the escalator.

RESTAURANTS

You may have occasion to go to a restaurant with a blind person. There is nothing wrong with reading the menu to him, unless he already knows what he wants. When the waitress takes your order, be sure she takes the blind person's order from him and not from you. If he needs the salt shaker or an ashtray, it is easier to touch the ashtray to his hand than give elaborate verbal directions. If he requests help cutting his meat, do so inconspicuously. At the end of the meal, give him the check for his dinner and let him pay the cashier himself. This is one small example of how you can help the blind person maintain his dignity as an independent human being, even though in certain practical respects he must depend on others.

GIVING DIRECTIONS

If you are in a situation where you have to give directions to a blind person, use concrete, simple words. Pick out the outstanding landmarks on the trip you are describing, and don't get bogged down in a lot of detail that can confuse more than help. Avoid using compass directions unless you are sure about them and in your judgment the blind person understands your references to north and south. This is also true about using the simple terms left and right; it is surprisingly easy to stumble over these apparently easy directions and say exactly the opposite of what you mean. After giving a set of directions, it is a good idea to ask the blind person to repeat them to you, so that you can correct any errors before he begins the trip.

Mobility Aids and Devices

It is likely that some blind people you meet will be carrying a cane. While being led by you, he may touch the ground occasionally in order to have some contact with the environment and to add to his feeling of confidence. This does not mean that you have any less responsibility for him; it is just another sensor for him. Usually he will not use the cane when being led. He may cradle the cane on his elbow, keeping it out of his way and yours. The blind person may have a folding cane which can easily be folded and put in his pocket when not in use. If the cane does interfere with your guiding the person, discourage its use. When walking in crowded areas, see that the cane does not extend so far ahead that it trips other people.

If the blind person has a dog guide, follow basically the same procedures that apply to a person without a dog. Ask if he needs help, even though he may appear to be totally independent with his dog. If he accepts your offer of assistance, have him hold on to your arm in the usual manner. In this case, it will require more attention on your part because you are now concerned with three body widths. Be sure not to go up escalators with a dog guide because his paws might get caught in the moving stairs.

Electronic devices are slowly coming into use by blind people as travel aids. If you encounter a person using one of these devices, don't be intimidated by its novelty. He is still a human being and can be approached just as though he were using any other kind of travel aid. The electronic device and the dog guide may serve as an interesting basis for a conversation.

One final idea that might be helpful in developing your understanding of blindness is to put on a blindfold and perform some of the tasks mentioned in this paper and other ones you can think of that a blind person must cope with in his everyday life. Because there are obvious dangers involved, especially for the fearless beginner, be sure to have proper supervision when you do so. Such experiences may prove more valuable than any reading you may do on the subject.

In conclusion there are no fixed rules for being with blind people. They are simply people who do not see well or do not see at all. Relating to them with common sense and sincerity will enable you to deal with nearly any situation. The ideas and pointers presented here are not absolute, nor do they touch on all possible situations you may encounter. But they may encourage your first moves in the direction of a blind person, and serve as focal points for your own thinking on the subject. In time, you will develop your own procedures which work for you and for the blind people you get to know.

At the time this article was published, William Goodman was an instructor in the Department of Habilitative Sciences, College of Education, Florida State University, Tallahassee, and a doctoral candidate in special education there.

35.
Visual Impairment Is Not Blindness
BENJAMIN WOLF

*In what ways are the needs of the visually
handicapped person significantly different from
those of the blind person?*

It is generally accepted that most individuals who
are labeled "blind" have varying degrees of vision. Nevertheless, those in
agencies for the blind, as well as members of the general population, often
act, talk, and think as though individuals are only either blind or not blind.
In the case of agencies, this kind of stereotyping results in services that
are geared largely for totally blind people; further, it is assumed that visually limited persons can benefit from these same services. The emphasis
in such programs is on helping people to compensate for their lack of sight
through the use of their other senses with little or no attention to the use of
their remaining vision. The framework of agency services will in general
involve mobility instruction, dependence on tactual usage, and aural reading even though what may be needed is attention to the actual visual potential of individuals. Obviously there are exceptions to this generalization,
yet the prevailing attitudes are such that the subject does merit re-exam-
ination.

First of all, there are very basic differences in the attitudes of sighted
people toward those who are blind and those who have limited vision.
Blind persons are generally objects of pity and, without going into the
many psychological factors involved, it is apparent that there is an overwhelming desire to aid and comfort blind persons. That is why blind beg-
gars can make a go of it on city streets and why agencies for the blind are
reluctant to change the word "blind" in their names to "visually impaired"
or "visually handicapped." "Blind" has money appeal, while the latter
phrases do not. Visually limited people, on the other hand, often arouse irritation and annoyance. They seem unnecessarily awkward or boorish. They
bump into things and do not seem to see where they are going at times.
They often have unusual postures, cock their heads, or twist their faces.
All of these characteristics seem to stimulate distaste and annoyance even
though they are simply a result of the individual's determined efforts to
make use of what vision he has.

Speaking very generally, there are differences between partially sighted
and totally blind persons in addition to their differences in visual acuity.
Blind children, for example, are often rather placid and unmotivated. They

From *The New Outlook for the Blind* 65 (December, 1971): 334-36. Reprinted
by permission of the author and *The New Outlook for the Blind.*

seem to accept their plight, especially if they have no memory of sight, and must be motivated from the outside in order to grow and develop. Whatever tragedy there is in their lives is usually a result of their emotionally upset parents providing them with a tense and critical environment. Partially sighted children, on the other hand, are often irritatingly persistent and searching. They try to relocate and capitalize on whatever bit of vision that they have. They will often deny their problem and try to keep up with their peers. They and their parents never give up the search for improvement or cure. If their condition involves a gradual deterioration of vision, they make continual adjustments to ever new visual situations.

Principles of Service

All of the differences between blind and visually limited persons need to be better understood and to be reflected in the structuring of services offered by agencies. Since these are more than quantitative differences in vision, each group will very often require a different complex of services. Unfortunately, there is little in the literature to guide the agency wishing to make this distinction, and much research, therefore, needs to be done in this area. Nevertheless, a number of basic principles upon which such services can be based have already emerged.

DIFFERENT SPECIALISTS ARE INVOLVED

First, it is clear that there is a difference in the kind of specialists that will make up the rehabilitation teams concerned with the two groups. Once the fact of total blindness is established, there is little need for any continued involvement by ophthalmological or optometric specialists. For partially sighted clients, however, there is a more or less continuous need for the involvement of ophthalmologists and optometrists, a need stemming from the variability of the remaining vision itself and from changes in the functional requirements of the individual as his personal situation is altered by the rehabilitation process.

KNOWLEDGE OF REMAINING VISION IS ESSENTIAL

Second, while blind clients usually require only behavioral services, partially sighted persons may need a combination of both behavioral and medical or physical services. The counsellor needs to know not only about the partially sighted person's social milieu, his interests, his motivations and needs, but also the specific nature of his vision—what he actually sees and under what conditions he sees best. This understanding is best achieved through the cooperative efforts of the entire team, ophthalmologist or optometrist, social worker, rehabilitation counsellor, and teacher. Detailed knowledge about an individual's sight has a significant bearing on how he is to be helped vocationally and even in the development of his life style.

Optical Aids and Eye Exercises

Third, whatever vision is available to the partially sighted person should be strengthened or augmented in every way possible, either through mechanical or physical means. Optical aids, which have been steadily improved over the years, are proving to be increasingly effective in assisting partially sighted persons to extend their seeing potential. Vision can also be strengthened through a regimen of eye exercises which help the individual to coordinate eye muscles and otherwise habituate himself to the most appropriate use of his remaining vision. While there is some difference of opinion about the value of this physical approach to the improvement of sight and a good deal of research and study needs to be done in this area, eye exercises under careful supervision have proved to be helpful to some individuals. Whether optical aids or physical exercises are used, however, careful follow-up is needed to assess improvement and to effect whatever changes or adjustments are needed to insure maximum visual functioning.

Using Remaining Vision

Finally, the development of a complex of services that is directly meaningful for persons with some vision must include a basic understanding of the differences between sight and perception. It is now generally acknowledged that a person should use whatever vision he has, not because such use effects any physical change, but rather because visual abilities improve with stimulation and use. When a partially sighted person makes full use of his vision, his perception increases in that what he sees becomes a more meaningful clue to his environment. For example, he may only see a small part of a street sign, but it is enough to tell him whether or not it is the street he wants. He may only be able to see the outline of a tree trunk, yet it tells him that the path to his house is a few steps ahead. Such an increase in the use of visual clues to the environment can be immeasurably important to the partially sighted person.

Summary

Visual impairment is not necessarily blindness and the requirements of visually impaired persons are in many ways significantly different from those of blind persons. All too often agencies for the blind have not distinguished between these different requirements in providing services. The essential difference is that blind persons must rely on their other senses in order to function, while partially sighted persons must be helped to use whatever vision they have in coordination with their other senses. In providing services to partially sighted persons, the following basic principles should be considered: (1) Full service requires the cooperation of medical, physical, and behavioral specialists; (2) Services for partially sighted clients should be individualized on the basis of their differences in degree and quality of sight; (3) Whatever vision the client has should be augmented or strengthened through either mechanical or physical means; and (4) Clients should be helped to enhance their perception to its maximum functional potential.

Benjamin Wolf is Regional Consultant for the Western Regional Office in San Francisco of the American Foundation for the Blind.

36.
Psychological Factors in Orientation and Mobility Training
PAUL J. SCHULZ

The training of a blind person to manage in his environment is of great importance. Try to identify the many problems involved in orientation and mobility training.

The emotional interaction between the mobility instructor and the student is an essential element in the successful outcome of mobility training. The teaching process does not consist merely of the transfer of information from the instructor to the student. Certainly the technical aspects of mobility training are the primary concern of the instructor, but the interplay of personal factors also can and does affect the outcome of instruction. As in all relationships between individuals, the positive and negative feelings, personality characteristics, beliefs, and attitudes of the instructor and the student may either interfere with or facilitate their interaction.

Transference-Like Situations

Of particular importance are the positive and negative feelings that are similar to those known in counseling or psychotherapy as transference and counter-transference. In simple terms, transference is the reaction of the patient to the therapist based on feelings which originate in his past close relationships with other persons. The feelings or perceptions may be positive or negative, but they will, in some

From *The New Outlook for the Blind* 66 (May, 1972): 129-34. Reprinted by permission of the author and *The New Outlook for the Blind.*

way, affect the therapeutic relationship. Counter-transference is a comparable feeling on the part of the therapist toward the patient.

Although, in a strict sense, the instructor-student relationship is not equivalent to that of the therapist and patient, it does include many of the same elements. The therapist deals primarily with the feelings, while the mobility instructor and student are concerned with the transmitting and acquisition of knowledge and a particular skill. Yet, because the process of mobility instruction also assists the blind person in developing self-confidence and renewed self-image as an adequate individual, it is similar to the therapeutic relationship.

INSTRUCTOR AS AN AUTHORITY FIGURE

The quality of the relationship, which is often a close one, will tend to arouse attitudes and feelings toward the instructor, such as resistance to the pressure of the instructor or dependence on him. In other words, by virtue of his position in the relationship, the instructor may be perceived as an authority figure. The student's attitude toward such figures and his perception of the instructor will therefore influence his reactions during instruction. In addition, the frequency of the contact between them will add to the intensity of these feelings.

The Problem of Dependence

These considerations are of particular importance when the relationship is between a professional and a person who is attempting to make an adjustment to the loss of sight. Such a person, during the initial stages of his blindness or severe visual impairment, is, of course, necessarily dependent. He may exploit this dependence or he may resent it; and his reactions may become focussed on the person with whom he has frequent contact and who is in a helping position.

INSTRUCTOR'S REACTIONS

Conversely, the mobility instructor may react negatively or positively to the feelings of the student. If the instructor resents the wishes of the student to exploit his dependent status, it will adversely affect the instructor's ability to teach. Similarly, if the resistance of the student irritates him, he may not be completely objective in his treatment of the student during the lesson.

The Benefits of a Deeper Understanding

If the instructor can understand his own motivation or the basis for his reaction to a particular student, he will be better able to deal with the feelings. If he understands the feelings of the student, he can be more objective in his work with him. Even if understanding is not possible, however, the awareness of his feelings may sometimes be sufficient; that is, if he is sensitive to his own feelings as well as to the feelings of his students, he can often control his reactions.

IMPROVED EVALUATION

A further benefit of such an approach is that the instructor can better evaluate the progress of his student. A student who is making little or no progress may be perfectly capable and the instructor may be applying all the appropriate principles and utilizing his technical knowledge to the fullest. If there is difficulty then, it may actually be related to the emotional interaction between them. Once he has determined this, the instructor can either use an alternative approach with the student or, if necessary, turn him over to another instructor. In either case, he facilitates the progress of the student.

Informal Discussions with Instructors

As part of an in-service training program at the Braille Institute of America in Los Angeles, a group of orientation and mobility instructors met with this writer for an informal discussion session. Each of these men and women was asked to present one or more questions concerning problems with students. Since our purpose was to explore the emotional aspects of the student-teacher relationship, we attempted to avoid technical material relating to mobility instruction. Instead, we concentrated on the feelings and attitudes of the instructors as well as on what they had been able to perceive of the feelings of the students toward them. The analysis of each question is here presented as a straightforward response, even though the format of the meeting was of a more general nature, including discussion, suggestions, and comments from the various participants.

Interference Produces Frustration

I seem to have an unusually intense negative reaction to sighted people who interfere with my orientation and mobility lessons. Why?

The situation that this instructor described usually involves a lesson in which the student is not aware of the instructor's presence. What often occurs is that the student is waiting to make a street crossing and some sighted passer-by first attempts to help the student, then notices the instructor, assumes that he has some connection with the student, and informs the student of the instructor's presence. When such a situation developed for this instructor, his anger would gradually increase, apparently as a result of the frustration he experienced when he found himself unable to cope with the situation.

While a number of practical solutions to this problem are possible (motioning to the person to move sufficiently far away from the student so that an explanation can be offered, having a note prepared with a brief explanation which could be handed to the person, etc.), the important point is to deal reasonably and calmly with the situation before the frustration and anger it produces interfere with its resolution. In this case, direct action is essential for another reason. If the instructor is unable to resolve the problem, the anger might be displaced onto the student. The instructor can then no longer be objective in evaluating the student for the remainder of the lesson; his overall effectiveness as an instructor is impaired; and ultimately the relationship with the student could be weakened.

Discontinuing a Student

How do you discontinue a student who is highly motivated to complete orientation and mobility training, but who is mentally unable to do so?

This instructor obviously had mixed feelings about the situation: he wanted to help the student but felt that he could not; despite his evaluation of the student, he did not wish to have the disagreeable and difficult task of informing the student of his limitations.

First of all, it is important to determine if such an evaluation is objective, to find out whether or not the instructor has negative feelings toward the student by, for example, having another instructor provide an independent evaluation. In this case, the other instructor concurred with the original opinion.

OVERCOMING A DIFFICULT PROBLEM

The major problem for the instructor, then, was his unwillingness to disappoint the student. He was sensitive to the feelings of the student, but in considering the student's needs and problems, it is evident that it would be more frustrating for him to continue with instruction than to stop. It is far kinder to help the student to deal with his limitations and to accept a more restricted goal than to subject him to the experience of constant failure. The instructor was helped to realize that this course of action was a more constructive and more realistic one.

Lack of Carry-Over

What can I do about a student who performs well on a lesson but who, when observed without his knowledge, does not use the proper techniques?

The apparent lack of carry-over from lessons to independent travel (a most frustrating situation, as this instructor also indicated) can be interpreted in a wide variety of ways. The instructor might interpret it personally, as a failure in his ability as an instructor. This in turn produces a feeling of inadequacy and decreases the objectivity of the instructor's evaluations of the student. On the other hand, the instructor might be contributing to the problem by providing too much support during the lessons and thus preventing the student from being adequately prepared to perform when he is off the lesson. In both instances, the attitude of the instructor toward the student and his evaluation of the student's potential for learning should be closely examined.

NEGATIVE FEELINGS

If, however, it is found that the instructor is not the direct source of the difficulty, then the possibility that the student may have negative feelings about mobility instruction should be considered. Although much can be learned from the close observation of a student's actions and comments, a direct approach is often much more productive. Naturally, such questions as "How do you feel about me as an instructor?" or "Do you like mobility training?" will often only result in evasions or a meaningless "Yes" or "No." On the other hand, asking "How do you feel about the way I'm teaching you?" or "What do you think or feel about mobility training now that you've been in it for a while?" might very well uncover positive or negative attitudes that are important for the instructor to know about.

Finally, the problem of insufficient carry-over may involve the student's increased use of residual vision. That is, certain techniques that have been taught are not necessary because the student is able to use his remaining vision instead. When this is suspected, the technical evaluation process that is a normal part of a mobility instruction program should be brought into play.

Preventing Overprotectiveness

How do I keep from developing an overprotective attitude toward my students?

This question implies that the instructor feels a potential for over-protective behavior toward her students. She knows that such behavior is detrimental and wishes to prevent herself from giving unnecessary help. On the other hand, this question may only be an overstatement of a simple wish to nurture. In fact, she may never demonstrate any serious degree of overprotection in working with mobility students.

REACTION FORMATION

When an instructor consistently provides help that a student does not need, however, his behavior may be a function of reaction formation. In other words, he has an unconscious wish to destroy a helpless object and reacts to this unacceptable desire by providing more help than the person actually needs. Since the unacceptable wish is unconscious, the person will usually deny that he is being overprotective.

Because this instructor was able to admit a potential for overprotection, it is unlikely that reaction formation is a factor. Furthermore, her ability to verbalize this potential is a good step toward a solution.

When the possibility of overprotectiveness exists, it is helpful to re-evaluate the student's ability and the instructor's goals for him, usually in consultation with another mobility instructor. If overprotective behavior is discovered, the instructor should obtain professional help to work through the feelings, especially if there is also evidence of reaction formation.

In either case, an instructor who is working through his feelings should perhaps work only with students who do not appear to be totally helpless. For example, he could work with partially sighted students.

Avoiding Over-Dependence

How can I prevent a student from developing feelings toward me that will lead to his fearing to travel when he is off the lesson?

It must be realized that the quite understandable and temporary dependence of a newly blinded person upon the sighted instructor may develop into an unhealthy over-dependence as a result of some personality trait or from extreme anxiety. Once the instructor realizes that a particular student is a dependent or anxious person, he can concentrate on minimizing the negative effects of the security that he necessarily provides. He can work to alleviate the anxiety while insuring that his support is realistic. In other words, the instructor should help the student to understand the value of traveling skills in permitting safe travel and discuss the problem with him, encouraging him to verbalize and deal with his feelings. If this approach does not work and if it is recognized that such fears are not a consequence of the student-instructor relationship, the best course of action would seem to be to refer the student for counseling or psychotherapy.

Severing a Strong Attachment

If a student becomes overly attached to and dependent on me, how can I best remedy the situation?

It is, of course, better to deal with this problem in its early stages—before a strong attachment has been formed. If the student has become unusually dependent before the instructor becomes aware of it, the situation can still be remedied and without a need for acting precipitously. The instructor's efforts should be directed toward a gradual reduction of the dependent status. While it exists, however, he can use it to the advantage of the student. This willingness to be dependent on the instructor usually dicates positive feelings. Knowing that these feelings exist, he can encourage the student to develop skills leading to independence. He can also help the student to develop motivation since the student wishes to please him.

The ultimate goal, of course, should always be the independent functioning of the student. Every consideration of the instructor should be directed toward this goal. For this reason, if all his efforts to sever the dependent relationship fail, he should refer to the student for counseling or psychotherapy.

Setting Reasonable Goals

During instructor training, perfection in cane techniques is stressed. How can the instructor best deal with the reaction he has toward a student who cannot or will not perform in the prescribed manner?

In this question, the instructor is referring to a reaction he had toward a student but is not specifying what it was. In response to further questioning, he indicated that his reaction was one of extreme irritation. The fact that the instructor reacted in this manner suggests that he had assumed that the student would not, rather than could not, perform. In other words, he felt that the student was resisting his efforts to help him achieve this high standard of perfection. If he had assumed that the student was incapable of performing, he would have reacted differently.

RELATING INSTRUCTOR'S TRAINING TO HIS EXPECTATIONS

During the discussion, this instructor also admitted that he had resented the stress on perfection in cane technique during his own training period. Now he saw that in expecting perfection of his students without regard for their ability to learn quickly, he had actually been displacing his resentment onto the students. Prior to the discussion, he had not been aware of the relationship between his feelings during training and his expectations of the students.

In a sense he had solved the problem once he became aware of the way he was expressing his feelings. The discussion, however, also helped him to take a more realistic approach to the problem. The group discussed perfection as a goal that need not be achieved overnight. They also considered it in terms of students' abilities and limitations.

Dealing with Fear and Anxiety

During training, the orientation and mobility instructor is required to spend many hours under the blindfold learning to travel with the cane. If he has certain fears himself when traveling under these conditions, this may affect his relationship with a student who has the same fears. How may we best deal with this kind of psychological reaction?

Undoubtedly, many persons experience anxiety when traveling without sight, whether the condition is temporary or permanent. The presence of anxiety varies in degree from one individual to another. Some may experience tremendous and incapacitating fear, while others experience only minimal anxiety. Sometimes severe anxiety can impede the progress of learning, but in most cases, the effects are not so pronounced. In fact, a minimal degree of anxiety may even facilitate the learning process: as a protective or defensive reaction it makes the student more sensitive to the various stimuli in his environment.

PROJECTING ONE'S OWN FEARS

Such projection, particularly when the instructor is unaware of it, can seriously interfere with his ability to evaluate events that occur during the process of teaching. The student may, in fact, be so anxious that he makes many mistakes on a lesson. If so, there should be other cues besides the feelings of the instructor. If these cues are not evident, then the mistakes of the student could be attributable to other factors.

Although this instructor stated that he experienced considerable anxiety while training under a blindfold, it did not interfere with his ability to travel or learn. According to his supervisor, he had been able to function quite efficiently. This knowledge helped him to consider the possible anxiety of his students more objectively.

MANY OTHER PROBLEMS COULD BE DISCUSSED

Certainly this discussion of the psychological factors in orientation and mobility does not exhaust the list of possible problems. The relationship between instructors and students is a complex one and there are many more situations and reactions that can and do occur.

Conclusions

What the discussion does suggest, however, is that the area of instructor-student relationships requires further consideration. It can be an interesting and useful part of the instructor's work and can help him to become more effective as an instructor. In addition, the consideration of the psychological aspects of the teaching process should provide a deeper understanding of those cases in which the student makes only minimal progress. For these reasons, it is imperative that the instructor not overlook this facet of the process. The emotional interaction between instructor and student will have its effect whether it is controlled or not. If considered and used properly, therefore, this interaction can greatly contribute to the independent functioning of the blind mobility student.

Paul J. Schulz is a consulting psychologist and counselor with the Braille Institute of America, Inc., Los Angeles.

37.
The Effects of Blindness
on Children's Development
JEROME COHEN

Within the group of children commonly consid-
ered as blind, there are great variations and
differences. What are some of these differences
that are especially significant to the teacher?

Human beings have a marvelous capacity for ad-
justing to a major handicap, such as blindness. But many factors can affect
the quality of adjustment. This became abundantly clear during a longitudinal, interdisciplinary study of children blind from birth recently completed at the Northwestern University Medical School. The children were
tested and observed, by various specialists in the fields of medicine, psychology, and social work, for an average of about twelve years from the
time of their birth. Detailed presentations of the medical findings have been
presented elsewhere.[1,2] But some generalized observations derived from
the study might be helpful to persons who work with blind children, particularly those handicapped both by blindness and real or apparent mental retardation.

A study of blind children in the Chicago metropolitan area had previously been undertaken by the University of Chicago, and a report of the
social and psychological development of preschool children was presented
by Norris and other.[3,4] Due to the cooperation of the Chicago project and
the children's parents, we were able to continue a follow-up study of fifty-
seven of the sixty-six subjects in the original group.

Eighty-five per cent (forty-eight cases) of the blindness within the
group was caused by retrolental fibroplasia (RLF), the result of over-oxy-
genation of premature newborn infants, which was the main cause of
blindness among newborns in this country between 1942 and 1955. Other
etiologic conditions were congenital optic atrophy, congenital cataracts, ret-
inoblastoma, and congenital absence of retinal receptors. Two-thirds of the
group had either no vision or light perception only, and the rest had partial sight but were legally blind.

Retrolental fibroplasia existed far more often in children who had had
very low birth weights and consequently had had to remain for many weeks

From *The New Outlook for the Blind* 60 (May, 1966): 150-54. Reprinted by per-
misssion of the author and *The New Outlook for the Blind*. Originally published in
Children (January-February, 1966), Washington, D.C.: United States Department of
Health, Education and Welfare. The report is based on research supported by a grant
(B-2403) from the National Institute of Neurological Diseases and Blindness, U.S.
Public Health Service.

in incubators. Over half of the forty-three children with this condition on whom we had original birth information weighed less than 1,360 grams (about three pounds) at birth, and 88 per cent were kept in the hospital for six weeks or longer. Twenty-five per cent were in the nursery for longer than ten weeks.

Most of this group have caught up with the height and weight norms of their ages; but the lightest prematures have tended to remain small for their ages.

As in other studies of premature births, a much higher incidence of other physical handicaps has been found in these children than is usually found in children with normal birth histories. Those of greatest psychoneurological significance are central nervous system disorders, such as seizures or cerebral palsy, which are found in 17 per cent of those who weighed under 1,500 grams at birth.

Intellectual Functioning

The group's present intellectual functioning ranges from 45 to 160 on the scale of Hayes-Binet IQ scores. Four children are unable to be tested with any degree of reliability and five are in institutions for the mentally retarded. Of the remaining 48 children for whom we have recent intelligence test data, eighteen score below 80 and twelve of those below 70. Twenty-four score between 80 and 120, and six above 120. The median score in the group is 93. The distribution is skewed toward the lower end, but there is also a slight piling up of scores at the high end.

The relationship between apparent mental retardation and the degree of vision and prematurity is particularly significant. Fourteen of twenty-seven children, or about 50 per cent, who are totally blind or have only light perception and who weighed under 1,500 grams at birth have IQ's below 70, whereas about 25 per cent of blind prematures with a higher birth weight have such low IQ's. Two out of six cases (33 per cent) of partly sighted children who weighed under 1,500 grams at birth have IQ's below 70. None of the full-term children in our sample are so impaired.

An analysis of the five verbal subtests of the Wechsler Intelligence Scale for Children (WISC) indicates that the average performance on each of the subtests is significantly higher than the mean for "comprehension." This difference holds for all children, both above and below the average IQ of 95. Also significant is the fact that the average-scaled score for "digit memory" is significantly higher in the group with below-average IQ's than the average of each of the other subtests.

According to the logic of the construction of the WISC, there should be no significant mean differences among the subtests. The lower scaled scores for "comprehension" could be due to a lack of social experience, to reduced applicability of the test problems, or to a reduction in abstract capacity of the children. The higher scores on "digit memory" among the below-average group could be the result of excessive emphasis which parents and teachers often place on verbal recall when the blind child displays few other intellectual accomplishments. The measures of intellectual level generally agree with ratings of school performance therefore appear to reflect the adequacy of personality fuctioning and adjustment, as well as intelligence *per se.*

The investigators found the WISC verbal scale to be a very good equivalent of the Hayes-Binet as an intelligence test for blind children. The correlation between the two sets of IQ's obtained on the tests is 0.95—very close to the reliability of either test.

A high incidence of abnormalities was reported in a study of the electroencephalographic (EEG) findings of twenty-eight children with RLF.[2] It is speculated, therefore, that a major correlate of behavioral retardation in these children is neurological abnormality.

The EEG abnormalities were located principally in the occipital lobes, but were often found in more anterior regions as well. Only one case exhibited sharply localized occipital abnormalities and produced an otherwise normal record. The prevalence of generalized high amplitude slow waves is consistent with the hypothesis of rather diffuse cortical damage. Twenty-one children showed spikes in the EEG, but only seven had epilepsy. It would thus seem that whatever brain abnormalities were present had more subtle effects on behavior, generally, than the production of gross seizures.

Two children with epilepsy were also spastic and four others were affected with a variety of cerebral palsy. Two children showed clinical and electroencephalographic evidence of generalized brain impairment in agreement with behavioral observations. One child had a mild neuromuscular deficiency because of poliomyelitis; four other cases showed mild neurological signs, either in exaggerated reflexes or weakness and flaccidity or certain muscle groups.

General Findings

A consideration of all of the factors with which the study was concerned— from social case histories, medical histories, parent's interviews, and neurological, psychological, and electroencephalographic examinations—leads us to the tentative conclusion that the majority of the children in the study who did not measure up to normal intelligence, and who consequently were not making a satisfactory educational adjustment, were children handicapped by generalized psychological impairments. Only in a minority of cases could we rule out physical factors and place the responsibility for poor development on an emotional basis. But it is difficult to tell what comes first. The parents of an organically impaired child may create emotional problems which obstruct the child's ability to compensate for his handicap.

The "constitution" of the child, for want of a better term, seemed to be the deciding factor in the outcome, if the basic neurological structures were intact. Behavior problems resulted in children who had had a traumatic upbringing, but in such cases we did not see behavior which simulated physical disability. On the other hand, brain impairment often resulted in low intellectual levels and inadequate adjustment even in families where all other factors were optimal.

We found no convincing evidence that prematurity coupled with oxygenation or blindness itself has resulted in a greater amount of brain damage than might have resulted from the same degree of prematurity itself and the prenatal conditions or possible trauma which contributed to prematurity. However, blindness, especially from birth, so limits the ordinary information flow available to the person that, in the absence of compensatory experiences, the child is not likely to reach the same functional level as he might have done with normal vision.

We have seen children with gross multiple handicaps make good academic progress and develop apparently normal personalities without serious emotional problems. Others either lacked within themselves the motivation and ability, or were too damaged by parental rejection and lack of opportunity for healthy growth.

Some Observations

The neuropsychological effects of visual deprivation may be due to impairments in any of three levels of functioning, or to a combination.

The first level is the organic. Impairment here may be due to damage of the brain by events similar to those causing blindness, such as those associated with a very light birth weight or severe illness. It may also be due to the reduction of neural impulses originating in the optic nerves and normally stimulating the brain at many levels. Generalized neurological impairments may limit general intelligence, and resulting learning and perceptual disabilities, with an overlay of emotional instability, may require unique educational procedures. The diagnostic team approach—as undertaken by the psychologist, the pediatric neurologist, the ophthalmologist, and the social worker, and aimed at understanding all the factors in the child's adjustment—is essential for the development of sound recommendations to educational specialists and parents about what the child can achieve through what approaches.

As yet we do not know how the deprivation of sight directly affects the child through changes in the brain's information handling capabilities—whether it is through the biological effects of a low number of impulses coming into the cortex, or through the effects of experimental limitations, or as a deleterious overlay of emotional deprivation.

The second level of impairment may be in perceptual integration, due to the direct psychological effect of the absence of visual input, from which most information about environment is normally received.

Vision is the dominant system for perceptual integration. While blind children appear to be highly sensitive to the attitudes of their parents, they tend to be less able to get independent confirmation of the appropriateness of their attitudes from those outside the close family. Blind children usually have endured some degree of social isolation and this, coupled with dependence on verbalization of experience as a substitute for visual integration and the inadequacy of perceptual data for intersensory confirmation of the environment, may lead to emotional problems and inadequate intellectual functioning. The psychological consequences of limitations in perceptual and learning experience when interacting with the consequences of minimal brain damage can produce severe intellectual retardation. However, if the child is able to compensate for his lack of sight by utilizing his other senses, and has experienced healthy emotional relationships, he may achieve a normal adjustment and a normal or even high level of intellectual productivity, despite complicated handicaps.

The third level of impairment is in emotional functioning and is the secondary effect of the unfavorable reactions from others, especially from the parents, to the visual handicap. This leads to distortions of normal social relationships.

When a mother brings home a blind infant—especially after weeks of initial separation from him because of his need for continued hospital care—she may have difficulty feeling the normal joy and pride in her newborn. Too often she is made to feel the pain and even the "curse" of having a handicapped child, by the expressions of sympathy or embarrassed false cheerfulness of friends and neighbors. Fortunately, many parents of blind children do establish a sound relationship with the baby and learn to love him and enjoy him despite his handicap and other people's reactions. But some parents feel a deep guilt which interferes with their ability to love the child. Others bear the burden of the child as a "cross," which brings them no closer to real love for the child.

Parental anxiety may result in either of the following damaging attitudes: perpetual overprotection; or expectation of more from the child than is realistic. Such attitudes, of course, affect the child's emotional growth, for one's self-concept is, to some extent, the internalization of the attitudes of others toward oneself.

Of course, as Allport[5] points out, it is necessary for the individual at some point to stop being a reflection of the opinions around him, and to form a self-concept based on his actual inner abilities, interests, and strivings. But to achieve objectivity requires confirmation of all the senses that the self is an individual, separate, and, to some degree, independent of others. Since vision is the sense which inherently presents the outside world as external, it is instrumental in the natural development of ego differentiation. Fortunately, but sometimes with difficulty, the interaction of the remaining senses in a blind person permits the verification of externality and thus ego differentiation.

Some Differences

Differences in the adjustment problems for the child born blind and the child who loses his sight even at an early age lie in both the social and the psychological spheres. Children blind from birth never have to adjust to blindness *per se,* and never have to accommodate to the loss of vision as do older children blinded by illness or accident. But the child who becomes blind realizes that he will never see again, and his feelings of hopelessness and despair may cause chronic anxiety and depression.

Blindness from birth may have less consequence for the child's own psychological self-concept, once formed, but children born blind tend to be more affected by other people's attitudes toward them.

Often a child may be educated as blind but have sufficient sight for easy travel and object recognition. We have concluded from our study that any degree of vision is a favorable factor for development, and, although we have not the supporting data, that the longer a blind child has had some vision the better. There is no evidence whatsoever that partial sight is a worse handicap than total blindness because of a conflict in whether the child behaves as a blind or sighted child. Each "blind" child with some vision who was questioned said that his vision was an advantage and in that way he was better off than his totally blind classmates. For the child who can see objects to be treated as blind may be an annoyance to him, but not a source of deep emotional conflict.

There is often less motivation for the partially sighted child to learn to use many of the aids for the blind, since to some extent he could depend on vision. This is especially true of training in techniques with the cane for travel. The partially sighted person may learn to rely on his other senses more readily if he is blindfolded during training.

One child with partial vision found it easier to read braille by sight than by touch. He never got to be a good braille reader, but the problem was solved by placing him in a class for the partially sighted in which he used books with large type.

Partially sighted children who lose what little vision they have tend to regress in their development. On the other hand, when a child who has been blind from birth has his sight restored by removal of congenital cataracts, he tends to rely upon the more familiar auditory and tactile-kinesthetic cues for a long time. Gradually, as what he sees conforms to his perceptions from his other senses, his vision takes precedence.

Von Senden[6] reports the case of a girl who for a long time after vision was restored had to stop at the top of a flight of stairs and feel her way down with her eyes closed.

The perceptual distortions reported by many blind people after sight has been restored are mainly due to faulty spatial perception mediated by the nonvisual senses. One glance tells the seeing person all the spatial relationships of the objects around him. If this kind of spatial sense is ever achieved by the totally blind, it is by painstaking serial exploration and may never be accurate.

Persons blinded in later life continue to use visual imagery and tend to imagine the world in visual terms, even though the information they receive is from the other senses. Visual imagery retains its organizing function and objects that are located by touch are fitted into the world of visual memory.

The mental picture of the world given in nonvisual terms as it must be to the blind person is beyond the imagination of a seeing person, just as it is impossible to explain to a person who never saw what it is like to see. The words we use are the same, but the meanings are different.

We evaluate the adjustment of the blind to a seeing world. Good general intelligence is the key factor to a successful adjustment, but it may be impaired by emotional problems arising from unsatisfactory affectional relationships with parents and other people significant to the child.

A blind child with neurological impairments faces even greater difficulty, both in adjusting to the social world of human relationships and to the physical world, and in obtaining learning experiences from the environment. However, there is evidence that many children with mild neurological disorders in infancy and early childhood tend to compensate, so that by adolescence little or no evidence of the earlier disability remains. The proper emotional background for a child, enabling him to overcome an impairment and make a good life adjustment, may alleviate the problem; and a deprived emotional atmosphere may aggravate it.

Professional understanding, based on the teamwork of several professions, is necessary for diagnostic evaluation of each child. The many blind children who achieve a satisfactory adjustment and function at an outstanding level of achievement demonstrate the power within human beings to overcome severe physical and emotional handicaps.

REFERENCES

1. COHEN, JEROME; ALFANO, JOSEPH E.; LOUIS D.; PALMGREN, CAROLYN. Clinical evaluation of school-age children with retrolental fibroplasia. *American Journal of Ophthalmology*, January, 1964.
2. COHEN, J.; BOSHES, L. D.; SNIDER, R. S. Electroencephalographic changes following retrolental fibroplasia. *Electroencephalography and Clinical Neurophysiology*, December, 1961.
3. NORRIS, MIRIAM; SPAULDING, PATRICIA J.; BRODIE, FERN H. *Blindness in Children*. Chicago: University of Chicago Press, 1957.
4. NORRIS, MIRIAM. What effects blind children's development. *Children*, July-August, 1956.
5. ALLPORT, GORDON W. *Becoming: Basic Considerations for a Psychology of Personality*. New Haven, Connecticut: Yale University Press, 1955.
6. VON SENDEN, M. *Space and Sight*. Glencoe, Illinois: Free Press, 1960.

Jerome Cohen is Associate Professor of Psychology in the Neurology and Psychiatry Department of Northwestern University and a member of Northwestern's Biomedical Engineering Center.

38.
The Blind in the Age of Technology:
A Public Discussion*

Modern technology has given us many aids for the education of the blind. As you review these aids, note how each aid extends (supplements, substitutes for) particular abilities or lack of abilities.

The following presentation of the remarks of the panel and of their discussion with the audience was prepared by the editors of the *New Outlook for the Blind* from a transcript of the meeting. In an effort to facilitate the task of the reader in following the rather free and broad-ranging discussion, questions that were directed specifically to an individual panel member and that were concerned with information presented by him in his remarks have been placed immediately after those remarks. Comments by other panelists on the same subject have also been grouped there. Miscellaneous questions and remarks have been placed after the discussion between the audience and the last panelist.

Remarks by Dr. Robert W. Mann: I am going to take a very pragmatic, provincial, and pedagogical approach in my presentation and I am going to limit my remarks specifically to the things that we have been doing at MIT. In our program at MIT, we have been concerned with devices not only for mobility and communication, but for vocational and recreational purposes

From *The New Outlook for the Blind* 64 (September, 1970): 201-18. Reprinted by permission of *The New Outlook for the Blind.*

*Five leading scientists in the field of sensory research and perceptual alternatives met together last spring, with an audience of about 300 workers for the blind and members of the general public, both sighted and blind, to discuss the role of technology in solving the problems of blind persons. This public meeting, held April 29, 1970, at the Ambassador Hotel, Los Angeles, was sponsored by the Los Angeles Area Committee of the American Foundation for the Blind, New York City. Miss Flora Marks, head of the committee, chaired the meeting; M. Robert Barnett, executive director of the American Foundation for the Blind, was the moderator.

The panel of scientists participating in the discussion included Robert W. Mann, Ph.D., Department of Mechanical Engineering, Massachusetts Institute of Technology, Cambridge, Massachusetts; Emerson Foulke, Ph.D., director, Perceptual Alternatives Laboratory, University of Louisville, Louisville, Kentucky; James C. Bliss, Ph.D., Bioinformation Systems, Group Engineering Techniques Laboratory, Sanford Research Institute, Menlo Park, California; Patrick W. Nye, Ph.D., Willis H. Booth Computing Center, California Institute of Technology, Pasadena, California; and Leslie L. Clark, director, International Research Information Service, American Foundation for the Blind, New York, New York.

as well. Participating in this program over the past decade have been many of my students (some of whom have gone on to work in the field of blindness—one at present is a technical advisor to the Commission for the Blind in Massachusetts), some of my faculty colleagues at MIT, and many of my colleagues in the medical profession with whom I have collaborated.

COMPUTER TRANSLATION OF BRAILLE

Our major concern over the past few years, and one which is now nearing completion, is computer automation for the translation of braille and the systems for the delivery of braille in environments that call for simultaneous availability of inkprint and braille. The computer program we are using is similar to the one that the American Printing House for the Blind, Louisville, has been using for a number of years for the production of braille books.

One of the complications of computer programming—for those who are innocent of its complexities and subtleties—is the great difficulty of transferring the computer program, that is, the directions for doing something, from one computer system to another. This problem exists not only between systems of different manufacturers, but between machines of the same manufacturer.

TRANSLATION PROGRAM IN COBOL

One of our current efforts, therefore, is the development of an English-to-Grade-2-braille translation program in a universally accepted computer language, in this case COBOL. This program, which is very close to fruition and which will be finished this summer, will be readily and easily transferable from any machine to any other machine. This means that environments that have access in any way to a computer of any of a wide range of sizes and kinds will be able to use this computer program to produce Grade 2 braille translations. Such access can usually be arranged, often at reduced rates or even for free, for use of a local insurance company computer or for equipment in a branch office of a computer manufacturer. The Atlanta public school system, which by late summer will be using our program to produce braille, has arranged for the use of the administrative computer already in use within the system.

TELETYPEWRITER BRAILLE

Much of our attention has also been directed to devices which will produce braille for the individual. Such a device, now in the process of experimental deployment and which we call the MIT BRAILLEMBOSS, is the size of a teletypewriter. It is designed to be interconnected with computers of various kinds either directly or through telephone lines. A BRAILLEMBOSS has been in operation for the last few months in the Perkins School for the Blind, Watertown, Massachusetts. If a teacher wants a braille version of an examination, he simply operates the keyboard and receives a Grade 2 braille version almost instantly via a telephone line connection with the MIT computer nearly 10 miles away. Similarly, several blind computer programmers in the Boston area get their computer outputs not in inkprint, which someone would have to read to them, but in braille. Before the year is out, we expect to have BRAILLEMBOSSES employed in a wide variety of typical situations: public schools, institutions for the blind, industrial and commercial settings for blind computer programmers, and a wide variety of others, including even broadcast stations so that blind radio announcers can get the wire service news in braille directly from the Teletype.

TELEVISION USED AS A READING AID

With the cooperation of colleagues not only at MIT, but at the Massachusetts Commission for the Blind and the Boston University Low Vision Clinic, we have under development a close-circuit television system for use by the partially sighted. This system includes an inexpensive television camera (like those used in banks and hotels for surveillance) which is focused on the reading material. The enlarged images of the letters then appear on an ordinary television set or monitor. The control of the movement of the camera and of the magnification, intensity, and contrast of the image are under the complete control of the reader. We have been very, very pleased with the fact that a wide variety of people with very low or tunnel vision have been able to use this kind of device and have been able to read with far less fatigue than when using telescopic or other kinds of optical aids.

Mobility Devices

Our interest in mobility devices ranges from the development of a more durable and practical folding cane to more sophisticated electronic sensing devices. The PATH SOUNDER is used in conjunction with a cane and reaches ahead of the blind traveler several steps beyond the reach of the cane to provide information about possible obstacles. Essentially an echolocation device, it hangs from a strap worn around the neck and provides audible cues to warn of obstacles at certain discrete ranges from the traveler.

WARNING SYSTEMS FOR THE DEAF BLIND

We have also been interested in the problems of deaf-blind persons, particularly the problem of adequate warning systems: fire alarms, paging systems, telephone bell, and doorbell enunciators that cannot ordinarily be sensed by individuals who can neither see nor hear such signals. The TAC-COM we have developed is a cigarette-package-size device that can be carried around in a person's pocket. It is essentially a radio receiver that, stimulated by a signal from a small transmitter at the point under "surveillance," produces vibrations and thereby provides an adequate tactile warning to the individual. By appropriate coding of various types and intensities of vibrations, it is possible for the deaf-blind person to identify the source of the warning signal, that is, he will be able to distinguish a fire alarm from a telephone call or a visitor ringing his doorbell. We are in the process of installing this kind of a system in the sheltered workshop and residential facilities of the National Center for the Deaf-Blind, Industrial Home for the Blind, Brooklyn, as well as in some private homes, in order to test its feasibility.

In addition to these devices, my colleagues and I at the Institute have undertaken studies for a variety of other devices that are also now being testing, including recreational equipment, such as a ball with a noise source that enables a blind child to locate it, and vocational devices, such as a steel tape measure which reads out in braille.

GENERAL AREAS OF RESEARCH

As I mentioned at the outset of my remarks, I have chosen to emphasize the pragmatic, the tangible things that are very close to realization, if not already available. I would, however, like to close my remarks by saying that this work is related to and derived from a much larger body of research in which my students and I have been engaged. This research, which is represented by a very substantial bibliography, is concerned not only with the problems of blindness, but is concerned generally with the problems of sensory and motor loss, with the whole question of human rehabilitation in the face of blindness, deafness, loss of cutaneous sensation, or loss of limbs.

In fact, a substantial part of my work has been directed towards artificial limbs and I have been associated with a prosthetic device known as the "Boston arm." This limb uses information from the central nervous system to control the artificial appendage. In other words, research of this kind is involved with the very intimate connections between the residual, virtually intact human system and machine, be it an artificial aid for the blind or an artificial limb. Clearly, there is a much brighter future ahead in which much more sophisticated devices will greatly facilitate the rehabilitation of those with sensory and physical disabilities of various kinds.

On the subject of using computers that have the capability of feedback in braille, couldn't libraries that have computers somehow provide this service to blind individual who would be willing to come into the library itself?

Dr. Mann: Certainly. For example, there is a blind graduate student in economics at MIT who gets all of his material in exactly that way, by using the MIT computer with an attached braille embosser.

What kind of equipment do you envision being needed for the computer-assisted production of braille, assuming that there is donated computer time?

Dr. Mann: The answer to that depends largely on the rate at which braille would need to be produced. The computer could be used in a batch process system or in an interactive system. In the batch system the input is a long stream of controlling commands. The computer then does its work uninterruptedly and the output is a continuous stream of braille. In an interactive system, a person types in a question to the computer and the computer answers in braille. Then he types in another and the computer replies in braille. The batch process system, which would be the obvious choice if the rapid production of braille materials is the aim, could use a commercial chain printer. These units, for which there are adaptation kits from IBM to turn them into braille printers, turn out about a thousand lines a minute. This would be quite good for turning out a single copy of something; mass production would be impractical because even though it is very fast it would tie up the computer for some time.

In the interactive mode you might just as well have a computer-driven embosser of the kind we are at present working on. This is much slower, about 120 braille cells per minute, but that is about as fast as anybody can read it. This kind of embosser could be used in a batch processing system where the demands on the system were modest and where the system could be used exclusively for braille production. For example, we have worked with the agencies for the blind in Denmark and have figured out that with one of our braille embossers working around the clock, they could produce all of the braille needed by the Danes. In this country, therefore, we expect that a volunteer group could very well use our braille embossers to produce braille at modest rates. For producers needing a higher volume of braille, however, the converted chain printer would probably be needed. One last note, neither of these systems has been adapted to produce interpoint.

I am sure that we are all very interested in experimental devices, but when, for example, will the collapsible cane that you mentioned be available to individuals?

Dr. Mann: That particular cane is available now from HYCOR, a manufacturer in Woburn, Massachusetts. I would, however, like to use this question to elaborate further on the whole problem of getting even a simple device to the point where it is commercially available. I will use this cane as a case in point. The final design for this cane was the result of extensive study, experiments, and testing over the period from about 1963 to 1968. At this point, Mr. Vito Proscia, the director of the Sensory Aids Center at MIT, took up the challenge of getting it into production. He went to the Northwest Foundation in Seattle and was able to convince them of the value of the cane we had designed. They awarded a grant to MIT, which MIT in turn used to provide a manufacturer with the nonrecoverable tooling and capital investment costs to produce the cane at a reasonable profit. The cane is made of a special grade of aluminum tubing which can be directly formed into conical members. This technique, called swaging, is a very new technique that requires a very special machine, a swaging machine. It was the grant from the Northwest Foundation that made it possible for us to buy the swaging machine for the manufacturer. This then is the tortuous path one has to go through these days to have a device manufactured in quantity.

Paradoxically enough, it is this business of mass production that Americans are best at. Of course, since the American free enterprise system operates on the basis of the highest return on an investment, manufacturers don't pick devices for the blind, or artificial limbs. It is by no means clear that such devices can make a profit. Who knows, perhaps they can. We simply have to figure out some way of achieving the transition from a laboratory prototype of a useful and reliable device to a level of production to meet the demand. The ultimate answer to the problem probably lies in the fact that production will require some sort of subsidy arrangement. Even so, we are faced with the problem of how such subsidy arrangements for private or public support are to be brought about.

You also mentioned an electronic sensing device when you were discussing mobility aids. Do you envision the traveler, when using both a cane and such a device, becoming more dependent on the device than on the cane?

Dr. Mann: I would see him sharing his dependence. We are all dependent on the sensory information that we receive through various channels. A person deprived of sight has to use other channels to supply the information normally received via the visual channel. The fundamental, theoretical problem is how to distribute information to these other channels. The cane is a superb instrument and we have an enormous scientific regard for the kind of information which a well-trained blind person receives from it. It is, unfortunately, only about an arm's length long. The intent behind the device I mentioned, and behind the several others that are under development, is to supplement or to augment the cane. None of the serious investigators of scientific aids for mobility are proposing a substitute for the cane.

Could one of you elaborate somewhat on the so-called laser cane?

Dr. Nye: The laser cane is essentially the familiar long cane into which is built three gallium arsenide lasers and three photocells. The lasers are small crystal devices which project a beam of reddish light within a very narrow frequency band in the visible spectrum. The principle of the system is simply what is called optical triangulation. The angles between the transmitter, the object reflecting the light, and the receiver indicate the distance of the object. When the angles between the transmitter and the receiver are correctly adjusted, only objects at a certain distance will be sensed. There are three beams of light scanning the area in front of the traveler, one for the area in the region of the head, one aimed at detecting objects at waist level, and one on the ground for detecting curbs, steps, and similar obstacles. The signals from the device are in two forms, one a tactile signal to the fingertip of the user for obstacles detected by the two lower beams, the other a warning sound for obstacles at head height.

Please elaborate on the television camera and receiver used as a low vision aid.

Dr. Mann: First, this is not a portable system. It consists of a television camera, a book stand, and whatever size of receiver that is most useful. With respect to distortion, there is very little regardless of the degree of magnification from inkprint to video that is desired. The greatest advantage of this system over optical aids is the question of glare. In all optical aids, the illumination required for reading the characters is directed at the paper, but it is also reflected back up into the eyes of the reader. In the television set-up, the page can be illuminated as much as required, because the reader does not look at it; he reads from the monitor. The degree of brightness and contrast on the monitor can be adjusted independently of the illumination on the page. In many cases, this means that the period of time which can be spent reading without discomfort is greatly increased. In addition, many individuals find that using the television set-up is not as physically tiring as using optical aids. The fact that the television camera does the scanning while the reader just sits back and reads from the monitor, obviously requires less effort than using optical aids and being forced to scan the page manually.

Are these devices available now?

Dr. Mann: No, they are not generally available. We are building 10 of them now for clients of the Massachusetts Commission for the Blind. The device was, however, specifically prescribed for each of these individuals. There are parallel investigations of this same system going on all over the country. For example, Dr. Samuel Genensky of the Rand Corporation in Santa Monica, California, is working in this area. I don't know if any other group is building these devices for the general public or not.

Mr. Clark: There have been proposed a number of closed-circuit television systems for aiding the reading of the visually impaired. In view of the marketing problems and the difficulties in maintaining the equipment in service, it has been suggested that a conference be held of those now involved in the design of such systems to help achieve a consensus among producers of the equipment. It is hoped that the National Academy of Engineering will soon sponsor such a meeting.

What is the cost of these devices?

Dr. Mann: We're aiming for about $1,000, although I must emphasize at this point that all of us represented here make every effort in designing and building such devices to keep costs down. We try, for example, to use only commercially available video cameras and monitors and to make the scan and control systems as simple as possible. One problem with sensory devices that must never be minimized is that they must be maintainable wherever they are being used. In the television reading set-up, which we call VIDEO VISION, the use of commercial elements enables standard television maintenance people to service the equipment.

Remarks by Dr. Emerson Foulke: The individual obtains information from his environment my means of his various perceptual systems. When one of these systems does not function properly, as in the case of visual impairment, the individual must obtain the same or equivalent information by means of some alternative perceptual system. What we are interested in investigating at the Perceptual Alternatives Laboratory, therefore, are these alternative ways of obtaining information from the environment. Although we are not limited in the laboratory to investigating perceptual alternatives that are appropriate for blind individuals, these do constitute most of our research effort.

MOBILITY

One area in which we are only in the process of formulating a research program is mobility, the skill of getting about independently. In order to perform a skill of this sort, the individual must obtain information about his environment, information for making the decisions necessary for safe and successful travel. Our interest is first of all in investigating the perceptual basis of mobility, in finding out what kind of information an individual needs in order to determine the states of the environment that are of concern to him when he travels as a pedestrian. Further, we want to know from what functioning sensory channels or perceptual systems he can obtain this information. If our experiments in this area produce useful data, it should be possible to indicate, for example, the kind of information that mobility devices ought to make available to their users. Such data would, of course, be useful in the design of such devices and, also, in indicating how procedures used in mobility training might be made more effective.

READING ALTERNATIVES

Another area, one in which we have done more work, is perceptual alternatives for reading. One such alternative is to obtain the same kind of information that is ordinarily obtained by reading visually through the sense of touch, that is, by some touch reading system. Specifically, we are interested in learning more about the relationship between man's perceptual capacity and the kind of dot patterns that occur in the braille code. There does not seem to be any reason for believing that man's perceptual capacity is exhausted by the 63 patterns that comprise the six-dot braille code. For this reason we have begun to explore his capacity for perceiving more complex patterns of the same general type, but formed of larger matrices or cells. We are at the present time, for example, exploring the perceptual characteristics of dot patterns that are formed by adding one or more columns to the two columns (of three dots each) of the existing braille cell. With each addition of such a column, the number of available dot patterns is increased eightfold. If it can be shown that such patterns are easily identifiable and easily learned, there then arises the very interesting challenge of deciding what meanings to assign to the new patterns that would be available. This is a little bit far out and we are not ready to make any proposals regarding augmented braille codes at this time.

Another kind of perceptual alternative to visual reading which we have been investigating is reading done via listening, particularly through recorded materials. Talking books are, of course, used very heavily by a great many blind individuals. The rate at which such reading is done is determined not by the individual's own reading requirements, but by the rate at which his oral reader happens to speak. This rate is usually much slower than the rate at which most individuals could conveniently listen. One goal, therefore, is to increase this rate so that it more closely or adequately matches the rate at which individuals can listen. Such an increase, because it reduces the time necessary to listen to a given reading selection, is often called "time compression."

Compressed Speech

Time compression can be accomplished in a variety of ways, some of which are relatively cheap, some relatively expensive. It unfortunately turns out in this case, as in many others, that the cheaper the method is, the poorer its general quality. For example, probably the cheapest method is simply speeding up a tape or record, that is, playing it at a speed faster than the one at which it was recorded. The distortion in vocal pitch and in voice quality introduced by this method, however, does not result in a very high quality listening experience. Word intelligibility is also very quickly degraded. Therefore, although it has some limited application, it is not really a satisfactory solution to the problem.

The Harmonic Compressor

Another means of compression currently available is the harmonic compressor developed at the American Foundation for the Blind using circuitry made available to it by Bell Laboratories. This device makes it possible to double the word rate of recorded speech while preserving vocal pitch and quality. Unfortunately, at present, the device can only double the word rate, that is, it has little flexibility. Yet another means of compression, one that is widely used at present, is the sampling method. In this method, only samples of the recording are reproduced in the final version and other very brief samples are periodically disregarded. This method works on the principle that when the samples deleted are short enough, the listener cannot detect their absence when the samples that are retained are played in succession. There is enough redundancy in speech signals to allow for this periodic deletion of small speech segments. The quality of the final recording is somewhat poorer than that realized with the harmonic compressor, but it does have the advantage of having the capacity to vary the rate of compression or, in other words, the word rate of the final output.

We have been doing research with compressed speech for quite a number of years. Although I won't attempt to review the research at this time, I will say that it has generally indicated that in a wide variety of applications, listeners ought to be able to cope successfully with speech presented in the neighborhood of 275 words per minute. This means that through the use of compressed speech, blind individuals will be able to read via recordings at rates comparable to the silent reading rates of high school and college students. We have also established the Center for Rate-Controlled Recordings, as a part of the Perceptual Alternatives Laboratory, University of Louisville, in an attempt to fill the requests of people interested in time-compressed recorded speech for use in research or for educational demonstrations. So far, we have been able to meet this demand. Unfortunately, we have not as yet obtained the kind of funding that would permit us to make such material available to individual readers.

One last area of research that I will just touch on before closing is investigating the process of visual reading to discover what operations the visual reader can perform that are not available to the person who reads by listening. The goal is to design a piece of equipment—an aural reading instrument—that will allow the individual who reads by listening to take advantage of these operations. I cannot, of course, go into this area in any detail in a presentation like this, but I can give an example of the kind of thing we are working on. The visual reader is able to search the printed page for desired information and retrieve it very easily. At present, the individual reading by listening to a tape or disc recording on existing equipment cannot easily do such scanning. There are ways, however, in which search and retrieval could be facilitated through the use of various types of auditory displays. Such a system, if it could be easily managed by a person who reads by listening, would provide one of the operations that are quite taken for granted by visual readers.

Since the speech compression devices you have mentioned are so expensive, is there any practical and inexpensive way of speeding up the talking book machines issued by the Library of Congress?

Dr. Foulke: Yes, if you don't mind the pitch distortion. One device for doing this is the variable frequency power supply manufactured by the American Foundation for the Blind. This can be connected to the motor of either a talking book machine or a tape recorder. Or, if you want to be a little more sophisticated, the American Printing House for the Blind has a small variable frequency power supply that is built into either a Sony 105 tape recorder or any of the talking book machines sold by them. In this case there is just a control on the deck that can be manipulated to change the speed of the record or tape.

In augmenting the braille cell, do you mean that additional dots would be added or that new kinds of compound cells would be formed?

Dr. Foulke: No, this is different from compound cells. The standard braille cell has three rows and two columns of dot locations, that is, six locations. What we are working on is what is called the "three by *n* cell," that is, three rows by any desired number of columns. This means that when you require patterns that cannot be formed in the current braille cell, an extra column of three dots would be added, giving you nine dot locations. Each time a new column is added there are eight times the number of characters that can be formed. Therefore, with two columns, the standard braille cell, there are 63 possible characters; with three columns, there would be 511 possible characters or 448 new characters. This, of course, would not be a replacement for the braille code and would be compatible with it.

Since present braille writers can only produce the six-dot cell, wouldn't such innovations as nine- or 12-dot braille require special equipment? And how, in the latter case, could one operate a braille writer with 12 keys?

Dr. Foulke: Existing equipment could be modified to produce nine-dot braille, but it is true that if you wanted to produce patterns in a cell with 12 locations, it would probably be necessary to form part of the pattern with one key operation and to complete it with another. I should note at this time that at present we are not even investigating the patterns that could be formed in a 12-location matrix. The kinds of schemes that we are considering, however, could be expanded to include 12 locations should the need for additional code characters arise.

Remarks by Dr. James C. Bliss: I am an electrical engineer and over 10 years ago I began working on what I thought was a basic research project to study the capability of the sense of touch. During this time, however, I have become more and more interested in practical problems, until today, my major concern is really trying to get some of the things that we have learned in the research programs out into use. Although that is really consuming most of my time, I am still involved in a few research projects.

When I first went to Stanford, I met Professor John Linvill, who has a blind daughter. The two of us have, since then, collaborated on the development of a device to help a blind person to read virtually any printed document. We have progressed through several experimental models of such a device and today I think we have one, called the Optacon, that represents a significant step toward the achievement of our goal.

THE OPTACON

The Optacon is about the size of a dictionary, weighs eight pounds, and operates on batteries. The probe, which is about the size of a lipstick case, performs much like a television camera, except that instead of handling images of 250,000 points it handles images of only 144 points. The probe has a little window through which it can "see" an area about the size of one letter. The image received through the probe is then magnified and displayed on an array, or mosaic, of 144 tactile pins. The activation of these pins produces a vibratory image of the letter from the page on about half the area of the finger. The probe is moved across the line of print, left to right, each letter being recognized through the moving vibratory image on the tactile display.

OPTACON IS BEING TESTED

We have built eight of these devices so far and for the past six months we have been experimenting to find out how well people can learn to read with them. At present there are five individuals who are quite good readers, but the best is John Linvill's daughter, Candy, who is now a freshman at Stanford. She can read at 60 to 70 words per minute and uses the device quite extensively for reading her mail, the notes and announcements that are passed out in her classes, and her German lessons. Although use of the Optacon has not eliminated her need to read braille, listen to recorded material, and use sighted readers, its area of usefulness does give her independent access to much material that formerly had often been a problem. Because of this, the device has become quite indispensable to her.

Two other Stanford students are also using the Optacon and are able to read between 30 and 40 words per minute. A computer programmer at the Stanford Research Institute, where I work, uses the device for many of the same purposes as others are using it, but in addition the device has been found to be useful in his work for reading computer listings and punched cards.

EXPERIMENTS WITH CHILDREN

One of the most exciting of our experiments at present is our work with six young children at a nearby elementary school. Ranging in level from the second to the seventh grades, these children have received individual instruction from us for about 15 to 30 minutes every day for the last month. Although this is our first experiment of this kind, it seems to be going rather well. One girl is able to read text material with the Optacon and is at the point where more access to the machine for practice would help boost her rather slow reading rate. An eighth grader outside this group is reading at about 30 words per minute. Some of the younger children in the group learned to recognize all the letters and are beginning to put them together to form words.

The Stages of Development

Before I go on to some of our plans for the future, I would like to speak briefly about the stages in the development of devices. In engineering and in research and development, devices first take shape in what is sometimes called a "breadboard" stage. At this point, the device is only something that almost works, but not quite. And even though you can't pick it up because if you do it will fall apart, the model does give you enough information to indicate whether or not you are on the right track and can go further. This is followed by the "prototype" stage in which the device will hold together. Often a number of copies are made of a prototype for experimental purposes. If the device looks good at this point, a large number of models are made for the "pilot run" stage. These can be field tested, that is, operated and used away from the laboratory and the people who invented and developed the device. This is an expensive stage because up to a hundred copies of the device are necessary for adequate testing. If the device performs well in the field, then it can be manufactured and made available more generally.

PROTOTYPES OF THE OPTACON HAVE BEEN BUILT

The Optacon is in the prototype stage, that is, we have made and tested the device and it looks very good at this point. My concern now, therefore, is in organizing and developing a pilot run so that the device can be tested more extensively in the field, in schools, rehabilitation centers, and other settings. My time, as I noted at the outset, has largely been devoted to trying to talk to anyone who might possibly help in getting the Optacon to this next stage.

EXTENDING THE USES OF THE OPTACON

There are, of course, other projects that are in the very early stage of development, the stage at which the Optacon was about six to 10 years ago. Two projects which are very promising are really extensions of the Optacon. We are, in other words, trying to answer questions like: Where do we go after the Optacon? What does the Optacon lead to? Is it a finished device in itself or not? It is my feeling that such research is part of the evolutionary process of a device and that we should not only continue to improve and refine such a device, but to extend its capability.

For example, we are studying the feasibility of connecting the Optacon to a computer via telephone lines. It may be possible to have the signals from the Optacon camera sent to a very sophisticated computer that is capable of recognizing the print and speaking words to the reader via the same telephone lines. We have simulated such a system in the laboratory and are now studying such design questions as what kind of character recognition error rates are needed and how well can an individual track a line of print.

Another possibility we are exploring is using something like an Optacon to look at the environment instead of the printed page. In effect, we would be applying the principles of the reading device to an orientation device. I must say, however, that with 144 points, or even a few hundred, the picture one would get of something would be only very crude. Clearly, there is a great deal of research to be done before there will actually be a practical orientation device based on these principles.

How difficult is it for a blind person to learn the forms of the letters of the alphabet as produced by the Optacon?

Dr. Bliss: I am sure there are a lot of individual differences in this matter. We have been fortunate in our work to have had average or above-average students to work with. When an individual does not know the shapes of the letters of the alphabet to start with, this can easily be taught though the use of an embossed or raised line alphabet with the Optacon. Because the patterns produced by the Optacon are so similar to the shapes of the printed letters, this problem has been only a very minor part of any of our training programs.

Once the basic use of the Optacon is learned, how long does it take to become proficient with it?

Dr. Bliss: There are several factors involved in proficiency that have little to do with the device itself, for example, an individual's facility with the language, how well he can spell, and his motivation to read. We have observed, at one end of the scale, that some individuals can read at 10 words per minute after one month's practice and up to 30 words per minute after two months. This is very fast and I think it is an exceptional person who can accomplish this. At the other end of the scale, there were individuals who, it was clear, would take a great deal of time to learn to do anything even closely resembling reading. Because of the nature of our research project, we have not had the time to train these individuals and have had to give up on them.

It is possible for an elementary school district to be included in the pilot program for the Optacon?

Dr. Bliss: If we had a pilot program, I am sure it would be possible. So far, we have only been doing research. We are now at the point where we are trying to bridge the gap between the research phase and the production and testing of a larger number of devices in a pilot program. At the moment, however, our plans are very fluid, which means that we have no formal plans, only hopes.

Remarks by Dr. Patrick W. Nye: My interest in this subject began about 10 years ago when I was carrying out some work in Britain at the National Physical Laboratory, work sponsored by St. Dunstan's, the blind ex-servicemen's organization in Britain. We were concerned with trying to find some solution to one of the basic dilemmas in providing reading and mobility aids for the blind. On the one hand, the best possible device is usually prohibitively expensive. For example, the system for reading that employs a computer which would produce artificial speech, as just described by Dr. Bliss, would cost somewhere in the neighborhood of a million dollars. On the other hand, we can conceive of devices which are less than ideal, but no one can predict whether, at the level of sensory perception, there is any chance that they would function successfully. For example, a reading device which generates a sound display might require that the reader learn what amounts to a new language of sounds. Can individuals learn such a system? And if they can, how well? Consider a mobility device which scans the environment and generates some kind of sound pattern. Such a device requires that the user extract from all the sounds generated by the device the particular signals which would indicate obstacles in his path. Again the question that must be answered is whether the user can acquire the necessary skill.

HUMAN PERCEPTUAL ABILITIES

Human beings can do some very clever things which machines cannot be made to do and this has led to the tendency, when working with less than totally ideal devices, to overestimate the degree of human sophistication and adaptability. Man's perceptual skills are, after all, limited largely to those required for survival and have evolved over a considerable period of time. One of the subtle things that a human being does, for example, is to extract or select information from a whole array of conflicting input signals. This is sometimes called the "cocktail party" problem, because one example of this ability is being able to select the voice of one particular speaker in an environment where many others are talking at once, to concentrate on what he alone is saying, and to reject everything else. An important question now is whether it is correct to conclude that dealing with the output of a machine is precisely analogous to the "cocktail party" problem. However, there are important differences in the way in which speech sounds are identified and an individual may very well not be able to select information from an arbitrary display as he would from an array of competing human speakers.

Our efforts were aimed at finding some solution that would be intermediate between the costly best solution and the inexpensive one that might prove to be too difficult to learn to use. One of the areas we investigated concerned the underlying reasons why some sounds are more difficult to learn than others and some new findings emerged. In any event, we never reached the point of actually building a device.

MOBILITY DEVICES

I am now associated with the California Institute of Technology and my work is centered largely on a study of mechanisms of vision. In addition I am active in a committee of the National Academy of Engineering that is concerned with sensory aids for the blind and the deaf. Dr. Mann is the chairman of the committee. More specifically, our interest has been in organizing the very fragmented sensory aids research efforts in this country and to that end I am organizing a research conference on the problem of mobility for the blind. By this means we hope to find the answers to two basic questions: How do we evaluate a mobility device? And, is it possible to say in advance what kinds of criteria a particular device should meet?

The first question would seem to be a rather easy one to answer. Set up an experimental situation with a set of obstacles and see if someone using the device can negotiate a course without bumping into anything. Such an approach, however, does not really determine if the device is of any practical use on a crowded, noisy street. But, to carry out tests in real-life situations is not without a great many hazards.

EVALUATING MOBILITY DEVICES

The second question is really a set of further questions. What kind of output, generated by the device, can a person easily anticipate and easily understand? What signals attract attention, that is, are more attention-getting than other signals? Can we, by process of simulation, generate or discover what are the best designs for an aid before the task of actually building it is begun? If such questions can be answered, what then is the best strategy for using such information to guide the design of better devices? I am hopeful that the conference participants will begin to provide answers to some of these crucial questions.

Remarks by Leslie L. Clark: I should like to consider two questions which I think are important to the context of the discussion which has taken place so far. One is simply, why technology? The other, what spectacular achievements can be expected in the next decade?

It seems quite natural in a culture such as ours, a culture in which we have reaped so many benefits from the applications of technology, to apply that technology to the problems of impairment. In fact, this has been a trend for some time in the field of work for the blind. It is said that it was the interest of the empress of the Austro-Hungarian Empire in providing some means of writing for her blind niece that led to the invention of the typewriter. The long-playing record was developed to aid in providing reading materials for the blind. Current advances in technology would seem to indicate that providing new links with the environment for the blind are possible.

It must be remembered that the population of blind people is far from uniform and that there are many subpopulations with special needs and requirements. It makes very good sense, therefore, to talk about an armamentarium of sensory aids so that many options are open to any particular individual for satisfying his needs and for getting at the environment in ways that are meaningful to him.

Artificial Vision

For the future, the possibility of artificial vision is the one spectacular idea that occurs to most people. Indeed, the question at the back of the minds of many blind people is: If technology is able to deliver some means for me to get direct access to my environment by providing me with a visual prosthesis, why then isn't all the money available for research devoted to such work and the work on other aids and programs of rehabilitation stopped? Clearly this attitude is a result of people having heard only of some of the successes in such research, but not of the many discouraging things that have been learned.

EXPERIMENTS IN THE UNITED KINGDOM

This view has been reinforced, for example, by the results of some rather extraordinary experiments conducted in the United Kingdom by Brindley, Lewin, Donaldson, and their associates. They inserted a prosthetic device within the skull of a blind nurse, placing it on the occipital cortex. The subject was able to perceive points of light, called phosphenes, about the size of a grain of rice held at arm's length, reliably, consistently, and stably in response to electrical stimulation. Such stimulation could be used to represent the features of objects in actuality in the form of duplicate, although simplified, patterns of these phosphenes.

I think it is important to realize that this is an experiment. It is a particularly bold and daring and courageous experiment because we know practically nothing about the nature of the electrical signal which stimulates phosphenes, about the long-term effects that such stimulation will have on the occipital cortex or the rest of the brain, or about the kind of information that the brain needs in order to make this a viable prosthesis. All that we do know from this experiment is that patterns can be stably and reliably generated and perceived. Even the most optimistic observer would not expect, even at the end of the decade, anything more than an extremely rough approximation to a visual experience, one whose nature and content cannot as yet be specified very well.

Another discouraging fact is that it has been estimated that even with the most optimum development of such a technique, fewer than 10 percent of those who are totally blind could be aided by it. Thus if one accepts the figure of 400,000 administratively defined blind persons in the United States, of whom 40,000 are estimated to be totally blind, perhaps 4,000 might be aided in an as yet unspecified way by a visual prosthesis.

DELIVERY OF TECHNOLOGY IS THE GREATEST CHALLENGE

There is, nevertheless, a real possibility for a specular achievement in the next decade in another somewhat different direction. If it would be possible for the developments that have just been described by the other speakers to be delivered in the quantities necessary to everyone who could use them, that would indeed be a spectacular achievement. The delivery of the technology for allowing persons to have direct access to the printed page when they need it and to navigate and orient themselves in both familiar and unfamiliar environments is the great challenge.

Is it true, as I have heard it said, that it is entirely conceivable that within our lifetime there will be an apparatus comparable to the human eye that will permit the blind to have a form of vision somewhat the same as sighted people?

Mr. Clark: Assertions have been made that, with an investment in time, talent, and money equivalent to the space program, a visual prosthesis could be produced. And we are all prone to believe that such a development is possible because we have all been conditioned to expect this kind of spectacular result from technology. These assertions, however, remain just that—assertions, no matter how prestigious the source. Even admitting the possibility, closer examination of the nature of such a device reveals that no one is really talking about providing a visual experience that is in any way comparable to the vision of sighted people. The devices so far are much more likely to provide an experience somewhat like watching a highly degraded, black-and-white television image in which there is some uncertainty whether or not an image or picture even exists on the screen. This is a very optimistic prediction and I am not sure that the result could even be called vision. It would probably depend on one's definition. Whether this kind of device is likely to occur in the decade we have entered, or in 25 years, or in 50 years, or at all, is difficult to say.

Would you please comment on the Russian experiments with artificial vision using dogs?

Mr. Clark: I have visited the Academy of Sciences in Moscow on three occasions and talked with the people involved in such experimentation. There is no reason to believe that they are any further along than the British or the Americans. In fact, they are probably not quite as far along as the British.

Experiments with artificial vision using animals is a very indeterminate sort of thing, because an animal cannot report to you on the success of the experiment. There has been a great deal of discussion, therefore, about the efficacy of using human beings in such experiments. This, however brings up the ethical question of using human subjects at this stage of the research.

Dr. Mann: I think an important point here is that when a normal person uses vision he transforms the physical space (what is happening in front of him) into a perception in his brain of what is happening in front of him. It is not at all clear, however, if, when one generates phosphenes by electrical stimulation of the brain, the perceptions one has are anything like the perceptual space that a sighted person "sees." The very sophisticated and very precise experiments of Drs. Brindley and Lewin are beautifully executed physiological experiments, but they do not begin to answer this question. We still have no idea of what that relationship is and, as Mr. Clark pointed out, it is unlikely that we will discover it by using animals.

General Discussion and Miscellaneous Questions

Mr. Barnett: I think this might be a good time to point out that a great deal of the research that has been described so far has been supported by federal money, that is, tax dollars. Federal grants to the states, to universities, and to other research centers, plus funds from private sources, have been extremely helpful in these efforts to advance our knowledge about sensory perception and the potential of devices that are of use to blind persons.

Dr. Nye: Dr. Bliss and I recently calculated that a total of about $900,000 per year is spent on research of the kind that we have been discussing here. This represents only about .2 percent of the $500 million spent on social welfare for the blind and visually impaired.

In his remarks, Mr. Clark said that there were 400,000 blind persons. Aren't there really more than that?

Mr. Clark: Yes, there probably are. I was taking a conservative figure for the number of totally blind persons in the United States. A rather more liberal one, one which may perhaps be closer to the truth, is 900,000. In both instances, the figures are only estimates.

Mr. Barnett: The world total is estimated to be between 15 and 25 million persons who meet the blindness definition, that is, individuals who are severely visually handicapped, but not necessarily totally blind.

Has there been any progress in presenting the charts and graphs found in books to talking book users and braille readers?

Mr. Barnett: As far as talking books are concerned, I don't think this problem has been solved. A recent meeting in Chicago to establish standards for the preparation of reading materials for the blind, called by the National Accreditation Council for Agencies Serving the Blind and Visually Handicapped, only discussed very basic questions, for example, tape speed and things of that sort. Don Staley, executive director of Recording for the Blind, New York, was the chairman of the committee on standards for recording. I am sure that the question of graphs and charts will be high on their list of priorities now that the really basic things have been established.

Dr. Foulke: In some instances, Recording for the Blind and other similar organizations and groups decide that some form of tangible representation of particularly important graphs and charts should be provided along with a recording. Some fairly standard procedures have been worked out for this. The group in Chicago, however, came to the conclusion that not enough is really known about the way in which tangible displays should be constructed for it to suggest standards. The Educational Research Department of the American Printing House for the Blind has done some research on how to choose symbols for diagrams that are easily discriminable and can be mixed. Dr. William Schiff, formerly with Recording for the Blind and now at New York University, has also done work in this area. The problem, however, remains that the translation of a visual display into a tangible form, into raised lines, for example, more often than not turns out to be a meaningless jumble of lines. There are several reasons for this. For instance, there are large differences in resolution for the two perceptual systems, sight and touch; also there has not been enough investigation to solve the problem of representing three-dimensional space on a tangible, two-dimensional surface. In addition, it must be noted that blind children, as they are presently being taught, receive very little systematic experience or training in learning to interpret information presented in the form of two-dimensional, tangible displays.

Have there been any advances in reducing the bulk of braille books?

Dr. Mann: One conceptual approach to reducing the bulk and the fragility of braille-embossed books is to store the information in coded form on magnetic tape. A machine then reads the tape and presents a continuous tactual display on what is known as a braille belt. A braille belt is a moving display of braille that is somewhat analogous to a moving electrical sign like the one that announces the news in Times Square in New York City. An extraordinary amount of such coded information could be stored on a very, very compact reel of tape. One could, for example, store several braille books on one tape cassette of the type used in portable cassette machines. Two groups that I know of are investigating this idea. Several of my students have made attempts at practical, economical, manufacturable devices; the more refined models are still under consideration. Arnold Grunwald at the Atomic Energy Commission Laboratory, Argonne, Illinois, is also working on a magnetic tape-to-braille belt system. The major drawback to this idea, of course, is that it does require this rather complex machine to read the tape and restore the information to a tactile form.

I have heard of a project to investigate the use of the enlarging capabilities of a microfiche reader as a low vision aid. What have been the results of that study?

Dr. Foulke: That research was being headed by Dr. Carson Nolan of the American Printing House for the Blind, Louisville. I do not recall the exact details of the project, but it seems that their experience was positive. I do not know what current plans they have for future implementation of the idea.

Nine

Neurologic,
Orthopedic
and
Other
Health
Impairments

The articles in Chapter Nine relate to problems of crippling among children and adults. Prevention of handicapping is discussed from the two points of view of genetic counseling and advances in medical practice. Psychological and educational problems relating to the broad field of crippling are discussed in detail.

Injury to man's brain and the resulting consequences are, of course, as old as man himself. However the handicapping condition now referred to as "cerebral palsy" is reported to have been first described as a syndrome in medical literature only a little over a hundred years ago. Dr. Winthrop Morgan Phelps, who is credited with being the first physician in the United States to devote full time to a specialization in cerebral palsy, is honored as a pioneer in this chapter. He, more than any other physician, has influenced the medical and therapeutic treatment of such children.

The first article in the chapter, entitled "Will My Baby Be Normal?" by Roland Berg, describes some of the recent advances in medicine which may be utilized by genetic counselors to reduce the frequency of handicapping among children.

Richard Masland's article, which follows, traces the progress which has been made in recent decades in reducing handicapping conditions. He appeals for additional research efforts in this field in order to provide the information which is required for greater success in prevention.

Unfortunately, there has been limited research on the educational problems relating to crippled children. Gloria Wolinsky reviews the status of educational research in the final article, and presents many problems which should be studied. The problems and issues described in this article should be of genuine interest to students who are specializing in special education since most of them have significance for all handicapped children.

Winthrop Morgan Phelps
1894–1971

PHYSICIAN
PHYSIATRIST
EDUCATOR

Dr. Winthrop Morgan Phelps was known in medical and educational circles as a pioneer in developing diagnostic and treatment techniques for children with cerebral palsy. His methods had a profound influence upon medical treatment and educational practices for these children.

As a young physician he became interested in a crippling condition which had received only minor attention since Dr. William Little, a London physician, had described the syndrome over a hundred years ago. The early medical description of cerebral palsy, or Little's Disease as it was originally called, associated it with such symptoms as feeblemindedness, cross-leggedness, lack of speech, and drooling. Dr. Phelps is credited with establishing the fact that mental retardation is not necessarily a component of the clinical syndrome. He created the term *cerebral palsy*, which may be loosely translated as a paralysis resulting from brain injury. He also developed the five-fold classification of cerebral palsy which is in wide use today.

Dr. Phelps received his medical degree from Johns Hopkins and later taught at Harvard and Yale. He left his comfortable teaching appointment at Yale University in 1934 to devote full time to the study and treatment of cerebral palsy. He founded the Children's Rehabilitation Institute near Baltimore where patients received care and thousands of professionals received training. In 1967 this institution became a part of the new John F. Kennedy Institute for Children at the Johns Hopkins Medical School.

39.
"Will My Baby Be Normal?"

ROLAND H. BERG

*This article discusses the benefits of genetic
counseling in reducing handicaps. As you read
the article note the importance of this service.*

"Is my baby all right?" Those words, anxiously
spoken, are the first a mother asks about her newborn child. An instinctive
dread of something going wrong haunts every woman during the long
months of pregnancy.

For most women, the fears prove false. But for many, the terrors are
all too real. Each year, as many as 250,000 mothers give birth to infants
with defects. These defects may mean an early death or a lifelong illness.
Not only does the infant suffer, but the life of the entire family can be
scarred.

Today, many of those tragedies can be predicted—and averted. Genetic
counseling can tell parents in advance the statistical odds of their unborn
children inheriting certain diseases. Even if the woman is already pregnant and the odds are likely that a birth defect may appear, special prenatal
tests can determine for certain. If so, under today's more liberal abortion
laws, the parents could then choose to have the pregnancy safely terminated. These prenatal tests also may alert the physician to a fetal disorder
that must be treated before or immediately after birth.

Recently, Dr. Henry Nadler, professor of pediatrics at Chicago's Northwestern University Medical School, and a leading geneticist, told about a
thirty-eight-year-old married woman who was a successful lawyer. Three of
her brothers and sisters were Mongoloids, and she was desperately afraid
the same fate awaited her children.

When she and her husband finally sought genetic counseling, a test dis-
closed she was carrying the family trait. The odds were 1 in 3 a child of
hers would be Mongoloid. She was also told that if they wanted to take
the risk, another test could be performed early in her pregnancy that would
tell whether her unborn baby was affected. Given this reassurance, the
couple risked pregnancy. But the prenatal test proved positive. The fetus
in her womb was Mongoloid. The pregnancy was terminated.

Four months later, the couple tried again. This time the test promised a
healthy child. And so it was—a lovely girl. Several years later, the wife—
now well past forty—again risked pregnancy. Once more the test promised a normal infant. Soon they had a fine healthy boy.

From *McCall's Magazine* (August, 1971): 52-55, 137. Reprinted by permission of the
publishers.

Although more than 150 genetic counseling centers recently have been set up in 44 states and Canada, not all are being overwhelmed with requests for guidance. Dr. William L. Nyhan, who heads such a service at the University of California at San Diego, says: "Not enough people are aware our service is available: we could help so many families if they'd only ask."

As well as providing patient services, most centers conduct genetic research. They are supported by grants of money from government bureaus and such voluntary philanthropies as the National Foundation–March of Dimes and the National Genetics Foundation. Both foundations conscientiously try to alert doctors and patients to the availability of counseling centers. Because some centers are more expert than others in testing for particular diseases, they may also advise the best place to go for specialized help. Anyone who needs guidance can contact the National Genetics Foundation at 250 West 57th Street, New York, N.Y. 10019, or the National Foundation–March of Dimes, which provides a list of all counseling centers in the United States.

A family pedigree is the single most important factor in genetic counseling. Given a family history, a geneticist can cite the odds on a child's inheriting the genetic disease in question. For some congenital defects, an examination of the chromosomes will disclose whether one or both parents carry a defect and the degree of risk to their offspring.

Chromosomes are tiny, rodlike structures—46 in number, enclosed in every cell in the body. Each rod houses thousands of submicroscopic genes, and each gene dictates a characteristic of a person's physical appearance and physiologic function. Every individual inherits a unique genetic package—half of the chromosomes donated by the father, half by the mother.

Genetically speaking, no one is perfect. Everybody harbors a few "bad" genes among the thousands that make up his personal blueprint, without apparent effect on himself. However, when defective genes from one parent are matched with similar defective genes from the other, risks of passing along a defect is high.

The 46 chromosomes present in every cell are arranged in 23 pairs, with only two exceptions: the woman's ova and the man's sperm. Each sperm and ovum contains a single set of 23 chromosomes. When the sperm unites with the ovum during conception, the two matching sets provide the fetus with its usual complement of 46 chromosomes per cell.

In the ovum, chromosome 23 is shaped like an X and carries only female sex genes. In the sperm, chromosome 23 can be an X, which also carries female determinants, or it can be a Y, which carries male sex genes.

In many inherited diseases, a baby's sex determines whether the child will be a symptom-free carrier or the true victim. Certain inherited diseases, such as muscular dystrophy and hemophilia, are what scientists call X-linked diseases. They mean the defective genes that cause those illnesses are housed in the X component of the sex-chromosome pair.

In the X-linked ailments, daughters run a 50-50 chance of being symptomless carriers; sons face a 50-50 risk of getting it.

An important tool in genetic counseling is a karyotype—an actual picture of chromosomes arranged according to size and shape. Karyotypes are prepared from samples of blood or skin cells grown in a laboratory culture. A technician then photographs them under a microscope, and arranges them according to a standardized pattern. Study by an expert can pinpoint the nature of certain congenital defects.

An unborn-baby karyotype can be prepared about the fourteenth week of pregnancy. A small needle is inserted through the mother's abdomen into the sac that envelops the fetus. With a syringe attached to the needle, the doctor withdraws a small amount of the fluid that contains cast-off cells from the fetus. These cells are grown, as adult blood cells are, and studied for chromosomal abnormalities. The procedure, called amniocentesis, is relatively painless and requires only a few hours' rest in a hospital. Thousands of expectant mothers have already undergone the test with remarkably few ill effects.

Because the majority of Mongoloid births occur in women over forty years of age, some geneticists believe all such pregnancies should be monitored by amniocentesis. If the fetus is Mongoloid, the karyotype is almost always unmistakable. At the parents' option, such pregnancies could be terminated.

According to Dr. Nyhan, "An amniocentesis done on every pregnant woman thirty-five years or older could save millions of dollars now spent annually on the care of these mentally retarded children, and, even more important, save parents untold heartbreak."

No one knows for certain why more Mongoloid births occur in older women, but statistics prove conclusively that genes are healthier at eighteen than they are at thirty-five.

At eighteen, a woman has only 1 chance in 2,500 of giving birth to a Mongoloid baby; by age thirty-five, the odds are 1 in 45.

Although most Mongoloid births are age-related, some younger women give birth to Mongoloid babies because they or their husbands carry a particular genetic defect. Dr. Arthur F. Mirkinson, director of the genetic laboratory at Long Island's North Shore Hospital, told me about a twenty-five-year-old woman whose first baby—now two years old—was a Mongoloid. Wanting more children but fearful of a repetition, she and her thirty-year-old husband sought Dr. Mirkinson's guidance.

From blood samples he did karyotypes on mother, father, and child. The mother's was normal, but the father's showed he was a carrier of a chromosome defect. The little girl's karyotype revealed the identical defect. Dr. Mirkinson told the couple the chance of it happening again was 1 in 10. He also told them if they risked pregnancy, the mother could be monitored from the fourteenth week on and a karyotype would reveal if the unborn was affected.

Unfortunately, the karyotype cannot predict all genetic defects. Hundreds of inherited diseases are known as "inborn errors of metabolism" and do not reveal recognizable chromosome patterns. Their defects involve the absence of key enzymes produced by the action of genes. Because some enzymes are essential to human growth and development, lack of a particular enzyme threatens life. Only a few of these metabolic diseases can be treated effectively; many are fatal.

Within the past few years, biochemists have devised tests that will determine whether the fetal cells in the amniotic fluid of a pregnant woman lack certain critical enzymes. Armed with these tests, geneticists can now monitor pregnancies and predict whether an unborn is affected by any one of more than a dozen metabolic afflictions.

Less than two years ago, Mrs. Allen Lynn of Los Angeles apprehensively faced pregnancy. Several years before, she had given birth to a baby who died of Tay-Sachs disease—a metabolic ailment that destroys brain, nerve cells, and vision. After the baby's death, the Lynns learned they both were carriers, and any child of theirs rated a 1 in 4 chance of inheriting the disease.

Early in Mrs. Lynn's pregnancy, the couple heard that Dr. John S. O'Brien, chairman of the neurosciences division at the University of California in San Diego, had developed a test that would reveal if an unborn baby lacked the enzyme that led to Tay-Sachs disease. Mrs. Lynn consulted Dr. O'Brien, underwent the test, and the verdict was a happy one: The fetus was normal. Almost afraid to believe it, Mrs. Lynn had the baby—a lovely little girl who recently celebrated her first birthday.

There is more to successful genetic counseling than family pedigrees, karyotypes, and biochemical tests of amniotic fluid. To Dr. Mirkinson, compassion is the most important ingredient. He will chat for an hour with a couple, getting their history, explaining the mathematics of inheritance. "It's vital that they—not you—make the decision whether to take the risk," he says. "And to do that, they must understand what the probabilities are, what the odds really mean. In this business, you're as much a social worker as a physician."

40.
The Promise of the Future in Relation
to the Crippling of Man
RICHARD L. MASLAND

Which types of handicapping conditions is science making greatest progress in controlling?

He who fails to consider the errors of the past is destined to repeat them. He who overlooks the successes of the past will never surpass them. Thus, if we are to look ahead, it is necessary first to look behind. The gains of the future may be most accurately predicted after a study of the gains of the past.

With this in mind, I have carried out a brief review of the advances in medicine during the 35 years since I was graduated from medical school. Some of these gains are summarized in Figures 1 and 2. There has been a 10-year prolongation of life expectancy. The death rate has declined, and maternal mortality and neonatal death rates are reduced to a fraction of their former level.

How have these tremendous health gains been accomplished? Study or changes in death rate in individual diseases reveals an interesting pattern. The infectious diseases have been almost eliminated. Tuberculosis and syphilis figures have dropped sharply. Pertussis, diphtheria, and measles are rare diseases. Poliomyelitis has almost been eliminated in this country. The devastating German measles (rubella) epidemic of 1964-1965 will never have to happen again.

However, the death rate from cancer, cardiovascular disease, multiple sclerosis, and parkinsonism remains unchanged. (The exciting new discovery of a treatment for parkinsonism will certainly create a break in this curve.) At present, over 70 percent of all deaths are from cancer or cardiovascular disease. The third leading cause of death—accident—is responsible for only 6 percent.

These curves dramatically demonstrate that those diseases for which we have a cure are being cured. *The change in pattern of disease results from new knowledge of cause and cure derived from research.*

The financial cost of the research program from which these advances have arisen is remarkably modest. Total expenditures are now running about $2 billion per year. It is less than 4 percent of the total health budget and only slightly more than we spend for beauty aids (*Figs. 3, 4*). A major share of this cost has been borne by the federal government (*Fig. 5*). However, industry, private, donors, and voluntary agencies have made im-

From *Rehabilitation Literature* 31 (May, 1970): 130-134. Reprinted by permission of the author and *Rehabilitation Literature*.

portant contributions. It is noteworthy that, even though heavily burdened with its responsibilities for the sick and crippled, the National Easter Seal Society for Crippled Children and Adults and affiliates has also made their contribution to research (*Fig. 6*).

The benefits of specific research accomplishments can be readily documented. The National Foundation for Infantile Paralysis spent a total of about $50 million on its entire research program, which led to the discovery of an effective vaccine. From this, about $5 million was for the vaccine. During this same period, the Foundation spent over $350 million to provide patient services. As a result of the $50 million expenditure, the $350 million will never have to be spent again. In 1955, the year the vaccine was introduced, there were 28,985 reported cases of poliomyelitis, of which 13,813 led to paralysis and 1,043 were fatal. This year, the total number of cases is less than 100.

In 1964-1965, an epidemic of German measles in the United States caused an estimated 20,000 babies to be born with disabling congenital defects—blindness, deafness, retardation, and palsy. Assuming that each child lives 50 years and that it will require $2,000 each year for someone to maintain such a defective person, the final cost to society will be 50 x $2,000

Figure 1. Mortality Rates and Life Expectancy Data for United States, 1930-1965. Mortality Rates for Total United States and Puerto Rico, 1940-1965. Also Rates for Maternal Mortality and Infant Mortality (Age 1-11 Months).

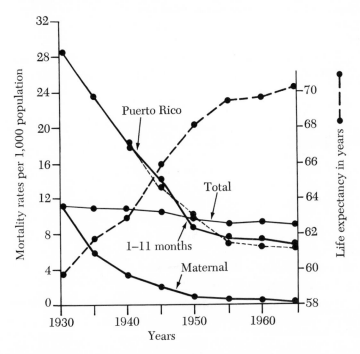

= \$100,000 for each defective child. The final bill for the 20,000 babies will be \$2 billion.

Since that epidemic occurred, a vaccine was developed and it was widely distributed last fall. It was believed that the anticipated epidemic of German measles would be prevented. The vaccine cost less than \$20 million to develop. It will save a billion dollars by preventing the next epidemic *and for every subsequent epidemic it prevents as long as our society is able to give the vaccine.*

I have been speaking only of dollars. Let heartache and misery speak for themselves. Truly, an ounce of prevention is worth a pound of cure.

However, we have only begun the job. The future holds even more exciting prospects, for we are on the verge of very important new discoveries. I can enumerate only a few especially crucial areas.

1. Immunity

The body is armed with a delicate mechanism through which it destroys or rejects foreign material, especially bacteria or other infectious agents. The mechanism is remarkably precise—the body

Figure 2. CHANGES OF DEATH RATE FROM SELECTED DISEASES IN THE UNITED STATES, 1945-1965. CURVES PLOTTED AS PERCENTAGE OF THE 1945 DEATH RATE.

Changes in death from representative diseases

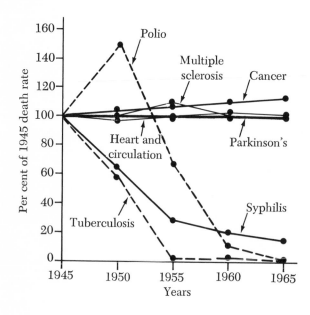

can and must distinguish between its own proteins and those from outside sources. Possibly it is this immunity that is a primary protection against tumor growths, which take on the character of a foreign substance and are usually rejected, the formation of cancer representing a failure of this mechanism. In a number of diseases, called "autoimmune," it is postulated that the mechanism becomes *oversensitized* and the individual's own tissues are attacked. The mechanism may underlie symptoms of such disorders as rheumatoid arthritis, dermatomyositis, multiple sclerosis, and nephritis. The *normal* operation of this process is now the major stumbling block to successful organ transplantation. Methods for the selective enhancement or suppression of the immune process are being developed.

2. Slow Viruses

It is possible that some of the autoimmune diseases result from an interaction between unusual infectious agents and the tissues of the body. An abnormal tissue is created, which the patient attempts to reject. New culture methods have recently led to the discovery of several latent viruses of the nervous system that have devastating symptoms. A new field is developing in the search for latent infectious inciting agents.

Figure 3. EXPENDITURES FOR HEALTH IN THE UNITED STATES, 1968. (NATIONAL ADVISORY COMMISSION ON HEALTH FACILITIES, GOVERNMENT PRINTING OFFICE, DOCUMENT, 1968, 0-327-238)

Allocation of health dollar–1968

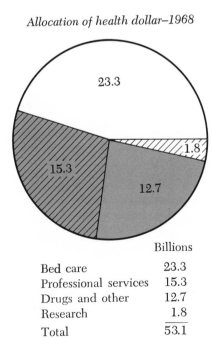

	Billions
Bed care	23.3
Professional services	15.3
Drugs and other	12.7
Research	1.8
Total	53.1

3. Metabolic Defects

The discovery of certain forms of mental retardation stemming from inborn abnormalities of body chemistry, some of which are treatable by dietary means, offers exciting possibilities. In addition, in some of these disorders, such as mongolism, the actual chromosomal defect can be demonstrated. To be treated effectively, these conditions must be recognized at birth. In some instances, prenatal diagnosis is accomplished by aspiration and study of amniotic fluid. Means are now being developed for systematic analysis of body tissues and fluids so that ultimately every person could be chemically characterized at birth and his susceptibility to disease properly dealt with from early infancy.

4. Cardiovascular Disease

Over 71 percent of all deaths are from heart disease and stroke. The latter is one of the most ravaging of the crippling diseases. Our ultimate objective is to determine the nature of the chemical and structural changes leading to narrowing of the blood vessels. It is probable that dietary or chemical means may be found to obviate these lifelong developments. Meanwhile, new refinements of surgical technic make it possible to restore the diseased blood vessels in some instances. The devel-

Figure 4. Expenditures for Medical Research in the United States, 1968, Compared to Other Expenditures That Year.

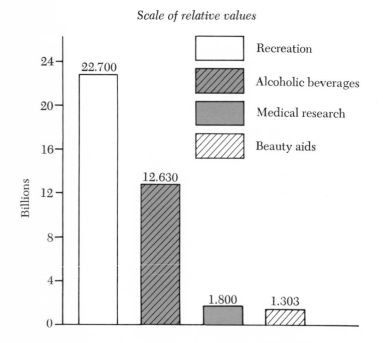

Scale of relative values

Recreation
Alcoholic beverages
Medical research
Beauty aids

22.700
12.630
1.800
1.303

Billions

opment of a safe and painless procedure for studying the circulation of the brain would make it possible to recognize the danger of stroke in time more often.

5. Restoration of Function for the Crippled

In spite of all foreseeable advances in preventive medicine, it is certain that we will continue to have to provide programs for the crippled and disabled. At present, there are an estimated 100,000 paraplegics in the United States—many as the result of spinal injury from automobile accidents.

Naturally, our first concern is to minimize the paralysis and achieve regeneration of injured nerves. A movement is now on foot to establish a number of paraplegic centers where methods of emergency care and rehabilitation can be developed. A great deal can be done by these centers to ameliorate the disability. Equally important, however, is the continuation of the research effort to find ways to help the brain and spinal cord pathways to regenerate. Regeneration does occur in the embyro and in some cold-blooded animals. The factors influencing such growth are only beginning to be understood.

Figure 5. Expenditures for Health Research Training, National Institute of Neurological Diseases and Blindness, 1954-1968.

NINDS grants and awards

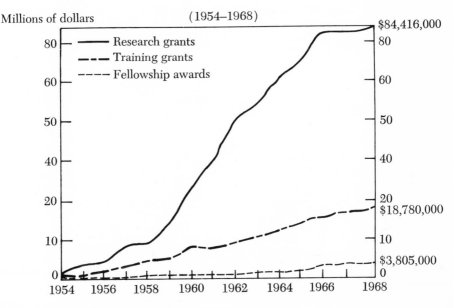

Compiled by Research & Training Manpower Section, PA, OD, NINOS, 4/23/69.

Since World War II, there have been striking improvements in our ability to help the paraplegic to follow a useful, satisfying life, and these efforts are being extended. The Easter Seal Research Foundation (ESRF) has played an important role in this field, having helped to support one of the first programs to develop a more scientifically designed brace for paralyzed limbs. Power-assisted devices have now been invented, and now, once again, the ESRF is supporting a pioneering undertaking to use signals from the muscles and nerves to activate and regulate the power-assisted movement aids.

In fact, a new concept is now being explored in a laboratory on neural control at the National Institutes of Health. To what extent might external devices actually be controlled directly from the brain or nerves? To what extent may information be channeled directly into the brain without passing through the sense organs? Can we find a substitute for the eye and ear? Realistic proposals for such devices are now being sought.

I have been able to mention only a few of the programs now under way that offer hope for the prevention and amelioration of crippling of children and adults. Judging from the successes of the past, the accomplishments I have outlined are reasonable expectations for the future.

However, these accomplishments are predicated on the assumption that we will continue and will expand our current research effort. What are the prospects for this? It is disturbing to note that serious cutbacks of the federal research effort are now in progress (*Fig. 7*). Under the pressures of fiscal restraint and the overwhelming domestic and foreign problems, efforts are being made to restrict current research and to limit the training of more

Figure 6. Expenditures of Funds for Services and for Research of the National Easter Seal Society for Crippled Children and Adults and the Easter Seal Research Foundation.

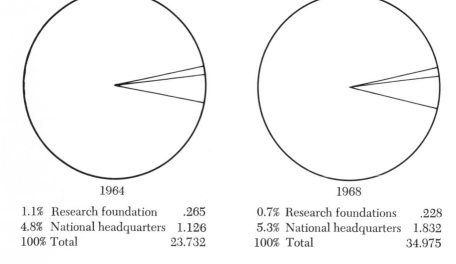

	1964			1968	
1.1%	Research foundation	.265	0.7%	Research foundations	.228
4.8%	National headquarters	1.126	5.3%	National headquarters	1.832
100%	Total	23.732	100%	Total	34.975

National institutes of health

Research institutes and divisions:

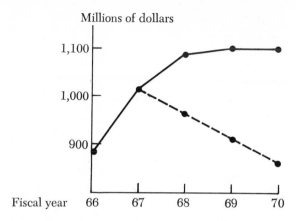

Millions of dollars

Figure 7. ALLOCATION OF FUNDS TO THE NATIONAL INSTITUTES OF
HEALTH, 1966-1970, FOR MEDICAL RESEARCH AND RESEARCH
TRAINING. DOTTED CURVE INDICATES ACTUAL TREND OF RESEARCH
SUPPORT, ASSUMING 8 PERCENT ANNUAL INCREASE IN RESEARCH COST.

scientists. With the desire for instant remedy, the cry across the nation is
"Treat us now, research can wait."

There have been serious cutbacks in the nation's research effort. Especially damaging has been the serious restriction placed on the research
training programs of the National Institutes of Health—the source of our
future research manpower. Truly we are borrowing from the future. It's
hard to believe our medical research structure, which has accomplished
so much, and which is the envy of the entire world, should be permitted
to fall apart. We cannot continue to recruit scientists for medical research,
we cannot maintain a solid research organization, we cannot achieve the
goals I have outlined unless there is a constancy of purpose not evident
at this time throughout the United States and in its administration.

The future of these programs is continually threatened within the
Congress. I urge you to contact the President and your Congressmen to indicate your support of the National Institutes of Health. Mr. Nixon has
emphasized the need for partnership and is asking the private sector to assume a greater responsibility. Possibly voluntary agencies, in spite of their
burden of patient care and service, could take on a greater share in research
and in this way express our commitment to the future.

*Richard L. Masland is professor and chairman, department of neurology,
College of Physicians and Surgeons, Columbia University, and is director of
the neurological service, Presbyterian Hospital, both in New York City.*

41.
Current Status and Future Needs in Research on the Orthopedically Handicapped Child
GLORIA WOLINSKY

On what phase or phases of care of orthopedically handicapped children do you think our research should concentrate?

A trend in any particular research area can be evaluated only in terms of a continuum. In 1953[23, p. 492] the following statement was made.

Three research trends may be noted in the literature on the orthopedically handicapped during the period from 1941 to the present: (a) a tendency to restrict investigations to fairly well-defined homogeneous groups of subjects, rather than studying general orthopedic populations; (b) an upsurge of interest in the cerebral palsied; and (c) an attempt to relate research projects to a frame of reference based upon psychological theory. This latter trend suggests that future reviews may list fewer contributions of a minor sort, and that major research undertakings which will make use of more sophisticated methods of sampling and analysis will provide a reliable body of information concerning the effects of orthopedic disability.

Seventeen years later a review of the research literature would reveal that, in spite of the considerable interest that has been displayed, the situation has not altered considerably. It is perhaps all the more interesting since the existing orthopedic population has substantially changed, in terms of clinical entities, in the organized school system. Wherein does the problem lie, that, in spite of changing populations, increased interest, and support, there has been no appreciable change in the direction of research in this area?

This presentation will attempt to answer this problem by analyzing certain factors operative on the investigative scene: first, the elements of the research situation; second, the complexity of the situation described as orthopedic; and third, a need for new approaches to research and the utilization of role theory. These three factors will be discussed in terms of their influence on current and future trends in research as it concerns the education of the orthopedically handicapped.

From *Rehabilitation Literature* 31 (October, 1970): 290-96, 318. Reprinted by permission of the author and *Rehabilitation Literature*.

New studies in the area of the orthopedically handicapped, while expressing continued interest in diverse clinical entities such as cerebral palsy, muscular dystrophy, arthritis, and congenital deformities, still are examples of discrete populations that tell us little more than how a segment of a specific group acted in terms of a measurement used at a particular time. The "major research" study in this area is still anticipated.

It is possible that a breakthrough in terms of a truly dynamic understanding of the basic problems to be "researched" has not been made because the proper questions have not been asked. Or if the questions have been asked, they have not been studied in a way that utilized the ascertained facts in the most efficient manner. In effect, research in this area, as in most of special education, is proceeding in the manner of classic analysis, reflecting the heritage of the physical sciences. Wholes are still being fractionated into a series of variables to be studied seriatim.[17] In spite of the verbal emphasis on the "total child," paradoxically the studies that are ultimately to benefit the "whole child" are carried out in fragmented fashion. Perhaps this is why, too often, the plaintive cry, "Good in theory, but not in practice," is heard.

The time of what Weaver calls "organized complexities"[50, p. 539] is very much with us, as it is with most other academic disciplines. The ability to establish research procedures in terms of complexities is not to be confused with the notion that the individual is lost in the process. For in any study of a complex entity, the parts must be analyzed and understood. But the study of parts can be understood only in terms of their relationships to each other and the entire system of which each is a component.[51]

The Complexity of the Situation Described as Orthopedic

The education of the orthopedically handicapped has more than its share of constituted parts. Indeed the realization that this discrete entity is not so discrete is, in itself, one of the more fruitful aspects of thinking in this area.

This "trend," which was not fully realized in the past, is reflected in several publications[7, 10, 53] acknowledging the complexity of the situation and the need for the pooling of information from various disciplines. No longer is this a problem for the exclusive domain of the doctor, the social worker, the teacher, or the psychologist. While each must perform a vital function in the total education of the orthopedically handicapped child, these are functions that are intimately interwoven.

Consequently, studies and discussions concerning perception, emotional development, problems of parents, duration of hospital stay, counseling, methodology, intelligence levels, and achievements appear ever more frequently in the literature. [5, 13, 25, 26, 28, 39] In perspective the studies emanating almost serve as a classic picture of Wiener's concern with entropy[52] and the disorganization and havoc caused by uncontrolled growth.

For these studies, surveys and researches appear to be strangely insulated from each other, touching tangentially for brief moments. The design or pattern that is basic to the common situation seems to be lost or at very best obscured. A working model or theoretical premise that would logically follow a concept of concerted action, i.e., interdisciplinary effort, is vitally needed. This model would form a conceptual basis for investigation that could be defined, refined, expanded upon, or even discarded if need be for future research and in clarifying many of the results that we have today.

In the past, many of our problems have dealt with events that would be of value in terms of prediction or use in imitation. But if, when a teacher used the result of such reports but found that Johnny did not want to sit behind a screen or Jane did not learn to read when the word was presented in its entirety, the tendency for bitter recriminations between those who worked with the theoretical and those who worked with the practical became quite evident. Whether these recriminations were part of mutual distrust or difficulties in translating theory into practicalities is still part of the unknown.

The Need for a New Approach to Research

Our research models as they are now constituted do not lead us to an understanding of failures and success. Life is not simply a cause-and-effect relationship. There are too many intervening variables. We have acknowledged this by utilizing diverse professional competencies for evaluation and treatment. However, the human situation is not a system where parts can be isolated for long periods of time for intensive study and then predictions made in terms of absolutes. The "real problem is to discover the actual operational mechanisms which govern such behavior, and not simply to measure it." [38, p. xviii] The world that the orthopedically handicapped child lives in is not simply a closed system, even though superficially it is circumscribed by the outline of the human form, limitation of mobility, and prejudices of society. This child, as any child, must come to terms with his environment. This coming to terms implies that an exchange of experiences is ongoing. No matter how circumscribed his life space, physiologically and psychologically he has to achieve homeostasis if he is to live. This homeostatic condition may have brought some confusion to our thinking, for this implies mobilization of resources only from within one's self. The problem may be clarified by utilizing von Bertalanffy's[48] discussion of "steady states" and "open systems."

The children we are concerned with present a visual picture of a system that remains constant as a whole, or in parts, but in actuality maintains a flow of its component parts. The component parts for this child extend beyond the immediate self to school and society, which in turn react in terms of their own component aspects. By realizing that this living organism is now a part of a "steady state," which implies a growth and development that is made up of anabolic and catabolic processing, both physical and psychological, we can begin to devise research models that will utilize these forces in an ordered way.[9, 22, 40]

Along with a new orientation to the problem must come new ways of analyzing a situation. This analysis must yield models for understanding, not simply numerical estimates of parameters. But, as we come to explore new models, there must always be the caution of realization of the representative symbolic use, for whatever methods and yardsticks that are used on a particular population. What is seen on paper is not an actual reproduction of events. If an understanding of the temporal meaning of research studies that are not based on universals can be truly realized, perhaps the disappointment at apparent failure in use will not be so acute. For then the understanding of failure will in reality be the first step towards a new approach to analysis.

Methodology and Value Systems

Can a start be made toward a new approach to this inspection of data? Have certain other academic areas been working along parallel lines?[16, 21, 40] Have we been blind to one area of research because of past commitments to another? Have we been sitting so long with inbred prejudices that we are not able to look around us and truly visualize what the progress in modern mathematics, statistics, and the physical and natural sciences will ultimately mean to those of us who work with the crippled. Our changing classroom picture reflects these great advances. While we still have fully to make use of these new concepts, or for that matter old ones, those who are immediately concerned with the technicalities and the consequences of contemporary theory and practices are looking rather closely at some of the results of increasing technical know-how.[2, 15, 30] For example:

What would this increase in mutation rate mean in terms of social burden: The answer is not known. Perhaps it cannot be, for social burden consists of diverse components that cannot be summed. . . . It is also important to remember that the more considerate of its unfit individuals a society becomes, the greater will be the burden of a given mutation rate. . . . [2, p.226]

Finally, assuming that medicine will have become highly successful in circumventing genetic death, will the net effect of medical practice have been unfavorable to the genetic capital of mankind? It is not inconceivable that by asking such questions man may one day find himself in the paradoxical position of searching for wiser and more humane ways than he now knows to counteract the undesirable evolutionary effects of too much success.[2]

It is important to add that this looking at the end results of a particular aspect of research is in terms of a value system[8, 12, 40, 45] that most of us are quite willing to brush off with "equal in his right to learn if not in his capacity." But from where does this noble enunciation of human rights spring? And, if this be the value system that we are part of, why in this time of great economic abundance do we still wrestle with the problem of support and proper care of the physically handicapped? A new approach to the problem must of necessity go beyond the immediate statistics. What is usually relegated to esoteric discussions in classrooms must be well understood, for these theoretical and sometimes idealistic statements are pragmatic in society. Theoretic statements, whatever their particular philosophic bent might be, lie at the very base of the statistics as we record and interpret them.

The question, then, is what theoretic construct of value shall be in use. The school population reflects directly society's concept of worth and value. Any change that is seen administratively results from other changes in the community. It, therefore, seems fruitless to undertake any research without a thorough understanding of this factor, either in research design as it relates to the topic to be investigated or in a particular aspect of a problem to be explored that must be related to a greater whole.

Role Theory and Its Implication for Research

Methodology and its close relationship to value theory lead to a second area of importance for future research: role theory. Very few of us come to understand the role of deviance as it concerns the sick or the handicapped. This is all the more strange since so many of us have chosen to work with deviant groups. So busy are we in the normative approach, that of education, that we forget the meaning of extremes of individual differences and its implications for organized groups. For though we meet together under the beneficience of a society that accommodates differences by designing education and training to minimize differences, its very accommodation is paradoxically a repudiation and rejection of deviance. This is reflected in the way it trains and licenses its teachers, creates curriculums, and assigns experiences for orthopedically handicapped children.

In the attempt to professionalize what was originally an expression of religious charity,[6] these children have been defined in well-meaning, but by now well-worn, clichés: "This child is like any other." "This child's needs are like any other child's needs." Far from clarifying matters, this, rather, presents an inconsistent picture of having to justify special classes and special equipment for a youngster who is supposedly like the "others." Since the appellation, "special," derives from a medical classification, this immediately places the child in a time continuum that includes a well-defined role of illness.[36]

Roles are rather interesting phenomena in that they evolve out of culturally defined systems of expectations:[43,49] systems of expectations that affect all who work with the handicapped. Again, the concern is with the superficialities of a situation when we just measure academic growth of cerebral palsied children or adjustment patterns of orthopedically involved youngsters. We have yet truly to view in an efficiently dynamic way the interrelationship in a situation that includes a role of sickness in a nonsick environment and its meaning for learning and living situation.

Barker and Wright's[1] classic study should have provided some creative insights for further work. For, while the disabled were not studied in an intimate relationship with the nondisabled, similar research designs were used for both. While it was found that "a surprising and significant result is the absence of clear-cut evidence that the physically disabled children differed appreciably from the normal children of Midwest in behavior structure,"[1, p. 465] the difference in the structured situation that surrounded these children in terms of the educational and social environment were marked. In other words the representative of the "normal" group, the teacher with the organizational system of which he is a part, forms a construct for this child that is symptomatic of society's idea of how the physically handicapped should be treated. If you would now recall the earlier discussion of "homeostasis" and "steady state" you can easily bridge the theoretic by noting that the youngster remains overtly the same, perhaps even employing similar defense mechanisms, as the normal child, but he will be reacting in terms of a system that changes its concepts about the functioning level of a member of its group because of an overtly manifested sign of deviance. This, then, will set off a reaction pattern that may be interpreted as different because of society's concept that this youngster is different, therefore he must act differently.

The Role of "Illness" and Its Meaning for the Orthopedically Handicapped

Why is this so? It has been stated that illness is part of a psychological continuum.[37] In order to safeguard itself against the liabilities of states of unproductiveness that illness can cause, society has institutionalized the role of illness and the roles of the people who must service these deviants. Whether we are consciously aware of it or not, we are not allowed to wallow in the inactivity that sickness may bring to us for too long a time. In order to make legitimate a nonproductive period of time, the sick are exempted from normal obligations, such as work, household chores, school, and other social responsibilities. One is told that "he ought to be in bed." Implicit is the need for help. Help and exemption from certain tasks are extended toward the patient as long as he wants to get well. His role is complementary to the doctor, who must make him well. Preventive medicine is, after all, a rather new concept in the history of modern medicine. The sick role is different from other deviant roles in that the person has come to it usually through no fault of his own. Sickness by definition is an undesirable state, so that, by institutionalizing it, "the sick role" becomes a mechanism in that the two most dangerous potentialities, namely, group formation and successful establishment of the claim for legitimacy, are avoided.[36] The development and consequences of the various organizations concerned with single clinical entities would be an interesting phenomenon to explore in terms of this analysis.

Perhaps one of the basic difficulties in ascertaining the questions that are to be answered lies in the fact that we have never come to explore fully at even a verbal level what this role means in its implication. An objection can be raised at this point by stating that the children with whom we work cannot be classified as sick, for we usually reserve this name for an acute state. But, while the acute state has passed for these children, they still bear the obvious stigmas of physical limitations that prevent them from performing certain tasks that we construe to be necessary for normal functioning.

We tend to ignore the deep feelings of inadequacy that the normal population projects onto a handicapped child. We overlook the more basic problem if overtly immediate needs are met. If we would use models that have as a basis an interplay of factors, we must understand this institutionalized role of acceptable deviance. We cannot afford to forget it because the child is in what is nominally a normative situation. Perhaps those of us who work in long-term treatment agencies understand this problem as we see the strain of accommodation as the child grows toward what is theoretically a self-sustaining status. It is apparent when a teacher in the regular grades objects to having a youngster who uses a crutch in her classroom. The roots of prejudice are very deep. The fear and anxiety that surround the malformed child are very much with us, for we must remember that it is only in relatively recent times that society has come to accommodate the physically deviant. The history of all groups tells of times when the malformed were left to fend for themselves or were destroyed. Though we know that different groups care for their deviants in diversified manners, they have come to this care only when they were able to control their immediate environment.[45]

Proper study of orthopedically handicapped children and youth is also impeded by the very fact that they are the young. In a sense they have a double role of dependency, that of the childhood dependency stage and the other of the "to be cared for deviant." But, whereas the so-called normal child by his passage through the school years at least in theory is helped to overcome this dependency stage, our handicapped children because of their isolation and limited mobility do not go through this developmental stage in an ordered fashion. Physically they are maturing, but, in regard to social and intellectual development, reports sometimes indicate that this is not always the situation.

When we attempt to explain low achievement levels, we discuss IQ's, interruption of schooling, and lack of facilities. Have we left out a rather important component—the staff that is part of the educational program?

Because staff members are viewing an entity that has a medical aura about it, and since they have grown up in a system that is permissive in demands at times of illness, perhaps unconsciously they extend the release from obligations to the learning situation.[16] Without intending this to be an indictment, may I say we all have heard, "Those poor things have suffered so much, why burden them with the discipline of truly learning how to read and write." In a sense we add an additional burden by not realizing that we have not demanded the most from these youngsters.

Another Look at Dynamic Psychology and Personality Theory

There is a third area in terms of developmental trends in research that is vital for us to look at. This is the broadly construed area of dynamic psychology and personality theory. All too often we still grapple with the question, "Is there a psychology of the physically handicapped?" Much effort has gone into the affirmation or the negation of this concept but we reflect basic conceptual weaknesses when we explore this in terms of a quantitative analysis, rather than its qualitative meaning.

We are still exploring the meaning of parent-child relationship. When we learn that there is much guilt feeling in parents of the handicapped, we hastily isolate this and use this for the cause, effect, and reason for the child's faulty personality development. We should remember that many parents of normal children have guilt feelings.[44, 46] The issue is not guilt feelings alone; it is rather how they operate in a given situation.

Future research in the general area of parent-child relations would do well to understand the basis of the research in Sears, Maccoby, and Levin, *Patterns of Child Rearing.*[44]

The importance of child-rearing as an object for study does not lie in any unique role that it plays as a determinant of personality but in the fact that in some stages of the child's growth it introduces some effect. The lesson for us clearly is not simply overprotection, rejection, or permissiveness. It is, rather, how this is operative in the life of the child and his parents and its commensurate effect on his training and education.

It seems important, too, for us to include the problems of research in perception and learning theory in our understanding of dynamic psychology. The last few years has seen a profound revival in studies and talks about perception and learning theory. While this research is directed at the present toward the understanding of the breakdown of "normal" processes, it is imperative for us to understand that perception is not a pathological state. It is the distortion or lack of perception that accounts for pathology in the learning situation. So that, while the problem of perception is one that may entail an analysis of an injured cerebrum, it may also involve an analysis of a person whose problem is an "injured" ego or faulty socialization.[3] The phenomenological self exists at all times in a state of perception, regardless of whether one is brain-damaged or not.

Those of us who work with the orthopedically handicapped often fail to realize the rich source of materials that we have available for study as to the effect of sensory deprivation and distortions of perceptions early in life. By this, I mean children who are born without completely formed limbs and are therefore unable adequately to explore their environment and children who are encased in casts early in a crucial developmental stage and must depend upon visual and auditory cues for orientation to their surroundings.

Some interesting work along this line has been done with respiratory patients[11, 20, 34] and with adults. The negative effects of hospitalization[41] on the emotional development of young children has also been recognized, but not found is a comprehensive study of young children who are determined early in life to have losses that interfere with normal developmental growth and affect later learning situations.

In the psychoanalytic literature, the early effects of locomotor restraint is discussed in terms of philosophic and generic concepts.[4, 19, 35] However, interest in research in the dynamics and interrelationship of visual, auditory, and locomotor deprivation was renewed when we were faced with the return of Korean war prisoners, the needs of the aerospace program, and the results of organized sensory deprivation. We are still to capitalize on this view of research endeavor.[54]

Cognition, language development, learning, and perceiving are all part of a personality structure. What effects does constraint of motor behavior in the life of a developing organism have on cognition, language learning, and even perceptual development? Therefore, the renaissance of interest in these areas may be of considerable assistance to us in understanding the problems with which we are concerned. But here again is the caution that these factors are a part of a greater whole. Theory of language, perception, learning, or cognition is not simply the cause and effect of an isolated laboratory situation but is functional in a complicated person who is a biological and psychosociological organism.

Concluding Remarks

We talk about the needed research in curriculum areas and we talk about the need to change teachers' and administrators' attitudes about the handicapped child. But do we know enough about the interplay of emotions between individuals to even begin to understand resistance to and accommodation of the physically handicapped? Do we understand the basic dynamics that are operative that make it more important to accept orthopedically handicapped children and adults as inferiors always to be protected and sheltered than to accept them as equals in their peer groups?

What is it that makes for acceptance? What is it that makes for choice of this particular field? What is operative in a situation that makes a previously poorly disposed teacher or administrator enthusiastically accept the child with cerebral palsy or a new approach to curriculum for these youngsters? Have we chosen to explore the relationships between teachers of the handicapped and those of the nonhandicapped? Do we know anything about life in a hospital for crippled children as it concerns the teaching situation? What thoughts have we given to teachers who must now face degenerative diseases such as muscular dystrophy and cancer in the classroom? What is the true implication of locomotor restraint in the life and development of a child? What is even operative in the social situation that makes some of us still call these children "crippled" and others shudder at the thought and, instead, call them the orthopedically handicapped? There are meaning and implication in all of this that must be a part of any organized research endeavor. If we are to prove worthy of our obligation both to our profession and to the culture that has chosen a specific way of handling a difficult problem, then it is incumbent upon us to really analyze the varieties of meaning and implications that a new picture of a very old entity presents.

Needed are propositions that would provide us with some oganized principles around which we could begin to explore the myriad of problems that are in the area of the orthopedically handicapped. We should not delude ourselves that we work in the exacting manner of some of the natural sciences. Even here there is the realization of the differences of the observational sciences such as astronomy and the experimental sciences like chemistry. Rather we should begin to identify variables, try to understand them, and then see their interrelationships. Since we cannot use the traditional test tube to any advantage, we must realize a permissiveness that would allow a certain elasticity in terms of changing and indeterminate variables. Implications of specifications and meanings of terms should be provisional, in terms of growing knowledge and changing fields.[27, 31] Meaning should correspond to neither the logical sum nor product of these regions, but rather to the pattern as a whole.[31]

If the next years are to prove more fruitful in terms of the proper utilization of resources than has the past, both in terms of research and application, then there must be a proper realization of the responsibility of proceeding within a research setting. There is the discipline of adhering to certain principles of research as applied to orthopedic problems and of spending long hours in learning about our subjects and learning how best to design meaningful models for research. We must also acknowledge our limitations and realize that it is also important sometimes to admit we cannot, for the time, explain certain phenomena. A caution, too, that in all our desires for knowledge we should not be misguided or enraptured with our findings that look so very significant on paper, but somehow lose their significance in practice. And, above all, in our search for understanding we must never lose sight of the fact that all our work is with what is perhaps one of the noblest expressions of the human situation, man's concern for his fellow man.

REFERENCES

1. BARKER, ROGER G. and WRIGHT, HERBERT F. *Midwest and Its Children: The Psychological Ecology of an American Town.* Evanston, Ill.: Row Peterson, 1955. 532 pp.
2. BEADLE, GEORGE W. Ionizing radiation and the citizen. *Scientific American* 201:3 (September, 1959): 219-32.
3. BEARDSLEE, DAVID C. and WERTHEIMER, MICHAEL. *Readings in Perception.* New York: Van Nostrand-Reinhold, 1958. 751 pp.
4. BERGMANN, THESI. Observation of children's reactions to motor restraint. *Nervous Child* 4:4 (July, 1945): 318-28.
5. BEST, GARY A. and FORCE, DEWEY G., JR. Orthopedic disabilities and special health problems, pp. 201-25: In Johnson, G. Orville and Blank, Harriett D. *Exceptional Children Research Review.* Washington, D.C.: Council for Exceptional Children, 1968.
6. BOCKOVEN, J. SANBOURNE. Some relationships between cultural attitudes toward individuality and care of the mentally ill: An historical study, pp. 517-26. In Greenblatt, Milton; Levinson, Daniel J.; and Williams, Richard H., eds., *The Patient and the Mental Hospital.* Glencoe, Ill.: Free Press, 1957. 658 pp.
7. BRADLEY, CHARLES. Interdisciplinary teamwork in special education. *Exceptional Children* 23 (October, 1956): 5-9, 38.
8. BRONOWSKI, JACOB. *Science and Human Values.* New York: Harper and Bros., 1959. 94 pp.
9. BUCKLEY, WALTER, ed. *Modern Systems Research for the Behavioral Scientist.* Chicago: Aldine Publishing Co., 1968. 525 pp.
10. CARDWELL, VIOLA E. *Cerebral Palsy; Advances in Understanding and Care.* New York: Assn. for the Aid of Crippled Children, 1956. 625 pp.
11. CATH, STANLEY H.; GLUD, ERIK; and BLANE, HOWARD T. The role of the body-image in psychotherapy with the physically handicapped. *Psychoanalytic Review* 44:1 (January, 1957): 34-40.
12. COHEN, MORRIS RAPHAEL. *A Preface to Logic.* New York: Meridian Books, World Publishing Co., 1957. pp. 168-791.
13. CONNOR, FRANCES P. and GOLDBERG, I. IGNACY. Children with crippling conditions and special health problems. *Review of Educational Research* 29:5 (December, 1959): 471-96.
14. DEUTSCH, KARL W. Communication theory and social science. *Am. J. Orthopsychiatry* 22:3 (July, 1952): 469-83.
15. Ethical aspects of experimentation with human subjects. *Daedalus* 98:2 (Spring, 1969): 219-596.
16. FRANK, LAWRENCE K. Psycho-cultural approaches to medical care. *J. Social Issues* 8:4 (1952): 45-55.
17. FRANK, LAWRENCE K. Research for what? *J. Social Issues Suppl. series, no. 10.* (1957): 5-22.
18. FREEDMAN, JONATHAN L. and DOOB, ANTHONY N. *Deviancy: The Psychology of Being Different.* New York: Academic Press, 1968. 158 pp.
19. FREUD, ANNA. The Role of Bodily Illness in the Mental Life of Children, pp. 69-81. In *Psychoanalytic Study of the Child. Vol. VIII.* New York: International Universities Press, 1952.
20. GLUD, ERIK and BLANE, HOWARD T. Body-image changes in patients with respiratory poliomyelitis. *Nervous Child* 11:2 (January, 1956): 25-39.
21. GRINKER, ROY R., ed. *Toward a Unified Theory of Human Behavior.* New York: Basic Books, 1956. 375 pp.
22. HILLIER, FREDERICK S. and LIEBERMAN, GERALD J. *Introduction to Operations Research.* San Francisco: Holden-Day, 1967. 639 pp.
23. HOLLINSHEAD, MERRILL T. The orthopedically handicapped. *Review of Educational Research* 23:5 (December, 1953): 492-507.
24. HUGHES, EVERETT CHERRINGTON. The study of occupations, pp. 442-548. In Merton, Robert K.; Bloom, Leonard; and Cottrell, Leonard S., Jr., eds., under auspices of American Sociological Association. *Sociology Today: Problems and Prospects.* New York: Basic Books, 1959.
25. HUNT, JACOB T. Children with crippling conditions and special health problems. *Review of Educational Research* 33:1 (February, 1963): 99-108.

26. HUNT, JACOB T. Crippling conditions and special health problems. *Review of Educational Research* 36:1 (February, 1966): 162-75.

27. HYMAN, HERBERT H. *Survey Design and Analysis: Principles, Cases and Procedures.* Glencoe, Ill.: Free Press, 1955. 424 pp.

28. JORDON, LAURA J. Children with orthopedic handicaps and special health problems, pp. 244-58. In Kirk, Samuel A., and Weiner, Bluma B., eds., *Behavioral Research on Exceptional Children.* Washington, D.C.: Council for Exceptional Children, 1963.

29. KEMENY, JOHN G.; SNELL, J. LAURIE; and THOMPSON, GERALD L. *Introduction to Finite Mathematics.* 2nd ed. Englewood Cliffs, N.J.: Prentice-Hall, 1957. Chapter VII, Applications to behavioral science problems, pp. 307-67.

30. LADIMER, IRVING. New dimensions in legal and ethical concepts for human research. 6. Social responsibility through communication. Concluding remarks. *Annals New York Academy of Sciences* 169: Art. 2 (Jan. 21, 1970). 584-93.

31. LAZARSFELD, PAUL F. and ROSENBERG, MORRIS. *The Language of Social Research: A Reader in Methodology of Social Research.* Glencoe, Ill.: Free Press, 1965. 590 pp.

32. LEIDERMAN, HERBERT and others. Sensory deprivation: clinical aspects. *A.M.A. Arch. Internal Med.* 101:2 (February, 1958): 389-96.

33. LUCE, R. DUNCAN and RAIFFA, HOWARD. *Games and Decisions: Introduction and Critical Survey.* New York: John Wiley and Sons, 1957. 508 pp.

34. MENDELSON, JACK; SOLOMON, PHILIP; and LINDEMANN, ERICH. Hallucinations of poliomyelitis patients during treatment in a respirator. *J. Nerv. and Mental Diseases* 126:5 (May, 1958): 421-28.

35. MITTELMANN, BELA. Motility in infants, children and adults: patterning and psychodynamics, pp. 142-77. In *Psychoanalytic Studies of the Child. Vol. IX.* New York: International Universities Press, 1954.

36. PARSONS, TALCOTT. *The Social System.* Glencoe, Ill.: Free Press, 1951. 575 pp.

37. PARSONS, TALCOTT and FOX, RENEÉ. Illness, therapy and the modern urban American family. *J. Social Issues* 8:4 (1952): 31-44.

38. PIAGET, JEAN. *Logic and Psychology.* New York: Basic Books, 1957. 48 pp.

39. REID, L. LEON. Children with cerebral dysfunction, pp. 226-43. In Kirk, Samuel A. and Weiner, Bluma B., eds., *Behavioral Research on Exceptional Children.* Washington, D.C.: Council for Exceptional Children, 1963.

40. RUESCH, JURGEN. Values and the process of communication, pp. 27-41. In *Symposium on Preventive and Social Psychiatry, April 15-17, 1957, Walter Reed Army Institute of Research, Washington, D.C.; sponsored by Walter Reed Army Institute of Research, Walter Reed Army Medical Center, and the National Research Council, Washington, D.C.* Washington, D.C.: U.S. Govt. Printing Office, 1958.

41. ROBERTSON, JAMES. *Young Children in Hospitals.* New York: Basic Books, 1958. 136 pp.

42. ROCKEFELLER BROTHERS FUND. *The Pursuit of Excellence Education and the Future of America; the "Rockefeller Report" on Education. (America at Mid-Century Series, Special Studies Project V.)* Garden City, N.Y.: Doubleday, 1958. 49 pp.

43. SARGENT, S. STANSFELD. Conceptions of role and ego in contemporary psychology, pp. 355-70. In Sherif, Muzaffer and Rohrer, John J., eds., *Social Psychology at the Crossroads.* New York: Harper and Bros., 1959.

44. SEARS, ROBERT R.; MACCOBY, ELEANOR E.; and LEVIN, HARRY. *Patterns of Child Rearing.* New York: Row, Peterson, 1957. 549 pp.

45. SUMNER, WILLIAM GRAHAM. *Folkways.* New York: Dover Publications, 1959. Boston: Ginn and Co., 1906. 692 pp.

46. SYMONDS, PERCIVAL M. *The Dynamics of Parent-Child Relationships.* New York: Teachers College, Columbia Univ., 1949. 197 pp.

47. VON BERTALANFFY, LUDWIG. *General System Theory: Essays on Its Foundation and Development.* New York: George Braziller, 1969. 289 pp.

48. VON BERTALANFFY, LUDWIG. The theory of open systems in physics and biology. *Science* 111:2872 (January 13, 1950): 23-29.

49. WARREN, RONALD L. Cultural, personal and situational roles. *Sociology and Social Research* 34:2 (November-December, 1949): 104-11.

50. WEAVER, WARREN. Science and complexity. *Am. Scientist* 36:4 (October, 1948): 536-44.

51. WERTHEIMER, MAX. *Productive Thinking.* Edited by Michael Wertheimer. Rev. ed. New York: Harper and Bros., 1959. 244 pp.
52. WIENER, NORBERT. *The Human Use of Human Beings: Cybernetics and Society.* Boston: Houghton Mifflin, 1954. 199 pp.
53. WOLINSKY, GLORIA F. Interdisciplinary action in special education. *Exceptional Children* 28:3 (November, 1961): 151-58.
54. ZUBECK, JOHN P., ed. *Sensory Deprivation: Fifteen Years of Research.* New York: Appleton-Century-Crofts, 1969. 522 pp.

Gloria Wolinsky is Associate Professor at Hunter College and Director, Regional Special Education Materials Center, Division of Teacher Education, City University of New York.

Ten

Behavior
Disorders
of
Children

Probably the most disturbing influence in a classroom setting for instructor and children alike is
behavior on the part of one child which is judged
to be inappropriate. The causes of such behavior
are numerous, and the behaviors themselves are
varied in significance. They range from a single
isolated incident to the manifestations of serious
and persistent psychiatric problems. The professional terminology referring to children whose
behavior in school settings is inappropriate
likewise varies; some common labels are: behavior
disordered, socially maladjusted, emotionally disturbed, educationally handicapped, etc.

Schultz et al., in the introductory article, report
on the extent of special programs for emotionally disturbed children in our public schools.
Their survey also includes data on such practices
as eligibility determination, program standards,
and exclusions. Their data represent programs in
the public schools under the direction of the state
education agency.

Knoblock, in the second article, relates the
trend in open education to the needs of emotionally disturbed children. His provocative article suggests a unique approach to meeting some
of these needs. In an article in Chapter Twelve,
Lord also discusses open education and its close
relation to the broader movement of individualized instruction. This emerging concept has
many implications for the education of exceptional children.

Behavior modification is a practice which is
currently being widely employed to change and
improve responses of children. MacMillan and
Forness, in the third article, analyze the

limitations and liabilities of the practice and provide a critical review which is particularly helpful at this time since the technique is often misunderstood and misused. Nevertheless, as the authors point out, behavior modification has a tremendous potential for use with atypical children.

In the final article of Chapter Ten, Morse describes a number of conditions which must prevail if the schools are to serve disturbed children. The author concentrates principally upon the environment of the classroom. The suggestions presented support many of the practices described in Chapter Twelve, *Special Education in Transition—Emerging Instructional Practices*, especially the importance of individualizing instruction and mainstreaming exceptional children.

Alfred Adler established child guidance clinics in Europe and the United States. His staffing pattern, which made use of a psychiatrist, a psychologist, and a social worker, is commonly employed today. He is recognized in this chapter for establishing the movement for child guidance clinics to serve disturbed children.

Alfred Adler

1870-1937

PHYSICIAN
PSYCHIATRIST
ORGANIZER OF CHILD GUIDANCE CLINICS

Alfred Adler was born on February 7, 1870, in Vienna, Austria. He received his degree in medicine from the University of Vienna in 1895. Adler joined Sigmund Freud in 1902, but in 1911, broke with him to found his own journal and school of psychiatry. He opened the first child guidance clinic in Vienna in 1920, and later moved to the United States where he was associated with the Long Island College of Medicine.

Adler maintained that man's dominant nature (motive) is a striving for superiority, usually in compensation for an inferiority. He believed that an individual's concept of himself influenced his behavior. His therapeutic approach, in contrast to Freud's, was flexible and probably more applicable to problems of children. His influence in the treatment of maladjusted and emotionally disturbed children has been widespread in child guidance clinics and schools in the United States. The tradition is carried on through the American Society of Adlerian Psychology and through the *Journal of Individual Psychology.*

42.
Special Education for the
Emotionally Disturbed
EDWARD W. SCHULTZ
ALFRED HIRSHOREN
ANNE B. MANTON
ROBERT A. HENDERSON

A questionnaire was sent to state directors of special education in each of the 50 states and the District of Columbia regarding the current status of public school services for emotionally disturbed children. Data of interest to the survey included: terminology and definitions, prevalence estimates, educational services available, program standards, eligibility and placement, termination of special services, exclusion procedures, and administrative organization of programs. Data were analyzed in two ways: (a) for the entire country and (b) by dividing the country into geographic regions. The highlights, both regional and national, are reported here to provide some current information pertaining to public school programing for disturbed children.

Educational programs for emotionally disturbed and socially maladjusted children have been in a few public school systems, primarily in larger cities, for well over 50 years (Haring & Phillips, 1962). Nevertheless, it has been only during the past few years, primarily due to Federal funds from the Office of Education, that such programs have been developed in smaller school districts. In 1948, there were a total of 90 public school districts operating special education programs for approximately 15,300 children characterized as emotionally disturbed and/or socially maladjusted (Mackie, 1969). With so few programs at that time, there was little apparent need to survey existing programs for such things as staffing patterns, types of services offered, and terms used. In 1966, the last year for which adequate statistics are available, approximately 875 public school systems provided some type of special education program for about 32,000 emotionally disturbed and socially maladjusted chil-

From *Exceptional Children* 38 (December, 1971): 313-19. Reprinted by permission of the authors and *Exceptional Children*. Copyrighted by the Council for Exceptional Children.

dren (Mackie, 1969). Today it is not unlikely that the number of children enrolled in special programs is closer to 100,000 in addition to the more than 65,000 children under the age of 18 years who are receiving treatment in public and private residential institutions.

However, the needs of emotionally disturbed children are far from being met. According to a recent report from the National Institute of Mental Health:

Various surveys conducted through school systems provide us with some estimates of how many children may really need mental health care. Several of these surveys indicated that approximately 2 to 3 percent of the children were in need of psychiatric care and an additional 7 percent in need of some help for emotional problems. Other estimates have ranged from 7 to 12 percent [Rosen, Kramer, Redick, & Willner, 1968, p. 50].

Use of the conservative prevalence figure of 2 percent results in the estimate of approximately 1,200,000 emotionally disturbed and socially maladjusted children between the ages of 5 and 19 who could probably benefit from some type of special education program.

Obviously, the growth of these special programs has been relatively late and until recently slow. This would appear, in part, to be the result of the lack of a clear definition of the problem. For example, Kanner (1962) noted that

... it is impossible to find anywhere a definition of the term "emotionally disturbed children" which had somehow crept into the literature some 30 years ago and has since then been used widely, sometimes as a generality with no terminologic boundaries whatever and sometimes with reference to certain psychotic and near psychotic conditions [p. 101].

Kirk (1967) also noted that there was no set pattern of organization or teaching for emotionally disturbed children.

Purpose and Methodology

Prompted by some of the above comments, the purpose of this survey was to clarify the current status of public school special education programing for emotionally disturbed children as required, permitted, and/or prohibited by laws, rules, and regulations in each of the 50 states and the District of Columbia. Specifically, it dealt with the following issues: definitions and terminology, prevalence figures and their derivation, patterns of service, case load for professionals, class size, diagnosis and placement, exclusion from school, administrative organization, and success of program.

A questionnaire was developed for use in this survey in consultation with the University of Illinois' Survey Research Laboratory. Copies were sent to the directors of special education in each of the 50 states and the District of

Columbia. (Data will be reported as if 51 states were involved in the survey.) The director was asked to either complete the survey form or to have his staff specialist in the area of emotional disturbance do so. The forms were mailed early in 1970 with the request that they be returned in approximately 1 month. Two weeks following the date for return of questionnaire a telegram and a second copy of the questionnarie were sent to those states not responding. This procedure produced 100 percent response.

Analysis included the development of data for the entire country and a subanalysis by four regions. Two sections of the country, the far west and the southeast, have formal regional organizations for educational purposes: The Western Interstate Commission of Higher Education (WICHE) and the Southern Regional Education Board (SREB). These two regional organizations consist of 13 and 15 states respectively. The remainder of the United States was divided into roughly equal halves, designated "east" and "midwest." Eleven states were assigned to the east and 12 to the midwest. A list of states by regions is contained in Chart 1.

Results

Because of the length of the report of results obtained in this survey it is not feasible to report tables and figures in this context; therefore, only the regional and national highlights are reported here. (Complete results are available in Hirshoren, Schultz, Manton, & Henderson, 1970.) While considerable care was taken to insure accuracy of information reported, contradictory information was sometimes supplied. The circumstances surrounding this problem arose when the state director or specialist in emotional disturbance elected to provide a copy of state laws, rules, and guidelines in addition to or in lieu of completing some parts of the questionnaire.

Chart 1. States Listed by Regions

WICHE	SREB	East	Midwest
Alaska	Alabama	Connecticut	Illinois
Arizona	Arkansas	Delaware	Indiana
California	Florida	District of Columbia	Iowa
Colorado	Georgia	Maine	Kansas
Hawaii	Kentucky	Massachusetts	Michigan
Idaho	Louisiana	New Hampshire	Minnesota
Montana	Maryland	New Jersey	Missouri
Nevada	Mississippi	New York	Nebraska
New Mexico	North Carolina	Pennsylvania	North Dakota
Oregon	Oklahoma	Rhode Island	Ohio
Utah	South Carolina	Vermont	South Dakota
Washington	Tennessee		Wisconsin
Wyoming	Texas		
	Virginia		
	West Virginia		

Six terms were used to identify emotionally disturbed children: emotionally disturbed, emotionally handicapped, emotionally maladjusted, educationally handicapped, emotional conflict, and exceptional children. Three-fourths of the states (N = 41) used either the term "emotionally disturbed" or "emotionally handicapped." The 3 states not including the term "emotionally" in their terminology were all within the WICHE region.

Most definitions provided by the states included some combination of the following terms: causal factors, normal intelligence, achievement problems, behavior and/or adjustment problems, and use of a diagnostician. The most common combination specified both academic achievement problems and behavior and/or adjustment problems. A few states included a statement concerning causal factors. Six states specified that in addition to other characteristics the child must have normal intellectual ability. Five states left the problem of definition entirely up to a diagnostician, and three other states mentioned a diagnostician together with one or more of the other factors. Overall, there appears to be a lack of consensus regarding the target population.

Some of the states' definitions were found to be circular. Circular definitions included: (a) those which only specified that the child was unable to profit from regular class and/or required special services and (b) those which defined emotional disturbance with another term such as emotionally handicapped.

One-third of the states (18) used a prevalence estimate of 2 percent, followed by 3 percent in 7 states and 5 percent in 6 states. The overall range reported was from .05 percent to 15 percent. The authors were unable to find any statement of prevalence for 7 states.

Four sources were identified from which states derived their estimates: national estimates, local or state data, Bower's California study reports (1961, 1962), and professional judgment. About one-half of the states seemed to rely on estimates provided from the United States Office of Education, while 13 states indicated that their estimates were based on local or statewide studies. Twelve states provided no answer to this question. It was also noted that some states relied on more than one source for their figures.

In seeking information about educational services for emotionally disturbed children, 12 services were specified: special class program, resource room program, crisis intervention, itinerant teacher program, academic tutoring, homebound instruction, guidance counselor, school social worker, psychotherapy by school psychologist, psychiatric consultation, public school transportation to nonschool agency, and payment by public school for private school. It was requested that each service be classified into one of four categories for the particular state: (a) required, e.g., mandatory by law or regulation; (b) authorized or permitted by law; (c) prohibited by law, rule, or regulation; and (d) not dealt with in law or regulation. A fifth category, "no response," was added during data analysis.

The general picture in the United States indicated that the vast majority of educational programs and services available to emotionally disturbed children were provided on a permissive basis. Regarding services, special classes were most often mentioned (47 states) followed by resource room programing (40 states), and then homebound instruction (38 states). Most of the 12 services for which information was requested were permitted, or at least not prohibited, by more than half of the states. Many inconsistencies were noted between states. For example, 8 states mandated payment by public schools for private school services while 9 states prohibited by law or regulation such payment. Lack of agreement was also noted in the relatively large numbers indicating that particular programs were not dealt with in law or regulation. The category of programs dealt with in law or regulation had more states included than the mandatory category in all but the special class program.

Regional differences were also noted in the data. The eastern states had the highest proportion of mandatory programs. The SREB states had no programs mandated. The SREB states also showed a relatively high proportion of states which either had not dealt with many of the types of services in their laws and regulations or did not respond to these questions. This same situation was present to a lesser extent in the WICHE states.

A thirteenth question about "other services offered" produced data on seven additional special educational services. Two states indicated that institutional programs were included in services available to their disturbed children, and two other states indicated that diagnostic programs were provided. One state each reported the following programs: work study, integrated classes, payment for any service not provided by the state, preschool program, and consulting teacher.

PROGRAM STANDARDS

With respect to standards, the authors were interested in determining three pieces of information concerning special classes in states where they were authorized: (a) the maximum number of students per class prescribed by law, (b) the maximum chronological age range per service, and (c) the maximum number of years a child could be enrolled. Further information was sought on the recommended (or prescribed) case load for the following professionals: resource teacher, crisis intervener, itinerent teacher, homebound tutor, school social worker, school psychologist, and school psychiatrist.

In indicating the maximum number of students per class it was noted that these varied as a function of level (primary, intermediate, secondary) with larger numbers being permitted for older children. The comments below are limited to the elementary level. In all regions, it appeared that 10 students seemed to be the modal figure for maximum class size. WICHE and SREB states indicated higher limits, 12 and 15 respectively, as their next most common limit. The east and midwest states dropped to 8 as their second most common maximum limit for special classes.

About one-half of the states reported that they placed some limitation on chronological age range in their special classes. Only three ranges were mentioned: 12 states indicated a 4-year range in age as maximum; 9 states used a 3-year range; and 2 states permitted a 5-year range.

A few states limited the number of years which a disturbed child could be enrolled in a special class program. Three states permitted a full 12 years. Two states indicated 2 years and two states indicated 3 years as the maximum permitted. One state limited enrollment to a single year. Another state permitted 6 years. Two states indicated an age limit of 21 years. Sixteen stated they had no limits.

There was marked variability among the states concerning number of students assigned to professional staff at any one time. Regarding case loads, data obtained from the 51 states indicated at one extreme that resource teachers had case loads of 60, crisis interveners had loads of 75, social workers carried loads of 250 students, and psychologists had 700 students. At the other extreme were those states with quite small case loads, usually in the case of teaching professionals.

ELIGIBILITY AND PLACEMENT

Responsibility for determining eligibility for special programs was divided about evenly in all regions between the superintendent of schools (or other administrator designated by him) and a committee usually including teachers, administrators, a psychologist, and a social worker. In fewer cases, a single diagnostician was specified, such as a school psychologist or psychiatrist. While over a third of the states (19) required a psychiatric evaluation, this was used as a single criterion in only a few (5).

Placement of children in a particular special education program seemed to be clearly the responsibility of administrators in eastern and midwestern states but tended to be shared by committees to a greater extent in WICHE and SREB. In addition, diagnosticians (school psychologists and psychiatrists among others) were not assigned authority for placement of emotionally disturbed children into special services.

Since administrators and committees constituted the most common authorities for eligibility and placement decisions, an attempt was made to determine whether decisions on these two aspects were made by the same people. Data on this question showed that in the majority of states the answer was no.

The authors were also concerned with whether a specific procedure for determining eligibility and placement existed. The majority of states (36) indicated that there was a specific procedure. Thirty-two states supplied sufficient information concerning this process and the personnel involved to undertake an analysis based on the model articulated by Morse, Cutler, and Fink (1964). Their model included some six steps or levels. Our data could not be differentiated into as many levels so it was possible to use only four: (a) initiation of process, (b) data collection, (c) screening and eligibility decision, and (d) placement decision.

In general, the data tended to show that various professionals and parents or guardians initiated the process. The data collection stage was also frequently an individual responsibility though the individual varied. Eligibility and placement decisions were heavily weighted toward administrators and committees. Usually the committees contained the same individuals who collected the background data, so some continuity did exist.

TERMINATION OF SPECIAL SERVICES

Questions were asked concerning the percentage of emotionally disturbed children receiving special education services who returned to regular class programs during the course of a year and the process by which this was accomplished. Twenty-one states were either unable to estimate the number of children actually returned to regular class programs, found the question not applicable, or failed to provide an answer. Regionally, the greatest range was found in the midwest. The SREB states had a similarly wide range, but reported over one-fourth of their states returning half of the children to regular classes each year. Overall, there was a wide range in the percentage of children returned to regular education from special programs: 5 percent to over 90 percent.

Responsibility for determining when a child identified as emotionally disturbed could be returned to regular class placement varied considerably. As was the case with eligibility determination, committees seemed to be the most popular procedure (21 of 51 states) with the special education teacher involved in at least 18 states.

The discussion of the role of various school personnel in the process of returning a child from special to regular education needs to be qualified due to insufficient data supplied by many states. The major difference between placement and return procedures seemed to be the greater involvement of the special education teacher in the decision making process.

EXCLUSION

State directors or their representatives were asked, "On what basis may a child in this category be excluded from school, and what procedures are required or recommended?" The most common answers were: (a) that the child could not profit from the educational services provided and (b) that the child's behavior was too disruptive and thus interfered with the educational program for other children.

The regional differences indicated that WICHE and SREB states more often cited disruptive behavior, while the midwest placed more emphasis on an inability to profit from an educational program. Eastern states responding tended to use both categories evenly. Twenty-one states failed to provide data regarding the basis on which a child might be excluded, with the largest number (9) from among the SREB states.

Concerning personnel and procedures involved in exclusion, it was noted that multiple designations were in evidence (e.g., more than one category of personnel were indicated as involved in a given state). School administrators were involved in only half of the states responding. The next highest category was diagnosticians including physicians, psychiatrists, and psychologists. Others indicated were: committees, parents and guardians, teachers, the courts, and other miscellaneous groups and individuals. Nine states did not respond to this part of the question and two states reported they did not permit exclusion.

ADMINISTRATIVE ORGANIZATION

In the great majority of states (41), local school districts bore major responsibility for providing special educational services to disturbed children. In 3 states, joint agreement or cooperative arrangements between districts were also used. Three other states had intermediate school districts at the county or parish level, and regional units had been established in 1 midwestern state. Two states in the east and 1 in the midwest provided direct state control. Non public school facilities were utilized by 1 state each in SREB, the midwest, and the east. Two states in WICHE and 1 in SREB found the question not applicable because of a lack of any program needing an administrative organization.

Discussion

In essence, the results of this survey on public school programing for emotionally disturbed children reflect anew the earlier findings of Morse, Cutler, and Fink (1964). Specifically the results seem to indicate that there are several problems apparent. Definitions of emotional disturbance tend to frequently be "quasi-psychiatric," and there seems to be a general lack of consensus regarding the target population in question. The wide range of prevalence figures may be attributable to inconsistency in terminology and definitions.

It appears that a broader range of service possibilities are needed but more importantly that evaluation of existing services should be conducted. At present, the primary service possibilities in existence are: special classes, resource rooms, and homebound instruction. These are usually planned for in states on a permissive basis.

Special class services are more prevalent at the elementary level than at the secondary level with more students enrolled per professional worker at the latter grade level. The same problems seem to be present here as discussed under terminology, i.e., that there appears to be a lack of consensus regarding special class guidelines.

With respect to eligibility of children for special programs, the trend appears to be away from having a single diagnostician determine eligibility to the use of a team composed of both mental health specialists and educators, and in a few cases parents. This is an encouraging sign. Though various professionals and lay personnel could initiate the referral processes, a definite plan was evident in many states regarding this process. Placement though heavily weighted toward administrators was also done by committees with the committees having the same composition as those responsible for collection of intake data.

Overall, there was a wide range of children returned to regular education from special education: 5 percent to 90 percent. This variation is difficult to explain. The large number of states which were unable to give an estimate or did not answer this question ($N = 17$) suggests the possibility of a lack of data on program effectiveness. This also points to the earlier mentioned need for evaluation of programs.

If the results from the field are a valid indication of the state of services for emotionally disturbed children, it would appear that many kinds of educational programs for such children exist and that these programs are in various stages of development. It is certainly a positive trend in education that services are beginning to be available to more children. It seems important at this time that educators seriously attempt to bring order into their efforts. An appropriate area for focus is evaluation. Programs for disturbed children need careful and systematic record keeping so that special educators can make special and meaningful programs.

REFERENCES

Bower, E. M. *The Education of Emotionally Handicapped Children: A Report to the California Legislature Prepared Pursuant to Section 1 of Chapter 2385, Statutes of 1957.* Sacramento, Cal.: Department of Education, 1961.

Bower, E. M. Comparison of the characteristics of identified emotionally disturbed children with other children in classes. In E. P. Trapp and P. Himelstein, eds., *Readings on the Exceptional Child.* New York: Appleton-Century-Crofts, 1962. pp. 610-29.

Haring, N. G., & Phillips, E. L. *Educating Emotionally Disturbed Children.* New York: McGraw-Hill, 1962.

Hirshoren, A.; Schultz, E. W.; Manton; A. B. & Henderson, R. A. *A Survey of Public School Special Education Programs for Emotionally Disturbed Children.* Special Educational Monograph No. 1-70. Urbana: University of Illinois, 1970. (ERIC Document No. 050540)

Kanner, L. Emotionally disturbed children: A historical review. *Child Development* 33 (1962): 97-102.

Kirk, S. A. Handicapped children. *Notes and Working Papers on Administration of Programs, Title III, ESEA.* Washington, D.C.: USGPO, 1967. pp. 232-33.

Mackie, R. P. *Special Education in the United States: Statistics 1948-1966.* New York: Teachers College Press, Columbia University, 1969.

Morse, W. C., Cutler, R. L., & Fink, A. A. *Public School Classes for the Emotionally Handicapped. A Research Analysis.* Washington, D. C.: The Council for Exceptional Children, 1964.

Rosen, B. M.; Kramer, M.; Redick, R. W.; & Willner, S. G. *Utilization of Psychiatric Facilities by Children: Current Status, Trends, Implications.* Washington, D.C.: USGPO, 1968.

*Edward W. Schultz is Assistant Professor, Department of Special Education,
University of Illinois, Urbana; Alfred Hirshoren is Associate Professor of
Special Education, Purdue University, Lafayette, Indiana; Anne B. Manton
is USOE Doctoral Fellow; and Robert A. Henderson is Professor, Department of Special Education, University of Illinois, Urbana.*

43.
Open Education for Emotionally
Disturbed Children
PETER KNOBLOCK

*What are the unique conditions in open educa-
tion that provide a favorable environment
for disturbed children?*

Personal Statement

*This is a passionate and personal statement grow-
ing out of my belief in the powerful skills and resources possessed by special educators and the children with whom they interact. This belief has
been reinforced countless times with many teachers and children. Undoubtedly, these skills have always been present, but it has been necessary
for me to make my own changes before I could look at others.*

*I began teaching at Syracuse University in 1962, and I suppose I ap-
proached my new role in traditional ways. As I spent more time with students and began to take them more seriously, I began to sense an extraordinary opportunity for me to be both a learner and a contributor to the
learning climate. I saw our students become creators of curriculum and
innovators of interventions, and in general they displayed fine instincts
for working with children and responding to others. I began to see myself
less as a teacher in the sense of a dispenser of information and more as
one who was both gaining and contributing to the learning and excitement
of others. In short, I began to trust the others with whom I spent my time.
As this happened, I felt less pressure to coerce, cajole, evaluate, and pre-
determine standards.*

*At Syracuse University, in our preparation program for teachers of
emotionally disturbed children, we gradually opened up our learning*

From *Exceptional Children* 39 (February, 1973): 358-65. Reprinted by permission
of the author and *Exceptional Children*. Copyrighted by the Council for Exceptional
Children.

environment so that more of the participants could have an input into their own preparation. No two years were the same for us. Over time we have developed our own form of a humanistically oriented special education preparation program, and it has "fit" us. For the past 4 years we have been funded by the Bureau of Education for the Handicapped to develop our model for working with inner city children who are labeled as disturbed and disturbing. This past year we created our own alternative educational setting for excluded children and youth (Knoblock, Barnes, & Eyman, 1972). Certainly, much of the material for this article and my own thinking has been influenced by our experiences during the past 10 years and most dramatically by our encounters last year in creating our own setting, which represented one example of an open education approach.

This article presents one alternative to existing approaches currently employed in special education. Open education approaches are currently being explored in regular education. There is much within this point of view which recommends its application to work with troubled children. Open education speaks to the basic humanity in everyone. It recognizes the growth potential residing in each person as he moves toward his goal of self realization. It attempts to impose less and explore more. The reader is urged to seriously consider both the human and educational implications of open education since our greatest resource is people and the development of each child and adult's effort to move toward his personal goal of self actualization.

Special education has a long history of concern for the intellectual and emotional development of children. This concern has grown out of a combination of actual needs of children and a set of beliefs, values, and attitudes that specify the directions in which children should move. The present emphasis on educating emotionally disturbed children, particularly those children in urban centers, has brought special educators to focus on many children whose problems, needs, and concerns fall into less classic and clinical categories. They are children and youth who are not fitting the existing structure of public school programs, and it is not clear what the proper interventions ought to be once they are in programs.

Due to the escalating expense of residential and institutional programs, the overwhelming number of children remain in school and community based programs. Furthermore, in recent years educators of disturbed children have seen the special class as somewhat limiting in that it often tended to be the only programing intervention within the public schools. There is a decided trend toward resource teacher approaches which emphasize keeping a child in a regular classroom and ultimately redefining and restructuring the classroom.

This article discusses open education for emotionally disturbed children as one alternative to redefining classrooms. Conceptualizing and implementing open education concerns values and beliefs about children and learning, as well as processes for supporting the growth of children.

Presently, there is a growing number of articles about open education. The term itself reflects the influence of British primary education, often in statements concerning their Infant Schools (Weber, 1971). Open education has often been associated with "informal classrooms" (Rathbone, 1971) and "open classrooms" (Kohl, 1970) and has been referred to as the "integrated day" or the "Leicestershire model."

Regardless of the name, there is an overriding belief in the growth potential of children and, in this case, of children called emotionally disturbed. There is a strong humanistic component to open education—the child is valued for what is already inside him and is not seen from the perspective of a deficiency model:

If we want to be helpers, counselors, teachers, guiders, or psychotherapists, what we must do is to accept the person and help him learn what kind of person he is already. What is his style, what are his aptitudes, what is he good for, not good for, what can we build upon, what are his good raw materials, his good potentialities? We would be non-threatening and would supply an atmosphere of acceptance of the child's nature which reduces fear, anxiety and defense to the minimum possible. Above all, we would care for the child, that is enjoy him and his growth and self-actualization [Maslow, 1968, p. 693].

Open education then is part or a focus on a more humanistic approach to the education of children. Needless to say, there are many opinions on what constitutes open education.

What Is Open Education?

Open education strives to be what its name states —open to all those participating in the environment. There is an opportunity for each person, child, and adult to have something to say about what is done and why it is done.

DEMOCRATIC PRACTICES

My experiences during the past 10 years in developing more open learning environments for the preparation of teachers and for the education of children and youth have convinced me that this is a model for a dynamic society. Open education can offer a way of spending time together which enhances the learning and development of everyone in that environment and at the same time lets each person live in an environment which fosters democratic principles (Sudbury Valley School, 1970).

These principles involve (a) respecting and valuing the individual rights of each person, (b) viewing the learning environment as a community in which those who are directly involved have control over what happens to them, and (c) guaranteeing equal opportunity without bias against the skills, viewpoint, or goals of each learner in the environment. These values are rooted deeply in our past and in our present rhetoric, and it is conceivable that learning environments can honestly reflect these values.

Open education is also a set of psychological propositions about how children learn. In her recent book, *The English Infant School and Informal Education,* Weber (1971) specified three such propositions:

1. Each child learns differently and has his own schedule and strategy for learning.
2. Children learn optimally in a rich and complex environment which encourages exploration.
3. Children learn best in a self directed fashion and in an environment which fosters their interaction with learning materials and with other people.

There are undoubtedly other psychological propositions which are equally relevant (Holt, 1967; Rogers, 1969; Featherstone, 1971), but those of Weber's point out the relationship between the values cited above and their translation into propositions about learning.

SET OF PRACTICES

This relationship becomes even more clear when open education is seen as a set of practices which tends to reflect the above values and propositions. In literature on education it is unprecedented to have so many detailed descriptions of actual classroom practices and interactions between teachers and children (Dennison, 1969; Herndon, 1971). Since a summary of these practices would be difficult, the reader is encouraged to read Rathbone's (1971) discussion of the implicit rationale of the open education classroom and Barth's (1971) discussion of the assumptions open educators make about children's learning. There are certain practices which find high visibility in many open classrooms. In an effort to convey what actually happens in open classrooms, a brief analysis of the behaviors and interactions of children and teachers follows.

Child Behaviors. The following list is representative of a wide variety of child behaviors encouraged in open education settings (Knoblock, 1970):

- A premium would be placed on the learning becoming self directed. Depending on the psychosocial development of the child and his interests, the environment of the classroom should allow him as much self choice about what he should learn and how he should learn it.
- Children are encouraged to specify their learning needs and interests and seek ways to meet these needs.
- Children engage in exploratory activity in an attempt to find the relationship between themselves and the materials in their environment.
- Children spend time with other children assisting them in learning activities and engaging in a variety of play activities.

- Children offer feedback to teachers, parents, and others concerning the viability of the learning environment.
- Children evaluate their own progress and contribute to the charting and analysis of their activities.
- Children play a vital role in working out their problems, disagreements, and conflicts with other children and adults.

Teaching Behaviors. Insights have been gained into the behaviors engaged in by teachers within open settings. Three followup studies of Syracuse University graduates have provided valuable information on what classroom teachers are actually doing with troubles children in open education environments. The following observations have been made in such settings:

- Adults function as partners and facilitators of children's learning. There is a tendency to respond to individual children and small groups.
- Adults function as organizers of the learning resources (materials, adults, and other children), making such resources known and available to the children.
- Frequently, the adults will design learning activities and encourage children to participate in them. There are a variety of teacher behaviors having to do with the initiation of activities. In one classroom I observed that a teacher had certain time periods for designated activities—free choice, reading, math, vocabulary development, or playground. Within several of these activities the teacher encouraged children to pursue the activity or task (finding words that begin with *th*, *cr*, etc.) in their own way.
- Teachers tend to ask many questions of the children and encourage them to solve problems rather than ask for or accept answers from adults.
- Teachers often view themselves as resources and catalysts for learning for the children and other adults. This implies that teachers need to be explicit about their skills and interests so that their skills can be used more efficiently.
- Teachers expend considerable energy assisting the children in committing their time and in setting reasonable and realistic goals for themselves.

"Behavior" of Curriculum Materials

The use of materials forms an integral part of open education learning environments. In a sense, these materials behave and speak to children and adults. In choosing materials, open educators typically prefer those that are more open ended, such as the activity based science approach of the Elementary Science Study under the direction of the Educational Development Center (EDC), the mathematics orientation of Biggs and MacLean (1969), and the reading approach known as reading through experience (Lee & Allen, 1963). This list is not all-inclusive since many teachers and children develop their own materials. In any event, the materials used tend to ask something of the learner. They are active and do not encourage passive encounters.

Open educators are intrigued with experientially based learning in which the child interacts with the learning material in a satisfying and thought provoking fashion (Hawkins, 1971). This "messing about" in a subject matter is often a personal matter, but it is thought essential to bring children and concrete learning materials into contact with each other.

One final comment on the use of instructional materials needs to be made. Learners and materials function optimally in learning environments that are arranged and designed to facilitate learning and communication between the child and his materials. Room arrangements, schools, corners of rooms, and so on all convey different messages to the child. In informal classrooms the expectation is that space will entice and respond to the creative urge of children and that it will respond to the varying needs for activity, exploration, and solitude (Hall, 1969; Sommer, 1969).

Responses to Children's Concerns

The point of view argued for in this article takes issue with any listing of characteristics of disturbed children. On a deeper level, there is the philosophical concern over the use of the label *emotionally disturbed* and the educational relevance of employing disturbance as a concept. Nevertheless, my experience during the past decade in focusing on children and youth in urban settings has bought me into contact with a variety of concerns and behaviors.

I have long believed in a psychoeducational model of teacher preparation and education of troubled children (Long, Morse, & Newman, 1971). Over the years at Syracuse University we have tried in our teacher preparation program to conceptualize and operationalize what is meant by this model (Knoblock & Garcea, 1969; Knoblock, 1971).

This present effort to explore open education for troubled children is, in my opinion, a logical extension of the psychoeducational model. The tenets of this model apply to open education, and in fact, by creating an open environment we may be enhancing the opportunity to implement approaches commonly thought of as psychoeducational. For example, both models advocate the integration of affect and content in the classroom. Both rely on acknowledging and responding to the feelings and behaviors of children. Both respond to the readiness levels of children for the implementation of academic skill development. Both believe that often learning will take place only if it is put in the context of relationships and only if the learner feels good enough about himself as a learner and person. Other parallels could be found, but the important point may be that open education approaches provide a learning environment in which the teacher can truly function as a diagnostician in the sense of seeing children operate in a variety of activities and with many other individuals.

Our clinical experience and extensive interviewing of troubled children has led us to focus on five concerns of these children. These are not meant to summarize a disturbed child but should be seen as examples of core concerns sufficiently troublesome to cause some children to act upon them. Many schools in turn have responded to these behaviors and feelings of troubled children. Borton (1970) discussed student concerns and focused on relationship concerns, self identity, and control concerns (a student's sense of his visibility and impact in the world). In many ways Table 1 and the following discussion incorporate some of the same concerns that Borton made reference to.

Conflict with Authority

The power relationships between teachers and children has tended to erode the potential for learning in many school environments. The win-lose focus of many teachers and children is no solution; no one wins in the ultimate sense. Informal classrooms (another designation under open education) tend to be places in which the participants want to be. This alone can contribute to a sense of ownership for what happens. When we take pride in our environments, we tend to make a commitment to working problems through. In our learning environment for children we focused on children and youth excluded from school. Initially, some students experienced considerable difficulty with the freedom and the choices. Adults functioned in ways which helped them become comfortable and active. To be sure, concerns existed between adults and children, but these became personal and intimate and had less to do with adults as roles or as authorities with con-

Table 1. Concerns of Troubled Children and the Response of Open Education

Concerns of troubled children	Response of open education
Conflict with authority.	Nonauthoritarian adults and environments in which less is decided for the child and more is done with him.
Tendency to move away from people and concerns; an unwillingness and inability to capitalize on their resources.	Emphasis placed on providing support to the child for becoming more active in self defining; provision of an environment that holds appeal to the child.
Concern with establishing relationships with adults who are trustworthy	Adults who firmly believe in the growth potential of children and communicate this in words and practices.
Feelings of loss of control over their own feelings and their learning environments	Mutuality between all participants in the learning environment thus enhancing active participation; response to the feelings and emotions of children.
Deep feelings of inadequacy leading to negative self concepts	Provisions for a variety of activities and behaviors which supply the child with many ways to self evaluate.

trol over them. Once contact between child and adult is put in the context of a relationship, there is an even greater opportunity to respond to issues of limit-setting, aggression, and interpersonal concerns that invariably spring up in the classrooms.

MOVING AWAY FROM OTHERS, SELF, AND INNER CONCERNS

Traditional education has placed a premium on children's becoming dependent on the adult, and in turn, there has been a diminution in many children's willingness and ability to be active in their own behalf. Disturbed children are frequently described as having behavior problems, but there is also a heavy preponderance of children who become passive learners and function below their potential in learning activities.

Open education offers many forms of support to the child in an effort to put him on a path toward self realization. Basic to this support is developing an environment which appeals to children. Such aspects as learning materials which respond to the variety of children's learning styles, opportunities to manipulate materials and to engage in experientially-based learning, choices of what to learn and when to learn it, and an opportunity to have a voice on how time is spent all contribute to a child's becoming more intrinsically motivated to partake in his learning environment and to shape it in productive ways.

ESTABLISHING ADULT RELATIONSHIPS

There is much in the behavior of adults in open education environments which reassures the child that he and the adult can trust each other. The teachers believe that direct experience is essential, and therefore, the child is asked less frequently to believe on faith that a particular subject matter or activity is important. He has a chance to experience it himself, to modify it, and to decide how and where it fits in this "curriculum." Writers who feel deeply about children, such as Redl and Wineman (1951), Cole (1970), and Rothman (1970), have shown how each child carries with him his own "curriculum" in the form of skills and observations of adults and other children.

Open education values each child's agenda and hopes to enable the child to build on his own personal agenda. If a child is involved in karate, an entire curriculum can be built around this activity ranging from learning self control, to learning physics, to buying boards which are used to break in half, to following systematic procedures, to reading karate books and magazines, and so on.

Furthermore, each child learns that the adults are not involved in the external evaluation of his performance. Adults in this environment make the assumption that knowledge is idiosyncratic and, therefore, highly personal. Thus, no one can truly judge whether one child's learning is "better" than another's. Also, the adult is seen by the child as a person who can also be turned on to learning.

Finally, the entire issue of trust is looked at and explored by those in open education environments. The participants explore this concern in a variety of ways—discussions, group meetings, and perhaps most significantly of all, observation of daily behaviors of adults who communicate an unconditional positive acceptance of who the child is and what he does.

Feeling of Loss of Control

The literature is filled with descriptions of children whose feelings of powerlessness mire them in confusion, lethargy, and self doubt. In open education classrooms one of the first processes engaged in by teachers and children is that of developing a learning community in which a partnership exists between all those present. We begin by assuming that in any group of children and adults there is an extensive reservoir of resources and skills. If we accept this assumption then our goal is to assist participants in specifying both their learning needs and resources.

In this learning community there is greater probability of a child's becoming involved in an activity reflecting his strength, as well as his limitations. It makes sense that one is more open to risk taking and engaging in learning activities in which he experiences difficulty, as in reading, if he has experienced success and a response in activities he does well.

A child learns he is not alone but is surrounded by a variety of adults. He can choose those with whom he is comfortable or those who can serve as resources to him. Open educators believe that many adults are needed to populate any learning environment. To rely on one teacher to transmit all that is necessary is to ignore the burden such a role places on that teacher.

Again, the feelings and concerns each child may have about his powerlessness are made a legitimate focus of his time in the classroom. By combining an approach which offers internally defined success and adults and children with whom he can talk, a child will come to feel a measure of control over his school and personal life.

Feelings of Inadequacy

Sensitive practitioners realize that how a child feels about himself is central to his engaging in learning activities. Open education acknowledges this concern and purposively sets about to create a responsive environment. Open educators typically ask troubled children to respond to the rules, to others, even to themselves, but it is imperative that a responsive environment be provided in which they can try out new skills, feelings, and behaviors. It is in the creation of a responsive and diverse environment that open educators hope to assist children in viewing themselves more positively.

Frequently, a child's negative evaluation of himself in school comes about because he either defines himself in narrow and rigid ways ("I'm no good in math") or because the school sets up an expectation of him in equally narrow terms. In open education the expectation is that the child will be exposed to a variety of ways to "do math" and hence will have more opportunity to see himself in positive ways. Open educators encourage children to view themselves not as good or bad but rather to discover their strengths, as well as their limitations.

An Environment for Everyone

Special education literature is filled with information about programs for handicapped children. What seems to be missing are programs that are responsive to the adults as well as the children. Open education approaches offer us an environment in which teachers, as well as children, can represent themselves as learners. It seems imperative for adults to also function as curious and vitally alive human beings in their learning environments. We have all experienced teachers who urged us onward to more efficient learning but who seemed drained of their own spontaneity.

In an open learning environment one of the major interventions a teacher can have is to present himself as an individual who is open to inquiry and knowledge seeking on his own. This can be seen when a teacher delves into a content area with a child and together they attempt to master the concepts.

There are many parallels between what occurs for teachers and for children in open education environments. Two of these are the need for communication in a learning community and the need for a focus on personal growth.

NEED FOR COMMUNICATION

During the past several years I have been involved with groups of teachers of troubled children. In one effort to find out the kinds of concerns teachers were experiencing, my associates and I designed a series of group meetings in which a small group of teachers shared their experiences with each other. We tape recorded each of our sessions, and along with an analysis of our meetings, extensive verbatim comments of the teachers were included in our statement. A colleague and I have written a book about this experience titled, *The Lonely Teacher* (Knoblock & Goldstein, 1971). The experience was profound because it helped me realize that any learning environment is incomplete unless the needs and concerns of teachers, as well as children, are valued and responded to. More and more teachers are now coming forward and talking about their isolation and their need to have contact with other adults in a learning and sharing relationship.

Open education is attempting to "re-people" the learning environment so that there are many adults who can respond as resources and catalysts for others, including other adults. Having a variety of adults with different skills enhances the probability that everyone will find some others with whom to relate and communicate. The role and authority dilemmas faced by so many teachers are dispersed and shared with other adults and children.

Open education environments encourage teachers to examine their own concerns and personal growth. The freedom represented in open education offers an unparalleled opportunity for a teacher to explore his own behavior.

The following statement is from one of our Syracuse University graduate students involved in creating an open setting in our Shonnard Street School Program (Knoblock et al., 1972). This student is responding to a question regarding how she felt about the freedom she experienced this year:

The freedom of this project to me means an acceptance of each person—student or staff—for what he is, where he is and where he wishes to go. There seems to be an implicit trust in each of us that we know what is best for ourselves —and that there are people around to help us figure it out, to give us a lot of feedback on our thinking, acting, relating, behaving, etc., that this kind of feedback is given and asked for freely—there are no strings attached (e.g., grades) nor pressures to do or be a certain way—that with this kind of freedom we will come to trust ourselves more and be more ourselves and that this is learning and growing.

In general I'm feeling very good about this kind of freedom. At times I feel scared, wondering where I'm going with all this, if I'm really OK or if I'm really just blowing the year. But these fears don't seem to be nearly as prevalent as my feelings of excitement and joy in finding this kind of freedom.

I think I've really *felt* this freedom—this acceptance of where I am and where I need to go. I've let go of a lot of reins I had on myself and am allowing myself to feel and experience all kinds of things I've never felt or experienced before. I feel like I've almost gone wild in a sense, because I'm doing so little reading and studying—but I've been doing a great deal of thinking and talking with people—and feel confident that I will again read and study—now because I want to and not because I have to [p. 11].

In the above quote one sees a young woman with a remarkable degree of insight into her changing needs and a willingness to assume responsibility for her decisions. Significant in her statement is a strong flavor of a learner —someone searching for more congruent ways for her behaviors to match her needs. This person and many others involved in open education look forward to a lifetime of learning in which they develop a process for learning. Each year is seen as just that—a year along the way to unlimited opportunities for personal growth and fulfillment.

REFERENCES

Barth, R. S. Open education: assumptions about children's learning. In C. H. Rathbone, ed., *Open Education: The Informal Classroom.* New York: Citation Press, 1971. pp. 116-36.

Biggs, E. E., & MacLean, J. R. *Freedom to Learn: An Active Learning Approach to Mathematics.* Ontario, Canada: Addison-Wesley, 1969.

BORTON, T. *Reach, Touch, and Teach: Student Concerns and Process Education.* New York: McGraw-Hill, 1970.

COLE, L. *Street Kids.* New York: Ballentine Books, 1970.

DENNISON, G. *The Lives of Children: The Story of the First Street School.* New York: Random House, 1969.

FEATHERSTONE, J. *School's Where Children Learn.* New York: Liveright, 1971.

HALL, E. T. *The Hidden Dimension.* New York: Doubleday, 1969.

HAWKINS, D. Messing about in science. In C. H. Rathbone, ed., *Open Education: The Informal Classroom.* New York: Citation Press, 1971. pp. 58-70.

HERNDON, J. *How to Survive in your Native Land.* New York: Simon and Shuster, 1971.

HOLT, J. *How Children Learn.* New York: Pitman, 1967.

KNOBLOCK, P. A new humanism for special education: The concept of the open classroom for emotionally disturbed children. In P. A. Gallagher & L. L. Edwards, eds., *Educating the Emotionally Disturbed: Theory to Practice.* Lawrence: The University of Kansas, 1970. pp. 68-85.

KNOBLOCK, P. Psychological considerations of emotionally disturbed children. In W. M. Cruickshank, ed., *The Psychology of Exceptional Children and Youth.* 3rd ed. Englewood Cliffs, N.J.: Prentice-Hall, 1971. pp. 565-99.

KNOBLOCK, P., BARNES, E., & EYMAN, W. *Preparing Psychoeducators for Inner City Teaching.* Syracuse University Final Report for US Office of Education, Bureau of Education for the Handicapped, 1972.

KNOBLOCK, P., & GARCEA, R. A. Teacher-child relationships in psychoeducational programming for emotionally disturbed children. In J. Helmuth, ed., *Educational Therapy.* Seattle: Special Child Publications, 1969, pp. 393-411.

KNOBLOCK, P., & GOLDSTEIN, A. P. *The Lonely Teacher.* Boston: Allyn & Bacon, 1971.

KOHL, H. R. *The Open Classroom.* New York: New York Review/Vintage, 1970.

LEE, D. M. & ALLEN, R. V. *Learning to Read Through Experience.* 2nd ed. New York: Appleton-Century-Crofts, 1963.

LONG, N.; MORSE, W. C.; & NEWMAN, R. *Conflict in the Classroom.* 2nd ed. Belmont, Cal.: Wadsworth, 1971.

MASLOW, A. H. Some educational implications of the humanistic psychologies. *Harvard Educational Review* 38 (1968): 385-96.

RATHBONE, C. H., ed. *Open Education, the Informal Classroom.* New York: Citation Press, 1971.

REDL, F. & WINEMAN, D. *Children Who Hate: The Disorganization and Breakdown of Behavior Controls.* Glencoe, Ill.: The Free Press, 1951.

ROGERS, C. *Freedom to Learn.* Columbus, Ohio: Merrill, 1969.

ROTHMAN, E. *The Angel Inside Went Sour.* New York: Bantam, 1970.

SOMMER, R. *Personal Space: The Behavioral Basis of Design.* Englewood Cliffs, N.J.: Prentice-Hall, 1969.

Sudbury Valley School. *The Crisis in American Education: An Analysis and a Proposal.* Framingham, Mass.: Sudbury Valley School Press, 1970.

WEBER, L. *The English Infant School and Informal Education.* Englewood Cliffs, N.J.: Prentice-Hall, 1971.

Peter Knoblock is Professor of Special Education, Syracuse University, New York.

44.
Behavior Modification:
Limitations and Liabilities
DONALD L. MACMILLAN
STEVEN R. FORNESS

This reading evaluates the use of behavior modi-
fication. As you read it, try to decide what use or
uses you would make of this technique in the
classroom.

The discussion concerns limitations inherent in the
behavior modification paradigm and common misuses of the strategy by
naive practitioners. The behavioristic explanation of learning often over-
simplifies the human situation. Some pure behaviorists view motivation as
extrinsic to learning and commonly separate the reward from the behavior.
The separation may be justifiable in early stages of a shaping program, but
desired behavior must come under the control of natural reinforcers as soon
as possible. Various programs have been adapted to incorporate some of the
evidence presented herein. Others have been less flexible, in which cases one
can only speculate about the benefits derived by those whose behavior was
modified.

Within recent years the application of behavior
modification techniques in classrooms of exceptional children has increased
greatly. Evidence abounds regarding the efficacy of behavior modification
with retarded children (Bijou & Orlando, 1961), learning disabled children
(Hewett, 1965; Lovitt, 1963), autistic children (Ferster & DeMeyer,
1961; Hewett, 1964; Lovaas, Freitag, Gold, & Kassorla, 1965), emotionally
disturbed children (Levin & Simmons, 1962a; Levin & Simmons, 1962b),
brain damaged children (Patterson, 1965), and assorted behavior problems in the classroom (Hively, 1959; Hewett, 1966; Valett, 1966; Whelan
& Haring, 1966). Hence, the contention that behavior modification is an
effective technique with atypical children appears to be well documented.

Hewett (1968) contends that behavior modification assigns the teacher
the role of a learning specialist, the role she is best prepared to assume.
Alternate strategies (i.e., psychoanalytic, sensory neurological) place the
teacher in the role of psychotherapist or diagnostician, roles which teachers
are generally ill prepared to assume. In light of successes in teaching atypical children with behavior modification techniques, Bijou (1966) contends

From *Exceptional Children* 37 (December, 1970): 291-97. Reprinted by permission of the authors and *Exceptional Children*. Copyrighted by the Council for Exceptional Children.

that one can no longer categorically explain the failure to learn in terms of a child's deficiencies, but rather must consider the tutorial inadequacies of the teacher. The combination of the factors above—teachers in roles of competence and the emphasis on what the child can do with properly sequenced and correctly reinforced material—provides a more positive approach to the education of exceptional children than did previous approaches which attributed the failure to learn to the child's defect.

By focusing on the consequences of altering and maintaining behavior, certain long-standing assumptions of educators have been questioned. One such assumption is that certain rewards, such as letter grades and teacher approval, have universal applicability. For certain children, the above rewards are ineffective. In attempts to identify rewards for children who do not respond to the traditional ones, investigators have utilized rewards considered unconventional by some (candy, check marks, tokens) with considerable success.

Research has further sensitized teachers to the power of their attention, and how their attending to misbehavior may have the effect of increasing its occurrence (Zimmerman & Zimmerman, 1962). Premack (1959) describes the use of activities the child prefers (high probability behavior) as an accelerating consequence for less preferred behavior (low probability behavior). Hence, if the child enjoys building model planes, the teacher can use this behavior as a reward for his performing tasks he enjoys less. Such evidence has had an impact on the ongoing practices in the special education classroom.

Enthusiasm over the reported successes of behavior modification with atypical children coupled with teachers' desperation for something that works may blind us to what behavior modification does not, or cannot, do. Mann and Phillips (1967) point out that a number of practices presently operative in special education are designed to fractionate global or molar areas of behavior. While their discussion did not include mention of behavior modification, their contention may also be valid with regard to this strategy. It is important that behavior modification be put in perspective with respect to the overall picture of education. Three limitations in the application of behavior modification to exceptional children will be discussed. Some of the limitations are inherent in the theoretical paradigm itself; others lie in the application, or misapplication, of that theory by practitioners. Specifically, the three limitations to be discussed are:

1. Learning theory does not guide the teacher in determining educational goals.

2. A view of motivation as exclusively extrinsic in nature is limiting in scope.

3. The operational definition of reinforcement ignores certain cognitive aspects of reinforcement.

BEHAVIORAL GOALS

Ullmann and Krasner (1965) state that the first question asked by the behavior analyst is, "What behavior is maladaptive, that is, what subject behaviors should be increased or decreased [p. 1]?" To the experimental psychologist this is a question answered only through objective analysis of behavior. Too often, however, the real question that gets answered is "What behavior manifested by the child most annoys me as his teacher," regardless of whether or not that behavior is interfering with the child's learning or development.

The behavior modification strategy does not determine educational goals for the child. This is not to suggest that the behavior modification strategy claims to determine goals, but in its inability to do so may lie the reason for its lack of acceptance in public school programs. Hewett, Taylor, and Artuso (1969) discuss the lack of balanced emphasis on goals and methods. They write:

> In general, selection of these goals is based on a desire to aid the child in changing maladaptive behavior to adaptive behavior. At best, these concepts of 'maladaptive' and 'adaptive' provide only the broadest of guidelines for selection of specific behavioral goals. In this sense the powerful methodology of the behavior modification approach is not matched by concern with goals in learning. Teachers are provided with an efficient means of taking emotionally disturbed children someplace but are not substantially aided in the selection of where to go.
>
> It is this lack of balanced emphasis on goals and methods that may preclude the acceptance of behavior modification in the field of education, particularly in the public school, and thereby may greatly limit its usefulness [p. 523].

Once the teacher has determined what the child is to be taught, the behavior modification techniques can be employed to achieve that end. Alternate developmental theories (e.g., Erikson, Piaget) may be more helpful for the determining goals in that they suggest to the teacher the developmental tasks that the child must master, and what skills he must acquire in order to achieve subsequent levels. Lacking a developmental framework, the teacher rather arbitrarily decides what the child must learn.

Wood (1968) expressed concern over the possibility that teachers are provided with a powerful tool in behavior modification techniques without simultaneously developing an understanding of its implications and potential misuse. In light of evidence suggesting that teachers, in general, are more concerned with maintaining power over students than in transmitting knowledge and skill, his concern seems well founded (Eddy, 1967; Henry, 1957; Landes, 1965; Moore, 1967). Implicit in the application of behavior modification techniques with children is the right of the behavior modifier to define what represents adaptive or appropriate behaviors. Wood (1968) described the teacher's role in such a relationship as follows: Having defined the child's present behavior as inappropriate *he* plans to shape it toward behavior *he* has defined as appropriate. In describing the teacher most likely to misuse this tool without considering the child's rights to participate in defining the goal behavior, Wood states:

These teachers may often be those against whose already abusive application of their authority pupils have the greatest need to be protected. Like many 'tools,' behavior modification techniques are themselves morally blind. Like a stout sword, they work equally well in the hands of hero or tyrant. Any person of moderate intelligence can, with assistance if not independently, apply them with great effectiveness for good or ill [p. 14].

In the case of many exceptional children, a number of their rights were abridged at the time of classification or labeling, thus making them more susceptible to abuse than had they not been so labeled.

ACADEMIC GOALS

When the educational goal is related to the teaching of subject matter, and the teacher employs a strict behaviorist strategy to achieve this goal, certain limitations inherent in the paradigm should be realized. The usual learning situation is much more complex than is suggested by the behavioristic paradigm. Enthusiastic proponents of behaviorism tend to be blinded by the framework and deny other possible explanations for human learning. The analysis of human learning in terms of discrete operational steps may ignore or violate the inherent logic in the material to be learned. Flavell (1963) explains Piaget's theory that schemata (organized information) develop as a consequence of assimilation and accommodation, and learning is facilitated by presenting materials in a manner amenable to reorganization of previously existing cognitive structures (schemata). In addition, Gagné (1962), operating within a different theoretical framework from Piaget, states that the nature and structure of the task to be learned is of greater importance than the behavioristic principles of learning, for example, reinforcement and practice.

It may be that behavior modification strategy fails to adequately consider the goals to which the shaped behavior is related. Determination of goals is left to the teacher who may, or may not, be a good judge of appropriate behavior. When the principles of behavior modification are applied to the teaching of subject matter the reductionistic conception of the learning process is a definite limitation. Autoinstructional techniques suffer from many of the same limitations, which are elaborated upon by Stafford and Combs (1967).

Motivation

EXTRINSIC

From the behavioristic point of view, motivation is seen as extrinsic to learning. Bijou and Baer (1961) stress the importance of behavioral scientists concerning themselves only with events which can be observed and quantified. In the application of reinforcement theory to behavioral management an attempt has been made to observe the suggestions of Bijou and Baer. In attempts to get children to read, sit in their seats, attend to materials, and develop other school appropriate behavior, the emphasis has been placed on the use of tokens, checks marks, and candy in association with the desired behavior. In programs developed to shape behavior through extrinsic rewards or consequences which are observable and able to be quantified, it is postulated that the child will ultimately want to engage in these appropriate behaviors because he will pair the social rewards of teacher or peer approval with the extrinsic rewards used during the shaping program. Inherent in such an approach is the belief that desire or motiviation can be manipulated by simply applying consequences when the organism behaves in a desired fashion. The theoretical approach described above is extremely limited, ignores much of the available evidence, presented in summary below, and discounts alternative explanations of motivation.

INTRINSIC

Piaget describes the equilibration process, wherein cognitive adaptation and growth result from the dynamic functioning of the processes of assimilation and accommodation Exploratory behavior is inherently interesting and rewards the child if it relates to the child's existing mental structures (schemata). Not only is it important to present material in a fashion commensurate with the child's previous level of cognitive development, but material thus presented can become a source of intrinsic motivation to the child (Hunt, 1961). There is no observable or quantifiable "pay off" for such behavior; however, when a match between schemata and task exists, the child finds the task inherently interesting.

Stimulation-seeking behavior appears to be another source of intrinsic motivation in higher order organisms. Festinger's (1957) "theory of cognitive dissonance" concludes that when incoming stimulation differs from existing perceptions or conceptions one is motivated to resolve the discrepancy. Festinger (1957) postulated that cognitive incongruities are a primary source of motivation in human beings, a source which is intrinsic in nature, and one which cannot be observed or quantified.

Although working outside of the two preceding theoretical frameworks, Harlow (1949, 1953) suggests that there may be an innate drive of curiosity, which is more likely to operate when the learners' primary needs have been satisfied (Maslow, 1943). Harlow (1953) explained that children and monkeys can enjoy exploration for its own sake. He cites the monkey who continues to solve problems despite the fact that his cheeks are full of food with which he was rewarded for correct or incorrect responses. Despite such unsystematic schedules of reinforcement, the monkeys increased their ability to learn how to learn (Harlow, 1949).

White (1965) offers another framework within which one can consider motivation. He contends that it is in studying the satiated child that one is truly able to understand human nature. In his paper critical of the traditional Freudian position which views motivation in terms of need reduction, White suggests that such a framework is unable to explain satisfactorily the apparent play behavior of the infant, or the one-year-old who tries to spoon feed himself despite the fact that he could gain greater oral satisfaction by allowing his mother to feed him. It may be added that neither can the reinforcement theory explain this behavior is terms of the observable events. Rather, White contends, the child is concerned with achieving mastery over his environment. Regarding play behavior, he writes:

It is directed, selective, and persistent, and it is continued not because it serves primary drives, which indeed it cannot serve until it is almost perfected, but because it satisfies an intrinsic need to deal with environment [White, 1965, p. 15].

The goal of behavior which White sees as an attempt to achieve competence may be to effect familiarity with the environment, or in more global terms, autonomy. In other words, the "pay off" is a feeling or sense of competence.

The point to be made with regard to motivation is that the behavioristic viewpoint is not the only framework within which one can consider motivation. In fact, the behavioristic paradigm is unable to explain adequately the behaviors described by Piaget, Festinger, Harlow, and White. One is unable to observe the consequences for behaviors that result from exploration, cognitive dissonance, curiosity, and competence as motives. Yet these sources of motivation must not be ignored or discounted as one attempts to reach the atypical child, or any child for that matter. Certain programs, such as Hewett's (1968), which are essentially behavior modification oriented, have altered their initial approaches and now attempt to utilize intrinsic sources of motivation. To the extent that this is practiced, however, such programs violate the pure approach suggested by Bijou and Baer (1961).

Reinforcement

Within the behavior modification framework, reinforcement is commonly defined as "a stimulus which increases the probability of a response." The reinforcement does not have to be directly related to the behavior, and often the separation is intentional. An example of this separation is the use of candy to reinforce problem solving or seat sitting. Theoretically, such a definition does not adequately explain the verbal confirming response discussed by Jensen (1968). In addition, certain practical ramifications should be considered by the practitioner prior to the application of reinforcers which are unrelated to the behavior they are reinforcing.

VERBAL CONFIRMING RESPONSE

Jensen (1968) describes the "verbal confirming response" (V_c) or feedback, which is a type of self or symbolic reinforcement used by humans. It is extremely limited in lower forms of animals and young children. V_c is more than merely a secondary reinforcement. A secondary reinforcer is a previously neutral stimulus which has gained reinforcing power through being paired with a primary or biologically relevant reinforcer. Secondary reinforcers are known to extinguish very rapidly in animal studies. Such is not the case with V_c which has the effect of strengthening behavior even though the verbal confirming response itself has no reinforcing properties in the biological sense. "The V_c response is most often covert, especially in adults, and may even be unconscious. It consists, in effect, of saying to oneself *Good* or *That's right* or *wrong* [Jensen, 1968, p. 124]." The function of language in the above manner has been demonstrated by several Russian psychologists (Razran, 1959). An interesting feature of the V_c is that it must be self initiated. To the extent that it is necessary in efficient problem solving, the use of extrinsic reinforcers that are unrelated to the specific behavior they are reinforcing preclude the necessity for developing the V_c. In depriving the child of the opportunity of this V_c are we hindering his development as a problem solver?

ARBITRARY VS. NATURAL REINFORCERS

Turning to more practical considerations, Ferster (1966) distinguished between arbitrary and natural reinforcers in a paper on aversive stimuli. He pointed out that arbitrary reinforcers differ from natural reinforcers in two ways: (a) when arbitrary reinforcers are used, the performance that is reinforced is narrowly specified rather than broadly defined, and (b) in the case of arbitrary reinforcers, the individual's existing repertoire of responses does not influence his behavior nearly as much as is the case with natural reinforcers. Therefore, natural reinforcers lead to more integrated, general learning.

In the first case, a positive consequence is promised for a specific behavior, seat sitting, and a child can obtain that consequence only by conforming to specific demands. He sits in his seat to obtain the reward, but learning does not necessarily generalize to global behaviors, that is, adequate classroom behavior. In the second case, arbitrary reinforcers benefit the controller, not the controlled. The teacher who says, "If you sit in your seat, I'll give you 5 check marks" is arbitrarily reinforcing seat sitting, which is reinforcing to the teacher for employing the strategy. But the child is not being reinforced by a consequence that naturally exists in his environment. His natural environment has never reinforced his sitting in his seat with a check mark, nor is it likely to in the future. In fact nonsitting has probably been rewarded through satisfying the curiosity drive.

While check marks, tokens, M & Ms, and the like may be justifiable as initial means of bringing behavior under control, they must not represent an end in themselves. In several instances, teachers employing the behavior modification strategy, as they interpret it, have had their children on check marks for an entire year. When asked the reason the children were still functioning at this low reward level, the teacher indicated, "I'm not about to change something that is working." This teacher has failed in her responsibility to bring the child's behavior under the control of reinforcers that will exist in the child's natural environment (e.g., social praise). Whelan and Haring (1966) distinguished between the acquisition of behavior and its maintenance. The arbitrary reinforcers are useful in the acquisition stage, but in the maintenance stage they suggest:

When the behavior needs to be maintained, then it is no longer necessary to provide accelerating consequences to each behavioral response. Maintaining behavior requires that the teacher reduce considerably the number of accelerating consequences provided; indeed, it is a necessity if a child is to develop independent learning skills and self control. It is during this maintenance process that appropriate behavior is accelerated by consequences which are intrinsic to completion of tasks, social approval, feelings of self worth, and the satisfaction of assuming self responsibility. Therefore, dependence on numerous teacher applied consequences gradually loses significance to a child [Whelan & Haring, 1966, p. 284].

It is interesting to note that the above authors, two of the most commonly cited behavior modification advocates, refer to intrinsic consequences, feelings of self worth and satisfaction of assuming self responsibility. It may be that the problem lies with the practitioner who has learned the *how* of behavior modification and rigidly adheres to its doctrines. In training teachers to utilize the strategy, it seems essential that the instruction should include a heavy dosage of the possible misuse of this potentially useful strategy.

Conclusions

In conclusion, the behavior modification strategy has tremendous potential for work with atypical children. Its use with these children is promising; however, its misuse could be terrifying. It is not a panacea. It gives no direction in determining educational goals; it reduces constructs of learning, motivation, and reinforcement to simplistic terms on occasion. To the unsophisticated practitioner, it may be blinding to broader frames of reference regarding the constructs listed above. Furthermore, it may preclude children from learning how to learn and thus becoming independent of teachers as such—a major goal of education. It is time we admitted the shortcomings and limitations of the approach as well as extolling its virtues. In an address to a group of autoinstructional technique enthusiasts, Howard Kendler at the 1964 American Psychological Association Convention said the following: "You have a system called Socrates, but you don't have one called God." This statement applies to the present discussion, and should be heeded by the rigid behaviorist.

REFERENCES

BIJOU, S. W. & BAER, D. *Child Development.* Vol. I. New York: Appleton-Century-Crofts, 1961.

BIJOU, S. W. & ORLANDO, R. Rapid development of multiple-schedule performances with retarded children. *Journal of Experimental Analysis of Behavior* 4 (1961): 7-16.

BIJOU, S. W. A functional analysis of retarded development. In N. R. Ellis, ed., *International Review of Research in Mental Retardation.* Vol. I New York: Academic Press, 1966.

EDDY, E. M. *Walk the White Line: A Profile of Urban Education.* New York: Doubleday Anchor, 1967.

FERSTER, C. & DeMEYER, M. The development of performances in autistic children in automatically controlled environments. *Journal of Chronic Diseases* 25 (1961): 8-12.

FERSTER, C. B. Arbitrary and natural reinforcement. Paper delivered at the meeting of the American Association for the Advancement of Science, Washington, D.C., 1966.

FESTINGER, L. *A Theory of Cognitive Dissonance.* Evanston, Ill.: Row, Peterson, 1957.

FLAVELL, J. H. *The Development Psychology of Jean Piaget.* Princeton, N.J.: Van Nostrand, 1963.

GAGNÉ, R. M. Military training and principles of learning. *American Psychologist* 17 (1962): 83-91.

HARLOW, H. The formation of learning sets. *Psychological Review* 56 (1949): 51-65.

HARLOW, H. Mice, monkeys, men, and motives. *Psychological Review* 60 (1953): 23-32.

HENRY, J. Attitude organization in elementary school classrooms. *American Journal of Orthopsychiatry* 27 (1957): 117-33.

HEWETT, F. A hierarchy of education tasks for children with learning disorders. *Exceptional Children* 31 (1965): 207-14.

HEWETT, F. Teaching reading to an autistic boy through operant conditioning. *Reading Teacher* 17 (1964): 613-18.

HEWETT, F. The Tulare experimental class for educationally handicapped children. *California Education* 3 (1966): 608.

HEWETT, F. M. *The Emotionally Disturbed Child in the Classroom.* Boston: Allyn & Bacon, 1968.

HEWETT, F. M.; TAYLOR, F. D.; & ARTUSO, A. A. The Santa Monica project: Evaluation of an engineered classroom design with emotionally disturbed children. *Exceptional Children* 35 (1969): 523-29.

HIVELY, W. Implications for the classroom of B. F. Skinner's analysis of behavior. *Harvard Educational Review* 29 (1959): 37-42.

HUNT, J. McV. *Intelligence and Experience.* New York: Ronald Press, 1961.

JENSEN, A. R. Social class and verbal learning. In M. Deutsch, I. Katz, and A. R. Jensen, eds., *Social Class, Race, and Psychological Development.* New York: Holt, Rinehart & Winston, 1968.

LANDERS, R. *Culture in American Education.* New York: John Wiley & Sons, 1965.

LEVIN, G. & SIMMONS, J. Response to food and praise by emotionally disturbed boys. *Psychological Reports* 11 (1962): 539-46. (a)

LEVIN, G. & SIMMONS, J. Response to praise by emotionally disturbed boys. *Psychological Reports* 11 (1962): 10. (b)

LOVAAS, O. I.; FREITAG, G.; GOLD, V. J.; & KASSORLA, I. C. Experimental studies in childhood schizophrenia: Analysis of self-destructive behavior. *Journal of Experimental Child Psychology* 2 (1965): 67-84.

LOVITT, T. C. Operant conditioning techniques for children with learning disabilities. *The Journal of Special Education* 2 (1968): 283-89.

MANN, L. & PHILLIPS, W. A. Fractional practices in special education: A critique. *Exceptional Children* 33 (1967): 311-17.

MASLOW, A. H. A theory of human motivation. *Psychological Review* 50 (1943): 370-96.

MOORE, G. A. Realities of the urban classroom: Observations in elementary schools. New York: Doubleday Anchor, 1967.

PATTERSON, G. R. An application of conditioning techniques to the control of a hyperactive child. *Behavior Research and Therapy* 2 (1965): 217-26.

PREMACK, D. Toward empirical behavior laws: I. Positive reinforcement. *Psychological Review* 66 (1959): 219-33.

Razran, G. Soviet psychology and psychophysiology. *Behavioral Science* 4 (1959): 35-48.

Stafford, R. R. & Combs, C. F. Radical reductionism: A possible source of inadequacy in auto instructional techniques. *American Psychologist* 22 (1967): 667-69.

Ullmann, L. & Krasner, L. *Case studies in behavior modification.* New York: Holt, Rinehart, & Winston, 1965.

Vallett, R. A social reinforcement technique for the classroom management of behavior disorders. *Exceptional Children* 33 (1969): 185-89.

Whelan, R. J. & Haring, N. G. Modification and maintenance of behavior through application of consequences. *Exceptional Children* 32 (1966): 281-89.

White, R. W. Motivation reconsidered: The concept of competence. In I. J. Gordon, ed., *Human Development: Readings in Research.* Glenview, Ill.: Scott, Foresman & Company, 1965.

Wood, F. H. Behavior modification techniques in context. *Newsletter of the Council for Children with Behavioral Disorders* 5:4 (1968): 12-15.

Zimmerman, E. H. & Zimmerman. J. The alteration of behavior in a special classroom situation. *Journal of the Experimental Analysis of Behavior* 5 (1962): 59-60.

Donald L. MacMillan is Associate Professor of Education, University of California–Riverside, and Stephen R. Forness is Special Education Director, Mental Retardation Program, Neuropsychiatric Institute, University of California–Los Angeles. The research reported herein was performed in part pursuant to the University of California Intramural Grant No. 9109 USOE Grant No. 0-9-141269-3366 (031), and NICHD Grant No. HD 04612, Mental Retardation Center, UCLA.

45.
If Schools Are to Meet Their Responsibilities to All Children

WILLIAM C. MORSE

What do we ask children to adjust to? What are factors in the total school environments and in specific classrooms that contribute to emotional conflict?

Schools are pivots for multiple concerns about children and youth. As institutions they incorporate responsibilities to children, to teachers, to parents and to the community at large. Nowhere is resolution of this multiple accountability more muddled than in the case of socially and emotionally disturbed pupils.

Even as the number of such disturbed children increases, schools display loss of confidence in the traditional approaches to helping them. The great majority of disturbed children are to be found in seats among their peers in the regular classrooms across the country, and will continue to be. Consultation to teachers, though still essential, leaves a void in real support. Special classes have a helping role but are few in number and known to be of limited effectiveness. While outside referral is the dreamed panacea, waiting lists remain long and liaison weak. At the same time, in the midst of a confusing cultural upheaval that is altering teachers' roles, the individual teacher often finds the added expectations of helping disturbed children taxing to the point where he defends himself by rejecting the responsibility. More and more activist parents demand that the public school provide an education for socially deviant or even schizophrenic youngsters; while other parents, driven by anxiety, insist that all such pupils be excluded from school. And yet when youth go on emotional binges or drug abuse hits the headlines, the community issues ultimatums to the school to do its duty. Faced with a deluge of demands and a drouth of creative solutions, many schools are permeated with an atmosphere of futility. Something has to give.

To develop viable educational programs for disturbed youngsters, we need to recognize the essential concepts that must be incorporated therein. These concepts are available in the practices of good institutional schools for the very seriously disturbed whose home schools have finally given them up as impossible because of their deviant behavior. In such special school settings most of the children persevere at their tasks a good deal of the time. In crafts they are often creative. On the playground and in gym

From *Childhood Education* 46:6 (March, 1970) 299-303. Reprinted by permission of the author and *Childhood Education.*

they manage to play games. At passing time they make little more than natural "kid noise" in the hall. Some hang around to talk with teachers after school. To be sure, outbursts, fights, campaigns of resistance, defiance and despair happen too, and on some days much more often than on others. But such incidents are expected, and handled with an air of security and within a purposeful plan. Among these children, most are destined to return to the so-called mainstream; others will need a lifetime of societal protection.

How do these schools and regular schools differ? How can we begin to use some of their insights to meet the needs of disturbed pupils in the regular school?

A good place to begin is with the concept of diagnosis. *Adequate special schools have gone far beyond traditional individual diagnosis.* Despite a continuing deep investment in understanding an individual child's developmental deviation, they concentrate not on his history but on his current status, self-concept, resources, and imitations as presented behaviorally in the school matrix. Since the children come in unique configurations and usually exhibit multiple handicaps (viz. several skills, internal stress, learning adequacies), diagnostic categorizing is avoided.[1]

Really starting where the child *is* emotionally and educationally requires a dual diagnostic stance: (a) with the nature of the child and what he brings to the situation, (b) with the equally relevant study of the responding environment and the stress or support it provides him. On such a core concept of individualization, the surround or the ecology of the school in general and classroom in specific becomes the key to accommodation. Some special schools have shown that we can not only design a less abrasive match for disturbed children but can also devise basic supportive elements. As we shall illustrate, this simple statement implies a revolutionary change in how schools operate, what teachers do and what specialists do. While some of the flexibility required will cost more money, to be sure, the even greater cost is that of changing ideology, with a resultant loss to comfortable vested interests. Let us look now at a few examples.

In an Adequate Educational Setting for Emotionally Disturbed Children:

1. A LONG-TIME VIEW REPLACES AN "INSTANT CHANGE" EXPECTATION.

Disturbed youngsters did not learn their patterns overnight and they will not change them in a day. By reducing ecological provocation, we provide extensive opportunities for new learning, interspersed with acceptance of the need for forgetting and relearning. In the regular school, if the teacher or principal "talks at" a disturbed youngster once, some magical change is anticipated. When adults imply by their statements or innuendoes that the youngster can be "normal" if he would only try a little harder, they add to his sense of inability and defeat. Time perspective is necessary.

2. THE DISTURBED PUPIL HAS AN ACCEPTING AND TRAINED PROFESSIONAL AS
HIS TEACHER.

Teachers in the best special schools are trained to be sensitive to the covert
as well as overt needs of the pupil, and to have available a repertoire of
relevant plans and techniques. Part of this sensitivity is attitudinal: through
self-awareness a teacher learns to regulate his own counter-reactive tendencies so as not to take children's behavior as a personal affront. He seeks
to respond in an authentic, just and trustworthy manner that provides stability in the environment; is tolerant but not permissive, expecting but not
over-demanding. If schools are to provide this ecological resource, intensive pre- and inservice training for teachers will be mandatory, with no de-
marcation between regular and special education skills. Only in this way
can we provide the personal supportive environment required. At present
the pupil often faces a rejecting tone and low expectations born of teacher
futility, self-fulfilling prophecies and other actions which reinforce deviation.

Scapegoating of pupils by frustrated adults is a sinister process. By predicting and outlining failure, berating the child at his necessary times of
regression, decrying the failure and evidencing no hope, teachers prepare
themselves for psychologically rejecting and excluding the child on a
"justified" basis ("There is nothing we can do"). Looked at as produced
frustration rather than as innate rejection of children by a hostile profession, the focus can be put on remedies rather than blaming.

3. THE DISTURBED PUPIL IS PROVIDED A RELEVANT SCHOOL CURRICULUM AND
NOT ASKED TO FIT A LOCKSTEP, PREDETERMINED COURSE OR METHODOLOGY OF
TEACHING.

He is not forced to repeat situations that have produced intensive anxiety.
As William Glasser has so vividly described, fear of failure dominates
many.[2] Only the empathic teacher knows how much pupils are both afraid
to fail and yet reluctant to do that which they can because "it's baby stuff."
Gauging the educational experience correctly calls for subtle ability to free
the child to accept tasks as appropriate.[3] New methods may be required,
along with especial help for those with learning disabilities. Moreover,
change must come in attitudes that regard work-programs as second-best
education. For many disturbed adolescents, job-related education is the
only avenue open.

4. THE DISTURBED PUPIL IS NEITHER EXPECTED TO SUFFER FROM GROUP ABUSE
NOR ALLOWED TO PERPETRATE ABUSE ON GROUP MEMBERS.

Many of the deviant pupils' problems stem from social malfunction, and
oftentimes a fixed role of group scapegoat or bully evolves. The reactive
environment must neither ignore nor pretend about these interactions,
often the most potent factors in classroom life. Through individual and
group discussions and Life Space Interviewing, impact of such incidents

is mitigated, youngsters are taught to deal with these facts of life within the context of a minimum social code.[4]

But withal, the distraught child cannot be overexposed to group life when it is beyond his tolerance. When he can only use mornings, full days make no sense. Length of time and type of group experience are two variables that need continual exploration. Small group size is considered critical in special classes that serve the disturbed pupil; six to twelve pupils is a preferred range. Public schools which cannot help many of these pupils in classes of from twenty to forty are fortunately starting to explore the range from tutorial to large-sized groupings. Group-size variation, as practiced in some forms of team teaching and module scheduling, offers opportunity for at least occasional time in small groups with intensified teacher input. Public school concepts about grouping must change.

5. THE DISTURBED YOUNGSTER IS NOT EXPECTED TO SUSTAIN HIMSELF WITHOUT AUXILIARY SUPPORT.

The regular school has too long depended on one teacher for everything. Disturbed pupils need high inputs—sometimes even the totality of one teacher. The requirement of many helping hands can be accomplished by incorporating sub-professional personnel. Some already used in public schools to assist disturbed pupils are: teacher aides, lay volunteer "mothers," "grandmothers," "grandfathers," future teachers, cross-age groupings of older students, indigenous community personnel and peers used to "teach" peers. Role models in Big Brother and Big Sister persons may be the most useful adjuncts at times. Conclusion: disturbed children can be served only with more help. Our cries for more personnel may not be answered by the community for a long time. But a reservoir of human resources is ready to be incorporated if we really are in earnest about meeting the manpower shortage.

6. CLASSROOM OPERATION MOVES TOWARD A LESS UNIFORM, MORE INDIVIDUAL- IZED GOAL-SETTING FORMAT.

For examples from elementary through graduate school see Carl Rogers' new book, *Freedom To Learn*.[5] Note that he does not propose introduction of random "freedom." Many disturbed pupils especially need strong structure, and Rogers clarifies the fact that this structure may be one of the major individualization dimensions—more important than the I.Q. or achievement level. At the very least, the distraught child needs a variety of immediate support. We cannot ask him to do alone on his own that at which he has already failed. While the teacher may design a much more individualized goal-seeking program, structure for doing specific tasks is still required. Machines—typing, recording and self-tutoring devices—can play useful roles when personal interaction is too difficult. It is important to note that the flexible classroom is not laissez-faire, since needed structure can come from pupil purpose as well as from authority.

7. SPECIALIZED MENTAL HEALTH EXPERTS MOVE FROM THE WINGS TO CENTER STAGE.

The new pattern does not rest on giving advice alone but on providing direct service when the disturbed pupil cannot be maintained in the classroom. In the institutional programs the psychiatrists are available to help with on-the-line problems. In the regular school, guidance personnel, psychologists, social workers and administrative personnel will have to make themselves available to work with academic and emotional problems at times of crises as well as in the calm of scheduled therapeutic interviews. Their whole role will change.

Disturbed pupils require this second line of assistance. They need a person to go to, to drain off the acid of frustration, on the not-infrequent occasions when the regular teacher cannot do enough. Our experience has been that a "crisis teacher" is the most important correlate to the regular classroom. This person takes over the pupil in a cooperative venture with the teacher when the going gets too rough in the group. Some counselors have begun to reorient their role to this function. Since many children are acting out problems in school stemming from home and community, they clearly need counseling to separate in-school from out, to see their areas of progress, to unwind at times, to straighten out their feelings and their lives.

8. NEEDS ARE MATCHED WITH AVAILABLE RESOURCES.

Some teachers have natural talent to help certain types of pupils. Patience quotas differ, resiliency differs, limit-setting definitiveness differs. We should therefore make every effort to match what the pupils require with natural adult resources. We know that often a severe problem to one teacher is a mild one to another, but we ignore the fact in our planning.

Another major inherent resource is the classroom peer-culture. Some classes can tolerate a disturbing pupil with minimum contagion, while another cannot absorb the impact of one more volt of disturbance. We need to assess and utilize peer stability in grouping disturbed pupils.

9. THE SCHOOL DEVELOPS NEW MODUS OPERANDI WITH PARENTS, MORE PUPIL-PARENT-TEACHER-EXPERT JOINT PLANNING AND EVALUATION SESSIONS.

While a few parents are enemies of their children, most are frustrated, anxious and afraid of the future. Parent associations for those with disturbed youngsters have been a great asset in many communities.

10. THE PHYSICAL ENVIRONMENT, THOUGH PLANNED TO REDUCE DISTRACTIONS, DOES NOT ELIMINATE FUN AND HIGH GRATIFICATION OPPORTUNITIES.

Planning of space, from study carrels to small group areas to high gratification areas, is a must. Most disturbed children lack re-creation through recreation. Press for academics can intensify to the point of defeat. Most of these youngsters feel hard put-upon by their efforts, however minimal the actual product may be, and so anticipate some return for their exertion. A classroom needs places to do what you choose for fun part of the time. Many of these youngsters have missed normal pleasures other pupils have received from plays, trips and special events; they are left out because of their reputations. But a balanced diet is necessary, with considerable reward for little effort until the youngster begins to believe in his capabilities.

Conclusion

Not even the most hygienic school environment can do everything for all children. But meeting the responsibility to do all we can will give pupils their educational birthright. Schooling is a major "treatment" avenue for disturbed children. Success here can counteract some outside malignancies. Only after we have maximized our regular school environment can we consider the alternatives. And the alternatives of special classes and referral will still be required for some cases.

NOTES

1. This theme has been extended in William C. Morse, Disturbed youngsters in the classroom, *Today's Education* 58:4 (April, 1969): 31-37.
2. GLASSER, WILLIAM. *Schools Without Failure.* New York: Harper & Row, 1969.
3. DENNISON, GEORGE. *The Lives of Children.* New York: Random House, 1969.
4. REDL, FRITZ. *When We Deal with Children.* New York: Free Press, 1966.
5. ROGERS, CARL. *Freedom To Learn.* Columbus: Chas. Merrill Publishing Co., 1969. (*Ed.'s note:* See review by Mary Jo Woodfin in February, 1970 *Childhood Education,* p. 276.)

William C. Morse is professor of Education and Psychology in the School of Education, University of Michigan at Ann Arbor.

Eleven

Special Education in Transition: Part One

Categories and Variables

Educational programs from the kindergarten to the university have undergone major revisions in the last decade. The revolution has encompassed educational programs for the handicapped and has resulted in major innovations, many of which have been discussed in previous chapters.

The issues before the profession may be illustrated by the titles of recent articles which have appeared. Here are some examples:

Special Education: A Teapot in a Tempest

Special Education for the Mildly Retarded—Is Much of It Justifiable?

Programs for Individually Prescribed Instruction

Special Education for the Mentally Retarded— A Paradox

Special Education Students—How Many Are Misplaced?

In this chapter the readings will concentrate upon suggestions for restructuring educational programs for the handicapped from an organizational point of view.

Historically speaking, most handicapped children in our public schools have been served in special classes, each of which has provided for one category or type of child. There has been limited use of resource rooms, except for partially-seeing children. The clinical or tutorial approach

415

was, however, used almost universally with children who had speech disorders.

In the past decade many alternative systems for delivering services have been developed and used effectively. Among these is the general resource room, which serves a variety of mildly handicapped children. A variety of auxiliary personnel has been used to supply technical assistance to the regular classroom teacher who serves handicapped children, such as the special education consultant, the crisis teacher who assists with disturbed children, the media specialist, the specialist who designs individual programs for children, and so forth. Most of these innovations have come about as schools have returned many mildly handicapped children to regular classrooms.

It is difficult at this early stage in history to pinpoint the conditions that produced these changes. Certainly our knowledge of children in general—their abilities and disabilities—has greatly increased; hence the profession has greater insight into their educational needs. There has been an increase in the respect for and tolerance of individual differences on the part of regular classroom teachers. Improvement in instructional material has made it easier for regular teachers to individualize instruction and thereby serve a greater range of individual differences. The impact of these influences is very positive, and improved services will continue to be derived from them.

The problem of devising an effective plan for grouping children for instruction has been a perennial concern in education. Traditionally, special education has classified children into what were thought to be homogeneous groupings—the blind, the deaf, the gifted. In recent years there have been very legitimate questions raised regarding these rigid classification arrangements. It has been pointed out that these labels placed upon children are not descriptive of the relevant instructional variables.

In the first article, Lord traces the development of special classes in the United States and the accompanying categorical grouping of exceptional children, and describes the trend toward mainstreaming. This article provides historical perspective relating to the current controversy.

The second article by Reynolds and Balow considers variables in special education and suggests the employment of instructional systems to meet the needs of exceptional children. These authors provide a discussion of theoretical and practical considerations in restructuring the field of special education.

In the third article, Oliver Hurley discusses the categorical/non-categorical issue from the point of view of its implications for teacher preparation. These three articles provide a balanced presentation of one of the most discussed problems in special education. While all the answers may not be included in these articles, the issues are presented clearly and convincingly.

The concept of accountability is also being widely discussed in our society today. Its application to public education has been advocated by many professionals and laymen, and it is clearly worthy of careful examination since it is modifying our educational practices. In the final article, Vergason examines accountability and points out several applications. His suggestions for personal accountability for the classroom teacher will be especially valuable for those who plan to enter the teaching profession. There is little doubt that one of the practices discussed—the voucher system—will be used extensively to purchase training for severely handicapped children in private schools.

Ray Graham, the former Director of Special Education for the State of Illinois, is featured as the pioneer in this chapter. His distinguished leadership at the national and state levels was instrumental in developing many of the current practices in the education of exceptional children.

Ray Graham
1898-1961

TEACHER
ADMINISTRATOR
EDUCATIONAL STATESMAN

Ray Graham served as a teacher, principal, and superintendent of schools in Illinois before he was appointed Director of Special Education in the Office of the Superintendent of Public Instruction in Springfield, Illinois in 1943. He is presented as a pioneer in administration because his "dynamic and effective leadership in Illinois and in the nation has left a lasting imprint on all who labor to make life more meaningful to children who are in some way 'different.' "* He invited consultants in specialized areas to assist him in decision making and mobilized parent groups as well as social agencies to assist schools in developing efficient programs. The Illinois Plan which he developed became widely known and was, in the 1950's, copied by many states. In addition to his unique contributions to the organization and administration of programs throughout the United States, Panama, and Canada, he served as President of the Council for Exceptional Children in 1948. He was also the driving force in Illinois behind the organization of the Institute for Research on Exceptional Children at the University of Illinois, a cooperative research organization of the State University, the Department of Public Instruction, and the Department of Mental Health. The book *Educating Exceptional Children* by Kirk is dedicated to the memory of Ray Graham and quotes Lao-Tzu to characterize his efforts: *"Of a good leader, who talks little, when his work is done, his aim fulfilled, they will say 'We did this ourselves.' "*

---

*From the dedication to Samuel Kirk's *Educating Exceptional Children*, Boston: Houghton Mifflin, 1972.

46.
Categories and Mainstreaming in Special Education: Perspectives and Critique

FRANCIS E. LORD

Can you trace the origin and development of our common labels?
In what way does mainstreaming seem to be a natural consequence of our earlier practices?

Two of the major concerns today of leaders in special education relate to the validity of the rigid categories or grouping of handicapped children for instruction and the concern regarding the assignment of mildly or moderately handicapped children to special classes. The movement to transfer some children from special classes to regular classes has come to be referred to as *mainstreaming*. These two movements will be reviewed in the introductory article in this chapter on restructuring special education.

Labels and State Programs Emerge

Special classes for handicapped children, which carry some of the labels used today, have been in existence since before the turn of the century. The first classes were in the larger cities of that period—Boston, New York, Philadelphia. These were isolated classes and could be found within the public school systems. However, by the third decade several states were providing services for at least three or four groups of handicapped children. Leadership and supervision were provided and statewide programs were well under way. Elizabeth Farrell's address (1923), which was reproduced in Chapter One, calls attention to these emerging developments.

The following are excerpts from descriptions of development of public school programs for exceptional children in three states. These brief summaries illustrate the emergence of state programs, including state aid to support special classes.

In Minnesota special classes in the public schools had their inception in 1915 when the legislature encouraged the establishment of special classes for defectives by granting fixed amounts to districts for each child enrolled in any of the four types of classes recognized by law: Deaf, Blind, Defective Speech and Mentally Subnormal.

Based upon a lecture, "Medical classifications of disabilities for educational purposes —a critique," delivered at the Fifth Annual Distinguished Lecture Series in Special Education, Summer 1966, University of Southern California, Los Angeles.

In 1940 Ohio's Code had legislative provisions for the special education of physically handicapped children: Deaf, Blind and Crippled. By 1941, the law was broadened to include those children "whose learning is retarded, interrupted, or impaired by physical or mental handicaps. . . ."

Before October 1945 only seven public school speech and hearing therapists were employed in Ohio school districts. . . . The provision of the $750 state subsidy for each approved teaching unit for retarded children (1945) has given impetus to the establishment of such classes.

Differences in the educational needs of children attending California public schools is first noted in *Codes Relating to Public Education of 1905*. At this time the 1903 compulsory attendance law requiring children from the ages of eight to fourteen to attend school regularly was amended as follows:

> Provided that should it be shown to the satisfaction of the Board of Education of the City or the City and County, or the Board of Trustees of the School District, in which the child resides, that the child's bodily or mental condition is such as to prevent or render inadvisable attendance at school, or application to study, a certificate from any reputable physician that a child is not able to attend school, or that its attendance is inadvisable, must be taken as satisfactory evidence by any such Board or that such child is being taught in a private school, or by a private tutor, or at home by any person capable of teaching, in such branches as are usually taught in the primary or grammar schools of the State.

This legislation implied a responsibility to physically and mentally handicapped children by boards of education, and in 1907 a law was passed making it permissive for districts to establish in the elementary grades an oral system of instruction for deaf pupils between the ages of three and twenty-one. During the next ten-year period, special education classes for deaf, as well as blind, speech handicapped, and hard-of-hearing pupils, were instituted in several of the larger school districts in the state. And in 1921 school districts were granted legal authority to establish special classes for mentally retarded students.

In 1927 the California State Legislature enacted laws on behalf of handicapped children which set the stage for successful future developments in special education, the most important of which was the appropriation of state funds to be used to reimburse school districts for the excess costs in educating such children.

Legislative enactments by the states that first developed special education programs were frequently duplicated in other states. Somewhat similar definitions were used from state to state which led to a uniform vocabulary to describe groups of handicapped children. A clear example is the definition of partially seeing children set forth by the National Society for the Prevention of Blindness which dominated practice for decades.

The principle of allowing compensation to districts to help pay for the added costs of special classes was established before the turn of the century. No doubt this practice of support was fairly easy to "sell" to a legislature since most states were accustomed to paying for the education of handicapped children who attended residential schools. In fact, the emerging day school program might have appeared to be a money-saving device.

The establishment of state support for special classes brought with it the question of eligibility for admission. A state wanted to be sure that the money that was appropriated was spent to educate children who qualified for a given service. Hence, states developed legal definitions of disabilities and established well defined regulations relating to eligibility for admission to special classes. Again the eligibility standards were tied to disability categories. The child had to be "in the category" to qualify for a given service.

In order to control the qualifications of special teachers, the states issued requirements for credentials or certificates. With few exceptions, separate requirements were set up for teachers of each of the categories. In the early 1920's it was clear that credential patterns would be directly related to the types of special education classes. Most states today prescribe a somewhat separate set of course requirements for each special education preparation program.

With the enactment of legislation in 1958, the federal government initiated support of leadership training for personnel in the area of mental retardation. Later legislation extended support to all areas of preparation for teaching exceptional children. At first, funding was made available to colleges for categorical programs. In recent years, however, there have been some changes which provide more flexibility in support patterns.

Questioning of Labels and Categories

The use of labels, medical labels in particular, has been generally criticized in the past few years by special educators. It is indeed fair to note that our labels are not all medical in origin or connotation. If one took the list of terms commonly used to describe groups of exceptional children, and then classified these terms as *medical* or *educational* or *psychological*, he would find some terms under each heading. While *crippled* may be medical, *gifted* has an educational connotation. *Learning disabilities* may be educational or psychological. *Educationally handicapped* is easy to classify. Labels, when applied to groups of children, are always misleading. The teacher who refers to her third graders knows, and would readily admit, that some of her children are really in the second grade and others are in the fourth, and even higher, in achievement. It appears that we will always have labels, so the challenge to those of us who use them is to understand their limitations as descriptors of groups.

There are at least two legitimate objections to labeling. First, labels are meaningless as descriptions of the educationally relevant factors in the education of the children so labeled. If one says that a child is crippled, we know little about his abilities and disabilities from such a characterization. In fact, most of our terminology referring to the handicapped (deaf, blind, emotionally disturbed, and so on) is clearly limited in revealing meaningful information about the true dimensions of the educational problems.

The major questioning here must be placed upon the adequacy of categorical labels *in general* when diversified populations are being described. Perhaps the most valuable aspect of the controversy will come from an insistence that the profession try to pinpoint factors (abilities and disabilities) which are significant for therapy in education. Education does focus upon learning characteristics, behavioral patterns, aptitudes, interests, etc. It would be helpful to have labels which are truly descriptive of these relevant variables.

Another objection to labels centers around terms which imply a social and/or psychological stigma (Jones, 1972). When the school classifies a child as mentally retarded, for example, it places him in an inferior social group in the eyes of most of society. The label remains with the individual throughout his entire life. Obtaining a job may be difficult in many instances. Recently the objections to school classification have been taken into the courts, as the reader has noted in the article by Ross et al. in Chapter Two.

It is difficult to deny the validity of the objection to terms which place a stigma upon a child. Certainly the child knows when he has been reclassified and assigned to a special class. In fact, his entire neighborhood is likely to know his status in school. One would expect some impact upon the personality and self-concept of children assigned to classes for the retarded. The special class instructors, however, try to develop desirable attitudes since they consider this to be one of the major objectives to be achieved.

A number of psychological problems relating to the adjustment and personality development of exceptional children in special classes have been investigated. Much of this research has been discussed elsewhere in this volume. Handicapped children (mental or physical), when assigned to regular classes, do not seem to enjoy a level of social acceptance afforded most normal children (Johnson 1950, Force 1956). It has also been difficult to demonstrate that early placement of young retarded children into special classes where personal development is stressed necessarily results in better positive self-concept (Mayer 1966).

But Our Knowledge Continues to Grow

Most of the services for exceptional children about which you have read in the accompanying articles have developed during the past five or six decades. This is a limited time for the development of knowledge and insight essential for a full understanding of the pathology, psychology and critical educational variables. The current reactions to many practices of the past are due to new insights and revised convictions, and are therefore really landmarks of growth.

We no longer view mental retardation as solely an inherited condition which is subject to limited influence by training. It is not a simple condition which can be identified by performance on a single verbal intelligence test. We now know that retardation is caused by a great variety of conditions—social, biochemical, genetic, and developmental. The influence of training may be profound on the development of capacity for self management. The condition is identifiable only by information from several sources, including psychological test results, medical data, and critical observation of skills and adaptive behavior.

We no longer believe that all cerebral palsied children are mentally retarded per se and capable of little or no improvement in the use of extremities, ability to speak, and so forth. Etiology is not limited to brain injury *at* birth. We now know that cerebral palsy results from many conditions before, during, and after birth, and includes such conditions as the RH blood factor, lack of oxygen, infections, and so on. Many children with this handicapping condition have average or better intelligence and are capable, as a result of well-planned education and therapy, of leading fairly normal lives.

The profession now knows that the goal of conservation of sight which was generally advanced for classes designed for children with low visual acuity was not valid. This view was widely accepted in the earlier years of such classes. Ophthalmologists have pointed out more recently that sight is not damaged through normal use. Consequently, today children with low vision are encouraged to use their sight and, in addition, special drills are employed to improve their visual efficiency.

As a result of over a half-century of medical study, educational testing and observation in school settings, special educators are well aware of the tremendous heterogeneity of abilities and disabilities within each category. A single label is inadequate in describing any group of exceptional children. In our attempt to describe "gifted" children more adequately, the profession now uses a number of modifiers such as creative, talented, academically gifted, or artistically gifted, for example.

This brief discussion may provide some perspectives concerning categories and the associated labels. Another article in this chapter by Oliver Hurley provides further analysis and some implications for teacher preparation.

Mainstreaming as a Reaction

The degree to which handicapped children should be segregated into special classes has always been a matter for open controversy in American schools. In the late 1960's a nationwide movement toward mainstreaming was well underway. It is well to note, however, that some handicapped groups were handled in the schools with little or no segregation. Speech therapy has always been given as an auxiliary service to regular class instruction on a tutorial or clinical basis. Many partially seeing children were substantially integrated under plans generally promoted by the National Society for the Prevention of Blindness. Some special schools operated on integrated plans in conjunction with regular classes which were housed in the same building.

Numerous studies were made of the influence of segregation upon such considerations as academic achievement, personal and social adjustment. Often the design of the study was questionable and the instruments used to measure differences were inadequate. Consequently, helpful conclusions are difficult to make. However, the degree of integration achieved varies with the different handicapped groups—yes, indeed, with each individual child in a group. The social acceptance of the handicapped by the nonhandicapped appears to be a major problem and is often only partially achieved in regular classes. Nevertheless, the force of the argument is on the side of those who advocate as normal an education as possible for all handicapped children.

Federal funds which were made available by grants from the Bureau of Educational Personnel Development, U.S. Office of Education, have been instrumental in initiating numerous conferences and projects which focus entirely upon mainstreaming. These projects related to such important considerations as: (1) development of new delivery services—ways of getting services to the children; and (2) training of a variety of auxiliary personnel to provide support services to children who are trying to make it in the regular class. Examples of such personnel are: resource teacher, clinical teacher, consulting teacher, crisis teacher, diagnostic specialist, and prescriptive teacher. Well developed statewide programs have been developed in some states. Texas, for example, has adopted "Plan A," which is designed to return as many handicapped children as possible to regular classes and to provide the necessary supplementary services to assist them in handling the new demands made upon them. Many of these programs are described in the references which follow.

There is little doubt that many marginally handicapped children assigned to special classes could have survived in regular classes. Also, perhaps advances in adjusting to individual differences of children in regular classes have made such classes a more satisfactory instructional environment. Improved teaching materials in particular have helped individualize instruction. When instruction is completely individualized and teachers are given adequate support personnel, perhaps one-half to two-thirds of the handicapped children who had to be assigned to special classes in the past to receive adequate instruction may then remain in the regular grades.

REFERENCES

COMBS, D. N. and HARPER, T. H. Effects of labels on attitudes of education towards handicapped children. *Exceptional Children* 33 (February, 1967): 399-403.

FORCE, DEWEY. Social status of physically handicapped children. *Exceptional Children* 23 (December, 1956): 104-7, 132.

HAMMILL, DONALD and WIEDERHOLT, J. LEE. 1972. *The Resource Room: Rationale and Implementation*. Philadelphia: Buttonwood Farms, Inc. 68 pp.

JONES, REGINALD L. *Problems & Issues in the Education of Exceptional Children*. Boston: Houghton Mifflin, 1971. 424 pp.

JONES, REGINALD L. Labels and stigma in special education. *Exceptional Children* 38 (1972): 553-64.

JOHNSON, G. O. A study of the social position of mentally retarded children in the regular grades. *American Journal of Mental Deficiency* 55 (July, 1961): 60-89.

MAYER, LEMAR C. Relationships of early special class placement and the self concepts of mentally retarded children. *Exceptional Children* 33 (October, 1966): 77-81.

REYNOLDS, MAYNARD C. and DAVIS, MALCOLM D., eds. *Exceptional Children in Regular Classrooms*. Washington, D.C.: A publication of the Leadership Training Institute/Special Education, sponsored by the Bureau of Educational Personnel Development, U.S. Office of Education. (This is available from the Council for Exceptional Children.)

Francis E. Lord is Professor of Special Education, The University of Arizona, Tucson.

47.
Categories and Variables in Special Education

MAYNARD C. REYNOLDS

BRUCE BALOW

What changes in our attitudes and practices should be made if we accept the analyses and recommendations by these two authors, who are leaders in the field?

In all of society there is a rising revulsion against simplistic categorizations of human beings. The field of special education has been especially vulnerable to attack because in defining itself it has tended not only to list various categories of exceptional children but to use negatively loaded terminology to do so: the mentally *retarded,* the visually *handicapped,* the hearing *impaired,* the emotionally *disturbed,* and the socially *maladjusted.* The use of such categorical language has been especially evident in legislative and parent groups and in teacher education and school programs.

Fallacy of Categories

A number of problems may be created by the categorizing of people and programs. (a) There is a tendency to stereo-

From *Exceptional Children* 38 (January, 1972): 357-66. Reprinted by permission of the authors and *Exceptional Children*. Copyrighted by the Council for Exceptional Children.

type or to ascribe characteristics of the group to individuals. The practice, crude at best, is frequently in error and prejudicial to the interests of the individuals. (b) The category labels tend to become stigmatic and to be attached indelibly to the individuals, often resulting in scapegoating. Sometimes the child's label becomes an excuse for poor educational programs. (c) People who work with exceptional children may associate the categories with negative expectations and then carry them into their relationships with the children and into curriculum planning. A degree of diagnosogenic or prophecy fulfilling inadequacy in the child's development may result. (d) An assumption is made frequently about an easy isomorphism between categorical and educational classifications. For example, it may be assumed that all partially sighted children should read expanded print—which just is not so—or that because a child is "mentally retarded" he should get the "primary life needs" curriculum—again, not necessarily so.

Researchers who contrast groups of handicapped children with groups of so-called normal children often add to the problem. On the basis of such studies, the mentally retarded, for example, have been described as being cognitively rigid, being unable to think abstractly, showing stimulus trace or cortical satiation abberrations, exhibiting disassociation of verbal and motor systems, and being deficient or abnormal in many other ways. One could easily come to the absurd conclusion that a sharp discontinuity in mental ability occurs somehow so that people with IQ's of 76, for example, have entirely different characteristics from those with 1 point lower. Comparable problems abound in other areas of special education as well.

It is unfortunate that anyone should ever think of individual children and plan for them mainly in terms of categories although, undoubtedly, the extent of such practices may be somewhat exaggerated. We are all familiar with the caricature of the itinerant psychometrist, WISC kit at hand, who categorizes a child as mentally retarded after a 50 minute test and recommends special placement in a school about which he knows nothing. He represents a grotesque oversimplification of professional service that, hopefully, has no basis in fact. When the examiner phrases his conclusions in categorical language one hopes he does so as a kind of "shorthand" for a complex set of variables.

Flexibility of a "Variables" Approach

The perception of children through variables emphasizes the continuous differences among them on certain dimensions and permits us to try to quantify the differences in some way. Most of the variables that we find interesting in studying exceptional children are of interest also in the study of other children, which is to say that the distributions are continuous and include both exceptional and normal children. This continuity suggests that even if we attend to only a single variable, so-called exceptional children are children "only a little more so" in some one or several aspects and are not special types.

The convenience of using categories as a "shorthand" need not be eliminated if they are recognized as representing complex sets of variables. The category "mental retardation," for example, is a general term referring to a wide range of kinds and degrees of attenuation in cognitive development. Recently, so called "creative" children have been discussed as a kind of category, yet measures of creativity show continuous distribution. Most blind children are not totally "blind" but have different degrees of sight. An analogy can be drawn between the variables in one of these categories and the variables with which a weatherman deals. Temperature, barometric pressure, wind velocity, and cloud cover (his variables) are not static but combine uniquely at any moment over any place. "Weather" in itself is an abstract term; it takes on concrete meaning only in terms of the variables of which it is composed at a specific time and place. So it is with the categories of exceptional children; mental retardation, blindness, and creativity, for example, are abstract terms until they are given concrete significance by the particular constellation of variables in a particular child. Thus, the emphasis should be on variables and particularly on those variables that meet the test of educational relevance.

Two Kinds of Variables

It is useful, in considering their educational relevance, to distinguish between two general classes of variables—*source* or surfacing variables and *decision* variables. Most of the traditional variables dealt with in special education, such as those relating to mental retardation, vision, hearing, and emotional disturbances, are source variables. They are the sources or indicators of educational problems. While they may serve to alert us to problems or to potential problems, they do not indicate appropriate educational procedures. Consider, for example, the child who appears in school regularly with many bruises. It is clear that something should be done; but it is not clear whether the child is being abused by a parent, is showing the adverse physical effects of learning to skate, or is mutilating himself. The bruises evidence that something is wrong; they offer very little with respect to what should be done about them. They are source variables, not decision variables.

As another example, consider very low visual acuity. Certainly it is a problem that can be viewed as a quite reliable source or indicator of special education interest. However, poor sight in itself is not a good indicator of what educational procedures should be used with the child. The relevant variables in deciding on educational procedures might include tactual discrimination abilities at fingertips, intelligence, age, motivation, parental desires, and the low-vision aids available in the local schools. Similarly, mental retardation may be a child's problem, but judging whether he is likely to profit from a specialized school program may depend more on the sociopsychological climate of his home than on the immediate level of his cognitive functioning. Some of the decision variables, it should be noted, do not refer to the child but to his life situation.

The difference between source and decision variables is that the first provide the basis for identifying the problem and the second are the basis for making the educational decisions. Clearly, the variables on which decisions are based will change as educational technology improves and expands; thus, one should not think of decision variables in static terms.

Classification for Educational Purposes

One of the assumptions of the preceding discussion is that schools should be able to present alternative programs to accommodate all children. It is necessary, consequently, to allocate the children among the different programs or, in other words, to classify them. To develop this point of view it may be well to spell out the purposes of educational classification.

As a start, it may be useful to consider the purposes of classification in settings other than the school. Zubin (1967) cited three purposes of the diagnosis and classification of what he terms behavior disorders: (a) to search for etiology, (b) to make a prognosis, and (c) to select a therapy. Physicians and clinical psychologists tend to be oriented to these purposes. In anticipation of the discussion that follows, it can be stated immediately that none of the three is the chief concern of the special educator, yet our information systems tend to become distracted and cluttered by them.

Certainly it is clear that classification merely according to Zubin's first purpose, etiology, is not a useful approach in education. The cause of poor sight gives little help in deciding how one should teach a child. Similarly, it may not matter in educational planning whether the attentional problems of a child stem from brain injury or from other causes. Etiological variables may be useful in education but only in the context of the educational decisions to be made.

Similarly, prognosis has limited usefulness as an educational approach. Educators are employed to influence children's learning, not simply to predict it. One of the great errors in education is that general or broadband variables such as IQ test results, which predict academic achievement moderately well in almost all situations, are overused in decision making. Precisely because general intelligence test results predict learning and performance in many situations, they are virtually useless for making choices among educational situations. Educational decisions require attention to variables that produce interaction effects with educational treatments, that is, variables that help educators to make a difference rather than a prediction. This requirement is far beyond the content of psychological reports written in simple terms of "capacity," "expectation," or "underachievement," all of which are prognostic in orientation.

Zubin's third purpose, the selection of treatment, cannot be dismissed lightly in the present context because an important purpose of educational classification is to select treatment. Two general classes of treatments should be distinguished, however. The first is oriented to negative criteria, in which case we use terms like prevention, cure, or amelioration, and the second to positive criteria, in which case we use terms like development, competency, or achievement. In the second case, the concept of prevention is not meaningful in any full sense.

Educational treatments are always positive. They are concerned with teaching and learning, not with the recovery from defects or the simple prevention of problems. The educator "prevents" reading failure not by building antibodies but by teaching reading or its prerequisites with greater resourcefulness and better effect to more children. To be educationally relevant and to engage the teacher, the treatment must involve development, which is to say that the criterion is positive and that the concept of prevention is superfluous. To use Bruner's term, education is a growth science. Insofar as mental health and other fields succeed in specifying positive, health-giving, life-fulfilling goals and they orient themselves to pursuing such goals, there is little disparity between their concepts and those of education. One might also predict that the more fields such as mental health become oriented to positive criteria, the more they will find it useful to join forces with the school.

In short, the view proposed here is that special educators should stop talking about dysfunctions, deficits, impairments, and disabilities as if these were the starting points in education and recovery from or remediation of them were the goal. Obviously, one prevents problems or creates a kind of invulnerability to insult whenever competencies are engendered, but the competencies themselves are the goal.

Thus it can be said that Zubin's third purpose of classification is not suitable to education to the extent that its concept of treatment is oriented to prevention or cure. Education in a free society is predicated upon a commitment to enhance the development of all children in definitely positive ways. Special educators are concerned that absolutely no child is omitted from that commitment.

The approach to classification of children proposed here is concerned with the allocation of children among positively defined alternative instructional systems. For example, there are many different systems by which children may be taught to read; the problem of educational classification is to allocate each child to the system most likely to serve him effectively. Within this framework, one does not speak of children as "learning disabled" or "remedial cases" just because they require atypical method of instruction. Furthermore, the purpose of introducing greater variety in reading programs is not to "prevent" reading problems but to teach reading more effectively to more children.

Instructional Systems

The term "instructional system" refers to integrated sets of procedures, curricula, and materials that may be used to achieve certain major learning goals with children. The systems are themselves complex and require definite, systematic application by well oriented teachers. As already indicated, examples of instructional systems are provided by the several systems that can be used to teach reading. Some methods are highly oral-phonetic and others are completely nonoral; some use modified orthography in introductory teaching; and some assume and others do not assume linguistic sophistication at the starting point. There are methods that assume normal vision and ordinary libraries and others that depend on tactile discrimination and special braille libraries. Presumably, the schools should offer all systems that might be needed by any pupil.

The concept of instructional systems is open to the developments of the future as well as to the many procedures now used in the schools. The field of special education may be defined in terms of its responsibility to help develop and install highly differentiated school programs (many instructional systems) and to see that the related plans and decisions about children are made effectively. The particular systems for which special education carries primary responsibility include many in the categories of language learning, cognitive development, psychomotor training, socialization, and affective learning. Systems of language and speech instruction that do not assume hearing or normal auditory feedback are also quite specialized. Similarly, methods of teaching for mobility and orientation without sight require specialized efforts.

The application of behavior management procedures to produce basic responding, attending, and exploring behavior requires specialized efforts. The offering of especially intensive preschool language instruction to children who have unusual cultural backgrounds presents its own special aspects. Similarly, the management of curricula oriented to "primary life needs" requires specialized attention. One can view the crisis teacher model as a special system for interventions in school operations to serve both pupils and teachers at times of emotional crises. College departments of special education must define the particular competency domains they wish to emphasize in order to help build highly differentiated school programs of these kinds.

It should be noted that the concept of instructional system does not use child category language. Rather, the emphasis is on specifying competency domains and specific instructional goals. Allocation of children to specialized instructional systems should be approached openly, with the decision always resting on what is judged to be the best of the available alternatives for each child. One does not start or end with simple categories of children. Similarly, it is proposed that specialized teacher preparation carries labels reflecting the special competency domains rather than the categories of children.

Relations of Special and Regular Education

To the maximum extent possible, of course, special educators seek to develop the attitudes and skills necessary to accommodate pupils' unusual needs within the regular school framework. When it is not possible to achieve the necessary climate and individualization of

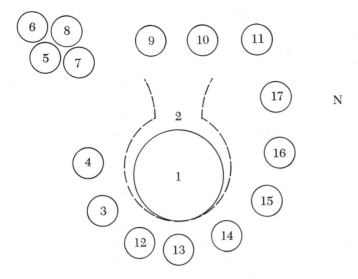

Figure 1. THE RELATIONS OF SPECIAL INSTRUCTIONAL SYSTEMS
(3, 4, 5 . . .N) TO REGULAR EDUCATION (1 AND 2)

instruction in regular classrooms taught by regular teachers, then special arrangements are made. Hopefully, every special educator sees himself as a resource for his entire school and not simply as one who takes his own little group to some isolated room.

In this framework, one can think of special education as an aggregate term covering all specialized forms of instruction that ordinarily cannot be offered by unassisted regular classroom teachers. The relation of "special" and "regular" education may be represented schematically as in Figure 1. The relatively large circle (1) symbolizes the teaching competencies possessed by regular classroom teachers. Competencies vary, of course, but the symbol is useful because regular teachers fall into a kind of modal pattern with respect to the range of their teaching resourcefulness. For example, most regular teachers do not know braille reading methods or the Orton-Gillingham procedures but they are able to teach reading to most children assigned to their classes by using other approaches.

It is incumbent upon special educators to help create as much resourcefulness as possible in regular teachers. The dotted portion (2) of the figure tends to enlarge the first circle (1) and represents the efforts that should be made to extend the specialized abilities and sensitivities of regular teachers. The dotted configuration is left open to indicate continuing consultation with and assistance by specialists. Colleges and universities and special education administrators need to exert themselves to devise and implement ways through which this growth of regular teachers and assistance to them may be accomplished. The major part of this growth will probably have to come through inservice education.

All of the remaining small circles (3, 4, 5 . . . N) are intended to represent special instructional systems that most often are offered by specially trained personnel. These instructional systems tend to fall into certain clusters, suggesting that several of them are likely to be learned and vended by one person. For example, some teachers become quite adept in handling combinations of lipreading, auditory training, fingerspelling, and special systems for language instruction without audition.

Because of the tremendous range of systems or curricula now in existence and likely to emerge in the future, teacher candidates can be equipped to handle only parts of them. Even if teachers could be given an introductory knowledge of all fields, it is patently clear that they could not keep up to date over the years in several such diverse fields as auditory training, braille, and cooperative work-study programs. Thus Schwartz's (1967) proposal to train undergraduates in everything from braille to specialized auditory training seems to go much too far. However, it should not be prejudged that teachers should be limited to a single system or a given number of systems. In accord with an idea launched several years ago in Minneapolis under the leadership of Professor Evelyn Deno, one of the ways in which many exceptional children may be served is by training "general resource teachers," who would be prepared to serve children with a variety of special needs in a team relationship with regular classroom teachers and who would be backed up by a corps of highly specialized consultants traveling around a city or a broad rural region.

The specialized systems or aspects of the school program can and perhaps often should carry labels reflecting their characteristics. Teachers might also carry the label in some cases as, for example, the "orientation and mobility instructor" or the "preschool language teacher."

In stressing systems of instruction, it is not intended that the concern should center exclusively on technicalities of methods and materials for cognitive learning at the expense of affective learning, motivation, or other topics. Nor is it intended in this discussion to diminish the importance of a teacher's clinical skills. All that is possible ought to be done to increase the abilities of all teachers to make detailed educational assessments of children and to follow through with precise educational programs as needed. Similarly, it will be helpful to have all teachers more thoroughly grounded in the psychologies of learning and individual differences.

Allocation of Children to Special Instructional Systems

A key consideration in conceptualizing special education as the aggregate of highly specialized instructional systems is the problem of allocating specific children to the various systems. Allocation can be thought of as a special case of classification, what Cronbach and Gleser (1965) call a "placement" decision. In essence, the placement decision involves maximizing the payoff for individuals within an institu-

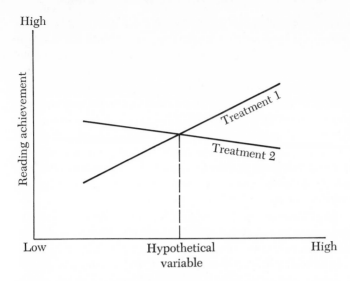

High

Reading achievement

Treatment 1

Treatment 2

Low   Hypothetical   High
variable

Figure 2. INTERSECTING REGRESSION LINES OF READING ABILITY AS PRODUCED BY TWO DIFFERENT TREATMENTS AGAINST A HYPOTHETICAL VARIABLE

tion in which several alternative treatments are available (assuming that all individuals are to be retained, or that no decision for rejection is made). The traditional predictive model of the school is not useful in making the placement or allocation decision and neither is simple categorization by handicaps; rather, educators must learn to interpret variables that produce interaction effects with instructional systems. In other words, children should be placed in special programs on the basis of demonstrated aptitude by treatment interactions (ATI).

Assuming, for example, that two treatments for teaching reading are available, one finds at least ordinal interaction (Bracht & Glass, 1968) when a variable is discovered that produces an intersection of regression lines, as is shown in Figure 2. At about the point of intersection, noted by the dotted line, it would be best to shift from treatment 2, used for pupils scoring low on the hypothetical variable, to treatment 1, used for pupils scoring high on the hypothetical variable. Note especially that it is not zero-order prediction that is important for the placement decision but, rather, the interaction effect. Although this example stresses a quantitative model, the general point of view goes to the philosophical and clinical roots of special education programs. It requires a specification of the alternative educational programs and a careful choice among them—not according to simple predictions or categories of children, but according to variables that help to make the necessary decisions.

The logic of the approach is quite different from now commonly used procedures which tend to depend upon certain broad-band variables such as IQ or decibel loss in the speech range to make placement decisions. To put this another way, variables that produce similar slants of regression lines for all approaches do not help to choose *between* approaches. When we have learned to specify the variables that should be used in allocating children to special programs we will, of course, have something quite unlike the present simple systems of categories of exceptional children.

There is a great need for research that shows how aptitudes and instructional systems can be joined optimally in educating exceptional children (Reynolds, 1963). A limited beginning has been made on the extensive work necessary to clarify relationships between the many possible educational treatments and aptitudes, or personological variables, suspected to be of consequence in educating the handicapped. Bracht (1969) has reviewed 90 ATI studies, and contributed an additional one of his own, of which few were specifically concerned with the handicapped. Only 5 of the 90 studies met his criteria for acceptable evidence on which to prescribe differential treatments for different subjects based on subject aptitudes. While interpretations of these studies could be made for handicapped children, none actually used handicapped children as subjects. Of the 85 with ordinal results (which are not fully satisfactory, statistically speaking) or with no results, 5 included handicapped children in their samples. Two studies utilized emotionally disturbed children and the remaining 3 were concerned with the mentally retarded.

In general, Bracht found that factorially complex measures, such as IQ, which correlate substantially with achievement were unlikely to produce differential performance among alternative treatments on achievement tasks. In his judgment, the more likely areas of payoff are to be found among specific abilities, personality, interest, and background status variables. Following their extensive review of research on ATI, however, Cronbach and Snow (1969) were somewhat more optimistic about the possibility that broad-band ability measures might produce interactions with educational treatments. Indeed they cited suggestive evidence that general intelligence produces more regressional slant with rough or scrambled instruction than with smooth (small, carefully sequenced steps) educational programs (Cartwright, 1971), also that methods requiring overt responding may show less correlation with general intelligence than those involving only covert responding.

The famous Illinois efficacy study of programs for educable mentally retarded children also produced an apparent interaction effect between IQ and educational placement (regular class vs. special class, using the Illinois curriculum guide and teachers prepared in the University of Illinois plan in the special classes) (Goldstein, Moss, Jordan, 1965). An intersection of regression lines occurred at about IQ 80, suggesting that children below IQ 80 achieved academically at a superior level when in the special curriculum while those with IQ's above 80 were better off in the regular program. A major challenge to special educators is to design educational programs which do not depend heavily on general intelligence and to apply them to children low in such general ability.

Studies completed at the University of Minnesota by Arnold (1965), Dietrich (1967), and Shears (1970) are beginning to illustrate the general approach necessary to identify effective differential treatments for children who are homogeneous on a specific relevant aptitude variable. The Arnold study (1965) grew out of a two-part study by Burt and Lewis (1946), in which slow learning children (IQ 76 to 83) were taught reading via alphabetic, kinesthetic, phonic, visual, and mixed methods. Over a 12-month period there were significant differences among teaching methods (treatments), but, perhaps surprisingly in view of Bracht's conclusions, differences in age, sex, and social class were not significant. Although not tested statistically, the data suggested that the visual method was most effective and the phonic method least for these slow learners.

Arnold (1965) chose a sample of adjudicated delinquents who were poor readers and grouped them for age, IQ, and word pronunciation level. Unfortunately, the groups were not especially homogenous in actuality. Four reading treatments were applied to each boy: visual, auditory, kinesthetic, and combination following a double change-over design which allowed for assessment of direct effects of treatments. Overall, the kinesthetic treatment was least effective, with only small differences noted among other treatments. IQ differences among groups seemed to make little difference in outcome, while initial reading level was highly important. Unfortunately, in the search for interactions between treatments and group characteristics, no interactions were found although wide individual differences were noted in the data. Some individuals learned essentially the same amount by each of the four treatments, but others learned twice as much with one treatment as another.

Studying the effects of task and reinforcement variables on the performance of behaviorally disordered children, Dietrich (1967) analyzed her data by subject's behavioral type (conduct problem, personality problem, inadequacy-immaturity) for simple and complex tasks which were neutral or emotional in content, with verbal or material reinforcement to the learner. Her design also called for all subjects to receive all treatments, allowing direct, controlled comparisons of the effects of different treatments on different aptitudes.

Each of the behavior groups showed differences in performance patterns under the various treatments. On the simple task, which showed the greatest differences between treatments, the conduct problem and inadequate-immature groups performed best when given material reinforcement on emotional content. These groups showed relatively poor ability to attend to verbal and social cues and appeared to profit from a situation with maximum arousal value. However, quite by contrast, the personality problem group performed best when given verbal reinforcement on emotional content. This group appeared to reflect considerable sensitivity to feedback from the immediate environment.

Shears (1970) studied American Indian kindergarten children living on a reservation for aptitude by treatment interactions involving readiness level, visual and auditory treatments, and basal reader and familiar words. As in the Arnold and Dietrich studies, all subjects received all treatments in a double change-over design. Readiness level was the personological variable of concern in this study, with two treatments and two types of teaching material manipulated for possible interactions.

The results of Shears' experimentation showed, as expected, that low readiness children performed much less well than the middle and high readiness groups. More importantly, the familiar words were much more readily learned, particularly among low readiness children. However, while the visual method was significantly better for the low readiness group, there were no other treatment differences.

Cronbach and Snow (1969) cited an early finding in a program of studies by Stallings and Snow (unpublished) which is especially intriguing. Individual scales of the *Illinois Test of Psycholinguistic Abilities* (ITPA) appeared to produce interactions with alternative methods of initial reading instruction. For example, ITPA Scale No. 8 (Auditory Sequencing) appeared to "correlate" positively with look-say methods and negatively with phonic methods.

In each of these studies, the interactions between pupil characteristics, teaching methods, and material suggest that the teacher would be more or less effective depending on the decisions he made to match the teaching system to the pupil. The interactions in most studies are no better than ordinal, meaning that a treatment may have been better for one aptitude group at a statistically significant level, but was not necessarily supplanted by some other treatment, also statistically significant, for a group showing different personological characteristics. Thus, while a great deal of clinical and partial experimental support exists for the ATI philosophy expressed here, the experimental statistical proof remains to be more fully demonstrated.

It should perhaps be reiterated that the view of special education proposed here says little about administrative structure. The preceding discussion does not suggest that special education goes on only in special classes or other separated centers. On the contrary, the view espoused here is that "special" instruction should be conducted whenever possible in regular classes and otherwise with as little separation of children from normal school, home, and community life as possible. Many special systems of instruction can and should be offered by well oriented regular teachers or through team arrangements of specialists and regular educators.

Implications

In summary, it is suggested that we try to be more explicit about what special education is. The concept of specialized instructional systems is proposed as an approach to such a definition. It is also suggested that we study children in terms of variables that aid in making allocation or placement decisions within a highly differentiated school system. The identification of such variables requires research demonstrating aptitude-treatment interactions. This concept of special education and of placement processes radically revises present views of "categories" of children. It focuses attention on variables that produces interaction effects with alternative treatment systems rather than on simple descriptions or surface aspects of handicaps; it calls for a detailed educational definition of our programs and procedures.

If this proposed transformation in views is undertaken, instructional systems and teachers may need special labels, such as the lipreading program, the braille teaching laboratory, the crisis teacher, or the engineered classroom. However, children will not need to carry stigmatic labels or be considered defective, impaired, or disabled simply because the educational procedures needed are unusual.

In administratively organizing school programs, we should maximize the resourcefulness of regular classroom personnel by using teams of teachers and specialists, upgrading regular and special teacher training, and using resource rooms, for example, rather than using segregation systems for pupils. However, even with extraordinary efforts, some specialized facilities will nevertheless continue to be needed and it is no service to handicapped children to argue for a precipitous shutdown of all special schools and special classes. The pivotal concern should be the improvement of regular school programs as a resource for exceptional pupils and not the abrupt demise of any administrative arrangement.

Training programs for teachers and other educators of the handicapped should be made specific to instructional systems rather than to categories of children. In other words, we should train and identify teachers by their competencies rather than as teachers of the "blind" or "learning disabled." Training programs for ancillary decision makers, such as school psychologists, should be radically revised to provide explicit orientation to educational systems.

State and local regulations and procedures for special education should be centered on special programs and the people who conduct them, rather than on categories of children. School systems should be offered financial incentives to install several alternative systems for the teaching of reading or more open general approaches to curriculum, for example, rather than processes for the identification of learning disabled children. Leadership personnel in special education should center their efforts on improving the programs, rather than on regulating the boundaries of the categories of children.

Special education should shift major attention to ways of inserting itself back into mainstream educational structures. The legislation, the "earmarks," and the special bureaucracies produced over the past decade have made their point in strong fashion; but, in the process, special educators have failed to win the leadership and concern of most progressive leaders in general education. Categorical aids should be used to build special education into broad programs rather than to build separate systems and to excuse general educators from concern with the handicapped.

It is a distraction from the main issues to argue about who is to be blamed for the difficult educational problems of some children. It is no more sensible to argue the extreme case of teacher failure than the case that a child with problems is defective or inferior. It is analogous to the fruitless nature versus nurture debates. Neither does it add anything to say simply that both child and teacher are involved. What we must do is to understand the problems and deal with them in terms of the child in a specific environment as arranged by the teacher. Discussions that fall short of that level are mere rhetoric or emotion. The arguments presented here involve focus on specific child and situation interactions and not on child, system, or teacher failures.

Hopefully, the points of view espoused here, if implemented, could serve to take us in the direction of individualized early placement for pupils so that they need not experience long periods of failure before specialized resources are provided. Thus, perhaps we can gradually learn ways for removing the degrading terminology now applied to children simply because their education is proceeding badly. They will have been placed in special programs not because they have failed or because they are impaired, but simply because that is the most promising educational situation for them.

The legislative structure that undergirds special education is drawn in language that stresses categories or surface variables. Perhaps that is inevitable and certainly not unique. In health, for example, much legislation is drawn in general terms such as heart, stroke, mental health, or cancer; but program development does not proceed in such simple categories. Similarly, in special education we may be able to live with social-action groups and legislation organized according to simple categorical language, but we should not let programs and children be confined by such language. The late Ray Graham used to advise special educators to drive ahead in program development and to let legislative changes come when necessary to validate new approaches. There is great need now for action in special education that stretches legislation and concepts of the past to include new meanings and more flexible programs.

REFERENCES

ARNOLD, R. D. A comparison of four methods of teaching word recognition among adjudicated delinquents with reading disability. Unpublished colloquium paper, University of Minnesota, 1965.

BRACHT, G. H. The relationship of treatment tasks, personological variables, and dependent variables to aptitude-treatment interactions. Unpublished doctoral dissertation, University of Colorado, 1969.

BRACHT, G. H. & GLASS, G. V. The external validity of experiments. *American Educational Research Journal* 5 (1968): 437-74.

BURT, C. & LEWIS, R. B. Teaching backward readers. *British Journal of Educational Psychology* 16 (1946): 116-32.

CARTWRIGHT, G. P. The relationship between sequences of instructional and mental abilities of retarded children. *American Educational Research Journal* 1 (1971): 143-50.

CRONBACH, L. J. & GLESER, G. C. *Psychology tests and personal decisions.* 2nd ed. Urbana: University of Illinois Press, 1965.

CRONBACH, L. J. & SNOW, R. E. *Final report: Individual differences in learning ability as a function of instructional variables.* (Contract No. OEC 4-6-061269-1217, US Office of Education) Stanford, Cal.: School of Education, Stanford University, 1969.

DIETRICH, C. The differential effects of task and reinforcement variables on the performance of emotionally disturbed children. Unpublished doctoral dissertation, University of Minnesota, 1967.

GOLDSTEIN, H.; MOSS, J. W.; & JORDAN, L. J. The efficacy of special class training on the development of mentally retarded children. Cooperative Research Project No. 619. ERIC Document 002-907, US Office of Education, 1965.

REYNOLDS, M. C. A strategy for research. *Exceptional Children* 29 (1963): 213-19.

SCHWARTZ, L. An integrated teacher education program for special education—A new approach. *Exceptional Children* 33 (1967): 411-16.

SHEARS, B. T. Aptitude, content, and method of teaching word recognition with young American Indian children. Unpublished doctoral dissertation, University of Minnesota, 1970.

ZUBIN, J. Classification of the behavior disorders. In P. R. Farmsworth, O. McNemer, & O. McNemar, eds. *Annual review of psychology.* Palo Alto, Calif.: Annual Reviews, Inc. 1967. Pp. 373-406.

Maynard C. Reynolds is Professor of Special Education, University of Minnesota, Minneapolis; and, at the time this article was published, Bruce Balow was Director, Division of Training Programs, Bureau of Education for the Handicapped, Department of Health, Education, and Welfare, Washington, D.C., on leave from the University of Minnesota.

48.
The Categorical/Non-Categorical Issue: Implications for Teacher Trainers
OLIVER L. HURLEY

Many adjustments in teacher preparation are being made as a result of the issue discussed in this article. What are the major impacts of this issue as viewed by Hurley?

When one thinks of the preparation of Special Education teachers, there are four questions to which he must attend. The four questions are:

1. What are the areas of knowledge with which the teacher must be equipped?
2. What kind of experiences does the prospective teacher require?
3. In each of the areas of knowledge and experience what would be ideal?
4. In each of these areas what is practicable and possible?

I

The question of feasibility or possibility is important but I think reality should enter the picture only after decisions have been made concerning an ideal program. Compromises usually have to be made, but the word is compromise, not abdication. Abdication results when we begin by asking about existing rules, regulations, and customs without being concerned with giving students a good education which encompasses what we consider to be necessary for a person to later function competently as a teacher. If we consider the nature of the teacher-pupil transaction, we see that there are two kinds of knowledge a good teacher must have— "supportive" knowledge and "content" knowledge. "Content" knowledge is that which the teacher actively works on, the substance of the teacher-pupil transaction. "Supportive" knowledge is that which determines in what manner he works on that substance.

What is this "supportive" knowledge? First of all, he should have a good working knowledge of child development. He should know intimately the normal course of development as described in numerous texts and studies. He should have a good working knowledge of normal child devel-

From *The Categorical/Non-Categorical Issue: Implications for Teacher Education* (1971): 39-48. Conference Proceedings, University of Missouri-Columbia. Sponsored by the University of Missouri and the Bureau for the Education of the Handicapped, Washington, D.C.

opment because the teacher needs a standard against which to compare the behaviors of his exceptional children. Without a standard there would be a tendency to attribute to the exceptionality many behaviors which are found in the cross-section of normal children. In addition to a firm understanding of normal child development the teacher needs to know in what ways the exceptional child differs from the normal. He needs to fully understand the nature and quality of these differences. At the same time, he should know well the areas of similarity. Thus, as much emphasis should be given to range and distribution as is now given to averages. He should fully understand that we do not know the range of normal variation of many traits. The teacher should be fully cognizant of the fact that although the vast bulk of children develop certain skills in a certain sequence these sequences are not necessarily unchangeable. That is, because the vast majority of children usually develop skill A before they develop skill B, does not always mean a teacher cannot teach skill B before the child has developed skill A. This implies that our research has not yet defined hierarchies of skill development in which each stage is sufficient and necessary for the attainment of the next stage.

A second area of supportive knowledge that the teacher should have involves learning. A teacher should know how children learn; the rules and principles of learning. He should have a good working knowledge of how materials should be presented in order to facilitate learning on the part of the children. He should be conversant with learning research and its practical implications for programming, sequencing and presentation of materials. He should be aware of the many factors which can impair learning on the part of the children—factors which reside not only in the children but also in the materials or their manner of presentation or in the teacher himself. He should be aware of the rules of reinforcement, transfer, discrimination, memory and so on, if he is sincere in wanting to make a "fit" between child and materials. Such knowledge will help the teacher determine why he does certain things at certain times.

Thirdly, the urban teacher should be provided with an understanding of cultural and ethnic differences—made to confront his or her stereotypes. The sociological variables and their possible impact on learning, on linguistics, and on life styles need to be appreciated, if not fully understood, by our prospective teachers of the retarded.

Next, in order for learning to take place in any classroom, the children must pay attention. The means that the teacher needs techniques of behavior management. Since he is working with a class, he needs to know something about group dynamics and the manipulation of groups. He needs to be equipped with a repertoire of techniques with which he can manage surface behavior and be consistent while doing it.

The areas of knowledge discussed up to this point are some of those which impinge upon the teacher-pupil transaction but do not make up the substance of it. No attempt has been made to delineate the specific sub-competencies. They are areas of knowledge which, if intelligently utilized, enhance the teacher-pupil interaction. This should result in more effective learning on the part of the child because on the part of the teacher there would be more effective presentation. If the teacher is not well-grounded in these areas then what information will he use to plan his course of study or to evaluate what he is doing or materials he is using. We must provide them with a frame of reference which resides in a theoretical and philosophical attitude and view of kids and teaching.

Now, what about the substance of the teacher-pupil transaction? A teacher needs to have a very firm foundation and understanding of the structure of the content which he plans to lay before his students. For example, he should know that reading involves more than just getting meaning from the printed page. It also involves factors of memory, auditory and visual sequencing, immediate recognition of letters and so on. He should be fully equipped, in other words, with a knowledge not only of how you teach reading developmentally to children but perhaps more importantly what you do with a child when he fails to learn to read. The same holds true for the other content areas. The teacher should be equipped not only with knowledge of the usual sequence of material presentation, but also with a knowledge of what to do with a child who breaks down at some point in this sequence. (This implies educational diagnosis, remediation—the learning disabilities approach.)

Implied here, of course, is that the teacher know how to teach the various subjects. Beyond subject specific methodology, however, the prospective teacher needs to develop a style which is not subject specific. The style I have reference to is that of inductive teaching. He must not only know how to force the child to make connections between disparate bits of information (i.e., to think), he must also know when inductive teaching is contraindicated in favor of rote or deductive teaching. Minskoff (1967) found that in 20 classes, only 12.5% of the teachers' questions required productive thinking by the children as contrasted with 87.5% requiring cognitive-memory or rote responses. This is a sad state of affairs. We certainly need to teach our teachers how to question so that the children learn how to think.

A teacher needs to know the role of language in cognition, the role of language in learning. Language can play both a facilitative and an inhibiting role in learning. If some children speak, as Bernstein (1961) says, another language, a restricted language, then the teacher may be confronted with a situation of impaired teacher-pupil communication (Hurley, 1967; Minuchin et al., 1968). If the research of Hess and Shipman (1965), Deutsch (1966), Bereiter and Englemann (1966), and others, have any validity in their findings that language is a very important variable in a disadvantaged child's learning, then it seems to me it is at least important for the special teacher to be acquainted with this research and equipped with methods and techniques for overcoming linguistic deficiencies, or coping with language differences.

Now whether the field stays categorical or goes non-categorical, the prospective teacher will still have to have these knowledges and skills. But if the elimination of categories occurs, then we will have to change the way we accomplish the development of these knowledges and skills in prospective teachers as is evident from the many speeches you've already heard. Any teacher I prepare should be a remedial and learning disabilities specialist as well as a behavior management specialist no matter what the handicapping conditions may be. Even though we recognize the heterogeneity of children classified under our current labels, the degree of heterogeneity will increase when those labels are removed. Therefore, it will be even more incumbent on us to train persons capable of solving problems, educational problems.

II

I see the effect of going non-categorical as speeding up some of the directions that teacher-training has taken in recent years, such as micro-teaching, the use of videotape loops, prescriptive teaching, etc. But the major impact will be on program organization. I see it as both intensifying and broadening the practicum experiences required to produce a competent person. I see it leading to the dissolution of the course structure as we now know it.

Before we go further, we should recognize that there are two levels to this issue. On one level we could talk about the elimination of categories within education generally so that special education would concern itself only with the severely and profoundly handicapped youngster (Lilly, 1970; Deno, 1971). On the second level, special education remains relatively intact in terms of its present target populations, but within special education categories are eliminated. It is likely that both of these will occur simultaneously.

Level I is the more extreme of the two for it means the dissolution of the structure called special education as we currently know it. Special education would still exist but only for the most severely handicapped children.

We need to realize that there is little way to uncategorize the deaf or the blind. Teaching braille to the blind or speech-reading or language to the deaf is sufficiently different that these categories will always be with us. However, declassification may force us to find more efficient ways to teach them early so that they can later move into the educational mainstream. Likewise, a visit to any institution for the mentally retarded will convince you of the existence of profoundly impaired children; i.e., children who would stand out in any crowd, children who are 24 hour retardates. I am not too sure what the elimination of the label would do for these children. Eliminating the inhibiting aspects of the medical model would help more. Therefore, the remarks I will make have reference primarily to children now called educable, maladjusted, socially disadvantaged, learning disabilities, brain damaged, physically handicapped, and, to a lesser extent, the hard of hearing and the partially seeing. I will discuss the impact on various areas. These are not discussed in any logical or temporal order or in order of importance. Now, what would it mean to teacher preparation programs if these latter named children were suddenly declassified?

Impact Number 1: Role Redefinition

The first impact will be one of fear, mild panic and crash programs. Once the panic subsided, we would be tested to the utmost. There will be panic since special education developed because regularly trained teachers were unable to manage these youngsters. Therefore, many of us will have to become intensely involved in inservice programs. We will have to re-tool most of our teachers, regular and special. This, in addition to developing a different model for pre-service training. These two will have to go arm-in-arm, for the inservice component will validate the pre-service component and provide the vehicle for input into the system by the consumer. There will be panic because many of us will lose our comfortable jobs at worst. At best, we will have to redefine our roles. Our roles will have to change because we will indeed become part of the structure of regular education. Of course, we will still be needed, but we will have to convince our respective schools of that. The impact of this sort of declassification will reverberate throughout all of the halls of ivy and not just in the special education wing, for teacher training will have to respond with new models for training. In my view, this will be an absolute necessity since the traditional model has not taught teachers how to work with *any* child—only with children operating within a very narrow range of conforming behavior. If the traditional model had worked, we would not be now assembled discussing the category vs. non-category issue.

With the pressure on colleges to produce teachers capable of dealing with reality; that is, capable of working with children who show a wide range of behaviors, we will find that many incompetent teacher trainers will leave or be asked to leave. We will screen ourselves out because the job will become a much tougher one. We should not be able to "hack" it. Dare we speak of the concept of accountability as it applies to the teacher trainer? (I speak here in the collective sense, meaning the entire program at college, as well as of the individual instructor teaching a specific course.) I think that when school systems can no longer "cool the mark out" as Johnson (1969) puts it, through special education categories, they will begin to tell us loud and clear what they think of our products. Indeed, they have already begun to do so; how else can we interpret the mounting number of requests to enter into partnership with the colleges and universities in the preservice training of teachers?

Perhaps, however, there is a way to avoid the necessity for a sudden delabeling, legally mandated; that is, by using our knowledge to make general education more effective and efficient so that the category vs. non-category issue is defused. Deno's (1970) eloquent article in *Exceptional Children* makes this plea. In a recent discussion with a colleague working in a follow-through program using a great deal of programmed instructional materials, individual prescriptions and operant techniques, I heard a startling statement. He said that of all the children in the 14 classes he is working with, approximately 300-350 children, they had been able to reach AND TEACH only 3, a percentage of one per cent. This is 1% in an area where the usual figure ran closer to somewhere between 5% and 10% on a conservative estimate. Not only that, but on preliminary evaluative measures, the group is achieving at a higher rate than the children in some of the nearby highly touted suburban school districts. If these figures hold up in later evaluation, the issue on which we are meeting will become moot. Need I say more? Ghetto schools are not known for their children testing on-grade.

This amounts to a redefining of our roles from one of treatment to one of prevention. As Deno (1970) says:

The special education system is in a unique position to serve as development capital in an overall effort to upgrade the effectiveness of the total public education effort (p. 231).

She proposed, as I am—and I do not see any other alternative—that "special education conceive of itself primarily as an instrument for facilitation of educational change and development of better means of meeting the learning needs of children . . ." (p. 229); that we organize ourselves to provide a continuum of services in such a way that children are isolated from their peers only to the extent necessary—not beyond. Hewitt's work in Santa Monica surely demonstrated the viability of this notion.

Since we recognize that we deal with the failures of the educational system, we cannot decategorize unless we get involved in the whole system and not just special education. It means widening our horizons and the demise of our insularity. I can't stress this too much. For example, the September 1970 issue of the *Phi Delta Kappan* was devoted to eight of the major issues in general education.

State and professional licensure of educational personnel; reconstruction of teacher education and professional growth programs; accreditation of schools; the meaning and application of performance criteria in teacher education, certification, and professional growth; the meaning and application differentiated staff in teaching; the profession's quest for responsibility and accountability; and the developing program of self-determinism in Canada (Stinnett, p. 3).

I have failed to find any substantive discussion analogous to the PDK discussion of these issues in the Special Education literature; yet it is a truism that the resolution, in whole or in part, of the issues in general education will have an influence on special education. Nevertheless, we persist in inadequately discussing them. In fact, I would venture to say, hoping

I'm wrong but fearing I'm right, that most are not even acquainted with the dimensions of the arguments in the current controversies. This is insularity!

The point is that we must begin to involve ourselves in the world of education generally and contribute to the education of all children. We can't complain about the output if we don't attempt to provide some input.

Impact Number 2: New Models

If we do redefine ourselves, we will recognize an even more pressing need for the development of new teacher-training models. This search has already begun in elementary education (ERIC Clearinghouse on Teacher Education, AACTE, 1969) and in Special Education (BEH is currently supporting 30 special projects). Lilly (1970) mentions others. However, decategorization would necessitate the coming-together of these efforts, for, unfortunately, elementary education tends to neglect special education in its conceptualizations. Certainly, a plan such as Hewitt's (1971) Madison Plan will require a new or different training model.

No matter what model is arrived at, I think it will incorporate a great deal more experiences in the classroom and in the community. The schools have already begun to tell us that our graduates are not good enough. Of course, parents have been telling us that for some time: newly minted teachers are not renowned for their expertise in pedagogy. One direction we have discussed in the East is the reciprocal adoption of public school and college or university. The schools are asking us to move our training program into the schools. If we're willing, we will be assigned one or two schools where we will do all of our training of both regular and special teachers. Now, the implications are staggering. In effect, we will become the supervisors of instruction for that school. If our students are there daily and our courses are taught there, we must be there daily. We thus assume responsibility for upgrading the existing staff as well as for training our students. Universities will have to reward this labor as well as they reward publication if it is going to work, for there will be little time left for research and writing, although I recognize the need for evaluation and planning so data can be collected. Of course, with a permanent staff of students, we can arrange workshops, seminars, demonstrations, etc. for the teachers, since the students can fill in. And these will be necessary, for the teachers will have to be brought up to date, retrained and introduced to new ideas. Not only that, we will have to often prove that what we suggest will work. This means demonstrating and taking over classes; becoming a clinical professor, as Conant termed it. Most of us do a little of this but not to the extent that would be demanded in such an arrangement. It implies all of the interpersonal relations problems and a closer alliance with those in regular education. Some systems in my part of the country are already asking for this: are *we* ready for it? I hope they are asking for it from a sincere desire to improve teacher competence and not from a wish to decrease costs of substitutes and supervisors. No matter which, I view this as an awesome responsibility.

This is only one model. Recent authors (Deno, 1970; Lilly, 1970; Nelson & Schmidt, 1971) suggest other possible models or directions for special education. There are many others.

Impact Number 3: New Skills

As previously mentioned, most programs produce teachers equipped to deal with children who fall within a very narrow range of behavior. When the children differ culturally, physically, or in cognitive style, most of our teachers are unable to cope. They have been taught, consciously or unconsciously, that when they fail, special education is there to make things right. In fact, we might say that where there is failure, it is usually the child's fault—so we are taught—not ours. Our teachers, by and large, have not been supplied the skills which would prevent failure. These special education would now have to supply, for I believe that if we equip our trainees with the requisite skills, many of the negative attitudes toward "non-spontaneous learners" (Deno, 1970) will take care of themselves. What are some of these skills? I mentioned some of them earlier.

First, there are the necessary skills in behavioral management and classroom management. We seem to be much more successful in training new teachers in this respect than we are in retraining old ones. Old attitudes, not so useful philosophies, and inhibiting stereotypes get in the way. We will have to devise effective and efficient ways of retraining. Perhaps the school-university partnership may provide the lever and fate control necessary for effecting behavioral change in teachers.

Second, we will have to provide our students with alternatives. I am yearly amazed by teachers I meet who seem to think that there is only one way to teach reading or one way to teach math. We will be required, even more than now, to provide our trainees with alternatives so that individual differences can indeed be met.

Closely allied to this is the development of the skill of educational diagnosis. That is, each teacher will need more than ever the ability to plan and carry out a systematic formal and informal educational diagnosis of abilities and disabilities and to plan for children according to their individual profiles. In my estimation this will mean reversing our present order of things. At present, most training programs focus on the "how" of teaching, some fewer also emphasize the "what," but very few emphasize the "why." The "why," that is the theory, is more often the province of doctoral programs. But how can one become a good diagnostician without a firm grasp of what it is one is looking for and why; i.e., of theory. With this firm theoretical base as a guide and a thorough understanding of the development of children, materials become a tool and not a course of study.

None of these skills can be developed without adequate practice. These are the skills that special educators are supposed to have. These are the skills to be shared with non-special education teachers.

Impact No. 4: Practica

If the school-university partnership idea takes hold, then much will be accomplished; I see various real or simulated experiences as the hub from which curriculum, methodology, techniques, materials, behavior management, characteristics, educational diagnosis can all flow. But more is needed, namely, observational videotapes which have heuristic value. Each of us should develop a set of these videotape loops which portray the uniqueness of children, the range of behavior, good teacher-pupil transactions, poor teacher-pupil transactions, behavior management techniques, etc. I say each of us should develop our own loops because the classes should be available for visitation, for work. Thus we could further ensure a variety of experiences for our trainees, and fully implement the idea of performance criteria.

In addition to viewing tapes and working in the "lab" school, the prospective teacher can be involved in micro-teaching situations. The student is assigned a topic or lesson to teach to a group of 4 or 5 children brought to the college for this purpose. The lesson is taped. Then supervisor and student and classmates can view it together, critique it, suggest improvements. Then the student can try it again. What better way to teach a student how to teach inductively? What better way to reinforce ideas of hierarchical sequencing of content? What better way to discover differences and similarities than by using the same lesson across various groups of children of varying degrees of handicaps, or by attempting the same procedures with larger or smaller groups (Peterson, Cox, and Bijou, 1971).

While we are doing all of these things within general education, we will still have to train our specialists for the severely handicapped. I do not think, however, that we will continue to need all the special courses we now have. I think that from a differential practica, and the questions and discussions which will arise in seminar, we will be able to produce teachers able to work with the severely atypical child.

If this is to work, the teacher-trainer will have to be with the student almost continually, otherwise the heuristic value of the experiences will be lost. This is why I like the public school lab school idea, for it will provide greater degrees of freedom. One day a week or every 2 weeks won't do it if we are to serve as "developmental capital" (Deno, 1970).

III

These, then, are some of the implications for me of the categorical issue:

a. Intense involvement in inservice and preservice training of all teachers.

b. Intensification and broadening of practical real and simulated.

c. A dissolution of the course structure as we know it.

One comment! I don't think that the issue is categorization. I think the issue is one of the form of the delivery of services. If, however, we concern ourselves with the training of teachers and transmit to them the expertise found in Special Education and help in improving the efficiency of general education, this question will become moot. If we do not de-insularize ourselves, I predict the re-institution of special classes very quickly and a more severe hardening of the categories. In this respect, if special classes for the mildly handicapped are dissolved, we had better be ready to forego for a time our research pleasures and provide the help both the children and the receiving teachers will need, albeit it is research needed. We will have to supply the crisis help. Otherwise we will have chaos and more failure.

Another comment! We are dealing with attitudes. The attitude that a child has integrity and I will teach him no matter what symptoms he shows, a willingness to ignore whatever labels have been attached, a need *not* to know his label, but a need to know his assets and weaknesses and take it from there, an experimental attitude, an attitude of accountability to self for a child's failure to learn.

This is not hard to mold in new trainees. It is indeed very difficult to develop in older teachers who don't have it. They tend to be from Missouri—we will have to show them.

What all this means to me as a trainer is a great deal more work. Setting up a program from a problem-solving point of view requires the agonizing process of developing competency based modules, much more careful selection of classes for taping, a very careful and continuing development of tapes which will serve as the catalyst for the discussion of topics we now discuss in the abstract; obviously, a screening of these topics, for we can cover a great deal more in lecture than we would in this set-up, the logistical problems of getting children for the micro-teaching activities and the programming of students through them, the training of critic teachers and their selection, and so on. Nevertheless, if we wish to turn out teachers competent to teach a broad spectrum of children, we will have to arm them with an arsenal of knowledge, techniques, and experiences—an arsenal of alternatives.

REFERENCES

BEREITER, C. and ENGLEMANN, S. *Teaching Disadvantaged Children in the Preschool.* Englewood Cliffs, N.J.: Prentice-Hall, 1966.

BERNSTEIN, B. Social class and linguistic development: a theory of social learning, pp. 188-214. In A. H. Halsey, Jean Floud, and C. A. Anderson, eds. *Education, Economy, and Society.* New York: Free Press, 1961.

DENO, E. Special education as developmental capital. *Exceptional Children* 37 (1970): 229-37.

DEUTSCH, M. Nursery education: the influence of social programming on early development, pp. 145-53. In J. L. Frost and G. R. Hawkes, eds. *The Disadvantaged Child: Issues and Innovations* (1st Ed.). Boston: Houghton Mifflin, 1966.

ERIC Clearinghouse on Teacher Education. *A Reader's Guide to the Comprehensive Models for Preparing Elementary Teachers*. Washington, D.C.: AACTE, 1969.

HESS, R. D. and SHIPMAN, V. Early blocks to children's learning. *Children* 12 (1965): 189-94.

HEWITT, F. with E. R. BLUM. The Madison Plan as an alternative to special class placement: an interview with Frank Hewitt. CEC ERIC'S The Now Way to Know. *The Educational and Training of the Mentally Retarded* 6 (1971): 29-42.

HURLEY, O. L. Teacher language: key to learning? *The Education and Training of the Mentally Retarded* 2 (1967): 127-33.

JOHNSON, J. L. Special education and the inner city: a challenge for the future or another means for cooling the mark out? *Journal of Special Education* 3 (1969): 241-51.

LILLY, M. S. Special education: A teapot in a tempest. *Exceptional Children* 37 (1970): 43-49.

MINSKOFF, E. H. An analysis of the teacher-pupil verbal interaction in special classes for the mentally retarded. Final Report. U. S. Department of HEW, Office of Education, Project No. 6-8092, Yeshiva University, 1967.

MINUCHIN, S.; MONTALVO, B.; GUERNEY, B. G. JR.; ROSEMAN, B. L.; and SCHUMER, F. *Families of the Slums: An Exploration of Their Structure and Treatment*. New York: Basic Books, 1967.

NELSON, C. C. and SCHMIDT, L. J. The question of the efficacy of special classes. *Exceptional Children* 37 (1971): 381-84.

PETERSON, R. F.; COX, M. A.; and BIJOU, S. W. Training children to work productively in classroom groups. *Exceptional Children* 37 (1971): 491-507.

STINNETT, T. Recording goals and roles: an introduction. *Phi Delta Kappan* 52 (1970): 1-3.

Oliver L. Hurley is Associate Professor, University of Georgia.

49.
Accountability in Special Education
GLENN A. VERGASON

What valuable contributions might we expect from the employment of the principles of accountability? Do you see any negative or undesirable consequences?

There are probably as many theories on the development of the concept of accountability in education as there have been writings on the subject in the last 2 years. One who reads the literature soon finds that scarcely any other topic in the history of education has been so explosive, has spread so far so rapidly, or has been more universally accepted by parents, taxpayers, and legislators. Accountability is a topic which places fear in the hearts of teachers and administrators, fear on the part of many that the public school system cannot survive the present crisis. Lessinger (1971) attributed to Congress the asking of the questions and the pushing for the hard data which resulted in the accountability movement.

Lessinger was requested to prove that Title I of ESEA had worked, and when the US Office of Education could not produce adequate proof, Congress mandated evaluation systems in Titles VII and VIII of ESEA. Lessinger developed many of his ideas in his book, *Every Child a Winner* (1970). Lessinger maintained he was not responsible for accountability but was the implementer of accountability, as intended by Congress, in the Texarkana project. The Texarkana project was a performance contract initiated between the Texarkana School District and a private firm (Dorsett) for the improvement of reading and math skills of potential dropouts. The full request for proposals (RFP) for this project, published in *Educational Technology* (1970), can give the reader a good idea of what performance contracting is all about.

Lessinger attributed to parents a strong role in the support of the concept of accountability. Without parents' and/or taxpayers' support, this concept like many others would have been a fad which quickly faded away. The base of support for accountability is too broad to be soon lost. The Gallup poll (Gallup, 1970) indicated that 76 percent of the public wanted principals and teachers to be more accountable for the learning of children.

From *Exceptional Children* 39 (February, 1973): 367-73. Reprinted by permission of the author and *Exceptional Children*. Copyrighted by the Council for Exceptional Children.

This article is adapted from a presentation at the CEC Conference on "Emerging Models of Special Education for Sparsely Populated Areas," Memphis, Tennessee, December 3, 1971.

At this writing as many as 13 legislatures have or are in the process of passing laws relative to accountability. Currently, there are three bills before the Georgia General Assembly dealing with the topics of teacher competency and accountability of teachers.

What Makes Up an Accountability Program?

The definition and rules of the game are fairly simple. Accountability means the schools will be held accountable for producing results. Lessinger (1971) stated, "Accountability is a regular public report by independent reviewers of demonstrated student accomplishment promised for the expenditure of resources [p. 73]." No longer is it acceptable to say that, because of the child's environment, his poor genes, his lack of motivation, or his father's not being in the home, the child cannot learn or it is his fault or his parents' fault that he does not learn. Schools are called upon to teach every child, to make every child a winner, and to offer schools without failure. Thus, the first element of a program of accountability is for schools to state what their objectives are and to have their success judged by how well they reach these goals. Second, schools are called upon to have an outside or independent audit. This concept does not imply that a private corporation must test every child to see if the teacher has done his job. It may mean an outside observer sees what is done, attests to its accuracy, and lastly makes sure the results are published. Many schools have assessed and evaluated programs for years, but they never reported to the public their areas of strength or weakness or their plans for improvement.

How does the practice of performance contracting relate to accountability? Performance contracting is a technique which has been used to test one facet of accountability. It involves contracting with a group or company to increase the performance of children in specified areas which are deemed by the school system as needing remediation above and beyond what teachers can accomplish in the regular system. Performance contracting comes from the field of engineering. The building contractor is required to produce a certain amount of work on a building within a given period of time. If he does not produce the expected amount of work, he is penalized. In education the performance contractor is expected to produce a specified amount of gain in achievement, attitude, or some other dimension or be penalized.

How Do Performance Contracts Work?

A performance contract is stated in a manner which makes it appear that the contractor "guarantees performance." The contractor agrees that unless the students in his program gain a specified amount he will not be paid. If the contract calls for each underachiever in reading to gain 1.4 grade levels in 9 months of school, the contractor is not paid unless the child reaches that level or is paid a percentage if the child reaches a lower level of success. What most persons fail to realize is that if 75 out of 150 students in a program do not reach the 1.4 grade level improvement and if the contractor is not paid for 75 students, he does not lose his shirt. Performance contracts call for the contractor to receive payment for setting up the program, for delivery of hardware (teaching machines), and for software (teaching programs). The hardware and software items come at higher prices in a performance contract than the school system would ordinarily pay for the same equipment or program off the self. What school systems are paying for is the management system, training, and efforts beyond what can be exerted through reorganization of available resources.

Is Performance Contracting Legal?

There is some question as to the legality of performance contracting (Martin & Blaschke, 1971), but this should not concern the field. If performance contracting is successful in the long run, the laws assigning educational responsibility to local school boards will be changed. The performance contract negotiated in the Texarkana School District was the first time a public school contracted with a private firm to provide academic instruction, the first use of performance contracting within a public school system, and the first use of a management support group.

Whether performance contracting will survive or not is unknown at this time. Those persons who are most knowledgeable in the field say performance contracting is transitory, but that accountability will be with us from now on.

Performance contracting, however, can be used as one method for obtaining curricular and software development so that more adequate materials and programs can be made available for schools. Some observations indicate that publishers involved in performance contracts have discovered that their programs were poorly sequenced and lacked data on the success of the programs with all except normal and accelerated learners. Such discoveries on the part of publishers might prevent many poorly tested materials from getting on the market and lead to an accountability for publishers.

Performance contracts cannot be relied upon to solve the problems of all school systems because there are just not that many companies. However, changes have already occurred in systems using performance contracts. The Dallas school system designated the teachers for the performance contract or, wrote the objectives, and maintained complete control over the performance contract. Dallas used the performance contractor to develop the skills, materials, training procedures, and management system to "turnkey" one of the programs into other schools where regular teachers and others are now applying the techniques (Estes, 1971). The "turnkey" concept is important for it provides a way of experimenting and then implementing programs into the mainstream. At present many schools innovate, but few successfully incorporate new programs into their systems. Frieden (1971) indicated that the only long range benefit to schools using private firms is that they act as a catalyst to effect changes in their operation.

Philadelphia has gone the next step, using the same principles employed by private firms in performance contracting to set up a program within the school system. Teachers and administrators agreed upon a goal of the attainment of a 5.5 reading level by all pupils before entry into the sixth grade. The program involved extensive training of the teachers, the provision for use of up to 40 different reading approaches, and the addition of materials.

Further developments in performance contracting have occurred in Cherry Creek, Colorado, where the Board of Education through support from the Colorado State Department of Education, has contracted with "I Teams" of their own teachers for specified results. The system has contracted with groups of teachers to work with the educationally handicapped, potential dropouts, and most recently with emotionally disturbed children to integrate them into regular classrooms (Mecklenburger & Wilson, 1971). It may be that the freedom of organization and the added incentive of rewards and recognition cause some teachers to change their own expectancies. Since the initial preparation of this article the Office of Economic Opportunity (OEO) has announced the results of its extensive testing of performance contracting in 18 cities. OEO had placed great hope, faith, and over 7.2 million dollars into proving performance contracting would work. The recent announcement concluded, "The results of the experiment clearly indicates that the firms operating under performance contracts did not perform significantly better than the more traditional school system [Winter, 1972, p. 1]."

Effects on Special Education

Special education is a part of regular education and as such must be concerned with the same efficiency and effectiveness issues. Special educators must also be concerned with the attitudes and actions of its publics. Special educators can no longer assume that because it is special education it is good for everyone. Special education cannot rely on the sympathy of legislators and others but must produce hard data on its successes and failures. Special classes with inadequately prepared teachers and with little in the way of materials or techniques which would make them special or stimulating cannot be tolerated. Placement in special classes or programs must be carefully monitored. Just as educators have advocated individualized curriculum, so special educators must advocate an individualized placement and programing for each child.

Little has been done in the way of performance contracting or the application of accountability to special education until recently. It may be that special education is the most accountable part of the American school or maybe special educators convinced everyone else that only special education could handle some children. In any event, only two projects have been located. The Grand Rapids Public Schools (Whitecraft, 1973) has a performance contract under a Title III grant with educable mentally retarded students. The other project is operated by the Duval County Schools in Jacksonville, Florida, and is entitled "Accountability Model for TMR Programs."

Legal Actions

Some accountability actions in special education have taken the form of legal actions. In cases such as *Arreola vs. Board of Education* the court ruled parents must be informed and have a part in their child's placement. In *Corarrubias vs. San Diego Unified School District* and *Stewart vs. Phillips* there are elements of punitive damages being sought by the plaintiff for children being mislabeled. Educators who have tended to ignore court decisions should pay attention to these cases because dollar judgments could be made against administrators and school systems (Ross, De Young, & Cohen, 1971). In the case of *Diana vs. State Board of Education,* filed in North District Court of California in behalf of 9 Mexican Americans, the petition claimed the children were incorrectly placed in special education. This action should not be a surprise to special educators when 26.3 percent of the children in special classes had Spanish surnames while the same group made up only 13 percent of the school population. As a result of this suit, the court ruled that (a) children whose primary home language is other than English must be tested in both their primary language and English, (b) such children must be tested only with tests or parts of tests that do not rely heavily on items such as vocabulary or unfair verbal questions, (c) Mexican and Chinese Americans already in programs must be retested, (d) each district must submit a plan for retesting and reevaluating all children on a systematic basis, and (e) a plan for special supplemental individual training must be provided to help each child back into the regular school classes.

Another case with great implications is that of the *Pennsylvania Association for Retarded Children, Nancy Beth Bowman, et al. vs. Commonwealth of Pennsylvania, David H. Kurtzman, et al.* The decrees finalized by the court on May 3, 1972, in this case stated that school districts:

1. May not postpone or in any way deny to any mentally retarded child free access to a program of public education and training.

2. May not deny home instruction to any mentally retarded child merely because no physical disability accompanies the retardation or because retardation is not a short-term disability.

3. Shall provide for immediate reevaluation, for reevaluation every year if requested by parent, and for reevaluation of all children at least every 2 years.

4. Must allow each child access to a free public program of education and training appropriate to his learning capacities.
5. Shall provide, no later than September 1, 1972, for the education and training of children less than 6 years of age.
6. Shall secure such proper education and training outside the public schools of the district where it is not possible to form a special class in a district or to provide such education for any child in the public schools of the district.

The implications of the above decree are:

1. Testing or assessment services must be more extensive and more carefully administered, and personnel whose secondary responsibility is testing must be discontinued.
2. Regular reevaluation every 2 years must be instituted and more frequently if requested.
3. Advisory committees must be employed to make placements and judgments based on data reviewed by professional persons. Such actions will be acceptable to the courts. California requires unanimous vote, minutes, statement of policies, etc. (Ross, De Young, & Cohen, 1971).
4. Parents must be involved in placement and should be kept informed on all actions.
5. Failure to provide service for any handicapped child in sparsely settled areas or because of low incidence figures is no longer an acceptable excuse.
6. Claims of adequate services in the regular school programs are no longer acceptable unless services meet the parents' expectations.
7. Keeping students on waiting lists to get into programs is not acceptable.

This ruling implies that: appropriate education and training programs must be available; such programs must meet the approval of the court; and whenever a program is not in existence, it must be provided or provision must be made for education or training in nonpublic schools or other facilities. The Pennsylvania case, when followed by similar cases in other states, will function to kill all exclusion clauses or other attempts to keep even the trainable retarded from having a school program. Note should be taken that the Pennsylvania ruling does not require the closing of special classes or that children must be in regular classes, but it does require the system to demonstrate how and when a regular class placement is not the best plan.

Thus, it is clear that special educators must learn how to function to use the law to meet the needs of children and avoid doing anything against the rights of children or their parents. We should view the legal actions as one form of accountability against "the system" and be cognizant that the next step may be against individual teachers.

Special educators have had difficulty in providing service to certain children with severe problems or to those in low incidence areas. Although intermediate school systems have been successful in some states, there are situations where these will not work to provide a full range of services. It also is difficult to offer service if the number of children exceeds the allowable number in one unit but is insufficient for two units.

For these reasons the writer has given support to a voucher plan for special education. This idea is opposed within regular education since it seems to be full of pitfalls in terms of propagating segregation, of producing an educational elite, and of wasting tremendous educational resources. It could be the potential downfall of public education. Both the NAACP and NEA oppose the voucher plan and all modifications of it. The writer believes some of the dangers associated with voucher plans would not be a problem in special education. A voucher-like plan has been practiced in special education. Parents have been paid $4.00 an hour to secure tutors for homebound youngsters, and states have made allotments to pay for the education of multiply handicapped and blind children in other states. Some systems reimburse parents for transporting their own children.

The voucher plan would be of great assistance to special education in sparsely settled areas and in low incidence areas. It would be necessary for the voucher to cover at least the minimum cost of educating the child in any program. It would not be sufficient for the parent to be granted $800, as the Washington, D.C. schools did to parents of trainable retarded children, when the actual cost of schooling was in excess of $1,600 per year. Such a voucher system would require the parent to be accountable for the education of his child. Thus, if four parents of the deaf went together to start a program for their children, they would be held accountable and their program would be subject to the same evaluation as would any other programs.

Such a voucher program might also serve to facilitate the integration and assimilation of mildly handicapped children in regular schools. If a parent brought his child to a regular school with his voucher and asked if a program could be worked out to meet the child's needs, educators might be surprised to see what teachers and principals would do with $1,600 above and beyond their regular resources. It might change some situations—as where retarded youths are not allowed on the playground at lunch or in the gym at the same time as nonretarded youngsters. The practice of limited use of vouchers in special education might lead to the development of certification of children's handicaps. Psychologists and educators could attend to the child's need for service based upon the parents written request for determination of eligibility. Eligibility would not necessarily require a label, but eligibility would legally earmark funds for program use and development.

The next development will be one step beyond the parent, where interested individuals, CEC chapters, agencies, or others will become the advocates for any handicapped child against a parent, another agency, or even their own agency to bring about adequate services.

Accountability of Administrative Arrangements

Many special educators are now discussing the advantages and disadvantages of resource programs, special classes, and other administrative arrangements. The problems of delivery of services to students may be far more difficult than is generally considered (Bruininks & Rynders, 1971) but the major concern of this article is "who is accountable?" In the special class the answer has been clearly "special education." In the resource plan and programs where students are enrolled in regular classes and are served by supportive special education personnel, the responsibility has been transferred back to mainstream education.

Recommendations for Special Education

Special educators have been affected little in the past by accountability but they will be in the future. Some recommendations seem appropriate if special educators are to approach this in a professional manner.

Schwarz and Cook (1970) found little relationship between what a teacher said were her expectations for a pupil in special education and what the child had accomplished 8 months later. This suggests a need to examine the whole idea of expectancy, teacher planning, the application of behavioral objectives, and how these relate to teacher education.

The second area of concern relates to the use of aides since aides may not increase the quality of instruction as much as they increase the cost per student (Cook & Blessing, 1970). An increase in the number of students under one master teacher with several aides would be a cost effective and cost efficient use of educational resources.

Standardized terminology seems to be one area where the field can be more definitive about its programs. Before long there will be more studies reported in the literature claiming success or lack of success (Vacc, 1972) for resource programs. Articles such as the one by Glavin, Quay, Annesley, and Werry (1971), which describes the Temple Resource Plan, seem desirable. Anyone referring to a Temple Resource program can communicate a set of expectations and an instructional arrangement.

The profession needs to develop what is termed "standard practices." These practices, whether they be in medicine, engineering, or other professions, refer to the most accepted practices for approaching certain situations. Thus a child with certain learning characteristics would have a prescribed program initiated until something better was accepted by the field as the "practice of choice." If the initial practice did not work after a specified time it would be discontinued and the program of second choice initiated.

One of the problems in the country is the excess of special education personnel in some areas while there are scarcities in other parts of the country or even within a state. A voucher system for teachers or some method of moving teachers into other areas should be employed. The voucher would be given to an experienced teacher with the understanding that certain moving expenses and compensations would be forthcoming if he were successfully employed in certain priority areas. Such a procedure would be more economical for the states and the Federal government than educating more teachers.

The quality of special education personnel in some areas needs the accountability concept applied to teachers. The excess of regular teachers in some areas has resulted in regular class teachers moving into special education and this is most true in rural areas. Mandatory special education legislation, which so many states now have, has resulted in a push for special education personnel. Many superintendents have been under pressure for years to secure trained special education teachers but have been unsuccessful. A certified teacher of questionable competency is likely to be hired as a special education teacher, whereas he would not be hired as a regular class teacher.

Through accountability the profession itself should begin to exercise those management and review procedures which will result in improvement of those in the profession. It also is time to seriously consider competency based certification of teachers. Some states such as New Mexico, Colorado, and Oregon are now attempting this, and other state departments of education are exploring it.

The next step is the job of selling regular class teachers on handicapped children being assisted in their classrooms. This model is well suited for mild handicaps, but special educators must reverse the trend of teachers' believing that the best thing for the child is removal from regular classes. Although books and articles have been written on this subject, the goal is far easier to write about than to accomplish (Reynolds & Davis, 1971). The task will involve a changing of attitude as well as training in new skills and understandings.

Personal Accountability for Teachers

Teachers should begin certain steps to assure personal accountability. Assessment of children's strengths and weaknesses the first week of school is advisable. Unless a system provides assessment in terms of formal and informal tests, teachers should administer tests for each other or conduct educational evaluations and document children's proficiency levels for each other.

When inappropriate materials appear to have been used in the past, these errors should be documented and sent to the superintendent's office or coordinator's office (e.g., when a linguistic approach was used with children having auditory discrimination and blending deficiencies).

Whenever a program has been changed drastically, the teacher should state in writing to the area supervisor why the program was changed and report 6 months later on results, with available data included.

Each teacher should establish for each child levels of performance expected to be met within a specified time. These procedures are well described in the literature on behavioral objectives.

The teacher should request the consultative help, training experiences, and materials he needs from the superintendent or supervisor. Requests should be made in writing and a copy should be retained.

Parents should be kept informed of all activities. The teacher should specify to the parent what the child and parent must do to fulfill their part of the contract.

Teachers should emphasize followup of special class graduates of children served in special programs.

Teachers should make sure they know what to do before starting a new program. One system recently started resources programs only to learn they had ended up with 49 variations. The education of teachers must be continuous, and this training must go far beyond what we know as inservice education.

The responsibility extends beyond the teacher. Special education was started because of the mistreatment, lack of treatment, lack of concern, and lack of appropriate programs in regular education. Some people have forgotten this. It has been pointed out that special education may have been providing a respectable out to regular education for its failures. If we now transfer accountability back to regular education, how will this be received?

If special education is to be accountable, we must begin with its administrative action and policies. Many special educators believe special education has always been one of the most accountable of all programs. Lessinger said this on many occasions, indicating that special educators have specified for each child a set of expectations or an achievement goal. Even curriculum guides have been stated in terms of reachable goals. Curriculum and occupational expectations were relevant. Whatever special educators have done in the past is not good enough for the future. Two and a half million handicapped young persons will be leaving school or graduating in the next 4 years (Martin, 1971). Forty percent of these will be underemployed. Special education must resolve to improve this situation in spite of the added problems of trying to accomplish better vocational education and rehabilitation through the mainstream.

Lastly, there must be an accountability for the administrator as well as for the teacher, and the parents. If a teacher is to be held accountable, the administrator must provide the necessary tools and a working situation to allow him to be productive. Special education programs without materials, without trained teachers, without educational assessment, yet with overenrolled classes have not done the profession any service. In the day of accountability, of the child advocate, of parent involvement, the above situations can and must be prevented.

REFERENCES

BRUININKS, R. H. & RYNDERS, J. E. Alternatives to special class placement for educable mentally retarded children. *Focus on Exceptional Children* 3:4 (1971).

COOK, J. & BLESSING, K. R. Class size and teacher aides as factors in the achievement of the educable mentally retarded. Final report. (OEG 3-6-0626620-19) Madison: Wisconsin State Department of Education, 1970.

ESTES, N. *Proceedings of the Conference on Educational Accountability*. Princeton, N.J.: Educational Testing Service, 1971.

FRIEDERS, B. Motivation and performance contracting. *Journal of Research and Development in Education* 5 (1971): 49-61.

GALLUP, G. The second annual survey of the public's attitudes toward the public school. *Phi Delta Kappan* 52 (1970): 33-46.

GLAVIN, J. P.; QUAY, H. C.; ANNESLEY, F. R.; & WERRY, J. S. An experimental resource room for behavior problem children. *Exceptional Children* 38 (1971): 131-137.

LESSINGER, L. *Every Child a Winner*. New York: Simon & Schuster, 1971.

LESSINGER, L. Accountability: Its implications for the teacher, pp. 72-82. In D. W. Allen, ed. *The Teachers' Handbook*. Glenview, Ill.: Scott, Foresman, 1971.

MARTIN, E. New public priority: Education of the handicapped, pp. 4-8. In *Compact*. Denver, Col.: Education Commission of the States, 1971.

MARTIN, R. & BLASCHKE, C. Contracting for educational reform. *Phi Delta Kappan* 52 (1971): 403-06.

MECKLENBURGER, J. A. & WILSON, J. A. Performance contracting in Cherry Creek. *Phi Delta Kappan* 52 (1971): 51-54.

REYNOLDS, M. & DAVIS, M. *Exceptional Children in Regular Classrooms*. Minneapolis: University of Minnesota, 1971.

ROSS, S. L., DE YOUNG, H. G.; & COHEN, J. S. Confrontation: Special education placement and the law. *Exceptional Children* 38 (1971): 5-12.

SCHWARZ, R. & COOK, J. Mental age as a predictor of academic achievement. *Education and Training of the Mentally Retarded* 6 (1971): 12-15.

VACC, N. A. Long term effects of special class intervention for emotionally disturbed children. *Exceptional Children* 39 (1972): 15-23.

WHITECRAFT, R. Performance contracting with EMR's. Grand Rapids, Mich.: Grand Rapids Public Schools, 1973. (Mimeo.)

WINTER, P. School performance pacts earn no 'A'. *Atlanta Journal* 89: 1 (1972).

Glenn A. Vergason is Chairman, Department of Special Education, Georgia State University, Atlanta.

Twelve

Special Education in Transition: Part Two

Emerging Instructional Practices

Many new special education instructional practices have emerged in recent years. Teacher preparation programs have been modified. New tests have been constructed to describe and diagnose discrepancies in growth, and improved teaching materials have been made available. Some of these changes have been noted in previous chapters. The articles in this chapter will describe three instructional practices that are thought to be of great importance.

Perhaps the greatest modifications are taking place in regular classrooms where some mildly handicapped children are being given realistic instruction. Both the regular teacher and special auxiliary personnel are being asked to acquire new skills in behavior modification, task analysis, prescriptive teaching, and additional evaluation techniques.

Most of the classroom innovations in one way or another contain elements of individualization of instruction. Adapting procedures to the abilities and deficits of the individual is a common concern. The reader must have noted this emphasis in Chapter Three, which discussed children with learning disabilities. The emerging practice of the open classroom provides a flexible instructional arrangement which invites individualization. The merging of these innovations provides an effective model for mainstreaming some exceptional children, and its potentials are reviewed by Lord in the first article.

The resource room is becoming increasingly popular as an auxiliary service for a regular classroom that attempts to include some handicapped children. There are, however, many variations in such rooms. Traditionally, resource rooms have been used extensively for blind children and provided books in braille, talking books, readers, braille writers, and so on. Other resource rooms have served children with single handicaps, such as retardation, or, in some cases, children whose handicaps differed.

An itinerant resource teacher often serves several schools, especially if the limited enrollments dictate such an arrangement. Cooperative or interdistrict programs serving exceptional children find the itinerant model one of the most satisfactory delivery systems. Reger and Koppmann describe such an operation serving a cooperative in New York state. While this is a single example of the use of a resource room, many of the features described are found in programs in other settings.

A number of special techniques such as precision teaching have been developed which have added new dimensions to individualized instruction. The third article summarizes an interview with Ogden R. Lindsley, who was instrumental in the development of precision teaching. In this interview he relates this teaching and measurement strategy to the problems of exceptional children. The technique embodies principles of operant conditioning and the measurement of performance.

A number of innovative curriculum practices are aimed at managing materials and experiences in a fashion to facilitate learning. The developmental task approach to curriculum building, which has been stressed in recent years, is an illustration of this trend. More recently, task analysis has been advocated as a means of giving greater direction to the teaching process. Junkala, in the final article, illustrates task analysis and points out its relevance to special education.

The "Pioneer Profile" in this chapter describes the innovative work of Grace Maxwell Fernald, who developed many remedial techniques that are in wide use today. The kinesthetic techniques for teaching reading that she developed have become increasingly popular in recent years for use with children who fail to respond to visual and auditory methods.

Grace Maxwell Fernald
1879-1950

PSYCHOLOGIST
EDUCATOR
REMEDIAL SPECIALIST

Grace Maxwell Fernald is well known in education and psychology for the development of the kinesthetic method, a remedial method for children failing in reading. She first described her systematic method in an article in 1921, and later in a book, *Remedial Techniques in Basic School Subjects*, in 1943.

Grace Fernald received her A.B. degree and Master's degree from Mt. Holyoke College, and in 1907 was awarded a Ph.D. degree in psychology from the University of Chicago. In 1911, Dr. Fernald was appointed to the staff of the State Normal School in Los Angeles, where she became head of the psychology department and laboratory. She spent her career at the University of California Los Angeles, which developed from the State Normal School. The Clinic School at the University of California Los Angeles was founded by Dr. Fernald in 1921, and today bears her name as a tribute to her innovative and distinguished work.

50.
The Open Classroom and Individualizaton of Instruction— Reinforcing Practices

FRANCIS E. LORD

How does the older movement to individualize instruction supplement and reinforce the more recent practice of the open classroom?

It is easier to explain how handicapped children became segregated into special classes than it is to design programs to integrate them into the regular classrooms. Some fairly obvious forces that led to the instructional divergence include separate financing, the use of medical certificates for admission, and the importance of focusing on the special needs of children to obtain enabling legislation. Since it took fifty years to establish the separation that exists today in the public schools, we must be patient with the time it will take to modify practices significantly. It always seems to take more time to disentangle a fishline than it does to tangle it.

One of the common errors has been to discuss all disability groups in special education in relation to the application of a single reform. We are dealing with very diversified handicaps among the special education groups and with children who have individual uniqueness. The marked degree of heterogeneity makes meaningless a general discussion of educational planning for all such children. It is misleading to say the trend is to return all exceptional children to regular classes. The severely handicapped, in particular, will never fit into regular classes as they are now operated. A recent article by Dunn (1968) has been widely misunderstood as advocating complete integration. More careful readers note that the title of the article refers to the *mildly retarded.* Some educators and many laymen have tended to overgeneralize and interpret the suggestion set forth as applying across the board in special education.

It is only recently that we have recognized that there are some groups of exceptional children, notably the gifted, where several instructional approaches have merit. As we increase the number of instructional options or administrative plans for serving exceptional children, we introduce a flexibility that helps us to move out of the rigid practices of the past. This noticeable flexibility may well be the first step toward some fundamental

An earlier version of this paper appeared in *Exceptional Children in Regular Classrooms,* Maynard C. Reynolds and Malcolm Davis, eds. A publication of the Leadership Training Institute, Special Education, Bureau for Educational Personnel Development, United States Office of Education, 1972. (Available through the Council for Exceptional Children.)

reassessments of our practices. The major concern of this paper is centered upon ways of combining a number of trends into an effective program for handicapped children.

Educational programming for exceptional children should profit very directly from many current innovations as well as a few from the past. It is suggested here that at least three educational movements should be useful in making the regular classroom a more acceptable place for mildly and marginally handicapped children: (1) individualization of instruction, which has been stressed for years; (2) programmed instruction and recent related technology; and (3) the emerging practice of the open classroom at the elementary level. If these three innovations could all be employed in a single operation, we would have a flexible educational program which would accommodate a wide range of individual differences. In attempting to apply these innovations, three major assumptions are set forth:

1. Instructionally significant variables occur to some degree among *all* children. Some variables retard learning while others facilitate growth. These differences occur not only among individual children, but also among factors (deficits or potentials) within a given child.

2. School organization and instructional practices must become more flexible in order to serve the needs of all children more adequately.

3. Mildly and moderately handicapped children may be served in the modified regular programs outlined in this paper. Severely handicapped children, especially the cerebal palsied, the congenitally deaf, and most trainable mentally retarded children may not survive in the suggested program.

Individualization: A Goal for the Past Century

Handicapped children have many defects which interfere with learning and few assets which facilitate achievement. Their academic, physical, and social needs vary greatly from child to child. However, we must view all children as having at some time or other some unique learning problems. Indeed, the able child who is an advanced reader may well have problems in schools as they are currently structured. Some relatively normal children progress in the different subjects at uneven rates. These variations in growth have inspired numerous plans for the individualization of instruction during the past one hundred years.

Nevertheless, for well over a century the American schools have been grouping children into age-grade classes. This practice started in the Boston Quincy Grammar School in 1848. It has been the universal grouping arrangement in all schools, including the one-room rural school which was so common fifty years ago. Numerous instructional plans have been proposed and instituted which attempted to introduce flexible groupings and individualized instruction.

While the system of grading the elementary school was just being well established during the Civil War period, there were objections to it by some thoughtful educators. William T. Harris, a distinguished educator who was Superintendent of Schools in St. Louis (1867-1880), is credited with speaking out against the rigid grouping of children. He made an attempt to break the lock step by introducing a flexible promotion procedure—namely quarterly promotion in place of the annual or semi-annual plan. Note that this attempt at individualization occurred over a hundred years ago.

The Dalton Plan, instituted in some schools in the twenties, used a highly individualized contract plan for students in academic subjects and used class groups largely for social and physical activities. A child could proceed from contract to contract at his own pace. With some modifications, the plan is still used by some instructors.

The Winnetka Plan, which was developed at about the same time, permitted the students to progress individually through so-called common essentials such as arithmetic, reading, spelling and writing, and to participate in group activities in such areas as social studies, creative arts, and physical education.

These are but three of the many plans which have been advocated for a century to break the lock step in our schools. In some communities adaptations were instituted and flourished for a period of time. Minor instructional adjustments are practiced in many schools today. However, a total commitment to individualization is seldom found in our schools.

The current interest in programmed learning is another manifestation of the individualization movement. It may well be that the dream of individualization will be achieved in the future as a result of the advances in educational hardware, including the principles of programmed learning *No principle of instruction has had such universal support at the theoretical level and, at the same time, such limited genuine applicaton.*

Open Classroom Invites Individualization

Except for the severely handicapped, most exceptional children's instructional problems are not distinctly different from those of normal children. It is difficult or impossible to identify a learning principle or a teaching guideline that is uniquely applicable to exceptional children. Indeed, teachers of normal children often copy the drill devices and teaching aids that special teachers have worked out in desperation. There seems to be only one "type" of nervous system, which is stimulated by a set of somewhat similar receptors.

Schools are structured around artificial groupings of children and rather narrowly conceived approaches to meeting their needs. Rigid grading of children, accompanied by instruction based upon *prepared* instructional guides, provides an unrealistic setting in light of our knowledge of individual differences. Schools must be restructured around centers of learning (developmental, remedial, therapeutic) with specialists who are able to facilitate *all* types of growth.

In the past, individualization of instruction was carried on with only minor administrative changes within the school. The classroom structure and, to a degree, the teachers' roles were essentially unchanged. The major adaptations were in the materials used and the freedom given to the children to move at their own pace. In some programs, as pointed out earlier, special arrangements were introduced to provide opportunity for social development as a balance to the increased emphasis upon the individual.

However, with the advent of the open classroom, the profession has an added incentive for individualization. In this arrangement children from several traditional grade levels may be working in a large classroom under the guidance of several teachers and capable aides. Children may be grouped and regrouped informally in a variety of ways throughout the day. Tutoring by aides or peers is easily arranged. Strict grade levels disappear, and team teaching prevails in the open classroom.

Numerous learning and drill materials are made available. Choices of materials for the individual child may be made in terms of his particular needs—his learning rate, his learning style, and his deficits. In every sense the open classroom provides an instructional organization which invites and facilitates individualization of instruction.

Programing for Differences • Combining Technology and Open Classroom

Our present instructional materials and the supporting technology enable us to program for a wide range of differences among children. We can assess many abilities and pinpoint disabilities. Developmental and remedial teaching materials have been developed to cover most of the curriculum. The major challenge is that of matching abilities with suitable materials and motivating the child. If we recognize that every child is a unique individual, we do not need labels to classify him. Traditional grouping of children into grades also becomes meaningless.

Let us assume that our diagnostic techniques and ability to describe all relevant aspects of development continue to grow in sophistication and to become truly helpful guides to instruction. It is assumed here that additional instruments may be developed that will measure or describe such factors as motivation, cognitive styles, "storage" capacity, visual efficiency, language ability, and many other factors. If we acquire the skill to describe a child adequately in terms of his potential for learning and his status at any given time, we will have accomplished the first step in the proposed approach set forth here. We seem to be close to this stage now.

Assuming that we have all the relevant data on a child at age three to four—a desirable age for the first stages of formal education—we could then structure a program that relates to his development and potential. His potential for growth would be the center of focus. The challenge of individualization becomes the primary problem of the school. Since our

Children's growth data cards

Representing instrumentation which will relate growth data on a child to specific developmental tasks. The curricular printout details the modifications desired to meet the needs of each child in an open classroom which features individualized instruction.

Differences in children to be programed are symbolized by stick figures.

Figure 1. PROGRAMING INDIVIDUALIZED INSTRUCTION

descriptive data on each child would be profuse, we would be forced to use the services of a mechanical programer to store information and to assist in designing individualized programs. One may visualize the essentials of this proposal with the assistance of the simple diagram, Figure 1, above.

The personal inventory card which is fed into the device contains all the relevant educational data on a child at a given developmental stage.

Since all children are served by similar data cards, the traditional grouping —such as the superior, the normal, and the handicapped—are no longer appropriate. Each child's card is processed through the elaborate programming device in order to determine the next short-term placement (perhaps six weeks). The printout on each child will describe all appropriate educational services. Programs of needs and services have now replaced such groups as normal, slow, handicapped, and gifted. Developmental specialists, remedial technicians, and teaching aides now supplement teachers while instruction is carried on in an open classroom. Freedom to learn is the first rule of the teachers and aides. Exciting learning aids fill the classroom. Each child is recognized for his own worth, and no fixed groupings can be found. An aim of the past century— the complete individualization of instruction —may now become a reality. Efforts in the past hundred years have met with only limited success due to our inability to describe learning potentials and deficits completely, our limited individualized teaching resources, and the cumbersome age-grade structure. We have approached the stage of professional development where these limiting factors no longer prevail. Consequently, the payoff of the century-old dream may be near at hand.

REFERENCES

BLITZ, BARBARA. *The Open Classroom—Making It Work.* Boston: Allyn & Bacon, 1973.

DENO, EVELYN N., ed. *Instructional Alternatives for Exceptional Children.* Papers prepared for the Exceptional Children Branch of the National Center for the Improvement of Educational Systems by the Leadership Training Institute for Special Education under the Educational Personnel Development Act, 1973. Copies may be ordered from the Council for Exceptional Children, 1411 S. Jefferson Davis Highway, Arlington, Virginia 22202.

GIBSONS, MAURICE. *Individualized Instruction—A Descriptive Analysis.* New York: Teachers College Press, Columbia University, 1971.

PARKHURST, HELEN. *Education on the Dalton Plan.* New York: E. P. Dutton, 1922.

TYLER, FRED T., chairman. *Individualized Instruction,* Sixty-first Yearbook, Part I, National Society for the Study of Education. Chicago: University of Chicago Press, 1962.

WASHBURNE, CARLTON W. and MARLAND, SIDNEY P., JR. *Winnetka: The History and Significance of an Educational Experiment.* Englewood Cliffs, N.J.: Prentice-Hall, 1963.

WASHBURNE, CARLTON, ed. *Adapting the Schools to Individual Differences,* Twenty-fourth Yearbook, Part II, National Society for the Study of Education. Chicago: University of Chicago Press, 1925.

Francis E. Lord is Professor of Special Education, The University of Arizona, Tucson.

51.
The Child Oriented
Resource Room Program

ROGER REGER

MARION KOPPMANN

Resource room programs for children with problems are not new. But there seems to be a large degree of variation among programs and there is not universal understanding of this kind of approach. The following is a brief description of one program operated by the Board of Cooperative Educational Services (BOCES) in suburban Buffalo, New York.

Nineteen school districts participate in the special education programing offered through BOCES. The student population of these districts is approximately 85,000 public and 25,000 nonpublic school children. Five of the districts established a total of 11 resource rooms through BOCES in the 1969-70 school year, and in the 1970-71 school year the program grew to include nine districts and a total of 23 resource rooms.

During the first year of the resource room program there were 58 classes for children classified as mentally retarded and 55 classes for children said to have serious learning difficulties. The rapid expansion of these special class programs led to a search for alternatives to special classes for students with problems, and the resource rooms and a Child Evaluation Center were the result.

The Child Evaluation Center

The center was established to help children from regular classes. These children are seen for 3 days by the center's staff of teachers; then the classroom teachers spend a day going over results and recommendations. The fifth day is spent on followup visits. No diagnostic labels are placed on the children and no recommendations for placement are given. The center's purpose is entirely to help children by helping classroom teachers better understand problem children in their rooms.

There are several features that make the center unique. First, only teachers are employed—no psychologists, social workers, or medical personnel are involved. Second, nothing that takes place at the center is considered confidential or restricted. Parents and teachers are encouraged to see everything that has been noted about any child. The schools that refer children are asked to withhold any information that might be considered confidential since it would be of no use. Third, parents are invited to take

From *Exceptional Children* 37 (February, 1971): 460-62. Reprinted by permission of the authors and *Exceptional Children*. Copyrighted by the Council for Exceptional Children.

part in and observe everything that goes on in the course of the evaluation process, including the daylong conferences after initial evaluation has been completed. Fourth, no child in a BOCES special education program is eligible for referral to the center. Only children in regular classes whose teachers want help are eligible.

One novel aspect is that the program encourages parents to participate in the entire process of evaluating their children for educational disabilities and skills. Some liberal centers will allow parents to observe incidental behavior or the testing of small children—but they are not usually permitted to view the total testing process and they cannot usually attend or participate in staff conferences. The informality of the situation relaxes parents so they are not anxiety ridden about possible bad news. Any questions are immediately answered. Parents can see all tests the child has taken. The parents are encouraged to stay at the center throughout the evaluation period so that any questions can be answered while the child is observed in action.

TEACHERS

Each regular class teacher who has referred children to the center is given two rating forms to complete. One form may be anonymous and is returned to the center. The other is submitted by the teacher to the local district superintendent and is never seen by BOCES personnel. From the returns on these forms to date, about one-third of the teachers feel they have benefitted greatly and have been able to apply what they learned about their referred children to other students in their classes. Another one-third seemed to be unsure about what benefits accrued. Most of the teachers made routinely positive statements, but it is likely that they felt the period too short with too much happening for them to appropriately incorporate and apply the information available. One-third stated that they had been helped by the experience, but not to the extent of the first group.

During the 1969-70 school year, 99 students were seen at the center and 15 students were seen during the summer of 1970. This program, incidentally, comes to a per pupil cost of approximately $300. This must be compared with the cost of between $2,000 and $3,000 for each student placed into a special class. While not all children seen at the center would have been placed into special classes, some would have been and the net result is a financial saving to the schools—always a good argument for any special education program.

Resource Rooms

The resource rooms are located in regular elementary and secondary buildings. A space about the size of a small classroom is used. Each room is furnished with a teacher's desk and chair and one or two small tables with four to six small chairs. A telephone is accessible in each room. Equipment such as typewriters, tape recorders, phonographs, blackboards, mirrors, and storage cabinets is standard. A minimum annual budget of $1,000 is provided for materials and supplies.

CRITERIA AND ADMISSIONS PROCEDURES

Up to 15 students may be enrolled in the program at any one time. During the 1970-71 school year, it was decided that at the secondary level an additional five students could be enrolled at the discretion of the resource room teacher. Children are admitted by action of the chief school officer of the local district, the building principal, and the resource room teacher. All children admitted must attend the school building where the rooms are located. No children from other buildings, public or private, can participate in the program for just tutoring or similar activities. The teacher must have immediate access to each child's regular classroom teacher.

Any child handicapped in any way relevant to his educational needs is eligible for admission. The nature or degree of the handicap need not be spelled out, nor does the child have to fit any diagnostic category; in fact, the typical classification system used in special education is irrelevant. One child might be eligible because his abilities seem very low and he needs assistance in order to do his work. Another child might be eligible because he is considered very bright and is bored with school and thus has become disturbing and generally unproductive.

SCHEDULING

No child can be in the resource room more than a half day at a time. If it is determined that more time is needed, the child is then placed in a special class. Children may be scheduled for any combinations of time periods during the week (one hour each morning, 2 hours every Tuesday and Thursday, etc.). The scheduling is arranged by the classroom and resource room teachers.

As part of the association with the Child Evaluation Center, all resource room teachers and center staff meet for a 3 hour weekly staff meeting. The first several months of the meetings are devoted to discussion of various measurement instruments and their uses. Whenever children from buildings containing resource rooms are seen at the evaluation center, there is an opportunity for the resource room teacher and the center staff to work closely to assist the regular classroom teacher.

PROGRAM CONTENT

The first order of business for the resource room teachers is to evaluate all children enrolled in the program. After pinpointing problem areas the teachers design educational specifications of ways to assist the students. They may provide tutoring for individuals or small groups. They typically do not focus on remedial reading as such, but rather on basic perceptual-motor skills and similar fundamental areas.

To illustrate the kind of program a child might experience, the following is taken from a final report (June, 1970) prepared by a teacher from a resource room.

Sandy visited the resource room for approximately 75-minute periods four times a week. She worked in a group of three students. A total of 148 days were spent in the program. Goals to be reached with Sandy were:

1. Increase auditory and visual memory and sequencing;
2. Improve blending ability;
3. Improve identification of consonant and short vowel sounds;
4. Improve classroom behavior.

Sandy worked with the Frostig and Fitzhugh visual perception programs to help improve spatial relationships and figure-ground perception. A film-strip series and tachistoscope were used to develop figure-ground and form constancy. Cube designs, puzzles, and pegboard designs also were used. She worked on a walking beam, balance board, and bounce board to develop crosslateral and directional movements and to practice rhythmic patterns. She practiced the Cruickshank and Kephart designs and exercises at the chalkboard.

Rhythm instruments, tapes, and records were used to identify familiar sounds and to increase auditory memory and sequencing. The Peabody Language Development Kit was used daily with particular attention paid to those activities that developed auditory skills.

In the Gillingham Program much time was spent in the fall on the blending process. She studied the consonant and short vowel sounds, consonant diagraphs, consonant blends, silent *e* rule, soft *c* and *g* rule, and *er, ir, ur* patterns.

A behavior modification program was used to help control arguing, speaking out of turn, and interrupting others. A token reinforcement program was initiated. She earned points by displaying appropriate behavior and lost them when she violated a rule. The points accumulated to be exchanged later for a pre-selected prize. A similar program was initiated in the classroom by her teacher.

REACTIONS

There generally has been a very favorable reaction to the resource room program. This is displayed in part by the expansion from 11 units in 1969-70 to 23 units in 1970-71. In addition, directors of special education programs from other parts of the state have visited the rooms and at least six other Boards of Cooperative Educational Services are starting resource room programs in the fall of 1971 that are modeled after the program.

ALTERNATIVE TO SPECIAL CLASSES

For some children, the resource room can be an alternative to special class placement. On the other hand, it can be the alternative to no special assistance at all. But the program is not a total substitute for the special class approach. The resource room is not intended to take care of problem children in a disciplinary sense (as if the resource room were a "punishment room").

A major advantage of the resource room approach is that the children are assigned to regular classes and thus easily stay within the school's mainstream. In a special self-contained class, any involvement by regular class teachers such as integration for reading tends to represent an additional burden to the regular class teacher. In the resource room program it is the other way around; the regular class teacher is being helped by the special education teacher. The feeling is generated that the regular class teacher is the learning coordinator and the resource room teacher is an assistant who helps further the goals established primarily by the learning coordinator.

Roger Reger is Director and Marion Koppmann is Program Supervisor, Special Education Services, Board of Cooperative Education Services, Buffalo, New York.

52.
Precision Teaching in Perspective: An Interview with Ogden R. Lindsley

Precision teaching is a new technique in special education. Ogden R. Lindsley shaped and developed the idea in response to the needs of exceptional children as reported to him by the teachers of these special children. In this interview, conducted by Dr. Duncan, Dr. Lindsley described the origins of precision teaching, the difference between behavior modification and precision teaching, and the present and future implications of precision teaching for special and regular education.

Dr. Lindsley, we've heard a great deal about precision teaching, but we would like some answers to some questions, like where did precision teaching come from?

First, let me emphasize that precision teaching came about because of children in special education classrooms. If it had not been for these students communicating their needs to their teachers and the teachers sharing ideas with us, we could not have developed precision teaching as beautifully and quickly as we did.

In 1965, here at the University of Kansas, we decided to see if collecting daily frequency records of students' performance would be useful to classroom teachers. This idea of recording frequency of performance came from learning research. Dr. B. F. Skinner was the person who developed frequency to measure behavior. But Skinner's work was based on laboratory research and we wanted to see if recording daily frequency would be of any help in monitoring instruction and evaluating curriculum and teaching in special and regular classes.

So in 1965 we started having teachers record students' performances. Our first problem was that it was too much work for most teachers to record 2, 3, or 4 different daily frequencies on each child, especially if they had 12 to 30 students.

Then about 1968 many of our creative teachers began to involve the students in recording. We found that this was the answer to our economic and time problems—having the students record their own behavior. Now our kindergarten and first grade children are recording and charting their daily

From *Teaching Exceptional Children* 3 (Spring, 1971): 114-19. Reprinted by permission of *Teaching Exceptional Children*. Copyrighted by the Council for Exceptional Children.

classroom performances on Standard Behavior Charts. These records of performance are turning out to be very useful in curriculum design, behavior change, and handling discipline problems.

Is precision teaching different from or the same as behavior modification?

The thing they have in common is that the first people to use both originally were trained in the same academic discipline—operant conditioning. This was developed by Fred Skinner at Harvard and Fred Keller at Columbia and some of their associates and students.

The thing that makes them different is that behavior modification stresses the change procedures that were originally used in laboratory operant conditioning. It focuses on the use of extrinsic rewards or reinforcement with tokens or candy to bring about change.

Precision teaching on the other hand uses the measurement procedures that operant conditioning originally used but relies more on traditional change procedures that teachers and students invent and select. We're finding in precision teaching that the most effective ways of improving behavior, when we measure behavior frequency, tend to be curricular. They consume less classroom time and don't rely on synthetic rewards or some form of punishment to change behavior. In other words, in precision teaching we try to get the child doing more successful classroom work by making curricular changes which involve him in the learning process, rather than trying to jack up a dull curriculum with rewards for doing boring tasks.

Precision teaching involves daily recording of the frequencies of different classroom performances on a standard chart. This permits teachers and students to project the outcome of the procedures they are using. Standard charts facilitate sharing data.

Behavior modification tends to use procedures like reward and punishment in new and more controlled ways to affect instruction. The child's performance is usually measured by the teacher and does not necessarily include frequencies or the use of a standard chart. In behavior modification, measurement tends to be used to determine whether the reward system was effective or should be altered.

What implications do you think precision techniques have for exceptional children?

If we accept the fact, which most teachers do, that every child is different, then *every* child is exceptional. In the past we've labeled children as exceptional, or we've used specific labels like retarded or learning disabled. These children have dropped out of the bottom of a normal class. The gifted child has popped out of the top of a normal class. Gifted and learning disabled students are retarded by the curriculum assigned them in the average classroom. The gifted child is not stimulated to perform to his ultimate; the retarded child can't perform to the average.

Through individualized planning, we can give every child his own curriculum. In special education this is practically a necessity if we are to help students reach their educational goals and become functioning citizens.

Precision teaching gives the child, the parent, and the teacher a recording technique, a tool to select curriculum materials and involve the child in this selection. This makes it highly probable that you will find a curriculum that will be best for Tommy for October and one for February. If you tried two or three different curricular materials at the same time and made them as different as possible and involved the child in selecting his materials, you would probably soon find the best curriculum for him. If you try three each day and separately record his improvement on each, within 2 to 3 weeks (or in an extreme case, 4 weeks), both the child and teacher can see which of the curricula he shows the most improvement on and which one he should stay with to gain most educationally. Once you pick the best one, then choose a new curriculum as "insurance." You may find that it is even better. In this way every child can be working on different curriculum materials at a different acceleration, and we can have a constant record for the child and teacher that shows with which set of materials the student improved the most for that month.

Another built-in advantage is that precision teaching gives an ever ready, on-going report system to the parents. In addition, if teachers share with parents the techniques which succeed in the classroom, parents may be more willing to share home techniques with teachers.

Why is it important to chart daily frequencies of classroom behaviors? Don't children improve anyway?

There are hundreds of ways of improving a child's behavior; every child is unique and different. The problem is not to discover a new universal teaching method. I don't think one will ever be discovered. The problem is to use the excellent teaching methods we already have with the children whom they will work best with.

We discovered in our original work that to benefit from Skinner's greatest discovery (the use of frequency as a measure of behavior), frequencies had to be recorded in the classroom. Then we found that we had to make a standard chart, because without guidance and structure daily charting was just too complicated and consumed too much time for most teachers. When we tried to share those charts in inservice training meetings, we spent all of our time trying to figure out each others' charts.

When teachers made their own charts it took as long as 28 or 30 minutes for a teacher to make her chart clear to the other 20 to 30 teachers. The Standard Behavior Chart increases communication at least 10 times, since it only takes 2 to 3 minutes to share a project.

Also since equal percent gains get equal distance on the standard chart, you can project the future course of behavior by drawing a straight line through the middle of the daily frequencies you've charted. The direction of this line shows whether the frequency of performance is increasing, decreasing, or remaining the same.

The six cycle design of the chart provides an adequate range of behavior. Behaviors that occur once a day as well as those that occur as frequently as 1,000 times per minute can be charted. This feature of the standard chart insures that the types of behavior teachers would tend to measure are not biased by the nature of the chart.

Once teachers learned how to chart, it was clear that teacher- and child-invented change procedures were more fun, more effective, and less expensive than many reinforcement, reward, or punishment procedures that we might advise from a theoretical or academic point of view. It's very clear that what teachers need most is a way of comparing and evaluating the daily effects of the teaching procedures they already know, rather than advice on new ways of changing the behavior of students.

Where do you think precision teaching goes from here?

This is probably the most important question you have asked me. Around 1962 we recognized that future education desperately needed some way to handle unique differences among students. We needed some way to determine which curriculum format fitted which child best. So we set a strategy for the future. Probably one of the biggest advantages in the development of precision teaching is its future orientation.

The funny anachronism that faced us in the 1950's in human learning research was that the method which Skinner had developed to assess general laws of behavior was also the most appropriate one to study individual differences. And those studying individuals were using methods only appropriate for groups. Right now we have a similar problem where the most dynamic, and I think, the most efficient and exciting learning trends and ideas are those coming out of Piaget, Neil Summerhill, and the British Open School. However, the evaluation methods used for these new classroom ideas and theories are ones which *by design* can pick up only similarities and general trends among people. So a payoff area would be to take these highly unique and different types of open classrooms and use precision teaching techniques to monitor the improvement and growth of each child, working on his own custom tailored curriculum program. A beautiful wedding would be that of the best techniques for monitoring the performance of students with the best programs for maximizing dynamic curriculum and individual learning.

Measuring the frequency of behavior was developed to record the *outer* behavior of people. Recently we have been charting *inner* behaviors like success thoughts, anxiety feelings, joy, love, and compassion. How many times a day do you feel compassionate? How many ecology thoughts did you have today? Charting may be one of the few sensitive techniques that we have to keep track of these inner thoughts, feelings, and urges. It could be that precision teaching will ultimately provide man with the most good and the most help by being applied to his inner behaviors. It is one of the few ways to chart and change inner behaviors.

Thus, some future strategies include using precision teaching to monitor students in open dynamic classrooms and letting them chart their own social interaction and self-concepts.

Another use would be to accelerate the ability of students in our regular classrooms who are getting 90 to 100 percent correct every day and are nowhere close to their educational potential. With precision teaching charts we can show that some students have been in school 4 years, received straight A's, and are bored to tears. They have never shown any acceleration or improvement on their charts, which means the school has taught them nothing. They have simply performed at the top of their class. Those students should be put on a curriculum which could allow them to make a high frequency of errors. This may sound strange because we as teachers are generally pleased when our students make few errors. The errors, however, would show that a student is challenged and working towards improvement. In addition, a special curriculum could be selected for a child gifted in math but in nothing else. Then he could stay in his regular school activities, but he could be working on college math because his charts showed that was the only math that was challenging to him.

We can use these charts on daily classroom performance and improvement to design curriculum packages. Each child could possibly have 10 curricular choices. They all could be recorded on the standard charts. No students would ever be reading the same material each week; they would change to the curriculum alternative that they showed the most improvement on.

One problem will have to be solved to make this process work. We will have to learn to treat errors as learning opportunities, as a beautiful man named Caleb Gattegno does. We want to constantly increase the difficulty of the material so that errors are present and can be used not as social stigmata but as *opportunities to learn*. The whole idea is to challenge the myth that children have to be right most of the time, since this idea slows down the learning process terribly. By taking the onus from errors we may find that children dare more and try more.

It is essential for creative people to be allowed to make mistakes. Most creative people I have known are different from all the people around them, for they don't know when to quit. For them every failure is a success, because they then know how not to fail that way again.

Is there anything else you would like to add?

Yes. There's a lot of confusion about precision teaching. People think it's a new teaching approach, a new type of learning or reinforcement theory. In the past most new ideas about classroom instruction have literally been "approaches" or theories involving goals. *Precision teaching is not an approach;* it is an easy, inexpensive system of monitoring daily improvement —not performance, but improvement. Improvement is acceleration; performance is frequency of occurrence.

The difference is an important one, especially in view of all the talk we're hearing about raising teachers' salaries on the basis of how well the children in their classes perform. For example, if a teacher uses standard achievement tests with a group of children who are good achievers, it's not too difficult to get their performance up to criterion. The teacher can then qualify for a raise based on teaching output, measured by children's achievement test scores. The problem, however, is that if a teacher is assigned children who have great difficulty learning, the teacher would have an awful time getting the children up to criterion before the end of the semester.

You would have a very different situation if the teacher were being evaluated on the children's improvement or acceleration, that is the *change* or improvement in the frequency with which a particular behavior is performed. Then the teacher who had the most underachieving children would have the greatest opportunity to show pupil improvement. This kind of evaluation would directly reward a teacher for improving the behavior of children, not for trying to get them to reach some standard level of performance. In short then, precision teaching entails recording the acceleration or change in frequency of wanted behaviors or the deceleration of unwanted behaviors, as opposed to simply recording level of performance.

I'd like to again underscore that precision teaching is *not* an approach to classroom instruction. Any teacher who is now comfortable with her style of teaching, her hard learned way of communicating with her students, and the unique way she expresses her love for her students would not substitute precision teaching for what she is doing. She simply *adds* precision teaching techniques to her current style in order to become even more efficient. Precision teaching tools are designed to improve and refine current teaching methods and materials. That's a confusion I find in a lot of teachers. They fear that if they try this new thing they will have to temporarily put aside or abandon their trusted teaching skills. Precision teaching simply adds a more precise measurement instrument to present teaching, making teaching more economical, more effective, more enjoyable, and more loving.

Ogden R. Lindsley is Professor of Education at the University of Kansas. He was associated with the Kansas Center for Mental Retardation and Human Development.

53.
Task Analysis and
Instructional Alternatives
JOHN JUNKALA

*How is task analysis a major element in the
larger movement to individualize instruction?*

In the search for factors that might allow special
education to become truly special, the skills of task analysis seem to have
been largely overlooked. Teachers are still looking for the "right" materials
to use with children who have learning problems, on the assumption that
the materials, once found, will provide answers to instructional problems.
In another article, I have described the futility of this type of reasoning
and have written about the need for developing teachers' skills in the precise definition of instructional objectives.[1] Task analysis is an extension of
these skills because it identifies the demands that a task will make on a
child, and thus allows the teacher to prepare the child to meet each
demand.

Most educators acknowledge the readiness imperative, but many view
it as only a phase that occurs before the introduction of formal instruction.
Dolores Durkin points out that the question "Is the child ready?" is really
incomplete.[2] To make it complete one must add, "Ready for what?" Readiness is a state of preparedness for what is to come next. Ideally, in an instructional situation, the child begins with all the skills and concepts needed
before the next small step is introduced. We can see then that readiness
is really a continuous process, and that conclusions about readiness can
only be made in the context of the tasks contained in a specific activity. To
know whether a child is ready, the teacher must be aware of what the child
will have to be able to do.

One need not spend much time visiting special education programs before he hears such phrases as *"to individualize instruction"* or *"to take him
from where he is. . . . "* "Where he is" usually means grade level (he is reading at a 2.3 level). Yet we rarely find such a statement very helpful in
planning for a child who has a learning problem. These children often have
so many gaps in their skills that a grade-level statement, even though
yielded by a standard test, is almost totally useless for detailed educational
planning.

Typically, these children do not make steady progress through standard teaching materials. When progress stops, the search for instructional alternatives begins. The search is often of the type previously mentioned:

From *Academic Therapy* 8 (Fall, 1972): 33-40. Reprinted by permission of the
author and *Academic Therapy.*

looking for the "right" materials. If a look-say approach to reading is in use, the teacher might switch to a phonics or a linguistic approach, or perhaps to elements of all three approaches.

Educators often describe themselves as eclectics, subscribing to no single teaching approach but borrowing from all. "We use what works." Unfortunately for too many children, nothing seems to work.

Frustrated in their search for effective methods and materials, many teachers gradually lower their goals. Convinced that poor memory and short attention span are insurmountable problems, teachers find themselves espousing the affective aspects of their curricula and deemphasizing cognitive-academic components. (I would suggest that healthy social-emotional development flows in large part from the acquisition of basic academic skills.)

Methods and materials are often used as general treatments. They are employed as delivered by the publisher, with perhaps some modification of pacing. When they work, all is well; but all too frequently they do not work, and are discarded as just a few more futile experiences in the search for the right materials. Seldom do teachers attempt to look closely at the methods and materials they intend to use with a pupil in a given situation. Seldom do they attempt to *get inside* the tasks they are presenting.

With only a general awareness of the demands of a task (for example, "to utilize his listening skills") the teacher is able to conduct only a general search for instructional alternatives. With more precise knowledge of a task's demands, the search for alternatives can become more precise.

The ultimate operation in task analysis is a three-dimensional one that describes the cognitive, affective, and modality-processing demands to be made by a particular task on a particular individual in a given setting.

Doris Johnson has presented a very useful framework for the analysis of modality-processing demands.[3] This article, however, will limit itself to an explication of cognitive demands, although, as will be seen, it is impossible to discuss them in pure forms, as they are so intricately interwoven.

Cognitive Model

Figure 1 is a schematic representation of the relationship between the perceptual, coding, and conceptual demands of the cognitive dimension. Coding functioning presumes adequate perceptual functioning. Conceptual functioning subsumes both coding and perceptual functioning, although not every conceptual task need include a coding component.

Perceptual Level

Perception means selecting stimuli from the array of those that are impinging upon us, and then integrating and structuring them so that we can identify them accurately. Identification implies that

Figure 1. SCHEMATIC REPRESENTATION OF COGNITIVE DIMENSION

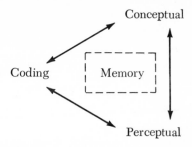

we are aware of the functions, characteristics, or meanings of the stimuli we structure. Identifying this picture as a church is an example of functioning at the perceptual level.

Identifying b as the letter *b* is a perceptual event. Pointing to a box on a table full of objects after hearing the word *box* is a perceptual event.

The look-say (or sight) approach to reading is largely perceptual in its demands, at least in its early phases. Children learn to read whole words by their total configurational patterns. The word *said*, for example, is just that, nothing more, nothing less. It is not a collection of sound symbols that equals the word. It is just *said*.

Coding Level

As soon, however, as we look at *b* and say "buh," or "*b* as in baby"; or as soon as we hear "book," and are required to know that it begins with *b*, we are functioning at a coding level. Letters and sounds, or letters and objects, must be associated with each other. At this level of cognitive functioning we are beginning to abstract the properties of objects and events. We are not dealing with things solely as they appear in concrete form (a church, or the letter *b*); rather, we are dealing with the letters that will graphically record the sounds of their names.

Conceptual Level

At the conceptual level, task demands are concerned with the development of meaningful relationships. Of course, there is meaning at the perceptual level, because a picture of a thing means the thing itself; and at the coding level, because a letter stands for a sound. At the conceptual level, however, the task requires the child to *relate*— that is, to classify objects or events, or to draw inferences from them, or to make statements about their value.

The "Perceptually Handicapped"

The term "perceptually handicapped," while not exactly a misnomer, has often been applied to all children with learning disabilities. Though it is undoubtedly true that many learning problems can be traced to inadequate perceptual functioning, many others occur at higher cognitive levels with no perceptual impairment whatsoever.

In working with children we sometimes get confused about the sources of our failures because we mix perceptual, coding, and conceptual demands in the same task. There is no reason why all three should not be present, as long as we are aware of their presence and as long as we are aware of what we are asking the child to do.

The way in which a teacher words the directions for a task plays a large part in determining the level of the task's complexity for the child. Teachers frequently compose their verbal directions on the spur of the moment without taking time to think through all of their implications. As an example, one teacher decided to give a quick drill on initial consonants to a child, and put the following list of words on the chalkboard:

| ball | cat   bird   dog   saw   bag

She then gave the following directions (with the indicated results):

1. "The word in the box is *ball*. Show me another word that begins with the same letter as *ball*." (The child pointed instantly to *bird*.)
2. "Show me a word that begins with the same letter as *box*." (The child was unable to do so.)
3. "Show me all the words that begin with the same letter as the word in the box." (The child did this successfully.)

The teacher concluded with some frustration that the child's performance was erratic. "Sometimes he knows it and sometimes he doesn't. He's probably perceptually handicapped."

An analysis of the teacher's directions and the child's responses yielded the following information. Task 1 can be placed either at the perceptual level or the coding level, depending on the clues used by the child in solving it. If he used the visual clue of the beginning letter of the word in the box, then he solved the problem at a perceptual level. If he used the auditory clue of the initial sound of *ball,* then he solved it at a coding level, as he was able to scan the row of words while remembering the sound, and then pick out a word that began with a letter denoting the same sound. It is also possible that he used both of the clues. Task 2 clearly demands coding skills. The child did not see the word *box.* He merely heard it and was then called on to visualize the letter denoting its initial sound and scan the row until finding a word beginning with a letter which stands for the same sound. He was unable to do this. We can infer, at least tentatively, that he solved Task 1 on the basis of visual-perceptual clues. Task 3 is conceptual in its demands on the child. He was required to sort out the words that begin with the same letter as the word in the box. This he was able to do.

We can see that the child is able to solve problems of conceptual complexity when given good visual clues. We do not know, however, whether his failure with the coding task is due to an auditory deficiency (memory or discrimination) at the perceptual level, or whether he is intact auditorily but deficient in the integration of auditory and visual (coding) information.

It would not be overly difficult to check these questions out in a very short time. For instance, to check for auditory skills the teacher might produce a row of pictures instead of words and say, "This is a ball. Show me another picture that begins with the same sound as ball." Or, "Listen, and raise your hand when both pictures begin with the same sound: ball-cat; ball-bird; ball-dog; ball-bag."

The point is this: through the ability to present a carefully worded, pre-analyzed task the teacher is able to look at the child's successes and failures and immediately choose alternatives to the instructional approach which has just failed. This skill places a teacher far ahead of those whose only explanation for failure is the child's poor memory or short attention span.

Instructional Alternatives

In the design of instructional alternatives the teacher can move in two directions, *lateral* and *vertical.* A lateral move keeps the activity at the same level of complexity (perceptual, coding, or conceptual), but changes the material to bring the task closer to the child's state of readiness at that level. A vertical move changes the level of complexity of the task.

As an example of a lateral move, a teacher working at the conceptual level asked a child to tell how the following three words on the chalkboard were alike:

stuff   laugh   paragraph

The child's ability to read and understand each word had been established earlier. When the child could not answer correctly, the teacher immediately eliminated the third word and changed the list to read:

stuff	laugh
if	trough
off	rough

The child was able to read each word correctly but was still unable to tell how they were all alike. He was unable to classify this information. The teacher made another change:

staff	laugh
off	trough
puff	rough

The child immediately answered that each pair of words rhymed. (In that section of the country, *laugh* is "laff.") The rhyming concept allowed the teacher to call the child's attention to the final sounds of the words, and the child was then able to conceptualize on that basis. The teacher had been ready for a vertical move if one had been needed. She could have switched to a coding task, associating the *f* sound with the appropriate letters. If necessary she could have moved to the perceptual level to work on auditory or visual skills.

A useful rule of thumb for moving laterally within a level is to change either the amount of material or the stimulus-signal characteristics of the material. In the case just cited the teacher chose the latter tactic.

Another teacher presented the following exercise in visual discrimination at the perceptual level:

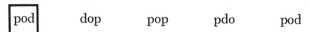

The directions to the child were: "Find a word that looks like the word in the box." When the child had difficulty in doing so, the teacher eliminated two of the three distracting words. If the child had failed with that, the material could have been further simplified by using single letters instead of words. Or the teacher could have altered the stimulus-signal characteristics of the material by using letters with more obvious differences. The following group is an example:

$$\boxed{\text{pod}} \qquad \text{fat} \qquad \text{cow} \qquad \text{sag} \qquad \text{pod}$$

As illustrated by the last example, a rule of thumb for making a perceptual task easier is to increase the differences until the child can cope with the material.

Group Instruction

The responses of a child working on preanalyzed tasks tell the teacher a great deal about the skills and levels at which the child can work successfully. In addition to serving as the basis for individual instruction, this information enables the teacher to *individualize* instruction in group settings. She is able to use a single activity as a framework for working with a group of children, each of whom may differ from the others in cognitive skills.

As an example, a teacher planned a language arts activity around a large colored picture of a farm scene. She based her questions and directions on her knowledge of each child's specific skills:

"What do we call this animal?" (*perceptual*)

"What color is it?" (*perceptual*)

"Point to another animal whose name begins with the same sound as *duck.*" (*perceptual*)

"What letter does *cow* begin with?" (*coding*)

"Show us all the animals that have wings." (*conceptual-sorting*)

"How are the birds, chickens, and ducks alike?" (*conceptual-classifying*)

"We can see that the sun is going down and the animals are at the barn door. Why are they there?" (*conceptual-drawing inferences*)

Task analysis is a major element in the individualization of instruction. An ability to analyze tasks allows the teacher to determine pupil readiness, to teach groups of children with varying skills, and to produce sophisticated alternatives to instructional failure. These skills should be placed in the professional repertoires of all teachers of all children.

NOTES

1. JUNKALA, JOHN. Teacher evaluation of instructional material. *Teaching Exceptional Children* 2 (1970): 73-76.
2. DURKIN, DOLORES. What does research say about the time to begin reading instruction? *Journal of Educational Research* 64 (1970): 52-56.
3. JOHNSON, DORIS J. Clinical teaching of children with learning disabilities. In *Successful Programming: Selected Papers on Learning Disabilities*, ed. John I. Arena. San Rafael, Calif.: Academic Therapy Publications, 1968.

John Junkala is Associate Professor of Education, Boston College, School of Education.

Appendix A

Excerpt from
Peter Mills et al., Plaintiffs
v.
Board of Education of the District
of Columbia et al., Defendants
AUGUST 1, 1972

Editors' Preface

Reproduced below is the Judgment and Decree *in the Mills case which resulted from civil action in the United States District Court for the District of Columbia. While findings and opinions apply only to the District, the primary issues in the case may have a profound influence upon the responsibility of districts to provide services to handicapped children and upon procedures for suspension, placement, and review of disputes between the school and the parents.*

The suit was brought by Peter Mills et al. against the District for denying publicly-supported education to certain handicapped children and for excluding, reassigning, or transferring exceptional children from regular public school classes without affording them due process of law.

The Memorandum section of the case, which is not reproduced here, gives details on each of seven children who were alleged to have been improperly served. While all these children were black, the class suit covered all children in the District who had also suffered from the alleged discrimination. School laws and regulations were cited by the plaintiffs in support of their case, and the District did not deny the charges.

From *In the United States District Court for the District of Columbia, Peter Mills, et al., Plaintiffs v. Board of Education of the District of Columbia, et al., Defendants.* 348 F. Supp. 866 (1972).

Judgment and Decree

Plaintiffs having filed their verified complaint seeking an injunction and declaration of rights as set forth more fully in the verified complaint and the prayer for relief contained therein; and having moved this Court for summary judgment pursuant to Rule 56 of the Federal Rules of Civil Procedure, and this Court having reviewed the record of this cause including plaintiffs' Motion, pleadings, affidavits, and evidence and arguments in support thereof, and defendants' affidavit, pleadings, and evidence and arguments in support thereof, and the proceedings of pre-trial conferences on December 17, 1971, and January 14, 1972, it is hereby ORDERED, ADJUDGED AND DECREED that summary judgment in favor of plaintiffs and against defendants be, and it is hereby granted, and judgment is entered in this action as follows:

1. That no child eligible for a publicly supported education in the District of Columbia public schools shall be excluded from a regular public school assignment by a Rule, policy, or practice of the Board of Education of the District of Columbia or its agents unless such child is provided (a) adequate alternative educational services suited to the child's needs, which may include special education or tuition grants, and (b) a constitutionally adequate prior hearing and periodic review of the child's status, progress, and the adequacy of any educational alternative.

2. The defendants, their officers, agents, servants, employees, and attorneys and all those in active concert or participation with them are hereby enjoined from maintaining, enforcing or otherwise continuing in effect any and all rules, policies and practices which exclude plaintiffs and the members of the class they represent from a regular public school assignment without providing them at public expense (a) adequate and immediate alternative education or tuition grants, consistent with their needs, and (b) a constitutionally adequate prior hearing and periodic review of their status, progress and the adequacy of any educational alternatives; and it is further ORDERED that:

3. The District of Columbia shall provide to each child of school age a free and suitable publicly-supported education regardless of the degree of the child's mental, physical or emotional disability or impairment. Furthermore, defendants shall not exclude any child resident in the District of Columbia from such publicly-supported education on the basis of a claim of insufficient resources.

4. Defendants shall not suspend a child from the public schools for disciplinary reasons for any period in excess of two days without affording him a hearing pursuant to the provisions of Paragraph 13.f., below, and without providing for his education during the period of any such suspension.

5. Defendants shall provide each identified member of plaintiff class with a publicly-supported education suited to his needs within thirty (30) days of the entry of this order. With regard to children who later come to the attention of any defendant, within twenty (20) days after he becomes known, the evaluation (case study approach) called for in paragraph 9 below shall be completed and within 30 days after completion of the evaluation, placement shall be made so as to provide the child with a publicly-supported education suited to his needs.

In either case, if the education to be provided is not of a kind generally available during the summer vacation, the thirty-day limit may be extended for children evaluated during summer months to allow their educational programs to begin at the opening of school in September.

6. Defendants shall cause announcements and notices to be placed in the Washington Post, Washington Star-Daily News, and the Afro-American, in all issues published for a three week period commencing within five (5) days of the entry of this order, and thereafter at quarterly intervals, and shall cause spot announcements to be made on television and radio stations for twenty (20) consecutive days, commencing within five (5) days of the entry of this order, and thereafter at quarterly intervals, advising residents of the District of Columbia that all children, regardless of any handicap or other disability, have a right to a publicly-supported education suited to their needs, and informing the parents or guardians of such children of the procedures required to enroll their children in an appropriate educational program. Such announcements should include the listing of a special answering service telephone number to be established by defendants in order to (a) compile the names, addresses, phone numbers of such children who are presently not attending school and (b) provide further information to their parents or guardians as to the procedures required to enroll their children in an appropriate educational program.

7. Within twenty-five (25) days of the entry of this order, defendants shall file with the Clerk of this Court, an up-to-date list showing, for every additional identified child, the name of the child's parent or guardian, the child's name, age, address and telephone number, the date of his suspension, expulsion, exclusion or denial of placement and, without attributing a particular characteristic to any specific child, a breakdown of such list; showing the alleged causal characteristics for such non-attendance (e.g., educable mentally retarded, trainable mentally retarded, emotionally disturbed, specific learning disability, crippled/other health impaired, hearing impaired, visually impaired, multiple handicapped) and the number of children possessing each such alleged characteristic.

8. Notice of this order shall be given by defendants to the parent or guardian of each child resident in the District of Columbia who is now, or was during the 1971-72 school year or the 1970-71 school year, excluded, suspended or expelled from publicly-supported educational programs or

otherwise denied a full and suitable publicly-supported education for any period in excess of two days. Such notice shall include a statement that each child has the right to receive a free educational assessment and to be placed in a publicly-supported education suited to his needs. Such notice shall be sent by registered mail within five (5) days of the entry of this order, or within five (5) days after such child first becomes known to any defendant. Provision of notification for non-reading parents or guardians will be made.

9. a. Defendants shall utilize public or private agencies to evaluate the educational needs of all identified "exceptional" children and, within twenty (20) days of the entry of this order, shall file with the Clerk of this Court their proposal for each individual placement in a suitable educational program, including the provision of compensatory educational services where required. b. Defendants, within twenty (20) days of the entry of this order, shall also submit such proposals to each parent or guardian of such child, respectively, along with a notification that if they object to such proposed placement within a period of time to be fixed by the parties or by the Court, they may have their objection heard by a Hearing Officer in accordance with procedures required in Paragraph 13.e., below.

10. a. Within forty-five (45) days of the entry of this order, defendants shall file with the Clerk of the Court, with copy to plaintiffs' counsel, a comprehensive plan which provides for the identification, notification, assessment, and placement of class members. Such plan shall state the nature and extent of efforts which defendants have undertaken or propose to undertake to

(1) describe the curriculum, educational objectives, teacher qualifications, and ancillary services for the publicly-supported educational programs to be provided to class members; and,

(2) formulate general plans of compensatory education suitable to class members in order to overcome the present effects of prior educational deprivations.

(3) institute any additional steps and proposed modifications designed to implement the matters decreed in paragraph 5 through 7 hereof and other requirements of this judgment.

11. The defendants shall make an interim report to this Court on their performance within forty-five (45) days of the entry of this order. Such report shall show:

(1) The adequacy of Defendants' implementation of plans to identify, locate, evaluate and give notice to all members of the class.

(2) The number of class members who have been placed, and the nature of their placements.

(3) The number of contested hearings before the Hearing Officers, if any, and the findings and determinations resulting therefrom.

12. Within forty-five (45) days of the entry of this order, defendants shall file with this Court a report showing the expunction from or correction of all official records of any plaintiff with regard to past expulsions, suspensions, or exclusions affected in violation of the procedural rights set forth in Paragraph 13 together with a plan for procedures pursuant to which parents, guardians, or their counsel may attach to each students' records any clarifying or explanatory information which the parent, guardian or counsel may deem appropriate.

13. Hearing Procedures.

a. Each member of the plaintiff class is to be provided with a publicly-supported educational program suited to his needs, within the context of a presumption that among the alternative programs of education, placement in a regular public school class with appropriate ancillary services is preferable to placement in a special school class.

b. Before placing a member of the class in such a program, defendants shall notify his parent or guardian of the proposed educational placement, the reasons therefor, and the right to a hearing before a Hearing Officer if there is an objection to the placement proposed. Any such hearing shall be held in accordance with the provisions of Paragraph 13.e., below.

c. Hereinafter, children who are residents of the District of Columbia and are thought by any of the defendants, or by officials, parents or guardians, to be in need of a program of special education, shall neither be placed in, transferred from or to, nor denied placement in such a program unless defendants shall have first notified their parents or guardians of such proposed placement, transfer or denial, the reasons therefor, and of the right to a hearing before a Hearing Officer if there is an objection to the placement, transfer or denial of placement. Any such hearings shall be held in accordance with the provisions of Paragraph 13.e., below.

d. Defendants shall not, on grounds of discipline, cause the exclusion, suspension, expulsion, postponement, inter-school transfer, or any other denial of access to regular instruction in the public schools to any child for more than two days without first notifying the child's parent or guardian of such proposed action, the reasons therefor, and of the hearing before a Hearing Officer in accordance with the provisions of Paragraph 13.f., below.

e. Whenever defendants take action regarding a child's placement, denial of placement, or transfer, as described in Paragraphs 13.b or 13.c., above, the following procedures shall be followed.

   (1) Notice required hereinbefore shall be given in writing by registered mail to the parent or guardian of the child.
   (2) Such notice shall:

(a) describe the proposed action in detail;

(b) clearly state the specific and complete reasons for the proposed action, including the specification of any tests or reports upon which such action is proposed;

(c) describe any alternative educational opportunities available on a permanent or temporary basis;

(d) inform the parent or guardian of the right to object to the proposed action at a hearing before the Hearing Officer;

(e) inform the parent or guardian that the child is eligible to receive, at no charge, the services of a federally or locally funded diagnostic center for an independent medical, psychological and educational evaluation and shall specify the name, address and telephone number of an appropriate local diagnostic center;

(f) inform the parent or guardian of the right to be represented at the hearing by legal counsel; to examine the child's school records before the hearing, including any tests or reports upon which the proposed action may be based, to present evidence, including expert medical, psychological and educational testimony; and, to confront and cross-examine any school official, employee, or agent of the school district or public department who may have evidence upon which the proposed action was based.

(3) The hearing shall be at a time and place reasonably convenient to such parent or guardian.

(4) The hearing shall be scheduled not sooner than twenty (20) days waivable by parent or child, nor later than forty-five (45) days after receipt of a request from the parent or guardian.

(5) The hearing shall be a closed hearing unless the parent or guardian requests an open hearing.

(6) The child shall have the right to a representative of his own choosing, including legal counsel. If a child is unable, through financial inability, to retain counsel, defendants shall advise child's parents or guardians of available voluntary legal assistance including the Neighborhood Legal Services Organization, the Legal Aid Society, the Young Lawyers Section of the D. C. Bar Association, or from some other organization.

(7) The decision of the Hearing Officer shall be based solely upon the evidence presented at the hearing.

(8) Defendants shall bear the burden of proof as to all facts and as to the appropriateness of any placement, denial of placement or transfer.

(9) A tape recording or other record of the hearing shall be made and transcribed and, upon request, made available to the parent or guardian or his representative.

(10) At a reasonable time prior to the hearing, the parent or guardian, or his counsel, shall be given access to all public school system and other public office records pertaining to the child, including any tests or reports upon which the proposed action may be based.

(11) The independent Hearing Officer shall be an employee of the District of Columbia, but shall not be an officer, employee or agent of the Public School System.

(12) The parent or guardian, or his representative, shall have the right to have the attendance of any official, employee or agent of the public school system or any public employee who may have evidence upon which the proposed action may be based and to confront, and to cross-examine any witness testifying for the public school system.

(13) The parent or guardian, or his representative, shall have the right to present evidence and testimony, including expert medical, psychological or educational testimony.

(14) Within thirty (30) days after the hearing, the Hearing Officer shall render a decision in writing. Such decision shall include findings of fact and conclusions of law and shall be filed with the Board of Education and the Department of Human Resources and sent by registered mail to the parent or guardian and his counsel.

(15) Pending a determination by the Hearing Officer, defendants shall take no action described in Paragraphs 13.b. or 13.c., above, if the child's parent or guardian objects to such action. Such objection must be in writing and postmarked within five (5) days of the date of receipt of notification hereinabove described.

f. Whenever defendants propose to take action described in Paragraph 13.d., above, the following procedures shall be followed.

(1) Notice required hereinabove shall be given in writing and shall be delivered in person or by registered mail to both the child and his parent or guardian.

(2) Such notice shall

(a) describe the proposed disciplinary action in detail, including the duration thereof;

(b) state specific, clear, and full reasons for the proposed action, including the specification of the alleged act upon which the disciplinary action is to be based and the reference to the regulation subsection under which such action is proposed;

(c) describe alternative educational opportunities to be available to the child during the proposed suspension period;

(d) inform the child and the parent or guardian of the time and place at which the hearing shall take place;

(e) inform the parent or guardian that if the child is thought by the parent or guardian to require special education services, that such child is eligible to receive, at no charge, the services of a public or private agency for a diagnostic medical, psychological or educational evaluation;

(f) inform the child and his parent or guardian of the right to be represented at the hearing by legal counsel; to examine the child's school records before the hearing, including any tests or reports upon which the proposed action may be based; to present evidence of his own; and to confront and cross-examine any witnesses or any school officials, employees or agents who may have evidence upon which the proposed action may be based.

(3) The hearing shall be at a time and place reasonably convenient to such parent or guardian.

(4) The hearing shall take place within four (4) school days of the date upon which written notice is given, and may be postponed at the request of the child's parent or guardian for no more than five (5) additional school days where necessary for preparation.

(5) The hearing shall be a closed hearing unless the child, his parent or guardian requests an open hearing.

(6) The child is guaranteed the right to a representative of his own choosing, including legal counsel. If a child is unable, through financial inability, to retain counsel, defendants shall advise child's parents or guardians of available voluntary legal assistance including the Neighborhood Legal Services Organization, the Legal Aid Society, the Young Lawyers Section of the D.C. Bar Association, or from some other organization.

(7) The decision of the Hearing Officer shall be based solely upon the evidence presented at the hearing.

(8) Defendants shall bear the burden of proof as to all facts and as to the appropriateness of any disposition and of the alternative educational opportunity to be provided during any suspension.

(9) A tape recording or other record of the hearing shall be made and transcribed and, upon request, made available to the parent or guardian or his representative.

(10) At a reasonable time prior to the hearing, the parent or guardian, or the child's counsel or representative, shall be given access to all records of the public school system and any other public office pertaining to the child, including any tests or reports upon which the proposed action may be based.

(11) The independent Hearing Officer shall be an employee of the District of Columbia, but shall not be an officer, employee or agent of the Public School System.

(12) The parent or guardian, or the child's counsel or representative, shall have the right to have the attendance of any public employee who may have evidence upon which the proposed action may be based and to confront and to cross-examine any witness testifying for the public school system.

(13) The parent or guardian, or the child's counsel or representative, shall have the right to present evidence and testimony.

(14) Pending the hearing and receipt of notification of the decision, there shall be no change in the child's educational placement unless the principal (responsible to the Superintendent) shall warrant that the continued presence of the child in his current program would endanger the physical well-being of himself or others. In such exceptional cases, the principal shall be responsible for insuring that the child receives some form of educational assistance and/or diagnostic examination during the interim period prior to the hearing.

(15) No finding that disciplinary action is warranted shall be made unless the Hearing Officer first finds, by clear and convincing evidence, that the child committed a prohibited act upon which the proposed disciplinary action is based. After this finding has been made, the Hearing Officer shall take such disciplinary action as he shall deem appropriate. This action shall not be more severe than that recommended by the school official initiating the suspension proceedings.

(16) No suspension shall continue for longer than ten (10) school days after the date of the hearing, or until the end of the school year, whichever comes first. In such cases, the principal (responsible to the Superintendent) shall be responsible for insuring that the child receives some form of educational assistance and/or diagnostic examination during the suspension period.

(17) If the Hearing Officer determines that disciplinary action is not warranted, all school records of the proposed disciplinary action, including those relating to the incidents upon which such proposed action was prejudiced, shall be destroyed.

(18) If the Hearing Officer determines that disciplinary action is warranted, he shall give written notification of his findings and of the child's right to appeal his decision to the Board of Education, to the child, the parent or guardian, and the counsel or representative of the child, within three (3) days of such determination.

(19) An appeal from the decision of the Hearing Officer shall be heard by the Student Life and Community Involvement Committee of the Board of Education which shall provide the child and his parent or guardian with the opportunity for an oral hearing, at which the child may be represented by legal counsel, to review

the findings of the Hearing Officer. At the conclusion of such hearing, the Committee shall determine the appropriateness of and may modify such decision. However, in no event may such Committee impose added or more severe restrictions on the child.

14. Whenever the foregoing provisions require notice to a parent or guardian, and the child in question has no parent or duly appointed guardian, notice is to be given to any adult with whom the child is actually living, as well as to the child himself, and every effort will be made to assure that no child's rights are denied for lack of a parent or duly appointed guardian. Again, provision for such notice to non-readers will be made.

15. Jurisdiction of this matter is retained to allow for implementation and enforcement of this Judgment and Decree as may be required.

Joseph C. Waddy
United States District Judge

Date: August 1, 1972

Appendix B

Books College Students Like to Read About Exceptional Children

ROBERT M. PORTER

What are the most interesting, just-for-fun books in the field of exceptionality? What will college students read, even if they don't have to? After several years of observation, I know some of them. For the past 4 years I have been teaching a well subscribed, elective survey course entitled "Exceptional Children," which has three sections totaling nearly 100 students each semester. Students in this course, juniors, seniors, and graduate students, are often highly motivated and sincerely interested in preparing to help other people.

I urge them to read widely, sampling the literature in each of the eight areas of exceptionality touched upon in the course—giftedness; retardation; brain damage; sight, hearing, and speech impairment; crippling and medical problems; and social emotional maladjustment. This is sometimes the only course in exceptionality that these future teachers will ever take. I give them a 250 book bibliography headed by a sentence from Milton's *Areopagitica:* "Books are not absolutely dead things but do contain a potency of life in them to be as active as that soul was whose progeny they are." I suggest the classics, the authoritative, definitive works such as those by Terman, Kirk, Ellis, Johnson, Frostig, Cruickshank, Van Riper, Dunn, McCarthy, and Lovaas. And they are read.

I also call attention to more "readable" books, many now in paperback editions. For possible help to students and others forced by time and proliferation of material to be selective in their reading, the top dozen books in reader appeal, based on the number of times mentioned in student reports, are listed below:

AXLINE, VIRGINIA. *Dibs.* Boston: Houghton Mifflin, 1964. (Paperback by Ballantine Books)

Says the cover, "His name is Dibs. He will not talk. He will not play. He is alone. This is the story of how he won his way back into the world of other children." One of the most popular books suggested in this course, this is a classic in which, in one student's words, "Miss Axline records her weekly sessions with a gifted, rejected little boy. Her account of her use of play therapy is very impressive." Another reader commented:

From *Exceptional Children* 39 (November, 1972): 240-42. Reprinted by permission of the author and *Exceptional Children.* Copyrighted by the Council for Exceptional Children.

One understanding I think I have come away with is that no matter how intelligent a child is or what his capabilities are, they will only be of limited value without the love, respect, and understanding of others. I've gotten my roommates so interested in it by talking about it that they are now reading and enjoying it.

BARACH, DOROTHY. *One Little Boy*. New York: Julian Press, 1952. (Paperback by Dell)

This is the story of 8-year-old Kenneth, who had an asthma problem and many problems with his mother and father. This book is narrated by the consulting psychologist who helped Kenneth understand his deep-rooted feelings, and it can help all of us better understand the minds of troubled children. One student's reaction was, "I liked it's message about the normalcy of Kenneth's feelings and its emphasis on accepting and channeling thoughts common to all children."

BETTELHEIM, BRUNO. *The Empty Fortress*. New York: Free Press, 1967.

More than one term paper has been held up because all available copies of this book were checked out of the library. The master therapist of emotionally disturbed children discusses his work and his therapy at his Chicago school. Included is his 1956 piece, "Joey the Mechanical Boy," and other case studies.

BLATT, B., & KAPLAN, F. *Christmas in Purgatory: A Photographic Essay on Mental Retardation*. Rockleigh, N.J.: Allyn & Bacon, 1966.

This is a pictorial study of visits to the restricted wards of five state institutions for the mentally retarded. It shows living conditions and the problems of policies, programs, personnel, and philosophy. It concludes with refreshing scenes from a well run institution.

BUCK, PEARL. *The Child Who Never Grew*. New York: John Day, 1950.

Wrote one student,

In a moving account of her own personal experience in rearing a severely retarded child, Miss Buck has successfully portrayed the pains of one who is unfortunate enough to give birth to such a child. I found this book to be extremely personal. The memory of my retarded sister's childhood has been indelibly imprinted on my mind. My mother constantly reassured me that my sister was not conscious of her condition and therefore was happy with herself. I am not sure my mother was convinced of this, however. I never was until I read *The Child Who Never Grew*.

GREEN, HANNAH. *I Never Promised You a Rose Garden*. New York: Holt, Rinehart, & Winston, 1964. (Paperback by New American Library)

One student described this book as follows:

This is the story of Deborah and her conflict with the world of reality that opposed her world of Yr. The author's merit was to delve into the inner mind and to portray the life of a schizophrenic. She has succeeded. Every aspect of hospital life is shown through the experiences of a pretty, bright, autistic teenager.

HERSEY, JOHN. *The Child Buyer.* New York: Knopf, 1960. (Paperback by Bantam)

"Wissey Jones is the child buyer. His job is to find gifted children and purchase them for United Lymphomilloid Co. He attempts to buy Barry Rudd and raise his IQ to 1000. This is the strangest book about a gifted child I've ever read," commented one reader. This book, by a Pulitzer Prize winner, is at once a satire, a prophecy, a good story, and a mine of information about intellectual ability.

HUNT, NIGEL. *The World of Nigel Hunt: The Diary of a Mongoloid.* New York: Garrett, 1967.

A remarkable book, this is supposedly the first and only one ever written by a mongoloid. One student made these comments:

A mongoloid writing a book is an achievement long considered impossible. The preface, by Professor Penrose, and the introduction, by Nigel's father, verify Nigel's mongolism and his authorship. The book is the record of his trips and adventures over a period of a few years. Nigel shows a good grasp of language with many creative expressions in his descriptions. He does become a little muddled at times, but on the whole, the book is very clear and fun reading.

Another student wrote, "Nigel seems to be a very happy person, which makes me wonder if the real victims of mongolism might be the parents." Still another asked, "Does this book really offer as much hope to parents of mongoloid children as it pretends?"

ITARD, J., & GASPARD, G. *The Wild Boy of Aveyron.* New York: Appleton-Century-Crofts, 1962. (Paperback)

Made into a 1971 movie, *L'Enfant Sauvage* directed by Francois Truffaut, this book is, as one reader wrote, "the story of Victor, a wild boy taken from the woods of Southern France and supposedly civilized. This was my first exposure to Itard and his work. It was very interesting, and although I found the language somewhat cumbersome, I felt the book was worthwhile."

KEYES, DANIEL. *Flowers for Algernon.* New York: Harcourt, Brace & World, 1959. (Paperback by Bantam)

First appearing as a short story, then as an award winning novel, and then as a television drama and finally a motion picture, this story describes an experiment whereby Charlie Gordon's IQ is raised from 79 to 185 in about 3 months. However, the change would not be permanent and Charlie knew it. He described day by day the burnout and the regression, and then finally he returned to his old job at Donner's bakery. One student's reaction was "the unique approach, an exploration of the world of the mentally retarded and the world of the extremely gifted by a person who experienced both resulted (for me) in an increased understanding of both worlds."

KILLILEA, MARIE. *Karen.* Englewood Cliffs, N.J.: Prentice-Hall, 1963. (Paperback by Dell)

In the words of one reader,

> This touching account by a mother of the struggle of a child suffering from spastic cerebral palsy is to be commended for its warm, realistic portrayal of the emotional trauma involved, but also for its factual explanation of this exceptionality and of what parents can do for such a child.

Another wrote,

> This book has a special warmth that carried over to the reader. . . . It helps one realize how much a child with cerebral palsy affects the whole family, and how much pain, effort, and hours of therapy are involved. What a miracle it is when such a child is able to do the tasks other people take for granted.

RUBIN, THEODORE I. *Jordi, Lisa and David.* New York: Ballantine, 1971. (Paperback)

This book combines the two stories of Jordi (1960) and Lisa and David (1961) into one volume. Wrote one student,

> Jordi is a fictitious story of a young schizophrenic, written as from the mind of the child himself. It is easier and more interesting than a textbook, and it revealed to me how through special care and training a disturbed child can be helped. The story of Lisa and David, from which a widely seen movie was made, is the account of two disturbed adolescents, how they found and helped each other in a residential treatment center.

Still another reader "found this book to be a deeply moving experience which captured and held me until I finished reading it. I actually became a part of the story. I became involved in the lives of these children."

Concluding Comment

In this author's experience, most college students who elect a survey course about exceptional children are enthusiastic about the subject. Therefore, they should be exposed to as wide a reading range as possible. This article has presented 12 books which (a) students find interesting, (b) are comparatively inexpensive, (c) are authoritative, and (d) thus recommend themselves for wide reading.

Robert M. Porter is Professor of Education at State University College, Oneonta, New York.

#93
2